The Archaeology of Kingston, New York

The Archaeology of Kingston, New York

JOSEPH E. DIAMOND

excelsior editions
State University of New York Press
Albany, New York

Cover credit: *Kingston, New York* by Len Tantillo. © 2015 by Len Tantillo. Used with permission.

Published by State University of New York Press, Albany

© 2025 State University of New York

All rights reserved

Printed in the United States of America

No part of this book may be used or reproduced in any manner whatsoever without written permission. No part of this book may be stored in a retrieval system or transmitted in any form or by any means including electronic, electrostatic, magnetic tape, mechanical, photocopying, recording, or otherwise without the prior permission in writing of the publisher.

Links to third-party websites are provided as a convenience and for informational purposes only. They do not constitute an endorsement or an approval of any of the products, services, or opinions of the organization, companies, or individuals. SUNY Press bears no responsibility for the accuracy, legality, or content of a URL, the external website, or for that of subsequent websites.

EU GPSR Authorised Representative:
Logos Europe, 9 rue Nicolas Poussin, 17000, La Rochelle, France
contact@logoseurope.eu

Excelsior Editions is an imprint of State University of New York Press

For information, contact State University of New York Press, Albany, NY
www.sunypress.edu

Library of Congress Cataloging-in-Publication Data

Name: Diamond, Joseph E. author.
Title: The archaeology of Kingston, New York / Joseph E. Diamond.
Description: Albany : State University of New York Press, [2025]. | Series: Excelsior editions | Includes bibliographical references and index.
Identifiers: LCCN 2025007525 | ISBN 9798855803969 (hardcover : alk. paper) | ISBN 9798855803976 (ebook) | ISBN 9798855803983 (pbk. : alk. paper)
Subjects: LCSH: Kingston (N.Y.)—Antiquities. | Excavations (Archaeology)—New York (State)—Kingston. | Kingston (N.Y.)—History. | Indians of North America—New York (State)—Kingston—Antiquities. | African Americans—New York (State)—Kingston—Antiquities.
Classification: LCC F129.K5 D53 2025
LC record available at https://lccn.loc.gov/2025007525

*For my grandfather Edward P. Moran (1908–1984),
a promise kept, my mom Joan M. Diamond (1932–2023),
and my supportive and talented wife, Rebecca P. Diamond.*

Contents

List of Illustrations — ix

Acknowledgments — xix

Introduction — 1

Chapter 1 Overview — 11

Chapter 2 Precontact/Contact Period Native American Sites in Kingston — 43

Chapter 3 Early Historic Background — 123

Chapter 4 Archaeological Sites in the Stockade District — 153

Chapter 5 The Matthewis Persen House — 193

Chapter 6 Later Historic Archaeological Sites in Kingston — 295

Chapter 7 Commemorating the Dead: The Cemeteries of Kingston — 305

Chapter 8 Enslaved Individuals in *Wiltwyck* and Kingston and African Americans in the Historical and Archaeological Record — 313

Chapter 9	Nearby Precontact Sites in the Towns of Ulster, Hurley, and Esopus	337
Chapter 10	Conclusions and Interpretations	359
Glossary		371
Notes		401
References		415
Index		443

Illustrations

Figures

Figure 1.1	Map of the city of Kingston showing corporate boundary.	12
Figure 1.2	Top row, left to right: Dalton point, Hardaway-Dalton point, three LeCroy points. Bottom row, left to right: LeCroy point, four Kanawha points.	27
Figure 1.3	Top and bottom rows: all Otter Creek points.	29
Figure 2.1	CR Collection, Kingston Point. Top row, left to right: two Kirk Serrated points, two Kanawha Stemmed points, two Neville Stemmed points. Bottom row, left to right: three Otter Creek points, one Beekman Triangle point, two Vosburg points.	60
Figure 2.2	CR Collection, Kingston Point. Top row, left to right; nine Sylvan Stemmed/Lamoka points. Bottom row, left to right; nine Sylvan Stemmed/Lamoka points.	61
Figure 2.3	CR Collection, Kingston Point. On left, two Genesee points. On right, seven Normanskill points.	61
Figure 2.4	CR Collection, Kingston Point. Upper row, left to right: two Snook Kill points, two Susquehanna Broad points, three Orient Fishtail points. Bottom row, left to right: one Adena point, two Rossville-like points, two Jack's Reef Pentagonal points.	62

Figure 2.5 CR Collection, Kingston Point. Selection of Levanna and Madison points. 63

Figure 2.6 CR Collection, Kingston Point. Top row, left: ¾ grooved axe. Below, left: gouge. At right: two pestles. All sandstone. 63

Figure 2.7 Hendrickson site/Turck collection. Fabricating and processing tools. Top row, left to right: denticulate, four scrapers, two drills. Middle row, left to right: three preforms, one biface. Bottom row, left to right: four bifaces. 72

Figure 2.8 Hendrickson site/Turck collection. Projectile points. Top row, left to right: one reworked Brewerton side or corner-notched point, one possible Vosburg point, three Sylvan Stemmed points, two Normanskill points. Bottom row, left to right: one Meadowood point, one Fox Creek Stemmed point, four Levanna points. 72

Figure 2.9 Hendrickson site/Turck collection. Prehistoric pottery. Top row, left to right: cord-wrapped stick decorated body sherd, four Jack's Reef Corded rim fragments, one Wickham Punctate. Bottom row, left to right: drilled mend whole from pot, three plain undecorated rim fragments, one Oak Hill/Kelso Corded, one incised Late Woodland fragment (c. 1400 AD–Contact). 73

Figure 2.10 Perry site 1985. Left to right: Dr. Leonard Eisenberg (SUNY New Paltz), Alvin Wanzer, Frank Parslow, Art Carver. 77

Figure 2.11 Perry site 1985. Left to right: Tom Turck, Frank Parslow, Richard Stewart. 78

Figure 2.12 Perry site projectile points. Top row, left to right: Charleston Corner-Notched point, Otter Creek point, two Vosburg points. Bottom row, left to right: two Brewerton Eared-Notched points, Brewerton Eared-Triangle point, an untyped point. 79

Figure 2.13 Perry site projectile points. Top row, left to right: three Sylvan Stemmed points, two untyped points, one Orient Fishtail point. Bottom row, left to right: two Meadowood points, one Fox Creek Stemmed point, two Jack's Reef Corner Notched points.   80

Figure 2.14 Perry site projectile points. All three rows: Levanna points. Point in lower right corner has been refashioned into a drill.   80

Figure 2.15 Perry site fabricating and processing tools. Top row: all scrapers. Bottom row, left to right: drill, netsinker.   81

Figure 2.16 Perry site fabricating and processing tools. Top row, left to right: three bifaces/knives. Bottom row, left to right: triangular biface, core. At far right is a large flake knife.   81

Figure 2.17 Perry site bifaces (six) made from maroon Indian River chert.   82

Figure 2.18 Perry site stone and ceramic containers. Top row, left to right: fragment of steatite bowl, three fragments of Jack's Reef Corded. Bottom row, left to right: Jack's Reef Corded, Wickham Punctate, terminal Late Woodland/Contact Incised pottery, child's incised pot.   83

Figure 2.19 Perry site ceramics. Top row left to right: CWS and punctated ceramic, three CWS impressed fragments. Bottom row, left to right: corded and dragged ceramic, two CWS, one incised fragment.   84

Figure 2.20 Kingston Armory excavation. Block excavation shot.   87

Figure 2.21 Abeel Street Precontact Site #1. Top row, left to right: Susquehanna Broad point, two Orient Fishtail points, untyped projectile point, projectile point frag (CX 74). Bottom row, left to right: Snook Kill point (CX 74), scraper (CX 77), Neville Stemmed point, Precontact pottery (both CX 78).   96

Figure 2.22	Abeel Street Precontact Site #1. Top Row, left to right: two bifaces (CX 23), muller (CX 24), biface and Sylvan Stemmed point (both CX 27). Bottom row, left to right: scraper, utilized flake/scraper (CX 28), biface fragment (CX 29), projectile point frag (CX 31).	100
Figure 2.23	Duck Pond site. Upper row, left to right: Neville Stemmed point, Brewerton Side-Notched point, Normanskill point, two Sylvan Stemmed points. Middle row, left to right; three Levanna points, one English/French flint utilized flake, one Precontact pottery. Bottom row, left to right: ground stone fragment, netsinker.	121
Figure 3.1	1695 Miller map from Fernow (1881, 84–85), with Bob Slater's overlay.	142
Figure 4.1	1695 Miller map showing uptown excavations.	154
Figure 4.2	Photograph of post-molds from Clinton Avenue site.	161
Figure 4.3	Photograph of post-molds from Clinton Avenue site.	162
Figure 4.4	Pot metal jetton/token inscribed "WTB" for Wessel Ten Broeck. The artifact is ¾ inches in diameter. From Clinton Avenue excavation/NYU.	163
Figure 4.5	From a 1687 survey map of the Ten Broeck property.	173
Figure 4.6	Senate House c. 1694 looking north.	174
Figure 4.7	Seventeenth-century Dutch roemer.	175
Figure 4.8	Senate House artifacts. Drawing of a stove tile or *Schüsselkachel* from Feister and Sopko (2003).	176
Figure 4.9	Early 16th century illustration of a stove composed of *Schüsselkachel*, the stove in the left rear of the room.	177
Figure 5.1	Plan view of the Persen House. Taken from Barricklo (2000).	195
Figure 5.2	Plan view of Phase 3 portion of Persen House showing floor joists and unit locations. Other house construction phases shown on edges of figure.	200

Figure 5.3	Persen House. Unit 1, west wall profile. (Note Context 3 not shown.)	202
Figure 5.4	Persen House. Unit 2, north wall profile.	205
Figure 5.5	Persen House. Units 4, 8, and 5, east wall profile.	207
Figure 5.6	Persen House. Units 5, 8, and 4, west wall profile.	211
Figure 5.7	Persen House. Planview of Units 7, 4, 12, and 9 showing palisade trench and post-molds.	214
Figure 5.8	Persen House. Units 4 and 7, north wall profile.	215
Figure 5.9	Persen House. Unit 9, west wall profile.	217
Figure 5.10	Persen House. Unit 9 and 4, south wall profile.	218
Figure 5.11	Persen House. Personal item. Bodkin (11.127).	222
Figure 5.12	Persen House. Unit 14, L-shaped excavation unit around doorway to Phase 5 portion of building.	229
Figure 5.13	Persen House. Yard clearing.	231
Figure 5.14	Persen House. Native American artifacts. Top row, left to right: small biface (3.160), quartz crystal (13.134). Center row: two Orient Fishtail points (11.127; 2.14), three Meadowood points (4.22; 5.26; 1.9). Bottom row: two biface frags (9.131; 10.98), drill (13.151), two Levanna Points (4.53; 2.11).	251
Figure 5.15	Persen House. Trade items. Top row, left to right: amber bead (7.168), large amber wire-wound bead (4.22), large black bead over large white wire-wound bead (13.149), bright blue bead (4.54), large bright blue bead (13.134), cassock button (12.159). Bottom row: large round black, med navy blue (5.28), tubular bead (9.116), very small white bead (13.150), tubular bead (4.72), red/black bead (10.98), wampum and copper bead (4.56).	252
Figure 5.16	Persen House. Waldglas. Top, left to right: coiled foot fragment (7.168), body/foot fragment (13.151). Bottom, left to right: raspberry prunt (9.102), two plain prunts (2.10; 5.30).	254

Figure 5.17 Persen House. Tin-glazed earthenwares. Six fragments on left, (Vessel #16), from a majolica charger. On right, majolica fragment (4.58). 255

Figure 5.18 Persen House. Tin-glazed earthenwares. Top row: blue and white decorated (13.156; 12.135; 4.38). Middle row: blue and white decorated (12.157; 4.16; 13.151). Bottom row, two blue and white (13.149; 13.134), and polychrome delft (9.94). 256

Figure 5.19 Persen House. Tin-glazed earthenwares. Top: white with two blue lines (12.159). Bottom: white with two blue lines (Vessel #6: 4.56). 257

Figure 5.20 Persen House. Stonewares. Left: Vessel #1, salt glazed stoneware plate (9.91; 6.41). Center: Westerwald fragment (13.150). Far right: two Bartmankrügge, top (2.10), and bottom showing portion of medallion (8.86). 258

Figure 5.21 Persen House. Slip-decorated buff-bodied earthenware. Plate/chargers with pie-crust edge. Left (13.150). Right example is Vessel #10. 259

Figure 5.22 Persen House. Slip-decorated buff-bodied earthenware. Tankards, plates, and porringers. Top row (4.90; 9.102; 13.149; 6.43). Middle row and bottom left (6.43; 6.43; 9.95). Bottom right porringer or posset pot, Vessel #9 (10.98; 13.134). 260

Figure 5.23 Persen House. Bat-molded wares. First two fragments on left: Vessel #11, charger/plate (9.96; 13.134). Center, left: Vessel #12, charger/plate (10.103). Center, right: Vessel #13, charger/plate (5.25). Two frags at right: Vessel #14, charger/trencher (9.95; 6.62). 261

Figure 5.24 Persen House. Large red earthenware pan. Vessel #2 (4.34). 262

Figure 5.25 Persen House. Unglazed redware with tooled decoration. Probably made by Cornelius Hoogeboom. Vessel #7 (12.159; 13.148; 11.124; 13.151; 9.102; 5.33). 262

Figure 5.26   Persen House. Red earthenwares. Top row: three kookpot rim fragments (13.134; 5.10; 14.178). Center row, left to right: two kookpot rim fragments (14.175; 14.176), kookpot foot fragment (14.176). Bottom: kookpot handle (7.170).   263

Figure 5.27   Persen House. Nonprovenienced artifacts. Top row, left to right: yellow- and brown-glazed kookpot handle, kookpot rim fragment, slip-decorated, buff-bodied earthenware bowl/plate with piecrust edge. Bottom row, left to right: kookpot foot fragment, green-glazed buff/salmon bodied earthenware, "EB" (Edward Bird) pipe fragment.   264

Figure 5.28   Persen House. Earthenwares. Top row, left to right: clear-glazed redware with speckles (4.58), green-glazed buff earthenware (13.151), brown-glazed redware (8.85). Center row, left to right: yellow-glazed redware (14.177), two green-glazed buff earthenware (9.102; 13.151), yellow-glazed buff earthenware (13.151), Bottom row, left to right: brown-glazed red earthenware (9.100), green-glazed buff earthenware (11.123), yellow-glazed buff earthenware (13.151).   265

Figure 5.29   Persen House. Tin-glazed, buff-bodied earthenware tiles. On left, three frags that mend to form ceramic Vessel #19 (9.91; 13.134; 12.132), a tile. Upper right, ceramic Vessel #20, (7.76; 4.18), a tile. Other fragments do not mend. Note red paint on tiles.   273

Figure 5.30   Persen House. Arms group. Top row: five gunflints (4.18; 5.30; 9.116; 7.74; 7.74). Bottom row: four gunflints (10.112; 4.23; 12.133; 7.142).   276

Figure 5.31   Persen House. Arms group/personal. Ivory whistle (found near stairwell).   277

Figure 5.32   Persen House. Tailoring. Top row: 32 pins and pin fragments. Second row, left to right: five metallic buttons, one clothing fastener, one pin. Third row, left to right: shell button, three glass buttons, one

	metallic button, one metallic button with glass insert, copper/brass thimble. Bottom row: eight bone buttons showing variations (all from context 13.134).	278
Figure 5.33	Persen House. Personal items (relating to hygiene). From top to bottom: toothbrush (7.81), toothbrush (12.133), toothbrush (13.134), toothbrush (12.132).	280
Figure 5.34	Persen House. Recreational items. Left to right: "EB" pipe (4.56), "JRTIPPET" pipe (14.177), "EB" trade pipe (9.102).	281
Figure 8.1	Three "Hudson Valley Flats" or early local Dutch bricks.	315
Figure 8.2	Two red earthenware pan tiles.	316
Figure 8.3	The interior back cover of Wessel Brodhead's family Bible.	322
Figure 8.4	Dr. John Rayburn (left) and SUNY New Paltz Geology Major Ross Hernandez conducting a ground penetrating radar survey at 157 Pine Street (January 16, 2019).	328
Figure 8.5	Section of bluestone road in front of Hurley Library, main Street, Hurley.	329
Figure 8.6	The gravestone of Ceazer Smith when it was first found.	331
Figure 9.1	Reconstructed pot of "Kingston Incised" type from the S-2 site (NYSM accession #A2014.03A.2.3).	339
Figure 9.2	Millens Quarry Phase 2. Locus 1. Estimated artifacts at surface.	346

Tables

Table 1.1	Precontact phases in the Hudson Valley.	22–24
Tables 2.1a-b	Sites in Kingston by phase/time period.	45–53
Table 2.2	Kingston Point Booth Collection/AMNH lithics.	55

Table 2.3	CR Collection of Kingston Point artifacts by type and lithic.	58–59
Table 2.4	Abeel Street Precontact Site #1. Lithic artifacts by lithic type.	98–99
Table 2.5	Kingston Meadows precontact loci.	109
Table 2.6	Duck Pond site artifact table.	119–20
Table 5.1	Persen House. Artifacts by function and strata group.	246–47
Table 5.2	Persen House. Native American artifacts by strata group.	249–50

Acknowledgments

This book could not have been written without the support of a great number of people. First, I would like to acknowledge the excavator of the Clinton Avenue site, the late Dr. Bert Salwen of New York University, and the late Dr. Leonard A. Eisenberg of SUNY New Paltz, who excavated the Hendrickson site. Both of these men were my professors at various points during my formative years as an archaeologist, and I owe a great deal to both of them. The same could be said for the late Robert E. Funk, a friend, a mentor, and a member of my doctoral committee. His publications are referenced throughout this book. Two other well deserving archaeologists who have taught me the fine art of excavation and stratigraphic interpretation are Jay William Bouchard and Dr. Joel W. Grossman.

For information concerning chapters 1 and 2, I would like to thank Dr. Jonathan Lothrop of the New York State Museum; Dr. Alex Bartholemew, Dr. Kaustubh Patwardhan, Dr. John Rayburn, and Dr. Frederick Vollmer of the SUNY New Paltz Department of Geology; Dr. Christopher Lindner of Bard College; Andre Krievs of Hartgen Archeological Associates, Inc.; Jay R. Cohen; Dylan Lewis; Jaime Meinsen; Amanda Ingarra; Al Cammisa; Dr. Philip LaPorta of the Center for the Investigation of Native American Quarries (CINAQ); Dennis Larios of Brinnier and Larios, PC; Ralph Swensen and Alan Adin of the City of Kingston Planning Department; Dr. Hope Luhman of the Louis Berger Group; and Dr. Robert Hasenstab of the University of Illinois, Chicago. Additionally, Jay Ciccone was instrumental in introducing me to the owner of the CR Collection as well as providing me with my third tour of Greene County chert outcrops on the same day that I photographed the CR collection for chapter 2. Sue Cahill, planning director for the City of Kingston, was kind enough to provide the map of Kingston for figure 1.1

For information on Tom Turck's collection from the Hendrickson site, I would like to thank Lindsay Jankovitz and Paul and Joanne Jankovitz. For information on the disparate collections that have been found at Kingston Point over the years, I would like to thank Mr. Peter Brill and Ms. Maria Martinez of the Smithsonian Institution, and Dr. Thomas Amorosi, Dr. David Hurst Thomas, Dr. Loran Pendleton, and Anibal Rodriguez for permission to work on the American Museum of Natural History collections.

For chapter 4, I would like to thank the late Robert Slater for information about his find at the Johnston House garden. Dr. Paul Huey and Lois Feister of the Office of Parks, Recreation, and Historic Preservation provided valuable information about the Senate House, Louw-Bogardus, and Clinton Avenue excavations. Paul Huey was kind enough to allow me to use his photographs of the stockade that was found by the New York University field school. Terrah Lindsay allowed me to use her drawing of the Wessel TenBroeck impressed metallic jetton (fig. 4.4). Len Tantillo not only provided me with a painting of the TenBroeck house (fig. 4.6) but was also kind enough to allow me to use one of his studies of c. 1694 Kingston for the book cover. Travis Bowman and Andrew Farry were extremely helpful in allowing me access to the Senate House archaeological collections at OPRHP. Andrew Farry and Stacey Matson-Zuvic were instrumental in moving the testing within the Senate House forward. Aaron Robinson, historic site manager for the Senate House State Historic Site, was incredibly helpful, as were other staff members Dena Preston, Rebecca Howe-Parisio, and Carl Harris. Special thanks to Laura Hertle for assisting me with screening on some very cold January and February days in 2020, and to Sean Seymour for carefully backfilling my excavation units inside the Senate House after I was done.

For the excavation in the DeWitt plot at the Old Dutch Church, I am especially grateful to Pastor Rob Sweeny, the consistory, and congregation of the Old Dutch Church for permission to do the excavation. Special thanks are due to Gage DeWitt and Justin DeWitt, as well as the DeWitt Family Association, for their tireless research to find the burial location of the progenitor of the DeWitt family. To undertake this excavation, a memorandum of understanding (MOU) between the DeWitt Family Association, Old Dutch Church, and SUNY New Paltz was drafted by Blaine K. Miller, Esq., and approved by Provost Barbara Lyman, Chief of Staff Shelly Wright, Dean of Liberal Arts and Sciences Laura Barrett, and Chair of Anthropology Kenneth Nystrom. Other folks who assisted us with the excavation (and backfilling) were Mr. John Quick, Taylor

Bruck, Gage DeWitt, Perry DeWitt, Schuyler DeWitt, Jamie Parsons, Doug DeWitt, Meade DeWitt, Annie DeWitt, Alan and Susan Glickman, Dr. Jeffrey Benjamin, Lindsay Jankovitz, James Decker, Lorne Montague, Alec Murillo, and Mark Saunders. The SUNY New Paltz students who excavated the site were Susan Fernandez, Paige Skeels, Sean Gallagher, Naomi Hertz, and Kevin Brophy. Other SUNY students that I had to borrow from the Pine Street African Burial Ground excavation included Rachel Drillings, Navneet Kaur, and Broderick O'Reilly.

For chapter 5, I would like to thank a number of people who assisted with the Persen House excavation. Special thanks are due to Mr. Marc Phelan, Mr. Harvey Sleight, architect Kenneth Barricklo, the late City of Kingston historian Ed Ford, as well as Dr. Paul Huey, Joseph McEvoy, and Lois Feister of OPRHP, who provided needed information on ceramics as well as information about Cornelius Hoogeboom. Thanks also to Mr. Robert Jury, an exceptional mason whose assistance with a sledge hammer was always needed. Most of the excavation at the Persen House was accomplished by the author along with Patrick Sabol and Frank "Eyeballs" Spada. Other field support was provided by Ken Jones, Mario Medalion, Rebecca Diamond, Alexis Waleski, and Alyson Faero. The faunal analysis was done by Dr. Thomas Amorosi. Lab work during the Persen House project was undertaken by myself, Trini deMunck, Rebecca Diamond, and my mom, Joan M. Diamond. Jon Palmer and Taylor Bruck were kind enough to allow me to rephotograph the Persen House artifacts for this volume. Mr. Keith J. Lehman of the Corning Museum of Glass was kind enough to rephotograph a *roemer* from the Jerome Strauss Collection (cat. #63.3.44) for this volume.

For chapter 6, I would like to thank Mr. William Rhinehart, who was kind enough to share his discovery of the N. C. Bell Pottery factory with me. Jane Kellar of Friends of Historic Kingston provided me with the excavation materials that the late Bob Slater and the late Ed Ford excavated at the site.

For chapter 7, I would like to thank Pastor Rob Sweeny, Eric Winchell, and Robert E. Haines, all of whom were kind enough to share information about Kingston's cemeteries, particularly the Houghtaling Cemetery.

For chapter 8, I would like to thank Susan Stessin-Cohn and Ashley Hurlburt-Biagini, who were instrumental in making this chapter more readable and also contemporary with the literature and terminology. Other readers who made helpful comments include Dr. Kenneth Nystrom, Phil Timbrouck, Tyrone Wilson, Ubaka Hill, and Carl Brown. Special thanks are due to the Kingston Land Trust for passing the Pine Street African Burial Ground to Harambee of Kingston, LLC, for permanent protection and preservation. Thanks also to Harambee of Kingston, LLC, for partnering with SUNY New Paltz to work toward the goals that Harambee has for the Pine Street African Burial Ground (PSABG). Rich Gromek has been instrumental in moving us forward with the PSABG National Register nomination. Town of Hurley historian James Decker provided me with the bricks and pan tiles for figures 8.1 and 8.2. Thanks also to the late Edwin Ford, former City of Kingston historian, who was with me on the day that we relocated the Pine Street African Burial Ground in 1990. Brad Jordan of Herzogs donated materials for the excavation at both PSABG and the DeWitt plot in 2022. Dennis Larios was kind enough to send his surveying team to the PSABG to set up a grid for us. From the 2022 SUNY New Paltz archaeological field school at the PSABG I would like to thank Kevin Brophy, Rachel Drillings, Susan Fernandez, Stefan Kloss, Regina Lufrano, Greg Aebi, Phillip Anson, Shawn Gallagher, Riley Goold, Navneet Kaur, Gavin Prescott, Paige Skeels, Jacquelyn Smillie, Makayla Williamson, Mikayla Dablan-Azony, Jessica Dankowitz, Naomi Hertz, Broderick Reilly, and Sara Saunders. From the 2023 archaeological field school, I would like to thank Eileen Corrales, Marcela Figeroa, Matthew Fredeman, Koby Weston, Samuel Whitehead, Caleb Berrios, Faith Davies, Nicole Dunne, Shelly Madera, Camellia Ostwald, Eoghan Rich, Madeline Todd, Allison Zuclich, Clara Chamorro, and Oren Teeter.

For chapter 9, I would like to thank Frank Spada for his assistance excavating the Millens Quarry site.

Thanks are due to Frank "Eyeballs" Spada for his careful work on sites such as Canal Path Trail, Colony Liquors, Abeel Street, Sailor's Cove, Kingston Meadows, Millens Quarry, and the Matthewis Persen House.

From SUNY Press, I would like to thank Richard Carlin, Julia Cosacchi, Sue Morreale, and Gordon Marce.

Special thanks are also due to my wife, Rebecca Diamond, who is responsible for the graphic design (figures) and photo editing in this book. Dr. Carol Raemsch edited the manuscript and made many insightful comments that improved the quality of the text. Without her amazing help, this project would never have come to fruition. Thanks also to Mr. Eli Basch, Esq., who was kind enough to assist with production costs. Special thanks are due also to an "anonymous reader" (Paul Huey) who pointed out several inconsistencies and spelling errors. I compiled most of the data discussed in this book during a SUNY New Paltz sabbatical leave for the Fall 2016 semester. That seems so long ago now, but then again, a lot of archaeological work has been happening in the city of Kingston and I wanted this volume to cover all of it. Finally, any errors in this book are my own.

Introduction

This book was written with the idea that not only archeologists but also the general public would be interested in the prehistoric (or "precontact," as is more commonly used today) and historic periods of the Hudson Valley, in general, and the Kingston area, in particular. Most of the existing information on precontact archaeology and historic archaeology in the Mid-Hudson Valley is contained within articles in academic journals, museum memoirs, and what archaeologists call the "gray literature," that is, reports compiled for local, state, or federal agencies when archaeological sites have the potential to be impacted by planned construction projects. For the general reader, many of these sources can be challenging to find, and even more difficult to digest, so I have attempted to change the tone of my writing to make the archaeological record more comprehensible and inviting.

While writing this book, I sent a copy of one of my recently published articles (Diamond et al. 2016) to some friends. One wrote back that by page 4 he fell into a "deep coma-like sleep."[1] Admittedly, he is not an archaeologist, but archaeologists would like to believe that our subject area is more interesting and valuable than simply as a cure for insomnia. That value lies in *Homo sapiens* interest in the past and, just as importantly, the fact that the past is all around us. We just need to be trained to see it.

This book, in a nutshell, is about people and the artifacts they have left behind. For almost 12,000 years, people have lived in the Kingston area, including Paleoindian groups and their descendants, the colonists who found their way to the New World and their descendants, and even some of you who are holding this book. All of humankind has left artifacts of one form or another, from stone projectile points and earthenware pottery to modern-day buildings, roads, train trestles, gravestones, advertising signs, and everyday trash.[2] All of these things can be considered artifacts, or what we call "material culture," which is the "meat and potatoes" of archaeology.

To find out about the groups of people who preceded us, archaeologists excavate "sites" in a careful and systematic manner using a grid pattern and documenting the evidence through various kinds of excavation forms, drawings, photographs, and now, more commonly, videos. Our analyses combine information about the artifacts with the soil strata (or archaeological context) in which they were found to make various inferences about the site: who lived there ("archaeological culture"), when they used the site (time frame), and what they were doing there (site function). For the precontact period as a whole, we seek to investigate how people changed from mobile hunters and gatherers to more settled horticulturalists and agriculturalists. We ask questions such as, when and how did lifestyles change and why? Was it because of environmental change, population increase, diffusion of ideas from other locations, the movements of people, a new technology, the spread of cultigens, or the introduction and spread of the bow and arrow? For what we refer to as the "Contact" period—primarily post-1609 in the Hudson Valley after Europeans colonized the area—we seek to understand the interplay between European colonists and Native Americans as they sought to interact with each other though trade and, ultimately, negotiated land deals in a landscape that became torn by warfare, colonization, and European-introduced endemic diseases. For the historical archaeologist, this time period is also a study of how Europeans brought with them a mental template—albeit a Dutch, French, English, Swedish, or Spanish one—to provide some semblance of order for themselves in the New World.

Historical archaeologists are also interested in specific ethnicities, social classes, class structure, power relations between classes, technology, raw material extraction, trade patterns, ideology, disenfranchised peoples, and material culture that reflect and legitimize power and control, among other things. They are also interested in material culture as commodities—in this case, items that are produced from raw materials, finished, marketed, and then traded or sold.

The kinds of archaeological studies that have been undertaken in the Kingston area include avocational archaeology, university-sponsored archaeology, New York State Office of Parks, Recreation, and Historic Preservation (OPRHP) sponsored archaeology, and cultural resource management, or CRM, archaeology. Lastly, there are accidental discoveries by the general public that are recorded and become part of the historical and archaeological literature.

One of these groups that has a knack for finding or reporting archaeological sites is avocational archaeologists. Avocational archaeologists are people who engage in archaeology in their spare time due to an interest in material culture and people from the past. Six sites discussed herein have been found and investigated, to a greater or lesser degree, by avocational archaeologists. University-sponsored excavations—such as those on Clinton Avenue and Green Street (by New York University), Ponchkockie (by the State University of New York [SUNY] New Paltz), the DeWitt Plot (by SUNY New Paltz), and 157 Pine Street (by SUNY New Paltz)—are driven by research objectives, restorative justice, and the desire to provide professional training to students. Three university-sponsored archaeological excavations in Kingston (Clinton Avenue, Green Street, and Ponckhockie) have produced trained archaeologists that went on to become CRM archaeologists, college faculty, and archaeologists working for the federal government in Washington, DC.

OPRHP excavations in the area have been limited to the Senate House State Historic Site, although individual members of OPRHP were also involved with the excavation and preservation of the Louw-Bogardus House on Frog Alley.

CRM is archaeology that is mandated either by the State Environmental Quality Review Act (SEQRA) of 1975 or by permits required by the New York State Preservation Act of 1980 (section 14.09 of the New York Parks, Recreation and Historic Preservation Law) or section 106 of the Federal Government's National Historic Preservation Act (NHPA) of 1966. These are also called "compliance" projects because they are mandated by these state and federal laws. Archaeologists who conduct CRM archaeology are required to have a master's degree in anthropology or history and meet the standards of 36-CFR-61, a set of federal guidelines and criteria. Throughout the course of my research on the area, I examined a total of 23 CRM reports documenting 53 archaeological sites that have been found thus far in the city of Kingston. For a more thorough explanation of CRM archaeology, see the glossary of terms included in the back of this book. The glossary provides short descriptions of some confusing, and often arcane, archaeological terminology, and at this point, it might be helpful to pause and review the glossary to become more familiar with terms and concepts as they occur throughout the text.

Based on my research, cases involving accidental discoveries in the area total only three, although it is probable that I have missed others due to a lack of sufficient information on my part. In addition to these, to round out the picture of the archaeology of Kingston, I have included four sites in the town of Ulster, one in Hurley, and one in Sleightsburg. All six are significant sites, and each can be viewed from the perspective that the people who lived on these sites spent a considerable time in what is now Kingston proper.

The sites discussed in this book are loosely organized by time period, although it should be mentioned at the outset that many precontact sites also contain historic materials and vice versa. For example, an initial archaeological survey that I conducted at Sailor's Cove was primarily focused on the 19th- to 20th-century Hutton brickyard, but during the course of the archaeological testing, we encountered remnant soils that were not mined by the brick industry and that still contained precontact Native American artifacts. Consequently, in what follows, I include the precontact artifacts as part of the Kingston Point analysis (chapter 2) and the historic brickyard in the historical archaeology section (chapter 6).

Throughout the book, I have used the metric system because American archaeologists have been doing so since the 1970s. We switched, but the rest of the country did not. For the sake of clarification, a 50 cm shovel test is 19¾ inches per side, a 1-meter square is 39⅜ inches, and a 2-meter square is 78¾ inches per side. In terms of square horizontal surface area, a 1-meter square is 1.196 yards, or slightly larger than a square yard, and a 2-meter square is 4.784 square yards. When discussing the amount of horizontal surface area that was excavated on a site, I have translated square meters into square feet to make it easier to contemplate the size of the excavations.

Also note that as one reads through site descriptions in archaeological reports, it becomes obvious that archaeologists generally do not excavate an entire site. In situations where the site is scheduled to be destroyed by construction, such as in CRM archaeology, we try to obtain as much data as possible by taking as large a sample as possible. In some situations, where archaeological data can be obtained by actually doing the excavation work for the project, we try to retrieve as much data as possible. For example, at local sites such as the Dutch Church Stabilization Project (Cohen 2005), a 100% sample was excavated, and at the Persen House, 87% of the interior portion of the 18th-century kitchen wing was excavated (see chapter 5). In certain research situations, such as those at the Senate House, Clinton Avenue, the Louw-Bogardus House, and the Hendrickson site, portions of the site are often left intact for future research. This was also the case at the Persen House, where, during the course of renovations of the kitchen wing inside the house, a 32-square-foot block of soil above the trench of the 1661 addition to the stockade was left intact and protected with sandbags, thereby preserving the original intact soils for later study.

As an archaeologist, one of the questions I'm often asked is how old an artifact is, followed by, "How do you know that?" For the various types of historic artifacts from sites such as the Persen House, Clinton Avenue, and the Senate House (to name a few), we gather information from documentary sources, technological patents, ceramic pattern registrations, and embossing on items such as coins, buttons, and bottles. For example, in an article entitled "Telling Time for Archaeologists," Miller et al. (2000) provide information on the earliest manufacturing dates for several hundreds of items, including the copper percussion cap for muskets (1816), shotgun cartridges (1850), Lineoleum (1863), toothpaste in a squeeze tube (1896), asphalt paving (1871), paper clips (1898), the popsicle stick (1922), aluminum foil (1947), and Velcro (1955). Any of these items, when found in an archaeological context, would provide a *terminus post quem* (TPQ) or "date after which" the archaeological context or soil layer was deposited. The same would be true for a group of coins in an archaeological context, where the latest coin would provide the TPQ for the deposition of the soil context. To clarify this, I have included both TPQ and the related concept of *terminus ante quem* (TAQ) or "date before which." TAQ is best represented by a burn layer. For example, at the Persen House, all of the artifacts within and below what we know is the June 6, 1663, burn layer had to have been deposited by that date and no later.

For older artifacts such as Native American items, radiometric or carbon-14 (C14) dating is utilized. In this case, we do not have written information regarding production dates, so we have to utilize another means by which to date the artifacts and the archaeological contexts they are found in. Carbon dating can be used on bone, antler, teeth, wood, charcoal, fabric, hide, and shell, although shell is a bit problematic because shellfish utilize older residual carbon in the water when constructing their shells. C14 dating can be either "direct," such as through scraping food residue off an excavated cooking pot and using the residue as a C14 sample, or "indirect," which refers to dating by association. In this case, artifacts found within in a cooking or storage pit containing a datable charcoal sample are assumed to be the same date, by association, as the C14 date of the charcoal. With this method, problems may occur when older artifacts are mixed in with fill from more recent soil disturbances.

Because specific kinds of artifacts, such as projectile points and pottery, change over time, the different types can be radiometrically dated to bracket their time range of use. Thousands of C14 dates over large areas of the northeastern United States have allowed archaeologists to pin down specific "type" artifacts to particular "archaeological cultures" and place them within a temporal and cultural framework. "Type" artifacts are known from the first published site where they were identified. For example, "Kingston Incised" pottery was first defined in former state archaeologist William Ritchie's 1952 publication on the Kingston site.

Most C14 dates are expressed in this book in the familiar format of years BC (i.e., "pre-Christ") and AD (*anno Domini* or after Christ), but for radiometric dates that have been found in Kingston and at other nearby sites, I have also included what are referred to as "calibrated" BP dates, that is, "years before present" dates, which refers to the date before 1950, when this technique was first used. BP dates are used by American archaeologists side by side with BC and AD dates. For a more detailed explanation of archaeological dating, see the glossary of terms.

To make the discussions in the text somewhat more comprehensible, I have included table 1.1 as a guide to radiometrically dated archaeological "cultures" throughout the Hudson Valley and the Northeast in general. The dates are referred to with the term "circa," which means that there is wiggle room for an archaeological culture to be a little earlier or later than the dates proposed. Some of the time periods and cultures overlap and are still somewhat confusing for several reasons, including a lack of adequate dates; the availability of only "legacy dates," which are older C14 dates from the 1960s and 1970s; or situations where multiple occupations on one site have clouded our ability to identify a specific occupation. Table 1.1 also provides diagnostic projectile point types, pottery types, and other classes of artifacts that characterize that particular archaeological culture or time period.

Tables 2.1a–b list the sites discussed in the text, with specific information on the precontact "archaeological culture" or time period identified at the site. One of the readily apparent trends in this table is that many of the precontact sites do not have temporally diagnostic artifacts (column 1). This means that we know it is a locus of precontact Native American activity, but we don't necessarily know which group or which time period the site originates from. This situation is common for sites where diagnostic artifacts sometimes do not get sampled as part of the excavation procedure, or alternatively, they are not present at all. Examples of this would be what are called "quarry sites" and "small lithic scatters." Quarry sites are where stone for making tools is extracted, whereas small lithic scatters are sites where a small range of activities have taken place, leaving only a minimal amount of artifacts as evidence. For other time periods such as the Paleoindian, Early Archaic, Late Archaic, Transitional Archaic, Middle Woodland, and Late Woodland, I simply have a presence/absence column denoting the presence of an artifact that is probably from that broad time period. More specific information is provided by "archaeological culture," or phase, which is tied to table 1.1. The last four columns concern the historic periods, which I have provided a general date. The very last column is the number of archaeological cultures or time periods represented at each site. The bottom row is a tally of the number of sites identified thus far in the city of Kingston and the seven sites surrounding Kingston that have artifacts from that particular time period. It should be noted that there are many more sites in the towns of Ulster, Hurley, and Esopus that could have been added here, but my focus is on the major sites that have been studied that surround the corporate boundary of the city of Kingston.

The referencing in this book follows standard anthropological style, and it is easy to become accustomed to. The reference list utilizes quotation marks for peer-reviewed literature (books, articles in journals, memoirs, research reports, etc.). Titles without quotation marks are CRM reports that are submitted to a town, city, or county; these are usually reviewed by state or federal agencies. These reports are referred to as the "gray literature" because of their limited distribution. Quite a while back, Karen Hartgen, an archaeologist from Troy, New York, suggested that archaeologists in New York State start a publication series called "Getting the Gray Out" in an attempt to publish more of the gray literature. While that never occurred on a statewide level, I hope to have done so for Kingston, portions of the town of Ulster, and for at least one site in the town of Esopus. As a result of this book, many of the CRM sites in the Kingston area will become familiar to people for the first time.

As a whole, this book attempts to put into a larger perspective the history of the human occupation of Kingston. Along the way, I summarize 23 CRM reports, 2 excavations by OPRHP, 6 avocational excavations, and 5 university-sponsored excavations: one on Clinton Avenue, one on Greene

Street by Dr. Bert Salwen and Sarah Bridges of New York University, Dr. Leonard Eisenberg's excavation at the Hendrickson site in Ponckhockie, my excavation at the DeWitt Plot in the Old Dutch Church graveyard, and Dr. Kenneth Nystrom's excavation at the Pine Street African Burial Ground at 157 Pine Street.

This monograph also serves as a vehicle for me to disperse the information contained in my Persen House report (Diamond 2004d), a somewhat unwieldy two-volume set, only one of which is readable, with the other containing raw data on the artifacts and strata groups found at the site. Many of the figures from the Persen House report are reproduced here for the benefit of readers interested in the full range of artifacts found at the site.

I have also included an extended discussion of the finds on Abeel Street that Frank Spada and I found during an archaeological monitoring project (Diamond 2014). "Monitoring" refers to working with construction crews to identify significant archaeological deposits, which can then be removed by careful excavation before they are destroyed. The discussion of what is referred to as Abeel Street Precontact Site #1 takes the reader through the process of finding, and then successfully mitigating, a small prehistoric site in the midst of backhoes, graders, trucks, and numerous construction workers.[3] It also makes the point that, like the Ingarra site on Wall Street, there is much to be learned through careful excavations under city streets and in people's backyards. To illustrate how CRM or "compliance" projects work in other situations, I have left some of the required archaeological details in my discussions of Kingston Meadows; Angstrom; the chert quarries at the Kingston Industrial Park, Ulster County Jail, and Millens sites; and the Persen House.

I have also included a chapter on the enslaved individuals of *Wiltwyck* and the presence of Kingston's African American community as represented in the archaeological record. These data appear in the form of transported artifacts, manufactured architectural materials such as bricks and pantiles, and buildings all over Kingston. African American history in the area is also evident at the Pine Street African Burial Ground and at cemeteries such as Mt. Zion on South Wall Street.

Lastly, as mentioned at the start of the chapter, this book is written for the general public as well as my colleagues in anthropology. In discussions with friends in the field, we have come to the conclusion (as have many others) that archaeologists don't do a particularly good job of educating the public about what we do, and how and why we do it. Additionally, for the five university-sponsored excavations I have discussed, these have provided professional training for students, data for descendants such as the DeWitt Family Association, and a form of restorative justice for those buried at the Pine Street African Burial Ground. University-sponsored excavations have also opened a window into Kingston's history as well as its deep past[4] for the city's residents. Many of the sites discussed here are CRM projects. In the area of CRM archaeology, there is a belief that if an archaeologist finds an "arrowhead," the project will grind to a screeching halt. That is not always the case, and it would be hard to imagine any kinds of new construction taking place if that were true. CRM archaeology is a phased procedure that locates, evaluates, and then mitigates (if necessary) the effects of construction projects on archaeological sites. In situations where an archaeological site is deemed incredibly important, or when human remains are found, avoidance of the site, whether though design changes or property transfers, can ensure the preservation of the artifacts or people buried there and also preserve the site for future research. With regards to Karen Hartgen's comment about CRM archaeology mentioned above, I hope I have finally "gotten the gray out" for Kingstonians.

Chapter 1

Overview

The Study Area

When conducting a formal archaeological research study, it is commonplace to provide a thorough description of the study area under investigation. This serves as a way of informing the reader or researcher about aspects of the geographical setting that can be used to tie into later. A background in the geology, pedology, and biology of the area within which the city of Kingston and environs is found provides a framework for why and how people have lived and thrived in this location for over a period of approximately 12,000 years. The environmental setting defines the kinds of resources that would have been available for survival of past populations as well as the kinds of materials and data researchers are able to identify archaeologically. For example, lithic quarries provided toolstone such as chert for Native Americans, which they relied on for hunting, food preparation, and crafting of other materials. Later, Dutch colonials mined clay for bricks and limestone, which were used in the construction of early houses. On Native American camp sites and habitation sites, the remains of precontact dietary data, called *ecofacts*, such as bones, seeds, carbonized nut fragments, and mussel shells, also become part of the archaeological record, and it is these seemingly mundane items that provide us with information about the lives of precontact groups.

The study area of focus in this book is defined by the corporate boundary of the city of Kingston. This is visible as a broken line on the Kingston East and Kingston West United States Geological Survey (USGS) quadrangle maps. However, several important sites along the edge and just outside of the corporate boundary have also been included to provide a more complete picture of precontact occupations in the Esopus drainage and along the Hudson River. Figure 1.1 does not include the location of all of the sites discussed in this volume for one major reason: the potential for looting of the archaeological sites and data. The Hudson Valley, like many areas of New York State and the world in general, has witnessed, and is currently experiencing, looting on an unprecedented scale. Archaeologists have been studying the effect that this has on our interpretations of the archaeological record, and we are not optimistic about the long-term preservation of numerous kinds of archaeological sites. The lack of a site location for some of the sites discussed herein just makes it that much more difficult for someone to locate the sites discussed in the text.

Figure 1.1. Map of the city of Kingston showing corporate boundary. *Source:* City of Kingston. Sue Cahill. Public domain.

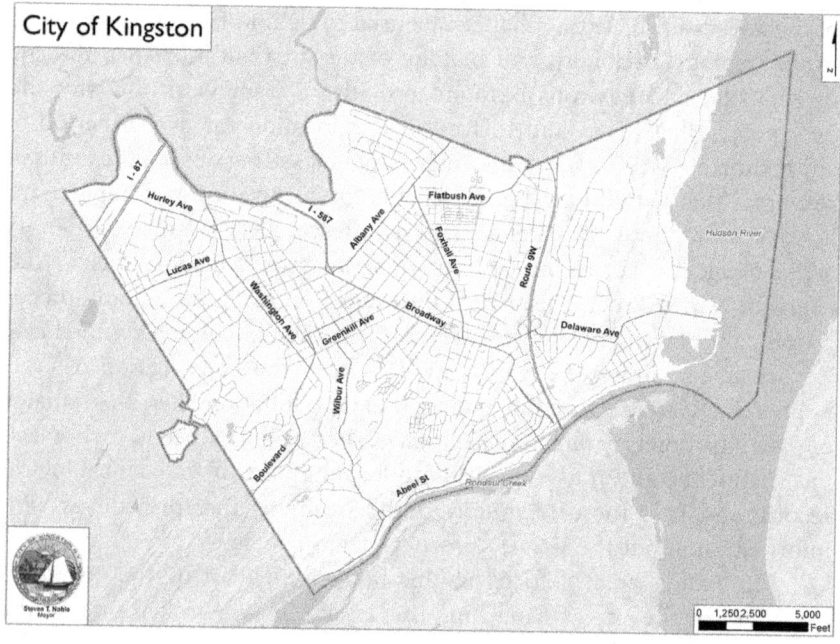

Geology

The city of Kingston (fig. 1.1) is composed geologically of several formations that break the surface from the Hudson River west through Kingston and into the towns of Ulster and Hurley. Proceeding from east to west, these begin with the Middle Ordovician (450–465 million years ago) Austin Glen formation of sandstone and shale. From a functional point of view, these rocks provide adequate stone for building walls or foundations for houses and industrial buildings. This is the case in the town of Esopus, just south of Kingston, where the major geological unit is the Austin Glen formation, which has provided the stone for all of the 18th- and 19th-century houses in the town. For precontact Native Americans, the Austin Glen formation also contains many thrust faults of Mt. Merino chert that was used as toolstone to make various forms of chipped stone implements. The thrust faults occurred during the Taconic Orogeny (c. 440 mya), a mountain-building episode that shaped the geography of the Hudson Valley. Running along the western side of the Hudson River, outcrops of Mt. Merino chert can be found just to the north of Kingston in the town of Ulster and to the south of Kingston in the town of Esopus. Just across the corporate boundary of the city of Kingston in the town of Ulster, I partially excavated a Mt. Merino chert quarry that was used extensively for thousands of years by the early residents of what is now Kingston.

Overlying the Austin Glen formation is the Helderberg group, which consists of the Port Ewen, Alsen, Becraft, New Scotland, Kalkberg, Coeymans, and Manlius limestones (c. 450–391 mya). In precontact times, these formations provided chert for stone tools, and later, in historic times, these same formations provided limestone and dolostone for building blocks as well as for lime and cement.

Overlying the Helderberg group is the Lower to Middle Devonian (c. 391–383 mya) Onondaga limestone and Ulster group of limestones and shales. During precontact times, the Morehouse Member of the Onondaga formation provided nodules of chert that make up the bulk of the toolstone used by early inhabitants in and around the area of today's city of Kingston. The Onondaga limestones also provided an available and more permanent form of building material for the Dutch and English inhabitants of Kingston during the late 17th to early 18th centuries. This was a time when Dutch, English, and French colonists were making the transition from wood-framed buildings and pithouses[1] to the more permanent stone structures that we see in Kingston and throughout Ulster County today.

Within and around the city of Kingston, the Onondaga formation is evidenced by the Morehouse and Edgecliff members, both of which include chert, as well as the Glenerie formation, which also includes chert, albeit of a poor quality for making stone tools. When I demonstrate stone tool making in my classes at SUNY New Paltz, I never use Glenerie chert because it is full of fossils and is not internally consistent. My predilection for better-quality material duplicates the choices of pre-contact Native Americans, who likewise did not find Glenerie chert a viable toolstone. Most Native American tools from the Kingston area are made from Onondaga chert (Morehouse member) and Mt. Merino chert, with very few being composed of Glenerie chert. Additionally, the Port Ewen formation produces usable cherts for toolstone. An archaeological study at the site of the Ulster County Jail revealed that Native Americans traversing what is now the southwestern portions of Kingston during precontact times stopped to exploit the Port Ewen limestone in this area for chert (see LaPorta et al. 2018).

During the 17th through 19th centuries, the exploitation of these limestone and dolostone formations resulted in the production of high-quality construction materials for shaped building blocks and, on a larger commercial scale, for mortar and cement. Archaeologically, this industry can be found along Hurley Avenue (Quarry Street) as well as the areas uphill on Pearl Street and Lucas Avenue for the exploitation of limestone in the 17th through 19th centuries, and then more visibly in Ponckhockie, where large mines of the 19th-century Newark Lime and Cement Company still exist below Hasbrouck Park. Lime kilns, which are large stone structures for processing raw limestone into powdered lime, are also still visible along Wilbur Avenue and on Abeel Street near the Rondout Creek.

The bedrock geology of the Kingston area, which would also include the town of Ulster, is rich in stone, clay, and sands that were exploited by Native Americans as well as European colonists from the Dutch colonial period right up to the present.

Soils

The surficial geology and resulting soils in the city of Kingston can be divided into several areas. In terms of overall square footage, the largest is a sand terrace that extends from North Front Street southeast past Greenkill Avenue to the edge of "Jacob's Valley,"[2] and then extends north to the corporate boundary and west to the drop-off to the floodplain of the Esopus Creek. This soil is called Riverhead fine sandy loam (3–8% slopes) and is described as "deep, well drained, nearly level soil formed mainly in water-laid deltaic deposits from streams that entered glacial lakes. It is on the top of deltas, and some areas extend more than one mile. Most areas are irregular in shape and are 25 to 400 acres in size" (Tornes 1979, 63). This relatively level sand terrace extends into the town of Ulster past the old IBM complex and begins to be broken up by other soil units north of Route 209 in Lake Katrine. Between this sand terrace and the Esopus Creek, the soils are generally classified as Unadilla silt loam, Tioga fine sandy loam, Raynham silt loam, and Canandaigua silt loam. These four soil units were formed in gravel-free water deposited material (Tornes 1979, 81), water-laid deposits (60), alluvium (77), and lacustrine deposits (20), respectively. The key in understanding the deposition of these materials is that the soils formed as the result of either postglacial lakes or later alluvial reworking by the Esopus Creek.

In the northwest corner of the city, uphill behind Dietz Stadium and further to the south as far as Linderman Avenue, the soils consist of the Plainfield-Rock outcrop complex, rolling, which consists of "about 65 percent Plainfield loamy sand, 15 percent rock outcrop, and 20 percent soils of minor extent"; areas of this soil consist "mainly of the Plainfield soil between a series of folded shale, siltstone, sandstone and limestone bedrock ridges" (Tornes 1979, 59). This unit also makes up the soils from along the ridge at the corner of Flatbush Avenue and East Chester Street bypass south to approximately the area of the train trestle on the Rondout Creek.

Wrapping around the inner corporate boundary of Kingston from about Route 32 to the Rondout Creek and around to north of Kingston Point (Tornes 1979) is a large grouping of soils, which include the Bath-Nassau rock outcrop complex, hilly; Riverhead fine sandy loam, 3–8% slopes; Stockbridge-Farmington Rock outcrop complex, hilly; Nassau-Bath-Rock outcrop complex, very steep; Bath-Nassau complex, 8–25% slopes; Farmington-Rock outcrop complex, steep; Stockbridge-Farmington gravelly silt loams, 8–15% slopes; and Williamson silt loam, 3–8% slopes.

Lastly, we can include an important soil unit that was specifically exploited by Native Americans, the 17th-century Dutch, and 19th- to 20th-century immigrants: clay. Exploitable clay appears in several locations in Kingston, most notably along North Front Street near Tannery Brook on Washington Avenue, where it was mined by Cornelius Hoogeboom for bricks, roofing tiles, and ceramic vessels in the 1660s through the 1680s (and possibly later). Clay pits can be found at Kingston Point, in East Kingston, in the town of Ulster, and into Saugerties, where it was extensively mined in the 19th century for stoneware and earthenware pottery as well as brick. Clay pits are also found at the same elevation in the town of Esopus along River Road. All of these clay deposits, which extend up the river to Albany and Troy, are vestiges of postglacial Lake Albany (see Hutton 2003, fig. 1).

The most important thing to keep in mind regarding soils, particularly with respect to Native American occupations, is that people generally prefer to live and camp on well-drained ground. Additionally, for past populations, well-drained sandy soils provided the perfect soil matrix for storing collected and cultivated plant foods in large storage pits. For the city of Kingston, as well as the towns of Ulster and Hurley, this is typically the Riverhead series of sandy loams. These soils commonly overlook the rich floodplain soils of the Esopus Creek, where Native Americans in the Late Woodland period grew maize, beans, and squash. Because the Esopus Creek floods in the spring and fall, Native Americans would transport their foodstuffs, whether cultivated or collected, to higher ground on these sand terraces for burial in storage pits to keep over the winter. Evidence of storage pits has been found at several archaeological sites in this area, including the Angstrom site (Cammisa et al. 2007, 2009) on Hurley Avenue, the Hurley site on Hurley Avenue (Funk 1976, 146; Hart et al. 2017), and at the Armory site near Manor Avenue (Louis Berger Group 2008). These sites are discussed at length later in the book.

Late Glacial History

The late glacial history of the Mid-Hudson Valley, and Kingston in particular, begins with the retreat of glacial ice and the colonization of the Northeast by plants, animals, and people. Feranec and Kozlowski (2016) recently dated over 45 Late Pleistocene animal remains from New York State in particular. They found that caribou (*Rangifer tarandus*) dated c. 17,970–16,450 cal. years BP (c. 16,020–14,400 BC), a time during which the Hudson Valley would have been part of a larger area comprised of an herb tundra environment. Mammoth (*Mammuthus sp.*) followed the caribou in time, with dates of c. 17,600–15,230 cal. years BP (c. 15,650–13,280 BC), at a point when the biota was herb tundra, followed by forest or park tundra. Herb tundra are open areas devoid of trees that are populated by grasses; although similar, park tundra environments have sparse numbers of trees such as spruce, fir, and alder. Mastodon (*M. americanum*) moved in at c. 14,540–14,080 cal. years BP (c. 12,590–12,130 BC) as the first boreal forests were established and the main food source for mastodon—spruce—dominated the forest. Feranec and Kozlowski provide minimal age estimates for the retreat of the Laurentide Ice Sheet at 17,250–16,640 cal. years BP (c. 15,300–14,690 BC) at 68% probability for the earliest estimate and 16,450 cal. years BP (c. 14,500 BC) at 95% probability for the latest estimate.

The Laurentide ice sheet covered what is now Kingston under approximately 2.5 miles of slowly moving ice and snow, which terminated in northern New Jersey and Long Island. Consider that most 747 jets travel at about 25,000 to 30,000 feet in elevation: the next time you see one, try to imagine an ice sheet extending from the ground to midway between the plane and the ground. That ice sheet would range from Long Island and northern New Jersey north to the Arctic.

After the retreat of the ice sheet, Kingston would have been surrounded or partially covered by a series of linked proglacial lakes at about the 240-foot elevation line, called Glacial Lake Albany, which extended from above present-day Albany south to the Hudson Highlands. The postglacial landscape would have been punctuated by large lakes, kettle ponds, and, between them, a series of high ridges running north–south that would have provided a migratory corridor for the first human inhabitants in the Northeast, the Paleoindians (see Bradley et al. 2008; Lothrop 2023; Lothrop and Bradley 2012; Lothrop et al. 2017; Lothrop, LaPorta, et al. 2018; Lothrop, Burke, et al. 2018; Peteet et al. 2009).

The Paleoindians who moved into the Hudson Valley after the glacier retreated hunted the previously mentioned animals as well as having at their availability now-extinct species such as the flat-headed peccary (*Platygonus compressus*), the giant beaver (*Castoroides ohioensis*), the musk ox (*Bootherium bombifrons*), and the extinct stag-moose (*Cervalces scotti*). Due to acidic soils, and the extended time interval between the Late Pleistocene and the present, most of these faunal (animal) remains would not survive in most of the soils that make up the archaeological record. Exceptions to this rule are localized bogs, and in Orange County, the "Black Dirt Area," which has produced the largest concentration of

Pleistocene fauna in New York State (see also Lothrop 2023; Lothrop et al. 2017; Lothrop, LaPorta, et al. 2018; Lothrop, Burke, et al. 2018).

Flora

The wild plant foods available to Native Americans in the Kingston area would have been numerous. Nuts are one such category, and these have traditionally been harvested in huge quantities during the fall. Several species of hickory (*Carya sp.*) and several species of oak (*Quercus sp.*), as well as black walnut (*Juglans nigra*) and butternut (*Juglans cinerea*) are found locally. The chestnut (*Castanea dentata*) was a major food source for Native Americans and European colonists until most of the chestnut trees succumbed to the chestnut blight (c. 1904–1940). Other foods gathered by Native Americans included wild grapes (*Vitus sp.*), staghorn sumac berries (*Rhus typhina*), raspberries/blackberries (*Rubus*), blueberries (*Vaccinium boreale*), strawberries (*Fragaria virginiana*), cattail roots (*Typha*), wild onion/leek (*Allium sp.*), Indian cucumber (*Medeola sp.*), water plantain (*Alisma*), amaranth (*Amaranthus*), and goosefoot (*Chenopodium*).

Cultivated foods utilized by Native Americans during the Late Woodland period were primarily corn (*Zea mays*), common beans (*Phaseolus vulgaris*), and several varieties of squash (*Cucurbita sp.*). These have been found archaeologically within the city of Kingston as well as on sites in Hurley (Diamond 1999a; Diamond et al. 2016; Funk 1976, 146; Hart et al. 2017) and Marbletown (Diamond 2004a).

Fauna

The wild animals available to Native Americans as sources of food, skins, fat, antler, bone tools, and decorative items such as teeth were very similar to what we see in the area today. Mammals included black bear (*Ursus americanus*), white-tailed deer (*Odocoileus virginianus*), raccoon (*Procyon lotor*), woodchuck (*Marmota monax*), porcupine (*Erethizon dorsatum*), eastern cottontail rabbit (*Sylvilagus floridanus*), beaver (*Castor canadensis*), river otter (*Lontra canadensis*), fisher (*Martes pennanti*), and several species of squirrel (*Sciurus sp.*). Birds included wild turkey (*Meleagris gallopavo*), grouse (*Bonasa umbellus*), various songbirds, and various species of ducks and geese, as well as hawks, peregrine falcons, and eagles, which were used primarily for their feathers. Reptiles such as the box turtle (*Terrapene carolina*), eastern mud turtle (*Kinosternon subrubrum*), painted turtle (*Chrysemys picta*), and snapping turtle (*Chelydra serpentina*) were also consumed. Box turtles were also utilized for their shells, which, when filled with small pebbles and outfitted with a handle, produced an excellent rattle.

Many archaeological sites have yielded samples of fish remains as well as species that are no longer extant in the Hudson Valley or that are totally extinct. One site, called the Wolfersteig site (Diamond et al. 2016), located in Hurley just 1.3 miles west of Kingston and overlooking the Esopus Creek, has given us a glimpse of the kind of fish that local Native Americans consumed c. 1300–1400 AD. This site had excellent small bone preservation, and thus a large sample of fish remains were collected from the site, particularly from several pits that were excavated. The fish included sturgeon (*Acipenser sp.*), eastern silvery minnow (*Hybognathus regius*), common shiner (*Luxilus cornutus*), creek chub (*Semotilus atromaculatus*), fallfish (*Semotilus corporalis*), white sucker (*Catostomus commersonii*), creek chubsucker (*Erimyzon oblongus*), white catfish (*Ictalurus catus*), brown bullhead (*Ameiurus nebulosus*), yellow perch (*Perca flavescens*), and sunfish (*Lepomis sp.*). Of special note, particularly given the site's location in Hurley, were three anadromous species that most likely spawned in the upper reaches of the Esopus Creek prior to construction of the Barclay Dam in Saugerties, New York, in the 19th century: sturgeon (*Acipenser sp.*), American shad (*Alosa sapidissima*), and striped bass (*Morone saxatilis*). These fish can no longer make it past the dam, which was constructed by Henry Barclay in 1826, primarily to provide waterpower for mill races and machinery (French 1860, 666). The presence of sturgeon in the upper reaches of the Esopus Creek has also been documented at other regional sites (Cammisa et al. 2009; Diamond 1999a, 47–50, app. 7; Diamond 2004b; Diamond 2023; Funk 1976, 146).

The Esopus Creek and the Hudson River provided another variety of food that is easy to gather: freshwater mussels (*Unio* and *Elliptio*). In Kingston, sites such as Angstrom (Cammisa et al. 2009) on Hurley Avenue, and Hendrickson (Eisenberg 1989) and Perry (Lewis 2018) in Ponckhockie, have yielded freshwater mussels as a portion of the Native American diet. The previously mentioned Wolfersteig site in Hurley as well as the S-2 site in the town of Ulster also contained evidence of freshwater mussels. Interestingly, two faunal species that have appeared in the archeological record as part of both the precontact period Native American diet and the Dutch colonial diet that no longer exist in the Hudson Valley are elk

(*Cervus Canadensis*) and passenger pigeon (*Ectopistes migratorius*). Elk once populated the Hudson Valley until they were exterminated locally, probably by the end of the 18th century. Processed elk remains have been identified at archaeological sites in Hurley, such as Wolfersteig, and in Kingston at the Angstrom site. The faunal collection from the Hendrickson site has not been examined by a trained faunal specialist; however, further work by a zooarchaeologist may indicate that elk is present in the Hendrickson collection as well. Elk pelts appear in a Kingston-area account book from 1712–1732, which described the exchange between Native Americans and colonials of 28 elk as peltry, meat, or animals (Waterman and Smith 2013, 52). The passenger pigeon, another component of the Native American diet, was hunted to extinction by Americans in the 19th century, with the last known bird perishing in a zoo in 1914.

Precontact Background

With the retreat of the Wisconsin Glaciation, the Mid-Hudson Valley became clear of ice by at least 14,500 BC (cal. 16,450 years BP at 95% probability; Feranec and Kozlowski 2016). As the glaciers retreated northward, a variety of plant and animal species began to colonize the glaciated landscape. Pollen analysis of the immediate postglacial landscape has indicated that an herb tundra environment characterized by occasional trees such as tamarack (*Larix laricina*), spruce (*Picea sp.*), pine (*Pinus sp.*), and birch (*Betula sp.*) was mixed with nonarboreal plants such as grasses, sedges, and herbs. The herb tundra environment would have supported a variety of Late Pleistocene mammal species such as the mammoth *(Mammuthus sp.)*, American mastodon (*M. americanum*), woodland musk ox (*Bootherium bombifrons*), stag-moose (*Cervalces scotti*), flat-headed peccary (*Platygonus compressus*), giant beaver (*Castoroides ohioensis*), Pleistocene bison (*Bison antiquus*), and caribou (*Rangifer tarandus*).

THE PALEOINDIAN PERIOD

The people who colonized the Hudson Valley during the Pleistocene, referred to as "Paleoindians," were initially thought to have been big game hunters, a premise based on earlier finds in the American Southwest. It is likely that these groups, who were highly migratory, exploited both big game such as caribou (Funk 1976, 210; Lothrop 2023) and smaller terrestrial animals and flora (Eisenberg 1976) that do not survive as well in the archaeological record. Their lifestyle, which has been gleaned through the discovery and investigation of hundreds of Paleoindian sites in the Northeast, has been characterized as "unrestricted wandering." This term implies that Paleoindians would not have had large base camps but instead traveled in smaller groups to take advantage of migratory animals and learn where resources were located on the landscape. Mental mapping probably took place as Paleoindians learned the skill sets to adapt to regional animal migration routes, lithic resource locations, and rising and falling postglacial lake levels (Lothrop 2023; Lothrop, Burke, et al. 2018). Paleoindian sites are relatively rare in the Hudson Valley. This is mainly because groups were small, and the materials they would have left behind while migrating across the landscape would have been minimal and highly scattered. Gramly and Funk (1990) defined five types of Paleoindian sites in the Northeast, with four of these being present in the Mid-Hudson Valley. These include quarrying sites, lithic workshops, possible habitation sites, and isolated finds of projectile points. Isolated finds are by far the most common (see Wellman 1982, 39–40).

Recently, there has been a more specific recategorization of northeastern fluted points that has moved us away from the simple term "Clovis," which was the projectile point named after the type site in New Mexico (see table 1.1). Bradley et al. (2008) examined numerous collections in the Northeast and regrouped fluted points[3] into eight variations over three relatively short time periods. The first is the Early Paleoindian period at c. 11,000–10,400 years BP (c. 9050–8450 BC). The projectile point types are Kings Road-Whipple, Vail-Debert, and the Bull Brook-West Athens Hill variety. The second is the Middle Paleoindian period at c. 10,300–10,100 years BP (c. 8350–8150 BC), with point types such as Michaud-Neponset, Crowfield-related, and Cormier-Nicholas varieties. The Late Paleoindian period dates c. 10,100–9500 years BP (c. 8050–7550 BC) and is characterized by two non-fluted projectile point forms: Agate Basin-related and Ste. Anne-Varney.[4] This reanalysis moves us away from simply assuming that all fluted points are "Clovis" and that they are all from the same time period and culture. Instead, we can investigate variations in Paleoindian points and flintknapping technology that reflect Paleoindian behavior over time as we attempt to map discrete movements, strategies, and the lifeways of the earliest colonizers of the post-glacial Northeast (Lothrop 2023; Lothrop et al. 2017; Lothrop, LaPorta, et al. 2018; Lothrop, Burke, et al. 2018; Rockman and Steele 2003; Spiess et al. 1998).

Table 1.1. Precontact phases in the Hudson Valley.

Phase	Dates BC/AD	RCYBP	Projectile point type(s)	Other diagnostics and pottery types
Contact	post-1609 AD	341 BP	Levanna, Madison	Glass trade beads, copper points, copper beads, white clay smoking pipes
				Kingston Incised, Munsee Incised, Wagoner Incised, Otstungo Notched
Garoga*	1500–1609 AD	450–341 BP	Levanna, Madison	Garoga Incised, Wagoner Incised, Otstungo Notched, Cayadutta Inciased
Chance*	1400–1500 AD	550–450 BP	Levanna, Madison	Chance Incised, Deowongo Incised pottery
Oak Hill*	1300–1400 AD	650–550 BP	Levanna, Madison	Oak Hill Corded, Kelso Corded pottery
Castle Creek	1200–1300 AD	750–650 BP	Levanna, Madison	Castle Creek Incised Neck, Castle Creek Beaded, Bainbridge Linear
Canandaigua	1100–1200 AD	850–750 BP	Levanna, Madison	Owasco Corded Oblique, Owasco Corded Collar, Owasco Herringbone, O-Platted
Carpenter Brook	1000–1100 AD	950–850 BP	Levanna, Madison	Carpenter Brook Cord-on-Cord pottery
Jack's Reef	600–900 AD	1350–1050 BP	Jack's Reef Pentagonal	Point Peninsula Corded, Wickham Incised, Wickham Punctate, Jack's Reef Corded
			Jack's Reef Corner-Notched	Kipp Island Crisscross, Carpenter Brook Cord-on-Cord, Wickham Corded Punctate
				Carpenter Brook Cord-on-Cord, Levanna Cord-on-Cord, Owasco Platted,
				Owasco Corded Horizontal pottery
Four Mile	c. 550–700	c. 1400–1250 BP	Greene	Petalas blades, rocker and dentate stamped pottery

Phase	Dates BC/AD	RCYBP	Projectile point type(s)	Other diagnostics and pottery types
Fox Creek	350–500 AD	1600–1450 BP	Fox Creek Stemmed	Ford Net-Marked pottery, Black Rock Trailed pottery, Petalas blades
			Fox Creek Lanceolate	Point Peninsula Plain, Point Peninsula Rocker Stamped pottery
Bushkill	400 BC–100 AD	2350–1850 BP	Rossville	Vinette Dentate, Vinette Complex Dentate pottery
Adena-Middlesex	600–200 BC	2550–2150 BP	Adena	Exotic artifacts from Midwest, Vinette Pottery, Point Peninsula Rocker Stamped
Meadowood	c. 1050–500 BC**	3000–2450 BP	Meadowood	Exotic artifacts from Midwest, Vinette 1 pottery
Orient	1100–750 BC	3050–2700 BP	Orient Fishtail	Steatite pots, Vinette 1 pottery
Frost Island	1500–1200 BC	3450–3150 BP	Susquehanna Broad	Steatite pots, Vinette 1 pottery
Snook Kill	1700–1500 BC	3650–3450 BP	Snook Kill, Mansion Inn blades	
Batten Kill	1800–1700 BC	3750–3650 BP	Genessee	
River	1900–1700 BC	3850–3650 BP	Normanskill	
Sylvan Lake/Lamoka	c.3100–1900 BC**	5500–3850 BP	Sylvan Steemed, Sylvan Side-Notched	
Vosburg	3000–2500 BC	4950–4450 BP	Vosburg, Beekman Triangle	Some ground slate points, knives. Occasional copper artifacts
			Brewerton Corner Notched	
			Brewerton Eared Triangle	
			Brewerton Side-Notched	
			Brewerton Eared Notched	

continued on next page

Table 1.1. Continued.

Phase	Dates BC/AD	RCYBP	Projectile point type(s)	Other diagnostics and pottery types
Vergennes	4600–3000 BC	6550–4950 BP	Otter Creek	Slate points, ground slate
Neville	5000–6630 BC	6950–8580 BP	Neville Stemmed, Stark Stemmed	
Kanawha	c. 6210 BC	c. 8160 BP	Kanawha Stemmed	
LeCroy	c. 6300 BC	c. 8250 BP	LeCroy bifurcates	
Kirk	c. 7200–6800 BC	c. 9150–8750 BP	Kirk Corner-Notched Kirk Stemmed/Serrated	
Charleston	c. 7900 BC	c. 9850 BP	Charleston Corner-Notched	
Palmer	c. 8050 BC	c. 10,000 BP	Palmer Corner-Notched	
Hardaway-Dalton	c. 8450 BC	c. 10,400 BP	Hardaway, Dalton	
Dalton	c. 8450 BC	c. 10,400 BP	Dalton	
Late Paleo-Indian	c. 8050–7550 BC	10,100–9,500 BP	Agate Basin related forms	Ste. Anne-Varney forms
Mid Paleo-Indian	12,250–12,050 BC	10,300–10,100 BP	Michaud-Neponset forms	Crowfield-related forms, Cormier-Nicholas forms
Early Paleo-Indian	12,950–12,350 BC	11,000–10,400 BP	Kings Road-Whipple forms	Vail-Debert forms, Bull Brook-West Athens Hill forms

* Denotes Iroquoian phases
**Hart et Al. (2023)

Again, because Paleoindians were believed to have been constantly on the move, specific site locations are difficult to find and, except in some notable cases, do not contain large numbers of artifacts or subsurface features. Isolated finds often occur as horizontally discrete finds, such as a lone projectile point in the middle of a plowed field or as one projectile point originating from a larger collection from a particular landform. That one artifact may be the only evidence that the site may have been occupied by Paleoindians during the Late Pleistocene.

The Archaic

"Archaic" is a term used to describe the time period from the end of the Paleoindian stage to the beginning of horticultural development in the Northeast. The Archaic generally began with the transition to the Holocene c. 8000 BC and continued to c. 1200 BC. The development of this term as a concept began in 1919, and, as it evolved, its meaning to archaeologists has changed over time (see Starna 1979). It is used here as a temporal bracket, with precontact adaptive changes relating to flora and fauna subsumed within three specific periods referred to as the Early, Middle, and Late Archaic.

The Early and Middle Archaic

The herb-park tundra environment in the Northeast was followed by a stage in which spruce, fir, alder, and pine overtook the park tundra and became the dominant arboreal species. This occurred after c. 10,000 BC and extended until c. 7500 BC (Fagan 1978; Salwen 1975). The Early Archaic followed the end of the Paleoindian stage at c. 8000 BC. It was characterized by a pine forest with mixed hardwoods, which, in southern New England, reached its maximum at c. 6400 BC (Beetham and Niering 1961). Early Archaic populations in the Northeast, including in the Hudson Valley, are thought to have engaged in a lifestyle called "restricted wandering," which means that they had adapted to certain river valleys or regions where they foraged for food. Because several modern forms of fauna were present in the Early Archaic, such as deer and moose, it is thought by some that the change from the Late Paleoindian to Archaic lifestyle was minimal, if it existed at all. From a material culture perspective, there appears to have been a technological change from the fluted points used by Paleoindians that were fitted to a bone foreshaft to projectile points that were hafted directly to the spear, dart, or javelin tip. These later forms of projectile did not have the capacity to be reloadable, as the fluted point would have been in the bone foreshaft. Two other artifacts that drop out of the tool inventory during the Early Archaic are scrapers with graver spurs at their corners and *pièces esquillées*. The first of these is a composite tool for scraping and engraving, which might have been used, for example, to outline the shape of a small tool, such as an awl or needle, on a larger bone, which would then have been removed for further refinement and use. The second is a tool that shows bipolar battering, meaning percussion marks at either end. This tool may have been used to "pop" the engraved shape or tool out of the larger bone or for splitting bone to access the marrow.

Historically, both the Early and Middle Archaic have been minimally represented in the archaeological record. These two time periods were initially suggested by Ritchie (1969a) and Fitting (1968) to be the result of a closed boreal forest environment,[5] where food was hard to come by for most forest dwellers (see Funk 1996). This is sometimes referred to as the "Ritchie-Fitting hypothesis" because both researchers developed this idea at about the same time (Fitting 1968; Ritchie 1969a). This particular environment would have existed from c. 10,500–9500 BP (c. 8500–7500 BC; Fagan 1978) and would have been composed mainly of spruce and fir, with slightly lesser amounts of hardwoods. These forests would not have been able to support a variety of large animals. However, Snow (1980, 168–69) has suggested that this is a simplification and that although Early Archaic forests were less productive than modern analogues, they probably held more potential than we realize.

For decades, several projectile point types, most notably the bifurcated-base forms (Ritchie 1971, plate 34), were thought to be early due their stratigraphic position on some sites, but it was not until these types had been found in the Carolina Piedmont (Coe 1964), West Virginia (Broyles 1971), and Staten Island (Ritchie and Funk 1973) with solid radiocarbon dates that patterns began to emerge. One of the most obvious trends was a change from fluted lanceolate blades with "ears," such as Dalton and Hardaway-Dalton points,[6] to corner- and side-notched projectile points. This might be indicative of the animals being pursued; of the method of hafting the stone projectile point to the spear, dart, or javelin shaft; or of a particular hunting method. Paleoindian fluted points were hafted to a bone foreshaft for quick reloading of the spear, and except for Dalton points—and a variant called Hardaway-Dalton, which are sometimes fluted—there is no evidence that this technology lasted particularly long into the Early Archaic. From this time period to the introduction of the bow and arrow, three kinds of projectiles with stone, bone, or antler points were likely used: spears, javelins, and darts.

Early and Middle Archaic cultures are often characterized in the Hudson Valley by diagnostic projectile point types and small assemblages of stone tools. From earliest to latest, these are Dalton at c. 8450 BC (cal. 10,400 BP); Hardaway-Dalton at c. 8450–8250 BC (cal. 10,400–10,200 BP); Charleston Corner-Notched at c. 7900 BC +/− 500 years (cal. 9850 BP); Palmer Corner-Notched at c. 8050 BC (cal. 10.000 BP); Kirk Stemmed, Kirk Serrated, and Kirk Corner-Notched at c. 7200–6800 BC (cal. 9150–8750 BP); Le Croy bifurcate points at c. 6300 BC (cal. 8250 BP); and Kanawha Stemmed at c. 6210 BC (cal. 8160 BP) (Broyles 1971; Coe 1964). Figure 1.2 illustrates some of these forms, although they are not from Kingston. Snow (1980, 160–66), in his discussion of Early Archaic projectile points and types, noted there are temporal overlaps in C14 dates between types from north to south as well as types that co-occur on the same site and in the same archaeological context. He suggested that some earlier south-

Figure 1.2. Top row, left to right: Dalton point, Hardaway-Dalton point, three LeCroy points. Bottom row, left to right: LeCroy point, four Kanawha points. *Source:* Photo by the author.

eastern points had longer use spans in New England (1980, 166), and this would probably hold true for the Hudson Valley as well.

The Early Archaic in the Hudson Valley is still poorly represented, but the identification of small sites has been increasing. One of the problems we face is extracting information from multicomponent sites where several thousands of years of later occupations have clouded the picture of what was happening in the Early and Middle Archaic. This is the case at Kingston Point as well as at the Ponckhockie, Hurley Avenue, and Abeel Street sites, where small numbers of Early and Middle Archaic projectile points have been found among huge numbers of artifacts from later periods.

The Middle Archaic in the Northeast (c. 6000–4000 BC) is often characterized by a mixed coniferous-deciduous forest consisting primarily of pine, alder, and birch, which eventually gave way to a pine-oak forest. This change began c. 7500 BC (cal. 9450 BP) and culminated c. 5000 BC (cal. 6950 BP). The Hudson Valley Middle Archaic is characterized by late Kanawha forms as well as two projectile point forms first identified in New Hampshire at the Neville site: the Neville point and the Stark point (Dincauze 1976). The Neville phase (or complex) dates c. 6630–5000 BC (cal. 8580–6950 BP). These two point types have analogs in the Southeast, where very similar points having relatively the same date ranges are referred to as Stanly and Morrow Mountain points, respectively (Coe 1964). Neville points and, to a lesser extent, Stark points have been found in the Mid-Hudson region (Diamond 2013; Eisenberg 1991 Funk 1991). Projectile points from this time period have been found at the Kingston Point, Ponckhockie, and Abeel Street sites. John Cross, working at the Annasnappet Pond site in Carver, Massachusetts, found both Neville and Stark points in association and produced a model of how larger points were likely reworked into smaller points after they were broken during hunting (Cross 1999). He postulated that Neville points "were atlatl dart tips, produced from bifacial preforms and maintained as hunting gear, while Stark points were 'thrusting spear tips'" (1999, 71).

The Late Archaic

The Late Archaic generally began c. 4000 BC (cal. 5950 BP) and continued until c. 1500 BC (cal. 3450 BP). It is commonly divided into three traditions. The first is called the Laurentian tradition. In the Hudson Valley, this tradition is characterized by groups adapting to a mast forest, where game, various species of nuts (such as acorn, hickory, butternut, walnut, and chestnut), and, eventually, shellfish became widely exploited. The

Laurentian in the Hudson Valley is composed of two phases: the Vergennes phase and the Vosburg phase. The Vergennes phase was first recognized in Vermont (Ritchie 1969b) and has been carbon dated at the Sylvan Lake Rockshelter in Dutchess County at 4610 BC +/− 100 years and 4030 BC +/− 120 years (Funk 1976, 306). It is characterized by the occurrence of Otter Creek projectile points along with a complex of other stone tools, such as ground slate knives and points, the *ulu*, winged bannerstones, plummet stones, adzes, celts, gouges, and small amounts of native (Great Lakes) copper artifacts. The latter are items that would have been traded, probably in a hand-to-hand manner, and originated from copper sources in the area of today's Michigan. A portion of this trade network has been documented in the Middle Ottawa Valley of Canada at the Morrison and Allumettes sites, where copper was being traded or obtained from the Michigan region during the Late Archaic (Chapdelaine and Clermont 2006). Both sites are considered workshops where native copper was turned into various items, including spiral beads, socketed harpoons, stemmed points, needles, and fishhooks. The large amounts of copper found at these two sites are not replicated on Late Archaic Hudson Valley sites, where native copper artifacts tend to be more poorly represented and typically consist of a single copper item among many lithic artifacts. Figure 1.3 shows the

Figure 1.3. Top and bottom rows: all Otter Creek points. *Source:* Photo by the author.

range of variation, flaking patterns, and toolstone common among Otter Creek points. These all have basal grinding and are not from Kingston.

The Vergennes phase was followed by the Vosburg phase, which incorporates several projectile point forms, most notably the Vosburg point as well as four variations of the Brewerton point (Funk 1988). This phase also included many of the tools from the Vergennes phase, including native copper. The Vosburg phase is characterized by at least six projectile point forms, including the Vosburg point, all four Brewerton points (see Ritchie 1971, 16–20), and a triangular form that has been called the Beekman Triangle (see Funk in Ritchie 1971, 121) or, alternatively, an "archaic triangle" (see Armory site below). There is no Brewerton phase as defined for Central New York in the Hudson Valley (Robert Funk, personal communication, 1999). Similar projectile points and stone tools have been found in Connecticut by John Pfeiffer at the Bliss site. This site, dating to c. 2750 BC (Funk 1988, 28; Pfeiffer 1984), included evidence of an oblong house pattern with a side entrance. Pfeiffer has referred to the site as part of the "Duck Bay phase," a regional Laurentian expression in Connecticut.

The second Late Archaic tradition is referred to as the "Narrow Point" tradition. In the Hudson Valley, this began with the Sylvan Lake phase (c. 3100–1900 BC/cal. 5500–3850 BP) and extended until the end of the River phase (c. 1900–1700 BC/cal. 3850–3650 BP). The Sylvan Lake phase was named after the type site at the Sylvan Lake Rockshelter in Dutchess County (Funk 1976, 148–72), and it is essentially coeval with the Lamoka phase in Central and Western New York. In many cases, sites that have Sylvan Lake phase artifacts also have projectile points that display the classic morphological attribute of Lamoka points, such as "the thick, 'unfinished' condition of the base" (Ritchie 1971, 29). This attribute is created during the flintknapping process as a result of using the original striking platform of the flake as the base of the finished projectile point. This somewhat unique process is a form of learned behavior that would have been passed on from one generation to another for the duration of the Lamoka/Sylvan Lake phase.

The River phase is the second phase of the Narrow Point tradition and is characterized by small to medium-sized side-notched points called Normanskill points, which date c. 1900–1700 BC (cal. 3850–3650 BP). These points do not have the unfinished base of the previously discussed Lamoka/Sylvan Lake type, suggesting a change in lithic reduction planning that likely had to do with a change in the hafting method. Sylvan Lake/

Lamoka points likely had more of a socket drilled out of the end of the javelin, dart, or spear, whereas Normanskill points were hafted using the side notch for attachment. The type site for the River phase is the River site near Cohoes, New York (Ritchie 1958a, 34–53), which was excavated by avocational archaeologists between 1941 and 1949.

The third tradition in the Late Archaic period is the Susquehanna tradition. This is sometimes called the "broad-spear tradition" because the projectile point types associated with it are larger, wider, and heavier than earlier projectile point forms. Two phases are most relevant to the Hudson Valley: the Batten Kill phase (c. 1800–1700 BC/cal. 3750–3650 BP) and the Snook Kill phase (c. 1700–1500 BC/cal. 3650–3450 BP). The first of the two is poorly represented in archaeological excavations and collections in the Hudson Valley. The second is more commonly represented in excavations in the Hudson Valley and in the Kingston area, in particular.

The Batten Kill phase has as its prime diagnostic artifact the Genessee point, which is a large-bladed point with a square stem for hafting. Although the Batten Kill phase is somewhat poorly represented in the Hudson Valley (Funk 1976, 261–63), the Snook Kill phase (259–60) is not. Most multicomponent sites with large samples of artifacts have at least some artifacts representing an occupation during the Snook Kill phase. Interestingly, the people of this phase also appeared to have preferences for certain kinds of lithics. Samples from archaeological sites show a clear preference for the maroon to light red cherts of the Indian River formation for the construction of projectile points and large knives. This may relate to the flaking qualities of the stone, which allowed for making large, broad projectile points, or it may relate to a cultural/ideological construct associated with the color of the stone.

A third aspect of the broad-spear tradition are finds of Perkiomen Broad points, which are rare in the Hudson Valley—so rare, in fact, that we have yet to determine how these fit into the overall picture. Currently, they are a minority projectile point form that co-occurs with other broad-spear types and may have had a specific function that we are unaware of.

The Transitional or Terminal Archaic

The next two archaeological phases are generally referred to as the Transitional or Terminal Archaic, signifying a gradual shift from a foraging lifestyle to a horticultural and, hence, more settled lifestyle. The two Transitional phases are the Frost Island phase (c. 1500–1200 BC/cal.

3450–3150 BP) and, slightly later (and probably related), the Orient phase (c. 1100–750 BC/cal. 3050–2700 BP). Around this time, at approximately 1500 BC (cal. 3450 BP) in the Northeast, we see a notable change in the way that people buried their dead. Instead of burials in base camps or in small seasonal camps, which had been the practice for thousands of years, people of the Frost Island and Orient phases began to set aside areas specifically for human burials and the rituals associated with them. These burials consisted of cremations with various kinds and amounts of artifacts broken and/or burned with the individual and then included with the cremated remains (Ritchie 1969a; Ritchie and Funk 1973, 344–45; Snow 1980).

These two archaeological phases in the Northeast are also characterized by the initial use of non-perishable containers: soapstone (or steatite) pots and pottery (Versaggi 2023). Sassaman (1999, 89) suggested that the use of soapstone vessels came into use very late in the Frost Island phase. Soapstone (talc-schist) pots were quarried from locations in Massachusetts,[7] Rhode Island, and Pennsylvania, and were probably traded via major waterways, as fragments of the pots are usually found along waterways navigable by canoe (see Sassaman 1999, 2006, 2010, 129–137; Truncer 2004; Truncer et al. 1998; Versaggi 2023). These pots were oval to slightly rectangular, with lugs or handles at the long ends, varying in size from 14 to 46 cm in length, and were probably made to resemble wooden prototypes (Snow 1980, 240). At the end of their use-life, pots were often included in burials (Ritchie 1969a; Snow 1980, 240) or turned into smaller items such as pendants or smoking pipes. Steatite pot fragments have been found on several precontact sites in and around the City of Kingston, such as the Hendrickson, Perry, Angstrom, Armory, and Sleightsburg sites.

Both the Frost Island and Orient phases are also characterized by the earliest known pottery in the Northeast, referred to as Vinette 1 pottery. This pottery is a relatively thick ceramic with a cord-decorated interior and exterior, sometimes with the addition of a small fillet of decorated clay at the lip. The use of soapstone and pottery provided other options for the way that people cooked their food. Prior to the introduction of pottery and soapstone vessels, skin bags were used to boil water. This was accomplished by using red hot stones that were dropped into the water, which cracked and gave off heat. These were then removed to be replaced by other stones until the water and the food in it were sufficiently heated and cooked. The result is what archaeologists call "fire-cracked rock," or FCR, which comprises a relatively large portion of many archaeological assemblages, particularly those from base camp locations. Pottery also served as a means for storing fats and oils, and may have been used later to store seeds for cultivation.

One other aspect of both the Frost Island and Orient phases is the increase in the use of yellow, red, and brown jasper as a toolstone for making artifacts. Many of these lithic types appear to have been traded from Pennsylvania, including steatite, which was used for making pots and ornaments. The movement of toolstone and cultigens from the southeast into the Hudson Valley was also associated with new ideas. As noted above, these had to do with changes in mortuary ritual (cremation) and the setting aside of specific locations for interring the dead away from habitation areas.

Orient phase groups probably lived in small circular or oval structures that could be easily taken down and moved or rebuilt. A probable Orient phase structure was found by avocational archaeologists James Burggraf and George Van Sickle just outside Hurley in Marbletown at the Guido site. Their excavations uncovered an oval structure that was 3.5 m long (11 ft, 5 in) by 2.74 m (9 ft) wide. Composed of approximately 22 or more posts driven into the ground, the house pattern suggested a shelter large enough for several individuals (Diamond 2004a).

The Early Woodland

The Orient phase appears to overlap in date with the Early Woodland Meadowood phase (Versaggi 1999; see also Versaggi 2023). Again, the Frost Island and Orient phases have provided evidence of the earliest use of burial ceremonialism in the Northeast, with cremations common and various trade goods being deposited with the dead or, in some cases, cremated remains. This continued in the Meadowood phase (c. 1050–500 BC/cal. 3000–2450 BP) and the succeeding Middlesex phase (c. 600 BC–200 BC/cal. 2550–2150 BP). Both phases were local components of large trade networks that spanned the country from the Midwest to the Northeast (Heckenberger et al. 1990; Spence and Fox 1986). The Meadowood phase is associated with the earlier Adena culture in the Midwest, and the Middlesex phase is part of a trade network with the Hopewell culture. These midwestern archaeological cultures were centered in Ohio, Indiana, and Illinois. During the Meadowoood and Middlesex phases, trade items included native copper from Michigan; mica from the Alleghenys; Indiana banded slate birdstones, bannerstones, and gorgets; and cultural ideas associated with these exotic items. In Kingston, several artifacts likely associated with trade with the Adena-Hopewell have been found at the Hendrickson, Kingston Point, and Abeel Street #2 sites.

In the Hudson Valley, a related but poorly understood phase is the Bushkill phase. Dr. Christopher Lindner of Bard College has viewed the Bushkill phase as a local expression of Middlesex and has documented chert microdrills during this period, which would have been used to make shell beads (Lindner and Folb 1996, 1998), as well as camp sites in the central portion of the Hudson Valley (Lindner 1992). Funk (1993, fig. 40) identified Bushkill components at both the Kuhr No. 1 site at c. 380 BC +/− 85 (I-7093; cal. 2σ 550–210 BC/cal. 2500–1740 BP) and the Westheimer site. These dates place the Bushkill phase in a period that overlaps with the Middlesex phase, indicating that it was most likely a local expression of that phase.

In the Hudson Valley, by about 450 AD (cal. 1500 BP), Adena-Hopewell-related artifacts are rare, potentially suggesting that the trade system established in the preceding Meadowood and Middlesex phases had collapsed.

The Middle and Late Woodland

The Middle and Late Woodland are time periods about which little remains known, and our assumptions about these periods rest on a few key sites. These sites are all located in New York State: the Fredenburg site near Otego (Hesse 1968), the Westheimer site near Schoharie (Ritchie and Funk 1973, 123–53), and the Ford site in Germantown (Funk 1976, 124–32). The Fox Creek phase (c. 350–500 AD/cal.1600–1450 BP) is known for its large lanceolate projectile points and net-marked pottery. The people of this phase and the Four Mile phase (see below) were probably the last in New York State to use large points for spears, javelins, and darts. These groups are thought to have practiced a centrally based foraging economy, which is best described as groups of people moving within a defined geographical area to certain locations at specific times of the year as resources in those areas became available.

Overlapping with the Fox Creek phase is a Hudson Valley phase or complex called the Four Mile phase. It is characterized by the use of Greene points, which are large lanceolate points similar to Fox Creek Lanceolates, as well as corded and smoothed-over corded pottery. Sites from the Four Mile phase include the Petalas and Tufano sites in Greene County (Funk

1976, 64–89). Food remains from the Tufano site included two sources of animal protein: sturgeon and white-tailed deer. Other animals such as turkey, bear, elk, woodchuck, turtle, and freshwater mussel were also identified. Floral remains included charred hickory nuts, acorns, berries, and seeds (Funk 1976, 89).

By about 600–900 AD (cal. 1350–1050 BP), and likely slightly overlapping with the Four Mile phase, is a phase or horizon called the Jack's Reef horizon (Rieth 2013), which is characterized by the use of corded ceramics and two projectile point types: the Jack's Reef Corner-Notched and the Jack's Reef Pentagonal. Arriving after the somewhat clunky Fox Creek Stemmed, Fox Creek Lanceolate, and Greene points of the preceding two phases, both Jack's Reef forms are thought to be the earliest "arrowheads" in the New York sequence. From an economic perspective, the Jack's Reef phase and the Four Mile phase (see also Snow 1980, 281–83) are characterized by large pits, likely used for storing acorns, other nuts, and possibly fish.

The time period c. 900–1300 AD has traditionally been divided into a number of phases in which distinct differences in pottery manufacturing techniques and decoration, as well as settlement patterns, have been used to define each phase.[8] Traditionally, the Late Woodland period began c. 1000 AD (cal. 950 BP) with the introduction of corn, beans, and squash as cultigens in a three-century time period called the "Owasco."[9] Until recently, this served as the model for Haudenosaunee (Iroquoian) development in northern New York State (Ritchie 1969a; Ritchie and Funk 1973; Snow 1980). This concept of a gradual series of archaeological phases at roughly 100-year time intervals between 900 and 1300 AD has been redefined based on updated data suggesting that there was no clear and gradual succession of phases (Gates St-Pierre 2001; Hart and Brumbach 2003). Dates for the introduction of corn and squash in New York State have now been pushed deeper into the past at the BC/AD boundary (Hart et al. 2007) and more commonly at c. 650 AD (Hart et al. 2003, 2011), while beans appear to be a relatively late introduction at c. 1300 AD (Hart and Scarry 1999). Most of these studies have focused on sites in Central New York and are based on older curated collections[10] made by the New York State Museum and the Rochester Museum and Science Center from the 1930s through the 1960s. Research into the spread and use of cultigens in the Hudson Valley is only now beginning.

By the late 13th century, settlement nucleation began among the ancestors of the Haudenosaunee in Central and Western New York State

(Hart et al. 2003, 745–46), and by 1550 AD, large, palisaded villages were the norm (Funk and Kuhn 2003; Ritchie 1969a; Ritchie and Funk 1973; Snow 1980). For about 300 years prior to European contact, the Haudenosaunee were living in small to increasingly larger palisaded villages.

In the Lower and Mid-Hudson Valleys, there is no evidence of this trend, with palisaded villages occurring only with the onset of European contact in 1609 and more commonly after c. 1650 (Diamond 1998, 1999a, 2023; Kraft 1989, 1991, 2001). During the time that the Haudenosaunee were slowly moving to larger and larger nucleated villages, the Algonquian speakers of the Hudson Valley were living in a dispersed pattern of small, unfortified hamlets composed of several longhouses each (Diamond 1999a, 2023). The tools used by Hudson Valley Algonquians from 1000 AD to European contact in 1609 are very similar to those used by their Haudenosaunee neighbors to the north. Hudson Valley projectile points are more commonly equilateral triangles (Levanna points) rather than the isosceles triangles (Madison points) used by the Haudenosaunee. Regarding pottery styles, the same similarities can be found, with high-collared, cord-wrapped, stick-decorated (c. 1300–1400 AD) as well as incised-decorated (c. 1400–contact) vessels being used by both groups. Additionally, both Hudson Valley Algonquians and the Haudenosaunee made pottery types referred to as "thickened rim varieties," which have a thickened rim with cord marked decoration, incised decoration, or notching on top and outside of the pot's rim.

European Contact

In September 1609, Henry Hudson sailed his ship the *Half Moon* into what was then referred to as the "north river" (Jameson [1909] 2010, 16–28). The Native Americans encountered by Hudson in the vicinity of the Mid-Hudson region included *Warranawankongs* and *Waornecks* (Esopus), *Wappingers* (Goddard 1978), *Catskill*, *Mohican* (Brasser 1978; Dunn 1994, 2000), and other Munsee speakers in the lower portions of the river (Grumet 1995, 2009; Kraft 2001; Ruttenber 1872). Trade between the Dutch and local Native American groups centered around the exchange of what Robert Juet, the first mate on the *Half Moon* (Jameson [1909] 2010, 21), called "trifles," which included glass beads, copper pots, knives, mouth harps, axes, and cloth. These trifles soon formed a basis for the exchange of maize, beaver, and other animal pelts—as well as land (Fried 1975; Grumet 1995, 2009; Lenig 1999; Vernon 1978). These European artifacts, when found in archaeological contexts, point to evidence of a Contact period site, feature, or "isolated find." Small but informative, they are the type artifacts for Native American sites occupied during the Contact period in Kingston and the surrounding area.

Types of Native American Sites

The kinds of sites that Native Americans inhabited were correlated with the time of the year, the size of the group, and the function of their activities. These sites can be divided, for simplicity's sake, into several basic categories, each of which is described below.

SMALL SPECIAL PURPOSE CAMPS

These types of camp sites would typically have been occupied for less than a day to several days. In most cases, the presence of stone tools and debitage, along with a lack of fire-cracked rock, would suggest that special activities were the focus and that cooking had not taken place on site. These clues suggest that the "occupation" may have been of very short duration. Small special purpose camps are typically characterized by artifacts that point to one function, such as fishing or nut processing. Alternatively, they might be represented by several hundred pieces of debitage and several formal tools, such as scrapers, utilized flakes, and projectile points. These types of sites are often referred to as "small lithic scatters" or "SLS" (see Rieth 2008). The Kingston Meadows sites, located on the floodplain of the Esopus Creek near the New York State Thruway, are classic examples of small lithic scatters. In many cases, the small amounts of debitage and the lack of even one diagnostic tool, such as a projectile point fragment, leave us wondering not only about the time period but also about the function of many of these sites. Another complicated factor is that, in many cases, what might have originally been a small special purpose camp appears archaeologically as a much larger site because of later use of, and disturbances to, the site area. Archaeological sites are often expanded horizontally by plowing and cultivation practices as well as other historic and modern activities impacting the landscape. Archaeological materials can become spread across a much larger area than the original site location, leading to potentially skewed interpretations of past human activities.

Extraction Sites or Lithic Quarries

Lithic extraction sites were of primary importance to hunter-gatherers who accessed crypto-crystalline stone for their tool kits. Several of these sites in the region include the Flint Mine Hill site in Coxsackie and more local examples such as the Millens Quarry in the town of Ulster, the Kingston Business Park, and the Ulster County Jail Prehistoric Quarry sites in Kingston. In each of these areas, groups would visit the lithic outcrops, or quarries, to remove toolstone and then work it into manageable "preforms" or "blanks" to bring back to a base camp or, alternatively, to carry it with them as part of a traveling kit on their daily rounds.[11] Related sites such as workshops and quarry-workshops were offshoots of the quarry and have been found both nearby and at a distance from the main lithic exposure. Artifacts typically found at extraction sites include large amounts of lithic debitage, hammerstones of varying sizes, stone picks, beaked tools, stone wedges, and anvil stones. Also typically found are bifacially worked pre-forms that result from removal of exterior cortex or rind to pre-prepare the material for transport and use elsewhere.

Reduction "failures" are also common on quarry sites. These are bifacial artifacts that have been roughly chipped out but where, during the course of flintknapping, the chert was impacted in a way that placed stress on a fracture plane or cleavage line in the stone and consequently broke the biface before the flintknapper had completed their process. The result is a mostly useless fragmentary biface that is usually discarded on site, and hundreds of these are typically found on quarry sites. Concerning quarry sites in the Kingston area, the black Morehouse chert visible in local limestone outcrops has extensive cleavage planes that make the production of tools a challenge (Diamond et al. 2022).

Base Camps

Base camps are usually found on deep, well-drained soils with a nearby water source. These areas were ideal locations for shelters, such as oblong, round, or oval wigwams, as well as features used in daily camp life. This would have included hearths as well as food-processing facilities such as drying racks for fish, roasting areas for nuts, and areas for hide processing. Archaeologists characterize base camps as sites that include a variety of tools with multiple functions, such as for hunting, hide processing, fishing, and plant processing, as these activities would have been carried out in locations where people spent most of their time. Base camps are a key component of Funk's (1993, 281) "centrally based wandering" settlement classification.

Seasonally Reoccupied Camps

These types of sites are in locations that were visited year after year, in some cases over centuries or millennia. The draw of these site areas likely related to water access, available foods or a specific kind of food within a wider catchment area, or simply familiarity with the site location. It is also possible that the consumption of berries, such as strawberries, black raspberries, and blackberries, when ingested and then dropped through defecation, would create seeded areas that people would return to for wild berries as well as animals that feed off them, particularly turtles.

Seasonally reoccupied camps are often difficult to interpret as associated with an individual archaeological phase or culture due to mixing of deposits. This is exacerbated in contexts such as plowed fields, where artifacts from many archaeological phases (read "cultures") are comingled by plowing. In these cases, based on projectile point forms and pottery types, we can identify which particular culture(s) used the site area, but we often cannot determine the functional use of the site for each individual culture that may have occupied the area. These types of camps fall into Funk's (1993, 281) category of "small camps" that may have been related to hunting, fishing, fowling, nut-harvesting, and kill-processing sites. Seasonally reoccupied camps in the Esopus drainage may contain from several thousand to hundreds of thousands of artifacts covering a 6,000-year time span.

Rockshelters

Rockshelters are locations where a natural rock outcrop or cliffs provide a windbreak or dry area for short-term habitation. In the Hudson Valley, most rockshelters that were utilized by Native Americans faced east, south, or southeast, away from the north and west winds. These natural structures provided a location for small groups of people to get out of inclement weather during their daily or seasonal rounds. One local Hudson Valley rockshelter in Hyde Park, the Huyler Rockshelter, faces west and may have functioned as an early to late spring site for harvesting anadromous fish, as large quantities of sturgeon and striped bass remains were found at the site (Diamond and Amorosi 2014).

In higher elevations such as in the Catskills, rockshelters provided a readily accessible location for small groups of hunters who may have been exploiting bear, elk, deer, or mountain lion from the fall through the spring (Diamond 1996a, 2013; Lindner 1998). These sites are somewhat rarer in the Kingston area, likely due to limestone mining in the 19th century, when rock overhangs and exposures would have been destroyed during extraction of building stone and lime for cement or mortar. As an archaeological resource, rockshelters have one defining negative, and that is their "visibility" (Deetz 1977). They were also used as camps during the historic period, and in the 19th and 20th centuries, many were drawn to them in search of artifacts (Lenik 1998; Schrabisch 1909, 1919, n.d.), which, in many cases, destroyed archaeological data (Sando and Johnson 2013) that would otherwise have been obtainable.

Horticultural Hamlets

Funk (1993, 281) characterized horticultural "hamlets" as "seasonal offshoots" of larger villages that would have been under one acre in size. These were typical of the Late Woodland period (c. 1000–1609 AD) and, from this time until the 1650s, would have been in and around the area of present-day Kingston. Settlements then likely moved to locations away from the stockaded Dutch encampment of *Wiltwyck*. Several village sites have been identified in the Mid-Hudson region, including within the city of Kingston, most notably at the Perry-Hendrickson and Angstrom sites. Recent collections donated to SUNY New Paltz (specifically, the George Van Sickle collection) have pointed to Late Woodland occupations on the floodplain of the Esopus Creek, which would have occurred from late spring to early fall for horticulture, with foodstuffs being moved to the well-drained soils overlooking the Esopus from the fall through the winter (see Diamond 2023, 13–22).

Horticultural Villages

Funk (1993, 281) suggested that horticultural village sites were present only in the Late Woodland to Contact periods. These sites are typically a minimum of one acre in size and are characterized as having house patterns, stockades, hearths, storage structures, refuse dumps, and a broad range of tool types. As mentioned above, this is not a common site type in the Hudson Valley, and at the current time, it is thought that it is more representative of the Haudenosaunee settlement pattern rather than an Algonquian one. Villages of this type appeared in the Hudson Valley after the onset of European contact in 1609 and appear to be modeled after the fortified villages of the Dutch (see Fried 1975). A precontact horticultural village in the Hudson Valley would likely have consisted of from one to four longhouses on a floodplain, with each structure separated by 100 to 300 feet of space between them.

Ceremonial and Mortuary Sites

Funk (1993, 282–83) described several variations of mortuary sites that have been found in the Northeast, including burial mounds, annular mounds, burials, cemeteries, ossuaries, and crematories. Individual burials and cemeteries are the two most applicable in this portion of the Hudson Valley. Native American burials have been found as isolates or as larger groupings of related individuals who were buried in the same location over long or short periods of time. In the Kingston area, they have been found primarily as isolates in association with base camp sites.

Summary

This chapter has provided the environmental setting for the introduction of the first people in the Hudson Valley and in Kingston in particular. These groups, the distant ancestors of today's Stockbridge-Munsee, lived in the Hudson Valley on tens of thousands of sites, from small special-purpose camps to larger dispersed hamlets. They extracted toolstone from local limestone outcrops as well as thrust-faulted sections of the Mt. Merino cherts that occur just outside the corporate boundary of Kingston. They also utilized glacially derived lithics such as granite, garnet amphibolite, gneiss, and cherts that were carried from north to south and were originally dropped locally as the Wisconsin Glacier retreated. Their diet consisted of all manner of mammals, fish, birds, and some reptiles. They gathered numerous kinds of nuts, berries, cattail roots, and wild plants, and, later, cultivated corn, beans, and squash. The fields they cleared for cultivation on the floodplain of the Esopus Creek became the impetus for Dutch expansion out of Fort Orange in Albany, as one of the motivations for the Dutch settlement of *Wiltwyck* was the large floodplain that could be used for the cultivation of wheat.

Chapter 2

Precontact/Contact Period Native American Sites in Kingston

Any review of precontact Native American sites in and around the city of Kingston should begin with mention of two classics from the early 20th century: William M. Beauchamp's *Aboriginal Occupation of New York* (1900) and Arthur C. Parker's *The Archaeological History of New York* (1922). These early works contain the first recorded reports of Native American sites in New York and, more importantly, the Hudson Valley and Kingston. Beauchamp (1900, 156) described two sites where artifacts were found early on in Kingston: a "village near Kingston Point" and a "village and cemetery at Ponckhockie." Parker, writing 22 years later, mentioned a "village site in the City of Kingston along the shore" and cited Beauchamp's description of the village and burial site in Ponckhockie (1922, 704). In the early days of American precontact archaeological inquiry, the only criteria for labeling a site as a "village" location was the discovery of large numbers of artifacts in a relatively concentrated area. In today's terminology, we might refer to such sites as "recurring camps" or "seasonally recurring camps," depending on the size of the site and the time period of the artifacts. However, these early works contained the first recorded reports of precontact artifacts found across New York State by collectors and farmers. The "village and burial site" documented by Beauchamp was likely encountered in two locations. The first is where clay and sand mining were common during the late 19th and early 20th centuries in an area overlooking the Hudson River. The second was in Ponckhockie proper, where streets and houses were constructed to provide housing for workers from the nearby Newark Lime and Cement Company and Hutton Brickyards.

These accounts by early New York State archaeologists formed the basis for future study of precontact archaeology in the Kingston Point and Ponckhockie areas of Kingston. Since the 1950s and, especially, the 1980s, additional precontact sites have been identified in these areas through investigations conducted by university, cultural resources management (CRM), and avocational archaeologists. The result of these studies is that this portion of Kingston, overlooking what would have been, at one point, a large postglacial lake, has been found to be characterized by Native American occupations reaching back over 11,000 years. Unfortunately, most of the occupation areas discussed by Beauchamp and Parker have been mined away for the overlying sand and underlying clay for brickmaking. In other locations, the sites have been destroyed by 19th- and 20th-century construction. What we have left in terms of data about this area of precontact activity is still somewhat sketchy, but I have attempted to track down as many extant collections as possible in order to provide a clearer picture of the precontact use and historic archaeology of the Kingston Point area. This chapter reviews the evidence for precontact Native American archaeological sites within the corporate boundary of Kingston (table 2.1a–b), beginning with Kingston Point and then moving through the city, eventually ending up at one site on the Boulevard and over 10 sites on Hurley Avenue. The first three collections discussed in this chapter provide some background on how and why collections from Kingston Point were assembled as well as where they are presently located.

Kingston Point

The site of Kingston Point has been a location for artifact collectors since the late 19th century. As already mentioned, clay and sand were mined from Kingston Point for the construction of bricks since at least the second quarter of the 19th century. This clay was deposited during the Late Pleistocene as fine silicates settled on the waters of glacial Lake Albany and sunk to the bottom. This clay layer extends up and down the Hudson River and into present-day tributaries that were once part of Lake Albany. The clay was a source of raw material for making bricks as well as ceramics. In the early 19th century, Egbert Schoonmaker and Nathan C. Bell had stoneware potteries on the point from c. 1805 to 1834 (Ketchum 1987, 129–31; Remensnyder 1963). Lying above the deep clays from the

Table 2.1a. Sites in Kingston by phase/time period.

Site	No diagnostics	Paleoindian	Early Archaic	Middle Archaic/Neville phase	Late Archaic (gen.)	Vergennes phase	Vosburg phase	Sylvan Lake/Lamoka phase	River phase	Batten Kill phase	Snook Kill phase	Frost Island phase	Orient phase	Meadowood phase	Adena-Middlesex phase	Bushkill Phase	Middle Woodland (gen.)	Fox Creek phase	Jack's Reef phase	Late Woodland (gen.)	Carpenter Brook phase	Canandaigua phase	Castle Creek phase	Oak Hill phase	Chance phase	Garoga/Initial Contact	Dutch Colonial period	British Colonial period	Colonial/Federal period	19th-century	Totals
Kingston Point		X	X	X		X	X	X	X	X	X	X	X		X	X		X		X											15
Cantines Island			X	X			X	X																						X	2
Rond. Riverpoint SSP			X				X	X					X																	X	5
Kingston Bus. Park																															
Locus 1	X																														1
Locus 2 (not exc.)																															1
Locus 3	X																														1
Locus 4	X																														1
Locus 5	X																														1
Locus 6	X																														1

continued on next page

Table 2.1a. Continued.

Site	No diagnostics	Paleoindian	Early Archaic	Middle Archaic/Neville phase	Late Archaic (gen.)	Vergennes phase	Vosburg phase	Sylvan Lake/Lamoka phase	River phase	Batten Kill phase	Snook Kill phase	Frost Island phase	Orient phase	Meadowood phase	Adena-Middlesex phase	Bushkill Phase	Middle Woodland (gen.)	Fox Creek phase	Jack's Reef phase	Late Woodland (gen.)	Carpenter Brook phase	Canandaigua phase	Castle Creek phase	Oak Hill phase	Chance phase	Garoga/Initial Contact	Dutch Colonial period	British Colonial period	Colonial/Federal period	19th-century	Totals
Hendrickson				X			X	X	X		X	X	X			X		X	X		X		X	X	X		X				X	16
Perry			X			X	X	X			X	X	X	X		X		X	X	X						X				X	15
Tammany Street								X																							1
Kingston Knolls			X																X												2
West Chestnut St. site	X																														1
Armory site						X	X		X		X	X	X																		6
Lipton St. site							X																								1
Canal Path	X																														1
Colony Liquors																															
Locus 1	X																														1
Locus 2	X																														1

Site	No diagnostics	Paleoindian	Early Archaic	Middle Archaic/Neville phase	Late Archaic (gen.)	Vergennes phase	Vosburg phase	Sylvan Lake/Lamoka phase	River phase	Batten Kill phase	Snook Kill phase	Frost Island phase	Orient phase	Meadowood phase	Adena-Middlesex phase	Bushkill Phase	Middle Woodland (gen.)	Fox Creek phase	Jack's Reef phase	Late Woodland (gen.)	Carpenter Brook phase	Canandaigua phase	Castle Creek phase	Oak Hill phase	Chance phase	Garoga/Initial Contact	Dutch Colonial period	British Colonial period	Colonial/Federal period	19th-century	Totals
Locus 3	X																														1
Locus 4	X																														1
Abeel Street (gen.)																														X	
Precontact Site #1				X							X	X	X				X														6
Precontact Site #2					X																										1
Sailor's Cove																														X	1
A11140.001248	X																														1
A11140.001249	X																														1
Ingarra site																	X														1
Ulster County Jail sites																															
Area 1	X																														1

continued on next page

Table 2.1a. Continued.

Site	No diagnostics	Paleoindian	Early Archaic	Middle Archaic/Neville phase	Late Archaic (gen.)	Vergennes phase	Vosburg phase	Sylvan Lake/Lamoka phase	River phase	Batten Kill phase	Snook Kill phase	Frost Island phase	Orient phase	Meadowood phase	Adena-Middlesex phase	Bushkill Phase	Middle Woodland (gen.)	Fox Creek phase	Jack's Reef phase	Late Woodland (gen.)	Carpenter Brook phase	Canandaigua phase	Castle Creek phase	Oak Hill phase	Chance phase	Garoga/Initial Contact	Dutch Colonial period	British Colonial period	Colonial/Federal period	19th-century	Totals
Area 2	X																														1
Area 3	X																														1
Area 4	X																														1
Area 5	X																														1
Area 6	X																														1
Area 7	X																														1

Table 2.1b. Sites in Kingston by phase/time period.

Site	No diagnostics	Paleoindian	Early Archaic	Middle Archaic/Neville phase	Late Archaic (gen.)	Vergennes phase	Vosburg phase	Sylvan Lake/Lamoka phase	River phase	Batten Kill phase	Snook Kill phase	Frost Island phase	Orient phase	Meadowood phase	Adena-Middlesex phase	Bushkill phase	Middle Woodland (gen.)	Fox Creek phase	Jack's Reef phase	Late Woodland (gen.)	Carpenter Brook phase	Canandaigua phase	Castle Creek phase	Oak Hill phase	Chance phase	Garoga/Initial Contact	Dutch Colonial period	British Colonial period	Colonial/Federal period	19th-century	Totals
Kingston Meadows																															
Locus 1	X																														1
Locus 2	X																														1
Locus 3	X																														1
Locus 4	X																														1
Locus 5	X																														1
Locus 6	X																														1
Locus 7	X																														1
Locus 8	X																														1
Locus 9	X																														1
Locus 10																				X											1
Locus 11 (not exc.)																															

continued on next page

Table 2.1b. Continued.

Site	No diagnostics	Paleoindian	Early Archaic	Middle Archaic/Neville phase	Late Archaic (gen.)	Vergennes phase	Vosburg phase	Sylvan Lake/Lamoka phase	River phase	Batten Kill phase	Snook Kill phase	Frost Island phase	Orient phase	Meadowood phase	Adena-Middlesex phase	Bushkill phase	Middle Woodland (gen.)	Fox Creek phase	Jack's Reef phase	Late Woodland (gen.)	Carpenter Brook phase	Canandaigua phase	Castle Creek phase	Oak Hill phase	Chance phase	Garoga/Initial Contact	Dutch Colonial period	British Colonial period	Colonial/Federal period	19th-century	Totals
Locus 12	X																														1
Angstrom				X		X	X	X				X	X					X	X				X	X	X						11
Duck Pond				X			X	X	X											X				X							6
Louw Bogardus House																												X	X		2
Behind 79 N. Front St.	X																											X	X		2
Clinton Avenue (NYU)																										X	X	X	X	X	5
Fred Johnston House								X																							1
Wall St./Fred Johnston																											X	X		X	3
DeWitt Plot, ODC	X																											X	X	X	4
Senate House								X					X																		

Site	No diagnostics	Paleoindian	Early Archaic	Middle Archaic/Neville phase	Late Archaic (gen.)	Vergennes phase	Vosburg phase	Sylvan Lake/Lamoka phase	River phase	Batten Kill phase	Snook Kill phase	Frost Island phase	Orient phase	Meadowood phase	Adena-Middlesex phase	Bushkill phase	Middle Woodland (gen.)	Fox Creek phase	Jack's Reef phase	Late Woodland (gen.)	Carpenter Brook phase	Canandaigua phase	Castle Creek phase	Oak Hill phase	Chance phase	Garoga/Initial Contact	Dutch Colonial period	British Colonial period	Colonial/Federal period	19th-century	Totals
Senate House (interior)																	X										X	X	X	X	5
Dutch Church	X													X														X	X	X	4
Persen House													X	X													X	X	X	X	6
Persen House garden																														X	1
Green Street/NYU	X																										X	X	X	X	5
N. C. Bell's pottery																														X	1
Reher bakery																														X	1
Twalfskill Brook																														X	1
Foundation #1																														X	1
Foundation #2																														X	1
Mary Powell																														X	1

continued on next page

Table 2.1b. Continued.

Site	No diagnostics	Paleoindian	Early Archaic	Middle Archaic/Neville phase	Late Archaic (gen.)	Vergennes phase	Vosburg phase	Sylvan Lake/Lamoka phase	River phase	Batten Kill phase	Snook Kill phase	Frost Island phase	Orient phase	Meadowood phase	Adena-Middlesex phase	Bushkill phase	Middle Woodland (gen.)	Fox Creek phase	Jack's Reef phase	Late Woodland (gen.)	Carpenter Brook phase	Canandaigua phase	Castle Creek phase	Oak Hill phase	Chance phase	Garoga/Initial Contact	Dutch Colonial period	British Colonial period	Colonial/Federal period	19th-century	Totals
Brick barges																														X	1
Pine St. A-A BG																												X	X	X	3
King. Point boats																														X	1
Kingston site	X		X				X		X	X			X												X	X	X				8
Manor site, Locus #1																										X	X				1
Manor site, Locus #2							X	X				X								X											4
Manor site, Locus #3								X				X																			2
Millens Quarry							X																								1

Site	No diagnostics	Paleoindian	Early Archaic	Middle Archaic/Neville phase	Late Archaic (gen.)	Vergennes phase	Vosburg phase	Sylvan Lake/Lamoka phase	River phase	Batten Kill phase	Snook Kill phase	Frost Island phase	Orient phase	Meadowood phase	Adena-Middlesex phase	Bushkill phase	Middle Woodland (gen.)	Fox Creek phase	Jack's Reef phase	Late Woodland (gen.)	Carpenter Brook phase	Canandaigua phase	Castle Creek phase	Oak Hill phase	Chance phase	Garoga/Initial Contact	Dutch Colonial period	British Colonial period	Colonial/Federal period	19th-century	Totals
Sleightsburg					X			X	X			X	X				X								X						7
S-2				X		X	X	X	X									X						X	X	X					9
Hurley site			X	X		X	X	X	X		X	X	X	X		X		X	X		X	X	X	X	X	X					19
# of Phases	36	1	6	8	2	6	13	14	8	2	6	10	12	4	1	4	4	6	5	5	2	1	3	5	6	6	8	11	10	24	230

Late Pleistocene Lake Albany were deep Late Pleistocene beach sands that were used to mix with the clay when making bricks (see Hutton 2003). During the Colonial period and extending into the 20th century, European immigrants brought with them their skills in brickmaking, which, when combined with the clay and sand of Kingston Point, provided a ready source for construction.

It was in these sand banks that collections of Native American artifacts were extracted in the 19th and early 20th centuries. For example, a Paleoindian projectile point—the type of spear point made by the earliest Native Americans in the region—was collected by Mr. Henry Booth from Kingston Point in 1908. This artifact is currently in the collections of the American Museum of Natural History (AMNH 20.0/2300; Diamond and Amorosi 2006). The projectile point was originally formed as a fluted point, a type dating to c. 10,000–8000 BC/cal. 11,950–9950 BP. Fluted points were made by Paleoindians for several thousand years and would have been used for big game hunting, most notably caribou. The points were made by taking one large flake (the flute) from each side of the point. This procedure made it possible to enclose the base of the point in a bone foreshaft, which was then loaded into a spear, dart, or javelin. The bone foreshaft made it possible to quickly replace the point/foreshaft after each throw. Bradley et al. (2008) have classified fluted points into early, middle, and late periods based on their morphology.

The fluted point in the Booth Collection (table 2.2) was later resharpened into a Neville point, a style characteristic of the time period c. 6630–5000 BC/cal. 6950–8580 BP. This artifact was made from good-quality waxy, mottled Western Onondaga chert and may initially have been made locally and then refashioned at a much later time. It is awe-inspiring to think that this artifact could have initially been left by a Paleoindian hunter and then found thousands of years later, to be reworked by a hunter in Middle Archaic times.

While this artifact was a stray find by Mr. Booth, other artifacts were collected during sand mining for clay, and yet other archaeological finds were more intentional. For example, during the 1920s, the principal of School #4, Mr. Ray Van Valkenbergh, brought school children out to the sand banks overlooking the Hudson River to dig and search for artifacts. The children found projectile points and knives made from chert as well as ground stone tools. The artifacts were then either sold or given to the Museum of the American Indian's Heye Foundation (1904–1990) in New York City, members of which traveled to Kingston to obtain the artifacts in

Table 2.2. Kingston Point Booth Collection/AMNH lithics.

Point Type/Tools	Green Mt. Merino chert	Black EO chert	Diabase	Red sandstone	Sandstone	Totals	% by row
Normanskill		1				1	3.3
Bare Island	1					1	3.3
Brewerton Side-Notched	1					1	3.3
Neville point	1					1	3.3
Endscraper	1					1	3.3
Reduction flake	1					1	3.3
Polished/Pecked Adze			1		1	2	6.6
Polished Adze	1					1	3.3
Beveled adze				1		1	3.3
Pitted stone/abrader					1	1	3.3
Bi-pitted stone					3	3	3.3
Spoolstone					1	1	3.3
Untyped PP's		1				1	3.3
Drills	1					1	3.3
Chert bifaces	1	9				10	33.3
Gouge					1	1	3.3
Hammerstone					2	2	6.6
Totals by lithic	8	11	1	1	9	30	
% by lithic	26.7	36.6	3.3	3.3	30		

order to add significant items to their collections.[1] With the movement of the Heye Foundation to Washington, DC, in 1990, some of these artifacts are now curated at the Smithsonian Institution.

The larger collection of artifacts from Kingston Point currently housed at the Smithsonian originated from two donors. The first was Mr. Joseph W. Keppler, who donated two chert bifaces (an artifact worked on both sides), two large Bare Island projectile points (18.8409), a "natural concretion, worked on one side, probably used as a fetish" (18.8192), and what appears to be a bear head effigy pestle made from sandstone (18.8465). The latter is very similar to a Late Archaic River phase example from the

Precontact/Contact Period Native American Sites in Kingston | 55

Bent site in Schenectady published in Ritchie's *The Archaeology of New York State* (1969a, plate 47). An equal number of artifacts ($n = 6$) in this collection were labeled "Kingston Point (Ponckhockie), Presented by School #4 of Kingston." These include a plain pestle (18.8341), a "stone implement blank with three notches" (18.8340), a sandstone gouge (18.8339), a slate bannerstone (18.8337), a "slate gorget with two perforations" (18.8336), and a drill (18.8338).

A variety of items were also found at this site by Mr. Frank Parslow, a member of the Mid-Hudson chapter of the New York State Archaeological Association (NYSAA). The artifacts that were still in his possession when I examined his collection in 2003 included a sinewstone, a bannerstone, and numerous projectile points from the Archaic (Otter Creek, Vosburg, Brewerton, Lamoka, Normanskill, Snook Kill), Transitional Archaic (Orient), Middle Woodland (Jack's Reef), and Late Woodland (Levanna) periods. The collection also included scrapers, knives, and pottery.

The collections at both the American Museum of Natural History and Heye Foundation are localized to "Kingston Point," but it is most likely that any artifacts with that provenience are from the sand banks overlooking the point rather than the low ground, which was referred to in the 18th and 19th centuries as "Cantine's Island." Another example, one of several Paleoindian artifacts from Kingston and probably one of the best known, was also found at Kingston Point. In his publication *Traces of Early Man in the Northeast*, Ritchie (1958b, 84) described the find spot as "on a high sand bluff overlooking Hudson and mouth of Rondout Creek. Dug from c. 4 feet below surface (2 feet dark refuse, 2 feet clear sand)." He added that the "overlying 2 feet dark refuse contained Laurentian and other artifacts." The Laurentian tradition in the Northeast is dated c. 4000–2500 BC (cal. 5950–4450 BP). The Paleoindian fluted point from Kingston Point is one of 33 from the Wallkill and Rondout Valleys that are currently under study (Lothrop et al. 2017, Lothrop, LaPorta, et al. 2018a). Jonathan Lothrop of the New York State Museum has suggested that the fluted point mentioned in Ritchie's 1958 volume has characteristics that would date it to either the Early or Middle Paleoindian time periods (c. 10,950–9650 BC/cal.12,900–11,600 BP).

The Booth Collection/Kingston Point

In the American Museum of Natural History archaeological collections is a set of artifacts from Kingston originating from the Henry Booth Collection.[2]

These are divided into artifacts simply labeled "Kingston," with no other form of provenience, and "Kingston Point," which is much more specific. Those labeled "Kingston" include two chert blades, one blade tip, two Genesee points, 20 bifaces, two Snook Kill points, one core fragment, one large flake, one flake knife, one Vosburg point, one large Levanna point, one Lamoka/Sylvan Stemmed point, and two projectile point fragments. These materials may have originated from Kingston Point or from anywhere along the Hudson River, or even from the sand pits at the Hutton Brickyards.

Artifacts specifically labeled "Kingston Point" are shown in table 2.2. This collection is heavily weighted toward large ground stone tools and pitted stones. The woodworking tools (adze, gouges) from this small collection of 30 artifacts numbers five, or almost 17% of the collection. This probably speaks to both the kinds of artifacts that Mr. Booth was acquiring during this time period and the kinds of artifacts that were being found around Kingston during the first decade of the 20th century.

The CR Collection/Kingston Point

In recent years, Mr. Jay Ciccone has investigated a surface collection of materials obtained from Kingston Point in the 1950s and early 1960s, called the "CR Collection." The collection includes 147 artifacts, with at least one Paleoindian artifact—a fluted point made of what appears to be pink chert.

An analysis of the CR collection provides us with our best glimpse of who may have camped on the terrace at Kingston Point (table 2.3) long before it was mined away for clay and sand. In addition to the fluted point, there are several types of Early Archaic points made from exotic materials (fig. 2.1). Two Kirk Serrated[3] are what appears to be Mount Jasper rhyolite, a New Hampshire lithic, while two Kanawha Stemmed points are composed of Kanawha, West Virginia, black chert[4] and an unknown gray chert. In *The St. Albans Site, Kanawha County, West Virginia*, Bettye Broyles (1971, 59) noted that most of the Kanawha points from the St. Albans site were black Kanawha chert, but some were made from gray chert. It is interesting that these five early projectile points ranging from the Paleoindian period to the Early Archaic were all made of lithics obtained from nonlocal sources. This points to two possibilities. The first is that it certainly represents the high degree of mobility that people experienced during these time periods (Lothrop 2023). The second is that small groups of hunters and gatherers transported previously accessed toolstone from the far Northeast and the Southeast into the Hudson Valley, a region

Table 2.3. CR Collection of Kingston Point artifacts by type and lithic.

Point Type/Tools	Green Mt. Merino chert	Indian River chert	Black EO chert	Waxy Gray WO chert	Brown chert	Black Kanawha chert (?)	Pink chert	Mt. Jasper rhyolite	Oriskany chert	Gray chert	Slate	Patinated chert	Quartz crystal	Grey quartzite	Silicified sandstone	Sandstone	Totals	% by row
Levanna/Madison	15	1	15	3					1	1			1	3			40	27.1
Jack's Reef Pent.	1		1														2	1.4
Adena	1																1	0.7
Orient Fishtail	2		3														5	3.4
Susquehanna Br.	2																2	1.4
Snook Kill	2																2	1.4
Genesee	2		1														3	2
Normanskill	4	1	5										1				11	7.5
Bare Island		1															1	0.7
Sylvan Stemmed	10	1	4		6									2	1		24	16.2
Beekman Triangle												2					2	1.4
Brewerton ET	1		1		1								1		1		5	3.4
Brewerton SN	2				1												3	2

Point Type/Tools	Green Mt. Merino chert	Indian River chert	Black EO chert	Waxy Gray WO chert	Brown chert	Black Kanawha chert (?)	Pink chert	Mt. Jasper rhyolite	Oriskany chert	Gray chert	Slate	Patinated chert	Quartz crystal	Grey quartzite	Silicified sandstone	Sandstone	Totals	% by row
Vosburg	2																2	1.4
Otter Creek	3																3	2
Neville	1				1												2	1.4
Kanawaha						1				1							2	1.4
Kirk Serrated								2									2	1.4
Fluted point							1										1	0.7
Untyped PP's	7		3								1		2				13	8.8
Drills	2		2														4	2.7
Chert bifaces	5		3														8	5.4
Pitted stone/HS																5	5	3.4
Pestle																2	2	1.4
Gouge																1	1	0.7
Grooved axe																1	1	0.7
Totals by lithic	62	4	38	3	9	1	1	2	1	2	1	2	5	5	2	9	147	
% by lithic	42.1	2.7	26	2	6	0.7	0.7	1.4	0.7	1.4	0.7	1.4	3.4	3.4	1.4	6	###	100%

Figure 2.1. CR Collection, Kingston Point. Top row, left to right: two Kirk Serrated points, two Kanawha Stemmed points, two Neville Stemmed points. Bottom row, left to right: three Otter Creek points, one Beekman Triangle point, two Vosburg points. *Source:* Photo by the author.

they may have been unfamiliar with. Archaeologists refer to these types of materials as "curated" artifacts, that is, artifacts that are kept, sometimes reworked into tools with new functions, and often carried for long distances. These materials are then sometimes found archaeologically in a location far from the original toolstone source.

The Middle Archaic is represented in this collection by two Neville points, one of local Mt. Merino Chert and the other of a brown chert that is likely from the Onondaga formation. From this time period on, all of the projectile points from this collection were made from locally derived toolstone (table 2.3).

The Late Archaic Laurentian tradition, composed of the Vergennes and Vosburg phases, is represented by three Otter Creek, two Vosburg, and eight Brewerton points, as well as two Beekman triangles (fig. 2.1). Other Late Archaic phases are represented by Sylvan Stemmed/Lamoka points ($n = 24$) (fig. 2.2), a Bare Island point ($n = 1$), Normanskill points ($n = 11$), Genesee points ($n = 3$) (fig. 2.3), and Snook Kill points ($n = 2$) (fig. 2.4).

Figure 2.2. CR Collection, Kingston Point. Top row, left to right; nine Sylvan Stemmed/Lamoka points. Bottom row, left to right; nine Sylvan Stemmed/Lamoka points. *Source:* Photo by the author.

Figure 2.3. CR Collection, Kingston Point. On left, two Genesee points. On right, seven Normanskill points. *Source:* Photo by the author.

Figure 2.4. CR Collection, Kingston Point. Upper row, left to right: two Snook Kill points, two Susquehanna Broad points, three Orient Fishtail points. Bottom row, left to right: one Adena point, two Rossville-like points, two Jack's Reef Pentagonal points. *Source:* Photo by the author.

The Transitional Archaic is represented in this collection by two Susquehanna Broad and five Orient Fishtail points (fig. 2.4). Artifacts from the Early and Middle Woodland periods include, respectively, one Adena point and two Jack's Reef pentagonal points (fig. 2.4). The Late Woodland is the most well-represented time period at this site, with a combined total of 35 Levanna (equilateral triangle) and Madison (isosceles triangle) points (fig. 2.5).

Other artifacts from this collection include fabricating and processing tools such as drills ($n = 4$), chert bifaces that are most likely knives ($n = 8$), one ground stone gouge, and one ¾-grooved axe (fig. 2.6). Plant processing tools are represented by five pitted nutting stones and two pestles (fig. 2.6). The presence of these tools points to the processing of food,

Figure 2.5. CR Collection, Kingston Point. Selection of Levanna and Madison points. *Source:* Photo by the author.

Figure 2.6. CR Collection, Kingston Point. Top row, left: ¾ grooved axe. Below, left: gouge. At right: two pestles. All sandstone. *Source:* Photo by the author.

which, at times, would have been stored in pit features in the well-sorted sands that likely characterized the site during that time.

Sailor's Cove

As part of a Phase 1B archaeological study of the Sailor's Cove housing project, located at the site of the former Hutton Brickyards, 39 shovel tests were excavated along the bluffs around the edge of the 19th- to 20th-century clay pit for the brickyard (Diamond 2004c). This testing sampled remnant soils on the site that had not been mined for brickmaking and still retained their integrity as a sand layer overlying clay. The shovel tests identified two prehistoric sites (Office of Parks, Recreation, and Historic Preservation #11140.001248 and #11140.001249). Neither of the two sites yielded temporally or culturally diagnostic artifacts, so the specific time period of the sites is unknown. What was found instead was a variety of lithic debitage (or waste flakes from tool manufacturing) along the edge of the clay pit.

Overall, one of the artifact types most conspicuously absent from the collections deriving from the Kingston Point sand banks is precontact pottery. Frank Parslow, cited above, mentioned that he had found some fragments, but given the large numbers of triangular points in the CR collection, there should also be pottery represented, as triangular points overlap in time with the use of multiple pottery types in New York State. Triangular points such as the Levanna and Madison types originated c. 900 AD and are commonly found with Late Woodland pottery. It is possible that collectors or others who were digging to look for stone tools were not looking for pottery or that the small fragments of dark brown ceramics were not noticed or not found interesting enough to keep.

Cantine's Island

During a Phase 1A archaeological reconnaissance of the city of Kingston (Diamond 1990), a walkover of what is referred to on historic maps as "Cantine's Island" was conducted. This is the somewhat rocky and bushy area of Kingston Point along the Hudson River, and it is separated from the mainland by an area of fill that is now home to playing fields and parking lots.[5] De Laet described this area c. 1625–1640 in his *New World*:

"This reach extends to another narrow pass, where on the west side of the river, there is a sharp point of land that juts out, with some shoals, and opposite a bend in the river, on which another nation of savages, the *Waoranecks*, have their abode at a place called Esopus. A little beyond on the west side, where there is a creek, and the river becomes more shallow, the *Waranawankougs* reside; here are several small islands" (Jameson [1909] 2010, 46). During the 19th century in this area, there was road construction, bulkhead building along the shoreline, industrial impacts, a railway line, and impacts related to the creation of a riverside park (see Blauweiss and Berelowitz 2022, 76–83). Although the ground in this area has been disturbed by mining activity, building construction, and stoneware production from the 18th century onward, there are still locations where intact soils retain archaeological sites and features. During a 1990 Phase 1A survey, small amounts of lithic debitage and one Neville Stemmed point were found on the surface (Diamond 1990; sites 10-P-59/USN #11140.001 and 10-P-60/USN #11140.001). The projectile point is a rare and early find within the corporate boundary of Kingston. The Middle Archaic Neville phase at c. 6630–5000 BC (cal. 8580–6950 BP) has been found only at the Hendrickson site, the Abeel Street Precontact Site #1, and the Angstrom site. These four sites are the only evidence for the Neville phase in Kingston.

Rondout Riverfront Shoreline Stabilization at Kingston Point

In 2019, in advance of Kingston's Riverpoint Shoreline project, a CRM study was conducted to examine a trail from near one of the exiting pavilions on site to the Hudson River at Kingston Point. A Phase 1A archaeological sensitivity assessment determined that three locations within the planned project area should be tested for archaeological resources through a Phase 1B investigation. This study identified evidence of Native American occupations buried below multiple layers of historic fill on the gravel road leading out to the point. A Phase 2 investigation was then designed to gather information about the site to determine whether it met the criteria for inclusion in the National Register of Historic Places (Gade et al. 2021). The archaeological study included the excavation of 25 shovel tests and four 1-meter units. The precontact components identified consisted of 26 projectile points, of which 21 were typable. These were one bifurcated base point, seven Brewerton points, six Lamoka points, five Bare Island points, one Wading River point, and one Orient Fishtail point. Also recovered during the excavations were 33 bifaces, 69 flake tools, 1,969 debitage, 42 cobble tools, and 9 cores, in addition to fire-cracked rock (FCR), organic remains, and faunal remains. This precontact site met the criteria for inclusion in the National Register of Historic Places under Criterion D, which requires that "the site must have, or have had, information to contribute to our understanding of human history or prehistory, (and) the information must be considered important" (National Register Bulletin 1997). The site had intact strata, features, and faunal and macrobotanical remains as well as excellent C14 dates.

In contrast, historic debris overlying the precontact component was not considered eligible for listing on the National Register. This collection of historic artifacts included 328 ceramics, 125 glass, 56 metal, and 17 tobacco pipe fragments that were all contained within several fill episodes. In general, historic artifacts found within fill episodes, because we have no idea where they originated, do not meet eligibility requirements for listing on the National Register of Historic Places.

In addition to the collections of artifacts retrieved during the archaeological excavations, 13 precontact features were also identified. This is a very high number of features considering the small area of horizontal exposure from the excavations. Six were identified as pits, two were pit/post molds, one was a post mold, two were FCR concentration/roasting pits, one was a burned soil stain, and one was thought to be midden (i.e., refuse) debris/fill from a slightly semi-subterranean precontact house structure. If confirmed through more expansive excavations, such as a Phase 3 data recovery study, it would be unique in the Hudson Valley and, in a larger perspective, all of New York State. The authors of the study (Gade et al. 2021, 27–28) drew comparisons between what they found at Kingston Point and similar structures at the Late Archaic Davidson site in Southern Ontario (Ellis et al. 2014). One structure at this site was about 5 meters (16 ft) in diameter, with a meter (39 in) deep basin, a sloping entranceway, and four support posts for a roof. There also appeared to be a narrow bench or shelf around the interior wall. We currently have no evidence of similar structures in the Hudson Valley, and it is worth wondering whether the features found at this site may represent a special-use structure designed to accommodate people along the Hudson River during the early to late spring when sturgeon, striped bass, shad, and alewives are engaged in their spring spawning run. In addition to riverine fauna representing a spring occupation, the presence of snake and turtle fragments from the excavation units suggest that these precontact occupations extended from spring into the summer.

Radiometric dates, similar to projectile points, place the features within the Late Archaic period. One feature, a circular basin-shaped pit, yielded a date of cal. 5753–5601 BP or cal. 3804–3652 BC at the 95.4% confidence level (Beta-581839). A Bare Island projectile point was also found in the matrix of this feature. Another feature, a post mold, yielded a date of cal. 4359–4150 BP or cal. 2410–2201 BC at the 95.4% confidence level (Beta-581840). After sorting out the stratigraphic relationships visible in the wall profiles and soil matrices noted during the excavation, the excavators concluded that "the Late Archaic midden at Kingston Point is a complex, layered array of FCR roasting features, house basin middens, and backdirt splays interspersed with superimposed and intrusive pit and post features" (Gade et al. 2021, 20).

An analysis of the collection of faunal remains from the site by Dr. Marie-Lorraine Pipes identified Archaic period faunal remains such as small-, medium-, and large-sized mammals, including white tailed deer; unidentified bird remains; Atlantic tomcod, sturgeon, and other unidentified fish; hard shell clam; and unidentified snake and turtle remains. To summarize the faunal remains, Pipes noted that

> all of the fish remains point to intensive fishing activities. Disposal of fish refuse by intensive burning may indicate that fish were being smoked or dried. The recovery of similar fish remains over an extended period of time reveals the importance of this location for fish procurement. The relatively small amount of mammal bone recovered from the same deposits as fish suggests that fishing was the primary reason for the site occupation. Aside from later historic domesticated mammal species, the majority of mammal bone fragments were not identified by element. The exceptions to this include the deer antler fragments, which could be tool-related, and a deer foot bone. The presence of two bone points, a bone scraper, and one other bone tool suggest that mammal bone raw material may have been used for making tools [Gade et al. 2021, app. F].

This excavation at Kingston Point is one of the most important within the corporate boundary of the city. Because of the historic fill layers overlying and protecting the precontact levels, the site provides an undisturbed window into Kingston's deep past. In addition to intact features, excellent faunal preservation, and a possible semi-subterranean house, this collection also includes a large assemblage of ground slate artifacts. Although six ground slate artifacts (projectile points, awl, abrader, and unidentified artifacts) may not seem like a lot, these were identified within a relatively small area. These ground slate objects, which are rare in the Hudson Valley, were tools used during the Laurentian Tradition and have sometimes been found associated with Otter Creek, Brewerton, and Vosburg projectile points.

Kingston Business Park Precontact Sites

The Kingston Business Park was initially tested for the presence of archaeological sites in 1995 by Hartgen Archeological Associates, Inc. (HAA), prior to the construction of the present industrial complex at the top of Corporate Drive. The Phase 1B study consisted of 190 shovel tests, which identified 412 lithic artifacts across six prehistoric site loci (HAA 1995a). The subsequent combined Phase 2/3 study (HAA 1995a) sampled larger areas within these six loci in an attempt to determine whether the site areas were eligible for listing on the National Register of Historic Places, and then to mitigate the impacts of the proposed construction on eligible sites. The focus of the Phase 2/3 study was (1) to establish the chronology of site use; (2) to determine whether the prehistoric loci represented "specialized activity areas, specific to procurement, reduction, or habitation, or do the activities overlap"; and (3) "how the lithic assemblages adhere to the typical quarry plan" (HAA 1995b, 11). To a certain extent, the archaeologists realized that, due to the large areas of exposed bedrock in the project area, the only kind of sites that would likely be in this location were those associated with lithic quarrying and reduction.

The artifacts from the six loci were classified into ten categories: chert flakes, chert trim flakes, chert block flakes, chert shatter fragments, chert cores, quarry debris fragments, matrix blocks, and Biface I, Biface II, and Biface III. The first seven relate to the extraction of chert and the initial processing of stone at the quarry site. The latter three are the developmental stages that a piece of toolstone takes during its transformation from a simple rock to a completed biface (Biface III), which can then be removed from the quarry and worked elsewhere. This reduction process removes unwanted limestone matrix and unusable cortex, ultimately leaving the flintknapper with a piece of worked stone that has gone through part of the reduction process and remained intact. One of the most common artifacts found at quarry sites are "reduction failures," or pieces in which the stone did not survive repeated attempts to remove unwanted matrix or cortex due to stress fractures or impurities in the stone.

Locus 1 was identified as a quarry site, which was sampled through a controlled surface reconnaissance by archaeogeologist Dr. Philip LaPorta. A total of 111 artifacts were found on the surface, most of which were shatter fragments (68%), flakes (16%), and trim flakes (12%) (HAA 1995b, 32). Of the total, 48 (43%) were Onondaga chert, 34 (30%) were Esopus chert and shale, 18 (16%) were Coeymans chert, 8 (7%) were Kalkberg chert, 2 (4%) were Normanskill chert, and 1 was Glenerie chert (HAA 1995b, 32). Of these types, 73% were locally available cherts and 27% were mined from the existing outcrops.

Locus 2 was identified as a rockshelter. Because it would not be impacted by the proposed construction, it was not tested as part of the Phase 3 investigation. This has become the preferred method for archaeologists and planners at the Office of Parks, Recreation, and Historic Preservation (OPRHP) to preserve sites for future research. This rockshelter is one of very few remaining within the corporate boundary of the city of Kingston. It is very likely that the limestone cliffs of the Newark Lime and Cement Company that were mined in the 19th century also contained similar precontact Native American deposits that were destroyed.

Locus 3 was thought to be a habitation site. A corner-notched projectile point was identified in this location during the Phase 1B investigation, and while it was not complete enough to be typeable, it may have originated from either the Late Archaic Vosburg phase (c. 3000–2500 BC) or the Middle Woodland Jack's Reef phase (c. 600–900 AD). The Phase 2/3 study identified 164 artifacts, 80 (49%) of which were shatter fragments, 31 (19%) of which were block flakes, 28 (17%) of which were trim flakes, 21 (13%) were flakes, and 4 (2%) were classified as quarry debris. Whereas Locus 1 yielded six types of lithics, Locus 3 produced 11 types. The cherts from this locus were represented by 106 (65%) Onondaga chert, 26 (16%) Coeymans chert, and 12 (7%) Esopus chert, with the remaining 12% consisting of a variety of others, including Normanskill, Kalkberg, Glenerie, Oriskany, Limeport, Epler, Rickenback, and New Scotland chert (HAA 1995b, 33).

Locus 4 was a workshop/quarry site located on a small knoll. Artifacts from the Phase 2/3 study totaled 170, with 72 (42%) shatter fragments, 39 flakes (23%), 30 block flakes (17%), 28 trim flakes (16%), and a quarry debris fragment (HAA 1995b, 34). The lithic materials included 82 (48%) Onondaga chert, 58 (34%) Esopus chert, 10 (6%) Coeymans chert, 8 (5%) Glenerie chert, and 6 (4%) Normanskill chert, with the remaining 3% consisting of Knaderack, Kalkberg, and Rickenback cherts. Of the debitage assemblage, 93% derived from the local area, 6% were extracted from existing outcrops, and 1% derived from the upper Wallkill Valley (HAA 1995b, 34–35). The latter was probably from a tool that was carried to the site and was resharpened while quarrying for other stone was taking place.

Locus 5 was a quarry site along a limestone outcrop. Artifacts from this location totaled 383, including 210 (55%) shatter fragments, 106 (28%) block flakes, 39 (10%) trim flakes, and 28 (7%) other flakes. According to the report, "the percentage of chert shatter fragments and block flakes (83%) to chert flakes and trim flakes was significantly greater indicating that chert block reduction and separation of chert from the matrix were the primary activities" (HAA 1995b, 35). The debitage consisted of 214 (56%) Onondaga chert, 75 (20%) Coeymans chert, 49 (13%) Esopus chert, 22 (6%) Kalkberg chert, 16 (4%) Normanskill chert, and the remaining 1% was New Scotland, Oriskany, Manlius, Glenerie, and Epler cherts. In total, 74% of the cherts were derived from the surrounding area and 26% were extracted from existing outcrops (HAA 1995b, 35–36).

Locus 6 was classified as a workshop. Artifacts from this locus totaled 745, including 127 (17%) shatter fragments, 72 (9%) block flakes, 144 (19%) trim flakes, and 384 (52%) other flakes. According to the report, "the percentage of chert flakes and trim flakes (72%) to chert shatter, block flakes and debris (28%) indicates that primary and secondary biface reduction were the predominant activities at this site" (HAA 1995b, 36). The debitage included 495 (66%) Normanskill chert, 157 (21%) Onondaga chert, 51 (7%) Esopus chert, and 27 (4%) Coeymans chert; the remaining 2% were from Glenerie, New Scotland, Oriskany, Becraft, and Epler cherts. In total, 95% of the materials were derived from the surrounding area and 5% were extracted from existing outcrops (HAA 1995b, 37).

Fifteen hammerstones, produced from locally available Oriskany sandstone, quartzite, and graywacke, were found during the study. One granite example was likely a glacial cobble originating from northern New York. Many of the Mt. Merino (i.e., Normanskill) chert[6] artifacts collected had exterior cortex, indicating they were fashioned from river or stream cobbles. These were probably from the shore of the Hudson River or from the Rondout Creek at a time when historic fill episodes had not yet covered the original shoreline of the creek. I have found similar large, water-worn "tested" cobbles of Mt. Merino chert along the Hudson at River Road in Port Ewen.

Overall, the archaeological investigation of the Kingston Business Park site documented a high-elevation location where Native Americans exploited natural exposures of chert-bearing Coeymans, Kalkberg, Manlius, Becraft, Glenerie, and New Scotland limestones for toolstone. Based on the percentages of locally available stone that was mined at each locus compared with regional stone, these site loci are thought to be areas where better-quality stone may have been cached or reduced. LaPorta (in HAA 1995b, 45–46) viewed the chert-bearing rock outcrops as likely providing some, but not necessarily good quality, toolstone. He interpreted these quarry sites as failed attempts to mine chert on a large scale but suggested that the mine locations still served as a focus for a combination of tool maintenance and small levels of chert extraction. Similar to the Ulster County Jail quarry sites discussed later in this chapter, the locations of these chert outcrops high above Ponckhockie were likely destinations for groups who were seeking additional toolstone for specific tasks such as cutting, scraping, and shredding of plant materials.

The Hendrickson Site

The Hendrickson site is situated on a sand terrace overlooking the Rondout Creek in Ponckhockie.[7] The site was initially found and excavated by Mr. Thomas Turck in 1971. In November 2016, I had the opportunity to study Mr. Turck's collection from the site. Although there were no site notes per se, the collection was curated in boxes labeled "Hendrickson Site 1971," and the collection still retained its original integrity.[8] The lithic collection consisted of fabricating and processing tools, including five scrapers, two drills, and eight bifaces/knives (fig. 2.7). The presence of one small netsinker suggested fishing activities, while hunting was represented by two projectile point tips, three preforms, six Levanna points, one untyped point, one Meadowood point, four Normanskill points, seven Sylvan-Stemmed points, one archaic corner-notched point (which is probably a fragmentary Vosburg point), one reworked Brewerton Side-Notched, and four untyped Archaic side-notched points (fig. 2.8). One deer antler flaker was also in the collection, along with several small bones. Pottery was relatively well represented in the collection, totaling 126 fragments that

Figure 2.7. Hendrickson site/Turck collection. Fabricating and processing tools. Top row, left to right: denticulate, four scrapers, two drills. Middle row, left to right: three preforms, one biface. Bottom row, left to right: four bifaces. *Source:* Photo by the author.

Figure 2.8. Hendrickson site/Turck collection. Projectile points. Top row, left to right: one reworked Brewerton side or corner-notched point, one possible Vosburg point, three Sylvan Stemmed points, two Normanskill points. Bottom row, left to right: one Meadowood point, one Fox Creek Stemmed point, four Levanna points. *Source:* Photo by the author.

could be divided into at least ten distinct vessels. These were four Jack's Reef Corded, one dentate-stamped vessel, one Wickham Punctate, one plain undecorated rim, two Oak Hill/Kelso Corded, and one incised pot that could be dated anywhere between the Chance phase (c. 1400 AD) and the Contact period at c. 1609–1654 AD (fig. 2.9).

In the fall of 1983, Dr. Leonard Eisenberg of SUNY New Paltz contacted Frank Parslow about possible locations of Late Woodland precontact sites in Ulster County. Parslow, and probably also Tom Turck, brought him to the Hendrickson site, which was then excavated by Eisenberg from 1984 to 1986 (Eisenberg 1989). Over the course of three field seasons, a total of 92 square meters (990 sq ft) of horizontal exposure was excavated. The deposits at the Hendrickson site were quite deep, with 12 to 24 inches (30 to 61 cm) of fill from 19th-century house construction capping the precontact Native American deposits. This historic overburden overlaid both a yellow sand about 8 inches (20 cm) in thickness in some excavation units and a brown gravelly sand about 10 inches (25 cm) in thickness in other units. Underlying both of these strata was a brown sand midden, with the latter stratum containing most (59%) of the precontact Native American artifacts. Below this was a mottled yellow and brown

Figure 2.9. Hendrickson site/Turck collection. Prehistoric pottery. Top row, left to right: cord-wrapped stick decorated body sherd, four Jack's Reef Corded rim fragments, one Wickham Punctate. Bottom row, left to right: drilled mend whole from pot, three plain undecorated rim fragments, one Oak Hill/Kelso Corded, one incised Late Woodland fragment (c. 1400 AD–Contact). *Source:* Photo by the author.

sandy silt, which extended to 4.5 feet (140 cm) in depth and accounted for 12% of the Native American artifacts found. In total, the excavations identified 2,424 stone tools, 10 bone and antler tools, 613 potsherds, and 41,739 debitage (Eisenberg 1989, 31).

Ninety-eight percent of the stone tools found at the site were produced from locally available toolstone, such as Mt. Merino chert, Indian River chert, and various colored and mottled cherts like the Morehouse chert from the Onondaga formation. Other toolstone utilized at the site included jasper, quartz, quartzite, and "chalcedony." The latter is a white toolstone that is most famous for its outcrops at Flint Ridge, Ohio. However, since the publication of Eisenberg's work in 1989, two outcrops of white chert, one called "Eppler chert" and the other called "Harmonyvale chert," which are very similar to the Flint Ridge chert, have been found in Orange County, New York (LaPorta 1996). Previously, the occurrence of chalcedony was assumed to imply long-distance trade from Ohio. However, the location of a more local chert source that is very similar to the Ohio material indicates that more caution should be taken when inferring long-distance trade. In fact, since the Wallkill River and Rondout Creek meet in Rifton, New York, it would have been an easy journey by canoe down the Wallkill River into the Kingston area, with high-quality toolstone sourced from the Orange County region.

Regarding the midden found at the site, because of the rich organic content, the presence of mussel shells, and the use of limestone for cooking stones, the brown sand layer in the midden, as well as the mottled soil below it, contained large numbers (at least for the Mid-Hudson Valley) of bone and antler tools. These two layers yielded an antler flaker, an antler projectile point, five bone awls, a bone bead, a bone needle, and an unidentified bone tool. The presence of bone and antler tools on any site in the Hudson Valley is a rarity due to soil acidity, which typically leads to quicker decomposition of organic materials. Interestingly, testing of the soils at the site found them to be slightly basic, with a pH range between 7.2 and 8.3.

Four items of a personal nature were recovered: an early glass trade bead (Kidd Type IIb31), a bone bead, and two stone pendants, the latter of which were ground and drilled. From the shape and size of these two artifacts, they could be interpreted as "gorgets," which are ovoid to rectangular ground and perforated objects. Gorgets were initially thought to be worn by Native Americans around the neck or chest area. However, Custer and Ewasko (2022) have made a convincing case that these may represent bullroarers, which are artifacts tied to a tether and swung in circles to make various sounds.[9]

Nineteen features were found at the site, 18 of which were in the brown sand midden. These features were characterized as "concentrations of debitage, discarded artifacts, refuse animal bone, and fire-cracked rock" (Eisenberg 1989, 46). These are the kinds of features that one finds at a campsite or base camp, where tool manufacture, tool maintenance, and cooking were often undertaken around the campfire. The fact that people appeared to have been living at the site full time suggests that features would be continually dug, filled, and refilled. This redeposition is a characteristic of base camps, since pits are continually reexcavated after fires, and artifacts such as debitage, food remains, and other assorted artifacts on the surface often get moved around and reburied. The collection of artifacts found at the site are likely a combination of items relating to specific functions within the features as well as items that were unintentionally included during backfilling or daily use.

Precontact pottery from the site totaled 613 fragments, likely representing 14 or 15 distinct pottery vessels. The earliest of these is the Vinette Dentate type, which dates to about 100 years on either side of the BC/AD boundary (Hart and Brumbach 2005). The latest type is Chance Incised (c. 1400–1500 AD), a late precontact type that evolved into a different incised decorative format (Kingston Incised) just prior to European contact with the Dutch (Diamond 1999a; and see Kingston site below).

The midden debris from the Hendrickson site yielded extensive dietary information on the inhabitants of the site. Again, because the soil pH was in the basic range, the midden had excellent bone preservation, which accounts for the large amount of faunal remains. Although the collection has not been examined by a zooarchaeologist, a cursory inventory of the fauna (Eisenberg 1989, 46–48) identified large numbers of white-tailed deer (*Odocoileus virginianus*), muskrat (*Ondatra zibethicus*), woodchuck (*Marmota monax*), raccoon (*Procyon lotor*), porcupine (*Erethizon dorsatum*), squirrel (*Sciurus sp.*), rabbit (*Sylvilagus floridanus*), snapping turtle (*Chelydra serpentina*), wild turkey (*Meleagris gallopavo*), sturgeon (*Acipenser sp.*), and freshwater mussels (*Eliptico sp.* and *Unio sp.*). Eisenberg (1989, 46) noted that deer remains were the most abundant mammalian remains at the site, which is common to most Native American archaeological sites.

The Hendrickson site produced evidence that several archaeological cultures utilized the terrace overlooking the Rondout Creek over a relatively long period of time. The earliest of these was during the Neville phase c. 6630–5000 BC (cal. 8580–6950 BP). Interestingly, this phase is also represented by a Neville Projectile point that I later found while walking around at Kingston Point as well as the previously mentioned fluted point that was reworked into a Neville point (Diamond and Amorosi 2006). A mile up the Rondout Creek, a Neville point was also found at the Abeel Street Precontact Site #1 (Diamond 2014).

Later occupations at the Hendrickson site included the Vosburg phase, the Sylvan Lake/Lamoka phase, the River phase, the Snook Kill phase, the Frost Island phase, the Orient phase, the Bushkill phase, the Fox Creek phase, the Jack's Reef "horizon," the Carpenter Brook phase at c. 1000–1100 AD (cal. 950–850 BP), the Castle Creek phase at c. 1200–1300 AD (cal. 750–650 BP), and the Oak Hill phase (at c. 1300–1400 AD (cal. 650–550 BP). Just prior to, and during, European contact, the site area was inhabited during the Chance horizon (c. 1400–1500 AD/cal. 550–450 BP) and the Early Contact period (c. 1609–1652 AD), that latter of which is represented at the site by the early glass trade bead (Kidd Type IIb31). This bead type postdates 1609 in the Mohawk Valley (Snow 1995, 33), and it is safe to assume that it was left at the site during the early years of Dutch colonization of the Hudson Valley. For the Kingston area, that time period could originate from c. 1609 and extend to the early 1650s. This may also have been one of the "trifles" traded by Hudson's crew to the locals they met as the *Half Moon* entered and left the river in September of 1609. Interestingly, this bead type is white with red and blue stripes. George Hamell (1983, 1987, 1996) and others (e.g., Zawadzka 2011) have written extensively on Native American color symbolism associated with places, otherworld beings, rituals, and the cultural metaphors connected to artifacts made of certain kinds of materials and of specific colors. For the Contact period Munsee speakers of the Hudson Valley, the preferred four main colors in the early Contact period were red, white, blue, and black (see also Diamond 2023, figs. 7.7, 7.16).

The Hendrickson site midden likely represents a series of base camps and special purpose camps that were occupied by various groups of Native Americans and that extended for several millennia from c. 6630 BC to AD 300. It was initially interpreted as a village site by Eisenberg, although he was likely referring to later occupations at the site after c. AD 600 to c. AD 1650. The range of stone tools from the site relate to hunting, stone fabricating and processing tools, butchering, fishing, nut processing, and tool resharpening and maintenance. This assemblage of tools covers most of the functional categories that would be needed in a base camp situation or, alternatively, where several thousand years of sites of multiple function were located in the same place.

The Perry Site

During Eisenberg's excavation of the Hendrickson site in 1985, the Mid-Hudson chapter of the NYSAA set up an excavation in the adjacent yard, owned by the Roscoe Perry family. The excavation extended for several months and was undertaken by NYSAA members (figs. 2.10 and 2.11) Art Carver, Tom Turck, Frank Parslow, Alvin Wanzer, Jack and Donna Vargo, Richard Stewart, Ed and Roslyn Stark, and David Wanzer.

The orientation and location of the units were tied to Eisenberg's grid in the Hendrickson yard, and the archaeologists used the same techniques, screen size, and archaeological recording forms as used by SUNY New Paltz students in the adjacent yard. The Mid-Hudson chapter's excavations amounted to 16 square meters (172.2 sq ft) of horizontal surface area. Like the Hendrickson site one backyard away, the Perry site proved

Figure 2.10. Perry site 1985. Left to right: Dr. Leonard Eisenberg (SUNY New Paltz), Alvin Wanzer, Frank Parslow, Art Carver. *Source:* Photo by the author.

Figure 2.11. Perry site 1985. Left to right: Tom Turck, Frank Parslow, Richard Stewart. *Source:* Photo by the author.

to have deeply stratified deposits and relatively similar stratigraphy. The soils consisted of a deep, mixed fill called "brown sandy sod," interpreted as originating from the excavation of a 19th-century house foundation, mixed with Native American artifacts. Below this was a dark brown sand containing some precontact as well as historic artifacts. The historic overburden was 14 inches (35 cm) thick and capped the precontact Native American deposits. Below this was a medium brown sand 14 to 23 inches (35–59 cm) in depth, which overlaid a medium yellow brown sand 23 to 35 inches (59–89 cm) thick that rested on a yellow sand ranging from 35 to 40 inches (89–102 cm) in depth.

Like many sites in the Mid-Hudson Valley, particularly those on major watercourses, most of the temporally diagnostic artifacts from the Perry site dated to the Late Archaic period (c. 4000–1400 BC). However, the Early Archaic (fig. 2.12) was represented by the presence of a Charleston Corner-Notched point dating c. 7900 BC (cal. 9850 BP). This projectile point type was first identified in West Virginia (Broyles 1971, 56–57) and is relatively rare in the Mid-Atlantic region. Points of this type, as well as the Kirk Serrated and Kanawha points found at the Kingston Point

Figure 2.12. Perry site projectile points. Top row, left to right: Charleston Corner-Notched point, Otter Creek point, two Vosburg points. Bottom row, left to right: two Brewerton Eared-Notched points, Brewerton Eared-Triangle point, an untyped point. *Source:* Photo by the author.

site, likely represent the movement of small groups from the Southeast into the Northeast as the biota evolved from a mixed boreal forest into a mixed deciduous forest.

The Perry site included several Late Archaic archaeological cultures common throughout the Hudson Valley (figs. 2.12 and 2.13), including those of the Vergennes, Vosburg, Lamoka/Sylvan Lake, and Transitional Archaic Orient phases. The Early Woodland was represented by the Meadowood and Fox Creek phases, the Middle Woodland by several Jack's Reef points (fig. 2.13), and the Late Woodland by Levanna points (fig. 2.14) as well as several kinds of precontact pottery.

The Perry site has a rich artifact inventory overall, with projectile points (figs. 2.12–2.14), scrapers, drills, netsinkers (fig. 2.15), strike-a-lights, bifaces, knives, flake knives (figs. 2.16 and 2.17), nutting stones, abraders, and debitage. Projectile points from the site included 1 Charleston Cornered-Notched, 4 Otter Creek, 2 Vosburg, 5 Brewerton, 4 Sylvan Lake/

Figure 2.13. Perry site projectile points. Top row, left to right: three Sylvan Stemmed points, two untyped points, one Orient Fishtail point. Bottom row, left to right: two Meadowood points, one Fox Creek Stemmed point, two Jack's Reef Corner Notched points. *Source:* Photo by the author.

Figure 2.14. Perry site projectile points. All three rows: Levanna points. Point in lower right corner has been refashioned into a drill. *Source:* Photo by the author.

Figure 2.15. Perry site fabricating and processing tools. Top row: all scrapers. Bottom row, left to right: drill, netsinker. *Source:* Photo by the author.

Figure 2.16. Perry site fabricating and processing tools. Top row, left to right: three bifaces/knives. Bottom row, left to right: triangular biface, core. At far right is a large flake knife. *Source:* Photo by the author.

Figure 2.17. Perry site bifaces (six) made from maroon Indian River chert. *Source:* Photo by the author.

Lamoka, 1 Normanskill, 2 Bare Island, 4 Snook Kill, 2 Orient Fishtail, 1 Meadowood, 1 Rossville, 1 Fox Creek Stemmed, 16 Levanna, and 29 untyped points and point fragments.

Chipped stone tools from the site included 26 knives, 52 bifaces, 240 utilized flakes, 29 scrapers, 8 drills, 3 gravers, 1 strike-a-light, and 8 choppers. Pecked and ground stone tools comprised 15 hammerstones and one each of the following: pestle, netsinker, nutting stone, and abrading stone.

Debitage totaled 12,505 pieces, the most common of which originated from Esopus (6321 or 50.5%), Mount Merino (1990 or 15.9%), Indian River and Eastern Onondaga (1165 or 9.3% each), and Western Onondaga (941 or 7.5%) cherts. Like the Hendrickson site, the Perry site had small quantities of Eppler/Harmonyvale chert (180 or 1.4%), likely from Orange County sources.

Prehistoric pottery was represented by 538 fragments, representing at least nine prehistoric ceramic pots as well as one made of steatite (fig. 2.18). There were three Jack's Reef Corded vessels, two pots that could

Figure 2.18. Perry site stone and ceramic containers. Top row, left to right: fragment of steatite bowl, three fragments of Jack's Reef Corded. Bottom row, left to right: Jack's Reef Corded, Wickham Punctate, terminal Late Woodland/Contact Incised pottery, child's incised pot. *Source:* Photo by the author.

be typed as Wickham Punctate, a crudely made pot that may have been crafted by a child, a possible salve or small grease pot, a nontypable pot, and one pot from the terminal Late Woodland/Contact period (c. 1400–1650 AD). Additionally, small fragments of punctate, cord-wrapped stick impressed, and incised fragments were found (fig. 2.19). This pattern is common on later precontact sites where pedestrian damage to pottery makes the fragments increasingly smaller over time.

The faunal remains from the site were analyzed by Dr. Thomas Amorosi. Domestic animal remains from the 19th- and 20th-century deposits included cattle, sheep/goat, pig, dog, chicken, and turkey. Imported bivalves from the coastal area that were probably imported during the historic period (i.e., 19th century) included hard-shell clam and oysters. Faunal remains from the precontact deposits that were likely consumed by Native Americans on the site included deer, black bear, red fox, porcupine, woodchuck, gray squirrel, various bird species, box turtle, snapping turtle, Atlantic sturgeon, striped bass, perch, and porgy.

Figure 2.19. Perry site ceramics. Top row, left to right: CWS and punctated ceramic, three CWS impressed fragments. Bottom row, left to right: corded and dragged ceramic, two CWS, one incised fragment. *Source:* Photo by the author.

The Perry site is important for several reasons. The first is that it illustrates the kinds of contributions that avocational archaeologists can make to our understanding of the precontact period. The second is that it documents the fact that intact archaeological deposits can be found in areas of 19th- or early-20th-century neighborhoods. The third is that it can provide us with a larger picture of the landform that the Hendrickson site is on. In this case, a larger excavated sample of soil (172.2 sq ft/16 sq m) informed us of an even earlier occupation that was not identified at the Hendrickson site just one backyard away. Lastly, the collection from the site is curated at SUNY New Paltz and thus serves as a hands-on source of archaeological data for students working in regional precontact Native American archaeology. The Perry site collection was initially processed at SUNY New Paltz by Cara Muniz, and reports on parts of the site were presented at the 95th Annual Meeting of the NYSAA (Meinsen 2011). The site collection was also recently reanalyzed for a master's thesis (Lewis 2018).

The Tammany Street Site

While undertaking testing for a proposed sewer system in 1980–1981, Hartgen Archeological Associates identified a small prehistoric site on Tammany Street in Kingston (HAA 1981). The site was found in garden areas that had not been previously subjected to cut-and-fill episodes for the construction of the street. The site consisted of only two debitage, one blockie flake, and one Sylvan Stemmed projectile point (c. 2500–1900 BC/cal. 4450–3850 BP). While this may not seem significant enough to call this location a site, one has to keep in mind that these artifacts are remnants of what would likely have been a larger site that has since been disturbed by both historic and modern construction events. In the archaeological report, it was surmised that this location may have been on the edge of what, during precontact times, was a small pond or marsh, which would have been suitable for hunting deer, beavers, muskrat, turtles, frogs, or waterfowl (HAA 1981). In addition, an environment such as this would provide an important carbohydrate source, cattail roots, which can be ground into flour and used to thicken soups into porridge or gruel. Cattail stems may also have been used for making baskets.

The Tammany Street site was found during archaeological testing for a proposed sewer system in Kingston. These linear surveys often produce what, at first, appear to be isolated finds, but when archaeological testing is expanded, particularly during a Phase 2 study, these finds often turn out to be larger, significant sites. The Tammany Street site is a perfect example of how Phase 1B testing can identify small sites that can later be examined for more information or protected from further disturbance. This is why archaeologists test impact areas in the first place.

The Kingston Knolls Site

In 1990, Bagdon Environmental Associates completed a Phase 1 archaeological survey of the proposed Kingston Knolls Townhouses at the end of West Chestnut Street overlooking Rondout Creek. The Phase 1 survey identified 105 artifacts, including 53 debitage, 2 bifaces, 1 endscraper, 22 FCR, 5 worked chert nodules, 10 ground stone fragments, and 12 sherds of Point Peninsula pottery, dating c. 600–950 AD/cal. 1350–1000 BP (Bagdon Environmental Associates 1990). The subsequent Phase 2 study located additional artifacts, including a Kanawha Stemmed point from the Early Archaic, dating to somewhere in the 6th to 7th millennium BC. Like the Charleston Corner-Notched, Kirk Serrated, and Kanawha points from Kington Point, this site is one of the few in Kingston that has an Early Archaic presence. Unfortunately, the client for the project backed out of the environmental process and did not pay for completion of the Phase 2 report. As a consequence, the report was never completed, and we have no knowledge of whether there was charcoal associated with the Kanawha Stemmed point. If this was the case, and the report was finished and submitted to OPRHP, we might have had the earliest radiocarbon date for a precontact site in the city of Kingston. This particular situation highlights the worst example of how the permit process can fall apart, and how known and important archaeological resources become lost forever.

The West Chestnut Street Site

During a Phase 1A study of the city of Kingston (Diamond 1990; Site #12-P-1/USN #11140.0011), I met a family at the western end of West Chestnut Street who had found a cache of five chert blades in their yard. Since their backyard overlooks the Rondout Creek, it is a similar site location to the Kingston Knolls site, just several hundred feet away. The blades were composed of Onondaga and Mt. Merino chert. There were no temporally diagnostic artifacts found with them, so this cache represents a deposit of stone tools that someone likely buried sometime in the last several thousand years to come back to but, for unknown reasons, did not return to retrieve their belongings.

The Kingston Armory Site

The Kingston Armory site was identified by the Louis Berger Group (LBG) during improvements to the Kingston Armory for the New York State National Guard from 2004 to 2008 (LBG 2008). In terms of total area excavated, this is, without doubt, the largest archaeological excavation conducted in the city of Kingston. The Phase 1B investigation consisted of excavating 104 shovel tests, which was then followed by 7 additional shovel tests, 21 1-meter squares, and 13 trenches during the Phase 2 study. The Phase 3 data recovery excavations consisted of 2,712 square feet (252 sq m) of block excavation (fig. 2.20) (LBG 2008, Figs. 2.21–23), the mechanical stripping of 12,486 square feet (1,160 sq m) of horizontal surface area, and two trenches excavated to examine the geomorphology of the site.

The sample size excavated, that is, the percentage of the site that was to be disturbed, was 6%. That 6% sample yielded almost 80,000 artifacts and 60 features. The research goal posed by the archaeologists was to "evaluate the functional role of this site in prehistoric adaptations over time" (LBG 2008, 102). Related to this were five separate research themes that addressed "site formation processes, chronology, community patterns and settlement systems, technology, and subsistence" (102).

The Kingston Armory site is located on a flat terrace or bench consisting of Riverhead fine sandy loam. As mentioned above, these terraces were probably formed by Late Pleistocene glacio-lacustrine deposits, and the authors of the report suggested that the terrace was likely associated with glacial Lake Quaker Springs or glacial Lake Albany. The original soils on the terrace were buried by varying amounts of clean fill, which essentially meant that the A-horizon and B-horizon soils were protected from various kinds of disturbances. Perhaps the most informative aspect of the excavation was the geomorphological analysis and interpretation of how and why Late Archaic contexts and features were buried so deeply, when there was no apparent origin for the additional soils below the

Figure 2.20. Kingston Armory excavation. Block excavation shot. *Source:* Photo by the author.

historic fill layer (LBG 2008, 240–42). The question was, how did artifacts from c. 6,000 years ago become buried so deeply, with later occupations ordered stratigraphically above them in the soil column, when there was no apparent geological cause for the soil buildup? The authors proposed three hypotheses: alluvial deposition from the Esopus Creek, aeolian or windborne deposits, and biomechanical processes. The first hypothesis does not make sense, as the site is well above the Esopus Creek floodplain. The second hypothesis also did not make sense, because the sands were not wind-blown. The last explanation, which seems the most logical, relates to the redistribution of soils from below ground to the surface by "conveyor belt" species such as ants, termites, worms, and other creatures (LBG 2008, 240). When ants and earthworms, for example, move soil or sand grains to the surface, they are taking soil content from lower down and moving it to the surface. As rain filters down through the soil and slowly compacts it, the small gaps created by the worms and ants are filled in. The result is that artifacts deposited by people over long periods of time retain their original location in the soil column vis-à-vis other artifacts from earlier and later occupations. As worms and ants bring soil to the surface, each assemblage of artifacts from a particular time period slowly moves downward in the soil column. Thus, the idea that conveyor belt species likely created the distinctive cultural stratigraphy at the site is likely the best explanation. This concept, referred to as "bioturbation," has been applied in other cases on sites that exhibit similar geological histories.

The earliest archaeological culture identified at the Armory site was the Late Archaic Vergennes phase, characterized by the presence of Otter Creek projectile points. Two features from the site returned strong radiometric dates. One yielded a date of 6170 +/− 40 BP (Beta-208977; cal. 2σ 5260–4940 BC/cal. BP 7200–6890), and the other produced a date of 5840 +/− 40 BP (Beta-208978; cal. 2σ 4780–4590 BC/cal. BP 6730–6540). The tools found at the site that were from the Vergennes phase levels were numerous and included 3 Otter Creek points, 2 untyped points, 11 cores, 2 drills, 27 bifaces, 13 endscrapers, 2 unifacial multipurpose tools, 2 bifacial cores, a chopper, 13 pitted stones, 5 hammerstones, 2 abraders, a mano, a pestle, 4 battered and pecked cobbles, a ground slate knife or preform, 7 utilized flakes, 7 retouched flakes, and 7,750 pieces of debitage. Overall, there seemed to be a preference among people of the Vergennes phase for Mt. Merino and Onondaga cherts. Subsistence activities suggested by the artifacts found at the site include hunting, hide processing, and plant processing. Botanical remains point to the exploitation of black walnut

(*Juglans nigra*) and, to a lesser extent, hickory (*Carya sp.*). Settlement pattern data such as post molds or house floors were not found, although most of the Vergennes phase artifacts were found clustered around several hearths and processing features (LBG 2008, 243), suggesting that the structures they occupied were temporary, at least temporary enough to not leave physical traces such as post molds in the soil.

Following the Vergennes phase occupation of the site was the Vosburg phase. Radiometric samples associated with this phase were identified from three separate features, yielding dates of 4550 +/− 40 BP (Beta-206389; cal. 2σ 3370–3100 BC/cal. BP 5320–5050), 4520 +/− 40 BP (Beta-206390; cal. 2σ 3350–3020 BC/cal. BP 5300–4970), and 5130 +/− 40 BP (Beta-210505; cal. 2σ 3980–3790 BC/cal. BP 5920–5740). The Vosburg phase assemblage consisted of 10 Vosburg points, 4 Brewerton Side-Notched points, a Brewerton Eared-Notched point, 1 Brewerton Corner-Notched point (?), 5 archaic triangular points, 3 point fragments, 18 bifaces, 1 drill, 1 trianguloid knife, 14 endscrapers, 1 unifacial tool, 3 utilized flakes, 10 retouched flakes, 26 cores, 15 pitted stones, 1 mano, 1 metate fragment, 1 pestle, 3 hammerstones, 3 ground stone tools, 1 plummet, 1 decorative object, and 6,603 pieces of debitage. Additionally, 34 archaic triangular points similar to Beekman Triangles (see Funk in Ritchie 1971, 121) were found. These are small triangular points that are one of the six projectile point types identified with the Vosburg phase. It is possible that each point type could have been used on a different-sized javelin, dart, or spear, or that certain projectile point types were preferred for hunting specific animals.

One comparison between the Vergennes and Vosburg phases on this site is that the number of lithic types utilized for chipped stone and ground stone tools decreased from 12 to 10, with a 90% decrease in argillite use.[10] There was also an increasing focus on Mt. Merino and Onondaga chert (LBG 2008, 203). Subsistence activities at the site, like the previous phase, appear to have been related to hunting, hide processing, and plant processing. One feature contained mostly carbonized bark, which was probably a liner for the feature, and another, basin-shaped feature contained 6,597 carbonized butternut (*Juglans cinera*) shell fragments and two hickory (*Carya sp.*) fragments. One additional feature contained two carbonized butternut, two butternut/hickory, and two hickory fragments. Consequently, these features may have been used for dry storage of nuts (LBG 2008, 244), which was common during the precontact period in the well-drained soils in and around Kingston.

The last archaeological cultures of the Late Archaic were represented at the site by two cultures commonly found in the Hudson Valley, neither of which provided C14 dates at the Armory site. The first culture is represented by the River phase (c.1900–1700 BC/cal. 3850–3650 BP), which yielded five Normanskill points, and the Susquehanna or Broad Spear tradition, a term that focuses on the size and breadth of the projectile points compared with smaller points of the previous Small Stemmed tradition (Lamoka/Sylvan Lake/Wading River/Poplar Island/Bare Island/Normanskill). The second archaeological culture is represented by the Snook Kill phase (c. 1700–1500 BC/cal. 3650–3450 BP), based on the presence of three Snook Kill points, all of which were made with maroon chert from either the Mt. Merino or Indian River formations.

Perhaps the largest component of the Susquehanna tradition, and one that is more commonly placed in the Transitional Archaic, is from the Frost Island (c. 1500–1200 BC/cal. 3450–3150 BP) and Orient (c.1100–750 BC/cal. 3050–2700 BP) phases. The Frost Island phase produced 28 Susquehanna Broad Spear points, 4 points reworked into awls or gravers, and numerous other tools and debitage. The Orient phase was represented by 29 Orient points, 8 scrapers, 1 celt, other tools, and debitage. Precontact groups from these two (probably related) archaeological cultures appear to have been the earliest in the New York State region to bury their dead in formal cemeteries and to cremate their dead, to engage in long-distance trade for steatite (soapstone) pots and jasper, and to make low-fired earthenware pottery. Eight steatite fragments were found at the site, as was earthenware pottery. A radiocarbon date associated with one feature and Frost Island/Orient phase Vinette 1 pottery from the site yielded a date of 2980 +/- 40 BP (Beta-208976; cal. 2σ BC 1360–1360 and BC 1320–1060/cal. BP 3310–3300 and cal. BP 3260–3000). No post molds or house patterns were identified from the Late Archaic or Transitional Archaic periods at the Armory site, a situation common for sand terraces throughout the Hudson Valley.

The Armory site appeared to have no archaeological remnants from the Woodland period (post-1000 BC), suggesting that the occupations at the site were represented entirely by Native American groups inhabiting the area during the Late Archaic to Transitional Archaic times. Over approximately four millennia, this well-drained landform, which was probably forested in nut species such as butternut, hickory, and black walnut, was extensively utilized for a combination of tasks, including hunting, hide processing, and the processing and storage of plant foods—specifically, nuts in large pit features that appeared to have been lined with bark or grasses. Due to the acidic nature of the soil, no faunal remains were found, so our inferences regarding what kinds of animals may have been processed and consumed on site are limited.

Another interesting aspect of the investigation of this site is the degree to which historic materials were not found. The Armory site was excavated at the terminus of Manor Avenue, the possible location of Thomas Chambers "Foxhall," which he built in the 17th century.[11] In the continuing search for Chamber's Foxhall, the presence of 17th-century ceramics, glass, pipestems, food remains, and architectural elements would have indicated proximity to the Manor House. None were found, however, and the search continues.

The Lipton Street Site

During a Phase 1A archaeological study of the city of Kingston (Diamond 1990; Site #5-P-1/USN #11140.0009), I was contacted by a local resident who had found two projectile points in their dog run on Lipton Street. The soil had worn away, leaving one Vosburg and one Brewerton Eared-Triangle point on the surface. This find suggested the Vosburg phase occupations found at the Kingston Armory site continued along the flat terrace along Manor and Kiersted Avenues, right up to the border with the town of Ulster, if not even further. In the Late Archaic, this level terrace was likely full of various species of nut-bearing trees, which, when harvested, could be processed and stored over the winter in pits, such as those found at the Armory site.

The Canal Path Trail

As a result of the city of Kingston's proposal to improve access and safety on a pedestrian right of way, I was tasked with shovel testing the Canal Path Trail, which leads from the Delaware and Hudson (D&H) Canal Company Office downhill to the Strand (Diamond 1999b). This survey consisted of a row of screened shovel tests that, for the most part, provided a profile of the many kinds of surface treatment, such as fine pea gravels, that had been added to the path since the 1820s. What was not expected, however, was the presence of Native American artifacts (debitage) mixed with very dark brown soils that appeared to be eroding from above the retaining wall on the trail. A closer inspection of open rain-washed soils indicated that the precontact artifacts were originating in the lot above the wall, which was a large, mowed lawn with obvious depressions from 19th-century house foundations across the lawn.[12]

Another portion of this project involved clearing the debris from the site of the D&H Canal Company's office at the top of the path for use as a pedestrian overlook (see Osterberg 2002, 122, bottom photo). Ford (2004) provided an idea of what this structure would have looked like, with a c. 1900 view taken from the tip of Island Dock (24). Also included in this volume are views of what the fully functioning coal depot at Island Dock would have looked like in the late 19th century (22–25). This location now serves as a small park that overlooks the Strand and the Rondout Creek.

Colony Liquors Precontact Site

This site, or series of small occupation loci that could be best described as "small lithic scatters," was identified during evaluation of potential construction impacts to a 29-acre parcel proposed for a warehouse being constructed by the Colony Liquor and Wine Distributors in the city of Kingston (Diamond 2007a). The project area was just inside the corporate boundary of the city of Kingston, with the town of Ulster line as its northern border. The area is an amorphously shaped parcel that borders an industrial site to the north, an apartment complex to the south, and woods to the east. It is level, with portions that are wet and portions that have been used as sand spoil piles.

The bedrock geology of this area consists of Lower to Middle Devonian Onondaga Limestone and Ulster Group or possibly the Lower Devonian Glenerie formation (Fisher et al. 1970, Lower Hudson Sheet). Both groups intersect near the project area, and both include various members that are chert bearing.

Shovel testing of the proposed project area targeted the entire property, with the exception of an area of deep sand fill and disturbance near the fence along the western edge of the project area. A total of 107 hand-excavated, hand-screened shovel tests produced 123 modern artifacts in 25 shovel tests and nine precontact artifacts in six shovel tests. A tenth precontact artifact was found on the surface. Because six to seven shovel tests produced evidence of precontact Native American activity, and because this area could not be avoided, a Phase 2 site evaluation was recommended.

Throughout the project area, forms of disturbance that might have affected the distribution of artifacts included forest clearing (likely during the 19th century) and movement of soils by four-wheeled vehicles, the trails of which crisscrossed the project area. Unfortunately, some forest clearing using a bulldozer had also been undertaken after the completion of the Phase 1B and prior to the Phase 2 study. In the locations that were disturbed by these activities, the soils showed a clear A horizon of about 10 to 12 inches (25–30 cm), with relatively undisturbed subsoil beneath it. The soils varied from sands to silty sands, with some locations including a bit of clay.

The Phase 2 investigation (Diamond 2007b) of the lithic scatters was undertaken as follows: each initial find spot from the Phase 1B was found and reflagged, and a baseline was set up on each. A series of 50-cm shovel tests was then set up at 5-meter intervals around the initial find spot. Excavation of the shovel tests then began in the vicinity of the initial positive shovel tests and proceeded outward. The testing and evaluation during the Phase 2 consisted of a total of 60 50-cm squared-off shovel tests and three 1-meter squares, which, in total, evaluated 18 square meters of excavated soil to a depth of 14 to 16 inches (c. 35–40 cm). These areas were divided into Locus 1 through Locus 4. Of the 60 shovel tests, only four yielded precontact artifacts. Three 1-meter squares were laid out within Locus 4, and of the three, only one produced precontact artifacts.

A total of eight precontact Native American artifacts were found in two loci during the Phase 2 study, including one tertiary flake from Locus 1 and five tertiary, one secondary, and one primary decortication flake from Locus 2. In total, 18 precontact artifacts were found during the Phase 1B and Phase 2 studies. No temporally or culturally diagnostic artifacts were found, but from a technological viewpoint, cherts from the Onondaga formations were utilized, as were pieces of green Mount Merino chert.

The site area appears to consist of a group of low-density lithic scatters that are quite sparse and difficult to define. Each area may have been a small work area where lithic reduction and some tool modification took place. The materials left behind after this process were then dispersed laterally by forest clearing and modern four-wheeled vehicles until most of the site varied in artifact density from one to five artifacts per square meter. This pattern is very similar in overall artifact density and horizontal extent to the sites found at the Kingston Meadows site (see below).

Abeel Street

In 2002, Hartgen Archeological Associates undertook a Phase 1A archaeological sensitivity assessment of Abeel Street prior to proposed water, sewer, and sidewalk work (HAA 2002a). The report proposed the need for archaeological monitoring during construction activities. Monitoring is a cost-effective technique that ensures that the archaeologists work with the construction crew when they are replacing or digging new water and sewer lines. If a Native American or historic Euro-American site is identified during construction, it is either temporarily bypassed or mitigated on the spot. Since water and sewer line trenches are relatively small and lineal, the impact area can be quickly assessed by an on-site archaeologist. The key idea here is that in situ information about a precontact or historic site is not relegated to a back dirt pile or taken away in a dump truck.

The archaeological monitoring of the Abeel Street project (Diamond 2014) consisted of an archaeologist who was available on-site for all phases of construction activities where the ground was being disturbed. The four main foci of the research design were to (1) document historic fill episodes and collect artifacts from those deposits, (2) carefully examine soils to determine whether precontact Native American materials were present, (3) mitigate any precontact sites or remnants of sites that were encountered, and (4) examine all soils for traces of human remains that may have been buried within the project area.

The monitoring was divided, for reporting's sake, into two areas: the portion of Abeel Street west of Wurts Street and the portion east of Wurts Street. Most of the time and effort expended on the project was in the area from Wurts Street west to the corner of Ravine Street. In total, 126 archaeological contexts were located between Ravine Street and Broadway. Due to the nature of the archaeological investigation in association with construction activities, these contexts are not in any kind of sequential or spatial order; instead, the numbers move from location to location where work was in progress and when collections of artifacts were made. This was in keeping with the concept that archaeological monitoring does not "slow down" or inhibit construction but, rather, is tailored to work with it.

Monitoring West of Wurts Street

Several archaeological contexts were found on Abeel Street between Wurts and Ravine Streets. This is primarily due to the amount of work that was done in this area. The first five archaeological contexts that were identified and sampled yielded only historic items, but one particular context alerted us to the fact that precontact Native American materials were also present. It was also apparent that many of the soil strata near the base of Hone Street included a combination of 19th-century and precontact Native American materials. In total, 369 Native American artifacts were found, including lithic debitage, cores, projectile points, bifaces, scrapers, utilized flakes, hammerstones, nutting stones, and muller/hammerstones. Of the two projectile points found, only one was diagnostic: a midsection and base of a Sylvan Stemmed point (see Funk 1976, 247–54), which have been radiometrically dated to c. 3100–1900 BC (cal. 5500–3850 BP) in the Northeast.

After the location of the precontact artifacts was ascertained, two 1-meter squares were excavated along the south side of Abeel Street. The on-site archaeologist, Frank Spada, concluded that because the soils looked relatively undisturbed, intact portions of an original site might be present. The site location was just above the drop-off above the old foundation of the Forst Meat-Packing Plant that was once located on the south side of Abeel Street (see Ford 2010, 4). This large, brick structure was demolished in the 1980s in order to construct new housing, which then never occurred. It was here, underneath the 19th- or 20th-century sidewalks, that remnant soils from the precontact (or pre-1609) era remained relatively undisturbed. Consequently, a grid of 1-meter squares was laid out on an east/west axis to sample what was left of the original soils in this location.

Abeel Street Precontact Site #1 (11140.002748)

Eleven units were set up on a long rectangular line to sample the soils under the sidewalk. The first stratum of Unit 1 was a strong brown silt with small pebbles, which varied from 3 to 7.5 inches (7–19 cm) in overall depth. It yielded 86 precontact artifacts, three of which were temporally diagnostic: one Susquehanna Broad point from c. 1500–1200 BC (cal. 3450–3150 BP) and two Orient Fishtail points from c. 1100–750 BC (cal. 3050–2700 BP) (Funk 1993, 157). The artifact-bearing soil was excavated to 7.5 inches (19 cm) in depth and ended when it was determined to be sterile soil with no cultural materials (fig. 2.21).

Units 2 through 5 contained similar soils and were excavated at similar depths as Unit 1. Unit 2 yielded 14 artifacts, one of which was temporally diagnostic: a Snook Kill point (fig. 2.21) from c. 1700–1500 BC

Figure 2.21. Abeel Street Precontact Site #1. Top row, left to right: Susquehanna Broad point, two Orient Fishtail points, untyped projectile point, projectile point frag (CX 74). Bottom row, left to right: Snook Kill point (CX 74), scraper (CX 77), Neville Stemmed point, Precontact pottery (both CX 78). *Source:* Photo by the author.

(cal. 3650–3450) (Funk 1993, 157), composed of black eastern Onondaga chert. Unit 3, placed west of Units 1 and 2, yielded 41 precontact artifacts, none of which were diagnostic. Units 4 and 5 were placed adjacent to Unit 1 as the row of 1-meter squares proceeded west, and each yielded small samples of nondiagnostic precontact artifacts, with three from Unit 4 and four from Unit 5.

Units 6 through 10 were excavated in the same row, but all were devoid of precontact materials and yielded only historic artifacts and brick, concrete, and bluestone fragments. It is likely that previous sidewalk and foundation construction destroyed any additional precontact archaeological contexts that might have once existed in this location.

Unit 11 was the easternmost and was situated to the east of Unit 3. This unit appeared to sample the last small portion of undisturbed soil east of Unit 3 and in front of a large concrete retaining wall. The soils ranged from slightly under and over 7 inches (17–18 cm) in depth. The first stratum yielded 26 precontact artifacts, two of which were temporally diagnostic. The most recent artifact was a fragment of coil-wound pottery (fig. 2.21), a manufacturing technique that was used throughout the New York State region from c. 200 BC–1000 AD (cal. 1150–950 BP). The second artifact was a Neville Stemmed projectile point (fig. 2.21).

The Neville phase was first identified in New Hampshire (Dincauze 1976) and, until the late 1990s, had bracketed dates of c. 5500–5000 BC (cal. 7450–6950 BP) (Funk 1993, 157; see also Funk 1991). One of the largest assemblages of Neville phase artifacts in the Hudson Valley originated from the Mohonk Rockshelter in the Shawangunk Mountains (Eisenberg 1991). Archaeological work at the Annasnappet Pond/Cranberry Bog Complex in Carver, Massachusetts, suggested that the dates for this projectile point type may extend back to 8580–8005 BP (Cross 1999, 63–64). Consequently, I have combined calibrated dates from (Cross 1999), Funk (1993), and Dincauze (1976) to suggest a bracketed range of c. 6630–5000 BC (cal. 8580–6950 BP).

To the west of Unit 10, headed toward Ravine Street, one 50-cm shovel test was excavated, which, while it did not produce any Native American artifacts, yielded sand and gravels along with strong brown silt that could potentially contain precontact materials. As a consequence, this shovel test was expanded into a 1-meter unit (Unit 12). This was excavated in two contexts, but only the first, from 0 to 28 cm, yielded cultural materials, which consisted of 14 precontact artifacts. None were culturally diagnostic and all related to stone tool manufacture or reduction. Because they were in mixed fill with historic artifacts, further investigation did not continue in this area.

In some locations, precontact artifacts were collected from fill that had been excavated by the construction crews, and each bag was given a unique context number—these were referred to as "grab bags." In all, 369 precontact artifacts were collected as "grab" samples. The total count of precontact lithics from what was labeled Abeel Street Precontact Site #1 was 565 (table 2.4). The breakdown by artifact types was 476 tertiary flakes, 15 secondary decortication flakes, 10 primary decortication flakes, 21 blockies, 5 cores and core fragments, 10 pieces of FCR, 1 pottery fragment, 9 projectile points and point fragments, 9 bifaces, 2 biface/performs, 2 scrapers, 1 utilized flake/scraper, 1 hammerstone, 2 nutting stone fragments (1 bi-pitted stone), 1 muller/hammerstone, and 1 muller. The fragment of coil-wound pottery brings the total to 566 artifacts.

Table 2.4. Abeel Street Precontact Site #1. Lithic artifacts by lithic type.

Point type/tools	Green Mt. Merino chert	Indian River chert	Black chert	Black EO chert	Waxy gray WO chert	Waxy brown Chert	Gray-brown chert	Gray-black chert	Mottled G &B Onon.chert	Pat. Mt. Merino chert	White quartzite	Brown quartzite	Pink quartzite	Gray chert	Oriskany chert	Argillite	waxy milky white chert	Sandstone	Totals
Orient Fishtail	1						1												2
Susquehanna Broad							1												1
Snook Kill				1															1
Sylvan Stemmed	1																		1
Neville Stemmed							1												1
Proj. pt. frags.	3																		3
Tertiary flakes	207	16	7	73	7	1	25	8	59	2				68	1	1	1		476
Secondary flakes	6	1	1	2				1	3					1					15
Primary flakes	4			2			1		1					2					10
Blockies	6		1	11	3														21
Cores	1			2			1						1						5
FCR											1	1						8	10

Point type/tools	Green Mt. Merino chert	Indian River chert	Black chert	Black EO chert	Waxy gray WO chert	Waxy brown Chert	Gray-brown chert	Gray-black chert	Mottled G &B Onon.chert	Pat. Mt. Merino chert	White quartzite	Brown quartzite	Pink quartzite	Gray chert	Oriskany chert	Argillite	Waxy milky white chert	Sandstone	Totals
Bifaces	2	1	1	2		1			2										9
Biface/preform	2																		2
Scrapers	1			1															2
UF/scrapers				1															1
Hammerstones																		1	1
Nutting stones																		2	2
Muller/ham.																		1	1
Mullers																		1	1
Totals by lithic	234	18	10	95	10	2	30	9	65	2	1	1	1	71	1	1	1	13	565
% by lithic	41.4	3.2	1.8	16.8	1.8	0	5.3	1.6	11.5	0.4	0.2	0.2	0.2	12.6	0.2	0.2	0.2	2.3	

From an overall perspective, this assemblage of artifacts points to a variety of site functions. The first was stone tool production and maintenance, which was represented by tertiary flakes as well as secondary and primary decortication flakes. Larger pieces of toolstone such as blockies, cores, and core fragments were also the products of tool manufacture, as were hammerstones, which were used for percussion during lithic reduction. When combined, these categories accounted for 532, or 94.16%, of the lithics found at the site. Hunting and butchering as a general category were represented by projectile points, knives (bifaces), and utilized flakes. These accounted for 19, or 3.4%, of the lithic artifacts. Hide preparation, which turns hides into clothing as well as shelter, was represented by scrapers ($n = 2$) and utilized flakes/scrapers ($n = 1$) (fig. 2.22). Numerically, these two categories combined accounted for only three artifacts, or .53%, of the total lithic artifacts. Plant processing was indicated by pitted nutting stones (fig. 2.22), mullers, and mullers that also appear to have been uti-

Figure 2.22. Abeel Street Precontact Site #1. Top Row, left to right: two bifaces (CX 23), muller (CX 24), biface and Sylvan Stemmed point (both CX 27). Bottom row, left to right: scraper, utilized flake/scraper (CX 28), biface fragment (CX 29), projectile point fragment (CX 31). *Source:* Photo by the author.

lized as hammerstones. This functional category was represented by only four artifacts, two of which mended to form one bi-pitted nutting stone. Overall, the count was four artifacts, or .7%, of the total lithic artifacts. These tools were most likely used to process black walnut, butternut, chestnut, hickory, or acorn nuts for food.

Cooking activities at the site were reflected in the presence of FCR and precontact pottery. Rocks were used in earth ovens to cook food, and FCR is the byproduct of boiling water in a skin bag by using heated stones repeatedly until the water boils and cooks the food. The archaeological evidence of these activities consists of fire-reddened stones that have fractured into sharp angles, usually with a smooth cobble exterior, since many boiling stones are river or stream cobbles. A total of 10 FCR were found at this site, which, when accounted for by weight, totaled 553.2 grams (1.22 lb). The FCR was found across five grab samples and one excavation unit (Unit 3). The precontact pottery sherd was a body fragment from a vessel that was probably used for cooking and storage of food.

Table 2.4 is an analysis of the lithics used to produce the stone tools from the Abeel Street Precontact Site #1. The first is Mt. Merino chert, which has been commonly called "Normanskill chert" in the literature. Several studies by archaeologists and geologists (Brumbach and Weinstein 1999; Kidd et al. 1993) have suggested that this lithic type is mislabeled and that most of the occurrences of this lithic originate within the Mt. Merino formation. The maroon chert is thought to be from the Indian River formation, which also has varieties of red and maroon shale (see discussion in Brumbach and Weinstein 1999, 6). Black chert may have several derivations, including the Mt. Merino, Esopus, and Kalkberg formations, or even the Onondaga formation. The fourth category is black Onondaga chert, which includes many of the Hudson Valley Devonian cherts from the Morehouse and Nedrow members that have small fossils and stress fractures and are characteristically found in Ulster County.[13] Other lithics included waxy gray Onondaga chert, gray-brown chert, gray-black chert, mottled gray and brown Onondaga chert (probably Moorehouse), patinated Mt. Merino chert (white patina), three distinct colors of quartzite (white, brown, pink,), gray chert, Oriskany chert, argillite, waxy milky-white chert (Eppler/Harmonyvale chert), and sandstone.

From an analysis of the lithics from this site, it is apparent that local extraction and utilization of the Mt. Merino formation was the most important source of toolstone. A total of 234, or 41.4%, of the toolstone derived from this formation. This would probably increase to 50% if the blacks and gray-black cherts that are also found in the Mt. Merino formation were included. Black Eastern Onondaga chert ($n = 95$) was the second most commonly used toolstone, at 16.8% of the total. The third most common are the waxy gray Western Onondaga and mottled cherts of the Onondaga series, which, when combined ($n = 75$), accounted for 13.3% of the total lithics. The fourth was a category of gray chert that accounted for 71, or 12.6%, of the total. The maroon chert of the Indian River formation accounted for only 18 pieces, or 3.2%, of the total.

Abeel Street Precontact Site #2 (11140.002749)

Abeel Street Precontact Site #2 was defined as a separate site for two reasons. The first is that the artifacts recovered, a total of three, probably relate to the small terrace just above the Company Hill Path where a prehistoric site eroding out of the hillside was previously identified (Diamond 1999b). The second reason is that this site is approximately 1,000 feet (305 m) from Abeel Street Precontact Site #1. Consequently, it seems prudent to split the two up, even if one of the sites yielded only three artifacts. The three artifacts include one biface with a drill bit broken off, a possible fragment of a catlinite pipe, and the tip and midsection of an Archaic period (4000–1500 BC/c. cal. 5950–3450 BP) projectile point of green Mt. Merino chert.

Abeel Street Precontact Site Summary

The archaeological monitoring program at the Abeel Street project was designed to examine intact soils and historic fill episodes to determine whether precontact sites existed within the project area and, more importantly, to assess whether any extant sites might contain human remains. Two sites were located. The first was located near the corner of Abeel and Hone Streets and yielded Native American artifacts ranging in age from c. 6630 BC to AD 1000 (c. 8580 to 950 cal. BP). Based on the artifact assemblage, which totaled 566 artifacts, the site appears to have been used as a camp location for activities related to hunting, butchering, tool maintenance, nut processing, and the cooking of food. Likely because of the acidity of the soils and the age of the site, no animal bones or human remains were found. This site, or what was left of it, was completely mitigated during the construction work on Abeel Street.

The second site, which was represented by only three artifacts, appears to be more enigmatic and probably relates to a larger site identified from Wurts Street to approximately Post Street. This site would now be located beneath the lawns on the relatively level ground that overlooks the Rondout Creek.

The Ingarra Site

After taking my archaeological field school at SUNY New Paltz, one of my students, Amanda Ingarra, decided to excavate a 1-meter square in her side yard on Wall Street in uptown Kingston. The first stratum (or layer) was a mix of 19th- and 20th-century artifacts and building materials. However, underneath that layer was a stratum containing precontact artifacts, including lithic debitage, several small chert tools, and pottery fashioned using the coil method. Coil-wound pottery tends to break in long rectangles following the direction of the coil. In cross section, the top usually has a convex profile and the bottom has a concave profile where the pottery was put together. This kind of technique was commonly used during the Middle Woodland period (c. 0 BC–1000 AD/cal. 1950–950 BP).

What is interesting about this site (at least to me) is that in the middle of uptown Kingston between rows of 19th- and early 20th-century houses, there are still intact archaeological deposits originating from one to two millennia ago. It is very likely that level ground along buried or abandoned streams running through Kingston still hold substantial evidence of precontact archaeological sites. In this case, Native Americans likely camped on the well-drained Riverhead series soils overlooking the location where Tannery Brook makes a turn at the base of the hill west of Wall Street and flows north toward the Esopus Creek.

In a larger sense, this also suggests that cities like Kingston, which has streets with large backyards on a sandy well-drained landform, contain the remnants of precontact Native American sites that were not disturbed during house construction. In this case, basement construction and the subsequent spreading of soil around the house during the initial construction acts to seal in the precontact layers under a protective stratum, which is what Amanda found to be the case on Wall Street.

Ulster County Jail Precontact Quarry Sites

As part of a SEQRA-mandated investigation, Hartgen Archeological Associates completed Phase 1A background work and Phase 1B testing on the site of the proposed new Ulster County Jail in 1999. Initially, 125 shovel tests were excavated on the 15.9-acre parcel, which produced evidence of hammerstones and aprons of chert debitage around several limestone outcrops in the study area. This study was the initial identification of several precontact lithic quarries and reduction areas that were formed by exposures of the Briarcliff facies of the Onondaga limestone and the Port Ewen limestone (LaPorta 2002). In this location, Briarcliff cherts are present as nodules that are filled with stress fractures that make the material quite brittle and difficult to work. The Port Ewen cherts produce larger tools and are a better quality of material to work with.

Because the identified precontact quarries were in locations that could not be avoided during construction, the SEQRA process moved from a Phase 1B directly to a Phase 3 data retrieval study (HAA 2002b). The questions the archaeologists wanted to answer related to (1) how the orientation of the bedrock influenced lithic exploitation; (2) what the organizational aspects practiced by the miners were; (3) whether fire was used and, if so, at what stage in the mining process; (4) whether there were differences in seasonal exploitation of the quarries; (5) what types of tools were used and whether different tools were used for various aspects of the mining process; (6) what types of tools were used to exploit the ore (chert); and (7) whether people were inhabiting the site or whether exploitation of the rocks was more impermanent (HAA 2002b, 3).

The Phase 3 investigation consisted of mapping, drawing, and photographing the chert-bearing outcrops. They were also raked clean of leaf cover, and artifacts lying on the surface were mapped. A total of 67 shovel tests and 30 square meters (323 sq ft) of units were excavated, with all soils screened through ¼-inch mesh. The study yielded 13,780 artifacts consisting of debitage (quarry debris), hammerstones, anvils, wedges, chisels, and two chert bifaces. The hammerstones were divided into several types: very large hammerstones weighing up to 30 pounds (which would have been used for heavy battering of the limestone), handheld hammerstones of 1–3 pounds (which would have been used for working the extracted chert), and beaked hammerstones, which had points for splitting the chert along preexisting fracture planes. The anvils were of two types: large stationary anvils that would have been used as platforms for battering chert and lap anvils that were placed on one's lap for finer and more controlled work. The wedges were composed of meta- or orthoquartzite fragments that were driven off larger cobbles and then used as a wedge for splitting the chert from its limestone matrix.

The Ulster County Jail site quarries were divided into seven areas. For the purposes of excavation and analysis, this method allows the archaeologist to view each location separately. Distinctions can then be drawn between the various outcrops as well as the means by which people did or did not exploit the chert contained within the limestone matrix. Area 1, which was found during Phase 1B testing, consisted of three limestone outcrops of the Middle Devonian Briarcliff facies. Due to the poor quality of the chert, and the fact that very little evidence for chert extraction was present, this location was not subject to further investigation during the Phase 3 investigation.

Area 2 yielded over 100 cobble hammerstones, some up to 30 pounds in weight, as well as debitage and lap anvils. Many had been piled up along the rocks as a result of 19th-century farm clearing. Like Area 1, this was another outcrop of Briarcliff facies chert, although the quality of the chert here was better than at Area 1. One 1 × 2 meter (39 × 79 in) excavation unit was placed near a location that showed extraction of the chert from its limestone matrix. The unit yielded 8 hammerstones and 662 pieces of lithic waste such as debitage and shatter fragments. LaPorta considered this location to be "the only outcrop of Briarcliff facies that developed into a successful extraction zone within the study area" (HAA 2002b, 16).

Area 3 was thought, after the completion of the Phase 1B testing, to have been a possible reduction station for the production of cores and bifaces from Port Ewen chert. Two 1 × 2 meter (39 × 79 in) units were placed in this area. Together, the two units produced hammerstones and 931 fragments of lithic waste, most of which was chert shatter. Most of the chert displayed fracture cleavages that would have made the production of large stone tools difficult, if not impossible. Other pertinent artifacts from this area included stone wedges and a lap anvil.

Area 4 had four quarry features, all for the exploitation of Port Ewen chert. Here were found stationary anvil stones, a large quartzite boulder used as a quarry hammer, and 29 chert blanks in a blocky format, which would have been produced for later reduction into preforms.

Area 5 was composed of three potential extraction zones of the Briarcliff facies; however, because they were still horizontal (and not angled or vertical), these exposures were not worked. All three were considered "failed extraction zones" because the amount of work necessary to extract the chert would not have been worth the results. From a study of the lithic outcrops at the site, LaPorta (1996, 1997) determined that the best outcrops were those that are angled or completely vertical.[14] Area 6 was composed of three bedrock outcrops of Briarcliff chert–bearing limestone. Aside from a few artifacts, and the possibility of a small pit to extract chert, this area did not yield extensive evidence of mining.

Area 7 was one of the most heavily quarried areas on site, probably because the lithic was the Port Ewen chert. This area yielded evidence of bipolar percussion and heat treatment, the latter of which is used to reduce the chert blocks to more manageable pieces. This area also produced the only formal tools found at the site: one complete biface and one biface fragment.

The Ulster County Jail quarry sites provide us with several kinds of information about the precontact use of these limestone formations. The first is that the Port Ewen cherts were preferred over the Briarcliff cherts, likely due to the stress and cleavage fractures in the Briarcliff chert. The second is that horizontal exposures of chert bearing limestones were not exploited due to a cost-benefit analysis on the part of precontact Native Americans, that is, the effort expended was not worth the material extracted. The upshot is that vertical and angled outcrops were exploited for their cherts, particularly cherts of the Port Ewen formation. Finally, were people living at the site? No. The archaeologists found no evidence of habitation, such as hearths or pits for cooking, suggesting that there was no associated habitation area or even a small camp near the chert outcrops. Rather, precontact Native Americans were likely using these outcrops as necessary during the course of their daily, weekly, or monthly excursions from larger base camps nearby. These sojourns are referred to as "task-specific activities" by archaeologists, and in this case, we have to imagine people having a "mental map" of where chert outcrops were located, their overall qualities for making different functional categories of tools, and, more importantly, which were the most easily accessible. A modern analogy would be something like this: on our daily rounds, we plan specific stops while traveling to shop for food, go to a hardware store, or shop for clothing (among other things). Our mental mapping would discourage us from going to a food store for plumbing supplies or to a clothing store for food. However, if we were going out to get plumbing supplies and then realized that we needed bread and milk, we might make a "pit stop" to obtain those items. Such is the case for the Ulster County Jail quarry sites.

The Kingston Meadows Precontact Sites

An archaeological survey was conducted to evaluate impacts resulting from the construction of the proposed Kingston Meadows Senior Residence in the city of Kingston (Diamond 2008, 2010b). The proposed construction location was a 19-acre parcel located on a terrace overlooking the floodplain of the Esopus Creek just north of Hurley Avenue in the city of Kingston. It is bounded on the west by the New York State Thruway, to the north by the floodplain and watercourse of the Esopus Creek, to the east by the floodplain of the Esopus Creek and several hotels, and to the south by the railroad tracks of the New York Central Railroad.

The location of the proposed Senior Housing building (Diamond 2008) was a large open field with woods along its edges. Along the southern edge of this portion of the project area is a small brook that flows under the railroad tracks and drains the residential area on the south side of Hurley Avenue. The woods continue along the brook and then hook around the floodplain to the far northern end of the project area. The entire project area would be considered as within the floodplain of the Esopus Creek—that is, prior to the construction of the Ashokan Reservoir system. This impoundment holds 131 billion gallons of water, which, during precontact times as well as the historic period, would have inundated much of the Esopus Creek floodplain during spring and fall floods. The Ashokan Reservoir was constructed from 1907 until 1916 (Steuding 1985), so it is relatively safe to assume that most of the soils that built up in the project area predate this. These soils consist of Riverhead fine sandy loam, 3–8% slopes along the bank overlooking the railroad tracks, Unadilla silt loam in the proposed senior residence location, and Tioga fine sandy loam along the Esopus within the 100-year flood mark (Tornes 1979, sheet 64).

In addition, soil borings by Gifford Engineering, Geotechnical, and Geoenvironmental Services documented a combination of brown clayey silts or silty clays overlying small deposits of sand. During the Phase 1B investigation, several large backhoe trenches were excavated in the open field but did not reveal any evidence of buried cultural materials or horizons. What we did find were several feet of fine soil strata showing evidence of specific flood events (Diamond 2008).

During the Phase 1B study, the project area was shovel tested at 50-foot (15.2 m) intervals, and nine sites were identified within the initial area of proposed construction (Locus 1–9). Additionally, backhoe testing was undertaken in the lower field, but no deeply buried cultural deposits were encountered. During an addendum to the Phase 1 study (Diamond 2009), three additional sites were identified (Locus 10–12) in the area of a proposed borrow pit for soil.

A Phase 2 site evaluation of Locus 1 through Locus 12 was undertaken to assess the original find spots for the loci encountered during the Phase 1B testing. This was done primarily to ascertain the size and extent of the sites, to determine whether significant deposits were associated with the sites, how old the deposits were as well as their horizontal extent and depth, and whether any prehistoric features existed below the A-horizon soil. These are the standard questions that an archaeologist looks to answer during a Phase 2 study to determine whether an archaeological site meets the criteria to become eligible for listing on the National Register of Historic Places.[15] Throughout the project area, forms of disturbance that might have affected the distribution of precontact artifacts included forest clearing (probably in the 17th or 18th centuries) and plowing for farming.[16]

The Phase 2 evaluation of the 12 precontact loci was undertaken as follows: each initial find spot or spots from the Phase 1B was found and reflagged, and a baseline was set up on the original grid or one closely approximating it. A series of 19-inch (50 cm) squared off shovel tests were then set up at 16.25-foot (5 m) intervals around the initial find spots. Excavation of the shovel tests then began in the vicinity of the initial positive shovel tests and worked outward. In most cases, we did two negative tests from each find spot to determine the overall horizontal extent of the site. In some situations, however, we felt that shovel tests with one artifact were probably representative of horizontal spreading of the locus by plowing,[17] which would be expected in a field that has been cultivated since the 17th century. In this case, sites that may have been small activity areas when they were formed have been dispersed to a wider area over the course of several centuries of plowing. In total, the Phase 2 site evaluation consisted of 411 19-inch (50 cm) shovel tests and 20 39-inch (1 m) squares, for a total of 122.75 square meters (1,321 sq ft) of excavation area. Table 2.5 shows combined artifacts from the Phase 1B and Phase 2 studies by function from Locus 1 to Locus 12.

Table 2.5. Kingston Meadows precontact loci.

Artifact Function	Loc. 1	Loc. 2*	Loc. 3	Loc. 4	Loc. 5	Loc. 6	Loc. 7	Loc. 8	Loc. 9	Loc. 10	Loc. 11	Loc. 12
primary decortication flakes	2		2					1			4	
secondary decortication flakes	18		9	2	1	3	9	32	2	4	7	5
tertiary and pressure flakes	3	1	44	2	4	1	1	21	1	17	36	1
blockies/blocky fragments			13		3					8	17	
blocky fragments/shatter												
secondary decortication flake/blocky							4					
primary decortication flake/blocky			1									
FCR/hammerstone											1	
projectile point frag(s)	1		1								1	1
utilized flake			3									
"micro" scraper			1									
Primary Decort. Flake/Utilized Flake											1	1
utilized flake/scraper						1						
biface on blocky frag.											1	1
biface fragment	1		1								1	
FCR	1		22	5	7	1	5	37			6	3
biface/shredder	1											
Pre-Contact pottery											9	
Totals: Combined Phase 1B and Phase 2 by Site:	27	1	96	10	15	6	15	95	3	29	82	12

* Limited Phase 2 evaluation

The Phase 2 study of Locus 1 consisted of 49 shovel tests and two 1-meter squares. Combined with the Phase 1B artifacts, the site consisted of 18 tertiary flakes, 2 secondary decortication flakes, 3 blockie fragments, 1 biface/shredder, 1 projectile point fragment, 1 biface fragment, and 1 FCR ($n = 27$). From the distribution of the artifacts, a suggested estimated site area of c. 240 square meters (2,583 sq ft) was proposed. Artifact densities within this locus ranged from one to three artifacts per square meter. Interestingly, this locus may be the southern half of a site that Mr. Frank Spada (personal communication 2008) identified through surface finds on the other side of the thruway in this area. This suggests the precontact site may have been horizontally dispersed by plowing from the 17th through the 20th centuries and was then bifurcated by the construction of the New York State Thruway.

Locus 2 was located during the Phase 1B investigation as an isolated find in one shovel test located on the 100-year floodplain. Artifacts were limited to a worked blocky fragment of black Onondaga chert. The Phase 2 evaluation of Locus 2 consisted of nine shovel tests placed around an initial positive shovel test pit. No artifacts were found in the additional tests, so formal excavation units were not added here.

The Phase 2 site evaluation of Locus 3 consisted of 69 shovel tests and two 1-meter squares. Combined with the Phase 1B artifacts, the site consisted of 44 tertiary flakes, 13 blockie fragments, 2 primary decortication flakes, 9 secondary decortication flakes, 1 biface fragment, 1 "micro-scraper" of mottled Western Onondaga chert, 1 projectile point fragment, 3 utilized flakes, and 22 FCR ($n = 96$). From the distribution of the artifacts, a suggested estimated site area of c. 600 square meters (6,458 sq ft) was proposed, most of which was likely the result of horizontal artifact movement due to plowing.[18] Artifacts were found in a number of "outliers" that may be from horizontal dispersion of plowed soils or precontact cultural activities on the edge of the high-density area. These artifacts may have stuck to the plow blades and eventually dropped off away from the main activity area. Artifact densities in this locus ranged from 1 to 17 artifacts per square meter.

The Phase 2 study of Locus 4 consisted of 29 shovel tests and two 1-meter squares. Combined with the Phase 1B artifacts, the site consisted of 2 tertiary flakes, 1 blockie fragment, 1 "shatter fragment," 1 primary decortication flake/blocky, and 5 FCR ($n = 10$). From the distribution of artifacts, a suggested estimated site area of c. 150 square meters (1,614 sq ft) was proposed. Artifact densities in this locus ranged from 1 to 4 artifacts per square meter.

Investigation of Locus 5 consisted of 20 shovel tests and two 1-meter squares. Combined with the Phase 1B artifacts, the site consisted of 4 tertiary flakes, 3 blockie fragments, 1 secondary decortication flake, and 7 FCR ($n = 15$). Based on the distribution of artifacts, a suggested estimated site area of c. 170 square meters (1,830 sq ft) was proposed. Artifact densities ranged from 1 to 5 artifacts per square meter.

Locus 6 was investigated through 14 shovel tests and two 1-meter squares. Combined with the Phase 1B artifacts, the site consisted of 3 tertiary flakes, 1 blockie fragment, 1 biface on a blocky fragment, and 1 FCR ($n = 6$). Based on the distribution of artifacts, a suggested estimated site area of c. 200 square meters (2,153 sq ft) was proposed, although this may have been overly generous, since some artifacts may have been dragged or moved by a plow. Artifact densities in this locus ranged from 1 to 2 artifacts per square meter.

The investigation of Locus 7 consisted of 32 shovel tests and two 1-meter squares. Combined with the Phase 1B artifacts, the site consisted of 9 tertiary flakes, 1 blockie fragment, and 5 FCR ($n = 15$). Based on the distribution of artifacts, a suggested estimated site area of c. 575 square meters (6,190 sq ft) was proposed, although, similar to some of the other loci, this may be an overgeneralization. Here, artifact densities ranged from 1 to approximately 5 artifacts per square meter.

Locus 8 was identified during the Phase 1B testing in three shovel tests on the eastern side of the small brook near the southeast corner of the project area. The Phase 2 investigation of this locus consisted of 31 shovel tests and two 1-meter squares. Combined with the Phase 1B artifacts, the site consisted of 32 tertiary flakes, 1 primary decortication flake, 21 blockie fragments, 4 secondary decortication flakes/blockies, and 37 FCR ($n = 95$). The distribution of artifacts suggested two estimated site areas: one of approximately 125 square meters (1,345 sq ft), with a low-density area between the two higher density locations, and a second area of approximately 100 square meters (1,076 sq ft). The northern edge of this locus was a wetland. Artifact densities ranged from 1 to 11 artifacts per square meter for one area, and from 1 to 41 artifacts per square meter for the other area.

Locus 9 contained artifacts that were not unexpected, as this was in an area where shovel testing of one of the alternate entrance routes to the site impacts an area near New York State Museum (NYSM) Site #729, a multicomponent site called the Duck Pond Site (discussed below). Artifacts found during the Phase 1B investigation of this locus included 1 tertiary flake of brown chert and 2 secondary decortication flakes, one each of mottled Western Onondaga and black Eastern Onondaga chert. Locus 9 was not tested during the Phase 2 study, as it was found to be just on the edge of the project area, with most of it being on an adjacent, unaffected parcel.

The Phase 2 investigation of Locus 10, combined with the earlier Phase 1B testing, consisted of 35 shovel tests and two 1-meter squares. Precontact artifacts included 4 tertiary flakes, 8 shatter, and 17 blockie fragments ($n = 29$). Based on the distribution of artifacts, a suggested estimated site area of approximately 150 square meters (1,615 sq ft) was suggested. Artifact densities in this locus ranged from 1 to approximately 24 artifacts per square meter.

The investigation of Locus 11 consisted of 72 shovel tests and two 1-meter squares. Combined with the Phase 1B artifacts, the site consisted of 36 tertiary flakes, 16 blockie fragments, 4 primary decortication flakes, 7 secondary decortication flakes, 2 biface fragments, one FCR/hammerstone, 1 projectile point fragment, 9 precontact pottery fragments, and 6 FCR ($n = 82$). The pottery sample consisted of body fragments that had a burnished exterior with no decoration and likely dates from the Castle Creek phase (c. 1200 AD) to sometime around European contact (c. 1609) and as late as c. 1652. Given the small number of Europeans in the area during the period from 1609 to 1652, it is possible that the deposition could be as late as 1652. However, since the site is only 3,000 feet from *Wiltwyck*, the date could be as late as 1658, the year that Stuyvesant moved the Dutch settlers to the bluff overlooking the Esopus floodplain. Based on the distribution of artifacts, a suggested estimated site area of approximately 630 square meters (6,781 sq ft) was proposed. Like some of the other loci, this may be overly generous, or it may simply be a guess, as there are many shovel tests that contained only one piece of debitage. This locus appears to be very spread out, and artifact densities ranged from 1 to 9 artifacts per square meter.

The investigation of Locus 12 consisted of 34 shovel tests and two 1-meter squares. Combined with the Phase 1B artifacts, the site consisted of 5 tertiary flakes, 1 projectile point fragment, 1 blockie fragment, 1 utilized flake/scraper, 1 primary decortication flake/utilized flake, and 3

FCR ($n = 12$). Based on the distribution of artifacts, a suggested estimated site area of c. 200 square meters (2,153 sq ft) was proposed, with artifact densities ranging from 1 to approximately 3 artifacts per square meter.

The testing procedure utilized during this study produced evidence that most of the site loci were quite spread out. This is primarily due to plowing, which disperses artifacts laterally and, in some cases, drags artifacts in wet soils on the plow blade and then drops them off at a distance from the original site of deposition. Originally, these sites may have started out as small quantities of artifacts in a relatively constrained area. Based on the small size of the sites, as well as the limited number of artifacts from each locus, these might be considered "small lithic scatters." With the exception of the Late Woodland (c. 1200–1652 AD) pottery found in Locus 11, no temporally diagnostic artifacts were identified. Several projectile point fragments were found, but they were not complete enough to identify with certainty. Additionally, there were no subsurface features such as hearths, storage pits, or post molds. Several loci produced FCR, indicating that cooking had been undertaken on-site, although the FCR was confined to the plow zone, and this points to individual short-term fires near the surface. All of the artifacts from Kingston Meadows were found near the surface or in the plow zone and not in undisturbed features below the interface. The latter would be more common if groups had been returning to reuse the site area (and their hearths).

The location and functions of the Kingston Meadows precontact loci provide us with data on the kinds of sites that are located immediately adjacent to the Esopus Creek on the floodplain within the corporate boundary of the city of Kingston. These are not seasonally reoccupied base camps with large numbers of artifacts (such as Hendrickson or Perry); rather, they are interpreted as short-term forays onto the floodplain to obtain food—such as cattail roots, berries, nuts, deer, turtles, turkeys, waterfowl, and fish—or perishable organic materials, such as cattail stalks for weaving baskets, wooden shafts for making darts, javelins or spears, and bark for making rope or twine. Most seasonal base camps would not be situated in locations prone to flooding; instead, basecamps were located on the sand terraces overlooking the floodplain of the Esopus Creek, and these types of sites have been found to extend from Saugerties to Marbletown. An example of a seasonal base camp to the south of the Kingston Meadows parcel is the Angstrom site (Cammisa et al. 2007, 2009), located just above the train tracks along Hurley Avenue.

The Angstrom Site

The Angstrom site was named after former homeowner Dr. Clement Angstrom and his family. The site was excavated to mitigate the effects of a housing complex (Hurley Crossing) on the archaeological resources present along the sand terrace just above the train tracks about 400 to 500 feet north of Hurley Avenue. This particular study is instructive for three reasons. The first is that it illustrates the contrast between the Angstrom site and sites on the floodplain just below it at Kingston Meadows. The second is that it is a well-studied site with multiple occupations as well as floral and faunal data that point to precontact diet. The third is that a description of the process, from finding the site during the Phase 1B reconnaissance to mitigation of the impacts during the Phase 3, conveys an understanding of how contract archaeology, or CRM, works.

During a Phase 1B field reconnaissance undertaken in 2007, 39 shovel tests were excavated at 50-foot (15.2 m) intervals across the terrace (Cammisa et al. 2007). A total of 41 artifacts, including two bifaces and one scraper, were found. The rest of the lithic material was debitage, but the important thing to keep in mind is that the Phase 1B investigation established the presence of a precontact site. This is the main point of the Phase 1 archaeological reconnaissance survey: establishing the presence or absence of cultural resources.

The Phase 2 site evaluation was also undertaken in 2007 (Cammisa et al. 2007). In this case, 30 close-interval shovel tests at 25-foot (7.6 m) intervals were combined with 10 1-meter (108 sq ft) excavation units. The Phase 2 investigation yielded 1,653 artifacts reflecting a variety of functions at this site. This assemblage included 1,234 debitage, 2 cores, 20 bifaces, 1 spokeshave, 1 utilized flake, 1 nutting stone, 11 projectile points, 4 scrapers, 2 hammerstones, 167 FCR, 2 sandstone ochre balls, 2 quartz crystals, and 237 fragments of precontact pottery. In addition to these finds, eight features were identified at the interface between the A-horizon soils and the subsoil. The soils at the site were described as a dark gray-brown loamy sand (A-horizon) overlying a yellow brown loamy sand (B-horizon or subsoil).

A Phase 3 mitigation of the site (Cammisa et al. 2009) was undertaken in the form of an additional 34 1-meter units (366 sq ft) combined with mechanical stripping of the A-horizon soil. Mechanical stripping, while it sounds incredibly destructive, is a relatively common method used by archaeologists to strip away the A-horizon soil, which is often a plow zone, and search for truncated features below it. "Truncated" features are archaeological features have been cut by the plow. The truncation line is the interface where the plow zone above (which is generally dark brown) and the undisturbed subsoil below (which is usually yellow brown) meet. The features appear as dark stains on a yellow background, and the soil inside or within the feature has usually remained untouched since the feature was filled in. Precontact features often hold dietary information such as faunal and floral remains, which can be used for radiometric dating of a site.

The Phase 3 investigation produced 3,500 artifacts, 435 faunal remains (shell, bone), and a large sample of floral remains. The artifacts included 2,102 debitage, 7 cores, 24 projectile points, 31 bifaces, 7 scrapers, 3 preforms, 2 hammerstones, 2 nutting stones, 3 other pitted stones, 1 pestle, 2 mullers, 2 drills, 1 knife, 1 plummet, 1 bolas stone, 1 anvil, 1 abrader, 1 spokeshave, and 1 adze. Additionally, 147 precontact pottery fragments and one Native American smoking pipe fragment were found. Cammisa (et al. 2009) also used flotation to determine whether botanical remains were preserved in the soils and within the features. Soil samples used for flotation are labeled, dried, and then "floted" in a tank to allow small botanical remains and dried bone to flot to the surface, where they are skimmed off with a small fish net. The sample is then sent to a paleobotanist to determine which plants, if any, are in the sample. Although flotation samples did not recover any seeds, Native Americans at the site were probably smoking *Nicotiana rustica*, a wild form of tobacco that was later domesticated by Europeans.

The occupations identified at the Angstrom site began in the Middle Archaic with the Neville phase c. 6630–5000 BC (cal. 8580–6950 BP) and included a number of Late Archaic archaeological cultures that are found throughout the Hudson Valley, such as the Vergennes phase at c. 4000–3000 BC (cal. 5950–4950 BP), the Vosburg phase at c. 3000–2500 BC (cal. 4950–4450 BP), and the Lamoka/Sylvan Lake phase at c. 3100–1900 BC (cal. 5500–3850 BP). The Transitional Archaic was represented by the Frost Island phase at c. 1500–1200 BC (cal. 3450–3150 BP) and the Orient phase at c. 1100–750 BC (cal. 3050–2700 BP). The Early Woodland was represented only by the Fox Creek phase at c. 350–500 AD (cal. 1600–1450 BP). The Middle Woodland was represented by a sample of Jack's Reef points (c. AD 600–900/cal. 1350–1050 BP), and the Late Woodland by both Levanna points and several kinds of precontact pottery (Castle Creek/Bainbridge forms, Oak Hill/Kelso Corded, Cayadutta-Otstungo Incised).

In their reports, archaeologists usually discuss features separately for several reasons. The first is that artifacts from a feature are below the truncation line discussed above, which means they have not been disturbed by plowing. We assume that the artifacts are in their original position, whether intentionally placed or used as fill in precontact times. Sometimes we find earthen ovens filled with FCR or reddened cobbles, and other times we might find the remains of a whole pot that was simply left in a hearth after it broke into fragments and was no longer usable. Of the 39 features that were found during the Phase 3 study of this site, six of these were very informative, particularly in regard to archaeological phase and diet. This once again points to the importance of Kingston's sandy Riverhead series soils for the construction of pits and hearths.

Feature 9 was a series of post molds that were radiometrically dated to 430 +/− 40 BP (Beta-261281; cal. 2σ AD 1420–1500). The post molds were found in a pattern suggesting a potential hide rack or a rack for drying skin during the tanning process. Tools associated with hide preparation would have been flensing (skinning) tools, which are usually made of bone or antler; stone scrapers; and bone punches or drills for making holes in animal hide to fabricate clothing. The stone scrapers are noted above, and were found at the site, but bone punches or drills would have decomposed in the soil.

Feature 36, which was likely a cooking pit, was radiometrically dated to 410 +/− 40 BP (Beta-261286; cal. 2σ AD 1430–1520). This pit produced Oak Hill phase pottery, hickory nuts (*Carya sp.*), a nutting stone, a bolas stone, a spokeshave, a biface, and lithic debitage.

Feature 42, most likely a cooking pit, was radiometrically dated 430 +/− 40 BP (Beta-261287; cal. 2σ AD 1420–1500). Macrobotanicals found during flotation analysis included corn (*Zea mays*), hickory nuts (*Carya sp.*), and walnuts (*Juglans nigra*).

Feature 44, a cooking or storage pit, produced Oak Hill/Kelso (c. 1300–1400 AD) and possible Bainbridge (c. 1200–1300 AD) pottery. Fragments of a Native American smoking pipe were also recovered from this feature.

Feature 45 was a shallow refuse-filled pit with numerous bone fragments, including elk (*Cervus canadensis*), white-tailed deer (*Odocoileus virginianus*), raccoon (*Procyon lotor*), squirrel (*Sciurus sp.*), unidentified bird (*Aves*), and sturgeon (*Acipenser sp.*). One of the deer bones had evidence that it had been chewed on by a large canid, probably a wolf or dog. Macrobotanical remains were limited to one bean (*Phaseolus vulgaris*), the only evidence for this cultigen on the site. This feature also yielded a small Oak Hill–like pot sherd that had a rim diameter of about 7 centimeters. As noted by Cammisa et al. (2009, 35–36), "It was probably used as a small salve or grease pot. Native American medicinal salves can often involve animal fat (grease) and/or vegetable salve, such as pine sap/resin (Moerman 2004). Animal grease could also be used to keep one warm during cold periods or swims, shine one's hair, disguise one's appearance and smell."

Feature 46, which produced a radiometric date of 550 +/- 40 BP (Beta-261289; cal. 2σ AD 1310–1360), was likely a cooking pit. Food remains included white-tailed deer (*Odocoileus virginianus*) and hickory nuts (*Carya sp.*). Two kinds of pottery were recovered from the feature: Oak Hill/Kelso Corded (c. 1300–1400 AD), possibly Bainbridge Linear (c. 1200–1300 AD), and a possible Castle Creek Incised-Neck pot. These combined Castle Creek and Oak Hill phase artifacts (c. 1200–1400 AD) were recovered along with an anvil, a preform, debitage, and FCR.

The Phase 3 mitigation of the Angstrom site produced evidence of many more archaeological cultures than the Phase 1 and Phase 2 studies, essentially pushing the occupation of the site back to the Neville phase and demonstrating that the site consisted of a series of short-term camps during the Late Archaic Vergennes, Vosburg, and Lamoka/Sylvan Lake phases as well as the Transitional Archaic Frost Island and Orient phases. However, most of the important dietary information originated from the Late Woodland period, between the 14th and early 17th centuries. According to Cammisa et al. (2009, 36), "most carbon-dated features fell close to or within the pottery dates recovered within them, from the 1200's to 1400's AD. Many of these features, could have been occupied simultaneously. If many, or just more than one of these features were indeed used simultaneously, then it appears that the site could have been functioning as a village or horticultural hamlet." Food remains such as nuts

> were recovered from a number of Late Woodland features and included hickory (most popular) as well as a chestnut/or oak, and oak. Chestnuts, besides being used to eat as nuts, can also be made into a flour. Hickory nuts can be also eaten as a nut or ground into flour. The nuts can be processed into oil, and the

tree sap into syrup or sugar. Acorn (oak nuts) can be eaten as nuts, although most need to be treated with a series of boiling in water to leach out the bitter tannin, usually roasted. They can also be ground in meal (flour) to make breads or muffins (Peterson 1977:190, 202, 204). Medicinally, astringent inner tree bark from white and northern red oaks can be used to treat chronic diarrhea, dysentery, bleeding, anal prolapse, piles, as a wash for skin eruptions, poison ivy, and burns, etc. (Foster and Duke 1990:278, 280 [citation in original]). (Cammisa et al. 2009, 36)

The wide range of tool types at this site—for hunting and butchering, fabricating and processing, plant processing, and cooking—demonstrates that people were using this terrace as both short-term or seasonal camps during the Archaic and probably as a series of small horticultural hamlets during the Middle to Late Woodland. The Angstrom site is situated on well-drained soils that overlook the Esopus Creek floodplain in a location where people can camp all year long. This site location is almost the exact opposite of the 12 Kingston Meadows loci that it overlooks: sites on the floodplain that are short-term procurement localities. It is also possible that the people who left artifacts at the Angstrom site were the same or related to the people who left artifacts at the Kingston Meadows sites.

The Duck Pond Site

The Duck Pond site (NYSM #729/USN #11140.000620) is located along Hurley Avenue near the tunnel under the New York State Thruway. The site was surface collected by Mr. George Van Sickle of Marbletown, New York, primarily in 1970. The site was registered with the New York State Museum in 1991, and it also has an OPRHP Unique Site Number (USN). Mr. Van Sickle's collection of artifacts included 103 lithic artifacts (table 2.6) and one piece of cord-wrapped, stick-impressed pottery. The lithics from the site (fig. 2.23) included temporally diagnostic artifacts from the Neville, Vosburg, Sylvan Lake, and River phases, and a sample of Levanna points from the Late Woodland period. Based on their small size, the latter appear to date c. 1400 AD to European contact. This would fit well with the one piece of pottery, which typically dates to c. 1300–1400 AD. One of the more interesting items, and one of the few lithics that confirms a Contact period occupation, was a utilized flake of either English or

Table 2.6. Duck Pond site artifact table.

Point Type/Tools	Mt. Merino Chert	Maroon Indian River Chert	Black Morehouse chert	Waxy Gray WO chert	Black & Brown chert	Gray-Black chert	Mottled Onondaga chert	Quartz Crystal	English/French flint	Gray Chert	Red Jasper	Metamorphosed Quartzite Sandstone	Sandstone	phyllite	Totals	% by row
Levanna			1							2					3	2.9
Triangle/w drill bit			1							1					2	1.8
Triangle /w scaper			1												1	0.9
Triangular preforms	1		2							3					6	5.9
Normanskill	1														1	0.9
Sylvan Stemmed							1	1							2	1.8
Brewerton Side-Notched												1			1	0.9
Neville						1									1	0.9
Proj. Point Fragments	1		1							2					4	3.9
Debitage	2	1	6				1			3	1				14	13.8
UF w/ graver spur	1		1												2	1.8
UF/spokeshave	1		3												4	3.9
Utilized Flakes	11		15				8		1	3					39	35.9
UF on blockie							1			1					2	1.8
Scrapers		3					1								4	3.9

continued on next page

Table 2.6. Continued.

Point Type/Tools	Mt. Merino Chert	Maroon Indian River Chert	Black Morehouse chert	Waxy Gray WO chert	Black & Brown chert	Gray-Black chert	Mottled Onondaga chert	Quartz Crystal	English/French flint	Gray Chert	Red Jasper	Metamorphosed Quartzite Sandstone	Sandstone	phyllite	Totals	% by row
ovate biface	1									1					1	0.9
biface fragments		4	4	2	1					2					14	13.8
Pitted Stone/HS													1		1	0.9
Netsinker													1		1	0.9
Unid. Ground stone														1	1	0.9
Totals by Lithic	19	8	35	2	1	1	12	1	1	18	1	1	2	1	103	
% by Lithic	18.6	7.7	34	1.8	0.9	0.9	11.9	0.9	0.9	17.6	0.9	0.9	1.8	0.9		100

French flint (fig. 2.23). This flake was too large to be from a gunflint and is probably derived from flint nodules that occur along the East Coast as ships' ballast, originating in Europe. This could have been a trade item between the Dutch and the local Esopus, or it may have been picked up along the shore of the Hudson River and traded inland.

One characteristic of this site was the large numbers of utilized flakes, utilized flakes on blockies, utilized flakes with spokeshaves, and utilized flakes with graver spurs. When combined, these totaled 47 artifacts, or 46.6%, of the collection. These materials may relate to the cutting of cattails and the processing of cattail roots and stalks. Alternatively, they could have been used for stripping the bark off plants to make spear, javelin, and dart shafts. Other artifacts included a small netsinker. The 21 projectile points and fragments point to hunting activities, or at least the reworking of spear, javelin, or dart tips, at the site.

Figure 2.23. Duck Pond site. Upper row, left to right: Neville Stemmed point, Brewerton Side-Notched point, Normanskill point, two Sylvan Stemmed points. Middle row, left to right: three Levanna points, one English/French flint utilized flake, one Precontact pottery. Bottom row, left to right: ground stone fragment, netsinker. *Source:* Photo by the author.

The artifacts from the Duck Pond site are suggestive of a location where Native Americans hunted, possibly fished for small freshwater fish, and potentially harvested cattail stalks and cattail roots as well as other plants to produce shafts for hunting. As mentioned above, the time period represented by the diagnostic artifacts ranges from c. 6630 BC to the time of European contact.

Summary

This chapter has discussed precontact sites within the corporate boundary of the city of Kingston. These sites represent the full range of precontact Native American cultures in the Hudson Valley, from Paleoindians to the ancestors of today's Delaware groups and the Stockbridge-Munsee Band of Mohicans. The sites range from base camps and later horticultural hamlets to smaller camps, extraction sites (quarries), and rockshelters. These sites are primarily Native American in material culture (artifactual) content.[19] Later chapters will discuss 17th- and 18th-century sites, particularly those in the stockade area, that physically overlap with earlier Native American occupations.

Chapter 3

Early Historic Background

A historic overview of the project area (*Wiltwyck*) reaches back to September of 1609, when Henry Hudson sailed up the river in his ship the *Half Moon*. Hudson was hired by the Dutch East India Company to find a northeast passage to the Orient, but when that was unsuccessful, he began to seek a Northwest Passage by sailing across the Atlantic. After reaching the New World, he sailed down the Atlantic Coast to Delaware Bay and then turned north to explore the area of present-day New York Bay. After spending over a week in the region of what is now Sandy Hook, New Jersey, and Staten Island, on September 12, he headed north up the river, eventually reaching as far as present-day Albany. Throughout the journey from Sandy Hook to Albany, the crew of the *Half Moon* met and traded with several Native American groups. Some of the meetings were less than friendly, and members of the *Half Moon* as well as several Native Americans were killed. Although not describing the Esopus per se, Robert Juet, the first mate of the *Half Moon*, offered a description of the Catskills as "other Mountains which lie from the Rivers Side" (Jameson [1909] 2010, 21).

One of the earliest forts set up in the Hudson Valley after 1609 was the short-lived Fort Nassau, in present-day Albany, which, from descriptions, appears to have been a small, palisaded fort with a moat. The fort was built specifically to facilitate trade with local Native Americans, particularly for furs and beaver pelts. The Dutch occupation of what is now Kingston did not occur until after the building of earlier forts in present-day Albany, that is, the construction and demise of Fort Nassau between 1614 and 1621, and then the construction of Fort Orange in 1624.

Later, in 1640, on a voyage up the river, David DeVries noted that he "came to Esoopes,[1] where a creek runs in; and there the savages had much maize-land, but all somewhat stony" (Jameson [1909] 2010, 206).[2] Other than a few individuals trading with Native American groups in the Kingston area, there was no substantial settlement of the area until after 1652, when Thomas Chambers and others purchased land from local Native Americans, hereafter referred to as "the Esopus."[3]

Interestingly, the idea of a trading post or fort in the location now known as Kingston Point, or Rondout Island, has been around for over a century and has recently reappeared in a pamphlet on Kingston's history. However, DeVries did not specifically mention a trading post or fort, and the historical record does not back up the claim. As Fried (1975, 155–61) has suggested, the idea of the fort was likely a misinterpretation of a later correspondence in 1664 describing not a fort on the Hudson but the village of *Wiltwyck* (now uptown Kingston). It is possible, however, that there was a small redoubt, or fortification, on the Rondout Creek at this time along what is now called "the Strand." This would have been used to store and protect goods moving to and from *Wiltwyck*. Today, the archaeological remains of this would likely be under several feet of 19th- and 20th-century fill, if it was not destroyed by construction. Also bear in mind that travel from *Wiltwyck* to the creek would have entailed heading down present-day Albany Avenue and turning right at Foxhall Avenue to begin the drop down lower Broadway to the creek. Both goods and people would have needed a place of protection as well as a location for storage of goods near the creek while ships' captains waited for a northerly or southerly breeze to take them upriver or downriver, respectively. There are numerous instances in the historical record, particularly the *Wiltwyck* court minutes, mentioning that ships could not sail either for want of a wind or a wind from the wrong direction. Remember that during the age of sailing, wind direction and speed could either move a ship along or prevent it from moving upwind, particularly within the narrow confines of the Hudson River's channel.

During the 17th century, the movement of goods and communications to both Fort Orange and New Amsterdam (today's Manhattan) would have been from the village of *Wiltwyck* to the Strand via the "Road to Flatbush," which is present-day Albany Avenue. From here, it would have bifurcated, with one branch leading to Saugerties, on what is now Route 32, and the other proceeding south, down what is now Foxhall Avenue. As tensions between the settlers and Native Americans grew, the road from present-day Foxhall Avenue to the Strand would have been a dangerous journey because of the possibility of attack by the Esopus.

Community Defense: The Stockade

In his *Early History of Kingston and Ulster County*, Marc Fried (1975, 15–18) carefully documented the first purchase of land in "Esopus" by Thomas Chambers in June 1652, with another addition purchased by Johannis Dykman near the Strand, or present-day Roundout Creek, on August 16, 1653. However, although these purchases from local Native Americans are recorded, there is no solid evidence to suggest actual settlement in the Esopus region prior to 1654. This is followed by land transactions by Christopher Davis (also called Cristoffel or "Kit" Davits) in 1653, Evert Pels (c. 1654), Juriaen Westphaelen (c. 1659), and Jacob Jansen Stoll, who also makes his first appearance in the literature in 1654 (Fried 1975, 15–19). Other early settlers were Johan de Hulter, who purchased land at Esopus (*Wiltwyck*) in 1654, and Cornelius Barentsen Slecht, who Fried first identified as appearing in the literature c. 1655 or early 1656 as a cook working for Thomas Chambers (1975, 20). Fried suggested that settlement by several of these individuals had positively occurred by June 10, 1653, but points out that Chambers and others could possibly have arrived after the deed of June 5, 1652 (1975, 24–25).

In 1657, due to warfare between local Native American groups and the Dutch in the vicinity of New Amsterdam, and particularly Staten Island, tensions also began to rise in the Hudson Valley. Many of these communications can be found in *Documents Relating to the Colonial History of the State of New York* (Fernow 1881). On September 15, in a letter from the directors of the Dutch West India Company (the Dutch trading company) to the director-general of New Amsterdam, Peter Stuyvesant, it was stated that "a redoubt at the Esopus for the defense and protection of our inhabitants there would be not only useful, but also necessary, as we have recommended it before to-day to your Honors" (Fernow 1881, 73). This apparently never occurred, as from what we know of the settlement pattern of the Dutch at the time, particularly from what we can gather from the historical record, the initial choice for house locations was in a dispersed pattern, making each household individually vulnerable to attack. Fried (1975, 27) suggested that the Dutch temporarily left the area out of fear of Native American attacks, a concept also mentioned by Chambers (cited below). On April 12, 1658, Jacob Jansen Stoll, in a letter to Stuyvesant regarding his debt of wheat (or Guilders) to Harman Jacobson, added,

> Besides, Sir, please not to take it amiss, if I ask, whether the people of Fort Orange have leave to sell openly brandy and distilled water to the savages, the barbarous people, as we, not only I, but all of the inhabitants of the Great Soopis see them daily drinking, while they say, that they get it from there; no good can come of it, but it must tend to the ruin of the whole country. They have also caused great inconveniences to Jacob Andriesen on the Strand, while they were intoxicated. (Fernow 1881, 76–77)

The "inconveniences" mentioned by Stoll were detailed in a later letter of October 15, 1658, where it was stated that "about a year or eighteen months ago they had wounded with a hatchet one Jacob Andriaesen on the head, while in his own house, in consequence of which he is still blind in one eye and that they also mortally wounded his little child" (Fernow 1881, 93). Over two weeks later, on May 2, 1658, Thomas Chambers wrote to Director Stuyvesant,

> To-day, the first of May 1658 great trouble has arisen here in the fearful intoxication of the cruel barbarians and I myself with one Pieter Dircksen and Hendrick Cornelissen came to-day to the tennis-court and saw that the savages had an ancre of brandy lying under a tree and have tasted myself, that it was pure brandy and according to all appearances they got madly intoxicated and about dusk they fired and killed Harmen Jacopsen, who was standing on the yacht of *Willem Moer*, and during the night they set fire to the house of Jacop Adrijansen, so that the people were compelled to fly; therefore I request, that we should receive assistance of troops, that we may make some stronghold for our defence; as we have been driven away once before and expelled from our property and it begins anew now, therefore, as long as we are under the jurisdiction of the Honble West-India Company, it is proper, that we should ask your honor for assistance, so that this fine country might be retained and we remain in our property,

for this Aesopus is a place, which if well peopled could feed the whole of New-Netherland and it would be, so to say, a sin, which could be avoided, if we should have to leave such a splendid country: hence we do not doubt, but your Honor will assist us speedily and I have informed myself among the savages, who or which savage had killed the aforesaid Harmen, and they have promised to deliver the said savage in bonds to myself and I shall send him to your Honor, but please to be careful and not begin the war to suddenly, so that we may first have a stronghold for our defense and as there is a good chance here, to inflict great damages to the savages, we hope your Honor will quickly assist us and not desert us in time of distress. (Fernow 1881, 77–78)

The next letter of Thomas Chambers, together with Stoll, Slecht, Dircksen, Broersen, Jansen, and Van der Sluys (May 18, 1658), to the Council of New Netherland (located in the city of Amsterdam) told the following story:

We now report that, that although we have done our best to apprehend the murderer, we are mockingly refused by the barbarians and as to the seller of the brandy the savages refer us to no one, but to many, now Peter then Paulus. But it is evident, that not only for the sake of selling their stock of beavers they all keep near Fort Orange, whereas the maker of the brandy-keg proves, the coopers have hardly sufficient time, to supply the demand by these people. The savages have, as we have previously communicated to your Honors, set fire to the cowshed, the pigsty and then the dwellinghouse of Jacop Adrijaensen and not being satisfied compelled us here, to plough for them, taking upon refusal a fire-brand and holding it under the roofs of the houses, to set fire to them; they use great violence every day, which we are not capable to relate to your Honors, and derisively say, that if they kill a Christian or more, they can pay for it in wampum and we have so far been obliged to carry out their wishes (Fernow 1881, 79).

The writers described the size of the Dutch population at Esopus (60–70 individuals), the amount of seed planted (990 schepels of seed), and the need for 40 to 50 additional men for defense (Fernow 1881, 79). These two letters yielded a positive response from Pieter Stuyvesant on May 28, 1658, when he agreed to go to *Wiltwyck* "forthwith, taking 50 or 60 soldiers with him as his body-guard, in order to make such arrangements, as he shall find necessary and the best advantage of the Company, this province and its inhabitants shall require" (Fernow 1881, 80). These documents give us a glimpse of the situation at this time, suggesting that, for many of the settlers and probably also for the Esopus, war was on the horizon.

Stuyvesant landed at Esopus (now the Strand in Rondout) on May 29, 1658. On May 30, at the home of Jacob Jansen Stoll, Stuyvesant and several settlers had a meeting with the community and a group of concerned Esopus. Several options were presented to the Native Americans, most of which related to reparations for Dutch settlers killed, buildings burned, and pigs slaughtered. Stuyvesant later stated,

> In closing the conference I stated and informed them of my decision, that to prevent further harm being done to my people or brandy being sold to them, all my people should move to one place and live close by each other; that it would be the best, if they were to sell me the whole country of the Esopus and move inland or to some other place; and that it was not good, that they lived so near to the *Swannekus*, that is white men or Dutch, so that the cattle and hogs of the latter could not run any more into the cornfields of the savages and be killed by them and similar reasonings after the customs of the savages to the same purpose, namely, that they ought to sell me all the land in the vicinity, as they had previously offered and asked us to do, which they took in further consideration, as the day was sinking and so we separated. (Fernow 1881, 85)

At this time, Stuyvesant also met with members of the Dutch community on several occasions. Due to the upcoming harvest, each family head tried, unconvincingly, to be the focal point of the proposed new settlement. In his journal, Stuyvesant stated,

> I told them then, that no protection was possible, as long as they lived so separate from each other, that it would therefore be for the best and add to their own safety, in fact absolutely necessary, as I thought that they should either immediately

move together at a suitable place, where I could and would help and assist them with a few soldiers until further arrangements could be made, or retreat to the Manhattans or Fort Orange with their wives, children, cattle and most easily moved property, so as to prevent further massacres and mischiefs; else if they could not make up their minds to either, but preferred to continue in such a precarious situation, they should not disturb us in future with their reproaches and complaints. Each proposition was discussed, but it would be too tedious to repeat the debates in detail . . .

The necessity of a concentrated settlement was conceded, although discussion ran high regarding this point as well as on account of the time, harvest being so near at hand and it being therefore thought impossible to transplant houses, barns and sheds before it, as on account of the place, where the settlement was to be made, for every one proposed his own place as being the most conveniently located; to this must be added, that they were to help in enclosing the settlement with palisades, which they apprehended, could not be done before harvest time. (Fernow 1881, 83)

The following day, an agreement was signed by members of the community, which provides us with information on community settlement patterns. On May 31, nine members of the community, among them Stoll, Chambers, and Slecht, wrote,

We the undersigned, all inhabitants of the Aesopus, having from time to time experienced very distressing calamities and felt and discovered, to our loss, the unreliable and unbearable audacity of the savage barbarous natives, how unsafe it is to trust to their promises, how dangerous and full of anxiety to live at separate places away from each other among so faithless and mischievous tribes, have resolved (upon the proposition and promise made by the Director-Genereal, the Honble Petrus Stuyvesant, that he will give us a safe-guard and further help and assist us in future emergencies) and deemed it necessary for the greater safety of our wives and children, to pull down our scattered habitations in the most convenient manner immediately after signing this agreement and to move close to each other to the place indicated by the Honorable General, to enclose the place with palisades of proper length with the assistance provided thereto by the Honorable General, so that we may protect ourselves and our property by such means. (Fernow 1881, 81)

The implications of this document are that prior to May 1658, the settlement pattern of the community could be classified as "dispersed," which made each family's houses, barns, and outbuildings an isolated and indefensible target for attack. Unlike the stone houses that many people associate with the earliest historic occupations, such structures were more likely wattle-and-daub houses or semi-subterranean houses with basements similar to those found by Paul Huey during archaeological excavations at Schuyler Flatts, near present-day Albany (Huey 1987, 1998). Remains of these types of structures have not been found in the area around Kingston, although we can still hope that, in the future, archaeological testing in previously undisturbed areas prior to proposed construction might locate them.

Considering that settlement would have occurred by 1654, and that movement to the hilltop location (discussed below) would have occurred in 1658, this means that archaeological evidence of the settlement would likely consist of a minimal amount of information reflecting the basic sustainment of life: shelter, a location for food preparation, a source of water, a location to eliminate human waste, and a garden or animal pen. South (1979, 228) has defined the basic components of British colonial life for various socioeconomic classes in the 18th century. For example, a "lower class household" would have been comprised of the minimum of structural components that a family or person would need to survive: a house and kitchen, a well, a chicken house, a privy (outhouse), a pig pen, a vegetable garden, and a toft or yard area. Adapting this concept to the 17th-century Hudson Valley Dutch would require few alterations. Homesteads would have likely included a house or kitchen, represented by part or all of a semi-subterranean structure; a well; possibly a privy (although even this is in doubt); posts for a Dutch-style adjustable corn crib; a pig pen; and a vegetable garden. Archaeologically, many years of accumulated fragmentary material culture within and surrounding these structures in the humic zone or about the first 10 inches (25 cm) of the soil is a common find. The types of material culture that survive in the soil and across a cultivated field for 300 years most often include smoking pipe fragments, wampum, European ceramics, glass cassock buttons, glass beads, copper or brass fragments, and personal items such as marbles, mouth harps, or metal buckles for shoes or belts. Animal bones (called "faunal remains" by archaeologists) that would have been commonly discarded in trash deposits outside of 17th-century houses would likely not have survived several hundred years of plowing and would otherwise have decomposed in the soil over a period of a few hundred years.

It is noted above that the use or presence of privies is questionable, and this is because none have been found from any 17th-century context to date. This suggests the likelihood that, during this time, as vividly portrayed in a chapter by Noël Hume (2003, figs. 3, 73), bodily wastes were collected in chamber pots and then disposed of outdoors, and not necessarily in the same place over a period of time. In this case, archaeologists may sometimes be looking for a category of features (i.e., privies) that may not exist archaeologically outside of urban situations.

Pig pens used historically may only be visible archaeologically as rows of posts associated with internal deposits of organic material, and these features may simply have been fences to keep pigs out of the garden rather than used specifically as pig pens. Fried (1975) noted that a major source of conflict between the Dutch and Native Americans, and a partial cause of the First Esopus War, was the Dutch habit of letting their pigs roam freely to forage, which often included forays into Native American maize and squash fields.

Corn cribs or hay ricks of the Dutch variety would be visible archaeologically at the interface between the humic zone and subsoil as a circle or square of large posts, which would vary in size depending on the circumference of the corn crib (see book cover, far right). Other structures relating to farming, specifically barns and sheds, may have lacked permanent footings. It is my opinion that early vernacular architecture that may have required stone footings (particularly Dutch barns) would no longer be visible in the archaeological record due to plowing and stone removal from fields in the 18th and 19th centuries. However, tool fragments and building hardware such as pintles, hinges, and nails might be found (although the Dutch were adept at building wooden hinges, which would not preserve so well).

Although the quantity of nonperishable items that would have been brought from Fort Orange to the Esopus during this time period is unknown, it was likely minimal, given a window of time between 1654 and 1658, the short period during when the Dutch lived in dispersed farms around what is now Kingston. Archaeologist James Deetz (1977,

94) described two specific concepts as they relate to archaeological interpretation of a site that are relevant here: focus and visibility. "Focus" is how well you can "read" or interpret an archaeological site. "Visibility" means how visible the site is when you come upon it. Is it at the surface, or does it have walls that are eight feet high? The latter would be an example of a very visible site. The very narrow window of occupation for these Dutch farmsteads would provide excellent *focus* because the material culture would be limited to a four-year time span of potential deposition. However, this short time span would also affect the amount of material culture observable on the surface, or in testing, thus making site *visibility* low. The location and excavation of one of these early farmsteads would provide us with detailed information on material culture inventory, diet, building construction, and use of space. Each homestead would also represent a defined "time capsule" given the short four-year occupation span.

Building the Stockade and the Beginnings of War

As more settlers arrived in *Wiltwyck*, friction between the Dutch and the Esopus grew. This caused Pieter Stuyvesant to travel to *Wiltwyck* to concentrate the settlers in one area, which is now uptown Kingston—or what we know as the Stockade Area. The construction of the fortified village by Stuyvesant and a group of soldiers from New Amsterdam began in June of 1658:

> On Monday, the 3rd of June, in the morning I began with all the inhabitants and the soldiers of my command to dig out the moat, to cut palisadoes and haul them in wagons. The spot marked out for the settlement has a circumference of about 210 rods and is well adapted by nature for defensive purposes. At the proper time when necessity requires it, it can be surrounded by water on three sides and it may be enlarged according to the conveniences and the requirements of the present and of future inhabitants. (Fernow 1881, 85)

On the next day, Stuyvesant noted,

> On the 4th of June I went to work again with all hands, inhabitants and soldiers. For the sake of carrying on the work with

better order and greater speed I directed a party of soldiers under Sergeant Christian and some experienced woodcutters to go into the woods and to help load the palisades on the wagons, of which there were 6 or 7; the others I divided again into two parties of 20 men each, under Captain-Lieutenant Newton resp. Sergeant Andries Lourensen, who were to sharpen the palisades at one end and put them up; the inhabitants, who were able to do it, were set to digging the moat and continued, as long as the weather and rain permitted. (Fernow 1881, 85–86)

Stuyvesant remained at *Wiltwyck* for a week, took a diversion to Fort Orange, and then returned to direct the movement of buildings and the cutting, hauling, and placement of palisades. While the villagers were relocating their homes to the stockade, Stuyvesant decided to keep his promise and employ the carpenters he had brought from Fort Orange:

Therefore I resolved to have them score some timber for a small house or barn at my own expense; the ridge of it was to lie on two beams and the people, who could not move their houses so quickly, were at first to be lodged there and afterwards I thought to use it according to circumstances as wagonshed or stable for horses and cows, for I had long intended to begin the cultivation of my bouweries in the Esopus, incited thereto by the fertility of the soil, but prevented so far by the audacity of the savages and because the people were so scattered. (Fernow 1881, 87)

By noon on June 20, "the sides of the stockade were completed and it was only necessary to stop up a few apertures, where roots of trees had been in the ground: this was accomplished in good time on that day" (Fernow 1881, 87). On June 21 and 22, with an unfavorable wind for a trip to Manhattan, Stuyvesant allowed his men to rest, although several helped Thomas Chambers and Jacob Jansen Stoll break down and remove their houses[4] as well as reconstruct portions of their barns within the stockade area. On June 25, Stuyvesant left *Wiltwyck* with what he considered to be a sizeable number of men to defend the village, "for they count themselves 30 fighting men, besides the 25 soldiers and 7 or 8 carpenters, who too are well armed: they are therefore, in my opinion, perfectly able to protect themselves" (Fernow 1881, 87). Although Stuyvesant left Esopus on June

25, not everyone had moved within the walls of the stockade by that time. On August 8, Andries Louwrens wrote to Stuyvesant:

> The savages here are becoming very arrogant and spiteful and have already killed a fine mare of Jacob Jansen's; they are very angry that your Honor had challenged twenty of their men to fight against us and would have accepted the challenge; they talk about it a great deal every day and to-day about 500 savages are assembled; their number is constantly increasing, God only knows, what their intentions are. . . . Thomas Chambers and all the people from over the kil have not yet come into the fort with their dwellings and I cannot well compel them. (Fernow 1881, 88)

In a letter from Sergeant Andries Louwrens to Stuyvesant on September 28, 1658, he communicated that (1) the bridge over the kil had been swept away except for one beam; (2) Stuyvesant's barn was just as he left it in June, although several people were willing to mow reeds and Jurryen Westfalen was willing to put the roof on; and (3) bricks were needed for the guardhouse for a chimney (Fernow 1881, 92). This tells us something about the early structures in *Wiltwyck*. The first is that the manner of roofing was mowed reeds, likely cattails, and second, bricks needed to be imported from either Manhattan or Fort Orange because, at this early date, there was no manufacturing of brick taking place at *Wiltwyck*.

On October 15, 1658, a meeting was called at the house of Thomas Chambers to discuss a proposal for the purchase of land and settlement of other issues with the Esopus. The meeting included "several Sachems or chiefs of the savages, namely *Pappequahen*, *Preuwamacken* and *Nachchamatt*, to whom the following propositions were made in the presence of Captain Martyn Cregier, Schepen Pieter Wolphertsen, Pieter Cornelissen van der Veen, Augustyn Heermans and others" (Fernow 1881, 93). Negotiations failed because of disputes over payments and the lack of desire on the part of the Esopus to make a decision in the absence of several important sachems, notably *Poenap* and *Caelcop*. When their comments regarding land sales to the Dutch and payments for property transgressions were delivered, they were in the negative. Immediately, Ensign Dirck Smith was given command over a force of 50 men, with instructions to "make secure the inclosed place, mount a proper guard at the two gates and the guardhouse in daytime, as well as at night," and was requested to "not act hostilely against the savages, unless they begin first and harm the Christians" (Fernow 1881, 96). Since it was October, and the crop of winter wheat needed to be planted, it was further resolved that

> the ploughing and sowing shall proceed and be kept up as far as possible and for the present only when a guard of about 20 or 25 men under the command of a sergeant can be given, according to the desire of the inhabitants each on his own land or all working together, to protect them against the hostilities of the savage; the inhabitants besides must take their arms with them, that in case of attack they may make a better stand against the savages. (Fernow 1881, 96)

On October 28, Jacob Jansen Stoll wrote a letter to Stuyvesant stating that the Esopus were stalling, only to be followed the next day with a very positive letter describing a change in attitude on the part of the sachems:

> The Soopus Sachems or right owners of a certain piece of land, which your honor well knows of, namely the large tract spoken of by your Honor, came to my house and have given one half of it as a present to me in recomensation of what they have done, saying they hoped, that now they need fear nothing and the soldiers would lay down their arms and live as good friends ought, and that it is not always their fault but also the fault of those, who sold intoxicating liquors to them, further that they were ashamed now before other savages, who might upbraid them, now that they have given their land away to the Dutch for fear and saying on the other side that they had now satisfied the General and would discover by this grand present, what the heart of our Sachem said, whether he would not make some present to them in return. (Fernow 1881, 96–97)

In the same letter, Stoll went on to say that the Esopus asked to be trusted and said, "We ought, Christian like, (to) give them some presents in return." A postscript for alcohol or tobacco was added to the letter by Stoll, Chambers, and Ensign Smidt: "All this talking has been done with dry lips. Your Honor may imagine, how zealously we have sat here with these kings, but we hope your Honor will remember his servants and give us something good for our lungs, which we could apply ourselves, if we had it" (Fernow 1881, 97).

Except for an action taken regarding payment for the reconstruction of the bridge in Esopus (April 5, 1659), the court minutes at Fort Orange were relatively quiet until Andries Laurens's letter of May 24, 1659, which read, in part, "I have received the goods on the 20th of May, 2 barrels of meat, one barrel of bacon, 50 pounds of powder, 915 bullets, 11 musket-matches,[5] 4 ells of duffels and the weights, 6 kettles, and the corn when measured, was found to be 29½. I have heard from Andries van der Sluys and Jacob Jansen Stoll, that your Honor had promised some presents to the Indians, and the Indians are said to murmur on that account" (Fernow 1881, 99). By the end of July 1659, Andries Lourissen was warned by a Mohawk Indian named *Amiros* of an impending conflict between the Esopus and the Dutch, which was reiterated to Lourissen by Stoll. He communicated his fear to Stuyvesant on August 4, 1659, with a description that some of the settlers, mostly notably Cornelis Slecht and Willem Jansen, had gone out to bring in the corn without an armed escort (Fernow 1881, 100). On August 17, the inhabitants of Esopus petitioned the Reverend Bloem to be their minister and to "make a good bouwery for him, provide it with a house, barns, cows and other cattle as proper, to tend the land" (Fernow 1881, 103).

An additional letter to Stuyvesant again described the fears of the inhabitants based on information they gathered regarding an impending attack (Fernow 1881, 104–5). In it, they requested a bell from Fort Orange, a drum "because there are now 40 soldiers here, besides the inhabitants," "2 or three little pieces for a present to the Indians," the need for building a redoubt of sod near the guardhouse, and musket fuses. In the same letter was a request for a court to be set up. It appears that the previously acephalous grouping of Dutch at Esopus desired a court system in a Dutch style similar to that of Fort Orange and *Rensselaerswijck*: "It is necessary, that some men were pointed, also a messenger, to hold some kind of a court, that everybody, no matter who, could be made to go along. They desire that an order be given regarding the thatch-roofs of houses, in which people live and make fire without chimneys" (Fernow 1881, 104). This is another indication of the kinds of building materials that were used in the houses that were moved from the fields surrounding *Wiltwyck* to the top of the hill in 1658. The houses had thatched roofs and, due to the shortage of bricks, did not have formal chimneys. It is most likely that, at this time, the frame houses within the stockade had jambless fireplaces with an iron fireback, or simply a wattle-and-daub wall, which would include a wattle (sticks) and daub (clay) chimney for venting the fireplace.

On August 21, Andries Lourissen, writing to Stuyvesant at Manhattan, stated, "These few words are to inform your Honor only, that the savages are rather quiet at present I trust, their hasty undertaking has been postponed: further, Cit Davis continues in his old tricks of selling liquor and tattling, as I with other persons have found a drunken savage there, called *Poenap*, on Tuesday, being the 18th of August of the present year" (Fernow 1881, 105). It appears that "Cit Davis" had "an in" with the Native Americans to whom he was selling liquor. Lourissen, writing to Stuyvesant on September 1, stated, "We were further advised by Cit, that the sachem *Caelcop* had said to him, he should move away from the strand for the savages, not only the barebacks but also the Sachems had resolved, to beat us" (Fernow 1881, 105–6).

On September 4, the Esopus offered several proposals to the Dutch at *Wiltwyck*. In doing so, they also paid 68 strings of white wampum for hogs and horses killed, "for capturing our four Christians," "that the soldiers shall not beat them any more," and to faithfully seal agreements that had been previously made (Fernow 1881, 106–7). On or around September 11, Stuyvesant sent men under command of Ensign Dirck Smith to *Wiltwyck* with "three light cannons and some other ammunition of war" as well as muskets, powder, and lead (Fernow 1881, 110). On September 17, Jan Jacobson Stoll wrote to Stuyvesant, thanking him for sending the soldiers and adding, "What regards the savages, they are very quiet, but we do not know, what intentions the Almighty has concerning us" (Fernow 1881, 111).

The First Esopus War

On September 20 or 21, warfare broke out between the Esopus and the Dutch at *Wiltwyck*, with the former laying siege to the village for eight days, which prevented news of the event from reaching Fort Orange. At this point, we must remember that news, in the form of handwritten notes and letters, was brought north by boat, requiring two positive factors: an unimpeded or defended movement to the Strand and a favorable or south wind for the trip. Ensign Dirck Smith's letter to Stuyvesant on September 29 described the situation, which centered upon the fact that the Esopus had fired first. When queried, Jacob Jansen said to Ensign Smith, "We wanted to slap their mouths, for the dogs have vexed us long enough." During the day, the Esopus attempted to burn grain stacks and barns, killed a number of horses and cattle, and then took 11 prisoners. From an account of one escaped prisoner named Harmen Hendrickson, over 400 Native Americans were counted. On September 26, Vice Director La Montagne at Fort Orange wrote to Stuyvesant describing the troubles, noting that "your Honble Worships ought not to allow any weak parties to land at the Esopuskil, for the savages are there with more than four hundred well-armed men and have taken possession of Kit Davits house, where they keep a good watch and a look out" (Fernow 1881, 116). Here, it is worth wondering why the group congregated at the house of "Kit Davits." Was he somewhat isolated, or did he have a large volume of the aforementioned brandy? Writing to La Montagne at Fort Orange on September 29, Ensign Smith stated, "It has been done through the liquor, that comes to the Esopus from Fort Orange, for we are very badly off at present, obliged to be under arms day and night and there have been so many savages of all sorts and we have skirmished with them continually for twice twenty-four hours, for they have openly declared us war and will not hear of any peace" (Fernow 1881, 118). The situation worsened, as letters to Stuyvesant from Slecht and Jansen attested to, with many of the villagers being besieged at the fort and animals being killed in the fields.

On October 3, at the insistence of the Esopus, the captive Andries Lourissen sent a letter to Stuyvesant stating, "Honorable General! I inform your Honor by this savage, that matters at the Esopus are in a bad condition; it is besieged by 500 to 600 savages, so that nobody can go in or near it. I am a prisoner with 9 men, Jacob Jansen is dead with 3 others. If Esopus receives no assistance, I am afraid, it will have no good end. Our people have taken one prisoner of them" (Fernow 1881, 119). At an Extraordinary session at Fort Orange on October 19, two *Maquaes* (Mohawk) sachems castigated the Dutch for calling the Esopus "dogs" and "rascals," and dispatched a *Mahikander* (Mohican) sachem "to the Esopus, to bring here the Christian prisoners and the Esopus chiefs, directing the messinger to give the three strings of wampum in the name of the *Maquaes*, that the Esopus savages should do no harm to the Dutch up here and down at the Katskil and release the Christian prisoners or else to proclaim war" (Fernow 1881, 122). The arrangement of two Mohawk chiefs and one Mohican chief sent to ransom the captives was copied to Ensign Smith by La Montagne at Fort Orange on October 21, who added, "but be on your guard and do not trust the savages" (Fernow 1881, 123).

In late October, the two Mohican sachems arrived, spent several days with the Esopus, and brokered an armistice between the Dutch and Esopus. Ensign Dirck Smith noted in a letter to Stuyvesant on November 1 that the Mohican sachems "came back to us and brought with them 2 prisoners, a soldier and free man. The soldier's name is Pieter Lamertzen and that of the free man Peter Hillebrantzen and some sachems came with the prisoners" (Fernow 1881, 126–27). Smith's next letter to La Montagne on November 13 stated, in part, "We behave ourselves as friends but they show themselves as rascals; it is true, we have got back 2 prisoners, but they keep the boy yet and have killed all the others; it is true we have made an armistice with them, but none of the principal sachems have been present" (Fernow 1881, 127).

Ensign Smith received a letter from Stuyvesant dated December 11, 1659, in which Stuyvesant directed him to lure between 12 and 20 Esopus into *Wiltwyck*, capture them, and hold them as hostages (Fernow 1881, 128). In a letter to the Directors in Holland on December 26, Stuyvesant noted that the poor weather, the approaching winter, and the potential lack of grain should a conflict arise "compel us to abstain from hostilities against the Esopus savages and their allies for the present and await a better and more suitable time" (Fernow 1881, 131). On February 12, 1660, Stuyvesant proposed taking an offensive rather than defensive posture. He stated, "A diversion is necessary and under cover of it an expedition, which must be entrusted to but few, whether successful or not: then we must make war and carry it on first against the Esopus tribe alone in their dwelling places and wherever they may retreat to" (Fernow 1881, 136). To this, Cornelius van Ruyven, one of the Burgomasters of New Amsterdam, added that the conflict should not begin before August or September, so that "they can be discovered more easily in the woods during winter by their foot-tracks in the snow." He also suggested that "in the meantime directly to disapprove of all separate habitations and farmbuildings and to assist and promote the establishment of hamlets as much as possible, either by lending negroes or carting out pallisades" (Fernow 1881, 141). Meanwhile, Stuyvesant wrote to the Vice Director at Curacao on February 17, 1660, requesting "negroes": "The Negroes, whom the Lords-Directors ordered to send hither, must be clever and strong men so that they can immediately be put to work here at the Fort or at other places, also if they are fit for it, in the war against the wild barbarians either to pursue them when they run away, or else to carry the soldiers baggage" (Fernow 1881, 142–43). Both of the aforementioned quotes address the Dutch's use of enslaved individuals to assist them in construction as well as warfare in early 1660.

Because soldiers were at a premium, in February, Stuyvesant and the other burgomasters of the city of New Amsterdam resolved to send a ship to Virginia to raise additional forces, which was done in March. It is interesting that the Dutch should turn to the English in Virginia for help, for in the last year, they had prevented English colonists from establishing themselves near the mouth of Wappingers Creek and to the north of Fort Orange. To further isolate the Esopus, on March 6, Stuyvesant and the burgomasters of New Amsterdam signed a peace treaty with the sachems of the *Rechkawyck* (Meautinnemin), *Hackinkasacky* (Oratum), *Najeck* (Mettano), *Haverstroo* (Correspin), and *Wiechquaeskeck* (Achkhongh). The response from the Esopus was delivered 9 days later when *Coetheos*, "chief warrior of the *Wappings*," informed Stuyvesant that he was sent by the Esopus chiefs *Kaelcop, Pegh, Peghquanoch, Pemmyyrawech, Preuwamach,* and *Semeckamenee*, "lest the Dutch should come to make war against them, but since they did not come and because the Dutch had made peace with all of the other savages, they too desired to make peace and they had wampum and bearskins ready to bring here, so that the Dutch and the savages at the Esopus might again be at liberty to plant; they would have come here themselves, but they were afraid" (Fernow 1881, 150). *Coetheos* was told by Stuyvesant at that meeting that "if the chiefs of the Esopus wished to make peace, they must come here themselves" (Fernow 1881, 150). On March 17, "about 3 miles inland," Ensign Smith "came upon a house with about 60 savages, who made no resistance, but started to fly; they saw the ensign and his troops too early, but nevertheless 3 or 4 have been killed on the flight" (Fernow 1881, 151). Whether this incident precipitated the First Esopus War, or whether it was already a foregone conclusion, is open to question.

On March 25, Stuyvesant declared "to begin a war, offensive and defensive, against the aforesaid Esopus savages and their supporters" (Fernow 1881, 152). The ensuing conflict lasted for several months, with incursions by the Esopus being repulsed by the inhabitants of *Wiltwyck*. In April, 15 important members of the Esopus were captured, and then almost all were sent as slaves to Curacao in June of 1660. A treaty of peace ending the First Esopus War was signed on July 15, 1660, with delegations of the Mohawk, Mohican, Catskil, Minquas, Wappingers, Hackensacks, and four Esopus sachems (*Kaelcop, Seewackemamo, Neskahewan,* and *Paniyruways*), even though the "10 or 11" members of the Esopus were still enslaved in

Curacao. The articles of peace included the statement that "the country for two or three miles on either side of the Esopus Kil is given to us for reparation of the damages," as well as clauses to prevent the killing of horses, cattle, hogs, "nor even a chicken"; to prevent alcohol consumption among the Native Americans; to prevent warfare from occurring as a result of local quarrels; to remain unarmed near Dutch houses or settlements; and to have the mediators act as bondsmen to keep the peace, and if not, to engage with the Dutch against the Esopus (Fernow 1881, 179–81).

On September 30, 1660, Surgeon Gysbert van Imbroch of Fort Orange petitioned the West India Company for payment for treating Dominicus, a soldier during the conflict.[6] Dominicus was brought to Fort Orange by Stuyvesant himself, "having eighteen different wounds," which were treated by the surgeon. The fee was paid for in "fifty guilders in beavers" (Fernow 1881, 188–89). On April 16, 1661, Stuyvesant wrote a letter to the Vice Director in Curacao, requesting that two members of the Esopus be sent back to *Wiltwyck*.

During the first week of May 1661, the village of *Wiltwyck* was expanded, with 13 lots being created:

> The lots were distributed by lot under the condition, that every one enclose its breadth on the outside with good, stout and suitable palisades. As the cross lots have a length of 14 rods on the outside, which is too much to bear for one person, whose parcel might by lot fall on the border of the garden, therefore the said 14 rods shall be enclosed by the owners of the four cross lots together, each marking 3½ rods. (Fernow 1881, 195)

This was a means for dividing a long section of the palisade between four adjacent landowners, thus making the construction of the palisade less of a burden on the individual landowner and ensuring its rapid construction. In this case, a long section of 14 rods (51.52 m or 169 ft) can be turned into four of 3.5 rods (12.88 m or 42 ft 3 in) each. Although it is tempting to think that, following the First Esopus War, each landowner would make the palisade a priority, this was not the case. Information drawn from the Kingston court minutes (cited below) indicate that many of those owning a lot backing the palisade had gaps large enough for people to climb through, if not to trade for liquor.

With lot 1 kept open, the following persons are recorded as drawing lots 2 through 13: Hendrick Martensen (2), Harmen Hendrick (3), Jan

Jansen from Amersfoort (4), Jacob Barentsen (5), Jan Lootman (6), Jacob Joosten (7), Willem Jansen (8), Pieter van Haelen (9), Matthys Roeleffs (10), Jan Willemse (11), Anthony Creupel (12), and Gerrit Jansen van Campen (13). This construction episode is shown in figure 3.1 as an

Figure 3.1. 1695 Miller map from Fernow (1881, 84–85), with Bob Slater's overlay. *Source:* Public domain.

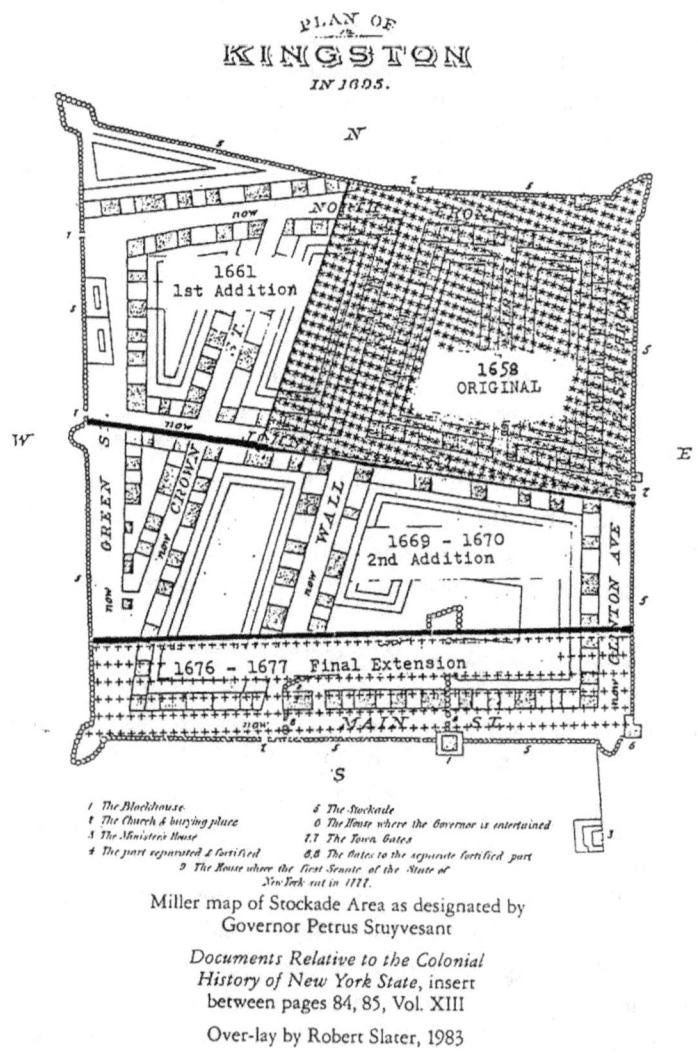

Miller map of Stockade Area as designated by Governor Petrus Stuyvesant

Documents Relative to the Colonial History of New York State, insert between pages 84, 85, Vol. XIII

Over-lay by Robert Slater, 1983

142 | The Archaeology of Kingston, New York

extension of present-day Green Street on the western edge of the terrace in uptown Kingston. It is within this 1661 addition that the predecessor of the present-day Persen House was constructed. Since the 1695 Miller map was originally lost and was then reconstructed "from memory" by Miller, it is unclear whether the number and location of houses on each block represents a reality. What is very likely is that the 13 lots set up in 1661 were subdivided within the stockade as areas that were originally intended for gardens but became prime and defensible real estate.

Fernow (1881, 212) includes an "Account of the Excise of the village of Wiltwyck, with the Names of those who Paid it" since October 24, 1661. The list is composed of 67 males who paid between 1 and slightly over 70 florins for the excise tax on wine and beer. This gives us an idea of the population that *Wiltwyck* had to defend itself.

On April 6, 1662, several members of *Beverwyck* (near Fort Orange, now Albany) petitioned the Governor General for permission to construct a new settlement at Esopus, stating,

> It is evident that the prosperity of this province of New-Netherland rest principally on agriculture and commerce; therefore the petitioners are very desirous to establish with many people a new village at the Great Esopus, where a great deal of uncultivated land lies. . . . The petitioners: are the first undertakers and settlers, to enter upon and cultivate the aforesaid lands on the Esopus, they respectivefully request, that your Honble Worships will please to give and grant each of them forty to fifty morgens of land, at and near the spot where the new village on the Esopus shall be laid out: the petitioners promise, each for himself, to enter upon the alotted lands immediately, to fence, plough, sow it, build on the lots in the village houses, barns etc. and furnish the cattle, necessary for such bouweries. (Fernow 1881, 220)

The petitioners were Phillip Pieterson Schuyler, Volckert Jansen, Gousen Gerritsen, and Andries Herbertsen (Fernow 1881, 219–20). The new village was leased in May 1662 (Fernow 1881, 220–21). Part of the agreement was that "all expenses and costs, arising on account of the village during the time of this lease, also the working on and repairing of the fortifications shall fall on the leesees." The new village, or *Niew Dorp*, was intended to be fortified, and one of the historical questions is whether or not this ever occurred. In a letter of August 16, 1662, Roeliff Swartout, the Schout of *Wiltwyck*, stated that "on the 11th of August one of Volkert Jansen's horses has been found dead in the woods, about half an hour's way into them, just back of the newly made fort" (Fernow 1881, 227). This would suggest that fortifications, if not a small redoubt, were being constructed in the New Village. In the same letter, Swartout requested 100 pounds of gunpowder and 200 pounds of lead. Shortly thereafter, on September 5, he informed Stuyvesant that the sale of liquor to the Native Americans was having a negative effect on relations with the Dutch. In addition to "the small still of Jacobsen Backer . . . the greatest mischief, which we have to expect herefrom, is caused by contraband-traders, who try to swallow up this place and sell a pint of brandy for a schepel of wheat" (Fernow 1881, 229).

Additionally, the need for some individuals to make money from the sale of liquor outweighed the possible dangers. From the Kingston court minutes of January 9, 1663, we find that "the Schout, plaintiff, demands from Mathys Roeloofson a fine of five hundred gldrs., because the savages were admitted to his house at night through the palisades, all of which the Sergeant and his roundsman declare" (Christoph et al. 1976, 1:52). Later in January, the officers of the Militia at *Wiltwyck* wrote to Stuyvesant, complaining that the court had allowed their ordinances to be pulled down with impunity (Fernow 1881, 235–36). The nine ordinances covered mustering of militia, possession of personal side and hand arms, mandatory appearance with no substitutions, and unguarded departure to the Strand. Of special interest are Ordinances 7 and 9. Ordinance 7 read, "Nobody shall be . . . allowed to load his musket with ball, wadding or paper, nor to discharge it at any window, gable or weathervane under a penalty of six guilders and reparation of the damage done." Ordinance 9 read, in part, "Nobody shall be allowed to mount guard or appear at the rendezvous, while intoxicated" (Fernow 1881, 237).

The need to keep the guards sober was as important as preventing alcohol sales to the Esopus. This was reiterated in a letter from the magistrates of *Wiltwyck* to Stuyvesant on January 24, 1663, stating, "The abuse carried on here in the sale of liquor to the savages . . . has come quite in vogue now at the new village, so that the savages have thrown each other into the fire" (Fernow 1881, 237).

In March of 1663, in a letter from the Commissaries at *Wiltwyck* to Stuyvesant, four nominations for Magistrates were listed: Thomas Chambers, Mr. Gysbert van Imbrogh (also "von Imbroch"), Jan Aersen Smit, and Cornelis Barentsen Slecht. The mention of Gysbert van Imbroch in March

1663 is his first appearance in the documents at *Wiltwyck*. According to Paul Huey (personal communication, December 30, 2004), before coming to *Wiltwyck*, Van Imbroch "was a merchant in New Amsterdam. In 1655, he obtained permission to sell by lottery 'a certain quantity' of books, and in 1657 he married the daughter of Dr. Johannes la Montagne. Apparently the books did not sell, and by reading the books and studying under his father-in-law, he became a surgeon. In 1660 he sold his house on the east side of Broadway north of Beaver Street in New Amsterdam." Because he is listed in Fernow (1881, 188–189) as a surgeon living in Fort Orange who petitioned for payment of a bill on September 30, 1660, it is probable that after he sold his house in New Amsterdam, he moved directly to Fort Orange.

By April, the overseers at *Niew Dorp* petitioned Stuyvesant for permission and help to erect fortifications around the new village and for "a few soldiers and ammunition of war, at least until the settlement has been put into a proper state of defense and inhabited by a good number of people" (Fernow 1881, 242). Those at *Niew Dorp* considered the construction of a palisade a necessity, whereas "the savages, who say, that they are willing to allow the erection of buildings, but that no fortifications must be made, which, if it should be done, would show that we had evil intentions" (Fernow 1881, 242). Stuyvesant wrote back on May 10, 1663, that "a considerable present should be made to the Esopus savages at the first opportunity, to wit, three or four pieces of duffels, some muskets, powder, lead and some Mercer's or Nuremburgh wares" (Fernow 1881, 243).[7]

The Second Esopus War

On June 7th, 1663, the Esopus attacked the settlement of *Wiltwyck*:

> They took a good time to strike, for the village was almost bared of men, who were pursuing their necessary occupations in the fields. They have burned 12 dwelling-houses in our village, murdered 18 persons, men, women and children and carried away as prisoners 10 persons more. The new village has been burned to the ground and its inhabitants are mostly taken prisoners or killed, only a few of them have come safely to this place, so that we find about 65 persons to be missing in general, either killed or captured, besides these 9 persons in our village are severely wounded. (Fernow 1881, 245)

The list of persons included Hey Olferts, who was "murdered in the gunners house." This would indicate that there may have been a house or structure specifically designed to hold a cannon or, if it was elevated, an arquebus.[8] A more detailed account of the attack was presented by the magistrates at *Wiltwyck* to Stuyvesant on June 20, 1663 (Fernow 1881, 256–57). Within this much more detailed document is a reference to Thomas Chambers, who issued an order to "secure the gates; to clear the gun and drive out the savages, who were still about half an hour in the village aiming at their persons, which was accordingly done" (Fernow 1881, 256–57). After the attack and by that evening, Chambers mustered 69 men "both qualified and unqualified" and "the burnt palisades were immediately replaced by new ones, and the people distributed during the night, along the bastions and curtains to keep watch" (Fernow 1881, 257). The magistrates also requested "carabines, cutlasses and gun flints and we request that the carabines may be snaphaunce, as the people here are but little conversant with the use of the arquebuse" (Fernow 1881, 257). What the magistrates were requesting were early flintlocks rather than the arquebus or matchlock. The flintlock had several distinct firing advantages over the arquebus. These included not needing a lit taper at all times to fire one's weapon, which made the soldier with an arquebus visible to the enemy at night. Additionally, the use of a lit taper also caused accidents with exposed gunpowder, often burning or wounding the soldier (Peterson 1956, 19–22).

One of the prisoners taken that day was Rachel La Montagne, the wife of Gysbert van Imbroch. She was later rescued in early July by a Mohawk delegation who had gone to the New Fort to attempt to rescue all of the prisoners. Mrs. van Imbroch then described in detail the defenses of the fort, its state of construction, and its location (Fernow 1881, 271–72). The information was then utilized by Captain Martin Cregier, newly commissioned to prosecute the war effort. Captain Cregier's account of his military operations in the Second Esopus War detailing the preparation, intelligence gathering, the attack on the Esopus fort, now thought to be in Shawangunk, as well as other events in and around *Wiltwyck* can be found in Fernow (1881, 323–54). For an excellent analysis of the New Fort's location, see Fried (1975, 87–102).

Although the aforementioned quote from Chambers suggests that the burned palisades were immediately repaired after June 7, this does not appear to have been the case. The need to repair the burned and fallen palisades surrounding the village appears to have been a major concern for the court as well as the military officers at *Wiltwyck*. However, an examination of the court minutes shows that motivating the villagers was a difficult task. More than a month after Cregier had defeated the Esopus at the New Fort, the palisades were still in a state of disrepair in September of 1663, as described in the following: "This Court resolves, in obedience to a previous request of the Captain Lieutenant and Council of War, to renew and replace the fallen and damaged palisades around the village, next Wednesday, September 26 with the assistance of all the inhabitants of this place, none excepted, under a penalty of twelve gldrs. for non compliance" (Christoph et al. 1976, 1:74). At an ordinary session on October 9, fines were meted out for noncompliance of the ordinance issued August 4, with the message that "no one should venture out to mow without consent and a proper armed convoy" (Christoph et al. 1976, 1:75–77). This suggests that even though the Esopus were "on the run," precautions regarding personal safety were still being enforced, even though these ordinances were often disregarded by the inhabitants of *Wiltwyck*. The court minutes show that for the next two years, this offense was one of the most common in *Wiltwyck*.

By mid-October, the repair of the palisades still had not been completed. In a session dated October 16, we find the need expressed in a resolution:

> Resolutions concerning the erection of the fortifications of this village of Wiltwyck. A note from the Captain Lieutenant, dated October 15, was read to the Honorable Court requesting that the palisades for this village of Wiltwyck be repaired and renewed, so as to serve for defense. After the reading the Honorable Court decides that there is an urgent necessity that this village be properly provided with good and new palisades, and therefore orders and directs every farmer to properly fence his lot, renewing the old palisades; and that the rest of the people, inhabitants or burghers, possessing thirty-nine lots in this village, shall from the watergate up and along the curtain walls to Aet Pietersen Tack's lot, properly repair and replace the old with new palisades of at least two feet in circumference, the thicker the better, and of a height of thirteen feet,[9] according the extent of the locality and as the Honorable Court may deem necessary. This renovation and enclosing shall commence next Monday, October 22. Wherefore, every inhabitant of this place

is notified to appear on said day at about seven o'clock, at the gate near Hendrick Jochemsens's house, there to be enrolled, for the purpose of commencing said work, and to remain at it until completed, on pain, for neglect or unwillingness, of three guilders for the first offense, twice as much for the second, and increasing so on three guilders. (Christoph et al. 1976, 1:88)

It is difficult to tell whether the resolution had the desired effect or what actually transpired on October 22. Whether the turnout was as expected, we may never know. However, the breaches in the palisades, and their overall integrity, remained an issue well into December: "December 4, 1663: The Honorable Court agrees to the proposition made by the Ensign, Christiaen Niessen, dated December 3, 1663, and to the resolution relative thereto passed by the Council of War, concerning the setting up of new and renewing of the old palisades around the village of Wiltwyck, within three days, and agrees to the same and will attend to its duty in the matter and notify the inhabitants thereof through the Village Messenger" (Christoph et al. 1976, 1:108). Although the inhabitants were probably notified, there does not appear to have been any strong motivation on the part of the villagers at *Wiltwyck* to repair the palisades. Whether this had to do with Cregier's attacks on the Esopus, the lower population and therefore visibility of the Esopus near *Wiltwyck*, or a false sense of security is difficult to judge. Problems with sealing up the exterior curtain wall remained throughout the winter and spring of 1664, as in the following, dated February 12: "In regard to the request of the Ensign, Christiaen Niessen, made to the Honorable Court, in reference to paying the woodchoppers, builders, and carters of the palisades for filling in the open spaces between the palisades near Cornelis Barentsen Slecht's and the main guard house, the Collector, Jacob Boerhans, is ordered, out of the excise money, to pay the Ensign aforenamed the sum of forty-one schepels of wheat" (Christoph et al. 1976, 1:126). And from the extraordinary session of March 1:

> The Honorable Court having seen and read the signed request of the Council of War, dated February 29, last, answers first, that the severity of the winter season does not permit any digging of the ground to fill in vacant spaces with palisades, though the palisades obtained for this purpose lie there ready,

and that the Honorable Court will do its duty by admonishing those on whose side the open spaces have to be filled in, and also by taking care to have the gates closed. (Christoph et al. 1976, 1:132)

At the end of August 1664, the threat was no longer strictly from the Esopus but also included the English, who were approaching from the south, as described in the following excerpts from the extraordinary sessions in July and September:

> The honorable Schout suggested that the fortifications be properly completed and repaired, as the savages are again gathering up the river. Also, that six or seven of the free men should watch, as the garrison at present is weak. It was resolved to commence work tomorrow. It was further suggested by Captain Thomas Chambers, that the free men are entirely unprovided with powder and shot, and he therefore requested of commissioner Beeckman that powder and shot be furnished. (extraordinary session, Monday, July 14, 1664; Christoph et al. 1976, 1:157)

> On the proposition made by the Honorable Schout what to do in case the English should approach our village of Wiltwyck, it is resolved that, at the discharge of a cannon, all the burghery shall repair to the head watch, there to receive further orders, and that in the meantime the Honorable Schout, together with the Honorable Court, shall seek to parley with said English beyond the gates. Meanwhile, the burgher officers are recommended to ascertain what powder and shot there are among the burghery, as we can not tell how the savages will act under these circumstances. (extraordinary session, Wednesday, September 4, 1664; Christoph et al. 1976, 1:161)

The English captured New Amsterdam on September 8, 1664. The English governor, Richard Nicolls, later signed a peace treaty with the Esopus on October 7, 1665, bringing the Second Esopus War to a close (Nicolls 2002). Concerns about conflict with the Esopus were still evident, however, in letters leaving *Wiltwyck*, such as the following from an ordinary session on October 21:

> Letter to Mr. Beeckman: Whereas, the Commissaries understand that your Honor has been ordered to send the Manhatans the powder and shot belonging to the Honorable Company still here, we, the Commissaries, therefore, deeming it necessary to the welfare of the village, request that your Honor be pleased to leave the packages of powder and shot here, until the English Governor at the Manhatans shall have sent us other packages of powder and shot, because, among the congregation of inhabitants here, no powder or shot can be found or procured, so that, in case of unexpected danger from the savages, the inhabitants may be provided therewith. Awaiting your Honor's written and immediate reply. (Christoph et al. 1976, 1:167)

And the following from extraordinary session of November 14:

> (Letter of October 26, 1664 from Governor Nicolls) stating basically that 1) no one shall sell brandy or liquor to the savages, and 2) that the Indians or savages be permitted to peacefully enter the village of Wiltwyck during the day to sell venison and merchandise and 3) that the inhabitants quarter the soldiers and 4) that the inhabitants and soldiers shall dwell together, in amity and friendship, so that in occasions of time or need, they may act together as one man. (Christoph et al. 1976, 1:168)

The latter refers to the quartering of English troops among the Dutch inhabitants. A perusal of the Kingston court minutes shows that this was not a particularly popular concept with the Dutch. The court minutes also continued to point to the need on the part of the villagers to fill in gaps in the palisades and to repair them in general. One of the most common problems, even after the attack of June 7, 1663, was the sale of liquor to Esopus through gaps in the curtain wall.

The New Village of Kingston

In September 1669, the village was given the name "Kingston," which held through present times, with the exception of a brief period during 1673–1674 when the Dutch temporarily retook the province and named the village *Swaenenburgh* (Fried 1975, 181). During the late 17th century and, particularly, the early 18th century, the area within Kingston that we now know as uptown Kingston grew considerably. People also spread out onto small farms within the vicinity of Saugerties, Esopus, Hurley, and Marbletown. A defining point in the 18th century was the burning of Kingston by the British army in October 1777. The British army dropped anchor near what is now Kingston Point and then proceeded up Foxhall Avenue to attack the city. A document put together shortly thereafter lists the "sufferers" or those people who had properties burned.[10]

Schoonmaker (1888) provided a glimpse of what the uptown area was like in 1820: "There were only to be found some seven or eight stone houses, at least one half of them unoccupied and falling in ruins, besides two dilapidated frame storehouses unoccupied on the dock." At this point, Kingston Landing, or the Strand, was more important as a point for import and export, having three dwellings, three storehouses, an inn, and a flour mill (Schoonmaker 1888). The late 1820s and 1830s saw an incredible expansion in the Rondout area as a result of the opening of the Delaware and Hudson (D&H) Canal, with Rondout as its terminus on the Hudson River. The D&H Canal, completed in 1828, was a 108-mile canal designed to bring the coal mined in Honesdale, Pennsylvania, to the Hudson River for shipment to metropolitan centers, particularly New York. The D&H Canal Company, whose main office was in Rondout (see Osterberg 2002, 120–23), provided fuel for the Newark Lime and Cement Company as well as for the Hutton and Terry Brickyards (Hutton 2003).

To the east of Rondout is Ponckhockie, a grouping of streets on a terrace overlooking the confluence of the Rondout Creek and the Hudson River. During the mid- to late 19th century, this area was a thriving neighborhood community made up of brickyard and cement company employees. The area of Ponckhockie, as well as Flatbush and East Kingston, were composed of communities of workers, many of whom were recent immigrants from Italy, Germany, and Ireland. Most were employed by the Newark Lime and Cement Company and the Hutton and Terry Brickyards. Blumin's (1976) volume on the urban threshold is an excellent resource for further information on 19th-century immigrants in the area.

Chapter 4

Archaeological Sites in the Stockade District

The earliest colonial Dutch settlement in the Mid-Hudson Valley, the Stockade District in Kingston, has seen little archaeological work considering its size and importance. To my knowledge, only 11 archaeological investigations have been undertaken within the district, and of these, only three have been the result of compliance with state and federal laws. This points to the need for greater involvement by the city of Kingston regarding soil disturbances and building permits within the National Register Stockade District as well as for the city to implement guidelines delineating potentially sensitive archaeological locations within the Stockade District (Diamond 1990).

This chapter is a summary of professional excavations conducted within the Stockade District in addition to two other locations in the district where important archaeological resources have been found. It should be noted that of these two, one *should have been* professionally tested and examined prior to soil disturbance that occurred during backhoe excavation for an electrical line trench along the northern edge of the stockade curtain wall. The other location was the two large parking lots on North Front Street that were stripped of the old macadam (from the early 1960s), graded out, and replaced with new and deep drainage channels. Those two lots had been waiting for archaeological investigation since the 1950s. However, both the City of Kingston and New York State agencies (the Department of Environmental Conservation and the State Historic Preservation Office) dropped the ball by not conducting a basic archaeological study prior to disturbing the soils. I was later informed that both Dutch colonial and precontact Native American artifacts were taken away with the fill. What is unfortunate is that we will never know how much of Kingston's archaeological history and precontact Native American archaeology were destroyed.

Figure 4.1 is the 1695 Miller map of Kingston showing the locations of archaeological excavations within the National Register Stockade District. The sites discussed in this chapter are the Louw-Bogardus House,

Figure 4.1. 1695 Miller map showing uptown excavations. Taken from Fernow (1881, 84–85). *Source:* Public domain.

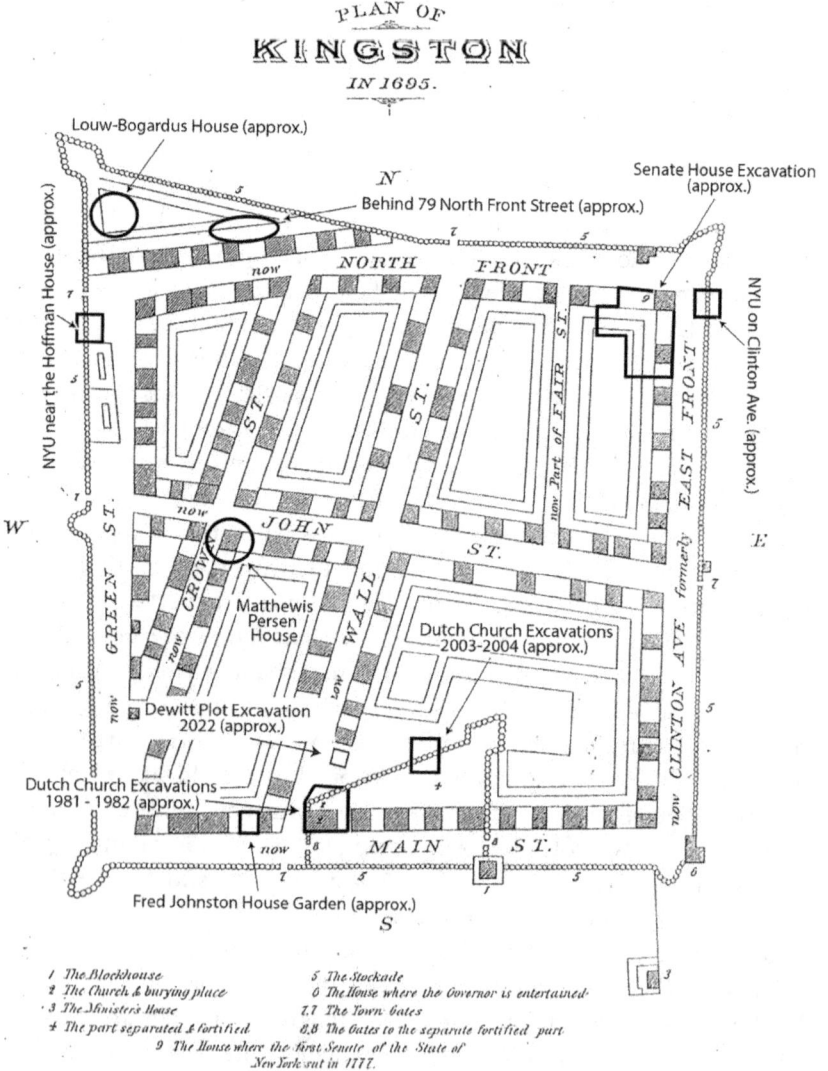

154 | The Archaeology of Kingston, New York

a site behind 79 North Front Street, New York University (NYU) excavations on Clinton Avenue, the Fred Johnston House Garden, the Fred Johnston House, the Old Dutch Church DeWitt plot, the Senate House and associated property, the Kingston Dutch Reformed churchyard, and NYU excavations on Green Street. Excavations within and outside of the Persen House have been set aside as a separate chapter, but these locations are also shown in the figure.

The Louw-Bogardus House

In 1969, a team of several local people, in conjunction with one member of the New York State Office of Parks, Recreation, and Historic Preservation (OPRHP), excavated four trenches in and around the Louw-Bogardus House ruin on Converse Street, also known as "Frog Alley" (Dolan 1969a, 1969b). The excavation was one of the first in the city of Kingston, and it eventually created a larger focus on the site as an important piece of Kingston's history. In 1974, a local urban renewal agency proposed to demolish it, but at a meeting of the Kingston City Council, because the Ulster Garden Club had an interest in acquiring the grounds, "it was decided that the local Urban Renewal agency would fence off the site until such time as a definite plan for the site has been agreed upon."[1] The site is now owned by the Friends of Historic Kingston. That small bit of public involvement saved one of the earliest structures in Kingston, something that did not happen for the gambrel-roofed Colonel Jacobus Bruyn house on the corner of North Front and Crown Street in the 1970s (Ford 2004, 11) or the birthplace of John Vanderlyn on Crown Street that was demolished by the City of Kingston in 2000 to 2001, only for the purpose of expanding the parking lot on Crown Street.

The Louw-Bogardus House was likely located on the original lot of Peter Cornelissen Louw, who, along with Pieter Jacobson, came from Holstein, Germany, to New Netherland in February of 1659 on the ship *Faith* (Huey 1981, 5; O'Callaghan 1850a, 53). Louw likely erected a structure on the property as early as c. 1661, although it is uncertain whether the present structure, which is composed of limestone, dates that early. Based on measurements of the original stone structure, Marc Fried (1975, 140–41) makes the argument that the earliest part of the house was built in 1676 by Cornelis Woutersen for Pieter Cornelis Louw. From our present knowledge of Dutch architecture in Ulster County, stone house construction likely did not begin until c. 1670–1680 (Paul Huey, personal communication, June 21, 2023), with a portion of the Senate House, like that of the Louw-Bogardus house, being perhaps two of the earliest buildings at c. 1676. Prior to this, most houses were likely frame structures with wattle and daub (sticks and clay) walls or, alternatively, had stone nogging (rocks laid with clay) between the posts. For the Louw-Bogardus House, future archaeological excavations will hopefully answer this question. Ford's (2004, 9) volume includes a c. 1922 photograph of the house when it still had a roof, doors, and windows.

The Louw-Bogardus House ruin is near the northwest corner of the stockade and was likely located within the northwestern bastion of the stockade. Pieter Cornelissen Louw ran a mill near the house beginning c. 1661 (Huey 1981, 5). The mill pond was created by damming up the small stream, called Tannery Brook, which drains the areas from present-day Linderman Avenue down to Washington Avenue and the base of North Front Street. Near the mill dam was a gate in the stockade known as the "Mill Gate," which allowed people to leave the stockade, cross the dam, and proceed down present-day Hurley Avenue to the village of *Niew Dorp*, or Hurley. The dam would have produced waterpower to mill grain from the flats below uptown Kingston as well as the flats up and down the Esopus Creek.

The four trenches excavated at the Louw-Bogardus house in 1969 produced evidence of a wide variety of 18th- and 19th-century artifacts relating to domestic use and food choices. Eighteenth-century ceramics (c. 1740–1780) found in the deposits included combed buff-bodied slip-decorated earthenware, coarse salt-glazed stoneware, creamware, porcelain, and finer salt-glazed stoneware. Faunal remains from the pre-1780 archaeological contexts suggested a reliance on beef, with pork, chicken, fish, and pigeon also present. Later deposits from c. 1780 to 1840 indicated use of pearlware, coarse salt-glazed stoneware, creamware, porcelain, red earthenware, and white earthenware or whiteware, which was developed in the 1820s. Faunal remains indicating diet were similar in the later deposits, except that mutton was also found and pigeon was missing from the sample. The sample also included a minimal amount of 17th-century materials, with mostly small red "Hudson Valley flats" or red Dutch bricks, several early pipestems, and a gray salt-glazed stoneware plate with cobalt blue decoration (Huey 1981, fig. 9). Fragments of a very similar plate were found at the Persen House site, discussed in chapter 5.[2]

In addition to this collection of artifacts, investigators found a reversal in the natural angle of the stratigraphy, suggesting there might have been a moat just to the north or west of the house. If this interpretation is accurate, this would be the only location where evidence of the moat mentioned by Stuyvesant during his visit to *Wiltwyck* has been found to date. The construction of a moat around the base of the hill in Kingston was mentioned at length in the journal of Director Stuyvesant's visit to the Esopus on May 29, 1658.

> On Monday, the 3rd of June, in the morning I began with all the inhabitants and the soldiers of my command to dig out the moat, to cut palisadoes and haul them in wagons. The spot marked out for the settlement has a circumference of about 210 rods and is well adapted by nature for defensive purposes. At the proper time when necessity requires it, it can be surrounded by water on three sides and it may be enlarged according to the conveniences and the requirements of the present and of future inhabitants. (Fernow 1881, 81–87)

On the next day, Stuyvesant noted,

> On the 4th of June I went to work again with all hands, inhabitants and soldiers. For the sake of carrying on the work with better order and greater speed I directed a party of soldiers under Seargeant Christian and some experienced woodcutters to go into the woods and to help load the palisades on the wagons, of which there were 6 or 7; the others I divided again into two parties of 20 men each, under Captain-Lieutenant Newton resp. Seargeant Andries Lourensen, who were to sharpen the palisades at one end and put them up; the inhabitants, who were able to do it, were set to digging the moat and continued, as long as the weather and rain permitted. (Fernow 1881, 85–86)

In modern times, the question has always been, did the stockade of 1658 have a moat on three sides? Because of the low elevation and silty clays that are found at the base of the hill from Tannery Brook around to Clinton Avenue, it is possible that *Wiltwyck* could have been additionally fortified with a moat. However, because the coarse sandy Riverhead series soils in the uptown area on top of the hill drain extremely quickly, the southern exposure of the stockade could not have been defended in this way. In fact, if the southern curtain wall of the stockade had a ditch, this would have been located archaeologically at the Persen House, approximately in the center of the Phase 3 addition of the Persen House (see chapter 5). Since this soil could not support a moat, excavation of a ditch could have been a possibility, although it appears this was also not the case. A defensive ditch would have presented itself archaeologically as a large soil anomaly (with a burn layer) filled with Dutch artifacts and probably capped with debris from the removal of the 1661 palisade and the backfilling of the ditch prior to construction of the 1669–1670 palisade to the south. That kind of soil anomaly has not been found inside or outside of the Persen House to date, although we would like to have found one. Additionally, Jacobs (2015, 59–60) suggested that the *grep* or ditch/furrow was not a moat but rather the ditch that was dug to stand vertical posts in.

Behind 79 North Front Street

During a Phase 1A archaeological reconnaissance of Kingston in 1990, Edwin Ford and I had the opportunity to view an open trench that had been backhoed from the rear of 79 North Front Street to the edge of the escarpment overlooking Kingston Plaza. Our visit was not part of a formal investigation, but Ed knew that a trench had been excavated, so we dropped by. Even though the excavation was undertaken in a National Register Historic District, no preliminary archaeological testing or monitoring was required by the City of Kingston. Our perusal of the soil from the utility trench identified precontact debitage and fire-cracked rock as well as 18th-century ceramics such as pearlware and creamware. A small foundation wall was also visible. This location is one of the most sensitive precontact and historic locations in Kingston, as it appears to be in a relatively undisturbed area that may include the remains of the north stockade wall as well as early house foundations inside the wall. Its soils, like most other locations in the uptown area, also contain precontact artifacts, although no culturally or temporally diagnostic Native American artifacts were found during our observations at this location.[3] Again, this simple, unregulated trench within the National Register district points to the need for formal evaluations by the Kingston Planning Board and archaeological work whenever ground disturbances are scheduled to occur.

NYU Excavations on Clinton Avenue

In 1970 and 1971, two teams of archaeologists from NYU, working under the direction of Dr. Bert Salwen, and then Sarah Bridges, excavated six test trenches (hereafter referred to as *units*) on Clinton Avenue in front of the Senate House. The Clinton Avenue excavation was the first university-affiliated excavation in Kingston, and it was the first time that evidence of the original stockade was identified archaeologically.[4]

The excavation is described in Bridges (1974) and Salwen and Bridges (1977), although the latter paper included only a discussion of the ceramic data from Clinton Avenue in comparison with other sites. The best description of the site and its contents is the former, which is Bridge's master's paper from NYU. Of the six excavated units, Bridges focused on the first three for analysis. This was because the last three units encountered construction and destruction materials, suggesting these units were in a location where previously intact soils were destroyed by later disturbances. In the first three units, totaling 165 square feet (15.4 sq m) of excavation area, several groupings of strata were identified. For the purposes of this study, the lower levels, or those referred to as Temporal Units 1 (pre-1620) and 2 (1620–1725), are the most significant (Bridges 1974). The first of these predated the occupation of *Wiltwyck*, while the second yielded evidence of one of the earliest wooden stockades in the Hudson Valley—the stockade constructed under the direction of Peter Stuyvesant in 1658.

Temporal Unit 1 produced evidence of historic use of this area in the form of artifacts such as white clay pipe stem fragments and oyster shells as well as Native American use of the area in the form of artifacts such as lithic debitage, preforms (blanks), and a projectile point. These artifacts were found in the lowest stratum, near the stockade posts. Temporal Unit 2 yielded the stockade posts as well as a *fleur-de-lis* stamped pipestem fragment and Dutch yellow brick fragments. There was a noticeable lack of Dutch earthenwares and a large (and unexpected) amount of English earthenwares. This finding may simply be the result of a lack of experience differentiating the two types of ceramics, however, as they are very similar. The years 1970 to 1971, when the work was conducted, were very early years for historical archaeology as a discipline in New York State, and archaeologists were only just beginning to acquaint themselves with 17th-century Dutch and English ceramics. Excavation at sites such as Fort Orange in Albany (Huey 1988) were contemporaneous with the NYU excavation, but other early urban sites such as the Stadt Huys site (Rothschild et al. 1987), Hanover Square (Rothschild and Pickman 1990), and the Broad Financial Center Project (Grossman 1985), all in Manhattan, were still years away. It wasn't until the late 1970s and early 1980s that archaeologists began to become more acquainted with early Dutch, English, French, and German ceramics, pipes, and glassware.

Units 1 through 3 of this investigation, located opposite the Senate House on the eastern side of Clinton Avenue, produced evidence of what is thought to be remains of the 1658 stockade, the construction of which was led by Stuyvesant in June of that year. This evidence comes in the form of "post molds," which are formed by the placement of a post in the ground with the refilled soil packed around it to keep it upright. When a post is eventually removed, the darker soils from the uppermost stratum fill in the hole, creating a mottled or very dark circle within the surrounding light brown soil, which can be identified archaeologically. Soil stains indicative of such features need to be carefully uncovered with a sharp trowel and drawn to scale to show their exact size and placement relative to other features and artifacts identified in association with it. In this case, archaeologists identified seven post molds on a north-to-south axis at 16 to 18 inches below the ground surface. The post molds varied in size from 8 to 12 inches in diameter and were irregularly spaced. Bridges explained this as "probably due to their several replacements" (Bridges 1974), meaning that whereas the original posts would likely have been relatively evenly spaced, when replacements were needed, a new post was placed immediately adjacent to the original post, which would have the effect of making them seem more closely spaced when identified archaeologically. An additional seven post molds, ranging from 8 to 11 inches in diameter, were identified in Unit 2 at the same depth as those in Unit 1, and eight more were identified in Unit 3 at a depth of 13–14 inches below the surface. The Unit 3 post molds were the only ones sectioned (cut in half) by archaeologists for profile drawings, as the post molds in Units 1 and 2 were preserved in situ and are likely still there. The post molds varied between 3 and 13 inches in diameter and were "tapered to round bases." It is likely that the smallest posts were used to plug holes in the stockade curtain. The post mold features also contained artifacts, which would have originated from the original excavation of the holes for the posts and from the post holes being filled back in with the surrounding soil. The artifacts recorded from these features included lithic debitage, brick and mortar fragments (including Dutch yellow brick), salt-glazed stoneware, white clay pipe fragments, mammal bone fragments, wood fragments, and large quantities of white plaster and oyster shell (Bridges 1974).

Interestingly, there is more than one method for stockade construction, which has been determined through comparison of soil stratigraphy across several historic sites. One method is the excavation of a trench, in which the posts are inserted, and then the trench is backfilled. The other method is excavation of individual holes for each post. In this location of the stockade on Clinton Avenue, it was determined that small post holes were excavated and the posts were simply pounded in. This can be observed in photographs taken by Paul Huey during the excavations, where there was no evidence that a ditch was excavated (figs. 4.2 and 4.3). Note that the shells and artifacts in the photo were simply placed there to make the post molds stand out for the photograph and were not found *in situ* (Paul Huey, personal communication, 2000).

One interesting find from the three units included what was thought at the time to be "Colono Indian Ware," a type of ceramic identified in the southeast and originally thought to be a Native American copy of British

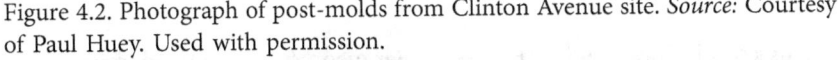

Figure 4.2. Photograph of post-molds from Clinton Avenue site. *Source:* Courtesy of Paul Huey. Used with permission.

Figure 4.3. Photograph of post-molds from Clinton Avenue site. *Source:* Courtesy of Paul Huey. Used with permission.

forms (Noël Hume 1962). However, Ferguson (1992) later demonstrated that this ceramic type is instead an African American copy of British forms, and he renamed the ceramic "Colono Ware," with the proviso that these ceramics could be made by Native Americans, enslaved Africans, or, later, enslaved African Americans (see also Cobb and DePratter 2012; Marcoux et al. 2023). This was not the case at Clinton Avenue, as none of the ceramic fragments imitated European vessel forms. I examined the "Colono Ware" found at Clinton Avenue and found it to be a heavily burnished Late Woodland Native American ceramic, probably body sherds with little or no decoration. From my experience at other local sites, it is probably Kingston or Munsee Incised pottery, and it would have dated to either just before or during the Contact period (c. 1550–1652).

Other finds included several white clay pipes, which were marked with various initials indicating makers' marks. From the Clinton Avenue collection these included "TW," "IC," and "RT" pipe marks. The latter is a Robert Tippett pipe, which is one of the most common pipes in the Northeast from the late 17th and early 18th century. As mentioned earlier, significant architectural items found at the site included small yellow

Dutch bricks, locally manufactured red brick of the same size ("Hudson Valley Flats"), and small amounts of red earthenware pan tiles for roofing.

One of the most interesting finds was a pewter or pot-metal disc or jetton that had the initials "WTB" embossed on it, as though a seal had been made. These would be the initials of Wessel Ten Broeck, the builder of what is now the Senate House. Ten Broeck probably had these seals made to affix to personal items or to items of value (fig. 4.4)

Anomalies noted by Bridges (1974) at the site include (1) the lack of Dutch ceramics from the time period of Dutch occupation; (2) large numbers of shellfish, particularly oysters (the latter are mentioned in particular because they are not discussed in any of the written records as being a primary food source); (3) the small amounts of Westerwald and other German stonewares; and (4) the high proportion of English slip-decorated earthenwares.

Figure 4.4. Pot metal jetton/token inscribed "WTB" for Wessel Ten Broeck. The artifact is ¾ inches in diameter. From Clinton Avenue excavation/NYU. *Source:* Courtesy of Terrah Lindsay. Used with permission.

Explanations for these anomalies were that "between 1651 and 1775 few Dutch painted wares could reach the colonies because of the restrictive British trade and navigation laws" (Bridges 1974; see also Noël Hume 1970, 140–41). In her report, Bridges noted that Huey suggested this was not the case based on data from Fort Orange. The question is, why were there so few Dutch wares? The same could be said for the small amount of Westerwald and Frechen stonewares, types that are also more common on other Dutch sites, especially Fort Orange. Coupled with the rarity of Dutch and German examples is the large amount of English slip-decorated earthenwares, particularly the combed and trailed wares that were often associated with the Staffordshire district after c. 1670 but that were made in other locations throughout England. Bridges (1974) explained the following:

> Throughout the paper, it has been emphasized that England influenced the other European countries in their trade through a strong position in the Triple Alliance, so that their navigation laws could affect non-English colonists in the New World. However, the Fort Orange site did not follow this pattern: the greatest proportion of ceramics from the seventeenth-century occupational levels are Dutch. This suggests some other factor operating to affect the importation patterns in the Dutch and Dutch-English settlements.

With regard to food consumption, Bridges was not able to locate any references in the literature (i.e., the Kingston court minutes) regarding the consumption of oysters. Perhaps the reason for the lack of information on shellfish in the Kingston court minutes is the mundane nature of shellfish (see also Kurlansky 2007). Most of the foods discussed in the court minutes and probate records were domestic animals (e.g., oxen, horses, goats, pigs, chickens, pigeons) or wild game such as venison, often brought in and traded by the Esopus. Shellfish, although an important part of the diet in the Netherlands, as often depicted in Dutch and Flemish genre paintings, was not mentioned in the Kingston court minutes or in any forms of local literature up to this point. On a broader level, several writers frequenting the Hudson Valley in the 17th century mentioned oysters in their descriptions of *Niew Netherland*. David DeVries, writing in 1642, stated that "there are fine oysters, large and small, in great abundance" (Jameson [1909] 2010, 223), an idea that Adriaen van der Donck reiterated in 1660 (Jameson [1909] 2010, 298). Oysters are well known as a favorite Dutch food and appear in numerous Dutch and Flemish genre paintings, particularly still lifes from c. 1600–1680. A compendium by the Albany Institute of History and Art showcased numerous Dutch genre paintings illustrating foodways, many of which included oysters in the paintings. The resulting catalog from the exhibit (Barnes and Rose 2002) included a cookbook containing recipes using oysters and other shellfish. Similarly, in an analysis of 17th-century genre paintings from the Netherlands, Fayden (1993, 131) categorized most of the oysters illustrated in paintings as those of Dutch middle- and upper-class interiors. Although they have not been analyzed in detail, the oyster remains found at Clinton Avenue likely originate from the New York Bay area. Additionally, Rose (2009) included a historical overview of Dutch recipes, foods, spices, and holidays that made up the Dutch colonial year.

Based on the archaeological data, in the form of garbage middens, it is evident that Dutch colonials brought with them their taste for and love of shellfish. This is a pertinent example of how one aspect of the historic past—in this case, foodways among Dutch colonials in *Wiltwyck*, and their descendants in Kingston—can only be accurately judged through an examination of the archaeological record.

The Fred Johnston House Garden

During garden planting and tree removal, the late Robert Slater documented several finds from the rear (western yard) of the Fred Johnston House at the northwest corner of Wall and Main Streets. These finds included numerous 18th- and 19th-century ceramics, such as pearlwares, creamware, stoneware, and Chinese export porcelain, as well as precontact artifacts. Of the precontact artifacts, one chronologically diagnostic projectile point was found: a Sylvan Stemmed/Lamoka point. These points have been dated in other portions of New York State and throughout the northeast as c. 3100–1900 BC/cal. 5550–3850 BP (Funk 1993, 157, fig. 25; Hart et al. 2023). Because a diagnostic projectile point was found in this location, it is most likely that there was a Sylvan Lake/Lamoka phase camp in the area near the corner of Wall and Main Streets. My perusal of Bob Slater's collection from the garden was sufficient to identify an occupation that could then be registered with the New York State Museum (Site #7975).

Archaeological Testing at the Fred Johnston House

I was contacted by the Friends of Historic Kingston in 1996 to conduct an archaeological examination prior to three trenches being excavated in and around the front and sides of the Fred Johnston House on Wall Street in Kingston (Diamond 1996b). The excavations took place prior to construction activities for stormwater drainage, a heating/humidity control system, and a buried electrical cable. The trenches were excavated in various locations around the western, southern, and eastern portions of the house. Soil strata revealed various layers of fill, with undisturbed sand at the base of each excavation trench. Fill typically consists of secondarily deposited soils that have been moved from somewhere else and that contain multiple kinds of artifacts that have a broad time range. Artifacts from the trenches ranged from the 17th through the 19th centuries and included ceramics, red Dutch bricks, clear lead-glazed redware, a white clay pipestem fragment, handwrought nails, window glass, an oyster fragment, and an animal bone fragment. Although this was admittedly a small sample of artifacts, the trench work provided a glimpse into the soil strata under the sidewalks along Wall Street, which is comprised of historic fill. The artifacts found in this location may relate to the occupants of the Fred Johnston House, or they may simply be items that were discarded and buried along Wall Street.

Excavations at the Old Dutch Church: the DeWitt Plot

In early 2020, I was contacted by Mr. Gage DeWitt of the DeWitt Family Association (DFA). Members of the DFA were attempting to find the burial location of the first DeWitt in North America, Tjerck Classen DeWitt, who was born in Friesland c.1626 and died in Kingston in 1700. Tjerck Classen DeWitt is the progenitor of all of the DeWitts in the United States and Canada. DFA members Gage and Justin DeWitt searched archival records as well as the DeWitt files at the New York State Museum in an attempt to find the location of the unmarked burial place of Tjerck. An 1894 *New York Times* article about this cemetery included this passage:

> The most interesting part of the cemetery is on the Wall Street side, for here the first stones were erected, and many of them still stand. These earliest relics are irregular slabs of bluestone,

with letters rudely and mysteriously cut upon them. Of these curious and ancient markers, the oldest one is that of Andreas DeWitt, the founder of the illustrious DeWitt family, which has been prominently identified with this country's history since long before America threw off the British yoke. The name was lost on the church records at the great conflagration, but was known by the descendants of the man who lies buried by this stone. As interesting almost as the stone itself is the worn and weather-beaten cedar post which has stood behind and supporting it longer than the memory of man. It is supposed that the post has been there almost as long as the stone. During the war of the rebellion, when the Ulster County regiments were quartered in the armory which stood across the street, many of the soldiers whittled off chips to keep as souvenirs. The marks of their jackknives may yet be seen on the tip of the old post.

Although the article indicated that Andreas (Andries) DeWitt was the founder of the lineage, this was in error. However, it did indicate that the post and stone were both standing together at that time.

An additional historical tidbit that the DeWitts encountered was a note from Reverend William Walsh in 1900 stating, "Tjerck Classen DeWitt died in Kingston, Feb 17th, A.D., 1700, and was buried in the burying ground of the Reformed Dutch Church. In the same grave was buried his son, Andries DeWitt, and a cedar post to which is attached a narrow flagstone, on which is inscribed, 'A.D.W., 22 July, 1700' marks the grave" (Historical Society, Newburgh Bay and the Highlands 1900, 41). The key term here was "attached," and subsequent historical research pointed to an iron strap as well as iron pins that held the stone to the post. The newspaper article and Walsh's comments led Gage and Justin DeWitt to focus on finding the location of the ADW stone, which was no longer in the churchyard proper but, due to preservation issues, had been removed for safekeeping to the interior of the church. In its place, a fragment of an unrelated marble gravestone was cemented in the ground. The original ADW stone was unique within the burying ground because the stone and its inscription faced south instead of on an east/west axis. This is unusual because in Judeo-Christian cemeteries, bodies are buried on an east/west axis with the head to the west and the feet to the east, so that on Judgement Day, the deceased can sit up and face the rising sun. The ADW stone, as well as its marble replacement, faced south and stood out among the other graves in the churchyard.

As a consequence of contacting the New York State Museum, the DeWitts were sent a photograph of the ADW stone c. 1850–1865 with the original wooden cedar post of Tjerck Classen DeWitt just behind it. This photo suggested that the location of the cedar post was just north of the original location of the ADW stone. At about that time, Dr. John Rayburn of the SUNY New Paltz Geology Department and several of his students undertook a ground penetrating radar (GPR) survey of the DeWitt plot. This work identified several "anomalies," which is not surprising in a graveyard, where each grave shaft will create a soil anomaly that appears as a parabola on the computer printout of the survey. On the same day, Dr. Rayburn pulled out his handheld metal detector and got a loud beep next to the marble replacement stone. I remember saying, "That's probably the iron strap."

At that point, the DFA designed a research strategy to "ground truth" the location of Tjerck Classen DeWitt's burial and to conduct a forensic analysis of any skeletal remains that were found. The research design entailed using three kinds of analysis: strontium isotope analysis, DNA analysis, and facial reconstruction. By examining different strontium signatures, strontium isotope analysis can provide information on whether a person grew up locally or in another region (see Nystrom et al. 2011). DNA analysis can provide information on family relationships to living people as well as to other archaeologically retrieved skeletal remains. Facial reconstruction is a forensic tool that allows the bioanthropologist, through anatomical knowledge and artistry, to reconstruct a person's appearance from their remains.

The research design was voted on and approved by the consistory of the Old Dutch Church. After several rounds of revised agreements with the Old Dutch Church and the DFA, the SUNY New Paltz archaeological field school began excavations in July 2022. Members of the DFA participated in the excavation from day one until the site was backfilled in August.

We began by excavating a 3 × 3 meter square, with the marble replacement stone in the southeast corner of the unit. Because the soils in uptown Kingston are so sandy, we decided to use arbitrary 10-cm (4-in) archaeological contexts, but at one point we switched to 20-cm (8-in) contexts. Arbitrary designations allow the archaeologist to set the size of the archaeological context as excavation proceeds downward. We did this simply to maintain control, because as we excavated, the sand dried out and we lost the ability to observe changes in soil color. The cultural strata that we found began with a very dark grayish brown sand about 25 cm (10 in) thick that had numerous modern artifacts in it, particularly coins dating from 1961 to 2007. Below that was a coal ash context that thinned out and disappeared to the east but got thicker toward the west (toward Wall Street), where it was 5–15 cm (2–6 in) thick in the wall profile. Below that was a dark brown sand that was 45–50 cm (18–20 in) thick. These three cultural strata overlaid a dark brown/very dark brown/dark yellowish brown sand that was the original soil surface for the 17th century through c. 1852, when the existing Old Dutch Church was constructed. This stratum was from approximately 85 cm (33.5 in) to about 120 cm (47 in), but in some locations it was as deep as 130 cm (51 in). The different soil colors relate to soil admixture due to grave excavation and backfilling, of which this stratum was a part. At the top of this stratum, we found stone chipping debris from the construction of the church in 1852 as well as a small piece of dressed limestone, which is very similar to the decorative bands of limestone in the church walls. In portions of the unit that were not disturbed during grave excavation, the soil was a sterile yellowish-brown sand that became increasingly gray as our excavation proceeded down to glacially sorted coarse gray sands.

The abovementioned strata reflect several behavioral patterns of uptown Kingstonians in the late 19th and early 20th centuries. In the ash deposit, we found a 1902 Indian Head penny, which provides us with a *terminus post quem* (or "date after which") for the deposition of the ash deposit. In this case, the deposit could not have been formed before the minting of the 1902 penny. Where the deposit deepened toward the sidewalk on Wall Street, it can be surmised that the contents of residents' ash buckets were being dumped into the graveyard, probably in the winter when the ash would blend in with the snow. The very dark grayish brown soil found above it, and also just under the lawn, was likely spread across the graveyard during the 20th-century. In the mix of sand in the third context, we found the iron strap and one iron spike that were used to hold the ADW stone to the post.

Below the ash layer and above the original 1852 surface was a layer of dark brown sand. The chipped stone debris found at the interface of the ash and sand suggests this soil was brought in to tidy up the graveyard after the existing church was constructed in 1852. Alternatively, it could be surmised that this soil originated from the inside of the church when the footings and foundation were constructed, but this would not be the case. The stratum overlying the 1852 surface had no evidence or fragments of human remains, which the soils from within the existing church would certainly have had, as this area was originally an early part of the graveyard before the church was built. Overall, the difference between the original ground surface and the churchyard's current lawn is about 85 cm or 33.5 inches.

As we continued the excavations, it became obvious that we had encountered the bottom of the original ADW stone, found near the 1852 interface. We cleared the soils around it and carefully troweled the surface, discovering a round soil stain immediately next to and north of the stone. We left the stone and soil stain in situ and continued working within the rest of the 3-meter unit. Once the excavation was deep enough to examine the full soil profile, we carefully cut back the soil and discovered the post mold, which contained an existing piece of cedar within the outline of the soil stain. The soil also contained the second iron spike, which, as mentioned above, was used to hold the stone to the post.

After locating the post, we then proceeded to search for evidence of grave shafts, which would occur as stains in the soil where the shaft was excavated and filled back in with a combination of yellow subsoil and dark humic soil from the top stratum in the graveyard. The goal of the excavation was to identify the burial of Tjerck Claessen DeWitt and his son Andries and, with the permission of the DFA and Old Dutch Church, to remove their remains for DNA analysis and isotopic analysis. DNA analysis can be used to construct a family tree, which, for the DeWitts, may conceivably go back into medieval times in Europe and could also reveal potential linkages to enslaved people buried at the Pine Street African Burial Ground. The isotopic analysis allows for determining which burial is which, since both Tjerck and Barbara (Andries mother) were born and spent the early portion of their lives in Europe and thus would have different isotopic signatures than their children born in America.

At c. 115–120 cm (45–47 in) below the ground surface, we encountered dark stains indicative of grave shafts. Before beginning to uncover the burials we were searching for, we had to enlarge our excavation to the east with a 2 × 2 meter unit (Unit 2) and to the west with a 1 × 1.5 meter unit in the western wall (Unit 3). Both endeavors were carried out by members of the DFA (Gage DeWitt and Perry DeWitt). In total, our investigation identified seven individuals within the confines of the 14.5-meter horizontal excavation unit. The individuals' skeletal remains were in very good condition, as they had been wrapped in burial shrouds and placed in wooden coffins. To the west and partially under Unit 3 were the remains of three people, stacked one on top of the other. While this would be unusual in a modern cemetery, it appears to be relatively common in the Old Dutch Church cemetery, particularly in family plots for large families of Dutch ancestry. In the new unit to the east (Unit 2), we found the remains of two people, one on an east/west axis at the northern end and one on an east/west axis in the southern portion of the unit. In the middle of Unit 2 (between the two previously discussed burials) and just to the east of both the cedar post and ADW stone, we located a male burial, with another male burial directly beneath. This confirms the Reverend Walsh's comments that father and son were buried in the same grave. Of the seven individuals identified, we exhumed six for further analysis. The skeletal remains were housed in the SUNY New Paltz bioarchaeology lab while being analyzed for information that can be gleaned from skeletal remains, such as overall health, cause of death, and stature. In addition, small samples of the remains were retained for DNA and isotopic samples before the remains were reburied in the churchyard.

The artifacts from the excavation unit above the human remains were very interesting and, again, pointed to the use of the graveyard as a repository for local Kingstonians' trash. The upper strata contained all manner of 19th-century artifacts, such as white clay smoking pipes, whitewares and ironstones, window glass, gravestone fragments, fragments of a Peter Barmann beer bottle, pearlwares, redwares, cream-colored wares, stonewares, bone buttons, ink bottle fragments, marbles, whiskey bottle fragments, tumblers, wine glasses, blacking/snuff bottle fragments, decanter fragments, mirror fragments, and lamp chimney fragments. Total faunal remains for the unit included over 350 bones, 13 whole clams, 112 clam fragments, 102 whole oysters, and 184 oyster fragments. Two contexts comprising a combined 8-inch-thick level contained a whopping 28 clam fragments, 60 whole oysters, and 91 oyster fragments.

The 17th and 18th centuries were represented in the assemblage by *Bartmankrügge* fragments, slip-decorated red earthenware charger or plate fragments, fragments of a gray salt-glazed stoneware mug or tankard with small cobalt blue rosettes, engine-turned redware teapot fragments, Jackfield-type redware, blue and white delft, yellow buff-bodied slip-decorated posset pot fragments, a lead glazed redware milk pan (?) fragment, and several fragmentary "Hudson Valley flats" or red Dutch bricks. The latter are probably from the late 17th to very early 18th centuries and were probably produced by enslaved individuals who toiled in the brickyard of Cornelius Hoogeboom, near the present location of North Front Street and Washington Avenue. An olive-green onion-shaped wine bottle likely produced in England c. 1670–1700 was also found.

A few Native American artifacts were found in the deposits, including a lithic biface fragment and a few fragments of debitage, made from Indian River chert ($n = 1$) and local Onondaga chert, mostly from the Morehouse member. These were all found relatively deep in contexts that were not composed of fill episodes from after c. 1852. There appeared to be a thin spread of precontact Native American artifacts in the southern Wall Street area that ranged from the eastern side of the Old Dutch Church property to the rear of the Fred Johnston House. These artifacts likely represent small encampments of people who were living on the sand terrace hundreds or thousands of years prior to the establishment of *Wiltwyck* in what is now uptown Kingston.

Excavations at the Senate House State Historic Site

The northeast corner of the original 1658 stockade is the location of the house of Wessel Ten Broeck (see fig. 4.1). Known locally as the Senate House, it is thought to have been constructed prior to 1695 (Reynolds 1929, 219–21) and most likely c. 1676 (Feister and Sopko 2003, 10), when it is thought that Wessel Ten Broeck built a house in that location. A 1687 survey map included a small sketch of the house with the gable end facing Clinton Avenue. This property, now owned and operated by OPRHP, was the subject of controlled excavations from 1970 to 1997 (Feister and Sopko 2003; Sopko 1991; Waite and Huey 1971). The primary purpose of the excavations was to test the area around the Ten Broeck House, particularly the lawn, in an attempt to find outbuildings or older structures related to the initial Dutch occupation of the area between 1658 and 1664. In addition, four other portions of the property have been archaeologically tested, and these are treated separately here in the same order as they are presented in Feister and Sopko's (2003) discussion of the excavations from 1970 to 1997. More recently, I was contracted to perform an excavation inside the Senate House before the floors were replaced (Diamond and Amorosi 2023).

The Senate House Lot

In total, 25 archaeological test units have been excavated on the site of the Ten Broeck House on what has been called the Senate House lot (Feister and Sopko 2003). The excavations traced building sequences and located dump areas and architectural elements from the 17th century that are no longer apparent as part of the building's fabric. As mentioned above, the 1687 survey map of the Ten Broeck Property (fig. 4.5) illustrated a house with its gable end facing what is now Clinton Avenue. From excavations in and around the building, it is apparent that the original structure likely had a pan tile roof, leaded glass casement windows, and chimneys partially built or faced with Dutch yellow bricks. To my knowledge, the only portion of the stockade area to yield evidence of Dutch yellow bricks is the northeast corner, where excavations were undertaken by OPRHP and NYU. Figure 4.6 is an illustration of the original first portion of the Senate House by painter Len Tantillo. The view is looking north from what is now Clinton Avenue.

The original Wessel Ten Broeck House is thought to be the middle section of the current Senate House, as this appears to be the oldest section of the structure. The growth of the Senate House closely parallels

Figure 4.5. From a 1687 survey map of the Ten Broeck property. Taken from Feister and Sopko (2003, fig. 4). *Source:* Public domain.

Figure 4.6. Senate House c. 1694 looking north. *Source:* Courtesy of Len Tantillo. Used with permission.

those of other late 17th- to early 18th-century structures in Kingston and in Hurley. For example, the Persen House and the Elmendorf House in Hurley (c. 1715), like the 1687 drawing of the Ten Broeck House, both began with a gabled front facing the street, which is a typical Dutch style of construction. In each case, the first or initial roof section was removed and the house was extended laterally along the street, with another section being added on. In all three cases, as the house grew over time, a kitchen wing was added onto the structure perpendicular to one of the sections.

Like many of the excavation areas in uptown Kingston, Native American artifacts were identified in many of the excavation units around the Senate House. The materials found in the excavations on the Senate House lot are similar to those from the nearby Clinton Avenue excavation, the Persen House, and the Fred Johnston House garden. In addition to lithic debitage, other artifacts such as drills, biface fragments, plant processing tools, and a steatite bowl fragment were found. Projectile points from the Sylvan Lake/Lamoka phase (c. 3100–1900 BC/cal. 5550–3850

BP), Orient phase (c. 1100–750 BC/cal. 3050–2700 BP), and Meadowood Phase (c. 1050–500 BC/cal. 3000–2450 BP) were found. A Late Woodland Madison point (c.1000–1658 AD) and Native American pottery with an incised decoration, dating c. 1400–1652 AD, were also found. Overall, the Native American artifacts from the Senate House excavations were spread relatively evenly across the property, with the likelihood that there are still precontact storage pits and dietary information to be found at the site.

Finds from the 17th century on the site of the house include combed buff-bodied slip-decorated earthenware (c. 1670–1795), small red and yellow Dutch bricks, red earthenware pan tiles, white clay pipestem whistles, turned lead (window casement or caming), faunal remains, tin-glazed buff-bodied earthenwares (delft), white clay smoking pipes, Iberian storage jar fragments, Frechen (probably *Bartmannkrügge* fragments) and Westerwald stoneware, glass prunts from *roemers* (fig. 4.7),[5] local redwares, and coral.[6] The coral was identified on the south side of the earliest part of the house in association with yellow brick and 17th-century white clay

Figure 4.7. Seventeenth-century Dutch roemer. *Source:* Courtesy of the Corning Museum of Glass. Catalog #63.3.44. CMoG 63.3.44. Image licensed by the Corning Museum of Glass, Corning, NY (www.cmog.org), under CC BY-NC-SA 4.0.

pipestems. Coral is particularly interesting because it may relate to the slaves of the Ten Broeck family (see chapter 7).

One ceramic type from the Senate House lot that has also been found at the Persen House and Clinton Avenue excavations is unglazed red earthenware,[7] which is relatively unique in the northeast. This particular vessel had a rounded base, which continued upward and was then squared-off at the top and decorated with wide incised lines (fig. 4.8). This vessel

Figure 4.8. Senate House artifacts. Drawing of a stove tile or *Schüsselkachel* from Feister and Sopko (2003). Illustration by Joseph E. McEvoy. *Source:* Public domain.

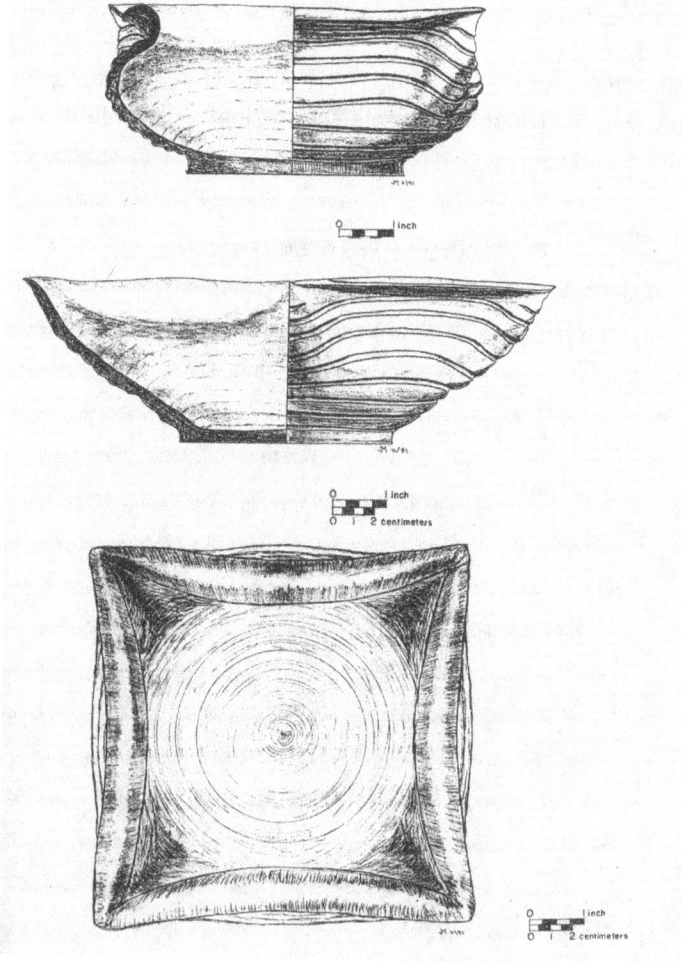

does not have any local analogues, but based on similar sizes and shapes of vessels depicted in paintings and found on other archaeological sites,[8] Feister and Sopko (2003) suggested this could represent an item such as drip pan, oil lamp, brazier, or *Schüsselkachel*. A *Schüsselkachel* is a tile for a brazier or stove that is composed of inverted tiles (fig. 4.8) that are mortared together to form a stove. The wavy lines on the ceramic function to key into the mortar to hold the stove together. Figure 4.9 is an early

Figure 4.9. Early 16th century illustration of a stove composed of *Schüsselkachel* in the left rear of the room. *Hausbuch der Landauerschen Zwölfbrüderstiftung*, Band 1. Nürnberg 1511–1706. Stadtbibliothek Nürnberg, 279.2. *Source:* Public domain.

illustration of a stove composed of *Schüsselkachel*. Because this vessel type is unknown outside of the Kingston area, Feister and Sopko (2003, 15) suggested it may have been manufactured by a local potter, specifically Cornelius Pietersen Hoogeboom. On January 20, 1665, Hoogeboom is noted in the Kingston court minutes (Christoph et al. 1976, 1:198) as applying for a lot to make bricks, and he likely also made pan tiles[9] and possibly redware vessels.

During the Van Gaasbeek (c. 1770–1797) occupation of the house, repairs were made to the building after the burning of Kingston in 1777. The main ceramic types from this period found during archaeological excavations were creamware (post-1762), buff-bodied slip-decorated earthenware (c. 1670–1795), redware, coarse stoneware, and pearlware (post-1780).

Excavations inside the Senate House

In 2020, limited excavations were conducted inside the Senate House State Historic site, in the form of two 3 × 3 foot squares (Diamond and Amorosi 2023). The excavations were conducted to evaluate two locations within the Senate House where floors had recently been removed while undertaking repairs in the house, making it possible to study parts of the property that have not been accessible since at least the late 19th century. The question I had, which was shared by the Senate House staff, was what was the extent of preservation of artifacts and faunal remains within the dried-in portion of the house? Conceivably, preservation could have been similar to the Persen House (see chapter 5), where intact soil layers within the house showed a layer cake of strata going back to c. 1200 BC. Although the Senate House was initially constructed c. 1676, the two rooms in which the excavations occurred were constructed in the late 19th century. One—the northernmost room, or "orientation room"—was an add-on for tour groups (post-1887). The other was a "reconstructed" kitchen, where the original was knocked down to make way for an "oldy-timey" looking kitchen (c. 1885–1887). Unfortunately, this is a common approach toward depicting the past: destroying the original and then rebuilding something that is thought to look more proper or appear more "original."

The excavation units were placed in locations of each room that were expected to yield the best data. The first excavation unit, in the north or "orientation" room, was placed between existing floor joists and several inches from a stone wall built c. 1751. It was hoped this would provide a sense of the soil strata and would sample some of the 18th-century builder's trench from the construction of the wall. Construction of basements to the south of this location would have required soil removal, probably to the north where the unit was placed. This location would have been outside an 18th-century addition that was likely added by the Ten Broeck family or, later, by the Van Gaasbeek family.

This excavation began with a level of fine dust and artifacts that was approximately 2 to 3 inches thick. This stratum contained red brick, mortar fragments, nails, white clay pipestems and bowl fragments, buff-bodied slip decorated earthenware (BBSDE) fragments, clear lead-glazed redware (RW), blue decorated salt-glazed stoneware (SGSW), blue-decorated hand-painted pearlware, window glass, olive green case bottle fragments, domestic cat, rat, bird, oyster, and Atlantic sturgeon scute fragments. One piece of precontact chert debitage was also found.

The next stratum was 4 to 5 inches deep and consisted of a dark gray brown silty sand mixed with construction debris that contained small red Dutch bricks, pan tile fragments, mortar, bone, smoking pipes, BBSDE fragments, window glass, a case bottle fragment, brown transfer printed whiteware (WW), gray SGSW, green-ginger glazed RW, brown glazed RW, Chinese export porcelain, delft, pumpkin seeds, nails, Atlantic sturgeon scutes, sheep, pig, dog, rodent, pigeon, a very small hard shell clam fragment, and oysters. One piece of brown jasper debitage was also found. This layer probably formed during construction activities when the orientation room was built (post-1887) and incorporated older materials that were mixed in during the construction process.

Below this stratum was a deep level of what appeared to be yard debris from the outside of the 18th-century house. This 8- to 9-inch-deep level of very dark gray brown silty sand was divided into two separate strata by an arbitrary break due to a drop off in artifacts such as mortar, brick, and pan tile fragments. The uppermost stratum contained significant quantities of small red Dutch brick fragments, pan tile fragments, charcoal, mortar, nails, BBSDE fragments, delft, glass, white clay smoking pipe fragments, cattle, sheep, pig, dog, turkey, duck, pigeon, fish, oyster, clam, case bottle fragments, redware, gray SGSW, Chinese export porcelain, and black Jackfield ware fragments.

The next underlying stratum consisted of the same soil as above and was approximately 4 to 6 inches deep. It contained less mortar, brick fragments, and pan tile fragments, suggesting that this was the lower portion of the stratum and that some of these construction materials were likely pushed down from above due to pedestrian activity around the outside of the 18th-century house. This stratum contained small red Dutch brick fragments, pan tile fragments, iron lumps (nails), white clay pipestems, sheet copper, 17th-century window glass, melted window glass, olive green wine/liquor bottle fragments, white-tailed deer, sheep/goat, pig, cat, fish, oysters, very small clam fragments, BBSDE fragments, brown glazed redwares, greenish-brown glazed redwares, ginger-glazed salmon-bodied earthenware, plain and blue decorated delft, Chinese export porcelain, Jackfield ware, and Whieldon ware. Precontact lithic debitage, a utilized flake, a chert core, and pottery were also found.

The next stratum was 4 to 5 inches deep and consisted of a compact mottled black, brown, and very dark brown sand that had significantly less construction debris than the strata above it. It contained pan tile fragments, mortar, nails, a white clay pipe bowl with shield design, devitrified 17th-century window glass, fish bones, oysters, brown-glazed salmon-bodied wares, ginger-glazed red earthenware, and blue-decorated delft, as well as precontact debitage, a utilized flake, and pottery. Also found were three fragments of what appear to be raw stone that may have been used for making precontact pottery temper. This has been identified by Dr. Fred Vollmer of the SUNY New Paltz Geology Department (personal communication, February 5, 2020) as garnet plagioclase amphibolite, likely originating from the southern Adirondacks. It was likely picked up locally in glacial gravels or along a waterway. This type of rock has been identified at many precontact sites within the Esopus and Wallkill Valleys. It is often found in situ in features, after having been heated to make it more friable and easier to reduce for pottery temper. In some cases, garnet amphibolite is also found scattered about on precontact Native American sites, where pieces of it were not heated or crushed for pottery temper.

At the base of this stratum, a more defined builder's trench line became visible along the southern portion of the unit. North of this, four round post molds from a precontact Native American structure were also visible. These post molds were at the base of the original A-horizon soil (the original topsoil from c. 1658) and were found with precontact Native American artifacts stratigraphically above and around them. The post molds were documented and then covered to protect them as the builder's trench was excavated.

The trench consisted of a very dark brown silty sand with small bits of charcoal and very small mortar fragments. It was 10 inches deep along the south wall and then angled up sharply along its northern edge in the unit. It also contained small amounts of pan tile fragments, mortar fragments, 17th-century devitrified window glass, handwrought nails, bone fragments from large terrestrial mammals, and oyster fragments, as well as precontact fire-cracked rock, debitage, and pottery. The pan tile fragments were limited to only the upper 2 inches of the builder's trench.

After the builder's trench was excavated, the post molds were individually bisected and profiled. The soil within each post mold was carefully inspected for charcoal or artifacts, but none were found. The post molds were composed of black to very dark brown humic sand, probably from the original A-horizon soil that was on the terrace when the posts were either removed or decomposed. All four post molds showed a profile between 2 and 3 inches wide and 4 to 8 inches deep, with a pointed base, or in the case of one post mold, a slightly rounded base. After the post molds were bisected, the soil around them was removed. This soil was 4 inches of a coarse to medium coarse yellow brown sand, which terminated on culturally sterile sand and pebbly hard-packed stratum that had no artifacts and only one bone: a medium terrestrial mammal fragment. Excavation ceased at 28 inches across the unit at the top of this stratum. The post molds were interpreted as remnant architectural remains likely from a wigwam or longhouse on the site at, or prior to, contact with the Dutch in this area c. 1652–1653. With Dutch settlers encroaching on Native American lands around *Wiltwyck*, it is most likely that this hilltop location was not occupied after c. 1652–1653. It certainly was not occupied by Native Americans when Stuyvesant moved the Dutch community to the hilltop and constructed the stockade in 1658.

The goal of excavating a second unit inside the house was to sample the soil underneath what would have been an early kitchen wing. For this excavation, window screen mesh was initially used to search for small items such as glass beads, pins, and other items that may have fallen through cracks in the floorboards or may have been pressed into the soil if the room previously had a dirt floor. Unfortunately, the initial part of the excavation in this location revealed a significant amount of prior disturbance as well as a large amount of soil likely brought in from other areas around the yard to fill in the room as the fireplace and hearth were being reconstructed c. 1887. As a consequence, ¼-inch mesh was used for screening when it became obvious that there were no intact strata with small items from either the Ten Broeck or Van Gaasbeek families or their slaves, who also resided here.

This unit was placed 7 inches in front of the southernmost limestone hearth support in an area that had a substantial amount of debris from the reconstructed fireplace and chimney support. Two strata were excavated before it became apparent (due to the whiteware in the deposit, which was late 19th century) that there were no in situ deposits relating to the 18th century, and that the deposits were a combination of building rubble from the 18th-century kitchen and fill that was brought in to level out and support the bluestone hearth stones in the remodeled kitchen. The initial stratum was an approximately 4-inch-thick powdery light brown sand mixed with debris (brick, mortar, plaster) that ended on a slightly darker soil that contained plant roots. One fragment of casement window glass that was slightly less than 2 × 3 inches was found. This fragment might give us information on the size of some of the original casement window glass inside the original detached 18th-century kitchen. Also found were one whole oyster shell, a chicken bone, four mammal bones, a fragment of a footed whiteware bowl, and two small red Dutch brick fragments.

The second stratum was a very dark brown silty sand that was about 10 to 12 inches thick and was excavated to a depth of 15 to 16 inches. This stratum contained whole oysters, oyster fragments, clam fragments, cattle, sheep/goat, pig, dog, cat, rat, muskrat, chicken, turkey, American shad, mortar, plaster, nails, galvanized sheeting possibly for roofing or roofing patches, anthracite coal, a peach pit, two bone buttons, white clay pipestems, a white clay pipe bowl marked "TD" within a wreath facing the smoker (c. 1755–1780; Paul Huey, personal communication, February 17, 2020), as well as fragments of a second pipe. The anthracite coal can be dated post-1828 based on the opening of the Delaware and Hudson Canal, which brought huge amounts of coal from Pennsylvania into the Hudson Valley and had its terminus on the Rondout Creek in Kingston.

Glass included window glass, patent medicine bottle fragments, and olive-green wine/liquor bottle fragments. Ceramics included blue, black, and brown transfer-printed whiteware, cream-colored ware, plain whiteware, plain pearlware, BBSDE fragments, clear lead-glazed redware, gray-brown salt-glazed stoneware, Jackfield ware, and hand-painted pearlware.

After excavation of the unit was completed, several samples of brick and mortar were collected from each stratum but were not washed and were instead left as found in the rubble. These materials serve as examples of the interior plaster walls and the variety of bricks used in the construction of the original kitchen. Only the small red Dutch bricks, probably used for the fireplace when the original was constructed in the

18th century, were collected. Common mid to late 19th-century bricks were not collected—these appeared to have been the preferred building material for the "reconstruction" of the kitchen, as they were found everywhere within this area.

The vertebrate remains collected during the excavations were analyzed by Dr. Thomas Amorosi. The Senate House collection from these two units is a small collection, numbering 318 bone fragments in total. The rate of identification of taxa was low (the NISP—number of identified specimens per taxon—was 15.5%) given the small size and fragmentary nature of this collection. Mammalian remains comprised 83% of this collection, followed by bird bones (9.4%) and fish (7.5%).

Even though the NISP was low, overall representation of taxa was quite wide-ranging for a site dating from the Dutch colonial period that continued to be occupied by Dutch descendants into the 18th century, and especially so given that only two archaeological units were excavated. Mammalian remains can be divided between the European domesticates such as cattle, sheep, goat, pig, chicken, turkey, and pigeon, with an occasionally supplemented white-tailed deer, and critters such as dog, cat, and rat species that would have been consuming this kitchen waste. The ratio of cattle to caprines (sheep/goats) for this period (17th–18th century) was one cow to 6–12 sheep (a northern European agrarian standard known as a "cow value"; see Amorosi 1996; Amorosi et al. 1996, 1998), and there is a hint of this same ratio within this faunal collection. Likewise, the cattle to pig ratio is the same as for caprines, which is evident in many late 18th- to 19th-century Mid-Hudson archaeofaunal collections.

The animals that would have consumed the kitchen waste are represented by evidence of domestic dogs, observed through bite scars and puncture wounds in the kitchen waste, and recovered house cats and rat species. The animal remains from Unit 2 had the highest incidence of gnawing from these three carnivores and thus are likely the result of what the dog, cat, and rats brought into the house from the kitchen waste pile. One novel pattern in the faunal collection is that the incidence of cat gnawing and puncture wounds were limited to chicken remains.

Avian remains in the collection were predominantly divided between domestic and wild fowl. Chicken remains were found to be of older ages, most likely beyond their egg-laying years. For the turkey remains, it was not possible to distinguish as either domestic or wild birds. Pigeon remains in the collection were fragmentary and could be assigned only to the genus level, but there is a good possibility that these were passenger pigeons

(*Ectopistes migratorius*). Very few waterfowl remains were recovered, and the one perching bird bone identified was likely something brought onto the site by the cat or rat consumers.

Fish remains were from local inland and brown water riverine species that are commonly found in the Hudson River and its tributaries. American shad and perch species were present, but the latter could not be further defined (i.e., yellow vs. white perch). Atlantic sturgeon not only frequent the Hudson but are part of the annual spring spawn (Smith 1985). Sturgeon remains were represented by small fragmentary scutes identifiable by the surface pore pattern (Desse-Berset 2011; Diamond et al. 2016; Halliwell and Spiess 2017; LeBreton et al. 2004; Williot et al. 2011; Wuertz et al. 2011).

The importance of the excavation of these two small units within the Senate House can be discussed through several important finds: evidence of both Native American and Dutch use or occupation of this parcel.

Evidence for Wampum Manufacture

In the orientation room unit, one stratum yielded a small piece of clam measuring 1½ × 15/16 inches in size and eight additional fragments of clam, which are thought to represent evidence for wampum manufacture. Wampum are small cylindrical shell beads that were manufactured and used by Native Americans to make treaty belts. Due to a lack of specie (coinage) in New Netherland, and later New York, the Dutch and English used wampum as a form of currency, and it was valued by its color and the length of the string. An additional stratum included six very small clam shell fragments that are thought to represent wampum manufacturing or at least preprocessing of *Mercenaria* on site. In size, they were 1⅛ × ½ inches, 1 × 9/16 inches, 9/16 × ¼ inches, ½ × ¼ inches, 7/16 × 7/16 inches (near the shell hinge), and 1¼ × ⅞ inches. These fragments, like those found in the strata above, appear to have been mechanically broken to be about the same size. These materials are likely associated with members of the Ten Broeck family in the 17th and early 18th centuries. Based on the lack of hard currency during this time period, the manufacture and use of wampum could probably be extended into the mid-18th century (Lesniak 2002; Pena 1990, 2006), and, in this case, the fragments may have been associated with the Van Gaasbeek family. Due to their small and consistent size, these small clam fragments are interpreted as representing wampum manufacture rather than food remains (Diamond and Amorosi 2023).

Further excavations in this area might recover more definitive evidence such as later stages of wampum manufacturing. Although clam shells are often ground down to make mortar or plaster, we do not believe this to be the case here. The area in and around Kingston is part of the Onondaga Limestone formation, and there are numerous lime kilns ranging in age from the 18th to 19th centuries throughout the area. These kilns produced a ready source of lime for making both mortar and plaster that was used to finish the interior walls of stone houses. Making these materials from clam shells would have been too labor-intensive, and because wampum was equivalent to currency, it would make more sense that this was the activity represented here.

Small Red Dutch Bricks/Pan Tiles

The orientation room stratum is also the first stratum in which significant amounts of small red Dutch brick fragments were found. Of particular interest is the possibility that many of these bricks, as well as the pan tiles found in the first unit, were likely made by enslaved workers in the nearby brickyard of Cornelius Pietersen Hoogeboom (see chapter 8).

Trade Items

In Unit 1, the stratum that consisted of 17th- to 18th-century yard debris contained one item that may relate to trade with Native Americans during this time period: a piece of sheet copper that appears to have been cut into a triangle for use as either a projectile point or to be rolled into a tinkler cone. This artifact could be viewed as a potential trade item, as failed copper and brass pots were often recycled into projectile points, tinkler cones, and beads, which were then often used for trade (Diamond 2023, fig. 7.15; Van Dongen 1996, 115–71).

Native American Features and Artifacts

This stratum also contained a larger amount of precontact Native American artifacts than other strata, particularly lithic debitage and pottery. This sample included fragments of two Native American pots: one that appeared to be a Black Rock Trailed vessel from the Middle Woodland period (Funk 1976, 315), and the other was a neck fragment of a smoothed exterior pot with a plat of six vertical cord-wrapped stick decorations. Based on what

I have observed from other sites in the Esopus drainage, this pot is likely Kingston Incised or Munsee Incised, dating c. 1550–1658 (Diamond 1998, 1999a, 2023). Similar smoothed-bodied and incised-collared ceramics were found outside of the Senate House (Feister and Sopko 2003) as well as during the 1970 NYU excavations across Clinton Avenue from the Senate House. Like the stratum above, precontact Native American materials were numerous. Here, precontact Native American artifacts accounted for 59% of the sample.

The builder's trench for the north wall of the building contained primarily architectural items and oyster shell fragments. Of the 33 artifacts from the builder's trench, 14 (or 42%) were precontact Native American artifacts.

The stratum containing the soil in and around the post molds yielded a total of 20 artifacts, of which 13, or 36%, were Native American in origin. Historic artifacts that had filtered down into this stratum consisted of five small pan tile fragments, one 17th-century devitrified window glass fragment, and one mortar fragment. However, the real find here was four post molds, likely from a wigwam or longhouse, which indicate that the soils within portions of the Senate House are still intact and retain cultural features that predate the Dutch period in Kingston. Other local examples of similar structures include a 110-foot-long × 29-foot-wide square-ended longhouse at the Grapes Site in Marbletown, New York, from the early Contact period (Diamond 1998, 1999a, 2023), and an approximately 32-foot-long × 15-foot-wide wigwam at the 230-3-1 site on the Wappinger Creek in Pleasant Valley, New York, dating c. 1575 (Cultural Resource Group 1993; Holt and Luhman 2007).

The Ten Broeck-Van Gaasbeek-Voorhies-Merrit Lot

The Ten Broeck-Van Gaasbeek-Voorhies-Merrit lot is located south of the Senate House and was owned by the Ten Broeck and Van Gaasbeek families from 1658 to 1850. Excavations were undertaken by OPRHP as part of an effort to determine whether significant deposits were located in this area (Feister and Sopko 2003, 41–47). A total of 15 units were excavated, totaling 136 square feet or 12.63 square meters, producing some evidence of Native American use of the area in the form of lithic debitage. However, most of the artifacts were of 18th- and 19th-century origin, such as food bones, early creamware, pearlware, and buff-bodied slip-decorated earthenwares, as well as architectural materials such as window glass, bricks, and nails.

The Abraham Masten House Lot

At the nearby Abraham Masten House lot,[10] 37 units of varying sizes were excavated, with a total of 146 square feet or 13.6 square meters of horizontal excavation area exposed. An archaeological study was undertaken by OPRHP as part of an effort to determine whether significant deposits were located on this lot (Feister and Sopko 2003, 48–69). Excavations identified lithic debitage, precontact pottery, and a possible hearth/fire pit. This indicates that undisturbed portions of the northeast corner of the original stockade area contained precontact Native American artifacts as well as intact features. Several areas yielded 17th-century materials, including red bricks, handwrought nails, delft, black glass wine bottle fragments, and early window glass. The lot also produced fragments of a Dutch tulip design delft plate (Feister and Sopko 2003, figs. 29a, 29b). In the 18th-century layers, common ceramics included slip-decorated buff-bodied earthenwares with joggled patterns (c. 1670–1795), "scratch blue" salt-glazed stoneware (c.1744–1775), creamware (post-1762), and red earthenware. These were probably ceramics that were thrown out of the Masten House during the 18th century and accumulated in the yard in what archaeologists call a "sheet midden."

Area West of Masten House Lot

In the area west of the Abraham Masten House lot, 27 units of varying sizes were excavated, with a total of 276.75 square feet (25.7 sq m) of horizontal excavation area exposed. This area produced evidence of artifacts ranging from precontact Native American items to 19th-century artifacts. Seventeenth-century artifacts included white clay smoking pipe fragments, small red Dutch bricks, handwrought nails, and delft.

West Half of the Senate House Property

The west half of the Senate House property from the Loughran House to North Front Street was also tested by OPRHP (Feister and Sopko 2003, 94–103). In all, 25 units of varying sizes as well as three trenches were excavated, covering 140 square feet (13 sq m) of horizontal excavation area. This lot produced evidence of a mid-19th-century privy, a modern dry well constructed of "Hutton" bricks, and 19th-century building foundations.

Excavations at the Old Dutch Church

From 1981 to 1982, the Friends of Historic Kingston hired archaeologist Theresa Murphy to locate the first Dutch Church in the city, which, based on the 1695 Miller map, was thought to be in the northeast corner at the intersection of Wall and Main Streets and southwest corner of the present Old Dutch Church graveyard. Excavations in the southwest corner of the present graveyard yielded ceramics, bottle glass, window glass, square cut nails, animal bones, and burned stone. However, no in situ archaeological remains of the structural elements of the original church were found, and a full report was never submitted.

In the fall of 2003, Jay R. Cohen was hired to test specific locations underneath and outside the present-day Old Dutch Church in the eastern portion of the churchyard to mitigate the effects of wall stabilization activities to support the east wall of the church. Eight units totaling 187.17 square feet (19 m) were excavated, producing 2,027 artifacts. Two units were inside the foundation and six were outside in the graveyard on the eastern side of the church (Cohen 2005). The inside units identified a brown sandy redeposited fill with architectural artifacts and stone footing supports. The outside units identified a series of fill and construction episodes, the latter being related to the construction of the present church in 1852 and a reconstruction of the church roof in 1853. Also found were previously used ground surfaces around the church that had been covered with fill.

Historic artifacts that were not architectural included 18th- and 19th-century materials such as animal bone fragments (cattle, sheep, goat, pig, horse, chicken), coal, bottle glass, wine bottle fragments, oyster fragments, clam fragments, lamp chimney glass, white clay pipe fragments, a belt buckle, and a straight pin. British and American ceramics such as whiteware (post-1820), pearlware (post-1780), creamware (post-1762), combed buff-bodied slip-decorated earthenware (c.1670–1795), brown Nottingham ware (c. 1700–1810), Jackfield-type refined red earthenware (c.1740–1850), white salt-glazed stoneware (c. 1720–1805), and gray salt-glazed stoneware fragments were found. Several fragments of Chinese export porcelain (c. 1790–1840) were also recovered.

The eight excavation units also yielded 47 precontact artifacts, including five rhyolite flakes, 41 flakes of Mt. Merino chert, and one chert core fragment. One of the chert flakes appeared to have been used as a graver. Cohen (2005) suggested that, based on an analysis of the debitage, random core reduction or "early and late-stage biface manufacture may have contributed to the production of flakes in the assemblage." Unfortunately, no temporally diagnostic precontact Native American artifacts were found during this study. However, because the Old Dutch Church is just across the street from the Fred Johnston House, it seems plausible to make the argument that the precontact materials identified here may be related to the Late Archaic (Sylvan Lake/Lamoka) site discussed above that was found by Robert Slater. When one views the entire uptown area as a level terrace with well-drained soils overlooking a major tributary of the Hudson, it is easy to understand why precontact Native American artifacts are found whenever controlled excavations are undertaken in Kingston's uptown area.

Cohen's (2005) excavations also revealed a buried A-horizon soil, the original graveyard, at approximately 68 centimeters (27 in) below the present ground surface. The additional 68 centimeters of overburden is probably related to soils removed during excavation of the basement for the church. This increase in elevation is also evident at the Persen House, discussed in the next chapter, where approximately the same amount of soil can be observed overlying the June 1663 burn level. It should also be noted that although one grave shaft was located archaeologically in the Old Dutch churchyard, no human remains were encountered in the excavated soils as isolated items or "stray finds." This is important because it suggests that no previous burials in this area of the churchyard were disturbed by the interment of the later burials.

NYU Excavations on Green Street

In 1971, NYU student Sarah Bridges undertook an archaeological excavation in the hopes of locating a portion of the 1661 stockade along Green Street in the Stockade District. The purpose of the testing was to locate the original soil surface in the area as it existed in the 17th century and, if possible, to find evidence of the 1661 stockade. The 1695 Miller map indicated the stockade in a location that would put it at the edge of the bluff overlooking Tannery Brook. From a 17th-century Dutch tactical perspective, by taking advantage of the drop-off, this method of construction would have added to the height of the stockade line, thus making it easier to defend and much more difficult to attack. Add to this the fact that Tannery Brook is at the base of the hill, which forms a natural moat.

Several test units and trenches were excavated, revealing highly disturbed soils in the area. Bridges thus concluded that much of Green Street has been disturbed and filled with later materials, most likely during the 18th and 19th centuries. She noted that "it is extremely unlikely that any traces of the west wall of the 1658 Dutch stockade will be found along this northern portion of Green Street. Since our excavations along Clinton Avenue in 1970 showed that the palisade posts were driven barely 2 feet into the ground, removal of the uppermost 2 feet would completely obliterate all evidence of these features" (Bridges 1972, 23–24).

In retrospect, there are a few issues with this conclusion. The first is that when the excavators from NYU found the portion of stockade in 1970 along Clinton Avenue, it was a part of the initial stockade built by Peter Stuyvesant in 1658. As Bridges mentioned, these were individual posts set about two feet into the sandy terrace along Clinton Avenue. This was not necessarily the case along the western wall for the first or 1661 addition to the original stockade. From Robert Slater's 1983 overlay of the original stockade (1658) and its three subsequent additions (1661, 1669–1670, 1676–1677), we noted that the west wall of the 1658 stockade probably cut across the parking lots just west of present-day Crown Street, with the 1661 addition extending past that to the bluff edge near Green Street. The 1661 addition can best be observed in the Phase 3 portion and interior of the Persen House as a deeply dug trench with upright posts in a line making a fortified stockade wall. The 17th-century stockade line may still be preserved in different locations along Green Street.

Summary

This chapter has briefly summarized the archaeological excavations that have been undertaken within the National Register Stockade District, commonly called "uptown Kingston." Since no colonial Dutch archaeological sites have been found outside of the stockade area, these excavations give us an inkling into the kinds of material culture, foodways, and burial habits that characterized the early colonial inhabitants of *Wiltwyck*. Since many of the early Dutch colonial occupations overlap Native American occupations and, in turn, are overlapped by later British colonial and

American colonial occupations, deposits, and artifacts, sorting out "slices of time" based on the archaeological record is difficult. The movement of soils, artifacts, artifacts in soil matrices, and the construction and filling in of pits creates a challenging puzzle for the archaeologist to piece back together. This situation, which is very common on urban sites, has recently been referred to by Olivier (2011, 129) as a *palimpsest*, or "a cumulative phenomenon of sequences of human occupation (that produced archaeological remains) thus recording memory in the land in the form of superimposed, stratigraphic layers." This concept can best be observed in the next chapter, the excavation in and around the Persen House at the corner of Crown and John Streets in Kingston.

Chapter 5

The Matthewis Persen House

For several reasons, the Matthewis Persen House site is one of the most informative sites in the Stockade District. The first reason is that intact 17th-century archaeological contexts have been found beneath the sidewalks on Crown and John Streets adjacent to the Persen House. The second is that intact strata have also been found beneath a portion of the house that was never previously disturbed, as it did not have a basement excavated under it. The third is that within an excavation conducted inside the house, a portion of the 17th-century stockade, along with evidence of the burn layer from June 7, 1663, were found. Further, below the burn layer were undisturbed contexts containing Native American and Dutch artifacts. Because of the significance of this site, I thought it was worth a separate chapter as a case study in this book. This case study is modified from the report that I wrote at the conclusion of the Persen House excavations and illustrates the kinds of information that can be gleaned through careful excavation and analysis of archaeological strata when combined with historical documentation.

The Matthewis Persen House is located on the southeast corner at the intersection of Crown and John Streets within the Stockade District in Kingston (fig. 4.1). The Persen House, having been constructed in five different phases, is set within the first expansion (1661–1663) as well as the second addition (1669–1670) of the fort. The house is shown on Miller's 1695 plan of Kingston (fig. 4.1), which is part of the *Documents Relating to the Colonial History of the State of New York* (Fernow 1881, 84–85). Robert Slater's map (see fig. 3.1), which is an overlay based on the measurements given in the Kingston court minutes and colonial documents, shows a conjectural plan of the three enlargements of the stockaded area.

Based on historic documentation, the first portion of the house appears to have been constructed c. 1663–1673 (Kenneth Barricklo, personal communication, January 14, 2004), and documentary sleuthing by Paul Huey (personal communication, July 21, 2003) identified that the lot may have been owned by Dr. Gysbert van Imbroch. The house and lot were sold by the guardians of van Imbroch's children on March 26, 1673 (Ulster County Deeds, bk. 2, p. 376). The deed was for "the sale of the childrens's house with everything fastened in the ground and fixed by nail and also the lot and garden" for 1,800 guilders (Netherlands traditional currency). At the end of the deed is added, "NB The guardians, also, will have to deliver the curtain appertaining to the same, at present in a satisfactory condition." As Paul Huey noted, "this 'curtain' would be the stockade wall; each householder was apparently responsible for the section of stockade wall, if any, adjoining his/her property." This tidbit is an interesting feature to visualize: If the southern portion of the stockade wall adjacent to the Gysbert van Imbroch house was still standing in "satisfactory condition" in March 1673, then it must have still been present when the 1669–1670 addition was placed to the south. This would mean that the village of *Wiltwyck* was made up of several zones based on the successive construction episodes of stockade building, until, of course, people later removed the palisade posts between their lots.

Gysbert van Imbroch was a surgeon who appeared quite often in the Kingston court minutes (Christoph et al. 1976). He died in August 1665, and his probate inventory (Christoph et al. 1976, 2:566–71), which was taken on September 1 and 2, 1665, provides us with not only the details of material culture in 17th-century *Wiltwyck* but also the contents of one of the largest libraries in the Hudson Valley at that time. At the end of the rather exhaustive list of items is the note that all of the articles were "stored in the deceased Gysbert van Imbroch's own house, standing and situated in the village of *Wiltwyck* with a garden annexed to it, surrounded with good palisades" (Christoph et al. 1976, 2:570). If the Phase 1 portion of the Persen House was indeed Gysbert van Imbroch's house, then the location of the garden annex is difficult to envision. During our excavations at the Persen House, we found that the June 7, 1663, burn layer surrounded the house under the sidewalks to the north and west. This would imply that the garden, if it was outside the 1661–1663 stockade, would have been located either south of the Persen House or in another lot within the 1661–1663 addition.

Kenneth Barricklo determined that the Persen House has gone through five major phases of construction. The first was during the time period c. 1663 to c. 1673 (Phase 1) when the house was probably a 1½-story wood-framed building constructed on a stone foundation, fronting on what is now Crown Street in the manner of most Dutch houses, with the gable end facing the street (fig. 5.1). Alternatively, the house may have been a wattle-and-daub frame structure with nothing more than a roughly dug

Figure 5.1. Plan view of the Persen House. Taken from Barricklo (2000). *Source:* Public domain.

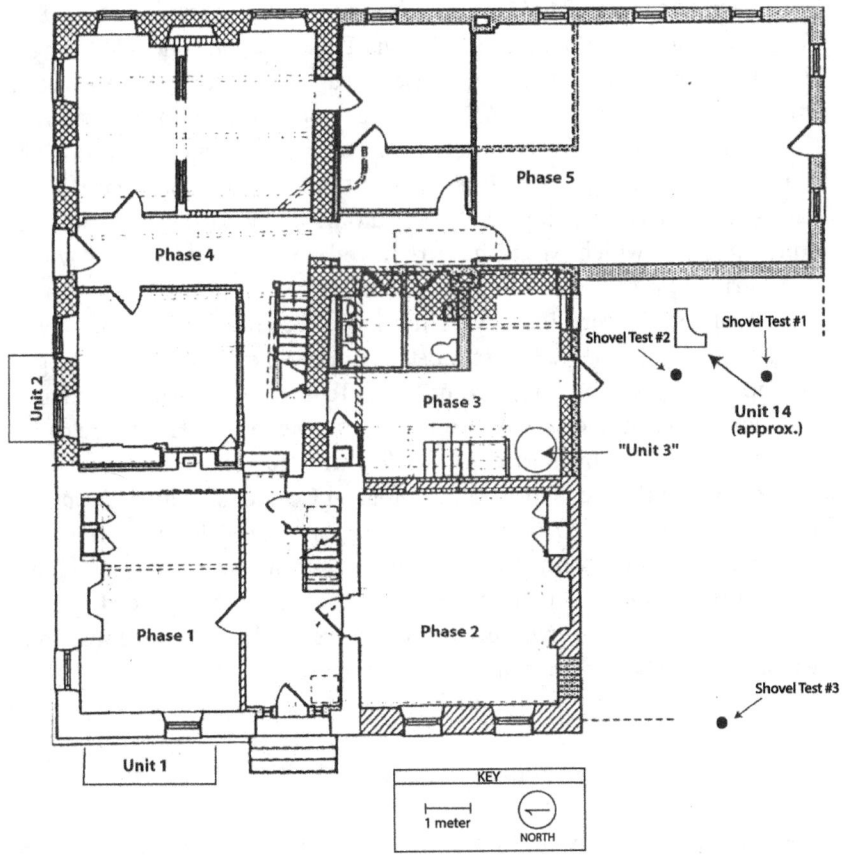

out basement for storage of root crops. These are the kinds of houses that have been found in *Rensselaerswyck* and are probably also the first types of houses constructed in *Wiltwyck*. Archaeologically speaking, as houses became more permanent and larger, particularly when construction involved the use of limestone, the construction of deep basements with stone walls for structural support often destroyed the earlier, more fragile architectural evidence. During the second phase of house construction (c. 1675–1730/35), the gable from the first phase was knocked down and a stone 1½-story was added to the south wall of the house, thereby extending it as a longer 1½-story house parallel with Crown Street. Phase 3 (post-1730–1735) was characterized by a two-story wood-framed "kitchen wing," which was added to the Phase 2 addition. This portion of the building appears to have been rebuilt after the burning of Kingston in 1777 (Barricklo 2000, 24–27), a fact attested to by Schoonmaker (1888, 307), who listed the house of Matthewis Persen as one included on the "List of Sufferers" from the fire. Phase 4 was a two-story stone addition to the Phase 1 section post-1777, which extended east along John Street. Phase 5 was a large two-story brick structure, constructed in 1922 by the County of Ulster, which intersects and abuts both the Phase 3 and Phase 4 portions of the house. This addition included the excavation of a full basement, which would have removed any exterior features within its footprint east of the Phase 3 addition.

At times, the terminology of the architect and the terminology of the archaeologist overlap. This is most common when concepts relating to time, however short or long, are utilized. To avoid confusion, particular construction events such as additions made to the Persen House are called "phases," as utilized by Barricklo (2000). This duplicates the use of the word "phase" in the New York Archaeological Council's *Cultural Resources Standards Handbook* (2000) and the way I have used it throughout the book to denote a precontact archaeological culture or a stage of archaeological investigation. For the purposes of this chapter, the word "phase" is used to describe the five building episodes of the Persen House, and these phases are keyed to figure 5.1.

The Persen House Excavation

In October 2000, two excavation units were placed adjacent to the Persen House to answer questions relating to structural problems apparent internally, most specifically in the basement. In order to determine the extent of foundation stabilization that was needed, the units were placed outside the limestone walls. Unit 1 was placed along the west wall of the Phase 1, or oldest, portion of the house on Crown Street, and Unit 2 was placed along the north wall about midway down the Phase 4 portion of the house on John Street (see fig. 5.1). Bob Jury, the mason who was working on stabilizing the wall, also did a shovel test, listed as Unit 3, in the interior of the house beneath the wooden floor in the Phase 3 portion of the house (fig. 5.1). This test was designed to answer questions that Bob had about specific structural elements inside the house. The shovel test revealed a large concentration of artifacts, in fact, many more than were found in the exterior units. At the time, this suggested that the interior portion of the house, an area that would have been an 18th-century kitchen wing, might hold substantial information about 17th- and 18th-century Dutch foodways and material culture.

Inside the Phase 3 addition, it was decided that, for several reasons, as large a sample as possible would be excavated. The first reason was that an exposed soil profile of the recently constructed (i.e., mid-20th century) stairwell leading down to the Phase 2 basement revealed an undisturbed column of soil. With the aid of a flashlight and a trowel, a series of stratified soils could be observed in the column, consisting of a clay mortar floor, various amounts of stone, brick, mortar, and, most importantly, the June 7, 1663, burn layer. This in situ stratigraphy pointed to the possibility of the Phase 3 addition, which was probably a summer kitchen, being an undisturbed "layer cake" of Kingston's history.

The second reason for undertaking a large excavation within the room was to obtain a large, controlled sample of 17th- and 18th-century artifacts from this portion of Kingston, which is important considering that a very limited amount of work has been done to date within the National Register Historic Stockade District. Excavations within the Phase 3 portion of the Persen House presented an opportunity to examine a large, undisturbed soil sample from which artifactual information about the Dutch occupation, as well as later periods, could be gathered.

The third reason for the excavation was that, as a consequence of my realization that the burn layer encountered in Units 1 and 2 was *not* from 1777, it also became obvious that 17th-century contexts from 1658 to 1664 could exist stratigraphically below the burn layer. The excavation of these kinds of contexts has the potential to provide tightly dated evidence from this time period. I had hoped that a privy, cistern, or well would be encountered within (and pre-dating) the Phase 3 addition. To my knowledge, no 17th-century features from these categories have been found in Kingston. A similar situation occurred at Fort Orange in Albany (Huey 1988), where garbage boxes, but no privies, were found. It is only in urban environments such as New Amsterdam (New York City), in which substantial amounts of horizontal surface area have been excavated, where evidence of backyard privy features containing primary deposits from the Dutch period have been found (Grossman 1985; Rothschild et al. 1987). This is not to say that all is lost but only that excavations have been few, and the key to obtaining this category of data is, as previously mentioned, broad, horizontal excavation areas.

To explain more clearly, an examination of the 1884 Sanborn Fire Insurance maps of uptown Kingston indicated that, at that time, there were several extant Dutch barns within the stockaded area, even as late as the last quarter of the 19th century. These were likely barns that were rebuilt in the Dutch vernacular style after the burning of Kingston by the British in October of 1777. This suggests that much of Kingston's late-18th-century archaeological and architectural features may still be preserved in the uptown area, particularly beneath parking lots (see Diamond 1990). This also points to the conservative nature of Kingston, discussed by Blumin (1976), regarding the apparent hold that old Dutch families had in the Kingston area as late as the mid-19th century, where Dutch vernacular architecture may have been the preferred construction type even into the 19th century.

In addition to excavations in the interior of the Persen House, various projects outside of the house were undertaken, most notably the reexcavation and replacement of an early 20th-century stairwell as well as pipe trenching.

Excavation Procedures

Because of the depth of the Persen House walls, it was necessary to excavate units that were wide enough to allow us access to approximately 5 feet (1.5 m) in depth. For this reason, a unit size of 1 meter in width was commonly utilized. All soil excavated from the inside and outside of the Matthewis Persen House was screened through ¼-inch hardware mesh, and the artifacts were removed, bagged, washed, and catalogued. All of the soil excavated from Bob Jury's "Unit 3" was screened and collected in the same manner. Since there was no record of stratigraphy, these artifacts were lumped together as one analytical unit.

The initial excavation unit (Unit 1) was placed on the west side of the Persen House and measured 1 × 3 meters. Unit 2 was located on the north side of the house (fig. 5.1), and due to problems with the steel reinforced concrete placed below the bluestone (in the 1970s), the unit's size was determined by the amount of concrete that could be removed. Consequently, Unit 2 measured 1 × 1.6 meters. Metric measurements were used because this is now standard, even in historical archaeology.

With respect to soil terminology (i.e., stratum, level, context), the terms utilized here are from the context method, or Harris matrix (Harris 1975, 1979a, 1979b). A Munsell Soil Color Chart was used to determine the color, hue, and chroma of the excavated soils. Documenting soil colors is an important part of archaeology, as different soil colors or textures may indicate whether a soil is intact or whether it was a mixture of several soils. This is particularly important for exposing and documenting features such as post molds or small pits. In some cases, such as inside the house, drier soils had to be moistened to determine actual color.

Sample Size

The size of the archaeological units excavated within and around the Persen House varied. This was related to several factors: the size of the sidewalk stones, which were removed from the sidewalk on the outside of the house (Units 1 and 2); the available working area on the inside of the Phase 3 addition; and the suggested impact area of the proposed trench around the door to the Phase 5 basement. The interior of the Phase 3 portion of the house (fig. 5.2) was undoubtedly the most difficult to excavate. Wheelbarrows were used to remove soil from the inside of the building, pushing them along pieces of plywood that were nailed into the floor joists. The soil was then taken off site to keep the yard area to the south of the Phase 3 addition unobstructed. This also cleared out the Phase 3 portion of the house for the restoration effort that was to begin after the archaeological work was completed.

As we excavated different portions of the room, our working space varied due to the placement of the floor joists and the fragility of the soils. This is the why the sample units depicted in figure 5.2 vary in size, shape, and number. Our primary concern was to keep a solid work platform

Figure 5.2. Plan view of Phase 3 portion of Persen House showing floor joists and unit locations. Other house construction phases shown on edges of figure. *Source:* Public domain.

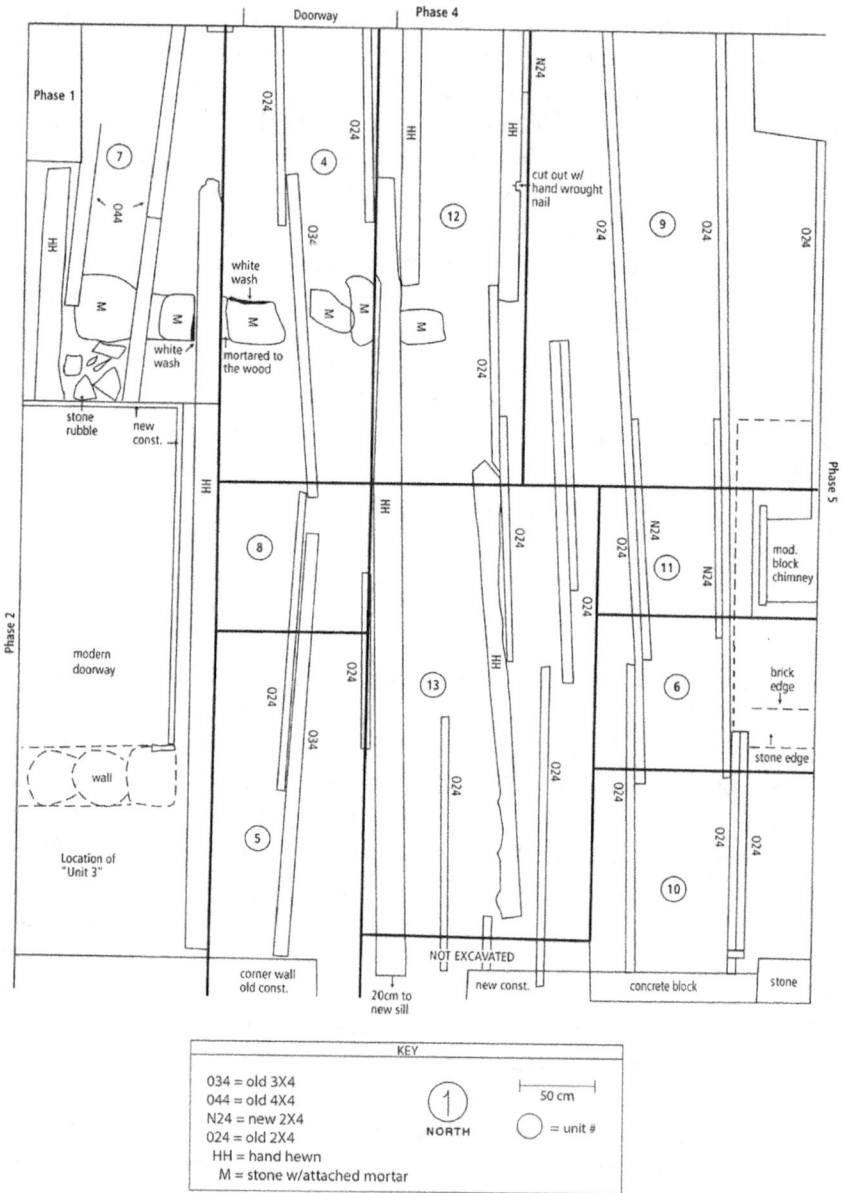

in the room as well as straight and solid walls leading down to the base of the excavation. This was a challenge, as the upper context was loose, consisting of a dusty fill overlying a clay/mortar floor, which overlaid loose sand. The added problem of numerous rat burrows and nests in every possible direction meant that to keep unit walls intact, vibrations from the excavation procedure had to be kept to a minimum.

The following list, keyed to figure 5.2, provides the unit sizes in square meters: Unit 1 (3 m), Unit 2 (1.6 m), Unit 3 (not applicable; this was a large shovel test and the walls later collapsed), Unit 4 (3 m), Unit 5 (2.5 m), Unit 6 (1.5 m), Unit 7 (2.36 m), Unit 8 (1 m), Unit 9 (5.675 m), Unit 10 (2.253 m), Unit 11 (.85 m), Unit 12 (3 m), Unit 13 (4.5 m), Unit 14 (2.035 m). The total excavated area was 33.273 square meters (358 sq ft). Unit 12 was only partially excavated, and most of the soils were left in situ.

Sidewalk Units

Unit 1

Unit 1 (1 × 3 m) was placed 83 cm from the corner of the building located at John and Crown Streets (fig. 5.1) on the west wall of the Persen House, which would have been the Phase 1 wall. After removing the bluestone sidewalk, approximately 10–12 cm of stone dust was encountered. This overlaid a 10-cm steel-reinforced concrete pad that supported the sidewalk. After the sidewalk was removed, the remaining concrete fragments were cleaned up and excavation began.

The Harris Matrix is a form of record keeping where each layer or stratum is given a context number beginning from 1 to the last context excavated. Each context is recorded in sequential order. Context 1 was a coarse sand mixed with rubble as well as materials relating to repairs done on the house. Artifacts from Context 1 included pipestems from c. 1660–1730 as well as ginger-colored red earthenwares and Jackfield-type red earthenware (1740–1850). Context 2 (fig. 5.3) was similar, being a mix of yellow-brown sand with mortar, plaster, charcoal, and brick debris. Artifacts from Context 2 included white clay pipe fragments, window glass, fragments of an earthenware storage jar, and creamware (post-1762).

Figure 5.3. Persen House. Unit 1, west wall profile. (Note Context 3 not shown.) *Source:* Photo by the author.

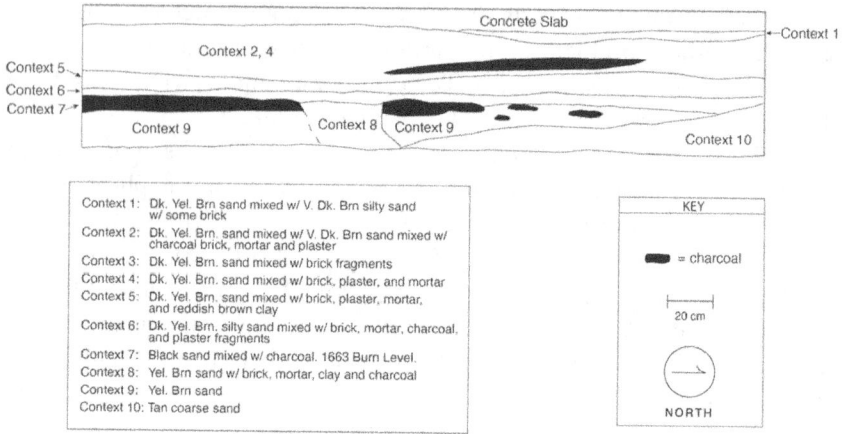

Context 3 (which is not shown on fig. 5.3) was a repair trench combined with a portion of the builder's trench for the Phase 1 portion of the building. It appears to have postdated the 1663 fire, as it cut through the burn layer and terminated at almost 152 cm (or 5 ft) in depth. Found within Context 3 in the south wall profile for Unit 1 were several pieces of bluestone, which appeared to be polished (via use or rubbing) and were hand-dressed. This may suggest that the repair trench is coeval with the bluestone addition above the front door on the Crown Street side of the house. Context 3 yielded numerous fragments of destruction and reconstruction rubble that, again, would have postdated the 1663 fire. Artifacts included creamware (post-1762), hand-painted pearlware (post-1780), and large amounts of small red handmade Dutch brick. The presence of hand-painted pearlware in the trench suggests that the repair to the wall occurred toward the end of the 18th century, if not the very early 19th century. In any case, it cut through the burn layer (Context 7), which is shown on the figures as a black line and described alternatively as either "charcoal" or "1663 burn layer."

Contexts 4, 5, and 6 were composed of dark brown sands with varying amounts of plaster, mortar brick, and charcoal. However, Contexts 5 and 6 held more reddish-brown clay, which is probably related to renovations or reconstruction of the walls. Although Context 4 did not produce large amounts of temporally diagnostic artifacts, Context 5 yielded fragments of several earthenware vessels, which can be conservatively dated to c. 1700–1750. Context 6, which directly overlaid the burn layer (Context 7), produced a 17th-century Dutch cooking vessel, combed slip-decorated buff-bodied earthenware from the 17th to 18th centuries, and a gunflint resharpening flake and white clay pipe fragments. Two of the latter are debossed with *fleur-de-lis* on the stems (see Dallal 2004, 221–26). One is similar to a specific pipe found at Fort Orange by Paul Huey (1988, 740, no. 2), and the other is generally similar in design to white clay pipe fragments found at Fort Orange. Context 6 also produced a pipestem with an embossed heel mark consisting of a crown with "H.G" below it, which is the mark of Hendrick Gerdes of Amsterdam, who produced pipes from 1668 to 1688 (McCashion 1979, 130–31). This mark has also been found at Fort Orange (Huey 1988, 740, no. 60), New York City, Huguenot Street in New Paltz, and at Haudenosaunee sites in central New York (Bradley and DeAngelo 1981, fig. 3.f; McCashion 1979).

Context 7 was a coarse black sand mixed with charcoal, which varied between 5 and 11 cm in thickness (fig. 5.3). This black sand is thought to be the burn layer associated with the June 7, 1663, burning of *Wiltwyck* by the Esopus. This context did not yield any datable European or Euro-American artifacts. Culturally diagnostic artifacts from Context 7 as well as from Context 8 below it consisted exclusively of Native American artifacts associated with cooking (pottery and fire cracked rock) and tool manufacture (debitage).

Cutting through the burn layer (Context 7) was Context 8, a roughly 27 × 27 cm square cut that extended 20 cm in depth. This square might have been a put-hole from scaffolding used to repair or extend the Persen House. The post would have been about 10½ inches (26.5 cm) on a side. Seventy artifacts were associated with Context 8, all of which were Native American in origin. These included nine lithic debitage, 59 fire-cracked rock, a "marginal" biface, and a blocky fragment of chert.

Context 9 appeared to be a portion of the original soil below the burn layer. It consisted of a yellow-brown sand that produced window glass, a white clay pipe fragment, and a projectile point. The latter is Meadowood-like (see Ritchie 1961, 35–36, plate17) and likely dates c.1050–500 B.C. or c. 3000–2450 BP.

Below Context 9 was a very coarse, tan, sterile sand (Context 10) that appeared to originate from a soil slump associated with a street drain near the corner. It was not excavated because it appeared to be clean fill associated with modern pipe trenches under the street.

Unit 2

Unit 2 (1 × 1.6 m) was located 7.34 meters from the northwest corner of the Persen House along the north side of the Phase 4 wall. In the opening soil stratum of Context 11 was a dark yellowish-brown sand with mortar, brick, shell, and stone debris. This context produced fragments of an undecorated green glass prunt associated with a *roemer* or Dutch drinking glass. A prunt is a small blob of glass that was applied to the outside of the vessel, and then a small stamp or mold was pushed against it to produce a raspberry-like appearance (fig. 4.7). *Roemers* that have rounded prunts without raspberry impressions generally date from the third quarter of the 17th century (see Baart 1984; Grimm 1984; Theuerkauff-Liederwald 1968, 1969) and were produced in Holland as well as Germany. Vreeken et al. (1998, 152–53) illustrated a similar *roemer* in the Amsterdam Historical Museum that dates to 1652. Context 11 also yielded a fragment of an English "onion" or onion-shaped wine bottle that dates c.1670–1710 based on comparisons with the shapes of dated examples (Dumbrell 1983; McNulty 1971, 1972; Noël Hume 1961, 1970).

Context 12 was a repair or builder's trench that cut through the 1663 burn layer on the north side of the Phase 4 portion of the Persen House. This context (fig. 5.4) is similar in nature to Context 3 in Unit 1 and included small red bricks, brick fragments, nails, glass, stoneware, Dutch ceramics, and a Levanna projectile point. Similar to the western side of the house, Context 12 also produced lumps of clay, which is probably from initial construction or reconstruction of the walls or chimney. Clay was used as the interior packing material between the stones in most stone houses, and the outside bonds were sealed with lime mortar.

Context 13 was a 12-cm-thick layer of sand (fig. 5.4) overlying the 1663 burn layer (Context 14). This sand yielded some burned clay but not nearly as much as the strata overlying the burn layer in Unit 1. Context 14, the 1663 burn layer in Unit 2, was very similar to that located in Unit 1 (fig. 5.3). It consisted of a 5-cm stratum of black charcoal mixed with coarse sand and produced no artifacts other than bone.

Below Context 14 was Context 15, a strong brown sand that extended from about 43 cm to 82 cm in depth (fig. 5.4). The upper portion of this context produced an Orient Fishtail projectile point, lithic debitage, and fire-cracked rock.

Figure 5.4. Persen House. Unit 2, north wall profile. *Source:* Photo by the author.

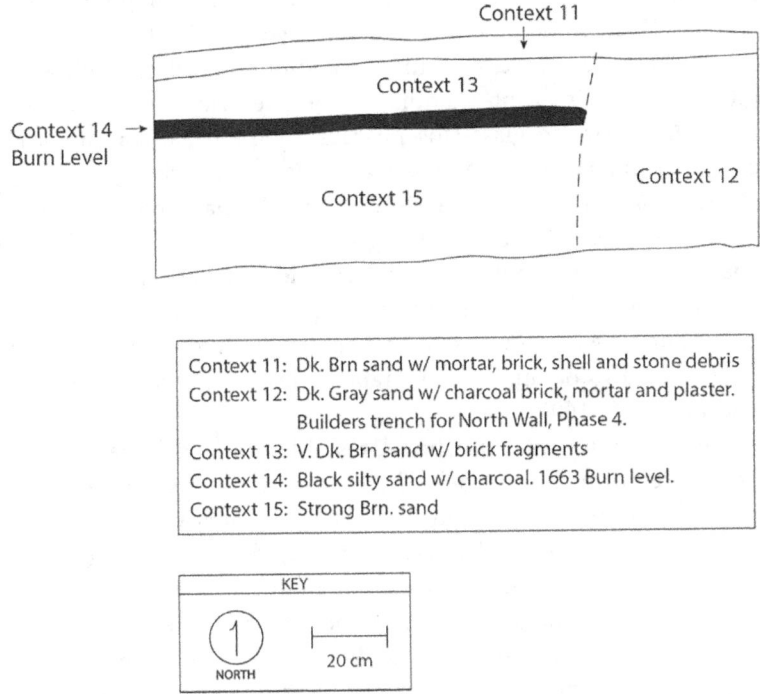

Interior Units

The interior units excavated in the Phase 3 portion of the Matthewis Persen House are discussed in numerical order, with details concerning their overall size (square meters) and shape. Many of the artifacts are discussed in this section in general terms. Artifacts pertinent to dating, European-Native American trade, and the Dutch and British Colonial periods will be discussed as they appear in the text.

Unit 3

As previously mentioned, Unit 3 was a large shovel test excavated in the extreme southwestern corner of the Phase 3 addition, between the south wall and the modern cellar doorway. The shovel test yielded 811 artifacts, of which 428 were bone and 42 were bivalve fragments (oyster and clam). When combined, this indicates that 58% of the artifacts from this shovel test were food remains. In addition, a colorless glass prunt was also found. This prunt is similar to the one discussed above but was made of clear, crizzled glass (Joseph McEvoy, personal communication, 2002) rather than the more stable aquamarine or deep green "forest glass" (*Waldglas*) that is characteristic of the German and Dutch vessels. This prunt may be from one of the glass vessels associated with George Ravenscroft's early attempt at making colorless glass in England during the last quarter of the 17th century (Charleston 1968). If so, it would be an early example when Ravenscroft was still experimenting with the ratio of alkali to lead to obtain his "christalline glasses," perhaps around 1676 (Charleston 1968, 160).

The excavation of this shovel test identified a large amount of cultural material in the soil near the rear of what would have been the backyard during the 17th century, and then the area within the Phase 3 construction after that. As discussed above, and in Barricklo (2000), the internal architectural details indicate that a kitchen wing was rebuilt after the 1777 fire, even though we did not find any evidence for the 1777 fire at the Persen House. Our only charcoal evidence dated from (1) the 1663 burn layer and (2) the charcoal associated with the brick chimney from the Phase 1 house when it was knocked down during the addition of the Phase 2 portion of the house.

Unit 4

Unit 4 was the first unit excavated inside the Phase 3 addition and was positioned between floor joists on a north/south orientation (fig. 5.2). The unit was excavated in 42 archaeological contexts, which ranged in depth from Context 16, the loose soil between the floor joists, to Context 73, a fine yellow-brown sand below the June 7, 1663, burn layer. The excavation unit was three meters in size and was designed to provide information about the interior north wall of the Phase 3 portion of the house. It was also appropriately placed so that two subsequent units could be linked with it, thereby creating a profile from the south wall of the Phase 4 addition to the south wall of the Phase 3 portion, thus giving us an idea of construction and destruction episodes (fig. 5.5).

Figure 5.5. Persen House. Units 4, 8, and 5, east wall profile. *Source:* Photo by the author.

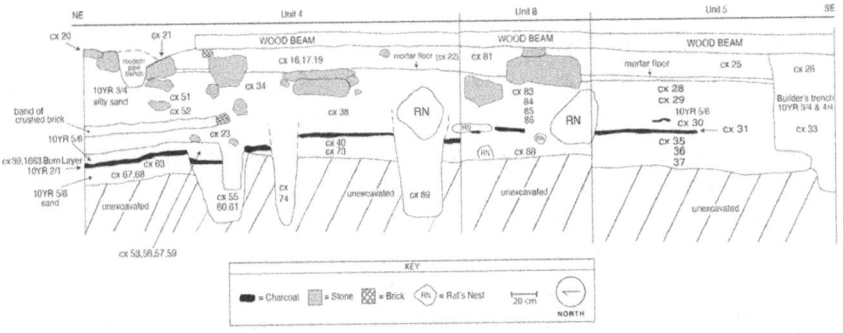

Contexts 16 through 19 were a combination of soils between the floor joists and above the clay/mortar floor, which appears to have been created to seal in the soils beneath (fig. 5.5). These contexts yielded creamware, pearlware, delft, Canton porcelain, blue transfer-printed pearlware (post-1800), white clay pipes with an "R. Tippet" cartouche, and various wine bottle fragments. Many of the bottle fragments have the shoulder mark indicative of the Ricketts three-piece mold, patented in Bristol, England, in 1821 (Jones 1983). Other interesting finds included a mouth harp (Context 16), a musketball (Context 17), two gunflints—one French (Context 18) and one English (Context 19)—and several fragments of delft tile. The latter are manganese-decorated, with a biblical scene and display and oxhead foliate corner decorations. These have been dated post-1700 based on Noël Hume's (1970, 293) discussion of manganese purple and biblical scenes. From other sources, such as de Jonge (1971) and van Dam and Tichelaar (1984), the date is also post-1700.

The presence of manganese-decorated delft tiles in this group of contexts indicates either soil movement from elsewhere or a revamping of the interior of the house. The tile fragments may have been part of the chimney and hearth surround at the east end of the Phase 3 portion of the house. Based on examination of the floor joists, it appears that when the chimney was taken down and replaced in 1922, the floor was also removed. At this time, the original pine boards were taken up, and 2 × 4 and 4 × 4 boards were added as floor joists and, in some cases, scabbed-on to existing handhewn joists. The original size of the Phase 3 portion of the house is shown in figure 5.2, where the handhewn joists end just above the row of stones used to stabilize the floor joists. This figure also shows a row of stones, which appear to be a wall running east/west, but this is simply a row of joist supports. The clay/mortar floor is between them and continued to Context 21, the original interior of the Phase 3 addition (fig. 5.5). Context 21, the north wall of the Phase 3 addition, was taken out at some point, likely c. 1922, and the floor was lengthened to reach the south wall of Phase 4; at the same time, the ceiling beams in Phase 3 (running N/S) were scabbed-on to reach the south wall of Phase 4. The add-ons are still clearly visible in the Phase 3 portion of the Persen House. Context 20, the rubble and stone debris associated with the construction of the Phase 4 portion, was identified at the northern end of the unit.

Below the clay/mortar floor (Contexts 22, 50) in Unit 4 were several archaeological contexts that produced combed slip-decorated buff-bodied earthenwares, white clay smoking pipe fragments, and window glass. In the narrow one-meter-wide trench, numerous red Dutch brick fragments and several whole examples were found. Below the rubble layer, another more concentrated rubble layer (Contexts 53, 56, 57, 59) was found, and we later learned this was the top of the trench for the 1661–1663 addition to the palisade. Contexts 53, 56, 57, and 59 yielded several items relevant to the third quarter of the 17th century. These include combed slip-decorated buff-bodied earthenware, a Levanna projectile point of local Morehouse Onondaga chert, an "EB" pipe bowl characteristic of the time period from 1655–1665 (Bradley 2007, 118–19; Dallal 2004, 226–30; De Roever 1987; McCashion 1979, plate 15), a *kookpot* handle, red Dutch bricks, several delft plate and bowl fragments, and pan tiles. Also found were one piece of wampum and one copper or pot-metal bead. The wampum was drilled from both ends, possibly indicating the use of a fine stone drill (see Diamond 2023, fig. 7.8) or an iron *maux*, the latter of which was used by the Dutch for making wampum. Wampum, or *sewan*, was a form of currency used by Native Americans, Dutch, and English, and its use might have extended into the last quarter of the 18th century (Burggraf 1938; Ceci 1977, 1989; Pena 1990). It was also used to create wampum belts, which were used to confirm and reaffirm treaties (Graeber 2001, 117–49). Numerous references to its use and value can be found in Fernow (1881) and the Kingston court minutes of 1661–1667 (Christoph et al. 1976). A Levanna projectile point of local Eastern Onondaga chert was also found in these contexts.

Below the rubble in the palisade trench was the soil fill. One of the most fascinating aspects of the palisade trench in Unit 4 was that there were several sections of the 1663 burn layer that had collapsed in neat chunks (fig. 5.5). These probably had to do with repairs to the curtain wall after the 1663 fire, or even later, as attested to by an examination of the Kingston court minutes.

Contexts 55, 60, and 61 produced a cannonball, melted copper and brass, early window glass, and pan tile fragments. The cannonball was examined by Colonel Paul Ackerman from the West Point Museum. Like the cannonballs from another unit during the excavations (Unit 5; see below), it appears to be the metric equivalent of a British four pounder (Paul Ackerman, personal communication, February 25, 2003). Colonel Ackerman suggested there might not be that much difference between an English and Dutch weapon from the same time period. The presence of the cannonball in the 1661–1663 palisade fill could point to several possibilities. The first is that it is a remnant from the June 7, 1663, conflict, although it is doubtful that it was fired in the conflict on that particular day. Based on the June 20, 1663, account of the attack by Roeliff Swartwout and others (Fernow 1881, 256–57), there appeared to be little time to utilize a cannon and no distinct force to fire upon. Rather, the cannonball might be part of a larger group kept near a gate or gun emplacement, or it could be the "light cannon" requested for defense and mentioned in various places in the Kingston court minutes. This idea is bolstered by the presence of three additional cannonballs of similar size from the southern end of Unit 5. Because only the later 1695 Miller map of the stockade has survived, it can only be presumed that a gate existed somewhere along the middle of the south wall of the 1661 addition to the stockade.

Outside the palisade trench, and below the June 7, 1663, burn layer, three contexts (Contexts 67, 68, 73) yielded a very small group of artifacts. This pattern was evident in both Units 1 and 2 on the outside of the Persen House. The small number of Dutch colonial artifacts from the contexts below the June 7, 1663, burn layer indicated the relative rarity of fragmentary material culture both inside and outside the fort. Except for several pits below the burn layer (Contexts 155 and 156 in Unit 13), which had small amounts of artifacts, most of the burn layer and soils below it contained primarily Native American artifacts.

Unit 5

Unit 5 was excavated to the south of Unit 4, with a 1-meter block of unexcavated soil (Unit 8) between them (fig. 5.5). Unit 5 consisted of 2.5 square meters of horizontal excavation as a long trench running to the south wall of the Phase 3 addition (figs. 5.2 and 5.5). It was excavated in 11 contexts. The soils were similar to those of Unit 4, yet Unit 5 did not have the complex situation near the row of stone supports (Context 21) or remnants of the palisade trench. One context of loose soil between the floor joists (Context 25) produced a large number of artifacts, notable of which were various forms of pearlware, creamware, Canton-style porcelain, English delft, an iron boat cleat, an English gunflint, and a number of glass fragments. Several fragments of table glass and an early English shaft and globe-type bottle finish (c. 1630–1680) were found. Providing important dates for the construction of the clay/mortar floor were blue transfer-printed pearlware (post-1800) and a copper cent from 1800–1809.

The clay/mortar floor (Context 27) covered most of Unit 5, except where the builder's trench for the repair of the south wall of Phase 3 was identified (fig. 5.5). One fragment of green shell-edged pearlware was found at the same level but was not imbedded within the clay/mortar floor, providing a possible *terminus post quem* (earliest date) of 1780 for the floor. Below the floor were two contexts, one of silty sand (Context 28) and the other of silty sand with white ash and charcoal flecks (Context 29). Context 28 produced two early trade beads (types IIa6 and IIa55; Kidd and Kidd 1970). Both postdate 1580 on Haudenosaunee sites (Snow 1980, 32), and several have been found on Munsee sites in the Esopus drainage (Diamond 1998, 1999a, 2023). Ceramics from Context 28 included delft, porcelain, and combed slip-decorated buff-bodied earthenware (c. 1670–1796). Context 29, a crescent-shaped deposit, yielded an "RT" pipe bowl from c. 1660–1720 (Walker 1977, 1732–39) and a molded or "silesian" wine glass stem dating either c. 1725–1750 (Vreeken et al. 1998, 187–91) or post-1730 (Hughes 1956, 88). The latter date is a better fit since the molded stem is eight-sided and fits Hughes's description as lacking "the precision and elegance of former types, reeding, shoulder outline, and bosses having lost their clear definition" (88).

Just above the burn level was a dark yellow-brown silty sand with clay and brick fragments (Context 30) yielding 5 fragments of coal*,[1] copper scraps, a twisted lead scrap, the plain prunt of a *roemer*, a French honey-colored gunflint, and a lead glass vial. Ceramics included 17th-century manganese-mottled pan fragments, delft, combed buff-bodied slip-decorated earthenware, and salt-glazed stoneware. Even at this depth, plain pearlware was found (post-1780), as was coal*, which generally dates post-1828, indicating the depth and degree of disturbance by rat's nests and burrows. The burn level (Context 31) yielded no artifacts, which was not at all surprising. Below this were three contexts of dark yellow-brown silty sand (Contexts 35, 36, 37) containing artifacts primarily of Native American origin (237 of 240; 98.75%). One diagnostic Native American artifact, a Meadowood projectile point, was found.

Cutting through the abovementioned deposits were a combination of builder's trenches and repair trenches for the south wall of the Phase 3 portion of the house (figs. 5.5 and 5.6). These were removed in two contexts or levels, simply to make excavation easier and to provide a base to work from. This is an arbitrary distinction and does not reflect differences in soil color or texture. Contexts 26 and 33 yielded large numbers of artifacts. From the uppermost context, these included coal*, an iron pintle, a 1966 Roosevelt dime, a patent medicine embossed "Balsam of Honey," a teal umbrella ink, a Reynolds soda water bottle from Kingston (post-1864), and a wine bottle seal embossed "Jan Eltenge 1754," with a pie-crust edge. Paul Huey (personal communication, August 21, 2003) informed me that this is probably the Jan Elting who was born in Kingston in 1709 and died there in 1762. He is buried in the Old Dutch Church cemetery two blocks away. For information on local wine bottle seals, see Veit and Huey (2014).

As previously mentioned, Unit 5, like Unit 4, yielded evidence of large weaponry. The excavation of Context 33 uncovered three cannonballs in a group. These are similar in size to the one found in Unit 4, suggesting that the four are from the same time period, if not from the same artillery piece. All are the equivalent of English four pounders. Again, similar to Unit 4, Unit 5 produced a large number of combed slip-decorated buff-bodied earthenwares as well as Dutch and possibly French wares.

Figure 5.6. Persen House. Units 5, 8, and 4, west wall profile. *Source:* Photo by the author.

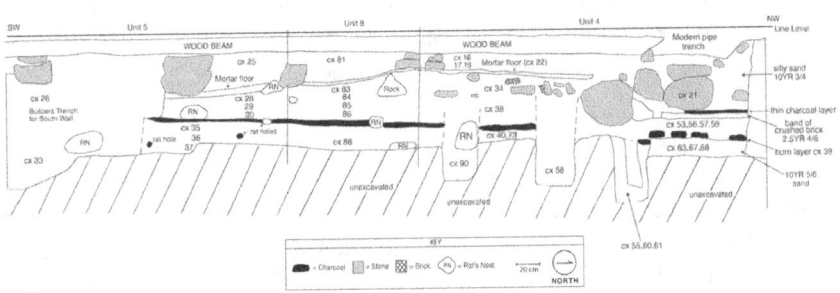

The Matthewis Persen House | 211

Lastly, figure 5.2 shows a half-timbered floor joist supporting the relatively new basement stairs (modern doorway). It was under these stairs that an ivory whistle was found prior to the excavation in the Phase 3 portion of the Persen House.

UNIT 6

Unit 6 was placed along the east wall (gable end) of the Phase 3 addition (fig. 5.2). It was designed to obtain a sample of soil in front, and to the south, of the original Phase 3 addition fireplace (fig. 5.2), which is shown as a dashed line along the east wall. Unit 6 sampled 1.5 square meters of horizontal surface and was excavated in nine archaeological contexts. Like previously excavated units, this unit contained loose debris between the floor joists, which apparently was impacted by destruction of the original Dutch fireplace and construction of the brick chimney (c. 1922). These early 20th-century destruction and construction impacts destroyed the clay/mortar floor in this unit but did not totally impact the 1663 burn layer.

The loose soil between the floor joists and some disturbed contexts underneath included Contexts 41, 42, and 43. A significant artifact from these contexts included fragments of a gray stoneware plate with cobalt blue decoration similar to those produced by the Crolius family of New York City (c. 1728–1848) and also similar to one found by Paul Huey at the Louw-Bogardus House (Huey 1981, fig. 9). Other interesting finds included a possible William Evans pipestem from Context 43 (c. 1661–1689), a possible copper projectile point, a possible fragment of *facon-de-Venise* glass, and several fragments of a *roemer*. Unit 6 also yielded several kinds of early ceramic, most notably slip-decorated buff-bodied earthenwares, Dutch whiteware, salmon-bodied earthenwares, and delft. The burn layer (Context 46) produced a large sample of Dutch artifacts, most notably a *roemer* fragment, three pieces of delft, and some lead scrap. Found in the yellow-brown sand below the 1663 burn layer was an Orient Fishtail projectile point dating c. 1100–750 BC/3050–2700 BP as well as three pieces of precontact pottery and lithic debitage.

UNIT 7

Unit 7 was an L-shaped excavation unit in the northwest corner of the Phase 3 addition (fig. 5.2), which was at the corner of the Phase 1 building. It included part of the builder's trenches of the Phase 2 and Phase

4 additions. It did not include the excavation of the Phase 1 builder's trench because the Phase 2 and Phase 4 trenches had virtually obliterated it, and it could only be observed in one small section of soil. Unit 7 was 2.36 square meters in horizontal extent, with 21 archaeological contexts defined and sampled. This large number of contexts was the result of several structural features coming together at this location, and each was segregated and excavated.

The loose soil between the floor joists in Unit 7 was excavated in three archaeological contexts (74, 75, 76) and combined as part of Strata Group 2. Artifacts from these three contexts included two French honey-colored gunflints, fragments of a Turlington Balsam bottle, a hexagonally cut bridge-fluted wine glass stem (c. 1760–1810), a small bottle with gold paint (gilding) inside, a stoneware marble, and two marked pipes. One is an "RT" facing the smoker (c. 1660–1720), and the other is a "TD" facing the smoker. This is the mark thought to be made by Thomas Dormer c. 1748–1770 (Oswald 1975, 135) and is thought to be more accurately dated at 1755–1780 (Paul Huey, personal communication, February 17, 2020).

Ceramics from the three contexts ranged from later wares such as blue shell–edged whiteware (c. 1820–1900) to early 19th-century wares such as green shell–edged pearlware and overglazed blue transfer-printed pearlware. Common, however, were 18th-century wares, including creamware, Canton style porcelain, manganese-decorated delft tile, and combed slip-decorated buff-bodied earthenware. Seventeenth-century ceramics in the upper stratum included potentially early combed slipware (as mentioned above), the foot from a ginger/brown-glazed *kookpot*, and Frechen tigerware, the latter of which was probably a *Bartmannkrügge*, a small-handled jug.

Below the loose soil was the clay/mortar floor (Contexts 78, 79), which did not yield a particularly large number of artifacts. A fragment of ironstone (post-1840) that was found might be from the matrix, although this is doubtful. Below the clay/mortar floor were several contexts of deeper sand and clay, which probably relate to the change in chimney orientation in the Phase 1 construction.

Artifacts from Contexts 141, 144, 146, and 147 included white clay pipestems (all unmarked), stoneware marbles, pan tile fragments, buttons, pins, early window glass, *roemer* fragments, wine glass fragments, and olive-green wine/liquor bottle fragments. Temporally diagnostic items were mainly ceramics. The four contexts yielded trailed redware, combed slip-decorated buff-bodied earthenware, delft, creamware, *kookpot* fragments, majolica, and a slip-decorated buff-bodied earthenware charger or plate (black with yellow dots). Chargers are large plates that often have two small holes in the foot of the plate that can be used to hang it as a decorative piece. Mixed among the early ceramics were later wares, such as black transfer-printed whiteware (post-1820), pink transfer-printed whiteware (post-1825), and "old blue" or "flow blue" transfer-printed pearlware (post-1815).

Underlying Contexts 141, 144, 146, and 147 was the 1663 burn level (Context 165), which yielded only 11 artifacts and 85 grams of Dutch red brick that had been pushed down from above. Physically below the burn level, but temporally the same, was the fill from the palisade trench. The upper portion (Context 166) yielded large amounts of Dutch red brick, stone debris, pan tiles, and an intrusive piece of blue hand-painted pearlware with a fish scale design (1780–1820). Context 166 is indicated in figure 5.7, a plan view of Units 7, 4, 12, and 9 assembled just above the burn layer. Context 167, a post mold filled with brick dust and small alternating bands of charcoal and brick dust is shown in figure 5.8. Below Context 166 was Context 168, the fill from the palisade trench. Artifacts from this context included a stoneware marble, "case bottle" fragments for

Figure 5.7. Persen House. Planview of Units 7, 4, 12, and 9 showing palisade trench and post-molds. *Source:* Photo by the author.

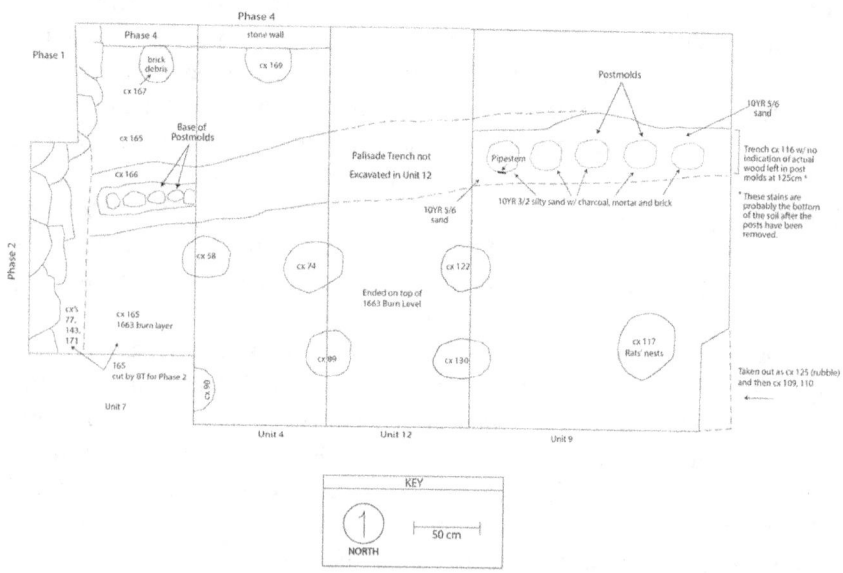

214 | The Archaeology of Kingston, New York

Figure 5.8. Persen House. Units 4 and 7, north wall profile. *Source:* Photo by the author.

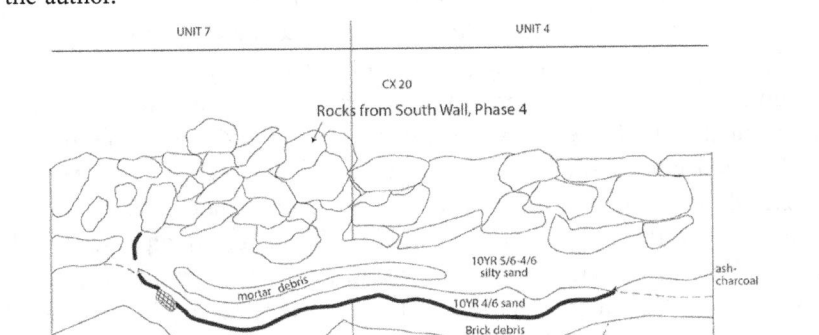

storing or dispensing gin, the coiled foot fragment of a *roemer*, burned ceramics, and a glass bead. The latter is an amber wire-wound bead of medium size (type WLB7; Kidd and Kidd 1970).

UNIT 8

Unit 8 was a 1-meter square between Units 4 and 5 (figs. 5.2, 5.5, and 5.6). Its excavation and wall profiles served to create a long trench, which extended on a north/south axis across the Phase 3 addition. This unit was excavated in a relatively straightforward way using eight contexts. Context 81 was the dusty soil between the floor joists, which, in this case, was excavated down to the clay mortar floor. Artifacts from Context 81 included an "RT" bowl with the debossing facing the smoker (c. 1660–1720), two 2-tined forks, a slate pencil, an olive-green wine/liquor bottle base, tumbler fragments, a bone toothbrush, a stoneware marble, buttons, pins, a large cent from 1800, and a white wire-wound bead (type W1B2; Kidd and Kidd 1970). Ceramics included delft, a combed buff-bodied slip-decorated earthenware charger and combed buff-bodied slip-decorated porringer fragments, plain creamware, various pearlwares, Canton style porcelain, and white salt-glazed stoneware plate fragments. The latter are the "dot, diaper, and basket" pattern from c. 1740–1765. Context 82 was the clay/mortar floor (figs. 5.5 and 5.6). Artifacts from this context were limited to an unidentifiable nail and the handle from a combed buff-bodied slip-decorated porringer (c. 1670–1795). Contexts 83, 84, and 85 were below the clay mortar floor and contained brick rubble. Artifacts from these three contexts included a white clay pipe bowl with eligible cartouche, coal*, a large brass pin, pan tile fragments, and early window glass. Ceramics from these contexts were all relatively early pieces of delft, combed buff-bodied slip-decorated earthenware, green and purple tin-glazed buff-bodied earthenwares (probably Portuguese/Spanish), and brownish-green-glazed redware. Context 86, just above the 1663 burn layer, was replete with rats' nests. Artifacts from this context were also early, including window glass, "case bottle" fragments for gin, and portions of a wine bottle of onion/apple shape c. 1680–1710. Ceramics included ginger-glazed redware, a glazed ceramic marble, plain delft, clear-glazed redware, and a *Bartmannkrügge* jug with partial medallion. Context 87 was the 1663 burn layer, which contained no artifacts. Context 88, the dark yellow-brown sand below the burn later, contained 199 artifacts, only one of which was historic, and this was likely intrusive.

UNIT 9

Unit 9 was the largest excavation unit within the Phase 3 portion of the house (fig. 5.2). It measured 5.675 square meters in horizontal extent and sampled 21 different archaeological contexts within the northeast corner of the Phase 3 construction. Contexts 91 and 93 sampled the dusty floor between the floor joists (fig. 5.9). Context 91 yielded fragments of an early window glass quarrel, a heavy tumbler or "firing glass," and a decanter with wheel engraved decoration. The "firing glass" gets its name from the sound it produces when slammed down on the table. Its "bang" was likened to the firing of a musket. A pressed glass goblet was also found, pointing to a *terminus post quem* of 1828 for these levels. The ceramics from Contexts 91 and 93 included more of the manganese decorated delft tile discussed above as well as another fragment of the salt-glazed stoneware plate, which might be attributable to the Crolius family. Like many other opening contexts, pearlware and whiteware were also recovered. A

Figure 5.9. Persen House. Unit 9, west wall profile. *Source:* Photo by the author.

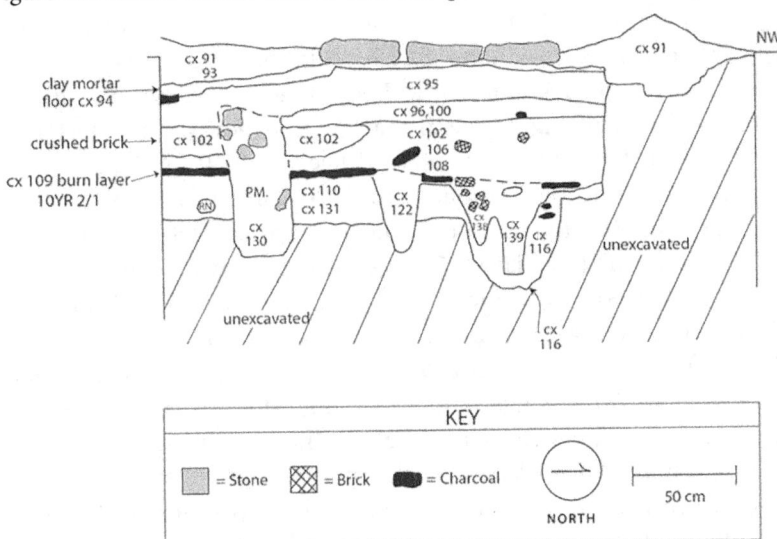

fragment of a glass syringe plunger was also recovered from Context 91. This may be part of the same syringe as the fragment recovered in Unit 10, Context 97.

Context 93, the lower context of loose soil immediately above the clay/mortar floor (Context 94), produced fragments of 17th-century artifacts, including combed buff-bodied slip-decorated earthenware porringer fragments and a burned plate or charger with a piecrust edge, as well as later ceramics such as blue transfer-printed pearlware (1800–1840) and black transfer-printed pearlware (1820–1900).

In Context 94, the clay/mortar floor was quite fragmented. Normally, the artifacts from within the matrix are not that common, but here it appeared that later artifacts may have been pressed into the matrix or combined with it during prior excavation. One notable example was an aquamarine bottle finish known as the "packer style," which dates c. 1850–1875. Also found was a faceted black bead and a small whetstone. Seven contexts of soil were found spread across the unit between the clay/mortar floor and the 1663 burn layer. Contexts 95, 96, 100, and 102 were thought to be a combination of sand and destruction rubble from the Phase 1 fireplace. Artifacts from these contexts included large quantities of combed buff-bodied slip-decorated earthenware porringer and plate/charger fragments, a trailed red earthenware pan or tray, Canton style porcelain, pearlware, a buff-bodied earthenware slip-decorated bat-molded charger, *kookpot* fragments, crown window glass (circular, handblown window glass), a 1749 British coin, fragments of a Frechen stoneware *Bartmannkrügge* jug, *roemer* fragments, and several marked pipe bowls. The latter, from Context 102, includes two "EB" marked heels c. 1630–1665 (De Roever 1987), an "RT" in beaded cartouche (c. 1720), and a "WE" mark facing the smoker. This was the mark of William Evans (c. 1682–1697).

Just above the burn layer (Context 109) were two contexts of sand (Contexts 106, 108), which included some brick and charcoal fragments in the matrix. Artifacts from these contexts included ginger-glazed earthenwares, a pipestem with a *fleur-de-lis* mark similar to that found by Paul Huey at Fort Orange (Huey 1983, fig. 113, no. 21), fragments of a *Bartmannkrügge* jug, delft, and majolica. The majolica is part of a dish with blue and white decoration on the interior and a clear glaze on the reverse, which dates c.1625–1650. The burn layer (Context 109) covered most of the unit except where post molds, rats' nests, and repair trenches to the stockade obliterated it (fig. 5.10). Two post molds (Contexts 122, 130) were found in the unit to the south of the curtain wall (fig. 5.9). The fill from the post molds did not contain many artifacts. Context 122 contained fragments of a white clay pipe with rouletted bowl, 11 pieces of lithic debitage, and *Bartmannkrügge* fragments. Context 130 contained a hammerstone, 40 pieces of lithic debitage, and pieces of a combed buff-bodied slip-decorated porringer (c. 1685–1795).

Figure 5.10. Persen House. Unit 9 and 4, south wall profile. *Source:* Photo by the author.

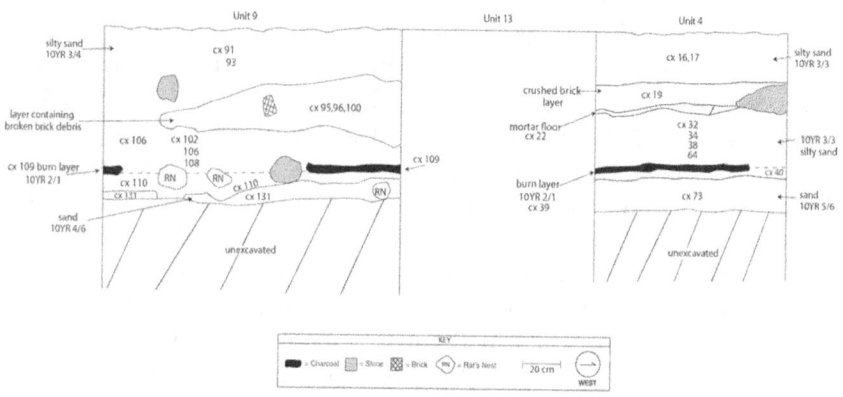

218 | The Archaeology of Kingston, New York

Two post molds (Contexts 138, 139) were found within the stockade trench, although their exact association with the curtain wall is unknown. Of the two, Context 139 is perhaps the most likely to be an original post mold from the curtain wall. Context 138 contained no artifacts, whereas Context 139 produced fragments of the red earthenware Hoogeboom vessel discussed above, a combed buff-bodied slip-decorated porringer, and fragments of a delft plate with double blue lines. Similar decorations occur on delft plates in Korf's (1981) *Nederlandse majolica*, dating c. 1655–1670.

Context 110 was the dark yellow-brown soil below the burn layer. This context produced pan tile fragments, a nutting stone, a stoneware marble, and 100 pieces of lithic debitage. The ratio of precontact Native American artifacts to historic artifacts in this context was 100:21, or 82.6%, of the total. Another context below the burn layer (Context 131) yielded debitage, a copper projectile point, cord-wrapped precontact Native American pottery, fire-cracked rock, and a hammerstone.

The excavation of Unit 9 was important for the archaeologists, because it was here that the palisade trench was easy to define and examine (fig. 5.7), and the excavations yielded artifacts from the Dutch colonial period. Context 116 produced early window glass, an "EB"-marked pipestem likely dating from c. 1650–1665 (De Roever 1987; McCashion 1979, plates 19, 20), and a French honey-colored gunflint. Also found was a tubular glass redwood and black bead (type IIIa1; Kidd and Kidd 1970) of the type that Snow (1995, 34) has dated to post-1626. Not surprisingly, a large collection of precontact Native American artifacts was found in the palisade trench fill. This is because the site of the Persen House was occupied by Native Americans prior to the construction of the settlement of *Wiltwyck* in 1658. One fragment of fire-cracked rock and 111 pieces of lithic debitage were recovered from the trench.

At the base of the trench was a row of dark soil stains originating from the soil that filled in the gaps after the posts were finally removed (fig. 5.7). There was no decomposed wood in the stains or large chunks of charcoal, indicating that the curtain wall had been removed rather than burned or left to decompose. While we might imagine that this could have been in 1669–1670, when the second addition of the stockade was constructed, we know from the probate records that the curtain wall next to Gysbert van Imbroch's house was in good repair. As mentioned elsewhere, this may indicate that some located within the fortified area retained their walls in the interior lots after the 1669–1670 expansion.

However, the stockade posts would have had to be removed prior to construction of the Phase 2 portion of the Persen House.

The disparity between the size of the Units 7 and 9 posts shown in figure 5.7 can be accounted for by two possible explanations. The first is that since the Unit 7 posts were deeper, they might represent the tips of smaller posts or, alternatively, a section of the curtain wall that was filled with smaller posts at some point. The sizes of the Unit 9 post molds are estimates based on soil color, curvature of the darker soils within the trench that partially outline the original locations of the posts, and scaled drawings recorded in the field.

Figure 5.10 illustrates the south wall of Unit 9 prior to the excavation of Unit 11 to its south. This figure does not include Unit 13, which was only partially excavated, but does include the south wall of Unit 4.

Unit 10

Unit 10 was excavated in the southeast corner of the Phase 3 portion of the Persen House (fig. 5.2) in 14 archaeological contexts. The first two (Contexts 97 and 98) comprised the soil between the floor joists and, given the size of the excavated unit, produced a large number of artifacts. The uppermost loose soil yielded fragments of crown glass, white clay pipestems, a clear glass "specie jar," another fragment of the clear glass syringe plunger found in Unit 9, a lead musket ball, mirror fragments, an iron skeleton key, precontact Native American artifacts, and an early trade bead. The latter is a round red bead with a black core (type IVa1; Kidd and Kidd 1970), a type dated by Snow (1995, 34) at Mohawk sites as post-1614. Considering its age, it is most probable that this bead was redeposited in a later context as a result of destruction and reconstruction activities, particularly trench excavations in the southeast corner of the Phase 3 portion of the house. Ceramics from the two contexts varied in date from plain ironstone (post-1840) to combed buff-bodied slip-decorated earthenware plate/charger and porringer fragments. Also found were pieces of the bat-molded charger discussed above, Rockingham ware, creamware, various kinds of pearlware, and white salt-glazed stoneware. The white salt-glazed stoneware consists of holloware, probably small bowl fragments, and "dot, diaper, and basket" pattern plates from c. 1740–1765.

Some of the diagnostic glass pieces from Contexts 97 and 98 included a snap case bottle base (post-1857), a wine glass or tumbler, wine/liquor bottle fragments, and clear and aquamarine vial fragments. Because of numerous construction disturbances, there was no clay/mortar floor or burn layer in this unit. However, given an identified change in soil color, it was possible to approximate where the burn layer would have been. The original soil was identified (Context 114) and two additional contexts of original soil (Contexts 118, 119) were excavated below it. Context 114 produced a variety of early materials, such as seven pieces of lithic debitage, an "RT" pipe bowl, and another pipe bowl with an "R Tippet" cartouche, both of which date 1660–1720. However, while it initially seemed that the first context below the burn level had retained its integrity, it also included creamware (post-1762), blue shell–edged pearlware (1770–1830), and stoneware with an Albany slip (1800–1900), indicating some bioturbation in the contexts with rat disturbances. Contexts 118 and 119 were better candidates for an "undisturbed" label, having only window glass, a *roemer* fragment, unidentifiable clear glass, debitage, and fire-cracked rock.

Unit 11

Unit 11, containing eight contexts, was the smallest of the units excavated inside the Phase 3 portion of the house (fig. 5.2). Measuring 0.85 square meters of horizontal surface area, this unit had been used as a balk between Units 6 and 9. Its upper two contexts (Contexts 120, 121) consisted of loose soil between the floor joists, but as in Unit 6 to the south, the clay/mortar floor had been destroyed by changes to the fireplace c. 1922 (fig. 5.2). Artifacts from these contexts included clear tumbler fragments, wine/liquor bottle fragments, buttons, a copper braid-end or bead, bone buttons, window glass, and pins. The only temporally diagnostic fragment was a wine/liquor bottle fragment from c. 1735–1770. Like Unit 9 to its north and Unit 6 to its south, it also displayed a well-defined 1663 burn layer (Context 126), with one context of original soil below it (Context 127). Just above the burn level were Contexts 123 and 124, two relatively intact contexts that produced coal*, stoneware marbles, early window glass, several *roemer* fragments, majolica, Canton porcelain, salmon-bodied earthenware with green mottling, delft, "Hoogeboom redware," combed slip-decorated buff-bodied earthenware porringer and plate or charger fragments, and two marked pipestems. One of the pipestems was a heel-marked "Tudor Rose," apparently a rare variant (see Dallal 2004, 211–17). The second marked heel was embossed "AI," for Andries Jacobz, an Amsterdam pipe maker c. 1686 (Huey 1988, fig. 114, no. 66; McCashion 1979, 136). Context 127 was the first context stratigraphically below the burn layer and contained one of the most interesting artifacts found during the excavation of the Persen House—a bodkin (fig. 5.11)—which was a decorative hair pin in style from c. 1610 to 1675. These appear in paintings and in probate inventories from 1611 until about 1673 (Paul Huey, personal communication, June 11, 2003). Most are highly decorative, with some including semiprecious stones or pearls. The bodkin found in Context 127 had engraved initials (likely of the owner), four small holes for stones, and a figure of a partially opened hand, which may have held a stone or pearl. A similar bodkin is shown in Caspar Netcher's painting *The Lace Maker* (1664), worn by the woman in her hair as a decorative piece (Nash 1972). Other examples of this were found during Boston's "Big Dig" (Lewis 2001, 33) as well as in a shell heap "at the very gates of Fort Massapequa" in the 1930s (Burggraf 1938, 54; for additional information, see Solecki 1985, fig. 3; Solecki and Grumet 1994). Writing about the shell heap, Burggraf (1938) reported that its chief interest lay in the amount of European white clay pipes and the occasional brass arrow point present. However, a solitary brass bodkin or needle, perforated midway between both pointed ends, was also found. Except for the material it was made of, it was identical with some bone specimens found at the Northport heap (Burggraf 1938, 54).

Interestingly, two almost-identical examples of the bodkin found in Context 127 were also found in the wreck of the *Kennemerland*, a Dutch East Indiaman ship that was wrecked on the Out Skerries (Shetland Islands) in 1664 (Price and Muckelroy 1977, fig. 17). The two examples

Figure 5.11. Persen House. Personal item. Bodkin (11.127). *Source:* Photo by the author.

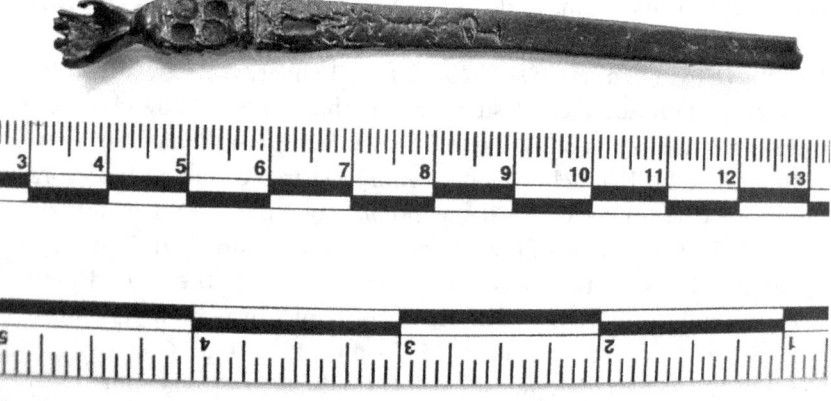

have molded hands, each with a hooked end with a slit, and one appears to have two or three small jewels or pearls embedded in the metal. That they were found in a ship that sunk in 1664 is significant, as the example from the Persen House was sealed below the June 7, 1663, burn layer and was therefore likely deposited within a year of those on the *Kennemerland*. Beaudry (2009) discussed several other archaeologically derived bodkins and their relationships to people as decorative items and as aspects of personhood.

Other interesting finds from Context 127 included delft, a *roemer* fragment, early window glass, debitage, fire-cracked rock, and a whole Orient Fishtail projectile point. A small post mold (Context 128) near the center of the unit yielded precontact Native American artifacts, including fire-cracked rock and lithic debitage, as well as a fragment of majolica (c. 1625–1650).

Unit 12

Unit 12 was located near the north central portion of the interior of the Phase 3 addition between Unit 4 to its west and Unit 9 to its east (fig. 5.2). It covered 3 square meters of horizontal surface area. The excavation of Unit 12 yielded nine contexts (note that the context description table lists 11, but this is because post molds 122 and 130 from Unit 9 were partially in Unit 12). Unit 12 sampled all contexts from the loose soil between the floor joists to the top of the 1663 burn layer. Excavation was temporarily halted at this point so that the burn layer could be preserved in situ. This is still preserved to this day within the Phase 3 addition of the Persen House. The excavation of Unit 12 yielded two contexts of dry loose soil between the floor joists (Contexts 132, 133) and the clay mortar floor below (Context 135), which contained a fragment of coral,[2] olive-green wine/liquor bottle fragments, a bone toothbrush, a clothespin, a spoon from a doll set, stoneware marbles, a copper/brass thimble, slate pencils, *Bartmannkrügge* fragments, delft tile with manganese decoration, creamware, pearlware, Derby stoneware, Canton-style porcelain, wine glass stem fragments, Jackfield-type red earthenwares, an English gunflint, a jackknife, and a copper/brass latch keep. A bracelet of elephant ivory was also found, as was a cut bridge-fluted wine glass stem c. 1760–1810 (Noël Hume 1970, 193) and a shoulder fragment from a Ricketts three-piece mold, which postdates 1821 (Jones 1983). A creamware chamber pot bowl rim (c. 1762–1820) was the only fragment of refined earthenware found during the excavation that relates to that particular aspect of personal hygiene. It should be mentioned that many of the small ceramic vessels that appear to be *kookpots*, or the English *pipkins*, can also function as chamber pots. The key to identifying the function of these pots is to have at least a mendable portion from base to rim. Noël Hume (2003, 138–49) defined a wide variety of vessels that served as chamber pots, the defining factor being the handle and base and the lack of feet.

The clay/mortar floor in this unit was somewhat hard to differentiate due to its fragmentary nature. As a result, the artifacts from Context 135 were not all within the clay/mortar matrix but instead had clay/mortar attached. Consequently, this context did not have the same integrity as other excavated contexts. Artifacts included stoneware marbles, an "EB" pipe heel c. 1630–1665 (De Roever 1987), an onion-shaped wine bottle c. 1680–1710, combed buff-bodied slip-decorated earthenware porringer fragments, a redware slip-decorated plate/charger, delft with blue floral decoration, and Canton porcelain.

Below the clay mortar floor were four contexts (157, 158, 159, and 162) loaded with brick debris, which extended down to the burn layer. Context 157 yielded a stoneware marble, a large wire-wound bead (type W1B2; Kidd and Kidd 1970), crown glass edge fragments, fragments of a slip-decorated, buff-bodied bat-molded charger, white delft with blue decorations, and combed buff-bodied, slip-decorated earthenware porringer fragments. Context 158 produced an iron pintle, an iron skeleton key, crown window glass edge fragments, a wine glass bowl fragment, "Hoogeboom redware," delft, and a redware jug with brown-glazed interior. Also found was one fragment of a pattern-molded and expanded (diamond pattern) pocket flask from c. 1790–1830. Pocket flasks were carried in one's coat pocket so that one might imbibe whenever the opportunity or desire arose. It should be noted that during the time period that this flask was blown, Americans "drank more alcoholic beverages per capita than ever before or since" (Rorabaugh 1979, ix). Context 159 produced case bottle fragments, olive-green wine/liquor bottle fragments, and pan tile fragments. In addition, a cassock button was found. These are relatively large, black glass buttons with embedded wire shanks, often found at Haudenosaunee and Dutch sites from c. 1575–1650 (Huey 1988, 254–55) as well as at local Munsee sites (Diamond 1996a, 1998, 1999a, 2023). Context 162, just above the burn layer, yielded a case bottle finish, early window glass, coal*, lithic debitage, fragments of a copper/brass candlestick base of cast metal (Joseph McEvoy, personal communication, June 11, 2003), and white delft with blue decoration. Context 162 yielded another cassock button similar to the one originating from Context 159. It should be noted that the burn layer (Context 163) was not excavated but only cleaned off for in situ preservation. After the excavation was terminated, a block of soil was carefully enclosed by a wooden box and subsequently wrapped and buffered with a layer of loose sand fill. Then, a platform was built above it to prevent pedestrian traffic from affecting the in situ burn layer. As a consequence, Context 164, the palisade trench, was given a number but not excavated. It appears in figure 5.7 as a dotted line linking the curtain wall in Unit 4 with the curtain wall in Unit 9.

Unit 13

Unit 13 was the second largest excavation unit, with a size of 4.5 square meters of horizontal surface area (fig. 5.2) and was excavated in 14 archaeological contexts. Unlike Unit 12, this unit was excavated well down into the original sands that underlay the 1663 burn layer.

The first context was the loose soil between the floor joists (Context 134) and the second was the clay/mortar floor (Context 136). Context 134 yielded a large number and wide variety of cultural materials, including an "RT" bowl (c. 1660–1720), an ivory and bone domino, a 1910 Lincoln penny, an 1820 large US cent, numerous buttons and pins, a quartz crystal, a slate pencil, a copper thimble, a wooden clothespin, and a bone toothbrush. Glass items from this context originated from the 18th through 19th centuries and included wine glass, tumbler, and goblet fragments as well as unidentifiable table glass. Several different bottles with either Ricketts mold marks or marks made by the lipping tool associated with Ricketts-style bottles from the 1820s were found, as were two additional dateable bottles: a clear bottle with snap-case base (post-1857) and a J. W. Reynolds soda water bottle from Kingston with an embossed patent date of 1864. A large bright blue round bead (type IIa55; Kidd and Kidd 1970) was also found. These have been found on Haudenosaunee sites in New York and Canada and have been dated by Snow (1995, 31) as post-1580.

Ceramics from Context 134 included plain creamware, hand-painted overglaze polychrome creamware, various forms of pearlware, whiteware, Rockingham yellowware, combed buff-bodied, slip-decorated earthenware porringer fragments, fragments of a buff-bodied, slip-decorated earthenware bat-molded charger, Jackfield refined red earthenware, Canton-style porcelain, white salt-glazed stoneware, and delft. The delft is represented by a shallow white bowl with blue decoration and a delft tile with a manganese-colored biblical scene.

The clay/mortar floor (Context 136) yielded 32 artifacts, none of which were temporally diagnostic. Below the clay/mortar floor were several contexts of sand with building rubble (Contexts 149, 150, 151). Overall, these three contexts displayed a minimum of vertical artifact displacement and yielded a large sample of 17th- and 18th-century items of interest. Pipestems included one embossed with "RT" (1660–1720), a smudged cartouche that might be a Tippet, and an "EB" heelmark c. 1655–1665 (De Roever 1987). Also found was one with a "Tudor Rose" heelmark (Context 151), similar to one found at Fort Pentagoet in Maine (Faulkner and Faulkner 1987, fig. 6.7, h). This is unlike any Tudor Rose heelmark found at Fort Orange (Paul Huey, personal communication, 2003). A second Tudor Rose heelmark was found in the same context (see also Dallal 2004).

Ceramics found in these contexts (149, 150, 151) included Westerwald stoneware, Fulham stoneware, white salt-glazed stoneware, creamware, various kinds of delft, green-glazed white-bodied earthenware, clear-glazed redware, Canton style porcelain, brown-glazed redware, combed slip-decorated, buff-bodied earthenware porringer fragments, and clear-glazed redware with manganese mottling. The two latest types are Rockingham yellowware and blue transfer-printed pearlware. Glass artifacts included crown window glass, fragments of the coiled foot of a *roemer*, and three glass beads. These included a large black round bead (type IIa6; Kidd and Kidd 1970), dated by Snow (1995, 32) as post-1580, and a very small white round bead (type IIa11; Kidd and Kidd 1970), dated by Snow (1995, 32) as post-1614. The third was a large white wire-wound bead (type WIB9; Kidd and Kidd 1970). At the base of Context 151 was the well-preserved 1663 burn layer (Context 153), which produced 57 artifacts, 15 of which were Native American in origin. Datable historic artifacts included combed buff-bodied slip-decorated earthenware porringer fragments and plates, a black slip-decorated buff-bodied earthenware porringer, and delft. Below this were three contexts of original brown sand (Contexts 154, 160, 161), which produced fragments of a combed buff-bodied, slip-decorated earthenware porringer, some handwrought nails, window glass, and an iron buckle. However, most of the artifacts were Native American in origin. Proceeding from the uppermost to the deepest context, in Context 154, the artifact ratio was 22 historic to 840 Native American; in Context 160, the ratio was 3 historic to 31 Native American; and in Context 161, all of the cultural materials ($n = 15$) were Native American in origin.

Located stratigraphically below the 1663 burn layer and within the yellow-brown sand were two features, labeled Contexts 155 and 156. These features predate the June 7, 1663, burning of *Wiltwyck*, and the artifacts are suggestive of this. Context 155 yielded pan tile fragments, handwrought nails, an iron spike or chisel, white clay pipestem fragments, early window glass, olive-green wine/liquor fragments, and clear lead-glazed redware with green specks, as well as fragments of an unglazed redware bowl and debitage. Context 156 produced pan tile fragments, black debitage, combed buff-bodied slip-decorated earthenware, and three fragments of blue and white majolica (c. 1625–1650).

SIDE YARD DEPOSITS

Because there was a new door proposed for the Phase 5 (brick) portion of the building, the decision was made to sample the deposits below the macadam in the driveway south of the Phase 3 portion of the building (fig. 5.1). At this point, the 1663 burn layer had been located as it extended from the sidewalk under John Street and through the Phase 3 portion of the Persen House. Here, it abruptly terminated at the edge of the builder's trench for the south wall of the Phase 3 addition. The question was, did the burn layer extend further to the south? Three shovel tests were placed in the driveway to answer this question.

Shovel test 1 (fig. 5.1) was placed approximately 4 meters south of the back door. It produced evidence of five distinct contexts. The first was 7 cm of macadam, underlaid by 10 cm of limestone gravel. This overlaid 79 cm of very dark brown silty sand with numerous historical artifacts, which ended in sterile subsoil (yellowish-brown sand), with no indication of a burn layer. Shovel test 2 (fig. 5.1) was placed 2 meters from the back door of the Phase 3 addition. It produced 9 cm of macadam, which overlaid 13 cm of limestone gravel. Below this was 58 cm of very dark brown sandy silt, again with numerous artifacts. The base of the very dark brown sandy silt was 80 cm below the macadam. The next 11 cm consisted of yellowish-brown coarse sand that did not produce any evidence of a burn layer. Shovel test 3 (fig. 5.1) was placed near the sidewalk and 2 meters from the corner of the house. This test produced evidence of 8 cm of macadam overlying 12 cm of limestone gravel. Below this was a mix of very dark brown sand mixed with silt, brick, various artifacts, limestone wall fragments, and bivalves (clams and oysters). Based on the limestone fragments, it was evident that a wall was here at one point, although it could not be determined whether it was related to a former shed or something more substantial. Below this mix was a coarse brown sand at 78–85 cm. Again, there was no indication of the burn layer. During excavations around the outside of the Persen House for curb work, as well as for utility trenches and the replacement of the sidewalk, it became evident that the burn layer was present in other locations around the house and that it likely extended under portions of the sidewalk both to the north and west of the Persen House. However, it was not found in the driveway area south of the Phase 3 addition. In my opinion, this is because the burn layer had no protection from the admixture of soils from both human and animal activity. The area of the driveway and yard likely would have been a quagmire in the early 18th century, thus mixing the black soils of the 1663 burn layer with the other silts and sands of the yard.

UNIT 14

Unit 14 was excavated in the yard area near the back door of the Phase 3 addition to both obtain a sample of artifacts and examine the stratigraphy of the yard prior to its disturbance during construction of a basement door in the Phase 5 portion of the house (fig. 5.12). Because of the shape of the construction trench, Unit 14 was L-shaped (fig. 5.12), and in terms of volume, it sampled 2.035 square meters of yard deposit. Four arbitrary contexts of 10 cm each were excavated. The reason for utilizing arbitrary distinctions was based on the dark soil of the yard deposit, which, when viewed in profile from the excavation trench, differed little in color or texture from top to bottom. Contexts 175 through 178 sampled the deposit and also took out a portion of the subsoil. A total of 1,272 artifacts were found, providing an assessment of the artifact yield in the yard area of approximately 636 artifacts per square meter. Context 175, the opening arbitrary context, produced one "RT," one "R. Tippet," and one "EB" marked pipe bowl. Since the "RT" and "R. Tippet" pipe bowls date c. 1660–1720, and the Edward Bird pipe bowl dates 1655–1665 (De Roever 1987; McCashion 1979, plate 18), this would indicate that 17th-century materials could be found at the very top of the soil column in the yard. This idea is bolstered by the recovery of delft, redware with manganese

Figure 5.12. Persen House. Unit 14, L-shaped excavation unit around doorway to Phase 5 portion of building. *Source:* Photo by the author.

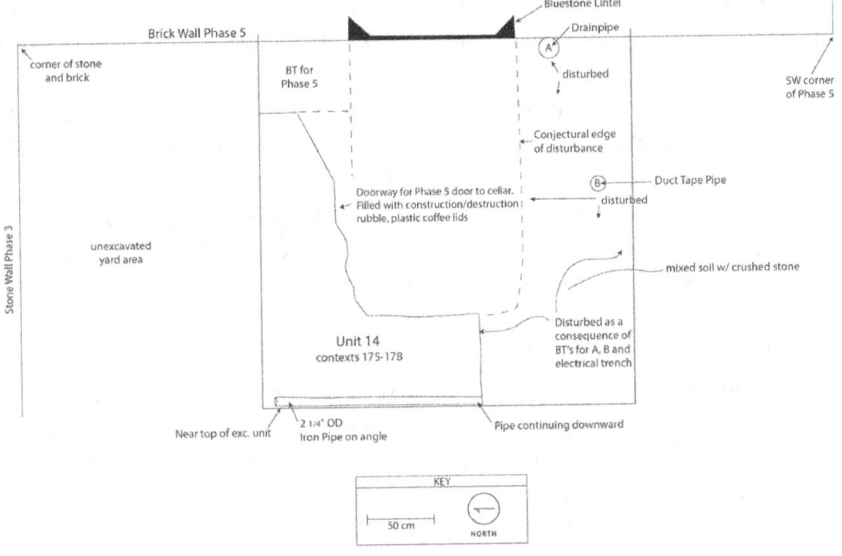

mottling, and combed buff-bodied, slip-decorated earthenware charger and porringer fragments. Later fragments from the mid-18th through early 19th centuries were also found, such as creamware, various pearlwares, lusterware, and Rockingham yellowware.

Context 176 also produced an "R. Tippet" pipe bowl fragment as well as 54 white clay bowl and stem fragments. Other finds from this context included early window glass, an iron knife, fragments of a *Bartmannkrügge*, white salt-glazed stoneware, delft, clear-glazed redware with manganese mottling, redware with both clear-brown- and ginger-colored glazes, combed buff-bodied, slip-decorated earthenware porringer as well as plate/charger fragments, and red-bodied trailed slipware. Later ceramics include creamware, pearlware, Jackfield refined red earthenware, and a Rockingham mug or tankard fragment.

Perhaps the most interesting find from Context 176 was a drilled circular shell bead. The bead is similar to those found on precontact sites on Long Island (Ceci 1977) as well as precontact Haudenosaunee sites (Hayes 1989; Sempowski 1989), Coastal Algonquian sites (Ceci 1989), and several local early Contact period Munsee sites (Diamond 1996a,

1998, 1999a). This shell was likely drilled from a whelk (*Busycon sp.*) columella, which was either traded whole or in fragments from coastal New York. Similar examples of whelk columella have been found locally at the Wolfersteig site (Diamond et al. 2016) as well as the Staubly and Grapes sites (Diamond 2023, 10–15).

Context 177, the third arbitrary context, yielded an "EB" and an "IR TIPPET" cartouche. The first refers to Edward Bird and the second is the cartouche of Joan and Robert Tippet, the latter having gone into business with his mother after the death of his father Robert. Walker (1977, 1493) has suggested a date for the death of the first Robert Tippet as between 1680 and 1687. Consequently, I have taken a conservative stance here and dated the pipe fragment as 1687–1696. Other artifacts from context 177 include coal*, salmon bodied earthenware with a "sick" green/mustard glaze, combed slip-decorated buff-bodied earthenware porringer fragments, redware, *Bartmannkrügge* fragments, delft, Oriental Export porcelain (European style), and later ceramics such as creamware (post-1762).

An important architectural artifact was a fragment of turned lead. Turned lead, or "caming," as it is sometimes called, was the structural support for glass quarrels in casement windows in the 17th and very early 18th centuries. Examples of casement windows can be found in Dutch genre paintings, such as Johannes Vermeer's *The Little Street* (c. 1658) and the *Kitchen Maid* (c. 1658), Pieter de Hooch's *Interior of a Dutch House* (1658), and Adriaen van Ostade's *Village Inn* (1660), with the latter displaying broken casements. Perhaps the most relevant scene, at least one that fits the context of the Persen House, is Pieter van Slingelandt's *A Tailors Workplace* (n.d.). The presence of turned lead in the yard deposits at the Persen House suggests the use of casement-style windows and hints to their use in other domiciles in *Wiltwyck* during the same time period.

Context 178, the deepest context in the soil column, produced far fewer artifacts than the previous three. Notable artifacts include a redware pan fragment with brown glaze, a combed buff-bodied, slip-decorated porringer fragment, and a plain pearlware plate. The latter dates from 1780–1840 and points to the vertical depth that later artifacts can move given the proper conditions.

Related to Unit 14, at least in general proximity, was several days of careful yard clearing undertaken in the south yard between Crown Street and the Phase 4 portion of the Persen House. Due to the finds from Unit 14, it was determined that original, undisturbed soils should be identified and protected from incursions by heavy machinery. Consequently, the yard area was meticulously hand troweled to reveal several features that were subsequently protected and have not since been disturbed. These included a pile of small red Dutch bricks (mostly brickbats), a partial stone foundation, and the probable base or shelf of a bread oven for the fireplace on the south wall in the Phase 2 portion of the house (fig. 5.13).

Figure 5.13. 13 Persen House. Yard clearing. *Source:* Photo by the author.

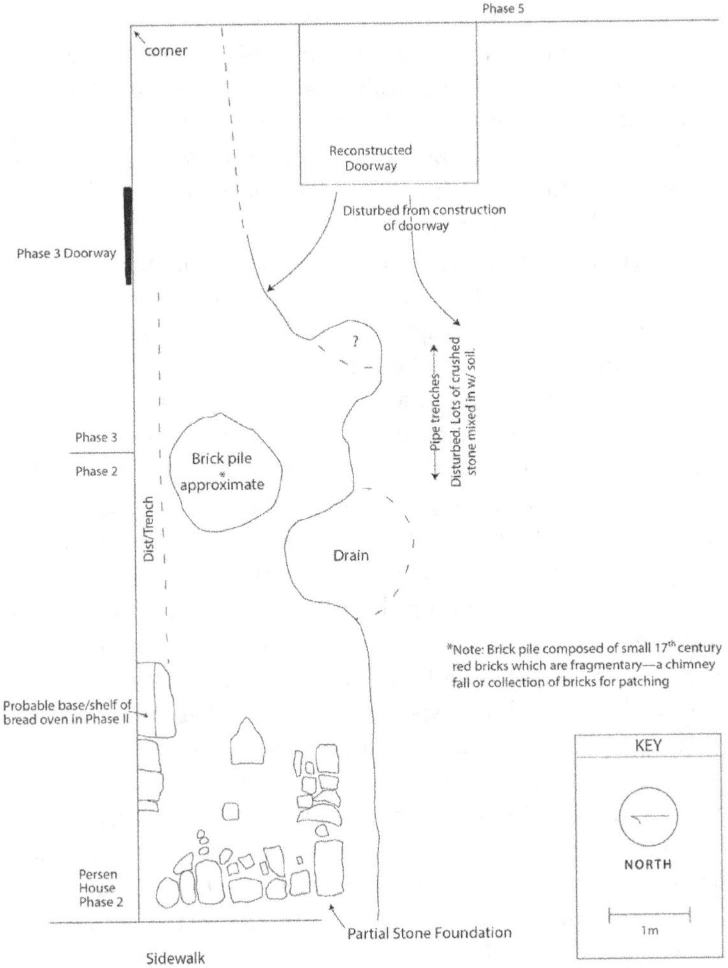

Strata Groups

The archaeological materials from the 10 excavation units on the inside of the Phase 3 portion of the Persen House ranged from 20th-century intrusions to the Transitional Archaic Orient phase. To better understand the changes that have taken place within the soil structure of the Phase 3 addition, similar soil strata from adjacent units have been "lumped" together to create larger, more meaningful analytical units. These large analytical groupings consist of (1) similar soils from adjacent units at the same depth that can be joined; (2) similar soils from units that are not adjacent to each other but where soil structures, artifact content, and visual interpretation of profiles suggest that they are one and the same; and (3) similar soils that have been vertically divided by arbitrary designations by the archaeologist. For example, the latter case is best illustrated by Strata Group 17, a series of four arbitrary divisions of a single deep yard deposit.

These analytical units can also be vertically demarcated by specific soils, such as the 1663 burn layer. For example, the soils below the June 7, 1663, burn layer are grouped together because the burn layer provides a *terminus ante quem* (latest date) for the soils stratigraphically below it. Those above the 1663 burn layer, especially those between the burn layer and the clay/mortar floor, can be dated post-1663 utilizing the burn layer as a *terminus post quem* (earliest date). The horizontal extent of the burn level away from the house, particularly to the north and west, would be reduced by pipe trenches along the edge of the sidewalk as well as areas underneath both Crown and John Streets. This was observable in Unit 1, where Context 10 appeared to be a large, clean fill layer of tan-brown sand that was likely clean pipe trench fill from underneath Crown Street.

The following strata groups have been defined based on relationship and location. Like the context system, there is no implied concept that one predates or postdates another due to the numerical sequence of strata groupings. The discussion of specific temporally diagnostic artifacts varies with strata group. In most cases, important artifacts or types are discussed by unit and context. Where strata groupings cross-cut units and, in some cases, are at opposite ends of the excavation, important temporally diagnostic artifacts are discussed by strata group. Normally, the assumption is that the *terminus post quem* for the latest artifact in a strata group, such as a builder's trench, provides the date after which construction or back-filling took place. For most of the excavation inside the Phase 3 portion of the house, it became apparent that the stratigraphy had been affected by several factors. The first factor was rat nests and burrows. The second was soil movement due to excavations during the Phase 3. The third, and equally problematic, was the difficulty in distinguishing soil color changes due to dryness inside the building. Conceivably, the swipe of a trowel in dry soil or a bump against the excavation unit wall can cause a late fragment of ceramic or glass to be included in an earlier deposit. If the excavator cannot distinguish the cut line of an archaeological context in the soil, there exists the possibility of contamination of early deposits by later deposits. Table 5.1 is a synopsis of the artifacts by strata group (note that this includes shellfish but not vertebrates).

Strata Group 1 (c. 1922)

Strata Group 1 included all soils related to the disturbance in front of the hearth at the eastern end of the Phase 3 addition (c. 1922). These soils were characterized as loose, with a mixture of both old and relatively new artifacts, particularly brick rubble. The disturbance in this portion of Phase 3 construction was related to several events. The first was the destruction and removal of the 18th-century fireplace at the eastern end of the Phase 3 addition. This likely included the temporary removal of the original pine floorboards during Phase 3 construction, as old 2 × 4, 3 × 4, and 4 × 4 boards were found underneath and scabbed onto the original joists. After the removal of the fireplace, a block-and-brick chimney was built (see Barricklo 2000, photos 148, 148j, 148k). Strata Group 1 yielded 573 (4.77%) of the total artifacts from the excavation. Most of the artifacts were kitchen (178 or 31.1%) or architectural (127 or 22.2%) in nature.

Strata Group 2 (post-1730–1735)

Strata Group 2 included all of the soils in original position above the clay/mortar floor and between the floor joists, as shown in figures 5.5, 5.6, 5.9, and 5.10. These ranged from one to three contexts of loose, silty, dusty sand with artifacts. These contexts were between and, in some cases, underlying the floor joists in the Phase 3 addition. Artifacts from Strata Group 2 run the gamut from 19th-century glass and ceramics to much earlier items that have been moved around vertically and horizontally as a result of wall and chimney repairs as well as rodent burrows.

This strata group yielded the largest number of artifacts from any of the groupings. It comprised 2,990 artifacts (24.9%) of the total—almost one quarter of the entire excavation. Like Strata Group 1, the kitchen category was relatively large, consisting of 998 items and 33.4% of the total. Architectural items, primarily nails, also accounted for a large proportion of the assemblage (758 or 25.4%). Nails were primarily of the cut variety, as modern nails were discarded and not included in the total count of artifacts. Two other functional categories that were well represented were the clothing (340 or 11.4%) and recreational (260 or 8.7%) categories. The former consisted mostly of buttons and pins, which were likely related to the tailor shop of Cornelius and Adam Persen from c. 1735–1769. From a quantitative point of view, this was the largest number of clothing-related items from the site and suggests that the clay/mortar floor was put down at the time of, or before, the Persen brothers used the house as a tailor shop.

The large number of recreational items, mostly white clay pipestem fragments, attests to the popularity of smoking at this time and also suggests that the Persens engaged in this pursuit while tailoring. Most of these pipes, with the exception of some Robert Tippet examples, were later types. However, as mentioned elsewhere in this chapter, the production, use, and distribution of RT pipes often extended into the 1770s. Other examples from this strata group were also later types. For example, Unit 7 (Context 76) produced a possible Thomas Dormer pipe, which dates c. 1748–1770 (Oswald 1975, 135), but which Paul Huey more recently identified as c. 1755–1780 (Paul Huey, personal communication, 2020). Interestingly, aside from the RT examples, there were no other pipes with 17th-century maker's marks.

Two other numerically large functional groupings, at least compared with quantities from other strata groups, were macrobotanicals and the arms category. From a total of 129 macrobotanicals recovered from the site, 64 (49.6%) were found in Strata Group 2. This large sample, most of which consisted of nut hulls associated with the holiday season, is an indication of rodent activity. Comparable in number are materials comprising the arms group, of which 14, or 53.8% of the total arms materials from the excavation, were represented.

Strata Group 3 (post-1730–1735)

Strata Group 3 included the walls and builder's trenches of the Phase 3 structure (see figs. 5.5 and 5.6). In his report on the Persen House, Barricklo (2000) provided the following information:

Phase 3 was built onto the eastern foundation wall of the Phase 2 section and was built without a cellar. There is no evidence of the original wood-framed walls for this addition. It was common in the Kingston Stockade area for a wood framed extension to be added across the rear of a house that would become a barn, kitchen, scullery wing or storage shed. Often the extension was a shed only, with one floor. The extant remains of the roof framing of this addition indicates that it was a double height structure with its ridge at right angles to the Phase one and two ridge. The kitchen or barn would have been entered from Phase 2 stepping down several steps. . . . The Phase 3 common wall to Phase 2 was built on top of the Phase 2 cellar wall. The separating wall is a hand-hewn stud wall infilled with soft hand-made bricks appearing to be used as an interior wall, which is fire-separating the house from the barn structure or kitchen wing. Phase 2 and Phase 3 could have been built at the same time; as a barn structure that became a kitchen with a fireplace. (27)

The idea that the Phase 3 wooden addition to the Phase 2 portion was planned and was coeval would make the dating of the Phase 2 and 3 somewhat easier, at least in theory. When, in 1735, Anthony Slecht transferred the property to Cornelius Persen, both his family and his brother's family lived in the house. This would have been an important point for enlarging the house and for extending a wooden frame addition for use as a tailor shop/kitchen wing. As mentioned in the discussion of Strata Group 2, most of the clothing and tailoring-related items (340, or 56%, of the clothing category) originated from here, indicating that it was in place and in use during that time period. One problem with this theory is the "Jan Eltenge 1754" bottle seal from Strata Group 3, which could conceivably be a *terminus post quem* for the Phase 3 construction. Unfortunately, due to construction and repairs along the south wall, this may have been part of the refilled soil matrix that also included pieces of an 1864 Kingston soda bottle and a mid-19th-century "Balsam of Honey" patent medicine bottle.

Because the builder's trenches for the Phase 3 portion of the Persen House witnessed substantial admixture, it is no surprise that Strata Group 3 had the third highest number of Native American artifacts. A total of

160 (20.7%) items of the entire total from this strata group were precontact materials. A comparable quantity was the kitchen category, of which 161 (20.8%) artifacts were found. Not surprisingly, the largest number of artifacts was from the architectural category (200 or 25.8%), and most of this sample was comprised of nails.

Strata Group 4 (post-1730–1735)

Strata Group 4 was the clay/mortar floor throughout most of the interior portion of the house (figs. 5.5, 5.6, 5.9, and 5.10). It was characterized as a hard mixture of clay and mortar, with some hay, faunal remains, and artifacts trapped within the matrix. It appears to have been used to seal in the deposits below and may have also been used to prevent the encroachment of pests such as rats, whose nests and skeletal remains were numerous throughout the excavation. Its extent is illustrated in the figures, although, in some cases, the edges are conjectural due to breakage of the clay/mortar floor by construction workers in 1922. The floor is thought to have been applied across the interior of the Phase 3 and underlying/abutting the stone floor joists that supported the wooden floor above. Along the northern wall of the Phase 3 portion, the floor was relatively intact. To the south, the clay/mortar was broken up for reconstruction or repairs to the south wall of Phase 3.

This strata group yielded a total of 270 artifacts (2.24%). Most of the artifacts were architectural materials (86 or 31.9%), shellfish (57 or 21.1%), or kitchen related items (44 or 16.3%).

Strata Group 5 (post-1730–1735)

Strata Group 5 included contexts from below the clay/mortar floor. Throughout most of the interior, but especially near the northwest, it generally began with a mix of small red Dutch brick fragments, clay, and mortar mixed with charcoal flecks. In Schoonmaker's *The History of Kingston* (1888, 306–8), Matthewis Persen is listed as one of the "sufferers" from the burning of Kingston by General Vaughn's British Troops on October 16, 1777. While some have suggested that these charcoal flecks are evidence of the 1777 fire, it appears that the brick debris may be the remains of existing soil mixed with the robbed remains of the fireplace along Phase 1's eastern wall. This strata group included large amounts of fragmentary red Dutch brick mixed with small amounts of charcoal and soot from the inside of the chimney. I do not believe that this small amount of charcoal, particularly given its context in association with brick fragments, is evidence of the 1777 burning of Kingston.

The soil matrix within which the brick and pan tile fragments were mixed was likely the soil excavated from the basement during construction of the Phase 2 addition, which would have been the logical point to (1) change the location of the fireplace from the east wall to the north in Phase 1, and (2) construct the Phase 2 and Phase 3 additions. This soil would also likely have had a level of midden debris, which was then incorporated into the fill of Strata Groups 5 and 6.

Major artifact categories from this strata group included the architectural (379 or 31%), kitchen (236 or 19.3%), shellfish (226 or 18.5%), and recreational (166 or 13.6%) categories. It should be noted that a total of 73.6 kg (160 lb) of small red Dutch bricks were removed from this strata group, which, if added to the numerical count, would have vastly increased the architectural category.

One artifact used for dating this stratum was the molded eight-sided wine glass stem from Unit 5 (Context 29), which postdates 1730. The presence of a sulfide buildup on the glass also suggests that it might have spent time, at least at one point, in a privy.

Strata Group 6 (post-1663–1730/1735)

Strata Group 6 included contexts that may have been related to Strata Group 5 but were deeper. These soils consisted of dark yellow-brown silty sand with brick, mortar, and clay pressed into them, but were still above the 1663 burn layer. Perhaps the best way to conceptualize this strata group is as a deeper version of Strata Group 5, in which, due to similarity of soils and pedestrian mingling of building debris during the robbing process, soils became homogenized. It should be noted that the combination of brick debris from Strata Groups 5 and 6 yielded 158.4 kg (354.5 lb) of brick, of which only seven were whole or partial (see discussion of Strata Group 5 regarding the content of this association of contexts).

The artifacts from Strata Group 6 were very similar to those discussed above. Architectural items accounted for 428, or 29.2%, of the artifacts, while the kitchen (305 or 20.8%), shellfish (236 or 16.1%), and recreational (189 or 12.9%) categories constituted the next three largest. This strata group also had the second highest number of precontact Native American artifacts (187, or 12.8%, of the strata group). The explanation for this occurrence relates to the nature and origin of the deposit. This strata group overlaid the 1663 burn layer and was primarily composed of soils that that were excavated from both the Phase 1 and Phase 2 portions of the Persen House. Any precontact Native American artifacts in situ in these locations would have been redeposited as fill just above the burn layer when the basements were excavated.

Strata Group 7 (c. 1674–1730/35)

This strata group consisted of fill within and overlying the palisade trench, the soils of which appeared to have compressed as a result, and consisted mostly of building rubble such as mortar, clay, and small Dutch brick fragments. One of the differences that separated it from the building rubble of Strata Groups 5 and 6 was the addition of large fragments of red clay pan tiles. This could either imply a construction/destruction episode or may relate to work around the chimney, which constituted most of the debris in Strata Groups 5 and 6. The three to four pan tiles that were recovered may have been the original roofing tiles for the Phase 1 structure, which may have been broken during the removal of the chimney. The palisade would have to have been removed for the pan tiles and debris to fill the trench. I have dated it post-1674 based on the fact that when the Van Imbroch children sold the house in 1674 (see above), the palisade was in good condition. If the pan tiles are from the hypothesized construction episode of Phase 2, the terminal date would be c.1730–1735.

Strata group 7 yielded only 204 artifacts, most of which were architectural (95 or 46.6%), followed by the kitchen (33 or 16.2%) and recreational (26 or 12.7%) categories.

Strata Group 8 (1661–c. 1674+)

Strata Group 8 consisted of the palisade trench and the silty sand matrix that filled it. This included artifacts from the dark soil stains, which were probably the post molds from the actual palisade, that is, from when the posts were removed and darker soil filled in the empty spaces.

The numerically largest category of artifacts from this strata group was precontact Native American artifacts ($n = 122$; 51.5%). This may be explained by the fact that when the palisade trench was excavated, the original soil was backfilled, in effect replacing the disturbed Native American materials. The precontact materials from this strata group constituted

1.01% of the total precontact artifacts from the full archaeological excavation. The next largest functional categories were architectural (48 or 20.3%), shellfish (16 or 6.8%), and fire-affected (12 or 5.06%) materials. The latter are thought to be artifacts that are related to the June 7, 1663, burning of *Wiltwyck*.

Post Molds: Strata Groups 9 and 10 (see discussion below for dates)

The division of post molds into temporally associated groupings within the Phase 3 portion of the Persen House is somewhat problematic (fig. 5.7). The earliest, based on artifactual evidence, appears to be Context 128, the small post mold in Unit 11. The very fact that two equidistant rows of posts ran through the Phase 3 portion of the house, and were below the clay and mortar floor (and contain brick fragments), points to the possibility that Contexts 58, 90, 74, 89, 122, and 130 were related to Phase 3 construction activities that predate the completion of the structure. These also penetrated the remodeling activities from the Phase 1 modification of the fireplace from the east wall to the north wall.

Although post molds 167 and 169 were close to each other and appear to form a row, the contents of each and the stratigraphy above indicate that they were not related. Context 169, the post mold at the north end of Unit 4, which was almost destroyed by the south wall of the Phase 4 builder's trench, contained very dark brown sand. Next to it, in the north wall of Unit 7, was Context 167, a post mold that was filled with microstratigraphic alternating bands of brick dust and soot (fig. 5.8). These bands covered Context 169, indicating that Context 167 postdated Context 169. A comparison of the soils also suggests that the two post molds were not open (or filled) at the same time.

The question remains regarding what construction activities these post molds were associated with. One possibility is a wooden shed addition on the back of the Phase 2 portion of the house. This would have predated the Phase 3 section constructed stratigraphically above it. If, in fact, there was another row of post molds, it might have been destroyed during excavation of the builder's trench along the south wall. Alternatively, the post molds could have been used as temporary supports to brace the post-and-beam portion of the Phase 3 during its construction. The post molds would have eventually been backfilled with nearby soil and covered with the clay/mortar floor when Phase 3 was completed. One other possibility is that the posts may represent the supports for one side of a trellis framework that would create an outdoor roof of grapes or other vine-like plants. These outdoor structures are common in Dutch and Flemish paintings from the 17th century, and would have provided a shady area to eat, drink, and smoke. In this case, the trellis would have been added on the rear of the Phase 2 portion of the house.

Strata Group 9 (c. 1730–1735)

Strata Group 9 consisted of posts cutting through the 1663 burn layer (fig. 5.7). These varied in size and shape and were found across the floor of the Phase 3 addition. Note that one potential post mold on the outside of the house (Context 8) was grouped with Strata Group 19—the soils on the outside of the house but above the 1663 burn layer—as it cut through the burn layer. The majority of the post molds identified inside the Phase 3 addition (Contexts 58, 74, 89, 90, 122, 130, 138, 139, 169) have been lumped into this strata group. Artifacts from this group were dominated by precontact Native American items (57 or 65.5%), with the kitchen category (14 or 16.1%) being the next largest. The kitchen category from these post mold contexts is one of the more pristine groupings of 17th- to early 18th-century artifacts on site. This includes majolica, *Bartmannkrügge* fragments, delft, Hoogeboom (?) redware, combed buff-bodied slip-decorated earthenware, and portions of an English onion-shaped wine bottle. The latest date of this grouping, or *terminus post quem*, would be post-1680 based on the shape of the wine bottle. The question is, was this part of a yard surface where artifacts from the surface were backfilled into the post molds after use, or were they part of the fill from the posthole and simply returned to the approximate location? The very fact that the post molds cut into Strata Groups 5 and 6 indicates that they had to be there for the post molds to have been excavated. Although the artifacts were early, the post molds were somewhat later. They may have been part of a wooden structure postdating Phase 2 but predating Phase 3, as they were sealed in by the clay/mortar floor on the inside of the Phase 3 portion.

Strata Group 10 (c. 1664–1730/35)

Strata Group 10 was a second grouping of post molds that was segregated from Strata Group 9 based on location, content, and point from which they cut down in the stratigraphic profile and their initial depth as indicated on plan views. This strata group included only one post mold (Context 167), which probably related to the destruction episode of the chimney on the east side of the Phase 1 portion of the house (fig. 5.8). I have dated it within a wide span, as it is difficult to ascertain exactly what was going on from a temporal perspective. Artifacts from this post mold included three architectural items and one precontact Native American item.

STRATA GROUP 11 (JUNE 7, 1663)

Strata Group 11 was the June 7, 1663, burn layer. This context was found in almost all of the interior units (Figures 5.5, 5.6, 5.8, 5.9, 5.10) as well as in exterior Units 1 and 2 (Figures 5.3, 5.4). It was not found in the yard area to the south of the Phase 3 addition. It was characterized by a black line varying from 6–10 cm in thickness, made up of charcoal dust mixed with sand. Strata Group 11 provides us with a *terminus post quem* for both the deposits above and those deposits sealed below it. It also allowed us to observe later construction or repair events, such as the posts in Strata Groups 9 and 10 that cut through the 1663 burn layer.

This archaeological context included several soil components that are usually found on precontact and historic sites. Excavations around the Persen House have not identified a humic zone, other than that identified in Unit 14, which took several hundred years to produce. The lack of a developed humic zone, or, as one would expect, a buried A-horizon soil, means that the burn layer penetrated the entire 1663 humic zone and actually represents it. This suggests that artifacts from the burn layer were surface scatter from June 7, 1663. Since this was the humic zone during the time that the settlement expanded, there should also be some earlier artifacts from c. 1661 to 1663 within this strata group.

Artifacts from the burn layer totaled 172, with the three largest functional groupings being the precontact (71 or 41.3%), architectural (42 or 24.4%), and kitchen (25 or 14.5%) categories. The precontact items were likely part of earlier Native American occupations contained within the humic zone. Evidence for these occupations would have been found around the 1661 stockade prior to the fire and were then sealed in by the fire. Regarding the date, I have suggested June 7, 1663. However, this may extend in either direction for approximately 2 years, because artifacts could have been trampled into the humic zone prior to the fire, and later would have been trampled into the black soil during the numerous attempts to repair portions of the palisade after the attack that precipitated the Second Esopus War.

STRATA GROUP 12 (PRE–JUNE 7, 1663)

Strata Group 12 consisted of the features below the 1663 burn layer. These can be characterized as small post molds (Contexts 115, 128, 129) that may have originated from the precontact period as well as two small pits (Contexts 155 and 156) that appear to predate the 1663 fire. During the excavation, it was difficult to determine the nature of the difference between the black sandy pit fill and the burn layer above it. Although we segregated them as pre–June 7, 1663, it is possible that they immediately postdate the fire. In any case, these appear to be pits, either for cooking or heat, that were immediately outside the palisade. Several contained 17th-century Dutch materials. Note that this strata group does not include features such as Context 117 that are thought to be large rat nests; these have been grouped into Strata Group 18. Artifacts from Strata Group 12 totaled only 112. Of these, the two largest categories were Native American (85 or 76%) and architectural (16 or 14%) items. Perhaps the most interesting items found in this cluster of features are the ceramics from the kitchen category: majolica, green speckled clear lead-glazed redware, unglazed redware, and combed buff-bodied, slip-decorated earthenware.

STRATA GROUP 13 (PRE-1663–TRANSITIONAL ARCHAIC, C. 1100 BC)

Strata Group 13 represented the original soils below the 1663 burn layer inside the Phase 3 portion of the Persen House. These consisted of from one to four contexts of yellow-brown silty sand grading into a coarse sand as depth increased. This was the soil matrix that the features in Strata Group 12 were surrounded by. It is the same sandy soil matrix (Riverhead series) that characterizes Kingston's uptown area.

This strata group had the highest number of precontact artifacts, with a total of 1,837, or 63%, of all precontact items from the site originating from this strata group. This number comprised 93.9% of all of the artifacts from Strata Group 13. The next largest categories within this group, in numerical order, were the architectural (58 or 3.0%), recreational (18 or 0.92%), and kitchen (16 or 0.8%) categories. Significant, temporally diagnostic Native American artifacts from this strata group included two Orient Fishtail projectile points (c. 1100–750 BC/3050–2700 BP) and five fragments of Native American pottery that were not temporally diagnostic.

Strata Group 14 (c. 1675–1730/35)

Strata Group 14 was the builder's trench for the construction of the Phase 2 portion of the Persen House. Artifacts from the builder's trench, particularly in Unit 7, exhibited the same problems with disturbances as in many other contexts. The year 1675 is used as a *terminus post quem* based on the information that when the house was sold by the children of Gysbert van Imbroch in March of 1673, it was the Phase 1 portion that was inside the curtain wall. This would indicate that the second half is later than c. 1675 but can extend to 1730–1735. While the Phase 2 addition to the Persen House should (could) be related to the change in gable direction, and may date from the first or second quarter of the 18th century, ceramics from this deposit included hand-painted pearlware (post-1780). Additionally, Canton Nanking porcelain, masonic pipe bowl fragments, and pipes with decorative fluting were also found, most of which became available in the last quarter of the 18th century. Again, this indicates the high level of disturbance to the deposits resulting from rats' nests and burrows.

A total of 91 artifacts were found in this strata group, most of which were architectural (29 or 31.9%), shellfish (19 or 20.9%), and kitchen (17 or 18.7%) materials.

Strata Group 15 (post-1777)

The date for Strata Group 15 is based on documentary evidence (see Barricklo 2000). This strata group comprised the builder's trench and wall segments for the Phase 4 portion of the Persen House. This included portions inside the building as well as the sample from Context 12 in Unit 2 on the north side of the Phase 4 portion. This strata group contained 56 artifacts, most of which were architectural (21 or 37.5%) and kitchen (10 or 17.9 %) materials.

Strata Group 16 (July 1663–c.1673)

Strata Group 16 was the builder's trench for the Phase 1 portion of the Persen House. This was encountered only in Context 3, Unit 1, underneath the sidewalk on the west side of the house. However, it does not appear to have been a pristine deposit that can tell us with any certainty, at least based on the artifactual evidence, when the first portion of the Persen

House was constructed. What we do know is that it cuts through the June 7, 1663, burn layer, and consequently, the existing Phase 1 portion of the Persen House must postdate the burning of *Wiltwyck*.

This strata group yielded 97 artifacts, the largest category of which was Native American items (38 or 39.2%). Like Strata Group 3, the explanation for this high percentage is the fact that after the basement and walls were excavated, the builder's trench appears to have been refilled with sand that contained everything from the burn layer down, particularly Strata Group 13, the original soil below the burn layer. Given the volume of the excavated soil matrix, the artifact content was quite low, indicating a relatively early context that did not contain large amounts of archaeological materials. Unfortunately, artifacts such as creamware (post-1762) and hand-painted pearlware (post-1780) were in the builder's trench, indicating the amount of soil redeposition around the house. Again, this points to the problems inherent in using strictly artifacts to date the contexts, because soil movement within and outside of the Persen House appears to have been substantial.

In his analysis of the Persen House, Barricklo (2000, 25) suggested that the Phase 1 portion of the house was outside of the 1661–1663 stockade. What we did not know at that time of his publication was that the lot encompassing the Phase 1 portion of the house was within the 1661–1663 stockade. It is most probable that the earliest portion of the Persen House was constructed from July 1663 to 1673, with a door facing present-day John Street and the early jambless fireplace along the east wall.

Strata Group 17 (c. 1674–c. 1975).

Strata Group 17 consisted of four arbitrary levels of yard deposits from Unit 14. The date is based on the knowledge that it is a yard deposit on the outside of the 1661–1663 addition to the stockade that would have been more accessible after 1674 (when we know that Van Imbroch's section of the palisade was still up), particularly when the southern stockade wall was extended to Main Street. The latter would have enclosed a much larger area, making the area in the south yard more accessible, particularly for garden plots and waste disposal. The terminal date of c. 1975 is an estimated date for the blacktop in the driveway.

With the vertebrate faunal remains removed, the quantity for this 2-meter excavated square was 657 artifacts. Of this number, the four largest categories were kitchen (196 or 29.8%), architectural (149 or 22.7%), recreational (144 or 21.9%), and shellfish (102 or 15.5%). Of the recreational category, all were either pipe bowls or stems.

Strata Group 18 (no date)

Strata Group 18 is a catchall designation for contexts that were disturbed, were interpreted as rats' nests or groupings of rats' nests, or were excavated and combined together, such as Unit 3, the large shovel test in the southwest corner of the Phase 3 portion of the Persen House. This strata group is comprised of 535 artifacts, most of which were architectural (218 or 40.7%) or kitchen related (110 or 20.6%).

Strata Group 19 (post-June 7, 1663–1730/35)

Strata Group 19 included all archaeological contexts above the 1663 burn deposit outside of the Persen House in Units 1 and 2, which included 461 artifacts The largest categories were architectural (222 or 48.2%), Native American (94 or 20.4%), and shellfish (47 or 10.2%). Both the kitchen and recreational categories were represented by approximately the same number of artifacts, being 33 (or 7.2%) and 35 (or 7.6%), respectively.

Strata Group 20 (pre–June 7, 1663)

Strata Group 20 consisted of all archaeological contexts below the 1663 burn line outside of the Persen House in Units 1 and 2. This strata group included only 36 artifacts, most of which were shellfish (18 or 50%) or from the recreational category (12 or 33.3%).

Artifacts by Functional, Temporal, and Faunal Groups

The artifacts from the excavation of the Persen House have been divided for analysis purposes into 14 broad groups. These are Native American (including precontact), European/Native American trade items, kitchen related, shellfish, architectural items, furniture, arms, the clothing group, personal items, "recreation," special activities, fuel, fire affected, and macrobotanicals. The three categories of kitchen, fauna, and bivalves are often included together as the kitchen category; here, they are divided. This makes possible the delineation of historic artifact patterns such as the Carolina and Brunswick Patterns, as outlined by South (1978). They have been separated here for clarity and tabulated in table 5.1 as such. They can then be recombined into one category so that numbers and percentages can be easily examined. When combined into one group,

Table 5.1. Persen House. Artifacts by function and strata group.

Strata Group	1	2	3	4	5	6	7	8	9	10	11	12	13	14	15	16	17	18	19	20	Sum	% of Total
(1) Pre-Contact	27	32	160	9	111	187	10	122	57	1	71	85	###	4	8	38	38	23	94	1	2915	24.29
% of SG	4.7	1.07	20.7	3.3	9.1	13	4.9	52	66	25	41.3	76	94	4.4	14.3	39	5.8	4.3	20.4	2.8		
(2) Trade Goods	1	3		1	6	3	2	2					3		1		1				23	0.19
% of SG	0.2	0.1		0.4	0.5	0.2	0.98	0.8					0.2		1.8		0.2					
(3) Kitchen	178	998	161	44	236	305	33	12	14		25	8	16	17	10	8	196	110	33	3	2407	20.05
% of SG	31	33.4	20.8	16.3	19.3	21	16.2	5.6	16		14.5	7.1	0.8	18.7	17.9	8.2	29.8	20.6	7.2	8.3		
(4) Shellfish	96	376	114	57	226	236	15	16	4		7		14	19	8	7	102	64	47	18	1426	11.9
% of SG	17	12.6	14.7	21.1	18.5	16	7.4	6.8	4.6		4.1		0.7	20.9	14.3	7.2	15.5	12	10.2	50		
(5) Architect.	127	758	200	86	379	428	95	48	4	3	42	16	58	29	21	30	149	218	222	2	2915	24.28
% of SG	22	25.4	25.8	31.9	31	29	46.6	20	4.6	75	24.4	14	3	31.9	37.5	31	22.7	40.7	48.2	5.6		
(6) Furniture			1		1									1							3	0.02
% of SG			0.13		0.08									1.09								
(7) Arms		14	5		1	2	1	2				2							1		26	0.22
% of SG		0.5	0.6		0.08	0.1	0.5	0.8				1.8							0.22			
(8) Clothing	49	340	17	6	43	62	14	7			3		10	8	3		2	45	3		612	5.1
% of SG	8.6	11.4	2.2	2.2	3.5	4.2	6.9	0.3			1.7		0.5	8.8	4		0.3	8.4	0.7			
(9) Personal	1	40	4	1	6	4	3	1					1	3				4			68	0.56
% of SG	0.2	1.3	0.51	0.4	0.5	0.3	1.5	0.4					0.1	3.3				0.74				
(10) Recreational	56	260	83	27	166	189	26	6	5		15	2	18	10	4	11	144	31	35	12	1100	9.2
% of SG	9.8	8.7	10.6	0.7	13.6	13	12.7	2.5	5.7		8.7	1.8	0.9	10.9	7.1	11	21.9	5.8	7.6	33.3		
(11) Spec. Activ.	12	25	7	2	23	15	3	3			2	1					3	5			101	0.84
% of SG	2.1	8.4	0.9	0.7	1.9	1	1.5	1.3			1.2	0.9					0.5	0.93				

Strata Group	1	2	3	4	5	6	7	8	9	10	11	12	13	14	15	16	17	18	19	20	Sum	% of Total
(12) Fuel	17	33	7	1	7	10	1	1								3	20	9	11		120	1
% of SG	3	1.1	0.9	0.4	0.6	0.7	0.5	0.4								3.1	3	1.7	2.4			
(13) Fire-affect.	7	47	10	28	4	5	1	12							1			26	15		156	1.3
% of SG	1.2	1.6	1.3	10.4	0.33	0.3	0.5	5.1							1.8			4.9	3.3			
(14) Macrobot.	2	64	5	8	14	19		5	3		7						2				129	1.07
% of SG	0.3	2.14	0.6	3	1.1	1.3		2.1	3.4		4.1						0.3					
Total	573	2990	774	270	1223	###	204	237	87	4	172	112	###	91	56	97	657	535	461	36	12001	
% of Total	4.8	24.9	6.44	2.24	10.2	12	1.7	2	0.7	0.03	1.4	0.9	16	0.8	0.47	0.8	5.47	4.5	3.84	0.3		

the kitchen category is often the largest group in each context. Another reason to segregate shellfish specifically is to examine the numbers and weight for shellfish from various contexts in an attempt to answer questions such as those posed by Bridges (1974) regarding the presence and use of shellfish in early contexts at Clinton Avenue (see chapter 4). Since the faunal remains have been analyzed separately by Dr. Thomas Amorosi, these will be discussed in conjunction with the shellfish and the different strata groupings.

Native American (All Precontact)

Artifacts from the Native American category were found in a high percentage in all of the archaeological contexts that were excavated and in all of the 20 strata groups (table 5.2). This is primarily because there is substantial soil admixture in this area and because the earliest Dutch occupations directly overlie, or are mixed, with soils that contain Native American artifacts. The 2,915 precontact artifacts found during the excavations make up 24.29%, or almost one quarter, of the total artifacts excavated in and around the Persen House.

The range of tools found on the site of the Persen House included projectile points, chert bifaces, scrapers, cores, drills, hammerstones, and utilized flakes (fig. 5.14). By far the most numerically preponderant precontact artifacts were lithic debitage. Of the 2,915 precontact artifacts recovered, 2,663, or 91.4%, were debitage, equivalent to a ratio of 89:1 debitage to chipped stone artifacts. These fragments comprise 11 categories of chert. Twenty-five hundred, or 93.9%, were composed of local black Eastern Onondaga chert in its nonblocky state. Blocky fragments of Eastern Onondaga derived from local limestone outcrops, and glacial till accounted for 1.9% of the debitage. Found in smaller quantities on the site were gray and brownish gray cherts similar to Western Onondaga chert. When combined, these total 47, or 1.8%, of the chert debitage found. Other colors represented included greenish varieties of Mount Merino chert (39, or 1.5%, of the debitage), Indian River chert (16, or .6 %, of the debitage), and other varieties such as milky gray Harmonyvale chert (7 combined, or .26%), quartz debitage ($n = 2$), and debitage with cortex or exterior rind ($n = 2$). The high percentage of black Eastern Onondaga chert indicates that the Native American catchment area for lithics was distinctly local. Cherts similar to these could have been recovered from nearby outcrops of the Lower to Middle Devonian Onondaga (Morehouse formation) and the Lower Devonian Schoharie, Esopus, Glenerie, and Port Ewen formations.

Table 5.2 Persen House. Native American artifacts by strata group.

Strata group	1	2	3	4	5	6	7	8	9	10	11	12	13	14	15	16	17	18	19	20	Sum	% of total
Black EO chert deb.	24	21	152	7	84	168	7	79	50	1	44	79	###	4	7	5	29	19	15		2500	85.8
Black EO blockys		1	2		12	4		13	3		1	3	11				1				51	1.7
Green chert deb.	1	2			8	4	1	1	3		7		10					2			39	1.3
Brn/gr. brn Blocky											1										1	0.03
Brn/gr.brn deb.		2			1			21			6		2			2	1		10		45	1.5
Milky grey deb.		1			1	2							1						1		6	0.2
Milky grey blocky																			1		1	0.03
Grey debitage		1																			1	0.03
Maroon debitage			1	1	3	3	1						2			1	1	1	2		16	0.54
Deb. w/ cortex		1											1								2	0.06
Quartz debitage																		1			1	0.03
Quartz crystal	1	1	1													1			3		7	0.24
Projectile point	1	1	2	1			1				1		3			1			1	1	13	0.45

continued on next page

Table 5.2. Continued.

																							Total	
P.P./biface														1									1	0.03
Biface (general)						3		1					2								2		9	0.31
Scraper	1																							1	0.03
UF/scraper													1											1	0.03
Utilized flake			1											1										2	0.06
Drill							1																	1	0.03
Core													2											2	0.06
Pitted nutting stone													1											1	0.03
Bi-pit. nuttingstone													1											1	0.03
Hammerstone						1				1			1											3	0.1
Pestle																1								1	0.03
Pottery									1				5			2								8	0.3
Fire-cracked rock			1		2	1		7		9	3		87	1		25	6		59					201	6.9
Total	27	32	160	9	111	187	10	122	57	1	71	85	###	4	8	25	38	6	23	94	1			2915	
% of total	0.9	1.1	5.5	0.3	3.8	6.4	0.3	4.2	2	0	2.4	2.9	63	0.1	0.3	1.3	1.3	0.3	0.8	0.3	0				

Figure 5.14. Persen House. Native American artifacts. Top row, left to right: small biface (3.160), quartz crystal (13.134). Center row: two Orient Fishtail points (11.127; 2.14), three Meadowood points (4.22; 5.26; 1.9). Bottom row: two biface frags (9.131; 10.98), drill (13.151), two Levanna Points (4.53; 2.11). *Source:* Photo by the author.

Plant processing was represented in the collection by a pestle fragment and two nutting stones. Symbolic artifacts were represented by the presence of seven quartz crystals, which are often found on Native American sites (fig. 5.14).

European Trade Items

This category of artifacts included glass, shell, and copper beads; wampum; copper projectile points; and cassock buttons. European trade items are segregated from precontact items due to their location of manufacture and time period (see table 5.1). The trade items found at the Persen House were not great in number, but they are informative. Of the 14 glass beads, most were probably produced in Amsterdam in the Venetian style (*façon de Venise*). Nine are from the grouping that Kenyon and Fitzgerald (1986) have called the Dutch Trade. These include bead types IIa6, IIa11, IIa43 (or IIa45) IIa55, IIa66, IIIa1, and IVa1 (Kidd and Kidd 1970), but this category does not include wire-wound beads. Here, the beads were dated using Snow's (1995) correlations to Haudenosaunee sites with the same types of trade beads. The five wire-wound beads from the Persen House excavations were not faceted forms. These types of beads likely postdate 1675 (see Snow 1995, 35) and were found well into the 18th century (see Huey 1983, 96; Karklins 1983, 125). Figure 5.15 illustrates the beads and includes unit and context information.

Two shell items were found. One was a piece of wampum that was drilled with a *maux*, an iron drill-like tool introduced at the time of European contact that greatly facilitated the production of wampum (fig. 5.15). The *maux* allowed the complete drilling of a finished wampum bead from one end to the other. Prior to this, either a fine chert drill or fine sand with a reed was used. In this case, the distinguishing technological

Figure 5.15. Persen House. Trade items. Top row, left to right: amber bead (7.168), large amber wire-wound bead (4.22), large black bead over large white wire-wound bead (13.149), bright blue bead (4.54), large bright blue bead (13.134), cassock button (12.159). Bottom row: large round black, med navy blue (5.28), tubular bead (9.116), very small white bead (13.150), tubular bead (4.72), red/black bead (10.98), wampum and copper bead (4.56). *Source:* Photo by the author.

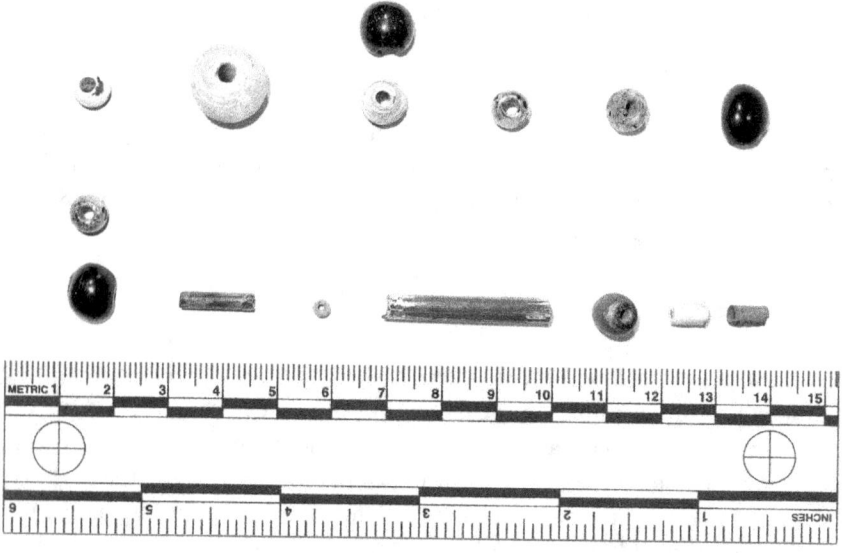

252 | The Archaeology of Kingston, New York

difference was whether it had been drilled all the way through or whether two drill holes met in the center (see Burggraff 1938, for drilling techniques associated with shell bead and wampum production). Wampum or *sewan* was a common monetary unit from the early 17th through 18th centuries in the Hudson Valley (see also Pena 1990), and it is mentioned in the *Wiltwyck* court minutes numerous times as a unit of exchange.

The other shell item was a circular shell bead (not shown). These types of beads may also have been utilized for monetary exchange, although production would not have entailed the same amount of time expenditure as wampum. Circular beads and shell beads (excluding wampum) that have been found in the Hudson Valley have been made by drilling through a *Carica* or *Busycon* columella. *Busycon* or whelk are known from several early Contact period sites in the Esopus drainage within three miles of the Persen House. Whelk is a saltwater species, so this implies trade with the coastal area of New York. Circular shell beads have been found at Haudenosaunee sites in New York (Hayes 1989; Sempowski 1989; Snow 1995) as well as Algonquian sites along the coast (Ceci 1977, 1989) and in the Hudson Valley (Diamond 1998, 1999a, 2023; Diamond et al. 2016).

I have examined in detail the fragments of saltwater clam or *Mercenaria* from the Persen House but did not find any indications of shell bead or wampum production. This activity is usually represented by fractured shell, long shell blanks, polished blanks, sandstone abraders or fine whetstones, and bead blanks broken during the drilling process. Although none were found at the Persen House, the possibility exists that such a deposit, or even midden scatter, could indicate the dwelling of original Lot 8 in the first portion of the stockade owned by Henry Zeewant Ryger, wampum maker (Fernow 1881, 230).

Two copper projectile points or point fragments were also found. These, as well as brass projectile points, are often found on Contact period sites in the Mid-Hudson Valley (Diamond 1996a, 1998, 1999a; Diamond et al. 2022, 2023; Lindner 1998, 50–53). They were often cut from copper or brass scrap, most commonly kettles traded from the Dutch (see also van Dongen 1996).

Kitchen Category

The kitchen category is kind of a catch-all that encompasses kitchen-related functions, such as cooking and the ceramics associated with cooking and serving, but also includes artifacts related to medical care, alcohol consumption and beverage presentation, lighting, and food storage. When combined with faunal remains, it is often the largest category of artifacts on domestic sites. When making comparisons with other historic sites, the numbers of faunal remains from each context or strata group should be added to this category. The kitchen category from the Persen House site has been subdivided into several categories, one of which is artifacts used for serving and eating, such as spoons, knives, forks, and bone handles (all eating utensils). These items totaled 23, or 60.5%, of the kitchen-related items.

Glassware was subdivided into seven large groups. Of the 847 nonarchitectural glass items, the majority was olive-green wine/liquor/beer glass, which amounted to 336, or 39.6%, of the glass total. "Other glass," representing a combination of functions, totaled 314, or 37.1%. When all of the subcategories relating to the storage and consumption of alcoholic beverages (i.e., wine/liquor/beer, case bottle, *roemer*, drinking glasses) are added together, the total was 464, or 54.8%, of the total nonarchitectural glass. Lamp chimney glass comprised 45, or 5.31%, of the total. Fragments of the *roemers* found in and outside of the Persen House are shown in figure 5.16, and an intact *roemer* from the Corning Museum of Glass is shown in figure 4.7 for comparison.

Figure 5.16. Persen House. Waldglas. Top, left to right: coiled foot fragment (7.168), body/foot fragment (13.151). Bottom, left to right: raspberry prunt (9.102), two plain prunts (2.10; 5.30). *Source:* Photo by the author.

The second largest category within the kitchen group of artifacts was ceramics. During the ceramic analysis, a list of crossmends, or fragments that matched up and represent one item, was made. A total of 18 ceramic vessels and two tiles were found to have crossmends or related fragments, with the majority being early 17th through mid-18th-century examples. This is not because these fragments were more numerous but simply that more time was spent on the earlier materials rather than the well-known pearlwares and transfer-printed whitewares of the 18th and 19th centuries.

The ceramics were divided into several large groupings reflecting ware type. These are tin-glazed buff-bodied earthenwares, which were subdivided into delft and majolica based on descriptions of the ware types in Wilcoxen (1987a, 1987b). A total of 22 majolica and 148 delftware fragments were found at the Persen House. Specific examples included a blue and white majolica charger (Vessel 16; fig. 5.17, left group), another majolica charger (fig. 5.17, right), multiple small delft fragments with

Figure 5.17. Persen House. Tin-glazed earthenwares. Six fragments on left, (Vessel #16), from a majolica charger. On right, majolica fragment (4.58). *Source:* Photo by the author.

blue and polychrome decoration (fig. 5.18), and several delft plates with two thin blue lines (fig. 5.19). Two delft tiles, both manganese in color, were assigned numbers 19 and 20, even though they are architectural in nature, in order to keep track of them. Both were probably used around the jambless Dutch fireplace in the eastern end of the Phase 3 portion of the Persen House.

The majority of tin-glazed buff-bodied earthenwares originated from Strata Groups 5 and 6, the two fill layers above the burn layer but below the clay/mortar floor. A total of 96, or 56.5%, of the 170 fragments found were from these two groups. The next largest occurrence of tin-glazed wares was from Strata Group 11, where 14 delft (but no majolica) fragments were found.

Figure 5.18. Persen House. Tin-glazed earthenwares. Top row: blue and white decorated (13.156; 12.135; 4.38). Middle row: blue and white decorated (12.157; 4.16; 13.151). Bottom row, two blue and white (13.149; 13.134), and polychrome delft (9.94). *Source:* Photo by the author.

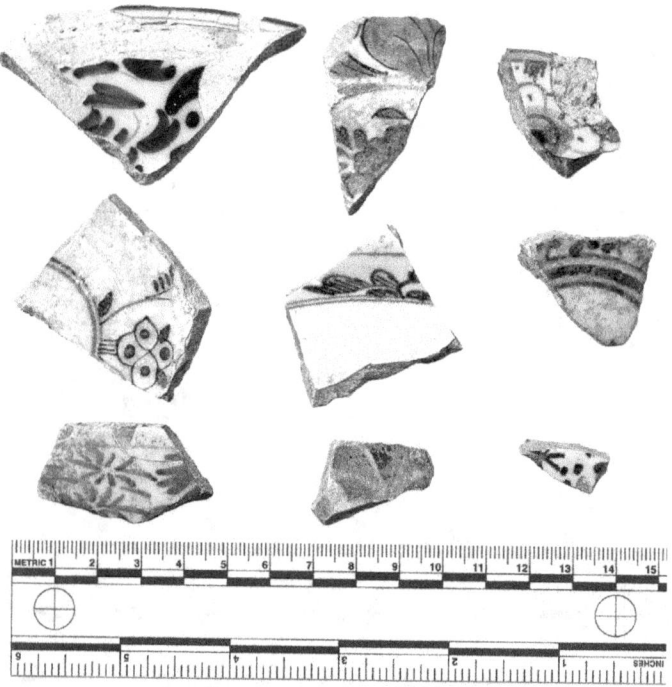

Figure 5.19. Persen House. Tin-glazed earthenwares. Top: white with two blue lines (12.159). Bottom: white with two blue lines (Vessel #6: 4.56). *Source:* Photo by the author.

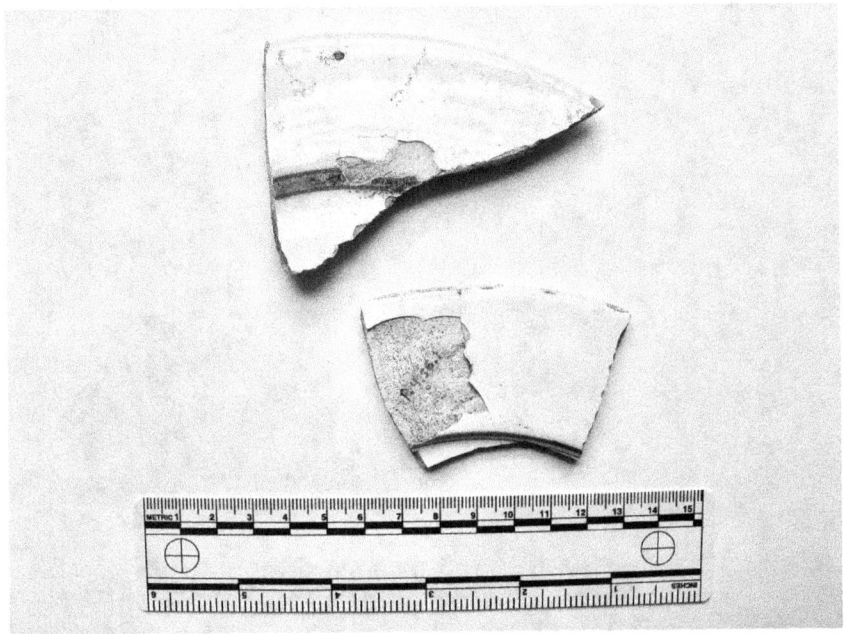

The stoneware category (fig. 5.20) was divided in the catalog into as many fine distinctions as possible. For the big picture, however, these have been tabulated by the following categories: Frechen/Tigerware, Westerwald, white salt-glazed stoneware, gray salt-glazed stoneware, and "other" (a compressed category). Of the 11 Frechen fragments, 4 (36.4%) were found in Strata Groups 5 and 6. Two fragments that crossmended (Vessel 5; fig. 5.20, lower right, one fragment shown) depict part of a medallion, although it is just the edge and is barely diagnostic. This vessel, if it was in one piece, would probably have been a "Bellarmine" or *Bartmannkrügge*.

Like the Frechen stoneware, a similar distribution is observable when one views the Westerwald ceramics. Here, two of the three examples were also found in Strata Groups 5 and 6. A ceramic similar to Westerwald was Vessel 1 (fig. 5.20), a gray salt-glazed stoneware plate similar to that excavated at the Louw-Bogardus house in Kingston (see Huey 1981, 9).

Figure 5.20. Persen House. Stonewares. Left: Vessel #1, salt glazed stoneware plate (9.91; 6.41). Center: Westerwald fragment (13.150). Far right: two Bartmankrügge, top (2.10), and bottom showing portion of medallion (8.86). *Source:* Photo by the author.

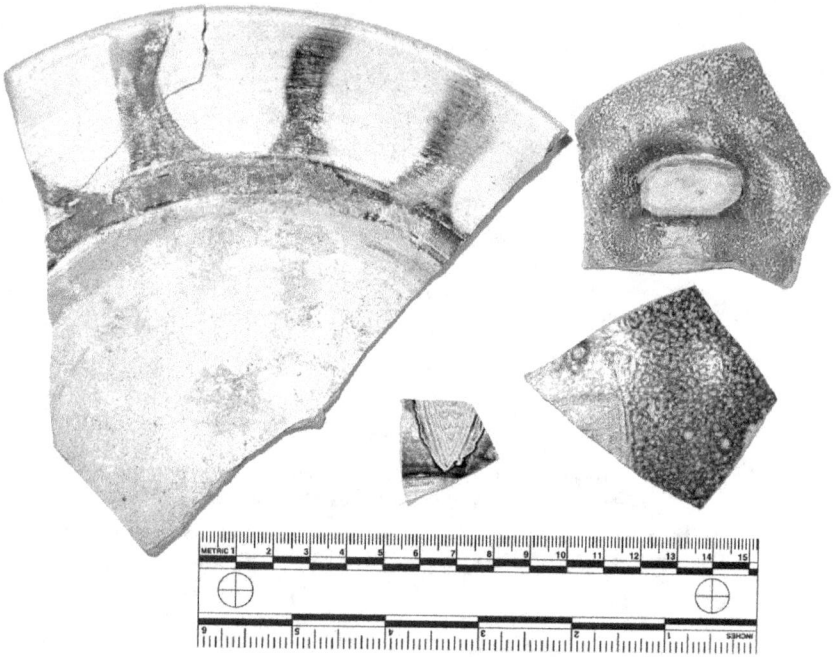

Historical archaeologist Meta Janowitz (personal communication, 1999) has suggested that these pieces may be from the Crolius factory in New York City.

One interesting category is white salt-glazed stoneware, which was developed c. 1720 (Miller et al. 2000) but became more common c. 1740 as molded examples became popular. This ware peaked in Strata Group 2, the loose soil between the floor joists, which would fit well with the clay mortar floor below it being installed c. 1735.

Several kinds of porcelain were compressed into one category. A total of 92 fragments were found at the Persen House, most of which (49 or 53.3%) came from Strata Group 2, the soil above the clay/mortar floor and between the floor joists.

Slip-decorated buff-bodied earthenwares (usually combed) make up a sizable portion of the late 17th- and 18th-century ceramics from the site. Combed and trailed vessels (fig. 5.21 and 5.22) accounted for 318 fragments, most of which were probably small pots or porringers (fig. 5.22). Vessels 8 and 9 represent these types. A second grouping, similar vessels with brown or yellow dots (fig. 5.22), accounted for 26 fragments. Plates and charger fragments amounted to 133 fragments. Crossmends among the ceramics allowed for the partial reconstruction of several interesting small plates/chargers. Vessel crossmends indicate a trailed slip-decorated plate (Vessel 10; fig. 5.21, right), four bat-molded plate/chargers (Vessels 11, 12, 13, 15; fig. 5.23), and a bat-molded charger or trencher (Vessel 14; fig. 5.23, right). The construction technique for the manufacture of bat-molded ceramics is illustrated in Orr (2003), and the date of c. 1725–1750 is provided by Noël Hume (1970, fig. 29). These were identified and separated by the Munsell color of the main slip.

The buff-bodied slip-decorated earthenwares occurred predominately in six strata groups. These are the mixed Strata Group 1 (53 fragments); Strata Group 2, the soil between the floor joists (112 fragments); Strata

Figure 5.21. Persen House. Slip-decorated buff-bodied earthenware. Plate/chargers with pie-crust edge. Left (13.150). Right example is Vessel #10. *Source:* Photo by the author.

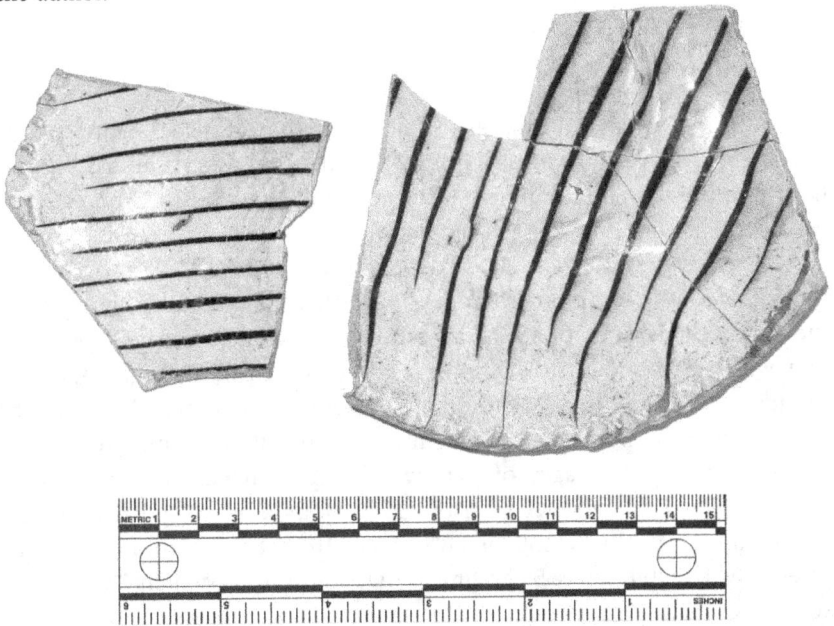

Figure 5.22. Persen House. Slip-decorated buff-bodied earthenware. Tankards, plates, and porringers. Top row (4.90; 9.102; 13.149; 6.43). Middle row and bottom left (6.43; 6.43; 9.95). Bottom right porringer or posset pot, Vessel #9 (10.98; 13.134). *Source:* Photo by the author.

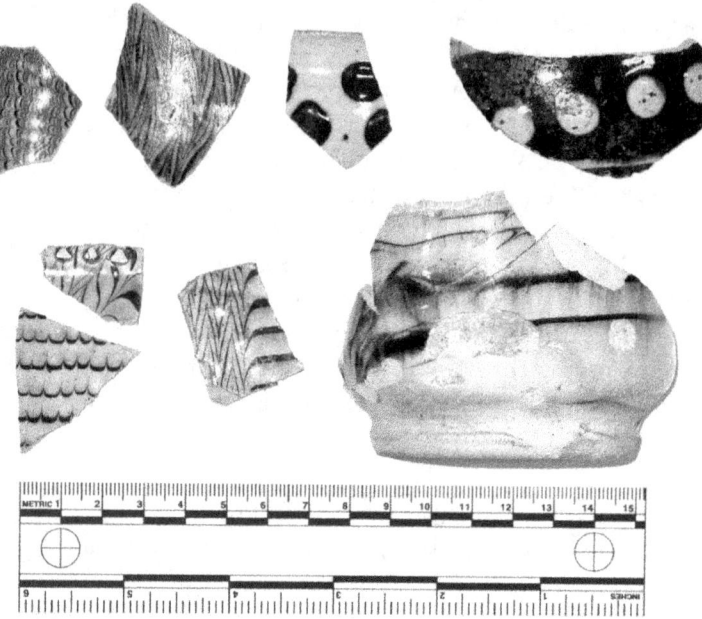

Group 3, the walls and builder's trenches of the Phase 3 portion of the house (55 fragments); Strata Groups 5 and 6, between the clay/mortar floor and burn level (combined-139 fragments); and Strata Group 17, the yard deposits in Unit 14 (92 fragments).

Creamware (1762–1820) and pearlware (1780–1840), two ceramic types that were very popular from the last half of the 18th-century until the first two decades of the 19th century, were each also grouped into one ware. A total of 181 various kinds of creamware fragments were found, most of which (111 or 61.3%) were from Strata Group 2, the soil between the floor joists. This kind of distribution is mirrored by the numbers and percentages of pearlware and whiteware (c. 1820–1900) from the Persen House. A total of 197 various kinds of pearlware were found, most of which (130 or 66%) were from Strata Group 2. For all categories of whiteware, 50 fragments were found, of which 31, or 62%, were found in Strata Group 2.

Figure 5.23. Persen House. Bat-molded wares. First two fragments on left: Vessel #11, charger/plate (9.96; 13.134). Center, left: Vessel #12, charger/plate (10.103). Center, right: Vessel #13, charger/plate (5.25). Two frags at right: Vessel #14, charger/trencher (9.95; 6.62). *Source:* Photo by the author.

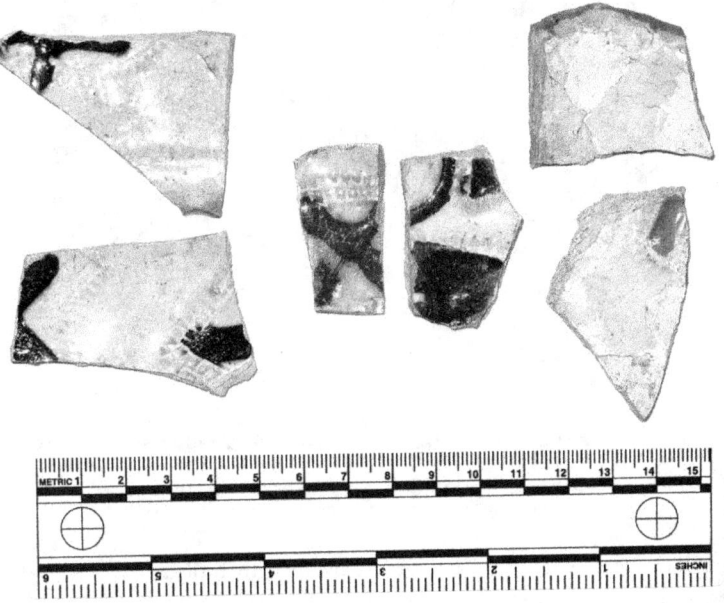

Redwares were sorted into 10 categories: clear-glazed/mottled, slip-decorated chargers/plates, ginger colored glaze, brown/black/brownish green glaze, Jackfield type, green glaze, green/yellow and white slipped Dutch whiteware, "Hoogeboom redware," and Buckley-ware. These are represented in the crossmend list by Vessel 2, a large pan (fig. 5.24); Vessel 4, a speckled milk pan; and Vessel 7, a probable Hoogeboom red earthenware vessel (fig. 5.25). The latter is one of only two or three known to date, with the others being from excavations at the Senate House and on Clinton Avenue. The three Hoogeboom pots are the only ceramic products (other than bricks and maybe pan tiles) that were manufactured in 17th-century *Wiltwyck*. Most of the red earthenwares in the black to brownish black to brownish green category are *kookpotten* fragments (fig. 5.26). It should be noted that the term *kookpot* is used in the text because it remains uncertain which of the ceramics are English (in which case they would be called a *pipkin*) and which are of Dutch manufacture

The Matthewis Persen House | 261

Figure 5.24. Persen House. Large red earthenware pan. Vessel #2 (4.34). *Source:* Photo by the author.

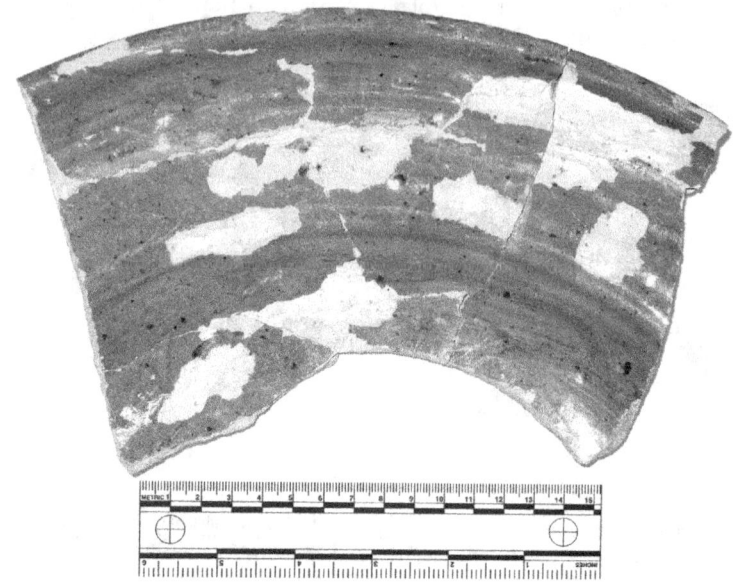

Figure 5.25. Persen House. Unglazed redware with tooled decoration. Probably made by Cornelius Hoogeboom. Vessel #7 (12.159; 13.148; 11.124; 13.151; 9.102; 5.33). *Source:* Photo by the author.

Figure 5.26. Persen House. Red earthenwares. Top row: three kookpot rim fragments (13.134; 5.10; 14.178). Center row, left to right: two kookpot rim fragments (14.175; 14.176), kookpot foot fragment (14.176). Bottom: kookpot handle (7.170). *Source:* Photo by the author.

(Janowitz 1993; Janowitz et al 1985; Janowitz and Schaefer 2019; Janowitz and Schaefer 2021). In either case, the description is of a small-handled vessel with an outflaring lip, often with three feet, that can be kept on a hearth or used to heat food on a hearth (figs. 5.26 and 5.27). Those that do not have feet may either be pans for food or chamber pots. Based on the small size of the fragments from the Persen House, it is difficult to differentiate. The Buckley-ware, dating c. 1720–1783, is represented by only one fragment from the site. Buff-white earthenwares were not particularly common, with several examples being found (fig. 5.28). Other related ceramics include one piece of an Iberian storage jar and one burned piece of buff-white earthenware.

SHELLFISH

The shellfish category from the Persen House site consisted of mussel, clam, oyster, marine gastropod, scallop, and snail. This category is import-

Figure 5.27. Persen House. Nonprovenienced artifacts. Top row, left to right: yellow- and brown-glazed kookpot handle, kookpot rim fragment, slip-decorated, buff-bodied earthenware bowl/plate with piecrust edge. Bottom row, left to right: kookpot foot fragment, green-glazed buff/salmon bodied earthenware, "EB" (Edward Bird) pipe fragment. *Source:* Photo by the author.

ant because it relates to the discussion by Bridges (1974) regarding the presence of shellfish at Clinton Avenue (see chapter 4). At the Persen House site, a total of 1,426 shellfish and shellfish fragments were found, which comprises 11.9% of the total (see table 5.1). Shellfish were found in every strata group except for two (i.e., Strata Groups 10 and 12) and were primarily from Strata Groups 2 ($n = 376$), 5 ($n = 226$), and 6 ($n = 236$). Strata Group 2 was the loose soil above the clay/mortar floor and probably dates post-1730–1735, and this might represent the tailor shop of Cornelius and Adam Persen. Strata Groups 5 and 6 were two portions of a deep deposit that overlaid the 1663 burn layer and was capped by the clay/mortar floor. The combined shellfish totals from Strata Groups 5 and 6 was 462 fragments, or 34.6% of the total shellfish from the site.

An interesting trend is the small quantity of shellfish from Strata Group 12, which had none, to Strata Group 11, which had only 7. The

Figure 5.28. Persen House. Earthenwares. Top row, left to right: clear-glazed redware with speckles (4.58), green-glazed buff earthenware (13.151), brown-glazed redware (8.85). Center row, left to right: yellow-glazed redware (14.177), two green-glazed buff earthenware (9.102; 13.151), yellow-glazed buff earthenware (13.151), Bottom row, left to right: brown-glazed red earthenware (9.100), green-glazed buff earthenware (11.123), yellow-glazed buff earthenware (13.151). *Source*: Photo by the author.

small quantity of shellfish evident prior to June 7, 1663, may only be a result of negative evidence. This is due to the small volume of soil (in features) that predate the fire. The area to the south of the curtain wall was relatively bereft of most European artifacts. Even the palisade trench (Strata Group 8) contained just 16 shellfish fragments, only one of which was a whole oyster. The increase in quantity can be observed in Strata Groups 5 and 6, which begins just above the burn layer (Strata Group 6) and continues above it (Strata Group 5). Although I have stated that there is no indication of a buried A-horizon soil here, this leads one to believe that this is midden debris from around the Phase 2 portion of the house, prior to its excavation. Strata Group 6, the deepest of the two, yielded 236 fragments (16.5% of total), of which 28 were whole oysters and two were whole clams. Just above this, Strata Group 5 yielded a total of 226

(15.8% of total) shellfish fragments, of which 33 were whole oysters and three were whole clams. Strata Group 2, the loose soil between the floor joists and just above the clay/mortar floor, was the most productive, with a total of 376 shellfish fragments (26.4% of total). Of these, 79 were whole oysters and 11 were whole clams.

The presence of large amounts of shellfish on the site, as previously noted, is a reflection of the Dutch love of oysters and clams. The question is, why are the quantities low in Strata Group 12 (pre–June 7, 1663) and Strata Group 11 (the burn layer)? As mentioned above, one factor might be location, particularly for Strata Group 12. For Strata Group 11, it might relate to volume of soil excavated, especially when compared to the deep and large deposits in Strata Groups 6 and 5 immediately above it. Strata Group 6, dating from post-1663 to c. 1730–1735, and Strata Group 5, which probably postdates 1730–1735, contained much larger amounts of shellfish. This is probably related to several factors: (1) popularity of shellfish for food, (2) possible use of burned shellfish for lime mortar, (3) the possible use of shell in animal fodder as a food supplement as utilized in the North Atlantic countries (T. Amorosi, personal communication, 2002), and (4) potential reuse of clam shells (*Mercenaria*) for wampum making. Although I have not examined the 18th-century documentary record in great detail, Pena (1990, 106) pointed to wampum manufacture in downtown Albany as late as 1750. As mentioned elsewhere in this chapter, the analysis of the *Mercenaria* fragments consisted of a comparison of the pieces, on a bag-by-bag basis as well as by strata group, with Burggraf's (1938) and Pena's (1990) discussions of wampum manufacture. None of the shell fragments conform to the typical pattern of shell breakage, reduction, grinding, and perforation associated with wampum manufacture, nor were any fragments of this process encountered.

The apparent discrepancy between the archaeological record and the documentary record, as noted by Bridges (1974), probably has several explanations, not the least of which is the mundane nature of shellfish as a category of data. In terms of popularity, oysters ($n = 1,078$) are more than three times more common than clams ($n = 311$) in gross total. When compared by whole examples from the excavation, the disparity increases markedly. A total of 227 whole oysters were found in the deposits compared with only 27 whole clams. This is more than an 8:1 ratio, which is likely an indication of a preference for oysters rather than clams. A distant third are mussels ($n = 29$), with scallops barely represented ($n = 4$). For convenience, I have lumped three other critters into see table 5.1:

coral, marine gastropod, and snail. The coral was probably picked up by enslaved individuals who originated further south, either coming from the Caribbean or areas south of North Carolina, which appears to be the northernmost limit for marine coral. Like the Senate House, the Persen House is one of two locations in *Wiltwyck* with evidence of artifacts that were likely owned and manipulated by enslaved individuals (2). These items were probably used as charms, jewelry, or gifts that may be associated with the ocean or water spirits or deities.

ARCHITECTURE

Artifacts from the architecture group provide us with some insight regarding early architectural details at the Persen House (table 5.1). Several categories of these items were identified during the excavations, with the largest categories being roofing or pan tiles, bricks, window glass, tiles, nails, and furniture-related parts.

Roofing or Pan Tiles

Evidence of roofing materials from the Persen House site originated from Strata Groups 5, 6, and 7 in the form of three or four unglazed red earthenware roofing or pan tiles.[3] These are similar to tiles found at the Senate House, Fort Orange, and most of the earlier sites in New Amsterdam. They have a lug that hooks under the purlin, a horizontal slat attached to the rafters, with an S-curve to overlap the adjacent tile. This is a common roofing material across most of Europe, especially the Low Countries. Although it is difficult to say for certain, the roofing tiles probably postdate the burning of *Wiltwyck* on June 7, 1663, even though there is ample evidence for plant-based roofing materials well after that. For example, in an ordinary session on January 26, 1666, it was stated that "the hon. schout proposes the necessity for this village that every house, covered with reed, straw or boards shall keep a fire-ladder near its chimney" (Christoph et al. 1976, 1:275). This suggests that although pan tiles may have been used, it is clear that other forms of roofing were still utilized. The roofing tiles were likely from the original roof of the Phase 1 structure. When the fireplace, probably a jambless, was moved from the east wall of the Phase 1 structure to the north wall, it is quite possible that several roofing tiles were broken in the process. A jambless fireplace has no sides, or jambs, as we are accustomed to. It is entirely open and the bricks that make up the chimney are supported by the rafter above the hearth, and the chimney extends up through the second floor and through the roof.

Dutch Red Bricks

Many of the roofing tile fragments were found in destruction rubble associated with a pile of small red Dutch bricks fragments.[4] Most of the whole bricks that would have originated from this deposit were likely collected and reused. The only whole or almost-whole bricks originated from Strata Groups 5, 6, and 7 and numbered only eight in total, again a good indication that the chimney fall was robbed and that the bricks were reused. The destruction rubble overlying the palisade trench in Strata Group 7 accounted for 33.2 kg (or 73 lb), whereas Strata Groups 5 and 6 together yielded 161.1 kg (or 354.5 lb), of brick debris. The 29.4 kg of brick debris associated with Strata Group 4 can also be added to this, as this count is primarily from disturbed areas and not the actual clay/mortar matrix. In total, 279.25 kg (or 613.4 lb) of small red Dutch brick were weighed and discarded. These small red Dutch bricks are the same as those found outside in Units 1 and 2. The bricks appear to fall into two minor variations. One is 3⅜ wide × 1⅜ thick × 7¼ inches long. The other is 3⅛ wide × 1¼ thick × 6⅞ inches long. Because these are handmade bricks, some variation is expected. Although describing the English method of brick making, Hutton (2003, 16) provided a visual picture of the process that is probably not that different than the Dutch method: "Before molding began, the surface of the mold was wetted and dusted with sand ['sanded'] in order to prevent adhesion of the clay. A molder shoved an eight-to-nine pound lump of clay into the mold, thoroughly forcing it into the corners and then 'struck off' the top of the mold to remove excess material." It is possible, and indeed probable, that this procedure produced slight or marked differences in the size of red Dutch bricks. When combined with the shrinkage, and sometimes twist associated with firing, this might account for the slight variation in brick size. These small bricks were used for the jambless fireplace in the Phase 1 portion of the house and can be found in the rubble in Phase 3. This type of brick has also been found at the Senate House, Clinton Avenue, in Hurley, and in excavations on Huguenot Street in New Paltz. The latter were probably transported from *Wiltwyck* to New Paltz for construction purposes after 1678, where they were used primarily for chimneys or ovens.

As previously noted, the small amounts of charcoal associated with the early brick rubble in the Persen House do not indicate a burn level. Rather, the charcoal flecks, and even small deposits, were probably the result of soot attached to the bricks. During the robbing and removal process, the soot was likely knocked off and created a few small bands in the soil as well as charcoal-flecked soil deposits.

The production of bricks in *Niew Netherland* was very important, if only to initially line chimneys. Venema (2003, 89–91) documented several brickmakers and tilemakers as early as 1630 at Fort Orange and extending until the mid-1660s. At Fort Orange, this endeavor was required because of the mandated change from straw to tile roofs, and it was also profitable due to the rich clay deposits in the area. During the construction of Dominie Blom's house at *Wiltwyck* in 1661, the need for 6,000 bricks was directed by Stuyvesant to Fort Orange, where Vice Director La Montagne reported that he had to purchase two groups of 3,000 to fill the order, apparently from New Amsterdam (Fernow 1881, 213). Between Fort Orange and New Amsterdam, there quickly appeared a market for building material. Cornelius Hoogeboom likely filled this void. The following was noted at an ordinary session recorded in the *Wiltwyck* court minutes of Tuesday January 20, 1665: "Cornelis Pietersen Hoogeboom requests that he may be granted a lot opposite the mill dam for a brick yard. The hon. court grants petitioners request and decides to grant him a lot of about ½ *morgen* in extent" (Christoph et al. 1976, 1:198). His output would have been the small red bricks that are now called "Hudson Valley flats," which were constructed to imitate the yellow Dutch examples of which he was familiar but were still several decades prior to the regulations to standardize the size of bricks. It also is possible that Hoogeboom provided more to the community than simply bricks. At an ordinary session on November 1st, 1667, Hoogeboom, as plaintiff, demanded of Reyner Van Coelen "11½ schepels of wheat for delivered stone and for wages" (Christoph et al. 1976, 1:369). This was probably local Onondaga limestone from the formations to the west of the stockade area in uptown Kingston. Hoogeboom may have been supplying this for basement or wall construction, particularly the gable ends of houses. From descriptions quoted and illustrated in Venema (2003), many of the extant houses that appear in paintings or descriptions of Fort Orange had stone and brick gable ends, with the long walls composed of clapboards. On April 25, 1671, at an ordinary session, Cornelius Hoogeboom requested "to be granted a lot to build a house on, across the dam near his brickyard, because there is a convenient place there," and his request was granted (Christoph et al. 1976, 459). It appears that his brickyard of over slightly one acre (½ *morgen*) was doing well enough to exhaust its resources within seven years. On April 1, 1672, at an extraordinary session, Hoogeboom requested "a lot for making brick, across the dam," and he was granted "as much soil as is necessary for house and lot and a brick yard, across the dam" (Christoph et al. 1976, 481).

After 1665, Hoogeboom was probably *the* producer of small red Dutch bricks for *Wiltwyck* as well as Hurley and, later, New Paltz. It should also be noted that in my excavation of over 1,000 square meters on Huguenot Street in New Paltz, not one fragment of small yellow Dutch brick was identified. This would further indicate the shift from yellow imported bricks to red local production between 1661 (the first *Wiltwyck* expansion) and 1677–1678, when the Huguenots settled in New Paltz. Hoogeboom is also probably the producer of the abovementioned unglazed redware vessel or *Schüsselkachel* (fig. 5.25), which appears to have a very limited distribution, being confined solely to the stockade area.

A total of 17 fragments of green-glazed brick were also found. These clustered (11 out of 17) in Strata Groups 5 and 6 and may indicate decorative elements on the Phase 1 chimney or gable end of the house.

Dutch or Flemish Yellow Bricks

One type of brick that was not found in any of the excavation units at the Persen House is the small yellow Dutch brick. Writing in 1726, Neve stated,

> Dutch or Flemish Bricks. I am informed by one that they are 6 and ¼ n. 2 and ½ broad and 1 and ¼ thick; another tells me that they are 6 n. long 3 n. broad, and 1 n. thick, as for my own part, I never measured any of them. They are of a yellowish Color. The Paveing with these Bricks, is neater and stronger than common. They must be layed in sand. They are commonly used here in England, to pave Yards and Stables withal, and they make a good Pavement, and are very lasting, and being laid edge-ways, look handsomely, especially if laid Herring-bone fashion. They are also used in Soapboilers Fats, and in making of Cisterns. (Neve [1726] 1969, 40)

These yellow bricks have been found in only two locations within the Stockade at *Wiltwyck*: at the Senate House (Feister and Sopko 2003, 11–21) and across from the Senate House on Clinton Avenue (Bridges 1974). This may be the case for several reasons. The first is that the northeast corner of the stockade is a portion of the earliest constructed and occupied portion of the stockade c. 1658, and as part of this early construction, the settlers used imported yellow Dutch bricks from either New Amsterdam or Fort Orange. It is doubtful that the bricks produced at Fort Orange (as discussed above) were yellow.

Yellow bricks have also been found in much larger quantities at Fort Orange and New Amsterdam. Their presence in large numbers at these two sites is related to easy access by water, a characteristic that *Wiltwyck* did not share with either of these two ports. Moving these bricks to *Wiltwyck* would have entailed off-loading them at the Strand near the mouth of the Rondout Creek and transporting them up present-day Foxhall Avenue and then down present-day Albany Avenue to the stockade area.

These small yellow bricks are generally thought to have been used for two purposes: as ballast in ships coming from the Netherlands and as an important building material prior to the establishment of brickmaking activities in *Niew Netherland*. Their absence at the Persen House may relate to the fact that it is more recent than the Senate House as well as the fact that by the time the Persen House was under construction, Cornelius Hoogeboom may have had his brickworks up and running.

Windows

Architectural glass from the Persen House included three types of window glass; early, deep aquamarine window glass; aqua, or later, window glass; and crown glass. From the glass assemblage from the site, we can get a glimpse of the kind of windows used in the earliest phase of the Persen House. One fragment of turned lead, also known as lead caming, was found.[5] Neve ([1726] 1969, 92) described these as "the small slender Rods of Cast-lead, of which the Glaziers make their turn d Lead. For their Lead being cast into slender Rods, of some 12 or 14 Inches long each, is called the *came* (and sometimes they call each of those Rods a *came*) which being afterwards drawn though their Vice, makes their turn'd Lead." During the turning process, a stamp was sometimes used to emboss the manufacturer and date. For example, Kenyon and Fitzgerald (1986, 35, plates 47 and 48) documented two maker's marks from Fort Albany in northern Ontario: "W.M. W.W. 1673" and "W*1690*D*P*."

The small fragment of turned lead points to the use of lead casement windows similar to those seen in Dutch genre paintings, as mentioned above. Although only one fragment of turned lead was found, the lack of more could be the result of the metal being scavenged and reduced to either musket balls or fishing weights.

Within casement windows in the 17th century were glass quarrels or panes. Several fragmentary examples were found in the Persen House excavations, although none were complete. The window quarrels have one dimension of 8.9 cm (3½ in), but there were no whole pieces to help determine length. The glass is of a deep aquamarine to greenish-aquamarine glass, which would be the same as used for making the common *roemer* or *passglass*. Throughout the cataloging process, it was noted that some of the window glass was early, or 17th century, and some was later, or 19th century. This was evident by both the color, with earlier glass being a deeper aqua or greenish aqua, and the greater degree of devitrification of the earlier glass. Later glass was often a clear to light aquamarine glass and had only a slight degree of glass patina. "Devitrification" and "patina" refer to the breakdown of the glass into small flakes, which eventually fall off.

Typically, the examination of window glass from domestic excavations provides only raw counts relating to breakage; however, at the Persen House, there was evidence of crown glass on site. Crown glass is a large pizza-like glass object from which individual window quarrels were cut. The size of the quarrel depends, of course, on the kind and design of the casement or sash being used in the window (Wilson 1976). At the Persen House excavations, seven fragments of crown glass were recovered, all of which originated from the outside edge or "crust" of the glass "pizza." This suggests that crowns were being transported to the site and then cut by a glazier to fit the windows. Six of the seven fragments were from Strata Groups 5 and 6. There were no fragments of the "bulls-eye" or middle of the glass crown where the pontil mark is located.

Tiles

Relating to both the kitchen and the architecture group were red earthenware hearth tiles and buff-bodied tin-glazed earthenware tiles. The former tiles cover a hearth and provide a fireproof insulation to protect the wooden joists under the floor. Typically, red earthenware tiles sit on, or are mortared into, stone or soil rubble in the arch built from the basement wall beneath the chimney. The arch is attached to the first-floor joist out into the room parallel to the wall. These tiles are often characterized as having a smooth, worn patina from use as well as slightly rounded edges. Only four red earthenware hearth tile fragments were found. Their distribution is not as informative as the delft tiles, as they occurred in Strata Groups 3 ($n = 1$), 4 ($n = 2$), and 5 ($n = 1$). Interestingly, each of these strata groups dated post-1730–1735, which suggests that the tiles might have been the hearth of the Phase 1 jambless fireplace, which would have been destroyed when the house was reoriented and expanded when Cornelius and Adam Persen acquired it.

Tin-glazed buff-bodied earthenware tiles with manganese decoration were also found at the Persen House (fig. 5.29). This kind of decoration began in the early 18th century (J. Baart personal communication, October 8, 2004), and consequently, I have dated them post-1700. These tiles are often thought of as surrounding only the fireplace, but they are often used as a decorative border above the floor moldings, thus providing an attractive

Figure 5.29. Persen House. Tin-glazed, buff-bodied earthenware tiles. On left, three frags that mend to form ceramic Vessel #19 (9.91; 13.134; 12.132), a tile. Upper right, ceramic Vessel #20 (7.76; 4.18), a tile. Other fragments do not mend. Note red paint on tiles. *Source:* Photo by the author.

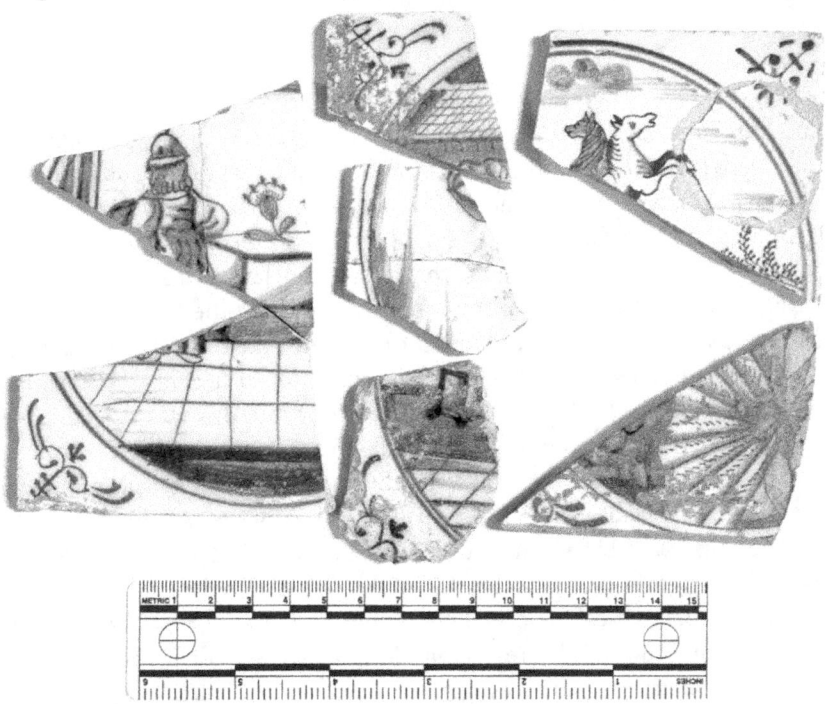

series of small vignettes surrounding the inside a room. Excavations on the inside of the Persen House yielded a total of eight fragments of manganese-decorated delft tile from three or four individual tiles. Based on this low number, it is probably safe to say that these were used only around the fireplaces rather than a combination of fireplace and molding decoration. Given the amount of reconstruction that occurred during the Phase 3 portion of the Persen House, these tiles probably came from the fireplace in that portion of the house. They were all found in Strata Group 2, scattered throughout the soils between the floor joists and the clay/mortar floor. It is probable that these were the tiles surrounding the fireplace, which were spread out during the destruction of the fireplace and then reconstruction of the floor during the 1922 remodeling of the room. Attached to several of the tiles was red paint similar in color to burnt umber or Venetian red, suggesting the color of the wooden moldings or the fireplace surround used to attach them to the wall (see fig. 5.29).

One partial blue-and-white tile was also found during construction activities in the yard area outside the Persen House. This tile had been reduced in size, ground down, and reused, perhaps around the jambless fireplace in the Phase 1 portion of the house.

Nails

Another large architectural category was nails. The three groupings of nails were handwrought (277, or 9.5% of total architectural), machine-cut (196 or 6.72), and unidentifiable (772 or 26.5%). As for most categories of architectural artifacts, Strata Group 2 yielded the largest count of nails ($n = 294$). Unidentifiable nails comprised the largest category mainly because, archaeologically, nails commonly appear in the form of bulbous iron lumps rather than typical straight nails. In some cases, a slight tap on the metal will allow enough surface encrustation to fall off to determine manufacturing method; in most instances, however, this was not the case.

Due to the large amount of construction activity in the Phase 3 portion of the house, modern wire nails were not saved, nor were small fragments of copper pipe, lead welding fragments, and bits of metal associated with 20th-century plumbing. Almost all of these occurred in the loose, dry dust between the floor joists, and most were probably associated with construction activities during rehabilitation of the building by the county.

Iron building hardware such as straps (possibly for hinges), pintles, and a general category including screws, hooks, eyes, and so on, are also included in the architectural grouping in table 5.1. Iron strap fragments totaled 10, most of which were from Strata Group 2. Three pintles were found, two of which came from Strata Groups 5 and 6. These may relate to changes in door locations or the adding or removal of Dutch-style doors.

Furniture

The furniture group was not well represented at the Persen House, as only three items were recovered. This might be due to several factors. The first is the longevity of furniture as opposed to smaller, more fragile items such as glass and ceramic. The second is that for most of its use-life, the Phase 3 portion of the house had a floor that would prohibit large items from entering the archaeological record. The third is that most of the items in a Dutch household would have been probated and then sold to local people who needed those items (see Gysbert van Imbroch's probate list [Christoph et al. 1976, 2:566–71] and compare with sold items [Christoph et al. 1976, 2:571–75]).

Arms Group

The arms category included all items of material culture associated with community defense and hunting. Of the 26 arms-related items found (table 5.1), perhaps the most visible archaeologically were four cannonballs. One was found in Unit 4 and three were found as a group in Unit 5, in the builder's trench for the south wall of the Phase 3 portion of the Persen House. Colonel Paul Alexander of the West Point Museum measured several of the balls and found that these varied from approximately 2.994 to 3.073 inches in size. An English four pounder is 3.053 inches in diameter, and this measurement is also similar to Dutch cannons of the period. Col. Alexander (personal communication, February 25, 2003) suggested that there would have been no difference between the English and Dutch guns, which would make a standard-sized cannonball usable in either.

The most numerically preponderant item from the arms category was gunflints (fig. 5.30), which can be divided into two types: English spall-type gunflints and French flake-technique gunflints. Each of these differs in terms of flint coloration and manufacture. English spall gunflints ranged from black to mottled black to gray. French gunflints are honey colored. A total of six English gunflints (23.07% of the arms category) and seven French gunflints (27% of the arms category) were recovered from the Persen House excavations and seemed to be rather evenly distributed among Strata Groups 2, 3, 6, 7, and 8.

Figure 5.30. Persen House. Arms group. Top row: five gunflints (4.18; 5.30; 9.116; 7.74; 7.74). Bottom row: four gunflints (10.112; 4.23; 12.133; 7.142). *Source:* Photo by the author.

Three musket balls were also found at the Persen House in Units 4, 5, and 10. These were not terribly diagnostic, as guns can be used for an extended period of time. The ivory whistle found underneath the stairs (fig. 5.31) could be included in the arms group because whistles were often used to signal a warning or attack. However, the whistle is not included in the tabulation of this category because it lacks provenience. Sulfur has been included in this category because it is an ingredient used in the manufacture of gunpowder. Paul Huey and Joseph McEvoy informed me (personal communication, June 11, 2003) that sulfur was also used during the historic period for fumigation purposes.

More recent arms-related artifacts included four 22-caliber shell casings and the brass from a shotgun shell. The former dated post-1846, while the latter dated post-1850 (Miller et al. 2000, 14). Four of the five were found in Strata Group 2, the loose soil between the floor joists and above the clay/mortar floor.

Figure 5.31. Persen House. Arms group/personal. Ivory whistle (found near stairwell). *Source:* Photo by the author.

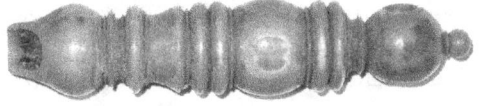

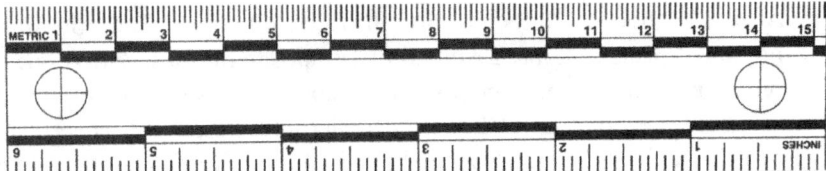

Clothing

The clothing category on most domestic sites is normally not large. South's (1977, 126–27) quantities for houses from 18th-century Brunswick, South Carolina, for example, ranged from about 0.3% to 0.6% of the total artifact inventory. However, at Brunswick, the Public House–Tailor shop yielded 5,574 artifacts from the clothing group, or 13.1% of the total from the site. The Persen House falls somewhere in between, with 612 artifacts from the clothing category (5.1% of the total), of which 341, or 55.7%, were pins. This number may have been larger if a smaller mesh size was used while screening soils during the excavations.

Of the 20 strata groups, five did not produce any artifacts from the clothing category (table 5.1). The strata group with the largest quantity of artifacts related to clothing and tailoring was Strata Group 2, the loose soil between the floor joists and above the clay mortar floor. Photographs 51 and 52 illustrate tailoring-related artifacts from two contexts within this strata group. The 340 artifacts from this strata group represent 55.6% of all of the artifacts from the site relating to tailoring. This indicates that (1) the clay/mortar floor was probably overlaid by the wooden floorboards of the Phase 3 addition, and (2) that it probably postdated 1735 to c. 1769 when Cornelius and Adam Persen were both engaged in tailoring at the house. Because no evidence of fire (i.e., charcoal, burned nails) was observed between the clay/mortar floor and the surface of the soil below the floor joists, this would also indicate that the Phase 3 portion of the Persen House was not burned in 1777. Although Matthewis Persen was on the list of "Sufferers" as having lost a house and barn to the British in October 1777, it is uncertain whether this was the house noted.

Since both Cornelius Persen and his brother Adam were tailors, the clothing category included a large sample of items relating to tailoring and clothing repair (fig. 5.32). From the total of 612 clothing-related items were 55 bone buttons and button-backs, 60 copper/brass buttons, 29 mother of pearl buttons, 21 metal or composite buttons, and 16 glass buttons. One artifact conspicuous for its absence was the bone button blank. These are portions of bone, normally long bones and ribs, from which buttons have been cut with the aid of a compass. They are then ground down and drilled with between one and five holes. The absence

Figure 5.32. Persen House. Tailoring. Top row: 32 pins and pin fragments. Second row, left to right: five metallic buttons, one clothing fastener, one pin. Third row, left to right: shell button, three glass buttons, 1 metallic button, 1 metallic button with glass insert, copper/brass thimble. Bottom row: eight bone buttons showing variations (all from context 13.134). *Source:* Photo by the author.

278 | The Archaeology of Kingston, New York

of button blanks indicates that Cornelius and Adam Persen had sources for bone buttons rather than manufacturing them in the house. Since many of the buttons may have functioned as bone button-backs, the back portion of the button attached to a metal decorative piece, these may have come with the buttons.

Bone button blanks, which are the processed rib bones from cattle, were also found in the uptown area at Clinton Avenue, where Bridges (1974) reported a total of nine, with one from an area associated with "debris from a burned wooden structure" and one from mixed strata supported by a late 19th-century retaining wall. This would suggest bone-button manufacturing somewhere near Clinton Avenue, with the possibility that the fragments may have originated from the Ten Broecks or Van Gaasbeeks, who occupied the Senate House.

Other artifacts relating to tailoring included 4 cufflinks, 5 decorative beads, 7 buckles, 7 thimbles, a pair of scissors, and 341 copper/brass straight pins. The straight pins constituted the largest number of any one type of artifact relating to tailoring. Their large number is partially a reflection of the kind of flooring used in the Phase 3 structure during the 18th century. Pins, buttons, and other items such as those found in Strata Group 2 would typically fall through cracks between ship-lapped floorboards, particularly if the floor joists were spaced far apart. Alternatively, these items would not fall through splined floorboards or, rarely, through tongue-in-groove flooring. Other artifacts from the clothing category included seven leather scrap and 25 shoe fragments, rolled copper wire for a clothing fastener, and a fancy pin.

Personal

Personal artifacts (fig. 5.33) are items associated with individual use. They can relate to various activities, such as personal hygiene (combs, toothbrush, mirror, syringes), bodily adornment (rings, bracelets, bodkins), education (slate pencils), personal and mobile alcohol consumption (pocket flasks), and utilitarian needs (a pocketknife and whetstone). They may also indicate the presence of children on site, such as doll or toy parts. A mouth harp that was found has been included in this functional category, although it could also have been placed in the recreation category.

A total of 68 personal artifacts were found in and around the Persen House. The most common personal items were copper/brass rings ($n = 17$) of various sizes. The greatest number of these (9, or 53% of the total)

Figure 5.33. Persen House. Personal items (relating to hygiene). From top to bottom: toothbrush (7.81), toothbrush (12.133), toothbrush (13.134), toothbrush (12.132). *Source:* Photo by the author.

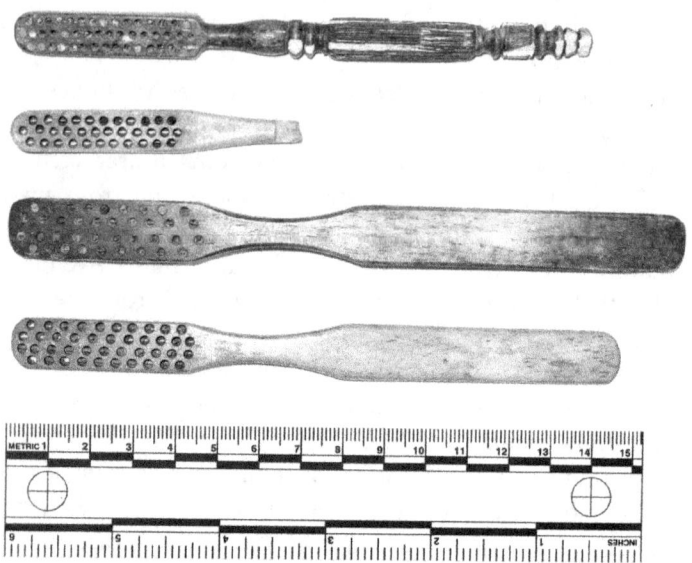

were found in Strata Group 2. The second most common personal item was slate pencil fragments, of which 13 (19.1%) were found. The third most prolific item from this functional group were coins, of which 11 (16.2%) were found. Most were copper and most came from Strata Group 2. Datable coins from this stratum included a large American copper cent (1800–1809), two US large cents (1800, 1820), and a 1910 Lincoln head penny. Three other datable coins were found in Strata Group 3 (1966 Roosevelt dime), Strata Group 5 (1749 British coin), and Strata Group 7 (1844 American half dime).

Other personal items included an inkwell fragment, three keys, and a newspaper fragment. Perhaps the most interesting personal item recovered from the Persen House excavations was the bodkin (fig. 5.11) found in Unit 11 (Context 127). Bodkins made their appearance in both the literature and in Dutch and Flemish genre paintings c. 1625 and became less common by 1675 (Huey 2015). Huey (2015, 1) noted that bodkins served a purpose for alerting potential suitors of the status of a woman: "Married women apparently wore them on the left side of the head, while they were worn on the right side of the head by unmarried women."

Also related to hair care and adornment were bone combs, of which three were found. One comb made of sea turtle carapace was also recovered. Some of the bone combs had the fine tines or teeth associated with the removal of nits or lice eggs from the hair. One item curiously absent from the rather large sample of artifacts in this category is the white clay wig curler (see Noel Hume 1970, 321–23), which was heated and used to curl the wigs of upper-class men. Paul Huey (personal communication, 2002) has informed me that these are rare on Dutch sites.

The ivory whistle found under the stairs prior to the Phase 3 excavation is illustrated in figure 5.31. As mentioned above, it could be included in either the personal or arms group, but because it was not in an excavated context, it is not included in the tabulation.

Recreation and Entertainment

Only three kinds of artifacts were included in this category: smoking pipes, marbles, and game pieces. An additional item that could have been included here was the mouth harp, although it has been classified in the personal category. The most common artifact in the recreation category was invariably the white clay smoking pipe, and it is here that the Persen House did not differ from other Dutch and/or English colonial sites of the period. A total of 1,064 smoking pipe fragments were found, and of these, 32 had maker's marks that can be associated with specific pipe-makers in the 17th and 18th centuries (fig. 5.34). Several also included small hints

Figure 5.34. Persen House. Recreational items. Left to right: "EB" pipe (4.56), "JRTIPPET" pipe (14.177), "EB" trade pipe (9.102). *Source:* Photo by the author.

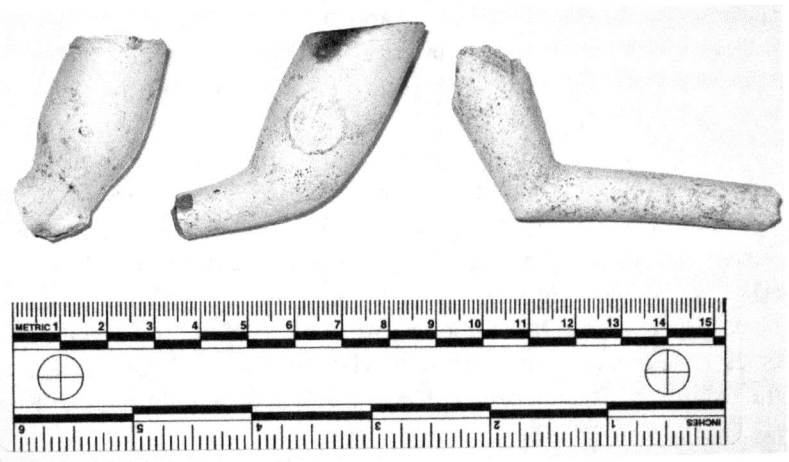

of marks that may be associated with specific pipe makers. In addition to these, there are also two variants of the Tudor Rose heel mark, one that has been identified at Fort Orange (Huey 1988) and one that is more enigmatic but shares similarities with an example from Fort Pentagoet in Maine (Faulkner and Faulkner 1987, fig. 6.7, h), which was occupied from 1635 to 1674. There are also four pipestems with debossed *fleur-de-lis*, an attribute often found on 17th-century Dutch pipestems (see McCashion 1979). Perhaps the largest inventory from one site showing the possible range of variation in *fleur-de-lis* marks are the pipestems from Fort Orange (Huey 1988, fig. 113).

Of the 32 marked pipes that can be associated with specific pipe makers, 18 (56%) displayed the makers mark of Robert Tippet. These marks varied from a simple "RT" facing the smoker as the pipe is used to several variations of the "R TIPPET" cartouche. These date from 1660 to 1720 (Walker 1977, 1732–39). One related pipe included the cartouche of "IR TIPPET," which was the mark of Joan Tippet and her son Robert (fig. 5.34), who went into business with her after the death of her husband Robert sometime between 1680 and 1687 (Walker 1977, 493). The presence of "R Tippet" and "Tippet" pipes on archaeological sites as late as the Revolutionary War still remains a mystery since production ended c. 1720 (Walker 1977) to 1722 (Diane Dallal, personal communication, October 26, 2003). Walker (1977) noted that Tippet pipes are found in later contexts, as did Stone (1974, 148–49), where R. Tippet pipes from Fort Michilimackinac were found in contexts dating 1740–1780. The appearance of these pipes on later archaeological sites and in later archaeological contexts can be attributed to several factors: the large number of Tippet pipes in circulation, a backlog of unsold pipes, counterfeiting, and later reuse of the molds of R. Tippet and his family. Since these factors are difficult to control for in the archaeological record, the date of 1660–1720 is used for the time span here, with the caveat that the pipes may in fact be associated with later use.

The next common pipestem mark was that of Edward Bird, an Amsterdam pipe maker who is represented in the Persen House collection by 9 (28%) of the marked pipes (fig. 5.27 and 5.34). Bird was born in Surrey, England, and produced pipes in Amsterdam from c. 1630 to 1665 (De Roever 1987). Furlow (2021) documented the spread of Edward Bird pipes as part of the Dutch trade network in the 17th century. Edward Bird pipes have been found in Scandinavia, Africa, Brazil, Curacao, Jamaica, the Dominican Republic, French Acadia (Maine), and throughout what are now the eastern United States from Maine to Charleston, South Carolina (Furlow 2021, 244).

All of the pipe marks relating to Edward Bird are heel marks. I have dated some of these at 1630–1665, and, where possible, I have used tighter dates from McCashion (1979) related to variations in mark and bowl profile, based on the presence of Edward Bird pipes on Haudenosaunee sites in central New York. The Persen House collection also included several examples of a funnel-shaped trade pipe made by Bird for export to *Niew Netherland*. The pipe mimics the shape and style of Native American trumpet bowl pipes from the time period and is thought to have been made specifically for trade with Native Americans (fig. 5.34, far right). These pipes have been found at Fort Orange (Huey 1998), Huguenot Street in New Paltz, sites in New York City, and on the "pipe wreck," a c. 1658–1665 shipwreck in Monti Cristi, Dominican Republic (Hall 2005, 152–55). This shipwreck was a Dutch vessel, which, among other cargo, carried an estimated 500,000 clay pipes for sale and distribution in the New World.

When Edward Bird died in 1665, his son Evert continued the business, calling it "The Rose" (De Roever 1987). Whether or not he was the maker of the two rose-marked pipes that were found at the Persen House may never be known. In 1668, Edward Bird's widow Anna van der Heijden, the stepmother of Evert Bird, remarried Hendrik Gerdes. De Roever (1987, 58) found that Gerdes was originally listed as a sugar bowl potter who later became a pipe maker. One pipe with "HG" and depicting a crown above it was found at the Persen House. This is one of at least three varieties of Hendrik Gerdes pipes. Another variant lacks the crown. These pipes date c. 1668–1688 (Huey 1988, 740; McCashion 1979, 130–31). Two similar variants have recently been found in deeply stratified deposits from the late 17th century on Huguenot Street in New Paltz.

Other marked pipes from the 17th century include done "AI," the mark of Andries Jacobz of Amsterdam from c. 1686 (Huey 1988, fig. 114, no. 66; McCashion 1979, 136), and one "WE," the mark of William Evans c. 1682–1697 (Alexander 1979, fig. 5, no. 1; Oswald 1975, 152–53). A possible William Evans stem mark was also found. Several 18th-century pipe bowls were found, the most notable bearing the mark "TD," possibly of Thomas Dormer (?) c. 1748–1770 (Oswald 1975, 135) but more probably post-1757 (P. Huey, personal communication, June 11, 2003). An 18th-century bowl with a serifed "T" in a diamond was also found. Serifs are the small projecting lines at the top of the letter "T," such as used in Times New Roman font.

Another form of recreation, and one common to the Dutch, in the 17th century was various games utilizing marbles (see Huey 2021). The 14 excavation units in and around the Persen House produced a total of 35 marbles, one of which was a large "shooter." Dutch paintings, such as Johanne Vermeer's *The Little Street* (c. 1658), often show children kneeling down, likely playing marbles on the sidewalk. Excavations at the Broad Street financial center in Lower Manhattan in 1984 similarly yielded a collection of marbles, where 17 were found in a basket with 17 marbles in the fill matrix (Dallal 1996). A bone and ivory domino (5+5) was also found during the Persen excavations. This could have simply been used as a domino or possibly in a game of *tric-trac*, as detailed in the left back room in Jan Steen's *Light Come, Light Go* (1661). *Tric-trac* is thought to be the precursor of today's backgammon.

Special Activities

The category of special activities, at least in this case, covers many possible functional categories, which are sometimes difficult to discern in the archaeological record. Although these types of artifacts are usually sporadic, in that they occur individually as one item among many, there is one grouping at the Persen House that stood out from the rest: copper and brass scraps, which may relate to cutting copper and brass kettles for trade items or to the process of reducing metals to smaller pieces to manufacture buttons.

One item, a cleat for a boat dock (or boat), appears to be out of context, and it is worth wondering how and why it found its way into the archaeological record beneath the Phase 3 portion of the house.

Fuel

A total of 120 fragments of coal as well as "clinker" (burned coal) were recovered from the Persen House excavations. Overall, the count was quite low, and, again, there are several explanations. Because most of the excavation units were either around the very edge of the house or inside of it, coal and clinker would be minimally represented. It is typically only when backyard deposits where coal buckets may have been dumped are investigated that large amounts of unburned coal and clinker fragments are recovered. I tend to view the presence of coal as an indicator of deposits, or at least associations of deposits, that postdate October 1828, when the

Delaware and Hudson (D&H) Canal opened (French 1860, 63). The D&H Canal ran from Rondout on the Hudson to Honesdale, Pennsylvania, and was built to open up the Pennsylvania coal fields to a larger target population in the Hudson Valley and, especially, New York City. The present location of Rondout Island was the D&H Canal Company's stockyard, a place where canal boats off-loaded millions of tons of coal for storage and transport.

Fire-Affected

This category includes all items that have been burned, melted, or affected by fire in any way. This does not include hearth tiles, which are, of necessity, fire affected. Because of an initial mix-up concerning the date of the burn layer encountered in Units 1 and 2, just one category of fire-affected artifacts was created. During the excavation of the interior, we had, for the most part, no problem finding the 1663 burn layer. What we were unable to locate, however, was an archaeological context associated with the October 1777 burning of Kingston by the British. I reasoned that fire-affected artifacts that were not pre-1663, and that were probably from the early to late 18th century might, by weight of numbers, indicate a context that could be correlated with the fire of 1777. The results were interesting, with fire-affected artifacts being the most numerically preponderant in Strata Group 2, the association of archaeological contexts below the floor and between the floor joists. A total of 47 of 156 (or 30.12%) fire-affected artifacts were found in Strata Group 2. This is slightly more than double the number from Strata Group 4 ($n = 28$) and Strata Group 18 ($n = 26$), which is simply an agglomeration of disturbed contexts.

Macrobotanicals

During the excavation of the Phase 3 portion of the house, it was noted that many of the rat nests contained dead rats in skeletal form, and nut fragments. The latter were saved, especially when they were encountered in mixed strata and especially just below and between the floor joists. Strata Group 2, the soil between the floor joists and above the clay/mortar floor, yielded 64 of the 129 (49.6%) macrobotanicals found at the Persen House site. The vast majority of all recovered nut fragments and seeds were in an excellent state of preservation, thus suggesting that they were not from the 17th through 19th centuries. At one point (during the holidays), we realized that, with the exception of peach pits, all of the sampled nut fragments were those commonly associated with a bowl of nuts at table settings and parties around the Thanksgiving and Christmas holidays. My hypothesis, although not a pleasant one, is that during the holidays, Persen House rats would steal little tidbits after hours from the Cornell Agricultural Cooperative Offices, which have been located in the Persen House since the early 20th century. When I broached this topic with Dr. Thomas Amorosi, the project zooarchaeologist (and *Rattus sp.* expert), he stated without a pause, "Oh, definitely." The seemingly large number of nuts in the strata group, then, are most likely not from soils that have been redeposited as a result of basement or builder's trench excavation, nor would they have been part of Colonial Dutch or English foodways. Rather, they are more likely an indication of food choice on the part of Persen House rats for most of the 20th century. The skeletons of the individual rats concerned, as well as their families, were found scattered throughout the fill, and their nests are illustrated in many of the figures in this report. The number of identified bone specimens of Norway rat and rat species combined is 680, of which 324 (47.6%) are from Strata Group 2, the soils under the floorboards and above the clay/mortar floor. The second largest grouping is 121 (17.8%) from Strata Group 6, the sands just above the 1663 burn layer, which appeared to be a favored location for nesting.

Discussion

The archaeological excavation of the two units on the exterior walls of the Matthewis Persen House has yielded important information about several facets of the history and prehistory of uptown Kingston. One of the most interesting of these is the depth from the modern sidewalk to the top of the 1663 burn level (Unit 1, Context 7), which was approximately 65 cm (27 in). This depth indicates that the street level in the 17th century was substantially lower than it is now. The burn layer provides a wonderful *terminus post quem*, or date after which, for those deposits above it, and a *terminus ante quem*, or date before which, for those deposits below it. The idea of a *terminus ante quem* for the burn layer allows us to examine the contents of the soil for a glimpse of street life (or at least sanitation) in *Wiltwyck* in the 17th century. From the Kingston court minutes, we have evidence that the situation, at different points, was pretty grim. Between late October and mid-November of 1664, we find,

It was also proposed, and thereupon resolved, that, by public notice to the inhabitants here of the mischief and damage that may result from fire, the householders living near the Mill gate shall be forbidden to carry their straw and rubbish, for the purpose of being burnt, close to the village palisades, but shall rather take the same across the Mill dam. Whereupon the following placard was posted: "Whereas, experience teaches us the impropriety of throwing out straw and rubbish and of burning the same close by the palisades, wherfrom great danger from fire may be expected, the Schout and Schepens therefore order that straw and rubbish shall be carted across the Mill dam by those living near the Mill gate, under the penalty heretofore fixed for that purpose. Further, all inhabitants here are directed to clear the streets, within four days, of straw and rubbish, so that, through the carrying of a light or the blowing out of a pipe of tobacco, a conflagration, such as the one at Amersfort on Long Island (God shield us), may not occur. And every one must attend every week to the said clearing and cleaning of the streets of the straw in front of his lot, under penalty of ten guilders' fine. Let every one guard against damage. (Christoph et al. 1976, 1:168–69)

The burning of straw in the streets was a means of disposing bed straw that was filled with lice and bedbugs, even though an order had been posted against this activity. This also extended to keeping the streets free from cattle and miscellaneous lumber, firewood, and wagons at night (Christoph et al. 1976, 1:240) so that people could traverse the streets without getting injured. A more involved decree from October 6, 1665 stated,

Whereas daily experience shows that the residents of this village, prior to this, did not only leave the dead bodies of their large and small cattle in the streets of this village, but that even some have brought the said dead bodies close by the curtains outside of this community directly upon and near the common roads, which decomposing bodies, on account of their stench, not only much inconvenience passers by, but may also be the cause of bad diseases, owing to said nasty stench, for the purpose of remedying and preventing which in the future, the hon. schout and shepen of this village of Wildwyck, in the name and by the authority of his Royal Majesty of Great Britain and the hon. Lord Ridsert Nicolls, gov.genl. at New York by the present order and command each and every resident of this place that, after this date, nobody shall further venture neither to leave his dead bodies of the cattle, however named, on the street of this village or to bring them near or about the curtains of this community on or about the common roads, but that said dead bodies shall be carried the distance of two rifle shots outside of the village. (Christoph et al. 1976, 1:253–54)

That *Wiltwyck* was, at times, a rather odorous hamlet is obvious. However, this does not necessarily translate into artifacts. What is striking about the outside deposits (Strata Groups 19 and 20) is the low density of historic artifacts found in the two excavated units. If we examine the artifacts in Context 9 from below the burn layer (Context 7) in Unit 1, the artifacts are exclusively Native American. This is also the case for the actual burn layer itself in Unit 1. The same is true for Context 15, the stratum of red sand below the burn layer (Context 14) in Unit 2. The burn layer in Unit 2 produced only one piece of bone. This would suggest that refuse deposition during the Dutch colonial and British colonial periods was confined to backyard areas, which would essentially become middens over time. An examination of the kinds and amounts of artifacts found in Unit 14 behind the Persen House confirms this. Here, 48%, or almost half of the artifacts recovered, were faunal remains. The other finds show an accumulation of artifacts from the 17th century, such as tin-glazed earthenwares and numerous redwares, to later ceramics from the 18th century, such as creamware (post-1762) and pearlware (post-1780), and, finally, 19th-century whiteware (post-1820).

It should also be noted that the Dutch ceramics and early earthenwares from the 17th- and early-18th-century contexts at the Persen House were very fragmentary. This supports Amorosi's evaluation of the bone as highly fragmented and suggests that the archaeological materials are from secondarily deposited contexts, if not sheet middens, where pedestrian action has taken its toll on the collection. At this point, it is difficult to determine vessel type conclusively as outlined by Baart (1994, 1997), Schaefer (1998), or Janowitz and Schaefer (2021) for Dutch ceramics from Amsterdam, and for 17th-century Dutch ceramics in general. In many cases, we are left with a tantalizing rim or body fragment that may be from either a pipkin (English), *kookpot* (Dutch), or even a chamber pot, which bears many similarities to these vessels (see Noël Hume 2003).

The presence of Native American materials in the archaeological strata surrounding the Persen House was expected. Of the 12,001 artifacts from the Persen House (not counting bone), 2,915, or 24.29%, were of Native American origin. Most of this was lithic debitage, which, as previously mentioned, was of local bedrock origin. The large numbers of Native American artifacts attest to the use of present-day uptown Kingston by precontact Native American groups for the last 3,500 years. The earliest occupations on site were from the Orient and Meadowood phases, both of which appear to overlap in time during the Transitional Archaic/Early Woodland during the first millennium BC. This was then followed by a gap in the archaeological record (at the Persen House) until the Late Woodland/Contact period.

The Levanna projectile points found in Unit 2 (Context 11) and Unit 4 (Context 53) were made by one of the groups encountered by the Dutch at Contact (*Warranawankongs* or *Waoranecks*), who were collectively called "Esopus." It is difficult to say whether either projectile point was directly involved with the events of June 7, 1663, when *Wiltwyck* was attacked and almost totally burned to the ground. Both, however, are in strata groups that either overlie the burn layer on the outside of the Persen House (Unit 2, Context 11) or are part of the palisade trench fill inside the house (Unit 4, Context 53). The plant processing materials, such as the pestle and nutting stone, represent indications of food preparation on site, although there appears to be no evidence for storage of nuts of cultigens in pits, as evidenced at other sites in the Esopus drainage (see Cammisa et al. 2009; Diamond 1999a; Diamond et al. 2016; Hart et al. 2017; Louis Berger Group 2008). In fact, except for several enigmatic post molds, there were no Native American features found at the site. This may indicate that later occupations just on the verge of European contact were occupying the bluff edge along North Front Street and Clinton Avenue.

The excavation of the Persen House materials were, as noted above, undertaken using the context system as outlined by Harris (1975, 1979a, 1979b). The analysis of the Persen House materials has proceeded by regrouping those contexts into strata groups that are temporally related based on vertical and horizontal stratigraphy and placement. A number of these strata groups deserve further elaboration and discussion, and some, due to their small size, are still somewhat problematic. The latter is a result of rat disturbances as well as small artifact counts, which make statistical comparisons difficult. This is a result of low artifact density and relatively small volumes of excavated soil from these contexts. Even when these contexts are joined, the resulting strata group has a paucity of artifacts. Strata Groups 9, 10, 14, 15, 16, and 20 could be considered difficult in this regard due to the small numbers of artifacts found in them. Strata Groups 1 and 18 are also problematic, since the first is the large disturbance in front of the hearth in the Phase 3 portion of the house, and the latter is simply a conglomeration of disturbed contexts. In the discussion that follows, it is assumed that the Norway rat (NISP = 130) and rat species (NISP = 550), as identified by Dr. Amorosi, are not culinary in origin. NISP refers to the number of fragments of a particular species that were identified. Consequently, other animal remains are referred to as "food-related" to distinguish them from the numerous rat remains found at the Persen House. It should also be noted that discussion of members of the pigeon family as a food source is a rarity in the Kingston court minutes. It must be remembered, however, that in the probate records, Gysbert van Imbroch had a pigeon rookery or "dovecote" (Christoph et al. 1976, 571).

Perhaps the most informative Strata Groups were 2, 3, 5/6, 7, 8, 11, 12, 13, and 17. Strata Group 2, as mentioned above, was the loose soil above the clay/mortar floor and between the floor joists. The greatest quantity of clothing- and tailoring-related items (n = 340) was found here, suggesting that the clay/mortar cap may relate to the Persens' construction of the Phase 3 addition and that this addition was likely used by the family as a business location. This "cap" would have effectively prevented many of the clothing-related items from migrating downward, except in rats' tunnels and other disturbances. Other indications that this may have been the case are the large amounts of creamware, pearlware, and whiteware in this stratum. Food-related mammalian faunal remains from Strata Group 2 consisted primarily of sheep/goat (NISP = 60), pig (NISP = 53), and, to a lesser extent, cattle (NISP = 27). Bird remains consisted of chicken (NISP = 304), turkey (NISP = 83), and pigeon (NISP = 49). Fish were primarily of the perch family (NISP = 27), perches (NISP = 11), and suckers (NISP = 18), which are common to the Esopus Creek. In addition, the only fragments of turtle found on the site were from this stratum.

One interesting nonfood mammalian artifact was an elephant ivory ring, approximately 5 cm (2 in) across, which was likely a piece of jewelry. It was the only artifact from the Persen House that originated in Africa.

Whether it belonged to Robin, a slave that Matthewis Persen "borrowed" from Benjamin Bogardus in 1782, or was acquired by purchase is unknown.

Strata Group 3, the walls and builder's trenches of the Phase 3 portion of the house, was also informative. Three cannonballs were found along the south wall of the house within this strata group, possibly pointing to its location near an artillery piece or opening along the curtain wall. Food-related mammalian faunal remains from this stratum included pig (NISP = 27) and, to a lesser extent, sheep/goat (NISP = 7) and cattle (NISP = 7). Bird remains included chicken (NISP = 30), pigeon (NISP = 23), and turkey (NISP = 13). The fish category, as in Strata Group 2, was dominated by perch family remains (NISP = 11) but also included sturgeon (NISP = 2).

Strata Groups 5 and 6, both located beneath the clay/mortar floor and above the 1663 burn layer, are lumped into one for discussion. Although Strata Group 2 yielded 340, or 55.6%, of the clothing-related items, Strata Groups 5 and 6 together totaled 105, or 17.2%, of the clothing-related artifacts from the site. Although this might be related to soil movement resulting from rats' nests, it may also indicate that a significant number of clothing-related (tailoring) artifacts were already present in the soils surrounding the Phase 1 portion of the house when the Phase 2 basement soils were excavated and eventually covered the burn layer. In this scenario, which will require much more historical research, both the Phase 2 and Phase 3 portions would postdate 1735. These two strata also yielded 96, or 56.5%, of all tin-glazed earthenwares (majolica and delft) from the site.

Mammalian food remains from these strata reflect a sharp increase in white-tailed deer (NISP = 15) compared with the strata above and below them. The most numerically preponderant domesticated animals were pig (NISP = 94), sheep/goat (NISP = 38), and cattle (NISP = 20). Birds were predominantly chicken (NISP = 127), followed by pigeon (NISP = 62) and turkey (NISP = 37). Strata Group 6 also had a relatively large grouping of marsh duck species (NISP = 13). Of the two strata, Strata Group 6 yielded the majority of the fish remains. Strata Group 5 yielded only perches and perch family (NISP combined = 5), whereas Strata Group 6 produced evidence of shark (NISP = 1), sturgeon (NISP = 1), perches and perch family (NISP combined = 32), and catfish (NISP = 1).

Strata Group 7, the fill overlying the palisade trench, produced a similar inventory of food-related mammalian remains. These included wild species such as white-tailed deer (NISP = 1) and gray squirrel (NISP = 1) as well as domesticated animals such as pig (NISP = 4), sheep/goat (NISP = 4), and cattle (NISP = 2). Chicken remains (NISP = 34) comprised the largest group of food items. No fish remains were found in this strata group.

Strata Group 8, the palisade trench and soil matrix, yielded few artifacts overall, which is informative in and of itself. Food-related mammalian remains consisted entirely of cattle (NISP = 3) and pig (NISP = 1), whereas chicken (NISP = 10), pigeon family (NISP = 7), and turkey (NISP = 1) comprised the bird remains. Fish remains were represented by just one fragment of sucker (NISP = 1).

Strata Group 11, the June 7, 1663, burn layer, yielded a total of 172 artifacts. Of these, 20 were early ceramics as well as food remains. This strata grouping, and those below it, provide the best view into what people were eating in and around the time of that event. Food-related mammals, like the species discussed in the Kingston court minutes, were pig (NISP = 4), sheep/goat (NISP = 2), and cattle/sheep/goat (NISP = 1). Birds consist of chicken (NISP = 6), turkey (NISP = 2), and pigeon family (NISP = 2). There were no fish remains from Strata Group 11.

Directly below the burn layer, and predating the fire, were several features lumped together as Strata Group 12. The artifact count for this strata group was low, reflecting the number of artifacts in general as well as the relatively small volume of soil that comprised this sample. The ceramics were all relatively early. Food-related fauna consisted entirely of four identifiable bones of pig (NISP = 1), cattle (NISP = 1), chicken (NISP = 1), and pigeon family (NISP = 1).

Strata Group 13, the original soils below the 1663 burn layer, had the largest number of Native American items from any strata group ($n = 1,837$). Even though a large amount of Native American artifacts was found in this grouping, with the exception of perch and perch family (NISP combined = 5), all of the food-related faunal remains were domesticated. These consisted of pig (NISP = 6), sheep/goat (NISP = 1), cattle (NISP = 1), chicken (NISP = 2), and pigeon family (NISP = 3).

Strata Group 17, the yard deposit in Unit 14, yielded an assortment of artifacts, 48% of which were faunal remains. This strata group gives us an insight into what relatively undisturbed backyard deposits in a small town/city (*Wiltwyck*/Kingston) should look like. Ceramics from this unit ranged from the 17th through 19th centuries. Food-related faunal remains included nondomesticated animals such as deer/deer family (NISP combined = 7) and black bear (NISP = 1) as well as domesticated mammalian forms such as cattle (NISP = 13), sheep/goat (NISP = 2), sheep (NISP =

1), and pig (NISP = 10). The backyard deposits also held large amounts of bird remains. These included chicken (NISP = 27), pigeon family (NISP = 47), and a perching bird (NISP = 1). The large number of pigeon remains from the yard deposits are duplicated only by a slightly larger number from underneath the floor in the Phase 3 portion of the house (Strata Group 2). This would suggest that pigeon remains were disposed of in the yard and were then likely dragged inside the house by rats or, alternatively, that the pigeon remains were those of Gysbert van Imbroch and were part of earlier fill from the third quarter of the 17th century. Fish remains from the yard deposits consisted of sturgeon (NISP = 7) and perch species (NISP = 1). The seven fragments of sturgeon make up the highest quantity of any strata group on site.

Recently, Marie-Lorraine Pipes analyzed the faunal remains from several Dutch colonial sites in the Albany area dating c. 1640–1668 (Pipes 2021). Similar to the food remains from the Persen House, the most numerous mammalian categories were cattle, white-tailed deer, pig, sheep, and sheep/goat (Pipes 2021, table 6.1). The most numerous birds were chicken, duck, goose, pigeons, and turkey. This would indicate that during the Dutch colonial period, and probably afterward in the English colonial period, major protein sources came from domesticated mammals, supplemented with deer and domesticated birds as well as wild/domesticated birds such as turkey and pigeon.

Excavations in the Proposed Matthewis Persen House Garden

In 2004, the County of Ulster proposed a garden area on the east side of the Persen House. Based on the findings of the earlier excavations, it was deemed necessary to conduct preliminary testing to determine whether the same kind of deposits found in the southwestern yard area under the driveway were also intact on the eastern and southern sides of the house. The county was proposing an ornamental fountain, two fence lines, eight trees, and an exterior air conditioning unit with associated electrical line. Jay R. Cohen (2004) directed the excavation of 12 backhoe tests, with a specific research design "to identify the horizontal and vertical extent of any existing fill deposits encapsulating the buried seventeenth and eighteenth century surfaces, and identify the depth at which intact archaeological deposits are likely to be encountered." The tests located a large disturbance relating to the previous burial of a tank but also found intact 19th-century deposits that should have had 18th- and 17th-century deposits stratigraphically below them. Not mentioned in the letter report of this excavation was that since Native American artifacts were found stratigraphically below the 17th-century Dutch artifacts inside the Persen House, these intact strata outside the house should have also contained precontact Native American artifacts. This suggests that there are areas around the outside of the Persen House that may still contain evidence of Native American occupations as well as 17th-century Dutch artifacts.

Summary

Archaeological excavations around the Matthewis Persen House have yielded information concerning Native American occupations in uptown Kingston that span the last 3,500 years. Added to this is evidence from the Dutch colonial and British colonial periods as well as artifacts that postdate the Revolutionary War. Although the excavations totaled only just over 30 square meters, this work has provided a window into Kingston's Native American past and hinted at historical information that might be obtainable from other investigations in and around the Stockade District. When the 20,508 artifacts (including faunal remains) are divided by 33 square meters, the result is that the soil around and inside the Persen House averages about 621 artifacts per square meter. These data concerning Kingston's past are probably also evident in other undisturbed locations in Kingston's uptown area. The key to saving and interpreting this information is to require testing of impacted soils within the Stockade District prior to construction projects such as gas, water, or utility lines as well as larger impacts such as building footprints. The archaeological deposits relating to Native American, Dutch colonial, British colonial, and early American occupations in uptown Kingston are a finite resource that cannot be duplicated.

Chapter 6

Later Historic Archaeological Sites in Kingston

The topic of this chapter has been separated from the Stockade District based on the proximity and age of the archaeological sites. Whereas sites in the Stockade District date to the 17th and 18th centuries, the examples discussed here are 19th-century sites. Although there are numerous historic archaeological sites outside of the Stockade District, here we review three specific locations where archaeological work has been carried out, an area where nine 19th-century industrial sites were identified, as well as maritime archaeological sites such as the *Mary Powell* steamboat, coal barges, and multiple small craft in the mud flats at Kingston Point.

Archaeology at Sailor's Cove/Hutton Brickyards

A cultural resources survey was conducted to evaluate a proposed 77-acre development in the area of the Hutton Brickyards, just north of Kingston Point, which was proposed for both housing and open space. This project was one of the few instances in which industrial archaeology was undertaken within the city of Kingston. The project area was somewhat amorphous in shape, bordering the Hudson River for approximately 1,600 feet and continuing north to a small cove, where the property ended, and was divided by North Street. To the east was a 28.7-acre series of brickyards spanning the time range from 1865 to 1980. To the west of North Street was a 48-acre pit where clay and sand have been mined since the 19th century (see Hutton 2003, figs. 67, 76; Gurcke, 1987).

At the time the survey was undertaken, there were 15 standing structures associated with the Hutton Brickyards within the Sailor's Cove project area as well as six historic archaeological structures such as foundations and a railroad bed. There were also three brick barges from the brickyards along the shoreline that were visible depending on the tide. Like the barge wrecks in the Rondout Creek, the sunken ships at Kingston Point, and the wreck of the *Mary Powell*, these barges are considered sites of nautical archaeological interest, as they embody a kind of construction that is no longer used.

Much of the 77 acres that made up this project area was previously mined for sand, which was mixed with clay to form brick. The value of this location for clay lies in its proximity to both the Egbert Schoonmaker Stone Ware Factory from 1805–c. 1815 and the Nathan C. Bell Pottery Factory from c. 1830–1834 (Ketchum 1987, 127–33). Both were located at "Columbus Point," now Kingston Point. The location of the factory was identified by Mr. William Rhinehart of Saugerties, New York, and is catalogued in Diamond (1990; site #10-H-56/USN #1140.001).

Within the proposed project area, four brickmaking companies previously utilized the site. The first was Cordts and Hutton from 1865 to 1890, which then became the Hutton Brick Company from 1890 to 1965. Eventually, it was sold to the Jova Manufacturing Company and then to the Staples Brick Company, until brick production ceased in 1980 (Hutton 2003, 111).

A collection of 10 historic maps of the vicinity were consulted to estimate the dates of historic structures within the project area. The 1854 Brink and Tillson map of Ulster County indicated no structures in the project area, with "D. Terry" in the vicinity of the present-day brickyards, while the 1858 French map indicated "W. Shaw" in the vicinity of the project area. These would have been brick producers, as "Terry" bricks are relatively common in the Mid-Hudson Valley. Lloyd's *Topographical Map of the Hudson River from the Head of Navigation at Troy to Its Confluence with the Ocean at Sandy Hook* (1864) shows "W. Shaw Brick Yd." in the location of the Hutton yard. This company probably made unmarked common bricks because the name Shaw does not appear in Van Der Poel's Hudson River Brick Collection (2023) whereas "19Terry24," "Terry," and "Terry Bros." are included. "Shaw" also does not appear in Gurcke's (1987) book on bricks and brickmaking.

The 1875 Beers map of Ulster County shows North Street simply ending at the "Brick Yard," which is illustrated as two long sheds on a north/south axis. Since the Cordts and Hutton Company began in 1865 (Hutton 2003, 111), this probably refers to this concern. The 1875 map also illustrates the "NY West Shore and Chicago Railroad" tracks running through the project area, just to the west of present-day North Street.

The 1878 map of the Cordts and Hutton Brickyards on file in the City of Kingston's Planning and Engineering Department simply shows a brick kiln, several small structures, including a smokestack and the wharf line. It is very probable that this is only a basic map, as it lacks many of the features necessary for the construction of bricks. It does show the location of the brick smokestack that is likely located near the engine house and puddling sheds seen in Hutton (2003, figs. 13, 14). This map also lacks any indication of brick kilns, which should be illustrated as being along the wharf line, or the frame puddling sheds shown on the 1875 Beers map. It should also be noted that when comparing the wharf line indicated in the 1878 map and the 1915 Codwise map, it is obvious that a large portion of the shoreline south of the wharf was filled in by 1915. This was probably done to extend the brick kilns further south along the wharf, which would have aided in the manufacturing process. Clay would have been mined and then mixed in the mixing sheds, molded and dried in the large drying yard in the center (see Hutton 2003, figs. 13, 14), fired in the kilns, and then loaded onto barges at the wharf's edge for transport.

The 1891 Beers map of the Hudson River from New York City to Troy shows only the "Brick Yard Wharf." This would refer to the Hutton Company that succeeded Cordts and Hutton in 1890 and produced bricks under that name until 1965 (Hutton 2003, 111).

The 1887 Sanborn Fire Insurance maps for the city of Kingston do not include the project area, as the maps cover only property to the south. The 1899 Sanborn Fire Insurance map provides much more information. The "Brick House" indicated on the 1878 map is here identified as a "Dwelling," and other structures that remained from 1878 include the "Open Top Kiln"; the "Office"; the "puddling sheds," which extended from near the office to almost the northern end of the property; and the 26 "Open Top Kilns," which extended along the full length of the wharf. Between the kilns and the puddling sheds was an open area that was likely used for the drying yard and the construction of "hacks," which were stacks of dried bricks.[1] Hutton (2003, 41, fig. 14) shows the puddling sheds to the left and the long row of kilns along the wharf. Also notable is a brick building indicated as "Eng," which was probably the engineer's or repair house that is later shown on the 1957 Sanborn map as the "Locomotive

House." Information regarding the "Brick Works" on this map indicates there was "no watchman," "no fire apparatus," "power steam," and "fuel wood under kilns & coal under boilers" at the locomotive house. The revised 1887 map of the map by E. B. Newkirk of 1867 shows the area of present-day Flatbush, called "Huttonville," an indication of the number of residents employed at the brickyard at this time. The Cordts mansion, built by one of the brickyard owners, overlooks the project area.

On the 1915 Codwise map, 16 buildings within the project area were no longer extant in 2004 when the archaeological survey was undertaken. These included a one-story frame structure near the road (which, if it was moved, might be the one-story frame building near the office), a one-story shop, two one-story brick buildings, five groups of mixing pits, a sand house, a frame kiln shed, a frame shed for mixing pits, two two-story frame structures near North Street, and the "2 Story Brick Dwelling" (mentioned above as a "Brick House"), shown with a two-story frame addition. Of these, only three might leave traces such as brick basements that could potentially be located archaeologically, while the other frame buildings may not have had substantial foundations. Most of the structures associated with brickmaking were frame buildings (see Hutton 2003, figs. 7, 13, 14, 17, 19, 20, 21, 23, 24), which would leave little, if any, traces, particularly on an industrial site.

The 1957 Sanborn Fire Insurance maps of the city of Kingston illustrate the Hutton Brickyards prior to being transferred to the Jova Manufacturing Company and Staples in 1965. Structures from the 1915 Codwise maps that were still standing at this time are the office, a one-story brick structure that might be the brick machine shop, the locomotive house, and the 16-foot-wide linear structure on an east/west axis to the east of this building.

Structures not on the 1915 Codwise map, and therefore constructed after 1915, include the brick structure near the office, the fuel tanks, the Lidgerwood crane used for putting bundles of bricks on barges, the centrally located iron frame structure used for drying brick, and, to the north, the three large bays of the brick kilns.

The project area also included three shipwrecks along the waterfront. All three were brick barges and varied with regard to state of preservation. Of the three identified archaeologically, one was in "good" shape and may, in fact, be the barge shown in Hutton (2003, 160, fig. 68). This barge still has an intact deckhouse.

A conversation with Mr. Mark Peckham of the Office of Parks, Recreation, and Historic Preservation (OPRHP; personal communication, February 4, 2004) revealed that all three would be considered eligible for the National Register of Historic Places as well as the State Register, as contributing structures in the historic brickyard complex. Mr. Peckham suggested that mitigation procedures as part of a Phase 2 or Phase 3 archaeological investigation would entail a complete photographic record with measured drawings of each wrecked vessel. He also suggested that the deckhouse on the best-preserved barge should be removed (i.e., salvaged) and made available to a local museum.

Overall, the brickyard complex is the culmination of 115 years of brickmaking technology and economic change in the city of Kingston. The existing structures represent portions of each of several company's tenures at the site and have since been rehabilitated for use as event space. The Hutton Brickyards complex is eligible for the National Register of Historic Places as well as the State Register, in the Industrial Complex Category. In an on-site conversation, coupled with a walk-over to evaluate the property, Mr. William Krattinger of OPRHP (personal communication, March 24, 2004) emphasized the need for viewing the site as a complex as well as the need for preserving the buildings that were structurally sound and could therefore still represent the complex. Coupled with this is the need to thoroughly document the structures that are deteriorated or structurally unsound, as these may be subject to removal in the future.

Nathan C. Bell's Pottery Factory at Kingston Point

In 1989, I was contacted by Mr. William Rhinehart of Saugerties. Bill had been engaged in a pedestrian survey around Kingston Point and had found the ceramic dump from N. C. Bell's pottery factory, which dates to c. 1830–1834 (Ketchum 1987, 129–33; Remensnyder 1963). We met at Kingston Point so that he could point out the location of his finds, which I then registered with the New York State Museum and OPRHP. His collection from the site included several wasters embossed "N. C. Bell, Kingston, NY," other fragments of pottery that were apparently wasters, which are broken pieces of pottery that did not survive the firing process, and numerous fragments of kiln "furniture" (Short 1982). Kiln furniture is used to create spaces between pots when stacked in the kiln prior to the firing process. The spaces allow an even flow of heat throughout the kiln. The kiln furniture from the site was constructed of ropes of clay about 6–10 inches long that were flattened and allowed to dry to facilitate the placement and stacking of the pots. All of the kiln furniture was glazed, most of which was either a clear lead glaze or, in some cases, a salt glaze.

In 2023, Jane Kellar of the Friends of Historic Kingston (FOHK) gave the SUNY New Paltz Anthropology Department a collection of ceramics obtained from the site of the N. C. Bell pottery works. The excavation was conducted in 1986 by former City of Kingston historian Ed Ford and FOHK member Robert A. Slater. These materials have given us a better idea of what Bell was producing, from large, handled preserve jars to low-handled jars and ovoid-handled jugs. Kiln furniture also makes up a large percentage of the excavated materials.[2]

Sites like N. C. Bell's pottery works are time capsules for future investigation. Archaeologists are one of the few groups that I am aware of that are interested, if not truly fascinated, by the broken pots in a pottery dump. Some of the questions that ceramic historians and material culture specialists would investigate focus on the kinds of glazes used, the kinds of decorations debossed or painted on the pots, and the range of pottery produced. The fragmented pottery that did not survive the firing process reflects the range of variation in ceramic forms produced by a particular potter. Although there are only about 20 to 25 whole ceramic vessels from this manufacturing site in collections throughout the Hudson Valley, careful excavation of the site in the future would provide us with a greater appreciation for the products that Nathan C. Bell produced.

Excavations at the Reher Bakery, Rondout

In 2013, Hartgen Archeological Associates conducted a Phase 3 archaeological study at the Frank Reher Bakery on Lower Broadway in Kingston (HAA 2013). The excavation located an "idiosyncratic brick cistern on two small outbuilding foundations, and a network of drainage features working to prevent the accumulation of water in the rear courtyard of 1010 Broadway" (HAA 2013, 24). During the 1860s through the 1870s, the house was owned by Edward Cloonan and Thomas Eubanks, who ran "Cloonan & Co," a firm specializing in soda water and sarsaparilla (HAA 2013, table 4). The two small outbuilding foundations were probably privies, and the cistern was filled in with household debris from the 1890s, most likely from the Jordan and Douglass families who lived there during that time period. Between 1904 and 1905, there was a short-lived saloon in the building. The Reher family ran the bakery at that location after 1908. Artifacts from the excavations included whiteware, eating utensils, buttons, smoking pipe fragments, doll fragments, condiment bottles, fruit jars, patent medicine bottles, beer bottles, lamp chimney fragments, and numerous food remains, mostly cow and pig.

This study gives us a glimpse into what late 19th- to early 20th-century life was like on lower Broadway. Key components of the site related to sewage disposal (privies), water storage (cistern), and multiple stone and brick drains to keep the building's basement dry. The latter would be particularly important since 1010 Broadway is currently at the base of a large stone wall, where water accumulation below it would be a problem.

The Archaeology of Twaalfskill Brook

In 1992–1993, as a result of proposed improvements to the Twaalfskill Brook on Wilbur Avenue, a Phase 1 and 2 archaeological survey was completed prior to drainage work to prevent flooding from the Twaalfskill Brook (Werner Archaeological Consulting 1993). Prior to the study, the archaeologists consulted the "Reconnaissance Level Archaeological Survey of Kingston" (Diamond 1990) to determine whether there were any previously known sites along the brook. In the 1990 study, I had not located any precontact Native American sites along the brook, mainly because I had not done any shovel testing. However, I had documented the remnants of 19th-century mills along the brook. The archaeologists initiated a shovel testing program along the new proposed right-of-way as well as the excavation of several deep trenches to the south of Abeel Street where the new culverts would enter the Rondout Creek. The deep tests were undertaken to look for deeply buried deposits and to access portions of the project area covered by asphalt. Both the deep tests and the shovel testing found no indication of Native American sites within the area of the proposed construction project. This is likely because most precontact sites are typically found on higher, well-drained ground, such as overlooking the Twaalfskill. Alternatively, these sites may have already been impacted by construction episodes in the 1830s and 1840s. At that time, Wilbur Avenue was the main route for bluestone quarrying companies along the ridge north and west of Kingston to access the Rondout

Creek to ship bluestone to New York, other ports along the Hudson, or Pennsylvania via the Delaware and Hudson Canal. The construction of Wilbur Avenue along the eastern side of the Twaalfskill Brook would have effectively destroyed any precontact Native American sites that were close to the brook. Small sites that may have been there include fishing stations to take advantage of the herring run during the spring, when the Twaalfskill would be at its highest flow.

While no precontact Native American sites were found, there were several potential historic sites in the project area that were evident from historic maps, my 1990 survey, and a simple drive down Wilbur Avenue. Of the nine sites that were located from my 1990 archaeological survey as a consequence of this project, two were to be directly impacted and therefore required further evaluation. These were two foundations that appeared to be the remains of early to late 19th-century mills that used the water from Twaafskill Brook to build up head to run the machinery. Each had a foundation, millrace, and mill dam to retain water until it was needed.

The first foundation, the furthest downstream of the two, was the bluestone and limestone foundation of a combined operation by two concerns. The 1887 Sanborn map of Kingston indicated the upper portion as the "Sweeney Bros Rubbing Mill" and the lower portion as the "G. Coutant Lime Mill." This mill was situated across present-day Wilber Avenue from the large limestone furnaces that still exist today on the east side of the avenue. The purpose of a "rubbing mill" is to grind down the surface of bluestone flagstones, making them less bumpy and thus more useful for sidewalks. The lime mill prepared limestone for its use in making mortar and cement. This product was then shipped out in large barrels.

The second foundation was slightly upstream on Wilbur Avenue and just above its intersection with Chapel Street. The archaeologists found that there was a mill in this location since at least the 1840s. On the 1887 Sanborn map of Kingston, the mill was indicated as owned and operated by "Jas Phinney" and was a "Feed Mill" for the production of flour and feed. This grist mill was later called "Twaalfskill Mills" on historic maps and continued into the early 20th century by S. Dubois Deyo and Anthony Lawatsch.

The Phase 2 evaluation of these two foundations documented their internal components, construction episodes, and the materials used to build them. However, since there were no intact working elements in either of the foundations, and the superstructures above the foundation walls were missing, the archaeologists ended their investigations, as the two structures therefore did not meet the criteria for National Register eligibility.

During the process of studying the Twaalfskill Brook, the archaeologists also documented several retaining walls that, not surprisingly, were constructed of bluestone. The bluestone industry in 1875 (at its terminus on Abeel Street at the south end of Wilbur Avenue) can best be observed on pages 53 and 54 of the 1875 Beers atlas of Ulster County, New York, which shows the Fitch Building, a large bluestone yard, and ships along the Rondout Creek (reproduced in Ford 2010, 3; see also Ford 2004, 72). An easterly extension of the yards, which would be the bluestone yard of Donovan and Sweeney, is shown as situated on Abeel Street under the train trestle crossing the Rondout Creek (Ford 2004, 73). These locations would have been the shipping point for bluestone from what is now Hurley, the town of Kingston, Sawkill, Woodstock, and Zena.[3]

More recently, an archaeological survey focusing on Ponckhockie and the hamlet of Wilbur was submitted to the City of Kingston (Audin and Audin 2023). Audin and Audin (2023, fig. 3), a Google Earth photograph, shows a large quarry east of Wilbur Avenue and terminating just before the railroad tracks near the train trestle. This is indicated on the 1870 Beers map of Kingston (reproduced in Audin and Audin 2023, map 5) as the quarry of "Briggs and Co., Lime Manufacturers." For those who have wondered why all of the lime kilns were located at the southern end of Wilber Avenue, this is the reason.

Maritime Archaeological Sites

Maritime archaeological sites are those consisting of shipwrecks or portions of shipwrecks. Due to the city of Kingston's location on a creek and on the Hudson River, multiple shipwrecks are located within and along the edge of the corporate boundary of Kingston.

OPRHP files indicate the location of the *Mary Powell*, a famous 19th-century paddle-wheeler, as along the waterfront in present-day Rondout. Apparently, the ship was docked and then began to fall apart and eventually sank.

The remains of coal barges are presently visible along the southern edge of Island Dock opposite Connelly, where they were last used and then eventually sank. Some are also across from the Strand on the Sleightsburg side of the creek. Several coal barges, as mentioned above, can be found submerged or partially submerged, depending on the tide, along the shore at the Hutton Brickyards.

Within the small bay at Kingston Point that was created by the railway in the 19th century are multiple boats that are visible at low tide. Most of these are about 15–30 feet long and were likely used for transporting goods across the river or for fishing. These small craft are considered maritime archaeological resources, as they provide data on 19th-century shipbuilding techniques and attributes for fishing vessels (shad, striped bass, and sturgeon),[4] small transport vessels, and ferries.

Summary

This chapter has outlined the current knowledge of 19th-century historic archaeological sites that have been examined or excavated within the city of Kingston. However, based on the small size of this chapter but the large number of extant sites within the city, it is obvious that there are many more sites to be investigated. These include domiciles, businesses, wharfs, other sites relating to limestone[5] and clay extraction, and mills and railroads, to name but a few. All of these were constructed, lived in, or worked in or on by former Kingstonians, and these are significant components of Kingston's history. In this chapter, I have attempted to scratch the surface of the literally hundreds of potential 19th-century archaeological sites within the city of Kingston. Those that have not been examined or excavated by an archaeologist still represent an archaeological resource for the future.

Chapter 7

Commemorating the Dead

The Cemeteries of Kingston

I have, to a certain extent, borrowed the title of this chapter from Rothschild and Wall's chapter 7 in *The Archaeology of American Cities* (2014), as it similarly focuses on the ways in which communities of people bury and commemorate their dead. In the city of Kingston, the treatment of the dead, as well as the material culture related to memorializing the dead, has varied considerably, from large landscaped, parklike graveyards such as Montrepose and Wiltwyck cemeteries, to lesser-known examples such as the Houghtaling, Pine Street, and Mt. Zion cemeteries. For each of the latter three, this is related to their location, such as Mt. Zion, or the lack of gravestones, such as at the Houghtaling and Pine Street cemeteries. A more visible burial ground is the Sharp Burial Ground, located on Albany Avenue, which, because it is more visible to the public, has allowed it to bear the brunt of vandalism, desecration, and removal of grave markers over the years.

Archaeologists use gravestones and their size, material, shape, inscriptions, decorations, and horizontal location and placement to make inferences about the people who were memorialized by them (Baugher and Veit 2104; McGuire 1988; Richards 2014). This is a noninvasive form of archaeology—gathering data about people who lived in the past without disturbing the soil or their remains. Archaeologists and other researchers study graveyards from several perspectives: as a cultural landscape (Francaviglia 1971), as commemoration of the dead (Parker Pearson 1999), as social statements about wealth and power (McGuire 1988), as an aspect of the growth of capitalism (McGuire 1988), as a dialogue with the living (Carroll 2006; Garman 1994), and as representing peoples' beliefs about death and an afterlife (Ames 1981; Baugher and Veit 2014; Deetz 1977; Deetz and Dethlefsen 1965, 1967, 1971; Dethlefsen and Jensen 1977; Parker Pearson 1999). Material culture researchers also view gravestones as folk art (Benes 1977a, 1977b, 1978). Most of these types of studies can be accomplished through horizontal spatial analysis coupled with inscribed gravestone data. The study of the commercialization of death—that is, the growth of embalming, the shapes and construction techniques of coffins (Crane, Breed and Co. 1858; Riordan 2000, 2.1–2.12), and the growth of the coffin hardware industry (Norris, C. Sidney and Company n.d.; Paxson, Comfort and Company 1877; Sargent and Company 1883; Strong and Company c. 1870)—can be studied from a documentary perspective (Mitford 1963).

Below-ground studies may provide us with the best data regarding the people who were buried in a cemetery, particularly when gravestones are missing or when they were not used to begin with. An additional method for gleaning the demographic aspects of past populations is the analysis of human remains by bioarchaeologists. "Below ground" studies can at times become controversial due to the overwhelming belief among the general public that the dead should remain at rest. However, cities expand, real estate becomes expensive, infrastructure needs to be built, and, very often, cemeteries are simply considered as "in the way." In these cases, they are sometimes "moved," for better or worse (such as the Houghtaling Cemetery mentioned below), depending on the situation and the level of government involvement. For archaeologists and bioarchaeologists, the most informative way to move a cemetery is through careful excavation,[1] followed by study of the human remains, and then reinterment elsewhere. This usually involves "stakeholders," who are oftentimes the direct descendants of those who were buried in the cemetery. In cases where an unmarked burial ground needs to be moved, the stakeholders may include descendants, interested individuals, or groups of people that have come together to have a say in the process (Cantwell 1994).

The graveyards of Kingston range from the earliest located at the Old Dutch Church in uptown Kingston to much later cemeteries that are still in use. An examination of each cemetery gives us insights into the growth of Kingston, land use, the "color line" in death, and the lives of previous Kingstonians. The cemeteries are discussed here in roughly temporal order and are referenced to Rhoads's (2003) book on architecture in Kingston.

The Old Dutch Church

The Old Dutch Church graveyard is the oldest graveyard within the corporate boundary of Kingston. It appears on the 1695 Miller map of Kingston in a slightly different outline from what we see today, and it holds the remains of many of Kingston's more illustrious inhabitants as well as many of its 17th-century settlers (see Rhoads 2003, 34–36; Richards 2014). Several excavations have been undertaken in this graveyard. The first occurred across the street from the Fred Johnston House in the 1970s and is somewhat enigmatic, as very little is known about the findings. Although artifacts found during the excavation are currently housed at the Old Dutch Church, the fieldnotes from the work unfortunately appear to be missing. In my initial perusal of the artifacts with Pastor Rob Sweeney, I was surprised by the large numbers of 19th-century artifacts and the smaller numbers of 17th- and 18th-century artifacts. It was not until I excavated the DeWitt plot in another part of the churchyard in the summer of 2022 (see chapter 4) that I began to understand why that might be the case. The second excavation was undertaken on the eastern side of the church prior to stabilization of the eastern wall. This excavation was accomplished by Cohen (2005) and is discussed in chapter 4 as an excavation within the Stockade District.

The Houghtaling Cemetery

The Houghtaling Cemetery is located on the east side of Pine Street between Clinton Avenue, St. James Street, and Franklin Street. It was "moved" beginning in March of 1965 for the construction of a medical clinic (see Haines 2021, 87). Some of the gravestones were brought to the Old Dutch Church, and most of them—except for that of John Converse, who was reburied with his gravestone above him—are kept in a corner of the churchyard. The records concerning the removal of this early graveyard are sketchy at best.[2] In a discussion with Mr. Robert E. Haines (personal communication, June 30, 2023), I was informed that the cemetery was moved by the two local funeral homes under contract with the Old Dutch Church. This was accomplished by what archaeologists refer to as "the coroner's method," which simply involves digging up the skeletal remains and putting as many bones as found in a bag for transport. It is usually done with heavy equipment, such as a backhoe, so that significant numbers of bones are likely missed as each individual is exhumed. Mr. Haines informed me that this process occurred behind a burlap sheet that was attached to the iron fence around the cemetery to prevent onlookers from viewing the removal of the burials. This may explain the skepticism on the part of some Kingstonians that I noted in footnote 2.

Although some of the gravestones were taken to the Old Dutch Church, the rest were brought to Wiltwyck Cemetery, where they were deposited in a pile. Over the years, they were broken up for use as foundations for the later gravestones in Wiltwyck Cemetery. One burial found with the casket intact, that of Lucas Elmendorf, was placed in a separate vault and buried on the Wall Street side of the Old Dutch Church under the stone of Martin Elmendorf, which was taken from Pine Street. Some of the remains that were removed from the Houghtaling Cemetery were buried in a vault at the Old Dutch Church. Those individuals that were not recovered via the coroner's method, or the numerous skeletal fragments that were not picked up from those that were moved, are still there within the bounds of the Houghtaling Cemetery and Pine Street medical clinic.

An archaeological excavation by Hartgen Archeological Associates in 2021 within the footprint for a new building at the Pine Street clinic found rows of intact burials with remains still within the coffins. A total of about 30 people were found within the building footprint during trench excavations to connect sewer and water lines from the medical clinic to existing service lines under Pine Street. The evidence points to the stones being moved and a small number of people being disinterred in 1965, with the bulk of the bodies being left *in situ*. As of this writing, the report is currently in progress (Matt Kirk, HAA, personal communication, September 2024).

A detailed inventory of the deceased was made by Dr. J. Wilson Poucher and Byron J. Terwilliger in the 1930s, at a time preceding the removal of the stones but when the cemetery was "not used for burial purposes" (Poucher and Terwilliger 1931). The inventory listed 299 individuals and indicated that the earliest gravestone was set in the 1830s and that the latest burials dated to the late 19th century. In addition to several Houghtaling family members, the graveyard holds the remains of many of Kingston's Dutch and English families from the 18th and 19th centuries.[3] I am certain that none of them were of African descent, since the Black community of Kingston would have been buried further up Pine Street behind what is now 157 Pine Street.

Sharp Burial Ground

This cemetery is located on Albany Avenue near its intersection with the hump over the railroad tracks near St. James Court (Rhoads 2003, 80). The cemetery is bounded by the railroad tracks, Albany Avenue, and the backyards of houses that front Elmendorf Street. In his memo of October 7, 1948, City of Kingston Engineer A. F. Hallinan, in an attempt to clarify the wording and responsibility of the city for three burial grounds (Sharp, Houghtaling, and the Pine Street African American cemetery), outlined the history of the Sharp cemetery. Although the cemetery includes earlier burials dating to at least 1810, it was not until November 18, 1832, that Jonathan D. Ostrander and his wife formally turned over the property to the City of Kingston as a burying ground (book 48 of deed, pp. 15, 16). In the deed, it is stated that the burial ground would be used "for the sole and express purpose of burying dead white persons therein, forever." This one sentence in the deed provides us with a view into Kingston's past. Only five years after manumission (release from slavery), white Kingstonians, and particularly ones of Dutch descent, chose to continue the practice of separate cemeteries for Whites and those of former slaves or free Blacks. The segregation and dehumanization that occurred during life continued in death. At this point in time, one of the few options for Africans, African Americans, and recently freed Black individuals would have been the small, scattered family plots of their enslaved ancestors in and around the city of Kingston or the Pine Street African American Burial Ground cemetery (discussed below).

Hallinan also noted that the construction of the Rondout-Oswego Railroad in 1868 cut through some burials at the Sharp Burial Ground, and as a consequence, the municipality required the railroad to build a stone retaining wall to protect the graveyard. He also described the erection of fences and maintenance undertaken by the City of Kingston to protect the graveyard. It has since been listed on the National Register of Historic Places in 2002. At present, the condition of the Sharp cemetery has fluctuated between having a well-groomed appearance and occasional episodes of vandalism that have included breaking and knocking over the burial markers of some of Kingston's earlier occupants.

Montrepose Cemetery

The Montrepose Cemetery is located southwest of Mary's Avenue and is bordered by West Chester Street, backyards fronting on New Street, portions of the Benedictine Hospital property, and the Twaalfskill Golf Club. More than any other cemetery in Kingston, Montrepose embodies the lawn-park cemetery movement and its incorporation of landscape architecture in the 1850s to create a parklike setting where people could visit and relax (see Rhoads 2003, 124–26). As one drives through the gate and comes to a fork in the road, there is a stone slightly to the left of the fork. This is the stone of Washington Laycock (1835–1899), one of Kingston's patent medicine vendors and producer of "Laycock's Worm Killer," a local late 19th-century cure for intestinal parasites. Further back in a large mausoleum of the Kennedy family lies Dr. David Kennedy (1932–1901), a former Mayor of Kingston and patent medicine vendor whose products, particularly "Dr. Kennedy's Favorite Remedy," have been found as far afield as Australia.

Mt. Zion Cemetery

The Mt. Zion Cemetery is located on South Wall Street in what I have described elsewhere as a "marginal" location (Diamond 2006). In general, and there are exceptions, the small graveyards of 17th- to 19th-century enslaved individuals in Ulster County are located on small hillocks, near steep ravines, or on the sides of hills—locations that could not be farmed and where the owner could keep an eye on his property (i.e., people). The earliest marked burial in Mt. Zion Cemetery, that of Samuel Tappen, is dated 1856. Two burials were then added in the 1860s, one in the 1870s, 12 in the 1880s, 16 in the 1890s, and 11 in the first decade of the 20th century. For each successive decade in the early 20th century, 6 were added between 1911 and 1920, 5 between 1921 and 1930, 9 between 1931 and 1940, 12 between 1941 and 1950, 5 between 1951 and 1960, and 2 after 1960, with the last marked burial in 1967. The cemetery also has 3 unmarked graves and 20 named graves with no information on dates of birth or death. The cemetery also holds the remains of 18 soldiers who served in the 20th Regiment of the US Colored Infantry during the Civil War and 14 who served in the First and Second World Wars.

As I have described elsewhere (Diamond 2006), the Mt. Zion Cemetery probably began as a small graveyard that became of primary importance to Kingston's Black community after the Palen lumberyard was constructed over the Pine Street African Burial Ground in c. 1877–1878. The increase in burials is most noticeable in the 1880s, 1890s, and early

20th century. The decrease in burials from c. 1911 on until 1967 probably relates to the lack of space at the graveyard for additional burials.

The Comforter Reformed Church Cemetery

The Comforter Reformed Church Cemetery is located on Wyncoop Place, with portions of the cemetery adjacent to the backyards of houses fronting Clifton Avenue and Highland Avenue. It is a small cemetery that dates from c. 1872 until its most recent inhumation in 2021.

Saint Mary's Cemetery

Saint Mary's Cemetery is bounded by Flatbush Avenue, Cemetery Drive, Farrelly Street, and several backyards of houses and businesses that front Foxhall Avenue. It is a good example of a large, level piece of ground that has been set aside specifically for burial. Rhoads (2003, 19, 122–13) mentioned that it was set aside primarily for the burials of Irish, many of whom have imposing monuments within the cemetery.

Wiltwyck Cemetery

Wiltwyck Cemetery is bounded by Cemetery Lane, Pine Grove Avenue, and West O'Reilly Street. It is composed of the Wiltwyck and Wiltwyck Rural Cemeteries. This cemetery was established in 1850 (Rhoads 2003, 96–97), and like Montrepose Cemetery, was set up in a street format with parklike portions.

St. Peters Cemetery

St. Peters Cemetery is located to the south of Pine Grove Avenue and to the west of Mary's Avenue. It is separated from the Wiltwyck Cemetery by one property and a forested area. It was established in 1887 as a German Roman Catholic cemetery (see Rhoads 2003, 97). One of the gravestones is a memorial for Peter Barmann (1844–1908), the owner of Barmann's Brewery, which was one of Kingston's largest breweries in the late 19th century. Barmann beer bottles are often found on local archaeological sites as well as yard sales in and around Kingston.

Mt. Calvary Cemetery

The Mt. Calvary Cemetery is near the corner of Route 32 and East Chester Street in a relatively hidden location behind a gas station. It is sometimes called the "Polish Cemetery" due to the large number of people of Polish and Eastern European ancestry interred there. One of the earliest dated stones is that of Stanislaw Augustyn, who died in 1922 and has a military marker next to his stone, which is likely from World War I. This cemetery is still in use.

Summary

The cemeteries within the corporate boundary of the city of Kingston hold the remains of Kingstonians from the 17th century to the present. The oldest marked stone is that of Andries DeWitt, who died in 1710 and was buried in the Old Dutch Church graveyard.[4] With that in mind, it is worth noting that we have over 300 years of Kingston's residents buried throughout the city. Their memorials are a reminder that, at any point, we can still walk through a cemetery to observe the legacy in stone that they, or their relatives, left for them. These stones range from large edifices to small bluestones that have inscriptions that are barely legible. For those of us that are familiar with Kingston's 19th-century products, that walk reminds us of Kennedy's Favorite Remedy, Kennedy's Cherry Balsam, Laycock's Worm Killer, and beer bottles with the name of Peter Barmann.

Chapter 8

Enslaved Individuals in *Wiltwyck* and Kingston and African Americans in the Historical and Archaeological Record

Just as with most other historically settled areas on the eastern seaboard, Kingston also has an early record of enslavement. The mention of enslaved individuals in the historical record can be found in town and city records, court cases, bills of sale, census data, tax records, wills, inventories, and newspaper accounts. Gravestones as a form of material culture also serve as a record of the presence of enslaved individuals in the community as well as of relationships between the enslaved and their owners. For example, there are many historic cemeteries, such as several in Rhode Island, where enslavers provided gravestones for their enslaved to let the reader of the gravestone know of their ownership (Garman 1994). In Kingston, we do not find examples of this, and most cemeteries for enslaved individuals of specific Dutch families were small, dispersed, and in marginal geographic locations. Larger early cemeteries that do include the remains of Africans, African Americans, and "free Blacks" tend to be characterized by a lack of formal markers. In some cases, a notation on a map or mention in a newspaper article is the only information we have that a cemetery exists.

Because in today's society we are accustomed to the use of large stone markers and mausoleums, we neglect the fact that burial ritual for Africans and African Americans in the 17th and 18th centuries was a participatory and active event that included storytelling and continual interaction with living descendants at the grave site. In this case, large stone markers were unnecessary and unaffordable, and only a general location or small marker would make it possible to locate one's relatives. This information was often then transmitted via oral tradition. This would make it possible to add recently deceased family members to a location near, or cutting through, the graves of their ancestors, the latter of which is a trait that was found to be commonplace in Black cemeteries in South Carolina (Combes 1974).

In 1974, John D. Combes wrote an article describing the burial practices among South Carolina's Black population, which included information on a wide variety of above-ground markers, many of which were wooden or repurposed house appliances. Grave goods or offerings placed at the surface consisted of bottles, lamp parts, ceramics, table glass, and other items. It was one of the first articles to call attention to "non-formal" above-ground markers in cemeteries. In that article, Combes, after finding over 100 grave pits, noted that "the graves themselves seemed to be placed throughout the cemetery with no order and many of the graves intruded through burials previously interred" (1974, 54). Based on ground penetrating radar, this appeared to be the case at the Pine Street African Burial Ground. However, excavations in 2022 and 2023 suggested that there was deliberate spacing between burials, although one juvenile was buried very close to an adult, suggesting a family relationship.

Historical Records on Enslaved Individuals in *Wiltwyck* and Kingston

THE KINGSTON PAPERS AND SENATE HOUSE RECORDS

Some of the earliest historical records available for the city of Kingston are two volumes translated as the "Kingston Papers," published under the direction of the Holland Society in 1976 (Christoph et al. 1976). The Kingston Papers cover the earliest court records for *Wiltwyck*, and then for Kingston, from 1661 to 1667. The names of several enslaved individuals present within the *Wiltwyck* community have come down to us from these records. These are "Bastien the Negro" (Christoph et al. 1976, 2:438, 473), "Dominicus the Negro" or Dominicus Manuel (Christoph et al. 1976, 2:449, 690–91), Mrs. Anna Brodhed's "negro" (Christoph et al. 1976, 2:468), "Barendt the Negro" (Christoph et al. 1976, 2:493, 509), and "Mingus the Negro" or Mingus Manuel (Christoph et al. 1976, 2:480, 526, 717–18). The presence of these individuals as well as how they are referred to in the historic records reflect the complex nature of slavery in early *Wiltwyck*.

The second tranche of historic documents for Kingston are the recently translated "Senate House Papers" (Mouw 2014), a loose collection of accounts, lists, and notes that are owned by the New York State Office of Parks, Recreation, and Historic Preservation (OPRHP).[1] These relate to the Senate House property, and many of the records refer to the Ten Broeck family. When discussing the "Senate House Papers," I refer to the documents in temporal order from the 17th to 18th centuries.

One of the earliest mentions of enslaved individuals relates to Cornelis Pietersen Hoogeboom's request for a lot, which was reviewed at an ordinary session on January 20, 1665, where the following request was noted: "Cornelis Pietersen Hoogeboom requests that he may be granted a lot opposite the mill dam for a brick yard. The hon. court grants petitioner's request (and decides) to grant him (a lot) of about ½ morgen in extent" (Christoph et al. 1976, 1:198). One half of a morgen is about one acre in today's terminology, and this would be in the area near present-day North Front Street near Washington Avenue.

Archaeologists believe that Hoogeboom produced bricks (fig. 8.1), hearth tiles, and pan tiles at the brickyard, materials that were needed by

Figure 8.1. Three "Hudson Valley Flats" or early local Dutch bricks. *Source:* Photo by the author.

residents for the interior of houses for heat and cooking purposes. The small bricks shown in figure 8.1 represent several sizes of the standard Dutch brick that was locally produced and used to replace the yellow Dutch bricks that were being imported from the Netherlands as ship ballast. They are small in comparison to today's bricks, and the variation in size reflects the difference in dimensions between the handmade brick molds from which the bricks were struck. Pan tiles (fig. 8.2) are roofing materials that replaced thatch and wooden shingles as Kingston began to upgrade its roofing requirements and as new buildings were being constructed.

From the SHP, we learn that Cornelius Hoogeboom purchased a 12-year-old boy named "Tromp" on March 26, 1681 (Mouw 2014, 110–11). The document was signed by Hoogeboom on March 26, and then sworn to by witnesses on April 10. The following legal document described the purchase:

> I, the undersigned, Cornelis Hoogboom, residing in the town of Kingstone in the Esopus, acknowledge in the presence of the witnesses named below, to be certainly and justly indebted

Figure 8.2. Two red earthenware pan tiles. *Source:* Photo by the author.

to Mr. Isaac Deschamps Marchand in New IJorck, for the sum of three hundred schepels of salable winter wheat, arising from a Negros, approximately twelve years old, sold to me and delivered to my satisfaction, which amount of three hundred schepels of salable winter wheat [I] promise to pay to that same Mr. Deschamps; specifically, two hundred schepels in February or March of next year, 1681, [delivered] to this place at my expense on the bridge [and] at the weigh-houses, and the remaining [one] hundred schepels in the month of Feb[ruary] or March 1682. Additionally, as has been stated, [it will be] at my expense on the same bridge; without exception, binding [my] descendants to the foregoing, all of my property, moveable and immoveable, especially the same Negros named Tromp. Everything without guile or cunning. In affirmation of the truth [of this, I] have signed this with my own hand, in the presence, as stated above, of the witnesses signed below, New IJorck, March 26, 1681 upon condition of [it being] delivered to the harbor.

We [being] present

A. De La Noy, Cornelis Hoogenboom, Clement Sebrah

New Yorke, April the 10th, 1683

Then the wittnesses heareunto subscribed appeared before mee and made Oath that they saw the above Cornelis Hoogenboom signe and Deliver this obligation as his Act and deede to Isaac Deschamps being sworne before mee the day and yeare above written. [Wilhelmus] M. Beeckman Depute Major. (Mouw 2014, 110)

The SHP also described the purchase by Mr. Hoogeboom of Esopus for one "*Noir*" (*noir* is the French word for black) in March of 1681 or 1682 (Mouw 2014, 112), whose name was Daniel. Because he was purchased, we can assume that he was enslaved.

The next earliest records that mention enslaved individuals include a list of debits (Mouw 2014, 218) for Jacop Dechker in 1684—"also one pair for *neger*-18"; for Jan Hondersrae in 1689—"also one pair shoes for his *neger*-f18"; and further down the list, another tally for Jacop Dechker—"also one pair for his *neger*-18" (Mouw 2014, 218–19).

In 1692, Cornelius Hoogeboom increased his ownership of men, women, and children, as outlined in the following:

> Be it known to everyone whom it concerns, in Kingstowne, on this, the twenty-first of April, sixteen hundre[d] ninety-two, being in the fourth year of the reign of Willem and Maria, by the Grace of God the King and Queen of Great Britain: I, the unders[igned], Cornelis Hogenboom, resident of Kingst[on] acknowledge and declare to have purchased from Capt. Arent Schuijler, residing in Albanij, his male Neger, named Jacob, for the amount of [one] hundred and sixty pieces-of-eight, to be paid in the month of Ma[y], in the year 1693, specifically, half the amount he is due, that is eighty pieces-of-eight in cash and the other half to be paid with bricks at the price at which they are purchased in Albany; half of the cost of delivery of the bricks to the strand shall be borne by each of the afore-mentioned [parties,] which, for the future, I oblig[ate], myself my heirs [and] the executors and admin[istra]tors of my estate to the payment of this, and I, the undersigned Arent Schuijler acknowledge that I have delivered the aforementioned Neger free and unencumbered, and I indemnify the afore[mentioned] Cornelis Hogenboom for all future claims now and fo[r]ever, pledging as security my person and my property, current and future, subject to that which is permitted by law, and without guile or cunnin[g], everyone for their own part, signe[d] with their own hands, and sealed at the afore[mentioned] place on the date [written] above.
>
> Signed, and sealed; Present [were] Corn[elis] Bogardus, Cornelis Hoogenboom Geijssebert Marcelis, Arent Schuyler. (Mouw 2014, 113–14)

Hoogeboom's purchase of "Jacob" from Arent Schuyler in 1692 was for 160 pieces of eight, with one half to be paid in pieces of eight and the other half to be paid in bricks, which Hoogeboom produced at his kiln in Kingston. In this case, Jacob might have been producing the products to pay for his own enslavement.

Next, a debit for Wessel Ten Broeck from 1693 from a shoemaker lists a variety of shoes made for his family as well as "one pair repaired for Jan Oots," who is listed by the translator as "slave" (Mouw 2014, 91–92, n497). The list of shoes also included "one pair for the *neger* boy—one pair (for) the other *negers* boy."

Another mention occurs in a 1696 list from a shoemaker, which indicated, "May, Aberham Hasebroeck repaired one pair for wife-5, also one pair for his *neger*-18" (Mouw 2014, 202). A second undated note mentioned the repair of shoes for "Aberham Hasebrouck, one pair for his son-15, also one pair for his *neger*-18" (Mouw 2014, 215).

An unsigned paper from 1698–1699 indicated "Antonio my *Negre* make (delivery of) one load of posts by agreement for twelve guelde" (Mouw 2014, 79). This may refer to the enslaved individual of John Cotton, for in April 1698; John Cotton rented out his enslaved individual "Antonio" to Wessel Ten Broeck for 5½ days (Mouw 2014, 79).

The next reference is a January 9, 1699, debit to Johannijs Wijnkop (Johannes Wynkoop) stated, "to one pair of handles for 18, also one pair for *negerijn* Sijnije for 15, also one pair for *neger* Wyl for 12" (Mouw 2014, 199).

No further mention of enslaved individuals was found in the "Senate House Papers" between 1699 and 1744. The next mention in the "Senate House Papers" of enslaved individuals comes in 1744 in a particularly lengthy entry describing an unnamed enslaved female individual being leased out to the author's sister or, alternatively, being leased out to others for 15 years. The author describes the birth of five enslaved children at her house, for which she charged a "daller" to deliver:

> Year 1744 the *negren* of my sister, Sara tot Broeck; she came to my house [the] first of May
> 1 for 3 pounds each year
> 2 for 3 pounds each year
> 3 for 3 pounds each year
> 4 for 3 pounds each year
> 5 for 3 pounds each year
> 6 for 3 pounds each year
> 7 for 3 pounds each year
> 8 for 3 pounds each year
> 9 for 3 pounds each year
> 10 for 3 pounds each year

> 11 for 3 pounds each year
> 12 for 3 pounds each year
> 13 for 3 pounds each year
> 14 for 3 pounds each year
> 15 for 3 pounds each year
> the years written above are years that she has gone out to work
>> another five years which she has been with me and has also given birth to her children at my [house]
>> the first was a year old when it died, named Robben
>> the second I have had for four years and five months and named Anna
>> the third I have had for one year and named Betty
>> the four[th I have] had for four[t]een gagen
>> the fifth I have [had] nine days
>> and five delivered by me for one daller
>> Blandina ten Broeck Blandiena. (Mouw 2014, 155)

The next mention of enslaved individuals in the SHP is from October 27, 1762, where a payment of 3 shillings for "one day having wood hauled (by) Johan ten Broek's *neger*" (Mouw 2014, 160) was noted. This entry, and the two discussed next, confirm the common practice that enslaved individuals were hired out by their enslavers for various projects that the enslaver was reimbursed for.

A debit-list of expenses for food, drink, wood, and hauling of wood for bridge construction on January 23, 1768, listed 32 people, along with "Mathijs Blansaien for expenses and work performed by his son and *neger* amounts to 11 lb, 16 shillings, 3 pence" (Mouw 2014, 141–42). A more cryptic notation concerned sales to Willim Mans: "1791 his *neger* had 2 loads of limestone" (Mouw 2014, 174). This telling notation informs us of who was quarrying and delivering limestone in the area of Kingston in the late 18th century as well as who was being reimbursed for the labor, in this case, Willim Mans. This suggests that many, if not all, of the extant stone houses in today's Kingston were constructed, in some part, with the assistance of slave labor.

Williams-Myers (1994, 24–35) noted that enslaved individuals engaged in domestic tasks as well as in grain production, milling flour and lumber, and iron production. In an impressive publication based on collecting and publishing 821 advertisements in Hudson Valley,

Connecticut, and New York City newspapers from 1735 to 1831, which document attempts by enslavers to recover runaway enslaved individuals, Stessin-Cohn and Hurlburt-Biagini (2023, table 6) generated a list of skills documented in these advertisements. These specialties included baker, blacksmith, brewer, brush maker, business, butcher, carpenter, chimney sweep, cook (kitchen help), cypher (math), dancer, doctor, driver, drummer, farmer (plough, mow), fiddler, flautist, French horn player, fuller (cloth), horse/oxen care, house servant, laborer, mason, miller, preacher, privateer/sailor, reader, scythe maker, shoemaker, singer, soldier, speller, tambourine player, tanner, waiter, and writer.

Historical documentation such as this and the other examples provided above illustrate that enslaved individuals contributed to the development of early communities in the Northeast (Fitts 1996), specifically including the construction and architectural heritage of *Wiltwyck* and Kingston. However, this aspect of the early history of the area is commonly unknown, forgotten, or ignored. These types of historic documents serve to more accurately piece back together the region's full and diverse history.

An Example of an Additional Record Specific to Kingston

An additional interesting piece of information specifically from Kingston's history relates to the practice of enslavers turning enslaved females into a source of revenue. This information comes from the last page of Wessel Brodhead's family Bible.[2] On the inside of the back cover (fig. 8.3), he noted "Dean," a female who he bought as a 22-year-old, and then, apparently, the seven children she later had who were born enslaved and then became commodities. What we do not know is whether he, or another one of his enslaved individuals, may have fathered these children. At any rate, he chose to keep track of their names and birth dates, even though he could not put this information in the front of the Bible, where white births, names, and deaths were recorded:

1791 Record & Memorandum

> 1791 June 4th have I Wesel Brodhead, bought my Negro wench Dean and Tom a Negro boy from Abraham Van Gasbeck whose age was the one, 22 years and the other 18 months pride 60 pounds.

1793. Nov 12th. Is born my Negro Boy Born, Name Henry
1796. March 12th-was Born my Negro Wench philis
1798 March 22nd was born my Negro Wench Mary
1801 May 12th. Was Born my Negro wench Eave
1805 April 22nd, was Born my Negro Boy Jack
1808 June 21st was Born my Negro Wench Rachel
1811April 22nd was Born my Negro Wench Harriatty

Figure 8.3. The interior back cover of Wessel Brodhead's family Bible. *Source:* Photo by the author.

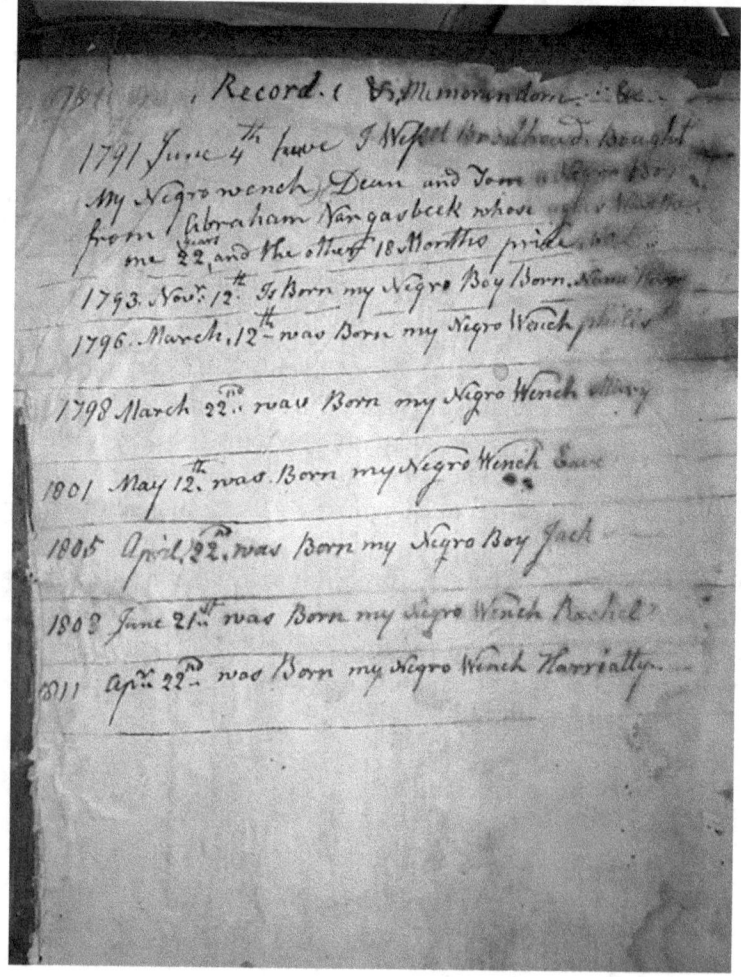

Census Records

Another common source of information for identifying the presence of enslaved individuals in the historic records is the census. The earliest local census documenting this for Kingston is the "Census of Slaves, 1755" (O'Callaghan 1850b). The entry for Kingston lists 236 enslaved individuals: 133 males and 103 females above the age of 14. Concerning who "owned" them, the following individuals, who relate to some of the archaeological sites mentioned in this book (i.e., Senate House, Persen House, Louw-Bogardus House), were listed as enslavers (numbers of enslaved individuals are in parentheses): Adam Paorsen (1), Widow Blandina Ten Broeck (2), Coenradt Ten Broeck (1), Benjamin Tan Broeck (1), Col. Abraham Van Gaasbeck Chambers (6), Col. John Tan Broeck (5), Lawrence Van Gaasbeck (1), Thomas Van Gaasbeck (5), Petrus Louw (1), and Johannis Masten (1). One portion of the 1755 census lists the names of the enslaved after their enslavers. From this, we can observe that common men's names such as Tom, Sam, Jack, John, Frank, George, Simon, Dick, Francis, Wil, Robin, Charles, Henry, Dan, and Ben were used, as were less common names such as Kellis, Bel, Gif, Smart, Quay, Trump/Tromp, Penney, Ebo, Prince, Caesar, Bal, Titus, Bris, Fort, Tone, Cato, and Bern. For females, the list includes common first names such as Mary, Anna, Jen, Catherine, Sue, Nan, Peg, Regina, and Sarah, and less common names such as Bet, Dijaen, Deen, Dien, Bat, Qussaba, Mat, and Gin.

By the time of the 1790 federal census, 711 enslaved individuals were listed as residing in the city of Kingston. At this time, the white population numbered 3,201, making the enslaved population 18.2% of the total, or almost one of every five people in the city. Of the 210 households who had enslaved individuals, those who held *more* than 10 enslaved individuals within their household included Andries DeWitt, Jr. (16), Henry Jansen (12), Jacob Ten Broeck (13), Wessels Ten Broeck (11), Peter van Gaasbeek (12), and Johannis Wynkoop (11).

Prior to the 1790 census, Matthewis Persen bought out his siblings' shares of the Persen House in 1770 and became the sole owner. He is thought to have died in 1819 at the age of 80 (Barricklo 2000, 15). During his tenure at the Persen House, it is probable that he had at least four enslaved individuals who were mentioned in the 1790 census. In *Olde Ulster: An Historical and Genealogical Magazine* (Brink 1910, 41–42), one can find reference to at least one of these individuals and the contractual situation by which Matthewis Persen obtained him:

This Indenture Witnesseth

    That I, Benjamin Bogardus of Dutchess County State of New York have let Matthew Persen of Kingstone County of Ulster and state aforesaid have a Negro slave Named Robin for the term of Nine years next ensuing, and said Matthew Persen his heirs or assigns will procure and provide for him the said Negro sufficient meat drink wearing apparel Lodging and Washing during the said term of nine years.

    And at the expiration of Nine years Next ensuing the date hereof, he the said Matthew Persen his heirs or assigns shall deliver the said Negro slave if alive unto the said Benjamin Bogardus his heirs of assigns. And for the true performance of the agreements aforesaid, the said parties bind themselves each unto the other firmly by these presents, in Witness whereof the said parties have hereunto set their hands and seals.

    Dated the fifth day of November, One thousand Seven Hundred and eighty-two.

Benjamin Bogardus (signed)

Matthew Persen (signed)

Sealed and delivered in the presence of us

Frantz J. Roggen

Petrus Roosa

Matthewis Persen probably utilized Robin for housework, construction projects, and other chores around the house and elsewhere. Based on the large amounts of tailoring equipment (buttons, pins, needles, and thimbles) found within the Persen House during archaeological excavations, it is also possible that Robin was engaged in tailoring for Matthewis Persen. We can only assume that he was returned to Benjamin Bogardus at the end of nine years. The Persen House, like many Dutch structures and historic sites in the Northeast, including the Ten Broeck House, was the home of numerous enslaved families as well as enslaved individuals at various points in time. However, their presence is often overlooked or marginalized because they commonly could not read or write, and hence could not participate in documenting their contributions to the historical record. This results in what Patterson (1982) has called "social death," a reference, in part, to the enslaved individual as a living person as well as the negligible content, and almost invisible quality, that history affords them (see also Jamieson 1995). "Social death" refers to the lack of social relations that are part of a reality for people who have been torn away from their families and larger social group and transported (against their will) to another location. Enslaved people could not (1) worship their ancestors, (2) form a cohesive family, (3) have social relations with other family members, (4) be worshiped as an ancestor, (5) have political power or authority, or (6) control their own destiny (Patterson 1982). Their only respite was the Pinkster Festival, a celebration over several days where they could celebrate their African roots (see Williams-Myers 1994).

Archaeological Evidence of Enslavement

Except for one piece of coral at the Wessel Ten Broeck House (Senate House) and one piece from the Persen House,[3] the artifacts collected as part of the archaeological record in and of themselves do not bear symbolic markings such as *cosmograms*, or associations that point to African usage, as has been found on other sites in the United States (Ferguson 1992; Klingelhofer 1987). Like many Dutch, French, and English sites where enslaved individuals lived, the artifacts they used (cooking pots, knives, guns, clothing, etc.) were the same as those of their owners, and it is difficult, if not impossible, to distinguish usage specifically by enslaved individuals except in cases of caches or the discovery of specific hiding places where items were kept.

One interesting piece of history that has been gleaned through the archaeological record is that, on large southern plantation sites in particular, artifacts used by enslaved individuals have been found to be horizontally distinct from those of their enslavers. These materials have been found associated with, under, and around dwellings, where they were deposited or hidden by enslaved individuals. Very often, as particular categories of artifacts (particularly ceramics) went out of fashion on large plantations, they were given to the enslaved individuals for use. This was the case at Drayton Hall, South Carolina, where I participated in an excavation by New York University in the cabin locations of the Drayton family's enslaved individuals. We found delft (tin-glazed buff-bodied earthenware), creamware, and pearlwares—high-style wares that, when initially purchased, would have been used by the Drayton family. As these wares were superseded by newer ceramic styles, they went out of fashion for the Draytons and were apparently given to the individuals whom they enslaved.

On northeastern sites, horizontal separation in archaeological contexts is more of a rarity. We can assume that many, if not all, of the ceramics, bottles, and cookware that we find archaeologically were probably handled by enslaved individuals during the course of their daily activities. It is a rare instance where specific markings on an item provide more specific and tangible information (e.g., see Goldberg and Witkowski 2006). For example, an "X" or "X" within a circle are African cosmograms called *dikenga*, most commonly found among the BaKongo of southern Zaire and northern Angola (Ferguson 1992, 110–20). The *dikenga* cosmogram represents "the crossroads between the world of the living and the world of the dead, day and night, and so on" (Lucas and Kirk 2023, 904; see also Fennell 2007) and has also been thought to be associated with water spirits.

In Albany, New York, Mike Lucas and Matt Kirk documented artifacts from the Bogart House excavation, most of which were basement finds relating to enslaved individuals. Most of the artifacts were found in two basement rooms as well as a barrel in one room containing a large number of artifacts, some of which included inscribed Xs (Lucas and Kirk 2023). Other artifacts from within the barrel included a cowry shell, a bone-handled knife with a carved X, a smoking pipe, a marble, and fragments of a "Turlington's Balsam of Life" bottle. Lucas and Kirk (2023) noted that "perhaps the Bogart basement was a place where agency and autonomy were expressed through the BaKongo *dikenga* and the arrangement of objects beneath the floor" (907). They concluded that "the contents of the barrel and other artifacts found under the floor of the Bogart House basement are rare and tangible evidence of a complex material world constructed by enslaved African Americans in Albany, New York" (907).

After manumission (release from slavery) in New York State in 1827, the census takers began to record the number of "free Blacks." From the 1840 census of Kingston, we learn that there were 288 free Blacks, comprised of 125 males and 163 females, who were living with 95 families. This number dropped by the 1855 census, which included 207 "free Blacks," comprising 66 families, and large numbers of single individuals, both male and female. As I have noted elsewhere (Diamond 2006), many of the surnames of Kingston's Black citizens were derived from the names of their former enslavers, either Dutch, French, or English—for example, DeWitt, Brodhead, and Timbrouck (from Ten Broeck). The census reports thus provide a glimpse into the number of Black citizens in Kingston at that time as well as their ties to their former enslavers.

The Pine Street African Burial Ground

I have chosen to discuss the cemetery at 157 Pine Street separately from the cemeteries discussed in the previous chapter for several reasons. The first is that this cemetery has no headstones, making it appear as though it is not a place of burial. The second is that it undoubtedly holds the remains of enslaved Black Kingstonians. Third, the graveyard was almost obliterated in the 1870s, when all of its stones were either removed or flattened when the property became a lumber yard. This destruction would have been finalized in the early 1990s when the cemetery was proposed as a parking lot (see Diamond 2006, 47–48). Fourth, after the lumber yard was defunct, the cemetery became a dumping ground for construction debris and household refuse. All four of these factors make the Pine Street African Burial Ground unique within the city of Kingston.

The Pine Street African Burial Ground is Kingston's largest African and African American cemetery (Diamond 2006); in fact, it may be one of the largest burial grounds of that category in the Northeast. It is located on the block between Pine, Fair, Franklin, and St. James Streets. It holds the remains of Kingston's African and African American population from the cemetery's founding as a burial location in the Armbowery in the mid-18th century. City of Kingston Engineer A. F. Hallinan noted in his memo of October 7, 1948, that the burial ground was set up by the trustees of the Corporation of Kingston on October 6, 1750. It continued as the main location for Kingston's Black community until its end as a burial location in c. 1877–1878, when it was sold and turned into Henry W. Palen's Lumber Yard (see De Lisser 1968, ii–iii).

The Pine Street African Burial Ground was "rediscovered" by the author, along with city historian Edwin Ford, in 1990 (Diamond 1990, Site 3-C-7). It is shown on several historic maps of the city as an empty lot (e.g., 1858 French map) and on the 1870 and 1875 Beers maps as "Cemetery." The cemetery was covered over in the late 1870s when it was sold and Palen constructed his lumberyard on it. At that point, the Black residents of Kingston had to find another location for the burial and commemoration of the dead, and they chose the Mt. Zion burial ground on South Wall Street.

In 1996, the property at 157 Pine Street was proposed as a parking lot for an uptown business. This would have entailed the destruction of one of Kingston's earliest unmarked graveyards. More importantly, it would have destroyed the burial locations of an invisible portion of Kingston's population: the Black population of Kingston from c. 1750 to 1877–1878. This community of individuals had no above-ground gravestones, no registered grave plot information, and only the backyards of several yards fronting on Pine, Fair, and St. James Streets as their final resting places. Thankfully, Mayor T. R. Gallo did not allow the parking lot project to proceed.

More recently, Dr. John Rayburn of the SUNY New Paltz Geology Department and I utilized ground penetrating radar (GPR) several times in an attempt to define the edges of the original cemetery and to estimate how many people may have been buried there (fig. 8.4). The GPR survey

Figure 8.4. Dr. John Rayburn (left) and SUNY New Paltz Geology Major Ross Hernandez conducting a ground penetrating radar survey at 157 Pine Street (January 16, 2019). *Source:* Photo by the author.

we initially undertook in 2019 revealed numerous soil "anomalies," which, after further investigation through archaeological excavation, turned out to be either stone markers or human burials. These were found in rows, with most anomalies on an east/west axis as well as many on a north/south axis. The stones were pieces of bluestone that appear to have been upright at one time and then laid flat and covered with soil. One stone showed the deep grooves characteristic of bluestone cart wheels (see Blauweiss and Berelowitz 2022, 52; Steuding 1985, 70), which would have been a fragment of the bluestone road that ran from Wilbur into the lower Catskills near West Hurley (fig. 8.5). The stones that were excavated were not inscribed but may have served as inexpensive markers whose position and affiliation with a particular family member in the cemetery was passed down through oral tradition.

Dr. Rayburn and I returned to 157 Pine Street in the early summer of 2022 and initiated a second GPR survey to locate the boundaries of the cemetery. Again, we found several anomalies and laid out a row of three 2 × 2 meter excavation squares along the southern edge of the original

Figure 8.5. Section of bluestone road in front of Hurley Library, main Street, Hurley. *Source:* Photo by the author.

property line indicated on the historic maps as the initial excavation units. In July, the SUNY New Paltz archaeological field school, in conjunction with Mr. Tyrone Wilson, founder and executive director of Harambee Kingston NY, Inc., the new owners of the property, began testing the cemetery to "ground truth" the historic maps. Dr. Kenneth Nystrom of the SUNY New Paltz Department of Anthropology directed the excavation. At the start of the excavation, we were informed that the sewer line to 157 Pine Street had failed and that a new line had to be installed. While this was being accomplished, Dr. Nystrom and I monitored the sewer trench for artifacts and human remains. Within the first couple of hours, we identified a gravestone and several gravestone fragments. The intact gravestone (fig. 8.6) gave us our first and, at this point, only name. Engraved in marble was

Ceazer Smith

died Jan. 26

1839,

aged 41 years 2

mo. & 5 days

Life's duty done, as sinks the clay

Light from it's load the spirit flies

While heaven and earth combine to say

How bless'd the righteous when he dies

Since he was born before 1799, Ceazer Smith may have been born into slavery in 1797 and died a free man in 1839. Research is currently being undertaken to find out more about him. The other identified gravestone fragments provided minimal information but were encouraging. Found among the archaeological units and during the sewer line replacement were two marble footstones—smaller stones that demarcate the eastern end, or foot, of an individual's grave—one engraved with "B.T." and the other with "D.T."

Figure 8.6. The gravestone of Ceazer Smith when it was first found. *Source:* Photo by the author.

The plan for encountering human remains consisted of the following: (1) human remains would be treated with the utmost respect from the time that they were encountered until the day they were reburied; (2) with the exception of recording photographs during excavation, visitors, the press, and students would be restricted from taking photos, and if this occurred, the photos would need to be immediately deleted; and (3) in consultation with Tyrone Wilson, samples of teeth and bone would be collected from every individual recovered during excavation for use in future bioarchaeological analyses.

During the study, the excavation of 26 square meters of backyard area located what we believed to be the southern boundary of the graveyard. Two post molds with cut bluestone bases were found along the lot line—a likely attempt to fortify the wood from termite and carpenter ant activity as well as provide a solid footing in a sand matrix. The excavation also located the remains of seven individuals: 5 adults and 2 juveniles. Near the southern boundary, the skeleton of a small New World monkey (*Cebus sp.*), with an iron and leather collar around its neck, was also found. This was likely someone's pet, possibly belonging to one of the people who the monkey was buried closest to. This discovery, while fascinating, is not unique. At the Five Points excavation in New York City, a stone-lined privy produced fragments of a New World monkey (*Cebus sp.*), which the authors suggested "associates at least a portion of this deposit with the Italian tenants who were employed as organ-grinders through the 1860's and 1870's" (Milne and Crabtree 2000, 173).

As students began excavating 2-meter squares at the back of the property, it became apparent that the graveyard was filled in during 1877–1878 and after the lumber yard years when the property reverted to backyards. Many of the units had significant quantities of brick and brick fragments, various categories of nails, window glass, concrete, bluestone, and large pieces of iron in the upper strata. Along with the destruction debris was a large amount of household items, which had been mixed in with the building materials. This included plain whiteware, blue transfer-printed whiteware, red transfer-printed whiteware, ironstone, flow-blue pearlware, red earthenware flowerpot fragments, porcelain, and various categories of stoneware.

Glass vessels included beer, soda, pharmacy, whiskey, liquor, wine, patent medicine, pomade, and perfume bottle fragments. One beer bottle fragment bore the partial embossed letters of the George Hauck Brewing Company, a brewery at the corner of Broadway and McEntee Streets that went out of business during Prohibition. Another included the embossed lettering "_R. BAR_" for the Peter Barmann Brewing Company, one of Kingston's most famous historic brewers.

Personal items included combs, marbles, syringe fragments, hair clips, buckles, white clay smoking pipes, buttons, slate pencils, and a lice comb. One Native American artifact, a Levanna projectile point, was found. However, this artifact was in an ash deposit, apparently having been discarded with coal ash when someone emptied their stove.

The archaeological study of the Pine Street African Burial Ground was intended to "ground truth" the fact that the property was indeed a burial ground as well as attempt to define the boundaries of the cemetery. In each case, the excavation succeeded, providing us with what was most likely the southern fence line of the cemetery as well as the remains of seven unnamed African American individuals from Kingston's past. Although we do have one name from the gravestone that was found,

Ceazer Smith, we are hoping through research and further excavations to discover many more names.

During the second field season conducted in 2023, 12 additional square meters were excavated across three units, two of which identified additional post molds, potentially indicating the southern fence line of the cemetery. The post molds were similar to those found the previous year, having a flat piece of bluestone at the bottom of the pit to support the post. Interestingly, the post molds were on a line heading to a current property corner stake. However, that corner is not the westernmost extent of the cemetery, which is shown on 19th-century maps as including portions of the property to the west of the stake. In one unit just inside the line of post molds, we found a juvenile burial that included a coin in the pelvis area. This was a copper penny with Draped Liberty Bust (facing right), but the date was not discernible. Since it did not have the Liberty cap and pole of earlier versions of the cent (1793–1796), we determined that it dates between 1796 and 1807. The copper coin is the only form of grave good/offering that we found in a burial at 157 Pine Street. After it was photographed and examined, it was placed in its original position and reburied with the individual.

In another unit in the middle of the lawn, a substantial piece of bluestone was found flat on an east/west axis above a burial. It is possible that this was laid flat when filling began in the backyard. Directly underneath the stone, a possible cache or offering of four items was found: a fragmentary smoking pipe in the shape of a fish (with scales), two ground glass perfume stoppers, and the lip and neck of a bottle with a cork stopper still intact. We are unsure what these items meant to the individual buried under the stone or, for that matter, to the person who placed them there. Additionally, this group of artifacts is different than the coin discussed above, which was placed inside the coffin and shroud of the juvenile burial, which would have occurred prior to or during the actual burial ceremony. The cache of items under the flat stone would have happened after the grave shaft had been filled in and could have occurred during or well after the burial.

At the end of the 2022 study, Professor Nystrom and I had discussed with Tyrone Wilson the feasibility of removing human remains from underneath the patio area behind 157 Pine Street, as it was agreed that having a small event space above people's graves was, at the very least, inconsiderate. During the 2023 study, our goals were to find additional evidence of the south boundary of the cemetery as well as locate burials immediately behind the house for removal. Consequently, we cleared the patio area behind the house at 157 Pine Street, uncovering an additional four burials.

In total, 10 individuals were identified during the 2023 field season, and on the next to last day of excavation, we encountered a set of coffin nails from the eastern end of a burial that we did not remove, as it was on the very edge of the patio area and the burial itself extended out into the lawn. In addition, during clearing of the area behind the house, a large nonfunctioning drywell in the form of a decomposed wooden barrel was replaced. The old barrel was filled with bluestone fragments and a fragmentary marble gravestone. Unfortunately, although the gravestone could be pieced back together, the inscribed portion was missing.

Overall, at least 17 individuals and one grave shaft (which we did not excavate) were identified during the archaeological study. From those 17 individuals, we collected 17 samples for DNA analysis and strontium isotope analysis. The individuals from the patio area were exhumed and brought to SUNY New Paltz for analysis prior to reburial. The remains that we encountered throughout the backyard of 157 Pine Street were analyzed in situ, and then bone, dental, and soil samples were collected by Dr. Nystrom prior to reburial.

The 2023 study gave us a broader perspective on the length of time the backyard had been used for refuse disposal. During the 2022 study, we found a significant amount of late 19th-century debris in the southwest corner of the lot. During the 2023 study, we found a brass faucet patented by "J. A. Vogel Co." on "Dec. 30th 1913" and a New York State dog collar #390480 with a date of 1931. These materials suggest that the southwest corner of the yard was being used as a location for refuse as late as the 1930s.

Ultimately, by locating gravestones and utilizing DNA analysis, we would like to give back to Kingston's African American residents the burial locations of their ancestors. This kind of study will entail comparing DNA from the individuals from 157 Pine Street with local Black Kingstonians to determine if there are genetic (i.e., family) relationships between them. This was accomplished for another recent study of an African American cemetery in Catoctin Furnace, an iron smithy in Maryland (Curry 2023, 472–77; Harney et al. 2023, 500; Jackson 2023, 482–83). Here, both enslaved and freed African Americans were disinterred during an archaeological excavation prior to highway construction in 1979–1980. The human remains and gravestones were removed and then curated until researchers undertook DNA analysis to identify whether any members of the local community were related to them, and, in fact, many were. More importantly, the descendants of the people from the cemetery were spread all across the country. This study is a model for 157 Pine Street as archaeologists, bioarchaeologists, and historians attempt to piece together the story of the cemetery and its occupants.[4]

Summary

This chapter has focused on characterizing the social and economic relationships between enslavers and their enslaved in the 17th and 18th centuries. From Christoph et al. (1976) and Mouw (2014) we learned that many of the enslaved were hired out to perform various construction projects throughout the city. While we sometimes think that the material culture of slavery is difficult to tease out of the archaeological record, we have only to walk down any street in the uptown portion of Kingston and walk past a stone building to experience a product of enslaved labor. The 17th- and 18th-century built environment of uptown Kingston was most likely produced by slave labor. Some of those enslaved individuals were buried at the Pine Street African Burial Ground,[5] and after the 1870s, their descendants turned to the Mt. Zion Cemetery on South Wall Street as a final resting place.[6] This is an example of how the color barrier enforced in life was also carried over into death.

Chapter 9

Nearby Precontact Sites in the Towns of Ulster, Hurley, and Esopus

The six precontact Native American archaeological sites discussed in this chapter were excavated from the 1950s to 2009. While they are not within the corporate boundary of the city of Kingston, the people who occupied these sites traversed this area and likely also left artifacts at many of the sites that have been found within the city that are discussed within this book. Each of these sites are just outside of the city in the towns of Ulster, Hurley, and Esopus. Additionally, two of these sites, the Kingston and Hurley sites, occur throughout the Late Woodland and Contact period literature of the Hudson Valley.

The Kingston Site

No discussion of Kingston's archaeological past is complete without mentioning the Kingston site, even though it is located in the town of Ulster. Our only description of the Kingston site is to be found in William Ritchie's *The Chance Horizon: An Early Stage of Mohawk Iroquois Cultural Development* (1952), even though the site is not Haudenosaunee (Snow 1980, 320–22). An interesting way to begin a chapter: the Kingston site isn't in Kingston, and although it occurs in a publication on Haudenosaunee archaeology, it is not a Haudenosaunee site.

The site itself is just north of the corporate boundary of the city of Kingston and was excavated by James Schaefer and Edmund Carpenter from 1945 to 1947, with state archeologist William Ritchie and Charles F. Wray spending several days on the site. Because the Kingston site yielded large amounts of Late Woodland incised pottery, Ritchie classified it with four other Mohawk Iroquois (i.e., Haudenosaunee) sites from the Mohawk Valley that had similar ceramics: Chance, Deowongo Island, Second Woods, and Oak Hill. At the time of its discovery, the Kingston site[1] was "the only member of the Chance series lying well outside of the Mohawk domain" (Ritchie 1952, 11).

Ritchie's (1952) trait list of the artifacts includes 32 Levanna and Madison type projectile points, 9 celts, 1 pendant, 2 hammerstones, 1 abrading stone, 1 pestle, 3 mullers, 2 multipurpose tools, 1 hoe, 3 net-sinkers, 1 hematite paintstone, 13 tools made from animal bone, antler, and shell, 15 bird bone beads, and 599 pottery fragments. In addition to the wide variety of Native American tools, the site is significant because it likely has the largest representation of Native American smoking pipes from a single site in the Hudson Valley ($N = 32$). The pipes were all made from locally sourced clay from areas around Kingston.

Of particular importance on this site was the presence of shell beads and pendants as well as European manufactured trade goods, which suggests the site is later than the Chance phase (c. 1400–1500 AD), as Ritchie had believed. Later artifacts dating from contact with the Dutch included two beads of conch or *Busycon* (whelk) columella, two white wampum beads made from *Mercenaria* (clam) shells, and two discoidal shell bead blanks (unfinished beads). European manufactured items included one triangular arrowhead, one irregular rectangular pendant, and one narrow rectangular scrap, all made from sheet brass. Seven glass beads, probably originally made in the Netherlands, were of two types: four were "small, ovate, light blue stripes on purple ground," and three were "small, barrel-shaped, red interior, end shows fine white star-like figure" (Ritchie 1952, 33). The first four could be any of three Kidd types (IIIm1, IVk3, or IVk4), and the second three beads could be Kidd Type IIIm1 or IVk4 (Kidd and Kidd 1970). These bead types are commonly found on early 17th-century sites in the Hudson and Mohawk Valleys (Diamond 1999a, 2004b, 2023; Fisher and Hartgen 1983; Lenig 1999; Pratt 1961; Rumrill 1991; Snow 1995) and are associated with Dutch trade for beaver skins, other pelts, maize, and land (see Karklins 1974). Lastly, five fragments of white clay smoking pipes were found on the site, another indication of trade with the Dutch.

Perhaps the most notable aspect of the Kingston site is that it has provided both a type site and a name for the most common form of precontact to Contact period Native American pottery in the Hudson Valley. "Kingston Incised" (fig. 9.1) was the name given by Ritchie (1952) to a particular form of incised pottery, the key attribute being small "ladder-like" patterns that fill in long vertical and oblique spaces between incised lines on the collar of the pot. The ladders would likely have been constructed using fingernails, twigs, hollow reeds, and stylus-like objects, the latter of which create a triangular impression not unlike those found on cuneiform writing in Mesopotamia. Kingston Incised as well as Hudson Valley Incised and Hudson Valley Crescent Incised were initially described and typed from the Bell-Philhower site in New Jersey (Ritchie 1949) and then used several years later at the Kingston site (Ritchie 1952). Currently, only the Kingston Incised type is widely referred to throughout the archaeological literature; the other two type names dropped out of use during the late 1950s.

One final notable feature of the Kingston site is that it yielded one of the largest collections of Native American pottery, when one considers the number of individual vessels present. Based on a study of the collection

Figure 9.1. Reconstructed pot of "Kingston Incised" type from the S-2 site (NYSM accession #A2014.03A.2.3). *Source:* Photo by the author.

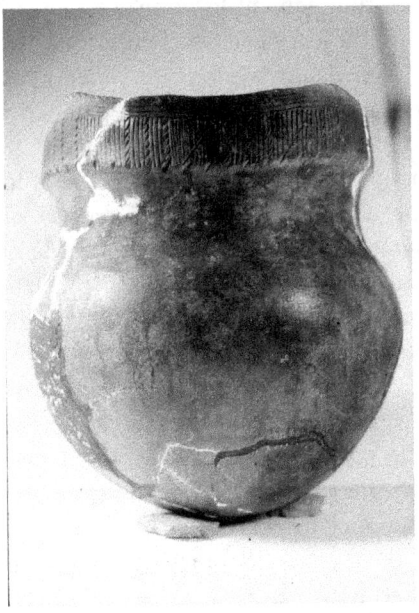

at the New York State Museum, I estimated that there were approximately 45 pots represented. A separate study of these pots undertaken by Hetty Jo Brumbach (1975) found two key attributes associated with Late Woodland to Contact period Hudson Valley pottery: the ladder design and, to a lesser extent (and percentage), a pointed rather than flat lip at the top edge of the pot.

One interpretation of the Kingston site is that it served as a series of small procurement camps during the Early and Late Archaic periods. This is evidenced in the New York State Museum collections by small numbers of projectile points such as Kanawha, Brewerton, Normanskill, Genessee, Orient, and Perkiomen points. However, I would argue that the site was used most extensively during the Late Woodland, after c. 1450 AD. The large numbers of pottery, smoking pipes, and the presence of plant processing tools would suggest one or more house structures, if not a dispersed horticultural hamlet. At the present time, the location of the Kingston site is still unknown. I have been looking for it since 1997 as part of my doctoral research, and I hope one day to conclusively pin it down.

The Manor Site

The Manor site is in the "general location" of the Kingston site, but as I mentioned above, it still has not been found and archaeologists are still trying to locate it. The Manor site was identified in 2004 during a Phase 1 archaeological survey of a 48-acre parcel planned for development of a housing community. The initial study identified an area of precontact Native American activity that was deemed worthy of further investigation; thus, a Phase 2 site evaluation was conducted (HAA 2005). The Phase 2 study recommended avoidance of the site, but due to the construction plan, this was not feasible; consequently, the construction impacts were mitigated by a Phase 3 data recovery investigation by Hartgen Archeological Associates in 2006 (HAA 2009).

The Phase 3 research design included several main questions to be addressed, which mainly centered on resource exploitation of the area by precontact groups. In addition, the study explored whether the Manor site might potentially be the location of the Kingston site that was described in Ritchie's (1952) publication.

The Phase 3 data retrieval, or mitigation, consisted of 72 shovel tests (18 sq m/193 sq ft), 43 units equaling 61.5 meters (661 sq ft), and four areas stripped by heavy machinery (86 sq m/925 sq ft), for a total of 165.5 meters or 17,787.7 square feet of excavated area. The stratigraphy of the site consisted of a fluvial gravel layer overlaid by a fine yellow-brown sand and an organic sandy forest mat (HAA 2009, 13).

The excavations focused on five loci that contained the most archaeological data. Locus 1 was the northernmost activity area and was examined through one unit and four shovel tests, yielding 78 debitage, 1 rough stone tool, and 9 fire-cracked rocks. Further work was not conducted on this locus.

Locus 2 was investigated through multiple tests that contained both high and low densities of artifacts. Eleven excavated units produced 4,094 debitage, 57 chipped stone tools, 1 ground stone tool, 17 projectile points, 18 rough stone tools, and 324 fire-cracked rocks, for a total of 4,511 artifacts. Of 16 diagnostic projectile points, five types were found at Locus 2: Brewerton Side-Notched, Sylvan Side-Notched, Susquehanna Broad, Perkiomen, and Madison. A piece of drilled soapstone was also found, probably relating to the Frost Island phase occupation that was represented by the Susquehanna Broad projectile points. Locus 2 also had several old back-dirt piles, likely from previous excavations, as well as several wooden stakes, leading the archaeologists to believe that the Manor site was indeed Ritchie's (1952) previously excavated Kingston site.

Locus 3 yielded a lithic workshop that was divided into three "production zones," where stone tool manufacturing would have taken place. Fifteen units yielded 11,281 debitage, 129 chipped stone tools, 10 projectile points, 34 rough stone tools, and 137 fire-cracked rock, for a total of 12,863 artifacts. The 10 projectile points include 9 that could be typed as Sylvan Stemmed and one that appeared to be a Susquehanna Broad point.

Production Zone #1 was categorized by "early stage reduction of chert on top of a stationary anvil," which weighed 18.1 kg (40 lb) (HAA 2009, 32). Stationary anvils are large rocks that serve as a platform for initial lithic reduction. This was also evidenced by large numbers of fragmentary limestone blocks from which the chert was removed. This area yielded "1,272 fragments of limestone, chert ore blocks, fragments of hammerstones as well as 26 used and unused pebble and cobble hammerstones" (HAA 2009, 32).

Production Zone #2 "was associated with the manufacture of tools out of silica-rich sandstone" (HAA 2009, 33). The horizontal production area for these tools was much larger than Production Zone #1, and because the lithic material was different than the cherts commonly used, it was easier to determine the overall size of the lithic reduction area. This production area yielded 6,243 pieces of debitage composed of silica-rich sandstone as well as 28 "failed" or broken ovate bifaces and one projectile point. Many of these artifact forms, as well as celt and adze preforms, were also found at other loci on the site, suggesting that the ovate bifaces found in Production Area #2 were preliminary tools that were to be later ground into finished forms[2] for woodworking tools. This production zone yielded only one projectile point: a Susquehanna Broad–like point made from silica-rich sandstone. This may give us an indication that the people who were using this stone occupied the area during the Frost Island phase (c. 1500–1200 BC/cal. 3450–3150 BP).

Production Zone #3 was "associated with the manufacture of bifaces, cores, and blanks from chert ore." The lithic debris scatter was centered on a cache (Feature 7), where 53 bifacial tools and blanks were discovered in a hole. The debris scatter was approximately 14 square meters (150 sq ft) in size (HAA 2009, 35). Associated with the cache were two narrow-stemmed projectile points of the Sylvan Stemmed type. Based on the color photographs in the report, the chert ore appears to be a combination of local brown and black Onondaga chert and green Mt. Merino chert. Although the report calls the Mt. Merino cherts "distant," there are quarries of Mt. Merino chert nearby (see Millens quarry below), approximately 2,590 meters (8,500 ft) away.

Locus 4 was examined with 15 units that produced 2,217 debitage, 45 chipped stone tools, 10 projectile points, 8 rough stone tools, and 139 fire-cracked rock, for a total of 2,419 artifacts. Diagnostic projectile points included a Vosburg point, Sylvan Stemmed points, Normanskill points, and an Orient Fishtail point.

Locus 5 was identified through shovel testing. One unit yielded 94 debitage, 1 chipped stone tool, and 5 fire-cracked rock, for a total of 100 artifacts. Further work was not undertaken at this locus.

The Manor site was interpreted as an open, backcountry camp. Although evidence of campfires was observed in the excavations, the charcoal associated with them was scattered and was not suitable for radiometric dating. There is also a clue suggesting that people returned to the site numerous times. This is based on the presence of several caches of lithic materials on the site. *Caches* refer to locations where items were purposefully stored so that they could be retrieved later upon returning to the area. One of the caches on the site included "53 bifacial preforms, cores, and lithic blanks in a small hole beside a flat piece of sandstone"

(HAA 2009, 78). These roughly made stone tools would have been reduced to provide readily available preforms to make formal tools such as scrapers, projectile points, and knives.

The study of the Manor site identified several important precontact loci from the Late Archaic period. One of the most interesting aspects of the study was the discovery of a lithic reduction area of silica-rich sandstone (Locus 3, Production Area #2), which was likely associated with the Frost Island phase. This locus appeared to represent activities focused on the production of bifaces for adze/celt blanks. The workshop produced roughly worked forms that had not been through the final stage of manufacture, which is grinding the blade edges down to produce a sharp edge for working wood.

The archaeological report on the site concluded with a discussion of the connection between the Manor site and the Kingston site that was excavated in the 1940s and published in 1952 (Ritchie 1952). The evidence presented for this is the two old grid stakes and several back-dirt piles found in Locus 2. The distance between the stakes was 5 feet, representing a common excavation size (i.e., 5-ft squares) that was used from the 19th century into the 1970s.

The Kingston site was described by Ritchie (1952, 11) as "situated on a wooded sand knoll bordered by a swampy area, just northeast of the corporation line of the city of Kingston." This description caused a great deal of controversy when the Manor site was mistakenly associated with the Kingston site in the Phase 3 report (HAA 2009). This led to numerous planning board meetings in the town of Ulster in 2010, as opponents of the development project used the information about human burials from the original report (Ritchie 1952) to prevent construction on the Manor site after the archaeological work (HAA 2009) had been completed. Other misinformation from these meetings suggested that I had completed a separate Phase 3 excavation of the Kingston site that I was, for some reason, hiding. This was not the case, as I have never been on the original Kingston site, even though I have been trying to pin down its location since at least 1997.

However, the Manor site cannot be the original Kingston site reported by Ritchie in 1952 for several reasons. The first is that the site reported in 2009 was entirely Archaic in date, based on the presence of artifacts from the Vosburg phase, Sylvan Lake/Lamoka phase, Orient phase, and Broadspear tradition/Perkiomen. Except for one Levanna point, it had no other temporally diagnostic Late Woodland artifacts and had no associated Late Woodland pottery. The original Kingston site had some Archaic components in the collection at the New York State Museum, as noted in the Manor site report (HAA 2009, 17), but it was overwhelmingly characterized by huge amounts of Late Woodland Native American pottery. It should also be emphasized that avocational archaeologists did not use archaeological screens in the 1940s when conducting their excavations; thus, the large amount of pottery at the Kingston site would have been picked up by hand, leaving many small fragments in the surrounding soil, which, if this was the original Kingston site, would have been found during the Manor site excavations. The Kingston site also had European manufactured items, whereas the Manor site did not. Although the Manor site was thought to be an associated earlier occupation area of Ritchie's original Kingston site (HAA 2009, 15–20), I believe that, based on conversations that I had with Edmund Carpenter in the late 1990s, the original Kingston site is almost one mile away from the Manor site, and that they are therefore two distinct sites.

The Millens Precontact Quarry

In 2009, I conducted a Phase 1 archaeological survey for a proposed 39-acre recycling center in the town of Ulster (Diamond 2009), which identified four precontact Native American sites. The most prolific in terms of artifact quantities was Locus 1, a quarry on the top of the hill directly within the building footprint of the proposed recycling facility. Here, the bedrock geology consisted of the Middle Ordovician Austin Glen formation of graywacke and shale (Fisher et al. 1970, Lower Hudson Sheet). The testing procedure during the Phase 1B study (Diamond 2009), in combination with consultations with a geologist, pointed to an interesting geological situation within the project area: the folded ridges comprising the Austin Glen formation appeared to contain a Mt. Merino chert thrust fault (Dr. Fred Vollmer, personal communication, November 25, 2009). This manifested itself in only one location within the project area, and that was an exposure of good- to poor-quality chert in Area A of Locus 1. From an archaeological perspective, the chert formation was evident on the surface and occurred as a line of small quarry pits, along with mining and workshop debris, indicating a chert-bearing formation in a linear pattern between the uplifted graywackes of the Austin Glen formation. The remaining portion of the chert in the project area had multiple stress fractures as well as quartz crystal inclusions, making it less desirable for toolstone.

Significant amounts of lithics found at the site have stress fractures with oxidation surfaces running through the stone. This is undoubtedly the reason for "production failures" as well as leftover portions of what initially appears to be good-quality chert but, on closer inspection, has size limitations based on the location and direction of the stress fractures. Production failures are caused by preexisting stress fractures in the stone that, when hit the wrong way, cause the artifact to break into unusable fragments. This is a topic discussed at length by Brumbach and Weinstein (1999) for stone tool failures and rejection at Flint Mine Hill, another Mt. Merino chert outcrop to the north in Greene County.

The colors of the chert lying on the surface, as well as those encountered during the Phase 1 study, varied from blue-black to black to the normal colors associated with Mt. Merino cherts, such as light or apple green to banded greens as well as mottled green and black pieces (Brumbach 1987; Brumbach and Weinstein 1999; Holland 2004; Luedtke 1992). We also found one portion of the outcrop that had a waxy grey Mt. Merino chert, a variety similar to what I have found at the Scott Farm quarry in Athens, New York.

A Phase 2 site evaluation was undertaken to determine whether the four precontact loci met the eligibility requirements for the National Register of Historic Places and for the State Register of Historic Places (Diamond 2010a). Specific and very different research designs were utilized for Locus 1 as opposed to the other three loci. Loci 2, 3, and 4 were each shovel tested and found to contain minimal artifacts, suggesting that they were isolated finds. Consequently, the emphasis on site evaluation shifted to Locus 1, where there was much more material. Because of the larger amounts of material found on the surface, the sampling strategy for Locus 1 consisted of gridding the site and utilizing several methods of data collection. Within the site area, we set up a series of 10 × 10 meter quadrants (fig. 9.2), which were labeled quadrants A through L. Within each quadrant, one square meter in each (fig. 9.2) was swept clean of leaves and surface sampled to determine overall weight of artifacts on the surface. These were not randomly sampled but instead were nonrandom and chosen to provide information on materials associated with the outcrop/quarry that could be used to determine the spread of quarry debris and locate specific locations where people were reducing lithics to make tools. Three of the visually examined units were then excavated and the

Figure 9.2. Millens Quarry Phase 2. Locus 1. Estimated artifacts at surface. *Source:* Photo by the author.

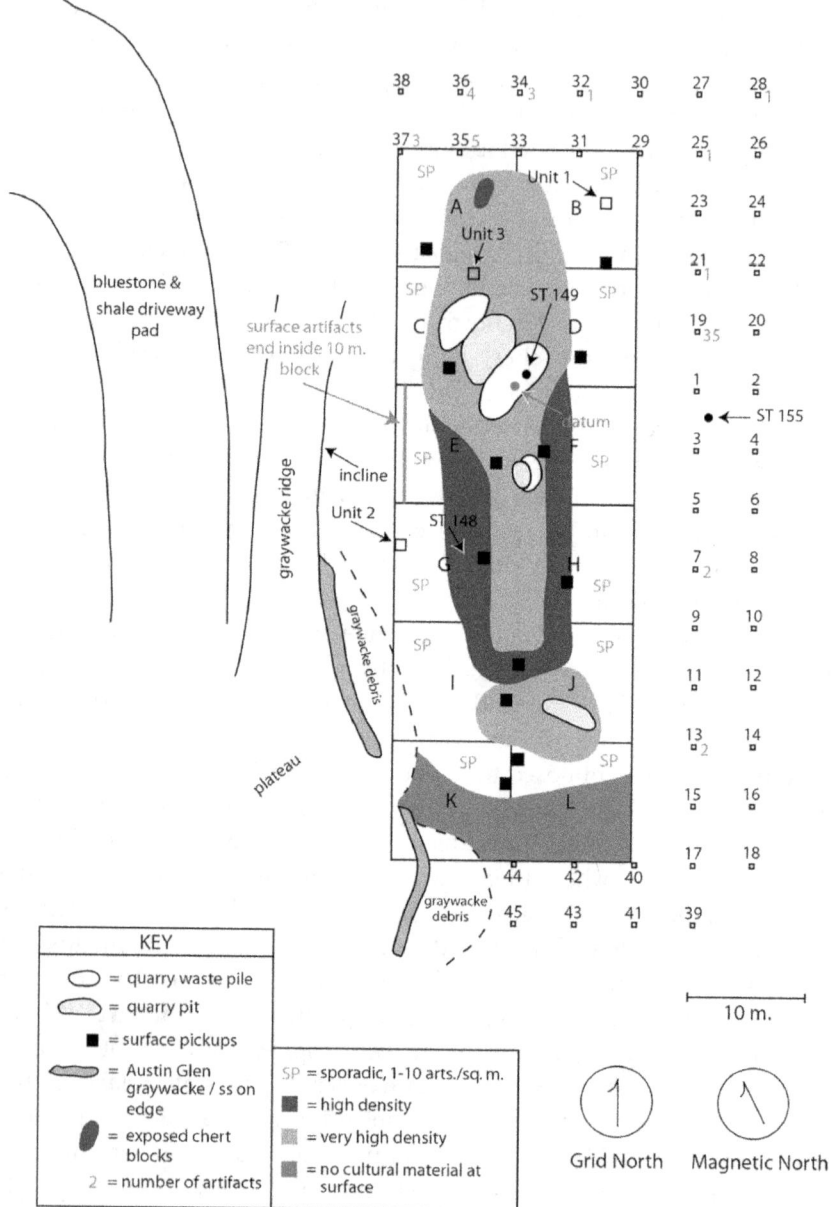

soil screened. Artifacts found through this method were then weighed to compare with the surface finds. The idea behind this sampling method was to get an idea of what was on the surface compared with what was subsurface. Additionally, we were looking for culturally/temporally diagnostic items that would provide information on which archaeological cultures exploited the lithic resources at the site. In areas where artifacts were not found, we utilized squared-off 50-cm shovel tests to define the site limits. After sampling the visually examined units, we completely sampled three excavated units.

During the Phase 1 investigation, precontact Locus 1 was represented by artifacts consisting mostly of debitage, several bifaces, cores, and a drill. These were found in 10 initial shovel tests, and artifacts were also located on the surface. Based on the debitage count, number of cores, and core fragments on the surface, at the conclusion of the Phase 1 study, we felt that the site was well documented and did not require supplemental shovel testing or excavation units.

The testing and evaluation of precontact Locus 1 during the Phase 2 study consisted of excavating 45 50-cm-squared shovel tests and three 1-meter squares (fig. 9.2). Additionally, 12 surface units were mapped and cleared of leaves, and all artifacts on, or protruding from, the surface were collected and weighed (fig. 9.2). Three of the 12 surface units were then selected for excavation. In this case, artifacts were weighed by stratum and then returned to the unit after excavation because the volume of lithic debris was enormous. We also excavated three units, two of which were completely sampled and one of which was simply weighed and backfilled. The Phase 2 testing and evaluation of the site examined a total of 17.25 square meters (20.6 sq ft) of excavated soil to a depth between 20 and 60 centimeters.

Of the 45 50-cm shovel tests in Locus 1, 11 yielded precontact artifacts and 34 failed to produce any precontact artifacts. However, the negative shovel tests allowed for the horizontal extent of the site to be determined. Along the southern border, 13 shovel tests failed to yield any debitage; thus, we were fairly confident that the site ended near the southern edge of quadrants K and L.

As described above, surface collection units were selected within each 10 × 10 meter quadrant labeled A through L (fig. 9.2). Each black unit in the figure represents the surface collection unit within that block, and the grid coordinates and artifacts (by weight) for each 1-meter unit are listed below:

Surface Collection A-1 (N11/W8): This unit yielded 11 lb or 4.99 kg of lithic materials at the surface.

Surface Collection B-1 (N10/E7): This was one of three units selected for surface and subsurface data collection. This unit yielded 3.35 lb or 1.7 kg of lithic materials at the surface. Below this, Level 1 yielded 63.75 lb or 28.9 kg of materials, and Level 2 yielded 5.9 lb or 2.68 kg of lithic debris. In this case, 5.38% of the lithics by weight were at the surface, and slightly under 95% were buried.

Surface Collection C-1 (N1/W6): This unit yielded 5 lb or 2.27 kg of lithic materials at the surface.

Surface Collection D-1 (N2/E5) and 1-meter excavation: This was one of three units that were surface sampled and then excavated. At the surface, 3 lb or 1.36 kg of lithic materials were recorded. This barely reflected Levels 1 and 2, however, as these yielded 144.25 lb (65.43 kg) and 140.75 lb (63.8 kg) of lithic materials, respectively. This unit yielded the only temporally diagnostic artifact found at Locus 1: a Brewerton Side-Notched Point. Unit D-1 provided invaluable information about the downhill, or eastern, side of the quarry in Quadrant D, and possibly Quadrants F and H further to the south. In this unit, only 1.05 % of the lithics were at the surface, and slightly less than 99% were buried.

Surface Collection E-1 (S7/W6): This unit yielded 11.75 lb or 5.33 kg of lithic materials at the surface.

Surface Collection F-1 (S6/E2): This unit yielded 3.5 lb or 1.59 kg of lithic materials at the surface.

Surface Collection G-1 (S15/W3) and 1-meter excavation: This unit, just to the west of what is probably the main outcrop, was surface sampled and then excavated. The surface yielded 3.5 lb or 1.59 kg of lithic materials. Level 1 produced 26 lb or 11.8 kg of lithics and Level 2 a total of 102.5 lb or 46.5 kg of lithic debris. The excavation of Unit G-1 suggests that just west of the centerline of the quarry, about 2.73% of the lithics are at the surface, and over 97% are buried.

Surface Collection H-1 (S17/E4): This unit yielded 1.25 lb or 0.55 kg of lithic materials at the surface.

Surface Collection I-1 (S27/W1): This unit yielded 16.25 lb or 7.36 kg of lithic materials at the surface.

Surface Collection J-1 (S24/E0): This unit yielded 6.25 lb or 2.8 kg of lithic materials at the surface.

Surface Collection K-1 (S34/W1): This unit yielded 0.5 lb or 0.23 kg of lithic materials at the surface.

Surface Collection L-1 (S32/E0): This unit yielded 1.75 lb or 0.79 kg of lithic materials at the surface.

In addition to the shovel tests and surface collections, two units (Units 1 and 2) were excavated, with all material saved and analyzed. One unit (Unit 3) was outside of the proposed scope of work and, like the others, was simply examined for bulk weight of artifacts.

Unit 1 (N15/E7) was placed to sample an area in the northeastern portion of the quarry that appeared to have a lower quantity of lithic debris than other portions of Quadrants A–D. Due to an immediate drop off in artifacts in the A-horizon soil (i.e., humus), the subsoil, which was a hard-packed silty clay, was not excavated.

Unit 2 (S13/W10) was placed on the western edge of Quadrant G to determine the density of lithics near the western edge of that quadrant. This was excavated to sterile subsoil, which, like Unit 1, appeared to be quite shallow along the edges of the site.

Unit 3 (N9/W4) was an additional unit (i.e., beyond the proposed scope of work) placed in Quadrant A. This was excavated simply to determine how much lithic debris was below the surface in this area, as there were large quartzite hammerstones partially buried in the ground, and the surface was littered with cores, biface fragments, and reduction flakes. We were not disappointed. Unit 3 probably had more lithics than soil and yielded 424 lb or 192.5 kg of lithic debris in the first level, and 117.5 lb or 53.31 kg of lithics in the second level. Level 1 was a dark reddish brown and Level 2 was a yellow brown silty sand that had a reddish tinge in some places, suggestive of strong brown soils that had changed color due to being heat-affected. In the southeast corner of the unit, a 50-cm block was excavated. This showed that the yellow-brown soil with a slight reddish tinge continued, as did moderate amounts of lithic debris. Although sterile subsoil was not reached, an estimate for the depth of lithic debris in this location would be on the order of 60 cm to approximately 1 meter, or about 39 inches. At 541.5 lb/245.81 kg, this was the most prolific location that we tested during Phase 2. This is not to say that Unit 3 would necessarily be the highest density location on site—that would most likely be the area around our datum, as it was elevated and appeared to be solid lithic reduction debris from the quarry pit to its northwest.

A total of 1,004 lb/500 kg of precontact artifacts were found in Locus 1 during the Phase 2 evaluation. These materials consisted of tertiary flakes, primary decortication flakes, secondary decortication flakes, blocky fragments of chert, marginal bifaces, utilized flakes, one Brewerton Side-Notched projectile point, bifaces, unidirectional cores, multidirectional cores, multidirectional cores/bifaces, prismatic cores, prismatic flakes, flake tools, and prepared flakes (flake blanks). Percussors (hammerstones) consisted of sandstone and quartzite cobbles ranging in weight from c. 100 grams to 4.1 kg. A large quartzite hammerstone/core of 4.55 kg (10 lb) was noted and is still in situ in the southeast corner of Quadrant A.

One culturally diagnostic artifact was found during the Phase 2 site evaluation. This was a Brewerton Side-Notched point, which is diagnostic of the Vosburg phase in the Hudson Valley and which dates c. 3000–2500 BC/cal. 4950–4450 BP (Funk 1988; 1993, 157).

The ore extraction activity at this site centered on a core zone of Mt. Merino chert extending roughly on a north/south axis down the baseline above and below the datum point. A subjective view of the site is presented in figure 9.2, where I simply walked over the site and estimated the concentrations of lithics at the surface. These are represented as colors, indicating no cultural materials at the surface, sporadic materials (1 to 10 artifacts per square meter), high-density materials, and very high-density materials. High density would be about 25 to 40 artifacts per square meter and very high density would be over 50 artifacts per square meter. The quarry waste piles would fall into the latter category.

Figure 9.2 also shows several quarry pits, one of which (Quadrant C) had a large debris pile to its northwest and southeast. Our datum was set on the southeastern of the two piles. To the north in Quadrant A, there was a section of exposed chert and a large area of lithic debris surrounding it, where we piece-plotted artifacts at the surface. This remaining outcrop did not appear to be of very high quality. It was extremely friable and had multiple stress fractures at the surface. At this point, we are unsure whether it was still in place or simply a large block of poor-quality material at the surface.

Proceeding south, there was one small quarry pit along the western edge of Quadrant F and a more linear example in Quadrant J that had a small, almost imperceptible, rise of quarry debris along its outside edges. This is shown on figure 9.2 as a very high-density area around this pit. As one moved to the east, the exposed lithic debris dropped off in quantity, and it was barely visible along the eastern margins of Quadrants B, D, F, H, J, and L. The same was true for the western side, which was demarcated by a vertical wall of Austin Glen greywacke. In Quadrant E, we indicated where surface artifacts ended just inside the western edge of the quadrant (fig. 9.2).

Along the outside edges to the east, there were several locations within the site that had higher amounts of cultural materials, indicating small activity areas or slope wash of small items. For example, five eastern shovel tests all had between one and two artifacts, making their densities 4 to 8 artifacts per square meter. One shovel test was more productive, locating 35 artifacts, for an estimate of approximately 140 per square meter in that area. All of the artifacts from this particular shovel test were patinated (i.e., chemically weathered) to a light apple green, with small white mottling. This may indicate an early but small activity area away from the main outcrop of toolstone. On the northern edge, several shovel tests yielded counts from one to five artifacts, indicating either a spreading of materials from the main area or work debris beyond Area A.

The Phase 2 evaluation of this quarry site found no indication of subsurface features such as pits or hearths, although, as mentioned above, the reddish-brown silty sand found in Unit 3 is suggestive of heat treatment in that area. Fire or a hearth may have been used to expedite removal of the chert from its matrix.

The Phase 2 study was designed to determine whether the site met eligibility requirements for the National Register of Historic Places and for the State Register of Historic Places, which it did. This site was a small quarry of c. 1,400 square meters, with at least one occupation during the Vosburg phase from c. 3000–2500 BC/cal. 4950–4450 BP

(Funk 1976; 1988; 1993, 157). The quarry retains high integrity because it has low archaeological visibility, and, consequently, it is doubtful that anyone has looted it in the search for precontact artifacts. Further work may indicate whether additional precontact archaeological cultures may have utilized the quarry. The quarry may also provide insights into lithic procurement, manufacture, choices of toolstone, and, ultimately, its role in the wider cultural context for the people utilizing it in this portion of the Hudson Valley.

The Sleightsburg Precontact Site

In 1979–1980, Hartgen Archeological Associates, Inc., mitigated the effects of sewer line construction on an archaeological site in the hamlet of Sleightsburg in the town of Esopus (HAA 1980). The archaeological excavation of the First Avenue site was confined to the linear impact area of the proposed sewer line. A total of 15.4 square meters (166 sq ft) of surface area were excavated during the archaeological investigation, with backhoe trenches connecting the excavated units to clarify stratigraphic relationships. Stratigraphically, the site consisted of six soil layers: (1) an asphalt and subsurfacing stratum, (2) a dark yellowish brown silty sand with historic road fill and precontact artifacts, (3) a dark yellowish brown silty sandy loam with buried historic topsoil and historic disturbances, (4) a yellowish brown sandy silty loam which is the precontact stratum, (5) a yellowish brown sandy silty loam with mottling, organic leaching and precontact artifacts, and (6) a strong brown compact mixed clay, sand, and silt with cobbles, gravel and no cultural materials (HAA 1980, 12–13).

The temporally diagnostic lithics found at the site consisted of 31 projectile points, which were divided by Dr. Robert Funk into a general Late Archaic category ($n = 15$), Normanskill ($n = 12$), Susquehanna/Orient Fishtail ($n = 1$), Orient Fishtail ($n = 1$), Squibnocket Stemmed ($n = 1$), and Madison ($n = 1$). Along with the projectile points, the archaeologists found 38 bifaces, 6 marginal bifaces, 12 unifaces, 107 utilized flakes, 9 cores, 85 blocky fragments of chert, and 5,260 pieces of debitage. The authors noted that of the chipped stone tools, 93 (or 81%) were composed of local Onondaga and Mt. Merino cherts. Several chert river cobbles with intact rind or cortex indicate that, like the two varieties of chert mentioned above, most of the materials were obtained locally.

Other artifacts included 9 rough and ground stone tools: 3 sandstone pestles, 1 bannerstone, 1 hammer-anvilstone, 1 hammerstone, 1 pitted nutting-stone, 1 stone bead, and 1 steatite (soapstone) pipe bowl fragment. The latter is particularly interesting, as it probably relates to the occupation by Orient phase peoples who were trading long distance for steatite.

A total of 62 precontact pottery fragments were recovered, representing, it is thought, at least 24 distinct pottery vessels. Based on an analysis of the pottery's decoration, paste, and temper (aplastic), many of these vessels are represented by only one or two pieces. Of the 62 fragments, 36% were decorated and 25% were less than 2 mm in size and often badly deteriorated (HAA 1980, 38). In terms of overall trends in ceramic technology, the authors noted that there was a greater variation in paste texture and aplastic in the Middle Woodland, with coarse to granular quartz/quartzite, "dark grit," and siltstone being used. By the Late Woodland period, the aplastic is confined to "dark grit," which I have found in pots of this period, and it is often determined to be garnet amphibolite. The Middle Woodland ceramics were also characterized by coil-manufactured construction. Of the sherds that were typable, two were classified as Point Peninsula Corded, and 29 sherds belonged to a Burnt Hill phase pot that was coil-manufactured and decorated with a dentate stamp (see Diamond and Stewart 2011). Later pots included incised fragments from the early Late Woodland (c. 1000–1300 AD) and two fragments of a possible Chance Incised pot (c. 1400–1500 AD).

This collection of artifacts indicates the presence of several archaeological phases on this site. The earliest would be the Sylvan Lake phase (c. 2500–1900 BC/cal. 4450–3850 BP), which was indicated by the presence of a Squibnocket Stemmed or Narrow-Stemmed point. The next would be a generalized Late Archaic presence, with a focus on the River phase (c. 1900–1700 BC/cal. 3850–3650 BP), as evidenced by 12 Normanskill points. Another would be the Frost Island/Orient phase (combined c. 1500–750 BC/cal. 3450–2700 BP), which is indicated by two projectile points and the steatite pipe bowl fragment mentioned above. Occupations in the Woodland period were the Jack's Reef phase (c. 600–900 AD/cal. 1350–1050 BP), the Early Owasco (c. 1000–1200 AD/cal. 950–750 BP),[3] and the Chance phase (c. 1400–1500 AD/cal. 550–450 BP).

One interesting development originating from this excavation was the possibility that the 15 projectile points discussed above as "generalized Archaic" are in fact not Archaic but are from a much later time period. They were found in association with the late Middle Woodland pottery, which caused Dr. Charles Fisher, one of the authors of the Sleightsburg report, to conduct a statistical analysis of the points, comparing them with other collections. Using discriminant analysis, Fisher (1982) compared the "Archaic" points to several samples of Lamoka, Normanskill, and Orient points from other collections. His analysis resulted in sufficient evidence "to support the interpretation of these points as members of another population of projectile points from eastern New York" (Fisher 1982, 62). So, what does this mean? It opens up the possibility that during the Late Middle Woodland, people in the Hudson Valley were still using side-notched projectile point forms even as they were moving to, and replacing them with, the better-known Jack's Reef Corner Notched and Jack's Reef Pentagonal points. It also suggests the possibility that we, as archaeologists, may be unintentionally dating some artifacts as "archaic" when in fact they may date much later.

The S-2 Site

The S-2 site is a large multicomponent site located on Hurley Avenue in the town of Ulster, between Kingston and Hurley. The site's name derives from Mrs. Simpson, the owner, who gave permission to Mr. Seward Osborne of Samsonville, New York, to excavate the site. The Simpson #1 site, which was excavated by Mr. James Burggraf, is discussed below as the Hurley site, the name under which it was published by Funk (1976, 146). In his excavation of the S-2 site, Mr. Osborne was assisted by Mr. Burggraf, who instructed him about site layout, recording plan views of the excavation, and notetaking.

The S-2 site is located on a terrace above the floodplain, overlooking the Esopus Creek. The soils consisted of a very dark brown to black humic zone overlying a yellow-brown silty sand. The site revealed evidence of occupations by most of New York State's precontact archaeological cultures, ranging from the Neville phase to the *Waornecks* at the time of European contact. The excavations consisted of 112 five-foot squares, which were laid out in sequential order on a north/south grid and yielded evidence of 45 pits and 5 post molds. Given the darkness of the soil, the site's location on a sandy terrace overlooking the Esopus Creek, and the excavator's lack of experience in defining small stains, it is very likely that many post molds related to house structures were missed. An examination of the field notes suggests that corn remains were identified, albeit sporadically, and that several pits were filled with freshwater mussel shells. The curated materials from these pits consist of two gallon-sized containers of freshwater mussel shells, which were likely harvested from the Esopus Creek.

A notable find from the site is perhaps the most complete example of Kingston Incised pottery that both Robert Funk and I had ever encountered (see fig. 9.1).[4] Found in a pit, the pot was associated with one Levanna point, one broken Levanna point, debitage, and other bits of fragmentary pottery.

The lithic collection from the S-2 site included pestles, pitted stones, one hoe, bifacially worked knives, drills, and scrapers. Faunal remains included one drilled shark's tooth, several bear canines, and a bird bone whistle. Ceramics included several Native American pipes and pipe fragments. One whole, unmarked trumpet-bowl pipe was also recovered. Ceramic vessels included Kingston Incised, Munsee Incised, Otstungo Notched, and Cayadutta-Otstungo Incised. S-2's last occupation was likely a habitation site for the Esopus in the Chance Horizon as well as in the decade during initial settlement of *Wiltwyck*. The collection of artifacts, site notes, and site map are curated at the New York State Museum.

The Hurley Site

The Hurley site is located on a high terrace along the eastern edge of the Esopus Creek, within the town of Hurley and just outside the southern corporate boundary of the city of Kingston. The site was excavated between 1958 and 1977 by Mr. James Burggraf of Samsonville (Funk 1976, 146). The site consisted of one of the largest excavation areas to date in the mid-Hudson region, approximately two football fields in extent. The excavations yielded hundreds of post molds, hearths, several large storage pits, and "fish roasting" platforms. The latter held the remains of partially articulated sturgeon and were called "sturgeon pits" by Burggraf.

Almost all precontact archaeological cultures in New York State are represented at this site by a collection of several hundred projectile points ranging from Early Archaic to the small Levanna points that are characteristic of the Contact period. Other tools included virtually all functional categories of chipped and ground stone. In terms of site function, this location was likely used repeatedly by people during the late fall to mid-spring, a time when precontact Native Americans would move away from the floodplain to higher, well-drained locations.

The Hurley site was described by Funk in seven short paragraphs on one page of his now-famous *Recent Contributions to Hudson Valley*

Prehistory (1976, 146), a New York State Museum publication that defined the precontact period of the mid-Hudson region for several decades. When I talked to him about the site (in 1997 or 1998), he mentioned that when he and William Ritchie first saw the collection, they were "overwhelmed" by the amount of artifacts and the size of the site. The result was the short description in *Recent Contributions*. The site notes, maps, and artifacts are currently curated at the New York State Museum, where I delivered them in 1994 after Mr. Burggraf's death (NYSM #A1994.52). The collection now serves to add to our knowledge of precontact Native American lifeways in the Esopus drainage and the area around Kingston in particular. I add this to the present volume to indicate how important curation is for the continual study, interpretation, and reinterpretation of archaeological materials to better understand the past.

Another example of this was reported in Hart et al. (2017), where the presence of maize found in large pits across the Hurley site and the associated radiocarbon dates were examined. A total of 22 radiocarbon dates were run on maize and charcoal from the same number of pits on the site, almost half of which ($n = 10$) also contained precontact pottery. The authors' conclusions were that "the groups that used the Hurley site were clearly concerned with storing resources. That at least some of the pits were used for agricultural crop storage is documented by four pits dating to the end of the sixteenth-century containing large deposits of charred maize kernels" (Hart et al. 2017, 154).

Although the Hurley site has occupations going back to the Early Archaic, I believe it represents a winter habitation site during the Chance horizon and contact periods. Its close proximity to *Wiltwyck* suggests that it may have been occupied as late as 1652. However, since it is located approximately midway between *Wiltwyck* and *Nieuw Dorp* (Hurley), it certainly was not occupied later than 1662 or 1663, when Hurley was settled, and then subsequently burned, during the Second Esopus War.

The Hurley site is one of a very few in the mid-Hudson region that point to maize cultivation and storage. The fact that it was located on a sand terrace at 180 feet above mean sea level, overlooking the rich floodplain of the Esopus, is no coincidence, as the rich alluvial soils of the Esopus Creek were the motivation for Dutch settlement in the valley. It is probable that the Terminal Late Woodland and early Contact period occupants of this drainage, the Munsee-speaking Esopus, used the site for habitation as well as for storage of corn, beans, and nuts.

Summary

The inclusion of these six sites from just outside the corporate boundary of the city of Kingston adds more information to an already robust database. The Kingston, S-2, and Hurley sites are primarily Late Woodland to European contact in age. The Millens Quarry, like the Kingston Industrial Park (HAA, 1995b) and the Ulster County Jail quarries (HAA, 2002b), provides information on toolstone extraction. The Sleightsburg site is a multicomponent Archaic and Woodland site, while the Manor site is primarily Archaic. The people who lived at these sites or utilized the stone that was quarried from these sites traversed the city of Kingston and its environs their whole lives, and it seems appropriate to include these archaeological sites in a discussion of Kingston's precontact past.

Chapter 10

Conclusions and Interpretations

Kingston's Precontact Past

The goal of this volume has been to place the city of Kingston in a deeper and more inclusive time frame than might typically be considered, as most people tend to consider only the present-day built landscape as representing the city and its history. However, this perspective overlooks the roughly 12,000 years that Native Americans have lived in Kingston. In the course of researching the content of this book, I have found over approximately 50 precontact sites composed of habitation areas, special purpose camps, tool caches, isolated finds, and lithic extraction sites within the limits of the city. To integrate these sites into a larger framework, and to address recent controversial excavations, I have included seven additional important sites identified just around the edges of the city in the towns of Ulster, Hurley, and Esopus (see table 2).

During the Paleoindian period, the most informative, and only, sites that have been identified are those overlooking the confluence of what is now the Rondout Creek and the Hudson River. Of the 51 phases or components summarized in table 2, the only presently known Paleoindian site is at Kingston Point. During the Late Pleistocene, this would have been a sand terrace overlooking a huge lake. Paleoindians likely camped on the well-drained sands above Kingston Point that were probably "beach-front property" during their search for wild game, plant foods, and new sites to exploit for toolstone as they mentally "mapped" the landscape (see Lothrop 2023). Due to the large expanses of today's eastern New York that were underneath these types of huge postglacial lakes, it is not out of the question, and was highly likely, that the Paleoindians constructed skin boats to cross waterways and large, connected lake systems.

One characteristic of Paleoindian groups—and this relates to the kind of projectile points they made—is that their tools needed to be constructed of high-quality stone. The examples from Kingston Point include Mt. Merino chert (sometimes called Normanskill chert); a high-quality, waxy Onondaga chert, and a high-quality pink chert.

During the Early Archaic, as the park tundra environment shifted to a boreal forest, the descendants of local Paleoindians would have encountered small groups of people moving up from the Southeast, as populations there began to grow during this time. While archaeological evidence of the Early Archaic is somewhat rare in Kingston, it is slightly more numerically preponderant than the Paleoindian period. Four sites within the city hold evidence of the Early Archaic—Kingston Point, Roundout Riverpoint SSP, Perry, and Kingston Knolls—with artifacts from Kingston Point providing evidence of movement of people (or lithics) from New Hampshire and possibly Virginia into this area. Just outside of the corporate boundary of Kingston, sites such as the Kingston and Hurley sites also provide evidence for Early Archaic occupations.

The Middle Archaic, a time when the boreal forest was transitioning to a mixed boreal/mast forest, is represented by six sites within Kingston: Kingston Point, Cantines Island, Hendrickson, Abeel Street Site #1, Angstrom, and the Duck Pond site. The key diagnostic artifacts from the Middle Archaic are Neville Stemmed and Stark Stemmed points, the latter of which are somewhat rare and often confused with later projectile point types such as Poplar Island and Rossville. Unless found together, as they were at the Neville site in New Hampshire (Dincauze 1976), or sealed stratigraphically between other soil matrices, Stark Stemmed points will probably continue to be underestimated in the archaeological literature. Around the edge of Kingston, the Middle Archaic is also represented at the S-2 and Hurley sites in the towns of Ulster and Hurley, respectively.

The shift to a fully developed mast forest during the Late Archaic likely led to population increases between 4500 and 2000 BC, and this is evidenced by the large numbers of sites from the Late Archaic in and around Kingston. In Table 2, the late Archaic is represented by a "general" category that is followed by six other columns: Vergennes, Vosburg, Sylvan Lake, River, Batten Kill, and Snook Kill. In total, 34 components, or 27%, of the prehistoric components within the corporate boundary of Kingston are from the Late Archaic period. Sites of this time period are well represented across Kingston in a variety of locations, many of which are near water, and several of which (i.e., the Armory, Lipton Street, Fred Johnston House, Senate House, and Persen House sites) are set back from and overlooking water. Many of the sites from the Archaic were likely special-purpose camps for plant processing, hunting, butchering, and/or fishing. Many probably included small structures that, after 4000+ years, have not left a trace in the soil. One site, the Rondout Riverpoint Shoreline Project at Kinston Point, may hold evidence of the earliest house structure (semisubterranean) in the Hudson Valley, if not in eastern New York.

The Transitional Archaic is represented by the Frost Island and Orient phases, of which there are 14, or 11.1%, of the prehistoric components in table 2. The Frost Island and Orient phases, like the Vosburg and Sylvan Lake phases before them, are well-documented archaeological cultures in the Mid-Hudson Valley. As mentioned earlier, the Guido site (Diamond 2004a), located in the town of Marbletown, has provided us with a rare view of an Orient house pattern that is c. 3000 years old. This is a rarity in Kingston, as well as other portions of the Hudson Valley, where the few house patterns that have been identified thus far date after c. 1400 AD.

The Early Woodland, which, I might add, temporally overlaps with the Orient phase, or vice versa depending on how one views it, is composed of the Meadowood, Adena-Middlesex, and Bushkill phases. As mentioned earlier, the Bushkill phase still needs further study to determine its relationship with the Middlesex phase. The three Early Woodland phases account for 7, or 5.5 %, of the prehistoric components in table 2.

The Middle Woodland period, which includes a "general" category and, extending from the Fox Creek phase to Jack's Reef, amounts to 11 components and comprises 8.7% of the prehistoric components in the city of Kingston in table 2.

The Late Woodland, which also includes a "general" category, covers the time period from c. 1000 AD to contact with the Dutch in 1609. It is composed of six phases that progress from the Carpenter Brook phase to the Garoga phase, with initial contact during that phase probably coming from the French along the Canadian border. A total of 17 components were found within the city of Kingston, or 13.5% of the precontact total.

Table 2 also shows 35 sites within the city of Kingston that did not include temporally diagnostic artifacts. This accounts for 28% of the total. Sites such as the 11 Kingston Meadows loci and the excavations done on either side of the Old Dutch Church, for example, consisted of only debitage and nondiagnostic tools.

Kingston's Contact Period

The time period just at European contact is represented archaeologically at three sites in the city of Kingston: Perry, Clinton Avenue and the Senate House. These all have late occupations dating c. 1550–c. 1609, and several have evidence relating to Dutch colonial period occupations. All are multicomponent sites with earlier occupations, attesting to the fact that these sites were important camp or habitation locations for Native Americans. The presence of Native American occupations in and around the city proper likely decreased after 1654, and it is highly likely that all of the Native American artifacts in the uptown area predate the 1658 movement of the Dutch to what is now the Stockade District.

Kingston's Dutch Colonial Period

The Dutch Colonial period in Kingston dates from c. 1652 to 1664. Fried (1975, 16–25) noted that settlers from Fort Orange had purchased land at Esopus in 1652 but that no formal settlement had been made until at least June of 1653. The draw was the large floodplain of the Esopus Creek, which, for the next several hundred years, would provide large amounts of grains, particularly wheat, for both Dutch and British colonists. The historic literature on the Dutch colonial period in the Kingston area is best exemplified by Fried (1975), portions of Evers (2005), Jacobs (2009), Jacobs and Roper (2014), Rink (1986), and, for the Munsee, Grumet (1995, 2009). For the lower Hudson and Manhattan, in particular, see Shorto (2004).

    The Dutch Colonial period is represented in Kingston by four sites that range from Contact period finds of glass beads, copper items, and smoking pipes on Native American sites (Hendrickson), to domestic sites (Persen House, Senate House), to garbage middens (Clinton Avenue). From a geographical perspective, the two sites associated with a mix of Dutch material and Native American artifacts are on the level terrace at Ponckhockie. Another just outside of the corporate boundary is the Kingston site. Evidence for the Dutch colonial period, not surprisingly, is most prolific within the stockade area in uptown Kingston. On these sites, coupled with the documentary evidence, we see the Dutch utilizing vernacular architecture to create a familiar environment that mirrors the one they left in Holland. Houses[1] were placed within a stockaded or fortified village, which was carved up into house lots with a fenced-in "toft," or garden area, behind or next to it. Initially, houses were probably post-in-ground structures (see Gall et al. 2011) with wooden frames that had wattle and daub (sticks and mud) walls and gabled ends that faced the street. The upper portion of the gable would have had a granary door and hoisting beam to lift food and seed into the garret above the living quarters. Many of these houses probably had dug-out cellars that were used for storing food at various times during the year. The cellars would have had dirt or flooring composed of wooden boards laid or nailed into joists placed directly into the soil. Windows came in three kinds:

> The *bolkozijn* was two side-by-side rectangles, one or both sides containing leaded glass panes in a hinged sash, with one or both sides covered by an outside shutter. Other windows were variations of the first: A *kruiskozijn* was a four-section unit divided by mullion, with stationary glass sections at the top, and shutters in combination with casement windows at the bottom; a *kloosterkozijn* was the left or right half of a *kruikozijn*. In the Netherlands, the fixed glass had an inside shutter (Dunn and Bennett 1996, 13).

Stevens (2005, 69–75) provides a more in-depth discussion of Dutch windows.

Roofing materials would have been thatch made from cattail stalks or tied grasses and, slightly later, wooden shingles (Stevens 2005, 61–64). Red ceramic tiles (pan tiles) were later used to replace the thatch, due to the possibility of house fires spreading from thatched roofs. At an ordinary session on January 26, 1666, there was a reiteration of a proposal from June 10, 1664, that "the hon. schout proposes the necessity for this village that every house, covered with reed, straw or boards shall keep a fire ladder near its chimney. . . . It is further ordered that every inhabitant here shall properly clean his chimney" (Christoph et al. 1976, 1:275). Reed or straw roofs continued within the village for at least 9 years, when another ordinance was passed in *Wiltwyck* to require changes. For example, on October 17, 1675, it was ordered "that all pea and straw roofs near the curtains which are to be found dangerous shall be made of wood" (Christoph et al. 1976, 2:535). It is most likely that by the end of the 1670s–1680s, the shift from wood had given over to tiles. This is observed in archaeological excavations at the Senate House and at the Persen House.

Heat, in most cases, would have been provided by a jambless fireplace that had a large open floor area to cook on as well as a location to sit around the fire to escape the cold. These fireplaces had square red brick hearth tiles as the flooring material. Another means by which to heat a house during medieval times into the 17th century was by using a brazier. These are stoves comprised of ceramic tiles that resemble bowls (*Schüsselkachel*) that have been mortared together to form a rectangular or square box. In Gysbert van Imbroch's probate inventory, there is reference to "the stove room." This may be the room that housed a brazier to provide heat, the fragments of which were found during the excavation at the Persen House. It is probable that Cornelius Hoogeboom was producing *Schüsselkachel* at his pottery works near the present corner of Washington Avenue and North Front Street. We currently have evidence of these ceramic vessels from only three locations in Kingston—Senate House, Clinton Avenue, and the Persen House—and all of these were located in the stockade area. Given the limited amount of excavation that has been undertaken within the stockade area, it is likely that more will eventually be found.

Decorations around the fireplace would have been various kinds of Dutch tiles, either blue and white, purple and white, or polychrome. The most commonly found kinds in uptown Kingston are the monochrome blue or purple manganese tiles.

The kinds of personal belongings that could be found within a Dutch house in *Wiltwyck* during the Dutch colonial period can best be illustrated by the probate inventory of Gysbert van Imbroch, the probable owner of the Persen House lot.[2] Although taken the year after the shift from Dutch to English rule (1664), it still provides us with a list of what would be found in a Dutch colonial house and, just as importantly, the ways in which "things" were used and stored.[3]

Many of the nonperishable personal items mentioned in van Imbroch's probate record are the kinds of items found at the Persen House and at the Senate House. These included glassware such as Dutch *roemers* (see fig. 4.7) and *berkmeiers*, both of which have small glass prunts as decorative elements. At Clinton Avenue, Dutch stratigraphic levels produced fragments of a *spechter*, a pattern-molded glass drinking vessel that was commonly produced in the Netherlands and Germany in the 17th century.

Ceramics from the 17th century included tin-glazed buff-bodied earthenwares such as majolica and "delft." These came in a variety of shapes: teacups, bowls, plates, chargers, decorative items, and tiles. Frechen and Westerwald stonewares were produced in Germany and were also copied in England. Fragments of *Bartmannkrügge*, handled vessels bearing the bearded face of a man, were a common serving vessel for beer and wine. *Bartmannkrügge* have been found at the Senate House, Clinton Avenue, the DeWitt plot, and the Persen House. Cooking and serving was accomplished in lead-glazed redwares in shapes that were common in the Netherlands as well as in England. Small pots with handles and three small feet called *kookpot* (Dutch) and *pipkin* (English) were used to heat and serve food. Redware ceramic trays of various shapes and sizes were used for collecting fat from meat over the fire as well as serving vessels. Fragments of these vessels have been found at the Persen House, the Senate House, and at the Clinton Avenue site across from the Senate House.

Food remains from the Dutch colonial period, both from written records and archaeology, point to a reliance on pigs, sheep, cattle, goats, and wild animals, some of which were obtained though trade with Native Americans. Crops such as wheat, peas, and maize were very important, with wheat being the primary food crop and unit of barter and payment of debts. Food remains originating from the Atlantic Ocean at Clinton Avenue included sturgeon as well as oysters. Recovered diet remains from archaeological contexts inside the Matthewis Persen House[4] included cattle, goat, sheep, pig, chicken, pigeon oysters, and perch. Most of the archaeological contexts had pigeon, and it should be noted that Gysbert van Imbroch, who once owned the property, had a dovecote. This was not mentioned in his probate inventory but was noted in the auction of his belongings. On September 9, 1665, under the list of his belongings and the prices realized was the statement, "Willem Beeckman, some pigeons, under condition that they shall remain in the cot, until the guardians shall find that they become a nuisance, 15 gldrs" (Christoph et al. 1976, 2:571).

Regarding personal hygiene, no archaeological evidence of privies in uptown Kingston has been found. This may be a result of sampling bias and the fact that large block excavations have not been conducted in the backyard areas of the 17th-century settlement. Alternatively, given the large number of deep 19th- and 20th-century basements in the Stockade District, it is highly probable that we have lost a significant number of them—if they were present. Another alternative is that chamber pots were used for human waste rather than in-ground refuse pits. This is a distinct possibility, as no privies were found during the excavations at Fort Orange (1624–1664) as well.

Trade items during the Dutch colonial period, as discussed in the Persen House section, included white clay smoking pipes, buttons, pewter, glass trade beads, copper and brass scrap, as well as shell beads called wampum or *sewan* (*Mercenaria*), and shell beads made of whelk (*Busycon*). Other trade items included ceramics, knives, hatchets, gunflints, shot, gunpowder, and muskets. Perishable items mentioned in trade accounts included cloth as *duffels*, as well as finished clothing.

The British Colonial Period

The British colonial period began in 1664, with the name *Wiltwyck* being changed to "Kingston" in 1669. During a brief period from 1673 to 1674, when the Dutch again took over the province, Kingston was renamed *Swaenenburgh*. After the British regained control of the province, it reverted back to "Kingston." Sites from the British colonial period would date from 1664 to 1783, with a small blip of 1673–1674 Dutch occupation within that time frame. Archaeologically, it is almost impossible to define this short period during which the Dutch regained control of the province. The problem is that many of the sites and archaeological contexts in uptown Kingston share a combination of Dutch and English—as well as German—artifacts, making clear definitions of time periods difficult. Another problem is the long use life of several categories of artifacts, particularly ceramics. In this case, clear lead-glazed redwares from colonial Dutch households could be used and discarded 20 or 30 years later. The same is true for tin-glazed buff-bodied earthenwares, such as faience (majolica and delft), which were probably used partially as decorative items in the household and did not see the intensive use life of the more common redwares. Related to this is the fact that many forms of utilitarian ceramics, such as Dutch and English lead-glazed redwares, continued to be produced in the same shapes and sizes, making estimations of date, and even attribution of country of origin, difficult.

In the later British colonial period (1700s–1770s), archaeological contexts across uptown Kingston contain the record of trade from England. Glassware such as leaded glass-stemmed drinking glasses and decanters, and ceramics such as creamware, basaltware, and pearlware, have been found and are used to provide relatively tight dates for archaeological deposits.

British colonial components have been found at the Louw-Bogardus House, behind 79 North Front Street, Clinton Avenue, the Senate House, the Dutch Church, and the Persen House. Probably the most informative are those from the Louw-Bogardus, Senate House, and Persen House sites, where, in addition to the Dutch and English material culture of everyday life, we also have evidence of dietary patterns.

At the Matthewis Persen House, a group of strata dated to the British colonial period. Because there was a large sample of excavated contexts, and because the faunal remains were examined by a zooarchaeologist (Amorosi, in Diamond 2004d), the dietary data is much more substantial and varied. Recovered mammal remains included cattle, goat, sheep, pig, squirrel, rabbit, elk, deer, and muskrat. Fowl were represented by chicken, swan/goose/duck, pigeons, wild/domestic turkey, goose, duck, and swan. Reptiles included a general turtle category as well as softshell turtle. Fish were represented by catfish, perch, suckers, shark, and sturgeon. The combined strata groups also produced huge amounts of oysters and hardshell clams (quahog). Without the fragments, a count of whole oysters and clams would be 873 and 22, respectively. It is most likely that the love for shellfish that is so commonly seen in Dutch and Flemish genre paintings of the 17th century also continued into the 18th century in Kingston, where many people still spoke Dutch and continued to conduct business transactions in Dutch. Oysters and clams would have been brought by ship from New York Bay, New Jersey, and possibly Long Island.

A recently translated account book from Kingston dating 1712–1732 illustrates trade between the local Munsee and a trader of Dutch ancestry (Waterman and Smith 2013). The account book lists trades for fabric, clothing, alcohol, ammunition, powder, knives/axes/swords, foodstuffs, kettles, smoking pipes, pots, pans, bells, glass beads, combs, guns and gun repairs, playing cards, mouth harps, money, silver, shoes, tobacco, and skins. Waterman and Smith (2013, 52) provided a list of animal skins that were traded, which included deer, marten, beaver, bear, elk, raccoon, pig, fisher, otter, wolf, mink, and cat, the latter of which is probably a mountain lion, bobcat, or lynx. Meat traded with Native Americans likely included all of these categories as well as turkey and hare. The importance of Waterman and Smith's (2013) volume is that it documents a significant Native American presence (at least 40 individuals) in the Kingston area in the first half of the 18th century, a time during which many scholars believed that Native Americans had been totally expelled from the Hudson Valley.

The New Republic and the 19th Century

There are very few archaeological contexts, if any, within the sites discussed above that can be pinned down to the time frame of 1776–1783. However, there are contexts that postdate the 1790s and many that are from the 19th century. There are also buried soil horizons from the late 18th through the early19th centuries. Examples such as the deposits at the DeWitt plot at the Dutch Church hold large amounts of dietary data, particularly the love for clams and oysters for those living on Wall Street during the late 19th and early 20th centuries. One set of faunal materials from this time period (post-1777), found at the Persen House, also included sheep/goat, pig, great blue heron, chickens, grouse, and perch.

The 19th-century history of Kingston has been well covered in the literature by Evers (2005), Thing (2015), Hutton (2003), Blauweiss and Berelowitz (2022), Steuding (1995), and, particularly, Blumin (1976), whose book *The Urban Threshold: Growth and Change in a Nineteenth-Century American Community* is an exhaustive and very fascinating study of the city, its growth, and its immigrant communities in the 19th century. William Rhoads's *Kingston, New York: The Architectural Guide* (2003) is also a must for those who want to understand the changing styles of architecture that can be found throughout the city. Ed Ford's books (2004, 2010) are required reading if one wants to observe the growth of the city as well as the historical background of any street in the city.

The 19th-century archaeology of Kingston can be found at 24 sites (table 1), and those are the ones that archaeologists have investigated. Nineteenth-century sites and artifacts have been found at the Cantines Island, Hendrickson, Perry, Abeel Street, Sailor's Cove, Clinton Avenue, Senate House, Dutch Church, Persen House, Persen House Garden, N. C. Bells, Reher Bakery, and the Twaalfskill Brook sites. This list would also include the shipwrecks of the Mary Powell (see Beers 1875, 49) and the brick barges and small boats that are found along the Rondout Creek and at Kingston Point.

The set of 24 sites listed above is not an exhaustive inventory. There are also boats along the south side of Island Dock that would be considered maritime archaeological sites,[5] as are the large barges on the south side near Connelly. There are sites across Kingston from the 19th century that are what archaeologists call "highly visible." These include the Newark Lime and Cement Company caves in Ponckhockie (see Beers 1875, 59; Ford 2004, 72); lime kilns all across Kingston, from Ponckhockie to the corporate border on western Abeel Street and on Wilber Avenue; and various foundations, mills, and factories. My archaeological reconnaissance report of Kingston (Diamond 1990) showed that many of the parking lots in Kingston hold the remains of archaeological sites below the asphalt. This is true for the two parking lots at the top of Wurts Street and Broadway, which were formerly the George Hauck Brewery Company (see Ford 2004, 84), as well as the numerous parking lots in and around the stockade area in uptown Kingston. Parking lots are time capsules where everything below them is sealed in by macadam, and where modern artifacts are routinely discarded regularly as litter on the surface. The asphalt protects the archaeological contexts both from incursions that are destructive and from the threat of recent artifacts mixing with older deposits.

Archaeological Opportunities in Kingston—Lost

In his book *Before Albany*, James Bradley (2007) described situations where significant archaeological sites have been destroyed when, in fact, they should have at least been investigated through the CRM process. A similar situation exists for Kingston. During the course of writing this book, two large parking lots on North Front Street were resurfaced, with the addition of below-ground drainage systems, as part of a Department of Environmental Conservation grant to the City of Kingston. The two lots are within the National Register Historic District and should have been tested to determine what was under the macadam and how deep the deposits were. The parking lots have been open since at least the late 1950s to early 1960s, and they were probably one of the most sensitive areas in the uptown Stockade District with regard to Native American and Dutch colonial archaeological materials. In my 1990 survey of the city (Diamond 1990), I flagged these areas as significant archaeological sites, and I also gave a talk about them, which was sponsored by the Friends of Historic Kingston. Because these sites were next to the trench behind 79 North Front Street, it was logical to assume that the deposits on the hilltop overlooking Kingston Plaza would have remained intact. A friend of mine walked the northern parking lot project area as it was being destroyed and found precontact artifacts everywhere as well as a Dutch trade pipe made by Edward Bird in Amsterdam c. 1630–1660. The parking lot construction should have been stopped and examined for archaeological deposits under New York State Law 14.09, but also by the State Environmental Quality

Review Act (SEQRA), if only the city would have initiated a review. Since the project was within a National Register Historic District dating to the Dutch colonial period in Kingston (1652–1664), this should have been a no-brainer. From what I have observed, the only SEQRA projects that are initiated in the city of Kingston are those that have significant public opposition.

Another similar situation was the construction of a large building on an empty lot in Ponckhockie. This was accomplished after I had (again) cited it (Diamond 1990) as one of the most archaeologically sensitive areas in the city of Kingston. It was a large lawn that likely had evidence for the Indian village cited by David DeVries (Jameson [1909] 2010, 206) in his early description (April 27, 1640) of Kingston and the area around Ponckhockie. It was also on the same landform and near the location of both the Perry and Hendrickson sites, both of which yielded significant archaeological features and were probably part of a horticultural hamlet in precontact and contact times.

There are numerous other circumstances where sites have recently been destroyed within the city, even after I identified them in 1990. This could be interpreted as "crying over spilled milk"; however, there are state laws in place meant to prevent these situations. As archaeologists say, "They're not making precontact or Dutch colonial sites anymore." Archaeological sites are finite resources: when they're gone, they are truly gone.

Glossary

activity area—A location where people used, broke, or discarded artifacts or trash relating to a specific task or multiple tasks.

adze—A ground stone axe-like artifact fitted into a wooden handle to facilitate woodworking; similar to a celt.

A-horizon soil—The very dark brown to black humic soil that overlies what is usually a yellow or yellow-brown subsoil (the B-horizon). The A-horizon is composed of more organic materials, which make the soil darker, whereas the B-horizon soils are usually undisturbed glacially deposited sands or mixed loams. Both soil types are common in most of the northeastern United States.

Ancre—An *ancre* of brandy is equivalent to 38.75 liters or 10.3 gallons.

anvil—A large stone used as a base for percussion when reducing stone blocks to smaller pieces or when attempting to remove chert ore from limestone. "Lap" anvils are flat pieces of stone (usually sandstone) that serve a similar purpose on the flintknapper's lap. Anvils are usually found in chert reduction or quarrying locations and are characterized by having large numbers of small impact pits on their surfaces.

archaeobotanist—An archaeologist that specializes in the identification and analysis of botanical remains recovered from an archaeological site or deposit. Archaeobotanists regularly work with pollen and macrobotanical remains from both wild plant species and domesticated cultigens (maize, beans, squash, amaranth, and chenopodium). More recently, they have used plant phytolith analysis to determine the types of plant silicates or phytoliths found on ceramics or stone tools. The focus on phytoliths now makes it possible for archaeologists to bypass the requirement of finding carbonized plant remains to infer plant tending or cultivation.

archaeological culture—An archaeological construct used to define a "prehistoric culture," now more commonly referred to as "precontact," in both time and space for analytical purposes. An archaeological culture is often called a "phase." Many archaeological cultures have a "type artifact" or group of type artifacts that are associated with them. These are commonly projectile points, steatite pots or fragments, certain ground stone tools, or, in later cases, specific pottery types.

archaeological excavation—The primary means by which archaeologists gather data about the past. Archaeological excavation destroys the archaeological record as one proceeds downward. Consequently, archaeologists document soil colors and textures as well as inclusions and artifacts within each soil stratum. This is done by bagging artifacts that are found together, as well as drawing wall profiles and floor plans to show the soil strata and relationships of soils from one archaeological unit (square) to another. Archaeologists excavate strata (or layers) through three different methods: *natural stratigraphy*, which is caused by nature; *cultural stratigraphy*, which is caused by the constructive or destructive activities of humans; and *arbitrary stratigraphy*, which is most commonly used when archaeologists encounter a deep stratum with no apparent changes in soil color or texture from top to bottom. In this case, the archaeologist might create artificial 5 cm (2 in) or 10 cm (4 in) contexts to control the collection of artifacts in distinct context bags from top to bottom. On large sites that have both historic and Native American occupations, this method provides a clear view of when historic artifacts decrease in number (and percentage) and the point where precontact Native American artifacts increase and become a larger percentage of the total artifacts in that context.

archaeological interpretation—The end result of the study of two main components: artifacts and soil matrix. The relationship between artifacts and soils provides the archaeologist with data that allows for higher levels of explanation or hypothesis testing, which serve to elucidate the archaeological record.

archaeological record—The combination of soil matrices and artifacts that make up archaeological sites all over the world. The archaeological record begins with the first stone tools during the Lomekwian (c. 3.4 mya), which was first identified at the site of Lomekwi 3 in Kenya, and ends every day as we deposit garbage into landfills.

archaeologist—An anthropologist who studies the human past as well as the material culture of the present. Archaeologists "don't do" dinosaurs or fossil shells such as brachiopods. This is a misconception that confuses archaeologists, who study the human past, with paleontologists, who study ancient plants and animals.

argillite—A fine-grained sedimentary rock that fractures like chert and flint; this material weathers and the edges dull rather quickly after flaking.

arquebus—A large musket that was fired from a supporting tripod or forked rest. The arquebus used either a flint against steel combination or a handheld powder fuse. A "snaphaunce" was one of the first firearms to use a locking mechanism to hold a flint in a clamp. The flint struck the frizzen (hammer) to create sparks that set off powder in the flash pan that then ignited the powder in the touch hole to fire the gun.

artifact—Anything made or altered by humans. An artifact can be made of any natural (such as bone, shell, or stone) or artificial (such as glass, ceramic, or plastic) material, and can be made at any size or scale. For example, artifacts can be as small as a coin or pin or as large as an 18th-century ship. The ship would qualify as a "feature," another form of artifact, albeit one that is not portable. In my Principles of Archaeology class at SUNY New Paltz, I sometimes place a round, unaltered stream cobble in the middle of the room. Unless a student has a similar cobble in their backpack, this would be the only object in the classroom that is *not* an artifact. It would be called, in Louis Leakey's terms, a "manuport," which are typically lithics that have been transported to a site but never used.

artifact density—The amount of artifacts found in an excavation (usually measured by the square meter). Artifact densities allow the archaeologist to observe activity areas on a site as well as to identify locations of the site that were not utilized as intensely. A fall-off in artifact density horizontally is often used to determine the relative boundaries of a particular site or activity area.

assemblage—A set of artifacts left on a site by a particular group of people or archaeological culture. The kinds of tools in an assemblage suggest site function, that is, plant processing, hunting, butchering, hide processing, fishing, lithic extraction, or tool modification. Where specific functions are represented or suggested, these are termed "task-specific." Where numerous functions are represented, these are often interpreted as "base camps."

atlatl—A throwing device consisting of long shaft with a handle and curl at the end to hold a spear that serves as an extension of the human arm, thereby increasing the distance, accuracy, and impact strength of a projectile.

avocational archaeologist—Someone who is not professionally trained or awarded a university degree (BA or BS) or postgraduate degree (such as a master's or doctoral degree). Avocational archaeologists can receive training and, with professional guidance, often make significant contributions to the field of archaeology and in anthropology. "Avocationalists" are known for their dedication, serious interests in archaeology, and the time spent helping professional archaeologists saving sites for the future.

balk—An unexcavated block of soil between two excavation units. Balks are usually left in place to facilitate the movement of excavated soil from a unit with wheelbarrows and also serve to keep large sections of the site intact so that soil profiles can be taken. Balks are sometimes left in place so that the excavator can carefully peel back the soil by archaeological context from the side.

bannerstone—The counterweight used on the handle area of an atlatl (also called a spear thrower or throwing board). This weight allows the thrower to increase the distance, force, and velocity of the of the spear or dart that is thrown with the atlatl. Perhaps the most common form is a "winged" bannerstone, but other types include birdstones (which are in the shape of a bird) and boatstones (which are shaped like a boat). While winged bannerstones are usually drilled through the middle to fit on the atlatl, both birdstones and boatstones have small holes drilled through them near the base for attaching the weight to the atlatl.

Bartmannkrügge—Often called a "Bartmann Jug" or "Bellarmine" in the literature, these are handled jugs with either a molded or impressed face on the shoulder, as well as a medallion impressed or molded on the body. The earlier faces are more pronounced and well made, while later examples are sometimes called "debased" since they are simply made with a stamp that is run up the neck of the vessel. The exterior is usually mottled, which gives the ceramic its other name, "tigerware." These jugs were produced primarily in Frechen, Siegburg, and Cologne, Germany, from the late 16th century through the end of the 17th century. Similar examples were also produced in England during the 17th century.

bastion—A fortified position at the corner of a stockade or palisade ("curtain") that allowed enfilade fire parallel to the outside of the curtain wall. Enfilade fire is also called "flanking" fire.

biface—A stone artifact that is worked by chipping on both sides. Bifaces go through a series of stages, from very rough Stage 1 bifaces, which are usually found at quarries or nearby workshops, to finished artifacts such as projectile points.

bi-pitted stone—A round or oval cobble that has a pecked pit on each side to hold nuts during nut processing. These tools often have lateral battering, which indicates that were also likely used as hammerstones.

birdstone—A ground stone artifact shaped like a bird, with drilled holes for attachment. Birdstones are thought to be atlatl weights.

blank—See *preform*.

block excavation—A large archaeological excavation area of connected or adjacent units. Block excavations are designed to uncover large horizontal areas of historic or precontact deposits. The largest block excavations undertaken in and around the city of Kingston are the Armory site, Persen House, and Hurley site.

blockie—A piece of chert that fractures or shatters into a blocklike shape or a series of small blocks. This is a very common characteristic of the Onondaga and Mt. Merino cherts in the Hudson Valley. Blockies often break along stress fracture lines or cleavage planes within the chert.

boatstone—A ground stone artifact shaped like a small boat, with drilled holes for attachment. It is thought that, like the winged bannerstone, these were weights for an atlatl.

bolas stone—A small, rounded stone or spherical stone that has been pecked to allow it to be tied to a leather thong or textile cord. Bolas typically use a two- or three-stone arrangement tied together using thongs or cord. Bolas are used in hunting game, both birds and small mammals. Larger stones that have 360-degree battering in the middle are usually hafted hammers or clubs.

Bowery (*bouwerie*)—A self-sustaining farm.

cache—A group of finished artifacts, preforms, or raw toolstone that have been purposefully buried or hidden so that they can be retrieved later. A cache can even be a hoard of coins or jewelry, which was a common form of storage prior to the introduction of banks and safety deposit boxes.

carabine—A musket with a short barrel.

carbonized remains—Burned or charred remains, usually those of plants. Carbonized plant remains are more resistant to decomposition and consequently serve as samples for radiometric (C14) dates and can provide details about diet.

catchment area—The area surrounding an archaeological site that is exploited for natural resources such as animals, plants, raw tool stone, firewood, and so on. Catchment areas can vary in size depending on the needs and number of people using them (see Kelly 2017). When resources are exhausted, mobile groups often move to the next catchment area. (More settled peoples, such as agriculturists, will rotate their fields.)

chaine operatoir—The chain of operation that an artifact (whether ancient or modern) is subject to from a raw material to a finished product. This can also be extended past use life of the artifact to include burial, discovery by archaeologists, and eventual curation or display in a museum.

chert—This cryptocrystalline stone is relatively common in the Hudson Valley and around Kingston. Chert is a sedimentary rock similar to flint.

It fractures conchoidally and makes a variety of what are called "chipped stone" artifacts. The most common varieties of chert in the Mid-Hudson Valley are Onondaga chert (specifically, Morehouse member chert), Mt. Merino chert (often called Normanskill chert in the literature), and Indian River chert. Onondaga chert from the Morehouse member varies from brown to black to a mottled appearance with small fossils and is found as nodules in the Onondaga formation. It often appears almost waxy. Another Onondaga chert from the Edgecliff member is grayish white to white and appears most commonly as blocks with multiple stress fractures throughout. Mt. Merino chert is usually found as thrust faults of chert into the Normanskill and Austen Glen formations of sandstones and shales. It varies in color from almost a turquoise green to deep green to black and even grey. Indian River chert is found primarily in Dutchess and Columbia counties and is a light red to deep maroon color. Chert is also called "toolstone" by archaeologists and "ore" by geoarchaeologists.

chopper—A stone tool, usually bifacially worked, that is used for heavy cutting or chopping.

columella—The interior column of the saltwater whelk (*Busycon sp.*), which is used for making white shell beads.

component—An archaeological culture or phase that is present on a site. Sites can be categorized as single component (one occupation at one point in time) or multicomponent (multiple occupations over time). Single-component sites are often the most informative, as they represent a "slice in time." This is particularly true for single-component precontact sites that are horizontally distinct in large cultivated fields. However, a well-preserved, deeply stratified multicomponent site can be equally informative if there are sterile zones of soil between the occupations. A classic example is David Hurst Thomas's work at Gatecliff Rockshelter in Nevada (Thomas et al. 1983). A riverine example would be the St. Albans site in West Virginia (Broyles 1971).

Contact period—For the Lower Hudson Valley, and especially the New York City Harbor area, a *terminus post quem* of 1524 has been argued based on contacts with Verrazano, when he described the inhabitants of New York Bay (Wroth 1970, 86). No matter what the starting point, the term indicates Native American contact with the first European explorers.

For most of the Hudson Valley, the term most commonly refers to the time period after 1609, and this extends almost until the end of the 17th century.

context—A soil layer or stratum that is differentiated from others based on soil inclusions, color, texture, and artifact content. Alternatively, a context can be arbitrarily assigned by the archaeologist to divide a deep archaeological stratum into multiple analytical units. These may be 5, 10, or 20 centimeters in depth, depending on what the archaeologist wants to achieve based on arbitrary designations. On Huguenot Street in New Paltz, 10-cm (4 in) archaeological contexts were used to break up the deep A-horizon soil. This allows the archaeologist to see the change in number and percentages of historic and precontact artifacts as one moves closer to the B-horizon soil. In the Persen House excavation, all soil had context numbers that were later combined to form strata groups of associated or coeval contexts.

core—A piece of chert (or quartzite or jasper) that has had repeated flakes removed from it. The flakes can be used for making formal tools or, alternatively, for expedient purposes such as cutting of various materials (see *utilized flake*). Cores can be pre-prepared so that the user has a small but effective piece of stone from which to drive off small bladelets for cutting.

cortex—The smooth exterior portion of a stream or river cobble, or the exterior of a piece of chert that is found in glacial soils. The cortex is also often called "rind."

crown glass—A large, round, pizza-like piece of blown glass. Crowns have a pontil mark in the center, which the glassblower uses to hold the glass while the edges are pulled out to make the "pizza" larger. As a consequence of this process, crown glass has an edge similar to a pizza crust. From the crown glass are cut different sized windowpanes or "quarrels." Although the interior of the glass is very thick around the pontil scar, and is usually thrown away, sometimes they are used for windows on either side of a door, simply to let some light in.

cryptocrystalline—Lithics that are silica-based and that fracture conchoidally. Examples include chert, argillite, jasper, quartz, quartzite, meta-quartzite, chalcedony, flint, silicified sandstone, and silica-rich sandstone.

cultigen—A domesticated plant such as corn, beans, or squash.

cultural resource management (CRM)—CRM is the largest employer of archaeologists in North America. "Contract archaeology," as it is sometimes known, is part of the planning process used by local, state, and federal agencies. The purpose is to locate, evaluate, and then avoid or mitigate archaeological sites. It is divided, for management purposes, into three phases. *Phase 1* is a background literature search, walkover, and subsurface testing (see *shovel test*) of the proposed impact area to determine whether any sites exist within the area to be disturbed. If no sites are found, then the process ends at Phase 1. If a site is located, then a Phase 2 study is generally recommended. The *Phase 2* is designed to determine whether significant deposits associated with the site can be located, how old the deposits are, their horizontal extent and depth, whether precontact features exist, and whether the site would meet eligibility requirements for the State or National Registers of Historic Places. A site would be considered eligible under Criterion D if it "has yielded, or may be likely to yield, information important in prehistory or history." If the site does not meet the requirements for inclusion in the National Register of Historic Places, the process ends at Phase 2. If the site is deemed significant, and avoidance is not possible, then a *Phase 3* mitigation or "data recovery" is undertaken. This is the final step in the process. It consists of the excavation of a sample of the site prior to its destruction by the construction process. In many cases, sites can be avoided through changes in a construction plan, or encapsulation, which is burying the site to preserve it for future research.

curation—The long-term storage of archaeological collections in a climate-controlled environment supervised by professional conservators. Often, such collections are housed in historical societies and regional, state, and national museums. The curation of collections makes possible further in-depth research, not only in archaeology but also in allied fields (i.e., zoology, botany, genetics, geology, climate change studies).

curtains—The walls of a stockade.

dating—Archaeologists use a wide variety of dating methods on sites. For precontact Native American sites, carbon-14 (C14) dating is used. For historic sites, dates are obtained by specific kinds of ceramics, glass, coins, or other forms of technology that require a patent, which can then be identified through the US patent office. Historic sites and historic archeological contexts can also be dated by reference to specific events or, in some lucky cases, newspaper fragments found in the archaeological context. Dating in the United States follows the traditional BC/AD format as well as a BP ("before present") date. The BP date is usually a C14 date that is given a date before 1950, which is the time that BP dates are correlated to, which is when radiometric dating was first developed. Other forms of denotation, such as BCE or CE, are not typically used in the United States but are commonly used in Europe and the Middle East.

debitage—Waste flakes produced during stone tool manufacturing (also referred to as "knapping"). On most precontact sites, debitage makes up the largest percentage of the total artifact count. Debitage is often divided into shatter (rocks that break along previously existing fracture planes), blockies, primary decortication flakes, secondary decortication flakes, and tertiary flakes. Primary and secondary decortication flakes are the initial stages of lithic reduction and, in many cases, show evidence of cortex or rind from a stream cobble or simply patina associated with being buried in the ground. Tertiary flakes are often the result of tool sharpening or modification in the last stages of stone tool manufacture. Depending on the quality of the toolstone, a fresh flake of debitage has an extremely sharp edge when produced. At times, and depending on the material, this may be close to 1 micron in thickness. These flakes are razor sharp and can be used for cutting a variety of materials (see *utilized flake*).

delft—This ceramic is a buff-bodied tin-glazed earthenware. When it is tin-glazed (white-bluish white) on both the obverse (top) and reverse (bottom), it is called *delft*. Plates or chargers that are tin-glazed on the upper portion and have a clear lead glaze on the reverse are called majolica. On majolica, this creates a kind of yellow-brown underside because one is looking through the clear glaze at the body of the ceramic. When an attribution is certain, a ceramic may be called Dutch majolica, if it is from the Netherlands. More recently, Dutch archaeologists have used the term *faience* for tin-glazed buff-bodied earthenwares that are white on the obverse and reverse and that are definitely from the Netherlands. Since many of the fragments discussed in this book are very small, I am using "delft" for those pieces and more specific terms for larger pieces that are more diagnostic, particularly majolica.

dendrochronological dating—Essentially, the counting of tree growth rings from a cross-section of a building timber such as a beam, header, or floor joist. This count is compared with a known regional series in order to provide a calibrated date. The reader might be amazed to discover that dendrochronological dates have been used even to calibrate radiocarbon dates.

devitrification—Glass devitrification is essentially a breakdown in the glass along its bonding planes. The result is a rainbow-like patina, which (especially in waterlogged examples) flakes off and the process then repeats itself with time.

DNA analysis—For archaeologists and bioarchaeologists, the two most pertinent forms of DNA analysis are mitochondrial DNA (mtDNA) testing, which traces ancestry through the female line, and nuclear DNA, which is packaged in the chromosomes. In the latter case, ancestral relationships can be traced through male and female lines.

drill—A stone artifact fashioned for drilling through stone, bone, antler, or wood. Precontact drill bits look very similar to those of today's steel examples. The base of the drill is usually made for hafting into a handle and is very often Y- or T-shaped.

duffels—A coarse heavy woolen material with a thick nap.

Dutch bricks—The term "red Dutch brick" or "Hudson Valley Flat" is used throughout the text when referring to the small red bricks that have been found in uptown Kingston at the Persen House, DeWitt Plot, Senate House, and the Elmendorph House in Hurley. These are modeled in size after the yellow bricks that were brought in from the Netherlands as ship ballast and used in *Niew Amsterdam* and Fort Orange. These bricks measure 6¼ × 3²/₁₆ × 1⅜ inches in size. They also vary somewhat around those measurements depending on how much clay was in the mold when the brick was struck. Like the 17th- and early 18th-century pan tiles (see below) found in uptown Kingston, the local examples are thought to have been produced by the enslaved individuals of Cornelius Hoogeboom at his kiln near the present corner of North Front Street and Washington Avenue. Consequently, these bricks are a very tangible item associated with historic slavery in Kingston.

Dutch rod—The Amsterdam rod is 3.68 meters or 12.07 feet.

ecofact—Plant or animal remains that have not been modified by humans.

ell—The Amsterdam ell is 68.78 cm or 27 inches.

English/French flint—These two categories of lithic are very similar to chert, but their coloring and mottling patterns distinguish them from northeastern cherts. As European-related artifacts, they occur as gunflints for both muskets and pistols. More rarely, they occur as artifacts of Native American manufacture that are made from flint nodules that have been shoveled out of the ballast or lower hold from Dutch, English, and French ships upon their arrival to the New World. The ballast, which is composed of river gravels and oftentimes artifacts, was shoveled into the ships along the river systems of Europe prior to their trip across the Atlantic. Ballast weight serves as a means of keeping a sailing vessel upright and seaworthy. When manufactured in England, the often-mottled grey flint is made using the spall technique. The French flint is usually honey colored and is manufactured using a blade technique, where individual flints are snapped off and then reworked to the desired size.

expedient tool—An alternative term for a piece of debitage that has been picked up or struck off a core and then used as a cutting tool (see *utilized flake*).

extraction site—The term commonly used for quarries (see below), where lithics are extracted from the parent rock and often reduced by flintknapping either on-site or nearby.

facon-de-venise—Glass in the Venetian style; a technique of glassblowing brought from Venice to the Netherlands in the 1500s. Many glass trade beads made during the Contact period were produced using this method.

feature—Features are nonportable artifacts that are destroyed by archaeologists during the course of excavation. Some are organic stains that contain charcoal or disintegrated organic materials. By the end of the excavation, they exist only as site notes, photographs, drawings, retrieved soil, carbon samples, and the artifacts that they contained. Examples of precontact features include storage pits, hearths, post molds, fire-cracked rock concentrations, and palisade trenches. Historic examples would include house or outbuilding foundations, post molds, palisade trenches, privies, garbage pits, wells, and cisterns.

fire-cracked rock (FCR)—Rock that has been heated in a fire and used to bake food or boil water in a skin bag. These are usually rounded and smooth river or stream cobbles that, when heated and thrown into water, break in an angular fracture. FCR is commonly found on sites that predate the introduction of pottery in the Northeast. It is also found in contexts where people have constructed earth ovens for baking food underground. For example, at the Hurley site on Hurley Avenue, avocational archaeologist James Burggraf (Diamond 2023, 9) found several "sturgeon pits." These were fully articulated sturgeon that had probably been caught in the Esopus Creek and were roasted in pits on a stone platform composed of previously used FCR and heated stream cobbles.

flintknapping—The process of turning raw stone into artifacts for various purposes. Flintknapping has become a popular pursuit for archaeologists who use it as a form of experimental archaeology as well as for hobbyists who want to learn the craft (see Whittaker 1994, 2004).

flotation—A process whereby soil samples (normally from a feature) are air dried and then placed in water with a flocculent (such as detergent) that attaches to small seeds, floral fragments, and small bones and causes them to rise to the surface. They are removed with a fine net (think of a tropical fish tank net) and are then dried and examined under a microscope. Most flot samples are divided for analysis into a light fraction (the part that floats), such as seeds, nuts, charcoal, and parasites, and a heavy fraction (the part that sinks), such as debitage, lithic artifacts, and pottery. After the process, the light fraction is divided and sent out to an archaeobotanist and a zooarchaeologist for their respective analyses. Flotation samples provide us with a wealth of information concerning precontact (and historic) diet, the presence and number of parasites and their eggs (Fisher et al. 2007), as well as the local environment during the deposition of the feature.

gorget—A ground stone artifact usually having two drilled holes to facilitate its being tied to clothing or worn around the neck. Gorgets are usually made from exotic materials. Those found locally are composed of soapstone or green-banded slate from Indiana. Gorgets made from Hudson Valley stone are often made from Stockbridge marble, which is the case for a gorget found at the Marbletown Rockshelter (Diamond 2004b, fig. 8). Recently, Custer and Ewasko (2022) have made a strong case for gorgets being used as "bullroarers," an artifact at the end of a short rope or cord that, when spun or rotated, gives off a variety of sounds in a wide range of sound intensities.

gouge—A stone tool with a ground-out sharpened hemispherical opening for working wood.

ground stone—Ground stone artifacts are produced by grinding one stone against another to create a desired shape and for a particular function. Ground stone tools include ulus, projectile points, knives, gouges, axes, adzes, celts, plummets, gorgets, bannerstones, birdstones, pipes, and boatstones. Ground stone tools area usually made of sandstone, diabase, graywacke, slate, quartzite, gabbro, metaquartzite, silica-rich sandstone, hematite, prophyritic felsite, Catlinite, diorite, periodotite, limestone, Stockbridge marble, and chert.

ground truth—In archaeology, this refers to finding hard (i.e., archaeological) evidence for something that may otherwise only appear on maps, in the historical literature, or on a GPR survey.

guilder—The national currency of the Netherlands.

hafting—The means by which a projectile point is attached to a spear, javelin, dart, or arrow. For the examples discussed in this book, the haft element is usually the stem of a projectile point, such as the Kirk Stemmed, Neville Stemmed, Stark Stemmed, Lamoka/Sylvan Stemmed, Wading River, Genesee, Snook Kill, and Fox Creek Stemmed types. Also note that some forms have a smaller stem with either side-notching (Otter Creek, Brewerton side-notched, Susquehanna Broad) or corner notching (Charleston corner-notched, Brewerton corner-notched, Brewerton eared-notched, Vosburg, Jack's Reef corner-notched). Triangular points such as the Brewerton eared-triangle, Beekman triangle, Jacks Reef Pentagonal, Levanna, and Madison forms would have been tied on near the lower end of their blade edges.

hammerstone—A rock, cobble, or pebble that is used for battering or flintknapping (i.e., stone tool manufacture and quarrying). The diagnostic attribute is usually small pecking or damage on the ends of the cobble. In some locations where percussion was used extensively (quarries, plant processing), the hammerstone may have bipolar, or even 360-degree, lateral battering around its edges. Hammerstones range in size from small examples that fit in your hand to some that weigh up to 60–80 pounds. The latter are usually found on quarry sites and are used to batter and break rocks into more manageable fragments to obtain chert.

honey wagon—The cart or wagon used to spread cow or horse manure on agricultural fields. Because many barnyards contain historic artifacts due to their proximity to domestic buildings, when manure is dug up, historic artifacts are often included and spread with the manure. These artifacts then appear in small quantities on precontact sites that are being excavated in plowed agricultural fields. The most frequently found of these are window glass, broken historic ceramics, white clay pipes, bottle glass, nails, domestic animal bones, brick and mortar fragments, and slate roofing shingles. It should be emphasized that these artifacts have been redeposited and are not in their original context around a historic structure. Related to this is the fact that, in many cases, it is not even known for certain where they originated from.

human burials—In the Hudson Valley, Native American human burials have been categorized into five "burial programs." The first is the extended burial, which is when the outstretched body was placed flat on its back with the face up. The second is the flexed burial, which is when the body was tied in a flexed or fetal position prior to rigor mortis setting in. Flexed burials range from tightly to loosely flexed. The third program involved the body being placed on a soil shelf in a seated position in a covered pit, with a very basic structure to cover it. This allowed for rapid decomposition of the corpse and prepared the bones for secondary burial. The fourth program is secondary burial, which involved the exhumation of any of the previous three methods of burial, with the sole purpose of cleaning off the bones for reburial. Secondary burials often involved a time gap to allow decomposition of the remains so that the individual's bones could be cleaned to white (which symbolizes purity). Secondary burials were often tied in a bundle or bag, which, after decomposing in the soil, appears archaeologically as a group of long bones together with the skull, pelvis, ribs, and shoulder blades that are no longer articulated, and typically lacks the small bones of the feet, hands, and vertebrae. Lastly, the fifth program is cremation, in which the remains were burned, leaving little archaeological evidence. In the regions of today's New York State, cremation appears to have been most common from the Frost Island phase at c. 1500 BC to the end of the Meadowood phase at c. 200 AD.

hunting and gathering—A form of economy in which people move to different locations during the course of the year as food resources become available, or, alternatively, task-specific groups disperse and exploit food resources, fuel, and lithics and bring them back to a temporary base camp. The trick is to stay mobile in order not to deplete resources, and this is why hunting and gathering is also called a "foraging" economy (see Kelly 2017).

in situ—An artifact still in its original location in the soil.

isolated find—An isolated find is an artifact that, after testing around it, is found to be unassociated with other artifacts or a larger site. Isolated finds can be any artifact category, but projectile points and debitage seem to be the most common.

isotope analysis—The study of stable isotopes in historical or ancient human tissues (bone and teeth) to determine diet, health, and origin of the individual. The most commonly used isotopes are hydrogen, carbon, nitrogen, oxygen, sulfur, and strontium.

Jacob's Valley—The small valley between Greenkill Avenue and Summer Street that extends down to Wilber Avenue.

Kidd Types—A classification system for historic period glass beads developed by Kenneth and Martha Kidd and published in 1970.

knife—A stone stool that has a sinuous to very sharp edge that is used for cutting. It is differentiated from a preform or blank (which has not been used) by the presence of fine use wear along the blades edge.

kookpot—Cooking pot. This term is used here instead of the previously used term *grapen*; the English version would be a *pipkin*.

lead glaze—A clear glaze formed by using lead oxide as the flux. Lead glazes prevent fluids from penetrating the body of the ceramic, but lead also enters the food and beverages being stored or served. Consequently, when eating from lead-glazed ceramics, the diner ingests lead and other heavy metals often associated with the lead oxide during the smelting process.

lithic—Lithic is another name for stone.

locus—A small site will sometimes be called a "locus of activity," especially when it does not have a significant quantity of artifacts. In some locations, a landform such as a large field may have several loci. In this case, it might be most propitious to call the whole field a "site," with breakdowns by locus within the field. Similar situations occur at quarry sites, where archaeologists will divide the quarry into different loci to gather specific data from each quarry location.

looting—The destructive process of digging for artifacts on archaeological sites and removing them from their original context. Looting may be considered the greatest threat to the archaeological record of humankind.

material culture—Another term for artifacts. Material culture includes this book as well as everything that has been made by humans that surround you as you read it.

midden—A deep (or shallow) soil stratum composed of numerous artifacts, very dark brown to black organic soil and decomposing food refuse. Middens are created intentionally as people discard food refuse in their living area, or in the case of 17th- and 18th-century historic sites, all around the house.

mitigate—Mitigation is either avoidance of an archaeological site, or a Phase 3 investigation, which is an excavated sample of the site (see *cultural resource management*).

morgen—A morgen is approximately 8,516 square meters or about 2.1 acres.

muller—A stone that is used for grinding plant foods such as nuts, corn, beans, amaranth, chenopodium, or cattail roots. Mullers often have a very smooth surface as a result of food preparation.

multipurpose tool—A stone tool that has been utilized for multiple functions. For example, at the Duck Pond site, there are several categories of tools that illustrate that one flake of debitage can be utilized (utilized flake) but can also serve as a spokeshave or have a small beak for use as a graver. Multipurpose tools can be thought of as the precontact equivalent of a Swiss Army knife.

native copper—A term used to describe copper from the Michigan Peninsula that was traded into the Northeast prior to European Contact. Native copper is most commonly associated with the Vergennes, Vosburg, Meadowood, and Middlesex phases. It can be differentiated from European copper fragments by the presence of zinc, tin, lead, silver, nickel, antimony, and arsenic that is present in the European examples.

NISP—The "number of identified specimens per taxon," or the actual count of bones that have been identified to a genus, or even a species, level. This nominal/ordinal statistical count is used by zooarchaeologists to mathematically describe a set of archaeologically derived animal bones. This is sometimes presented as a table that shows genus and species, followed by the common name of the animal. For example, if one were discussing *Morone saxatilis*, or striped bass, the NISP would be the number of identified specimens of striped bass skeletal fragments found in an archaeological deposit or feature.

nutting stone—A stone, often a rounded stream cobble, that has one or more depressions pecked on the surface. The holes keep nuts in place while they are being cracked for their meat. Commonly associated with the processing of hickory nuts, acorns, black walnuts, butternuts, and chestnuts (see also *bi-pitted stone*).

OPRHP—The New York State Office of Parks, Recreation, and Historic Preservation.

pan tile—Red earthenware tiles that were used as roofing materials in *Wiltwyck* and, later, Kingston. The tiles overlap each other on the roof and provide a much more waterproof, as well as fireproof, cover than the previously used straw. They are similar to red tiles seen in the Netherlands, Belgium, France, Spain, Portugal, Italy, Mexico, and California. Locally, they are thought to have been made by the enslaved individuals of Cornelius Hoogeboom near the corner of North Front Street and Washington Avenue. Pan tile fragments have been found in the Persen House, in the New York University excavations on Clinton Avenue, at the Senate House, and at the Elmendorf House in Hurley.

passglas—A Dutch and German drinking vessel with a long body that is punctuated on the exterior by rings of glass set at a particular interval. There are typically three to five rings. The tradition is to fill the glass with beer or cider, and the first person consumes the beverage down to one ring, and then passes to the next person, who does likewise before passing it on to the next person.

pestle—A stone tool used for grinding along its long edge and pounding at its ends. Precontact pestles are functionally the same as those used in today's kitchens.

pintle—An iron wedge with a vertical post that a strap hinge fits onto. Pintles are commonly driven into the wooden post within the door jamb to support hinges that hold up Dutch doors or batten-board doors.

plan view—A scaled drawing viewing down into an excavation unit from above. Used for the documentation of features, post molds, groupings of artifacts, or individual artifacts as they are found. Plan views include a north arrow, the scale of drawing, and information about the site name, unit number, grid coordinates, archaeological context, feature(s), date, and the person recording the information.

plow zone—The disturbed soil zone created through cultivation. Depending on the age of the field being investigated, the plow zone can be shallow (17th- to 18th-century plows) to very deep (modern plows and tillers). At the base of the plow zone, precontact features are often truncated and appear as very large dark stains in the sterile yellow subsoil. The significant point here is that only the soil and artifacts below the plow line are in their original position in the feature or pit.

plummet stone—A ground stone artifact shaped like a surveyor's plummet. Plummets may have a hole drilled to facilitate hanging, or, in many cases, they lack a drilled hole. From a functional perspective, they may have been used as jewelry, having been strung on a necklace.

porringer—A small ceramic pot with a handle that is used for eating porridge or gruel. Most of the porringer fragments found in the Kingston area are combed buff-bodied slip-decorated earthenwares that were produced in England. They occur as yellow-glazed with brown spots, swirls, or combed lines. Combed buff-bodied slip-decorated earthenwares date c. 1670–1795.

post mold—The soil stain, usually very dark brown to black, that remains of a wooden post buried in the ground. The delineation of post molds, and their careful plotting on a site plan, is the only means of determining the kinds and sizes of precontact Native American house structures. Post molds are also created when posts are removed from the ground. In this case, the dark A-horizon soil fills in the hole and leaves a circular black stain at the interface with the yellow subsoil. At the Persen House, palisade posts were formed when darker A-horizon soils mixed with the 1663 burn layer that gradually filled in the holes when the posts were removed. Post molds run the gamut from being very well defined to very difficult to discern.

pottery (Native American)—Low-fired earthenwares that are constructed by pinching, coiling, or luting. Decorations vary and include incising, rocker stamping with a dentate tool (see Diamond and O'Connell Stewart 2011), cord-wrapped stick impressions, cord-wrapped paddle impressions, trailing, check stamping, net impressions, punctates, and fabric impressions.

precontact—A term used to describe Native American cultures in the Hudson Valley prior to September of 1609, the year that Henry Hudson sailed up the river that now bears his name.

preform—A stone artifact that is in the process of becoming a formal tool.

privy—Another name for an outhouse; these can have from one to several "holes," depending on need, which is the size of the population using it.

procurement site—A site visited for collecting a specific item (e.g., nuts, fish, lithics, cattail roots, shellfish).

profile view—A drawing to scale showing the walls of an excavation unit or several units. The information recorded includes depths, soil colors, artifacts protruding from the walls, any features visible in the wall profiles, grid coordinates, and archaeological contexts. The profile also includes the site name, unit number, grid coordinate, scale, north arrow, date, and name or initials of the person recording the information.

projectile point—A projectile point is anything used to facilitate penetration on the business end of an arrow, javelin, dart, or spear. In the Northeast, projectile points come in a large variety of shapes and sizes over the 12,000 years of human habitation in the Northeast. For New York State, see Ritchie (1961).

provenience—Provenience (also called "context") specifically refers to the three-dimensional location of an artifact in Cartesian space. Often, piece-plotting of an artifact is expressed with X, Y, and Z coordinates within an excavation unit. Archaeological excavations are organized on a grid that is now typically demarcated in meters. For example, "Unit 42 has a grid coordinate location of North 18/West 10 at an elevation of 142 feet average mean sea level from a defined datum point." The datum point is located in this same space. In this way, a three-dimensional map can be created of the site and the artifacts that are recovered. Provenience also includes the context the artifact was found in, its depth, and its exact measurements from the south and west walls of the excavation unit.

prunt—Small application of glass to a roemer which is then flattened out with a device that gives the glass a raspberry appearance. Prunts are thought to be decorative as well as functional, making it easier to hold the glass vessel when imbibing.

quarry—A location, usually a rock outcrop, where people extract stone for use as tools. The toolstone is referred to as "ore" since it is being mined. In other cases, where the preferred toolstone is not accessible at the surface, pits are excavated in order to mine it. This is perhaps most famous at the "Grimes Graves" site in Norfolk, England, where Neolithic miners dug down at least 46 feet and excavated 435 horizontal shafts to extract flint from the limestone over an area of 98 acres (37 ha). Locally, it is most notable at sites such as Flint Mine Hill in Greene County and the Millens Quarry in the town of Ulster. Many quarries in the Hudson Valley have quarry pits or depressions, which are formed by excavations to get at buried deposits or to follow a vein of chert below the soil surface. Some quarries are surficial, which means that the bedding plane of the chert-bearing limestone is optimal for extraction of the chert, in this case, an angle of c. 20 degrees or more. Chert-bearing limestones that are still in their original horizontal position are rarely mined, due to the amount of labor that is needed to extract the "ore."

quarry tools—Quarry tools are commonly found at lithic outcrops where toolstone has been mined. These tools include hammerstones of various sizes, anvils, lap anvils, stone wedges, stone picks, beaked hammerstones, stone shovels, and stone chisels.

radiometric date—For the purposes of this study, all radiometric dates refer to carbon-14 dating. This dating method is based on the decay rate of an isotope of carbon (carbon-14) with a known half-life. There are two kinds of radiocarbon dating: standard and AMS. The latter, a more recent method that requires less organic material, is much more accurate. AMS dates are beginning to replace older "legacy radiocarbon dates" that were taken from the 1950s through the 1970s. Radiometric dates are probability statements that are expressed in radiocarbon years with a plus or minus value on either side of the date. The probability is expressed at 1 sigma (68%) or 2 sigmas (95%). For example, in the case of Feature 26 at the Armory site, wood charcoal yielded a date of 4550 +/− 40 BP (Beta-206389; cal. 2σ 3370–3100 BC/cal. BP 5320–5050). The initial date shown is BP or "before present," which, for us, is 1950, the date when C14 samples were first run. Beta-206389 is the name of the lab (Beta-Analytic) and the sequential lab number of the sample. The cal. 2σ is a 95% probability that the date for the sample falls between the BC dates shown above, and there is a 95% probability that the date falls between the BP dates shown above. Because most people do not think in terms of BP dates, I have included BC dates throughout the text. As an aside, American archaeologists do not use BCE (before the Common Era) or CE (Common Era) in the reporting of a date.

roemer—A Dutch and German style of drinking glass composed of a coil wound foot, a mid-section with applied prunts (see above; often called raspberry prunts), and a hemispherical bowl. Roemers were used for drinking wine, near beer, hard cider, and generally most of the alcoholic beverages available in the 17th century.

sachem—A paramount chief of a tribe or a group of bands.

sampling—The means by which archaeologists gather data. Sample sizes vary significantly depending on the level of effort and the budget available. Phase 1B surveys attempt to locate archaeological sites with a small sample of excavated and screened soil. Phase 2 evaluations increase this to answer several pertinent questions about the site. Phase 3 data recoveries (mitigation) are the last step in the process and can range from a 6% to 95% sample. The percentage of a site being sampled depends on whether the site will be preserved for future study or whether it will be destroyed by impending construction. In the latter case, the larger the sample, the better. Sampling can also be affected by screen size (see *screening*).

schepel—Dutch unit of measure equal to ¾ of a bushel.

Schepen(s)—A municipal or civic officer, similar to what we would call an alderman.

Schout—A local official appointed to carry out administrative, law enforcement, or prosecutorial duties.

scraper—A stone or bone tool that has a steep distal end that is used for scraping hides (hide processing) or plant materials. It can either be held with the fingers or hafted on a short handle.

screening—Archaeologists use various sized hardware mesh to screen soil for artifacts. The most common is ¼ inch mesh, although ⅛ and 1/16 are becoming increasingly popular. The size of the screen mesh determines the amount and size of artifacts that you are retrieving from a particular context, excavation unit, feature, or shovel test. As screen size decreases, the number of artifacts increases, as smaller items will be retrievable. For feature soils, some archaeologists use 1/32 inch, or window screen mesh. This vastly increases the probability that small faunal and botanical remains will be included in the sample. These samples are becoming much more relevant in the attempt to piece together precontact and historic dietary patterns.

SEQRA—The State Environmental Quality Review Act (1975). A set of guidelines that local government planning boards in New York State use to determine whether a construction project will impact various kinds of natural and cultural resources. Because it is self-enforcing, it is a relatively weak environmental law that rests on the pretext that municipalities and planning boards will participate. When it comes to finding and protecting archaeological resources, very often they don't.

settlement pattern—The locations, size, and function of precontact settlements on the landscape. Settlement patterns changed as Native Americans moved from an unrestricted wandering pattern during the Paleoindian period to a "restricted wandering" pattern in the Early and Middle Archaic periods, and then a "centrally based settlement pattern" during the Late Archaic period. By the Late Woodland period at c. 1300 AD, we begin to see fortified villages in northern and central New York. This was not the case in the Hudson Valley, where people lived in scattered clusters of longhouses (hamlets) up until the Contact period.

shovel test—A round or square "hole" dug to sample the soil to determine whether artifacts are present, or to determine the overall horizontal distribution of a site. The soil is typically screened through ¼ inch hardware mesh (see *screening* for more information). During Phase 1 surveys, round holes are usually excavated. I normally use 50 cm (19 in) square shovel tests during Phase 2 evaluations.

sigma (σ)—The Greek letter *sigma*, which, in statistics, represents a standard deviation. When shown as 2σ, this means two standard deviations or a 95% probability. That means that there is a 95% probability that the actual date falls between the two dates given.

sinewstone—A stone artifact that has one or more grooves along its edges from being used to work sinew into cord.

site—A site is any location where humans have left artifacts or features that can be examined and interpreted for aspects of human behavior. Sites can range from cities to foundations in the forest, bluestone quarries, historic houses, cemeteries, modern day camping locations, and college dorm rooms (Garvin-Jackson 1993).

site function—The kind of activities that were undertaken at a site, based upon an analysis of the artifacts found. For example, hunting and butchering, hide processing, lithic tool production, plant processing, burials, or lithic extraction. For historic sites, site function could include housing, fortifying, mining, docking, or constructing ceramic or glass kilns.

small lithic scatter—Small lithic scatters (or SLS) are small precontact sites that have few formal artifacts, and few to moderate amounts of debitage. Many small lithic scatters (often called a Locus) lack a temporally diagnostic artifact to anchor the site in time.

stage—There are several broad "stages" in northeastern and New York State archaeology. Most of these have been divided into early, middle, and late. The first is the Paleoindian stage, which covers the time period from the retreat of the Wisconsin Glaciation to c. 8000 BC. The next is the "Archaic" stage, which was a term that coined in the early 20th century and slowly developed over time (see Starna 1979). The Archaic ranges from c. 8000 BC to about 1300 BC. A temporally short stage after the Archaic is called the "Transitional," which refers to a gradual movement from a fully foraging society to economies marked by increasing plant domestication. The last stage is the Woodland, which begins c. 1000 BC and extends to European contact (c. 1609 in the Hudson Valley).

steatite—Also called soapstone. Steatite is a metamorphic talc-schist that has a hardness of 1 (very low) on Mohs hardness scale. It can be scratched with a fingernail. By comparison a diamond is 10, the highest, on Mohs scale. The Mohs hardness scale was set up by Friedrich Mohs in 1812.

storage pit—A large pit, usually circular, sometimes bell-shaped, that was excavated, lined with clay, bark, or grass, and used to store plant foods. Storage pits are usually found on sandy terraces, but may also be located on clayey soils, where the clay serves to protect the foodstuffs.

strata group—A strata group is a large (or small) number of different strata (or contexts) that have been lumped together to analyze the artifacts found within them. This has been made easier by computer programs such as Excel and Access. Strata groups are usually formed after the date of strata or specific contexts have been ascertained.

stratum—A stratum is a horizontal layer of soil that can alternatively be called a "level" or a "context" depending on the terminology one is using during an excavation.

strike-a-light—A chert tool that has been repeatedly struck against iron pyrite or another chert object to create a spark to start a fire. Strike-a-lights are often previously broken artifacts such as projectile points, or large heavy scrapers that will withstand multiple impacts along the distal edge of the artifact.

strontium isotope analysis—A scientific analysis based on the ingestion by people and animals of strontium isotopes (and their ratios) that become fixed in bones and teeth. After background isotope values are calculated by analyzing the strontium values from local critters that have died, it can then be applied to human skeletal data to determine whether people were local or nonlocal, or if they moved or were moved into the area under investigation. Strontium isotope analysis is being used to determine which people are local, and which people are nonlocal at the DeWitt plot at the Old Dutch Church and at the Pine Street African Burial Ground.

temporally diagnostic artifact—These are artifacts that have been dated in other locations in New York State or the Northeast by radiocarbon dating. Very often temporally diagnostic artifacts are related to an archaeological culture. The most common temporally diagnostic artifacts in the Northeast are projectile points and precontact pottery. Common artifacts that are not temporally diagnostic include debitage, drills, most scrapers, strike-a-lights, bifaces, nutting stones, pestles, axes, gouges, celts, adzes, and many other implements. For historic artifacts, temporally diagnostic might include artifacts with a patent date. For example, the crown closure found on present day soda and beverage bottles was invented in 1891. When found in an archaeological context, this means that the deposit could not have been produced before 1891 (see *terminus post quem* below).

terminus ante quem—The TAQ is the date before which an archaeological context or artifact was deposited. The TAQ is best observed as a burn layer, everything below which predates the fire. At the Persen House, this was the June 7, 1663, burning of Kingston, which provided a TAQ for all of the artifacts stratigraphically below it, and a *terminus post quem* (TPQ) for the artifacts above it.

terminus post quem—The TPQ is the date after which an artifact, stratum, or context is known to have been deposited. It is always the artifact with the latest date or latest beginning manufacturing date. For example, a historic archaeological context may include several hundred fragments of delft, Ehlers ware, white salt-glazed stoneware, combed buff-bodied slip-decorated slipwares, and creamware. But it is the fragments of creamware (post-1762) that provide the depositional date or TPQ of the context, because the deposit occurred after the invention of creamware, which is well documented.

tested cobble—Usually a large water-worn cobble that has been whacked by a hammerstone to determine the quality of the interior chert under the cortex or rind. Tested cobbles are often found along waterways and are characterized by having one or more large flakes taken off.

tin glaze—A glaze composed of tin that forms an opaque white glaze that often coats the interior or exterior of an earthenware vessel. Tin glazed ceramics usually occur on buff-bodied wares and are commonly called delft, majolica, or faience.

type—A group of artifacts within one functional category that share similarities in attributes such as overall form, raw materials, size, proportions, and weight. For lithic artifacts, this would also include chipping characteristics and various treatments such as basal or lateral edge grinding of the finished artifact. For pottery, this would include volume, decorative motifs, and tools used to create the decoration. For New York State projectile points, see Ritchie (1961).

type site—The first excavated and published site where a particular archaeological culture or temporally diagnostic artifact was found. The type site often provides the name for the archaeological culture. For example, William Ritchie's (1932) excavation at Lamoka Lake provided the name for the "Lamoka phase" in New York State as well as the Lamoka projectile point. At a more local level, William Ritchie's 1952 publication of the Kingston site was also used to define the ceramic type "Kingston Incised."

ulu—A semicircular knife, usually made of ground stone, that is made to fit a bone handle across the top as a handle. Usually called "women's knives" among Arctic peoples and people of the Canadian Shield area. Ulus are associated with the Vergennes and Vosburg phases in the Hudson Valley.

uniface—A stone tool that is only worked on one side. These are most commonly scrapers, where all of the flaking is done on the upper (or dorsal surface) of the artifact, leaving the underside (or ventral surface) unworked.

unit—A unit is an excavation square or rectangle that is placed on the grid or map of a site and is then excavated to sterile soil. Units vary in size between 50 cm (19 in), 1 meter (39.4 in), 1 × 2 meters, and 2 meters (78.8 in). Larger excavations of open areas that can vary considerably in size are called "block" excavations.

USN—The USN is the "unique site number" for an archaeological site in New York State that is registered with the Office of Parks, Recreation, and Historic Preservation. This is set up by township and sequential site number and includes both historic and precontact sites. For example, Locus #1 at the Kingston Meadows site has a USN of A11140.0001656, and Locus #12 ends in 1667. All of the sites on the floodplain at Kingston Meadows have sequential numbers in the OPRHP system. The New York State Museum has a similar system, but it is sequential for all of New York State (NYSM #___). Many sites have both a USN number and a NYSM number.

utilized flake—A flake of debitage or a specifically designed flake that is used for cutting various materials. Utilized flakes are characterized by having small, nibbled edges where very fine flakes have come off during the process of cutting.

vessel lot—Fragments of pottery that are thought to comprise one pot or ceramic vessel. Vessel lots are calculated based on the kinds of decoration, body treatment, and temper (aplastic) that one finds in an archaeological sample.

waldglas—Waldglas means "forest glass" and is a term that encompasses several 17th-century drinking vessels that have been found archaeologically in *Wiltwyck* and at other 17th-century sites such as Fort Orange (Albany), Huguenot Street (New Paltz), and *Niew Amsterdam* (New York City). Waldglas is common aquamarine glass that is used to make *roemers*, *nuppenbecher* (nippled beakers), and *passglas*.

wampum—Small shell beads made from the quahog or hardshell clam (*Mercenaria sp.*). Wampum can be found in three colors: black, purple, and white. It was strung and used by the Dutch and English as currency, and it was used by Native Americans to make belts for presentations to honor and reaffirm treaties. Because of their symbolic importance in wampum belts, black and deep purple wampum were considered more valuable than white wampum. An early and excellent article on wampum is by former Samsonville resident James Burggraf (1938). Early wampum and shell beads were produced using stone drills. Later postcontact wampum were produced with a *maux*, or iron drill. Elongated shell beads, as well as circular forms, can also be made from the whelk (*Busycon sp.*).

white clay—Used interchangeably in the literature with "kaolin." I have chosen to use "white clay" in this monograph. White clay is used to make smoking pipes, wig curlers, and porcelain. It can also be used as a slip during the manufacturing of slip-decorated earthenwares, which have various kinds of joggled, combed, and dripped designs on the ceramic.

zooarchaeologist—A specialized archaeologist that focuses on the identification, analysis, and interpretation of animal remains derived from archaeological sites.

Notes

Introduction

1. Dino Provenzano.

2. To decipher these artifacts, archaeologists are moving from "artifacts as text" (Hodder 1986, 2012) to the way that studies of the recent archaeological past intersect with human memory (Olivier 2011) and the ways that artifacts as "things" possess a dynamic presence that is made possible by us, but also by something that we respond to (Olsen 2013).

3. I would like to thank all of the members of the Argenio Brothers Construction Company of Newburgh, New York, for their interest, patience, and excellent sense of humor on the Abeel Street Project. Cooperation between archaeologists and construction crews should always be that easy.

4. As a local junior high school and high school student, I kept all of the newspaper clippings from the Clinton Avenue and Louw-Bogardus digs, as well as Len Eisenberg's excavations at Twin Fields and the Old Fort.

Chapter 1

1. It is worth quoting Cornelius van Tienhoven here regarding the first houses constructed by the Dutch when they entered the Hudson Valley. Writing in 1650, van Tienhoven provided construction details for temporary quarters: "Those in New Netherland and especially in New England, who have no means to build farm houses at first according to their wishes, dig a square pit in the ground, cellar fashion, six or seven feet deep, as long and as broad as they think proper; case the earth all around the wall with timber, which they line with the bark of trees or something else to prevent the caving-in of the earth; floor this cellar with plank, and wainscot it overhead for a ceiling; raise a roof of spars clear up, and cover the spars with bark or green sods so that they can live dry and

warm in these houses with their entire families for two, three or four years, it being understood that partitions are run through these cellars, which are adapted to the size of the family" (Van Tienhoven [1650] 1851, 27–35).

2. Jacob's Valley is the small valley between Greenkill Avenue and Summer Street that extends down to Wilbur Avenue.

3. A "fluted" point is a lanceolate projectile point that had as its last finishing stages the production of two flutes or channel flakes, one being taken off each side. The depression caused by each flute/channel flake allowed for the placement of two bone foreshafts (one on each side) that were tied together at and below the projectile point. This setup allowed for the foreshaft with attached point to be fitted into a spear or javelin. This meant that, during hunting, another point could be quickly reloaded when needed.

4. The projectile point types are named after their "type site," that is, the location where that variety was first found. For example, both the Kings Road and West Athens Hill sites are located in Greene County.

5. Closed boreal forests are characterized by having a "low carrying capacity," that is, they do not support a large number or variety of animals. For biologists and anthropologists, this is the most relevant argument for the disbelief in the existence of bigfoot or sasquatch. These creatures are most commonly associated with the closed boreal forests of the Northwest Coast of North America, a location that would not have the food resources to support a large hominin, much less large groups of these creatures.

6. Although both Dalton and Dalton-Hardaway points are fluted, they are not placed within the New York Paleoindian sequence due to their rarity in New York State and New England in general (Jonathan Lothrop, personal communication, March 16, 2022). West of Lake Erie, they are called Hi-Lo points and are found to have site distributions that "do not overlap with Dalton sites, thereby supporting the notion of contemporaneity."

7. For information on quarries in central Massachusetts, see Fowler (1943, 1955, 1969) and Turnbaugh et al. (1984). For Rhode Island, see Waller and Leveillee (1998) and Dann (1987). For Pennsylvania, see Wholey and Shaffer (2014). For an overview, see Truncer (2004).

8. During the time period AD 700–1600, ceramic styles and projectile points from the Hudson Valley were very similar to those from Central and Western New York. In fact, one of the most commonly asked questions in New York State archaeology is how we explain this commonality. It is understood that projectile point forms spread widely, since these are used for functional activities, such as hunting and, after 700 AD, warfare. However, the rapid spread of favored decorative tools, stylistic motifs, and patterns of decoration is more difficult to explain, especially across language boundaries such as those differentiating the Haudenosaunee (Iroquois) and Algonquians.

9. The use of the term "Owasco" was originally posited by William Ritchie to define a developmental stage of the Iroquois (Haudenosaunee), which

was named after a site at Owasco Lake in the Finger Lakes. It traditionally dates c. 1000–1300 AD and encompasses the Carpenter Brook, Canandaigua, and Castle Creek phases, each of which has about a 100-year time frame. The issue is that these were defined in Central and Northern New York State for the Haudenosaunee, but the terms are often used to denote similar time periods in the Hudson Valley, even though the people of the Hudson Valley were Algonquians, not Haudenosaunee. To compound this problem even further, ceramics are very similar and archaeologists have yet to figure out why. Additionally, there are no equivalent "phases" for the Hudson Valley that can be used. Herbert Kraft (1975, 2001) constructed a roughly analogous time frame for Algonquians in the Delaware Valley, but it is based on three large time periods. These are the Pahaquarra culture (c. 1000–1350 AD), an Intermediate period (c. 1350–1400 AD), and the Minisink culture (1400–1735 AD). For the most part, the ceramic types are the same or very similar to the Haudenosaunee types, but both Delaware Valley and Hudson Valley settlement patterns are completely different. To make matters more complicated, recent studies by Hart and Brumbach (2003, 2005) and Hart et al. (2003, 2007, 2011) have demonstrated that some of the evidence that Ritchie used to frame the "Owasco" stage, such as fortified sites and the "Three Sisters" (corn, beans, and squash), were not in fact present during this time period. Common beans (*Phaseolus vulgaris*) appear in the archaeological record in northern and central New York only after c. 1300 AD (Hart and Scarry 1999; Hart et al. 2002). Coupled with other ceramic studies (Schulenberg 2002), this has led to the demise of Owasco as an overall developmental concept (Hart and Brumbach 2003), although we are still left with the terminology for the material culture from c. 1000–1300 AD firmly entrenched in the archaeological literature.

10. Curated collections are one of the most valuable sources of previously excavated artifacts and data that can be used to test new hypotheses as new scientific methods are developed.

11. As an example, think of a Swiss Army knife. A preform or rough blank manufactured at a quarry could be turned into an artifact that might have several functions (spokeshave, scraper, or projectile point), all the while yielding razor-sharp cutting tools (debitage/utilized flakes) as the formal tool is produced through flintknapping.

Chapter 2

1. Mr. Frank Parslow, avocational archaeologist, Port Ewen and Kingston, New York, personal communication, September 30, 2003. Mr. Parslow was, for many years, a shad fisherman from River Road in Port Ewen. He was also a longtime member of the Mid-Hudson Chapter of the NYSAA.

2. The Henry Booth Collection at the AMNH is stored in Cabinet 224, Trays 4–7 and Cabinet 225, Trays 8 and 9.

3. I have chosen Kirk Serrated for these two artifacts following Coe (1964, 70), although Broyles (1971, 66, fig. 7) illustrated similar points as Kirk Stemmed. I have found them to be interchangeable in a number of publications depending on the amount of stem present on the artifact.

4. I have similarly labeled Kanawha black chert in our collections at SUNY New Paltz that were formerly the lithic collection of Howard D. Winters of New York University.

5. For views of what this area looked like during the late 19th through early 20th centuries, see Ford (2004, 34–43) and Murphy (2013, 109–16).

6. "Normanskill chert" and Mt. Merino chert are used interchangeably throughout this book where I am quoting from published sources. "Normanskill chert" is the original term used by archaeologists to classify the green to black cherts that are found running on a north/south axis in the Hudson Valley (Parker 1924; Wray 1948). They are actually mislabeled cherts that are part of the Mt. Merino formation, parts of which were thrust-faulted into the Normanskill shales and Austin Glen sandstones during the Taconic Orogeny. Unfortunately, the term "Normanskill" has had a wide and deep historical usage in the literature, and it is only more recently that some archaeologists are moving away from this term and substituting the actual geological formation from which the lithic originates.

7. "Ponck Hockie" is the name of a neighborhood at the south end of the city of Kingston. The name of Pokonoie Road, a street name of some long standing in the hamlet of St. Remy a few miles farther south in the town of Ulster, is probably a variant spelling of Ponck Hockie. Whritenour noticed that the name sounds much like a pidgin Delaware expression *pungw haki*, "dust land." Ponck Hockie may also combine a Dutch word for "point or hook" with the pidgin Delaware word *haki*, "land." The name first appeared in a February 22, 1667, reference to "the Ponckhachking path" west of present-day Kingston (Christoph et al. 1976, 2:636–37; Grumet 2014, 25).

8. One of the defining characteristics of great avocational archaeological work is the labeling of archaeological collections by site location and date. These two data points, when filled in with other information, provide the kind of provenience necessary for a professional archaeologist to use the data for analysis and comparative purposes. It should also be noted that, as mentioned in the text, these artifacts were curated. In this case, the boxes of artifacts were saved with their notes intact by the Jankowitz family, who realized the importance of the collection.

9. Argillite is a lithic that fractures conchoidally like chert and flint, but it weathers and the edges dull rather quickly after flaking. In the Mid-Hudson Valley, an area that includes many excellent quality lithic sources, one wonders why argillite is even used at all. One possibility, particularly in the case of the Armory site, is that Vergennes phase people preferred it for making large points such as Otter Creek points, which have broad flake scars and heavily ground bases.

10. Think of the scene where Crocodile Dundee is making a "phone call." He's using a bullroarer.

11. For an excellent discussion of Thomas Chambers, see Evers (2005, 88–91).

12. At the time of this writing, the site is being proposed for an Irish cultural center. Note that no historic or precontact testing or archaeology was undertaken prior to construction activities. This is another situation where testing would have most likely found precontact Native American materials as well as features such as wells and privies that would have been associated with the occupants of Abeel Street in the 19th century.

13. For other notes on Hudson Valley lithology, see Holland (2004) and Luedtke (1992).

14. This was also the case for the Montano project in Saugerties, New York (Diamond 2018). In 1994–1995, Hartgen Archeological Associates identified two chert outcrops/precontact quarries (A1115.15.000057 and A1115.15.00058) that consisted of angled Onondaga limestone (Morehouse member) that had been exploited for toolstone. Project archaeogeologist Dr. Philip LaPorta identified two kinds of limestone: those that were almost vertically bedded, and hence were exploited for toolstone, and horizontally bedded limestone, which was not exploited due to the work involved in getting at the seams of chert.

15. This is part of the stepwise process that archaeological sites go through as they are being evaluated during the CRM process. When sites do not meet these criteria, they are generally "written off." If data are found that meet these criteria, then the site is deemed "eligible." What that means is that it could be (1) avoided through changes to the site plan, (2) encapsulated under clean soil to preserve it, or (3) mitigated. Mitigation, or Phase 3, is a partial excavation undertaken to extract a sample of the site before it is destroyed.

16. The Kingston Meadows project area also yielded a sample of coal, clinker, and small fragments of whiteware, window glass, and bottle glass. These are randomly occurring 19th- and 20th-century artifacts that were spread by the "honey wagon" or manure wagon that spread cow manure across fields to fertilize the soils.

17. Cultivation of a field that contains an archaeological site is a common occurrence worldwide. Northeastern archaeologists as well as others around the world have been studying the effects of plowing since the 1970s. This has been undertaken by placing differently sized labeled items in a field in a known location, then keeping track of the number of times that the field gets plowed and disced (and its direction), and then relocating those items to compare with their original placement. What has been discovered is that larger items move farther, usually by being caught by a plowshare or disc and dragged down the field. Smaller items such as debitage, projectile points, scrapers, and so on have a tendency to move laterally as the soil gets flipped during plowing. Smaller items will also sometimes stick to the moist soil attached to a plow or disc and then

get dropped away from the main site area. This is one means by which artifacts from plowed-field sites can become dispersed horizontally, making sites seems much larger or more widespread than they originally were.

18. I would like to thank Dr. Alex Bartholomew and Dr. Kaustubh Patwardhan of the Geology Department at SUNY New Paltz (November 26, 2018) for identifying the fragment of ground stone (phyllite) and the Brewerton Side-Notched point (metamorphosed quartzite sandstone) from this site.

19. It is worth noting that no Native American palisaded villages have been found in and around Kingston. Various historical documents discuss the "Old Fort" (see Fried 1975, 66–84), which is thought to be located in Kerhonkson, whereas the "New Fort" (87–102) is thought to be located in Gardiner. Neither has been found archaeologically. For another Native American fortification that is thought to be similar to these two forts, see discussions on Fort Massapeag (Cantwell and Wall 2021; Solecki 1985, 1993; Solecki and Grumet 1994). For Hudson Valley settlement patterns c. 1400 to European Contact, specifically fortifications, see Diamond (2023, 17–22).

Chapter 3

1. "ESOPUS" (Greene and Ulster counties). Goddard (1978, 237; personal communication, 2012) suggested that *Esopus* is a pidgin word for *river*, whose Munsee form was apparently *sópsi w* or *wsó psi w*, "person from sópəs." Whritenour's analysis of an early orthography of Esopus, *Sypous*, evidently recorded by someone who spoke Dutch (the language has no palatalized "s" like the English "sh"), indicates that the name comes from a Munsee word, *shiipoosh*, "little river" (Grumet 2014, 11).

2. DeVries's description could very well have been of Kingston Point and Ponchockie, the latter of which probably had a Late Woodland to Contact period horticultural hamlet on sites such as Hendrickson and Perry.

3. The inhabitants of the Kingston area at the time of contact with Henry Hudson in 1609 would have been the *Waornaecks* and *Warranawankongs*, both of whom were Munsee speakers. By the third quarter of the 17th century, they had become associated with the place name "Sopus" or "Esopus," and their original names for themselves quickly dropped out of the literature and they became simply the "Esopus Indians." For ethnohistoric information on these groups, and the part that European introduced diseases had on them, see Grumet (1990, 1991, 1994, 1995, 2009).

4. Dutch structures from this time period were constructed using a mortise and tenon. One only had to knock out the wooden pin holding the joint together to take apart the posts, rafters, and joists.

5. These are probably for an arquebus, the precursor of a wheel-lock and flintlock.

6. Since Dominicus did not have a surname, he was most likely an enslaved individual.

7. The latter would be German stonewares either originating from Westerwald or Frechen, both of which have been found at the Persen House, the Senate House, and at other sites in Kingston. The Westerwald wares are usually grey or white salt-glazed stoneware jugs or tankards. The tankards commonly have molded designs and decoration in either cobalt blue or manganese purple. The Frechen wares are commonly handled jugs with a mottled brown "tiger" splotched exterior, often with a debossed bearded face on the neck and a cartouche on the body. These are also called Bellarmines or *Bartmannkrügge*. Of interest is the fact that Stuyvesant was suggesting gifts that were commonly used for alcohol storage and consumption. It should also be noted that similar stonewares were also produced in England to mimic the German wares.

8. Although we have no maps from this time period showing the location of defenses along the stockade, a "gunners house" may have been located near the Persen House. Given the fact that four cannonballs and an ivory whistle were found inside the Persen House, it is worthwhile postulating its nearby position during this attack.

9. This comment provides us with details of the fortification. Two Dutch feet were approximately 22 inches, while 13 Dutch feet, the height of the palisade, was approximately 12 feet.

10. For a succinct description, see Evers (2005, 141–45).

Chapter 4

1. Letter from Ellen T. McDougall to Lewis C. Rubenstein, July 12, 1974.

2. Meta F. Janowitz has informed me that the Persen House plate looks like a Crolius product from New York City. This may also be true for the Louw-Bogardus example.

3. During the summer/fall of 2016, both parking lots within the Stockade National Register Historic District on North Front Street were destroyed without archaeological testing or evaluation. A friend of mine went through the back dirt piles and found substantial quantities of Native American and Dutch colonial artifacts. The latter included an "EB" pipe, produced by Edward Bird of Amsterdam.

4. The artifacts from the Clinton Avenue site were initially stored at NYU and were then transferred to SUNY New Paltz under the direction of Dr. Leonard A. Eisenberg. The artifacts and site notes have recently been transferred to OPRHP since New York State currently owns the property where the post molds

were initially found. There are also artifacts from this site in Kingston City Hall, mounted on a piece of cardboard.

5. *Roemer* fragments were also found inside the Persen House (chapter 5) as well as outside underneath the modern bluestone sidewalks.

6. Coral has been found at the Persen House in a post-1730–1735 context as well as at the Abraham Hasbrouck House in New Paltz, where excavations by SUNY New Paltz during the summer of 2012 found several fragments in the northern extension (c. 1728) of the house. The northern extension has a basement cellar with fireplace and bake oven. The archaeological study examined the soils below the original floor of the slave quarters, and, in addition to coral, the excavation yielded large amounts of glass beads, needles, pins, ceramics, and faunal remains. In the Upper Hudson Valley, three pieces of coral have been found at the Van Buren Site (c. 1630–1686) in Papscanee Island State Park, four have been found at Schuyler Flatts (see Huey 1987), and two have been found at Fort Orange (downtown Albany) in the basement of the Van Doesburg House dating c. 1651–1664 (Huey 1988). Further south, coral has been found in the Van Horne House in Bridgewater, New Jersey, in archaeological contexts dating to the 1770s, and at the Clark Watson House (c. 1680–1700) in Perth Amboy, New Jersey (Richard Veit, personal communication, January 4, 2017). In addition, further away on the Caribbean on St. Eustatius, archaeologists excavated subsurface features in nine 18th-century slave cabins. Of the nine cabins, four had one or more pieces of coral within the pits and post molds underneath it (Stelten 2013).

7. Several fragments appear to be constructed from a white bodied earthenware similar to what archaeologists call "Dutch whiteware," which indicates that these fragments belong to a vessel that was not made locally.

8. Paul Huey (personal communication, 2000) has suggested that these fragments may be from a stove, which would have been constructed by stacking pots with the bowl side out, with the small grooves being utilized to grip mortar. Stoves of this sort are illustrated in drawings from c. 1500 to the present (see fig. 4.9). These stoves are still being constructed by potters in Westphalia, an area in northwestern Germany. The ceramic pots or tiles are called *shüsselkachel*.

9. Pan tiles have been found in uptown Kingston at Clifton Avenue, the Senate House, and the Persen House. Although rare in Ulster County, some have also been found in Hurley. The Elmendorf house on Main Street in Hurley has almost the same date, building history, and configuration as the Persen House. Its first phase (c. 1715) was as a building with its gable end facing Main Street. The pan tile roof was then removed and, like the Persen House, the building was expanded laterally along the street (c. 1730). Later, another lateral addition was added to the Elmendorf house as a tavern room c.1750, when it became the Half Moon Tavern. With the third expansion came a summer kitchen or kitchen wing (c. 1750) similar to that of the Persen House (Phase 3). During restoration

work on the upstairs first phase of the Elmendorf House, James Decker found pan tiles in the cracks around the original woodwork on the second floor. The pan tile roof was later corroborated by an excavation unit in the backyard that located the pan tile dump from the house. The pan tiles were used to surface the lane leading back to the Old Hurley Cemetery (Diamond et al. 2012). As an aside, at this point after 20 years of excavation on Huguenot Street in New Paltz, no pan tile fragments have been found. This suggests that this c. 1680 settlement probably used thatch or wooden shingles for roofing materials.

10. Torn down in the 1960s, this house is pictured in Ford (2004, 64).

Chapter 5

1. Coal with an asterisk is used throughout the text to remind the reader of a likely *terminus post quem* of 1828. In many cases, particularly at the Persen House, it represents vertical movement of soils as a result of rat nests, burrows, or collapsed tunnels.

2. Coral from the Persen House was found in Unit 12, Context 132. This is part of Strata Group 2.

3. See chapter 8 for examples.

4. See chapter 8 for examples.

5. Caming is also what holds stained glass windows together. However, in the case of the Persen House glass, the caming would hold together smaller quarrels cut into various shapes.

Chapter 6

1. For photographs of this area at the Hutton Brickyards c. 1900, see Hutton (2003, 40–41, figs. 13, 14).

2. The collection from N. C. Bell's pottery factory has been analyzed by Rachel Drillings, a student at SUNY New Paltz, for her senior capstone project in anthropology. During her research, she presented a paper on her findings at the 105th Annual Meeting of the New York State Archaeological Association in Oswego, New York (Drillings 2024). After further analysis and publication, the collection and notes will be donated to the New York State Museum, which, at present, does not have any artifacts or whole examples of N. C. Bell's pottery.

3. An informative pamphlet on local bluestone mining is *New York State Bluestone* (Conners et al. 2005). For a discussion of local mining in the Catskills and more, specifically Woodstock, see Evers (1972, 562–75; 1978).

4. For a discussion of fishing season, preferred catch, and local attitudes about these fish, see Lossing (1866, 144–46).

5. For local limestone mining and social history, see Werner and Burmeister (2007) and Benjamin (2022).

Chapter 7

1. Archaeological excavation, as mentioned elsewhere, is a slow process designed to obtain as much information as possible. One relatively new area of study is burial taphonomy, which involves studying the placement of the burial, grave goods, and the natural and cultural process that have affected the body since burial. This process stands in direct contrast to what is called "the coroner's method," which involves simply excavating a burial with heavy equipment to quickly rebox the remains for removal.

2. In section 8 of his locally produced pamphlet and under the title "Disappearing Burial Grounds," Roger Every stated, "The Houghtaling Cemetery was located on Pine Street in Kingston . . . until 1965. At that time all the bodies were supposed to have been dug up and re-buried in one mass grave in the First Reformed Dutch Church Ground. There were two-hundred and ninety-nine people buried in this cemetery. I don't really think they were all removed. This is a large part of history that has been removed and is now gone forever . . . in the name of progress" (Every n.d., 18–19).

3. This list would include Anderson, Auchmoody, Ball, Beekman, Beckman, Blackwell, Brink, Brown, Burhans, Cantine, Carter, Carle, Catlin, Cessell, Chambers, Cockburn, Cole, Cooke, Converse, Coon, Cranston, Crook, Davell, Day, Decker, DeWitt, DuBois, Demont, Dumont, Dunham, Elmendorf, Elting, Evans, Ferguson, Flinn, Folant, Frame, Fredenberg, Freer, Gibbs, Gould, Granger, Griffin, Hamilton, Hasbrouck, Harrier, Heermance, Hendricks, Higgins, Houghtaling, Houser, Hume, Hunt, Jackson, Jansen, Jennings, Joy, Keator, Kelham, Kiefer, Kiersted, Kinar, Krom, Langdon, Legg, Light, Long, Low, Luther, Martin, Masten, Maxon, McClune, McLean, Mead, Merritt, Milhams, Morgan, Morwood, Myer, Nichols, Teeple, Ten Broeck, Terry, Thompson, Thorp, Traphagen, Traver, Tremper, Trusdell, Valk, Van Anden, Van Buren, Van Etten, Van Gaasbeek, Van Keuren, Van Leuven, Van Schaack, Verplanck, Vignis, Vredenburgh, Weaver, Weeks, Wells, Wheeler, Whitaker, Wiltsie, Wyncoop, and Zendler.

4. This stone is no longer in the graveyard. It broke just below ground level at one point and was removed to the interior of the Old Dutch Church for safekeeping.

Chapter 8

1. My discussion here utilizes the terms as translated in both the Kingston Papers (Christoph et al. 1976) and the Senate House Papers (Mouw 2014). I have

followed the usage in the Senate House Papers and have italicized the term *negre* and *neger* as it was used for enslaved males, and *negren* for enslaved females. For many of the enslaved individuals in the SHP, we have no name but only this unfortunate term to indicate who they were and what they were (property or chattel), and how this small snippet of data informs us about their lives.

2. The owner of the bible, which was published in Amsterdam by Isaac van de Putte in 1718, wishes to remain anonymous. I would like to thank that person for providing me with access to this bible as a source of data.

3. Since coral does not appear naturally north of present-day North Carolina, the author believes that these items are personal/symbolic ecofacts that were carried by enslaved individuals and that they may potentially relate to water spirits.

4. Similar bioarchaeological studies in Schenectady, New York (Lee et al. 2009) and Charleston, South Carolina (Fleskes et al. 2020), have used DNA to determine the origins of enslaved individuals. In the South Carolina example, strontium isotope analysis was also used to differentiate African-born individuals from those born locally near Charleston. Closer to home, Nystrom et al. (2011) have used strontium isotope analysis to distinguish local versus nonlocal people in the Newburgh Colored Burial Ground (1830–1870).

5. A recent paper (Nystrom et al. 2024) presented the findings from the 2022 and 2023 excavations at the Pine Street African Burial Ground.

6. For a recent discussion of both the Pine Street Burial Ground and Mt. Zion, see White et al. (2024). For a description of the execution of Deyon, who in 1803 was executed in what is now Academy green, and who is most likely buried at the Pine Street African Burial Ground, see Harris (2024).

Chapter 9

1. At the time of its publication (Ritchie, 1952), it was believed that all ceramics that were decorated with incising were made by the Iroquois (Haudenosaunee). It should come as no surprise, at least after the fact, that the Kingston site was lumped in with the Haudenosaunee based on ceramic similarities. This was because, from the 19th century into the 1950s, most of the work in New York State was accomplished by the Rochester Museum and the New York State Museum. William M. Beauchamp's *Earthenware of the New York Aborigines* (1898) created a bifurcation in the way that archaeologists (as well as curio collectors) viewed New York State's Native American pottery. At the time, and proceeding up into the 1950s, all incised forms were "Iroquoian," whereas cord-marked pottery was considered "Algonquian." It wasn't until the advent of radiometric dating in the 1950s that distinct forms of pottery decoration, ceramic shape, and inclusions such as temper (aplastic) were pinned down to specific time periods. We now see incised decoration as a decorative technique that begins in the Bowman's Brook phase (c. 1100–1200 AD) and is used sporadically as a minor

form of decoration on the necks and shoulders of pots until the Chance phase (c. 1400 AD), when it became the prime method of decoration on the collar of the pot. This continued up until European contact on local ceramic types such as Kingston Incised and Munsee Incised.

2. The silica-rich sandstone found here may be the Upper Ordovician Quassaic quartzite, which, as mentioned in the report, makes up Hussey Hill (Snake Hill) in Port Ewen, and then portions of the ridgeline south to almost Middle Hope in Orange County. Alternatively, the silica-rich sandstone may also be from the Oriskany Group, which yields chert as well as a silica-rich sandstone/orthoquartzite. Because these lithics occur north of the Manor site, there is a possibility that the lithics utilized by Native Americans at the site were deposited by glacial action.

3. The use of the term "Owasco" was posited by William Ritchie (1969a, 272–300) to define a developmental stage of the Iroquois (Haudenosaunee), which was named after a site at Owasco Lake in the Finger Lakes. It traditionally dates c. 1000 to 1300 AD and encompasses the Carpenter Brook, Canandaigua, and Castle Creek phases, each of which has about a 100-year time frame. The problem is that these were defined in central and northern New York State for the Haudenosaunee, but the terms are often used to denote similar time periods in the Hudson Valley, even though the people of the Hudson Valley were Algonquians, not Iroquois. To compound this problem even further, the ceramics are very similar and we, as archaeologists, have not figured out why. Additionally, there are no equivalent "phases" for the Hudson Valley that can be used. Herbert Kraft (1975, 2001) constructed a roughly analogous time frame for Algonquians in the Delaware Valley, but it is based on three large time periods. These are the Pahaquarra Culture (c. 1000–1350 AD), an Intermediate Period (c. 1350–1400 AD), and the Minisink Culture (1400–1735 AD). For the most part, the ceramic types are the same or very similar to the Haudenosaunee types, but both Delaware Valley and Hudson Valley settlement patterns are totally different. To make matters more confusing, recent studies by Hart and Brumbach (2003, 2005) and Hart et al. (2003, 2005, 2007, 2011) have demonstrated that some of the evidence that Ritchie used to frame the "Owasco" stage, such as fortified sites and the "Three Sisters," were not in fact present during this time period. Common beans (*Phasolus vulgaris*) appear in the archaeological record in northern and central New York only after c. 1300 AD (Hart et al. 2002; Hart and Scarry 1999). Coupled with other ceramic studies (Schulenberg 2002), this has led to the demise of Owasco as an overall developmental concept (Hart and Brumbach 2003), although we are still left with the terminology for the material culture from c. 1000–1300 AD firmly entrenched in the archaeological literature.

4. This pot (A2014.03A.2.3) is currently in the New York State Museum. The NYSM site number for the Hurley site is A1994.52.

Chapter 10

1. For specifics on Dutch architecture in the Hudson Valley, see Blackburn (1987), Bradley (2007), Cohen (1992), Dunn and Bennett (1996), Fitchen (1968), Funk and Shattuck (2011), Huey (1988), Lacy (2013), McClure Zeller (1991), Meeske (1998), Reynolds (1929), Stevens (2005), and Venema (2003). For what might be the two earliest forms of architecture, see Gall et al. (2011) and Huey (1987). On a larger scale, looking at the Hudson Valley and Fort Orange, in particular, see Blackburn (1987), Bradley (2007), Funk and Shattuck (2011), Huey (1988), Lacy (2013), McClure Zeller (1991), and Venema (2003).

2. Here, I am not suggesting that the Persen House is the building occupied by Van Imbroch but that the house sites on the lot (or very near the lot) that was formerly owned by Van Imbroch.

3. Ceramic function can be determined by archaeologists through the study of use-wear analysis. Microscopic examination of ceramics allows us to see how ceramics were utilized. For utilitarian uses, scratch marks on the inside areas of pots, bowl, plates, and chargers indicate food serving and consumption. Use wear, such as chipping on the lower outside edges of the plate or charger, would indicate that the ceramic was used as a decorative element in the household and was probably displayed in an open cupboard with other colorful ceramics. Lewis Binford (1962) has termed these categories *technomic* (utilitarian), *sociotechnic* (social use or display), and *ideotechnic* (operating in the ideational or religious realm).

4. Here, I am not listing rat (*Rattus rattus*) as a food source. The excavation of the Matthewis Persen House found numerous rat nests and rat gnawings on bone materials. In fact, one strata was comprised of a rat colony or nest. As discussed, it is highly unlikely that rats were a food source, but they were a nuisance in terms of what they did to the stratigraphic relationships of soils in the Persen House. For obvious reasons, I am also not including several other finds, such as seagull, dog, cat, horse, fox, mouse, and elephant as food remains. The latter was present as a small bracelet.

5. Island Dock, or the large man-made island in the Rondout Creek south of Kingston, is a site unto itself and is not included in table 1. Island Dock was constructed in the 1820s and 1830s as a coal storage depot for the Delaware and Hudson (D&H) Canal Company. The coal was brought from the Pennsylvania coal fields via the D&H canal to Rondout and off-loaded. Nineteenth-century maps show a cross-shaped series of canals in the middle of the island where barges were brought in to load up to move coal up and down the Hudson River.

References

Alexander, L. T. 1979. "Clay Pipes from the Buck Site in Maryland." In *The Archaeology of the Clay Tobacco Pipe*, vol. 2, *The United States of America*, edited by Peter Davey. BAR International Series 60.

Ames, Kenneth L. 1981. "Ideologies in Stone: Meanings in Victorian Gravestones." *Journal of Popular Culture* 14 (4): 641–56.

Amorosi, Thomas. 1996. "Icelandic Zooarchaeology: New Data Applied to Issues of Historical Ecology, Paleoeconomy and Global Change." PhD diss., City University of New York. UMI Dissertation Services no. 9707064.

Amorosi, Thomas, Paul Buckland, Kevin Edwards, Ingrid Mainland, Thomas McGovern, Jon Sadler, and Peter Skidmore. 1998. "'They Did Not Live by Grass Alone': The Politics and Paleoeconomy of Animal Fodder in the North Atlantic Region." *Environmental Archaeology* 1 (1): 41–54.

Amorosi, Thomas, James Woolett, Sophia Perdikaris, and Thomas McGovern. 1996. "Zooarchaeology and Landscape Change: Problems and Potentials of Inter-site Comparison of Archaeofauna." *World Archaeology* 28 (1): 126–57.

Audin, Michael, and Maria A. Audin. 2023. Archaeological sensitivity assessment, Wilbur and Ponckhonkie neighborhoods, Kingston, Ulster County, New York. RFPK #22-11. Prepared for the City of Kingston Planning Department, Kingston, NY.

Baart, Jan M. 1984. "Der Gebrauch von Glas in Amsterdam im 17. Jahrhundert." In *Gluck und Glas: Zur Kulturgeschichte des Spessartglases*, edited by Claus Grimm. Verlag Kunst & Antiquitaten.

———. 1994. "Dutch Redwares." *Medieval Ceramics* 18:19–27.

———. 1997. "Post-medieval Archaeology in Holland." *Archeologia Postmedievale* 1:37–49.

Bagdon Environmental Associates. 1990. Stage 1 cultural resources survey, Kingston Knolls townhouse development, Kingston, NY. Prepared for Kingston Knolls, Inc.

Barnes, Donna R., and Peter G. Rose. 2002. *Matters of Taste: Food and Drink in Seventeenth-Century Dutch Art and Life*. Albany Institute of History and Art/Syracuse University Press.

Barricklo, Kenneth Hewes. 2000. "Historic Structure Report: The Matthewis Persen House." Prepared for the Ulster County Department of Buildings and Grounds, Kingston, NY.

Baugher, Sherene, and Richard F. Veit. 2014. *The Archaeology of American Cemeteries and Gravemarkers*. University Press of Florida.

Beauchamp, William M. 1898. "Earthenware of the New York Aborigines." *Bulletin of the New York State Museum* 5 (22).

———. 1900. "Aboriginal Occupation of New York." *Bulletin of the New York State Museum* 7 (32).

Beaudry, Mary C. 2009. "Bodkin Biographies." In *The Materiality of Individuality: Archaeological Studies of Individual Lives*, edited by Carolyn. L. White. Springer.

Beers, F. W. 1870. *Map of Roundout, Kingston and Wilbur from Recent & Actual Survey by Geo. P. Sanford C.E.*

———. 1875. *County Atlas of Ulster, New York, from Recent and Actual Surveys and Records*. Walker and Jewett.

———. 1891. *Atlas of the Hudson River Valley from New York City to Troy*. Watson and Co.

Beetham, Nellie, and William A. Niering. 1961. "A Pollen Diagram from Southeastern Connecticut." *American Journal of Science* 259 (1): 69–75.

Benes, Peter. 1977a. *The Masks of Orthodoxy: Folk Gravestone Carvings in Plymouth County, Massachusetts, 1689–1805*. University of Massachusetts Press.

———. 1977b. *Puritan Gravestone Art*. Dublin Seminar for New England Folklife, Annual Proceedings. Boston University/Dublin Seminar for New England Folklife.

———. 1978. *Puritan Gravestone Art II*. Dublin Seminar for New England Folklife, Annual Proceedings. Boston University.

Benjamin, Jeffrey L. 2022. "All Inhibitory Is Dream: An Archaeology of Anaesthesia." PhD diss., Columbia University.

Binford, Lewis R. 1962. "Archaeology as Anthropology." *American Antiquity* 28 (2): 217–26.

Blackburn, Roderic H., ed. 1987. *New World Dutch Studies*. Albany Institute of History and Art.

Blauweiss, Stephen, and Karen Berelowitz. 2022. *The Story of Kingston; Featuring 950 Images and Connections to the Catskills and New York City*. Blauweiss Media.

Blumin, Stuart M. 1976. *The Urban Threshold: Growth and Change in a Nineteenth-Century American Community*. University of Chicago Press.

Bradley, James W. 2007. *Before Albany: An Archaeology of Native-Dutch Relations in the Capital Region, 1600–1664*. New York State Museum Bulletin 509.

Bradley, James W., and Gordon DeAngelo. 1981. "European Clay Pipe Marks from 17th Century Onondaga Iroquois Sites." *Archaeology of Eastern North America* 9:109–33.

Bradley, James W., Arthur E. Speiss, Richard Boisvert, and Jeff Boudreau. 2008. "What's the Point? Modal Forms and Attributes of Paleo-Indian Bifaces in the New England-Maritimes Region." *Archaeology of Eastern North America* 36:119–72.

Brasser, Ted J. 1978. "Mahican." In *Handbook of North American Indians: Northeast*, vol. 15, edited by Bruce G. Trigger. Smithsonian Institution.

Bridges, Sarah. 1972. Excavations at the Green Street Site, Kingston, New York. New York University, New York.

———. 1974. "The Clinton Avenue Site, Kingston, NY." Master's paper, New York University.

Brink, Benjamin Myer, ed. 1910. *Olde Ulster: An Historical and Genealogical Magazine*. R. W. Anderson & Son.

Brink, P. Henry, and Oliver J. Tillson. 1854. *Map of Ulster County, NY*. Brink and Tillson.

Broyles, Bettye. 1971. *Second Preliminary Report: The St. Albans Site, Kanawha County, West Virginia*. Reports of Investigations, no. 3. West Virginia Geological and Economic Survey.

Brumbach, Hetty Jo. 1975. "'Iroquoian' Ceramics in Algonkian Territory." *Man in the Northeast* 10:17–28.

———. 1987. "A Quarry/Workshop and Processing Station on the Hudson River in Pleasantdale, New York." *Archaeology of Eastern North America* 15:59–83.

Brumbach, Hetty Jo, and Judith Weinstein. 1999. "Material Selection, Rejection, and Failure at Flint Mine Hill: An Eastern New York State Chert Quarry." *Northeast Anthropology* 58:1–25.

Burggraf, James D. 1938. "Some Notes on the Manufacture of Wampum prior to 1654." *American Antiquity* 4:53–58.

Cammisa, Alfred G., Thomas Amorosi, Felicia Cammisa, Justine McKnight, and Alexander Padilla. 2007. The Angstrom site: Phase IB and II archaeological investigations for the proposed Lloyd Park Commons, City of Kingston, Ulster County, New York.

———. 2009. Phase III data recovery excavations at the Angstrom site, City of Kingston, Ulster County, New York.

Cantwell, Anne-Marie. 1994. "'Something Rich and Strange': Reburial in New York City." *Northeast Historical Archaeology* 21/22:198–217.

Cantwell, Ann-Marie, and Diana DiZerega Wall. 2021. "Building Forts and Alliances: Archaeology at Freeman and Massapeag, Two Native American Forts." In *Dutch and Indigenous Communities in Seventeenth-Century Northeastern North America: What Archeology, History, and Indigenous Oral Traditions Teach Us about Their Intercultural Relationships*, edited by Lucianne Lavin. State University of New York Press.

Carroll, Maureen. 2006. *Spirits of the Dead: Roman Funerary Commemoration in Western Europe.* Oxford University Press.

Ceci, Lynn. 1977. *The Effect of European Contact and Trade on the Settlement Pattern of Indians in Coastal New York, 1524–1665: The Archaeological and Documentary Evidence.* University Microfilms.

———. 1989. "Tracing Wampum's Origin: Shell Bead Evidence from Archaeological Sites in Western and Coastal New York." In *Proceedings of the 1986 Shell Bead Conference, Selected Papers,* edited by Charles F. Hayes, Lynn Ceci, and Connie Cox Bodner. Research Records 20. Rochester Museum and Science Center.

Chapdelaine, Claude, and Norman Clermont. 2006. "Adaptation, Continuity and Change in the Middle Ottawa Valley: A View from the Morrison and Allumettes Island Late Archaic Sites." In *The Archaic of the Far Northeast,* edited by David Sanger and M. A. P. Renouf. University of Maine Press.

Chapman, Perry H., Wouter Th. Kloek, and Arthur K. Wheelock, Jr. 1996. *Jan Steen: Painter and Storyteller.* Yale University Press.

Charleston, R. J. 1968 "George Ravenscroft: New Light on the Development of His 'Christalline Glasses.'" *Journal of Glass Studies* 10:156–67.

Christoph, Peter R., Kenneth Scott, and Kenn Stryker-Rodda, eds. 1976. *Kingston Papers.* 2 vols. Translated by Dingman Versteeg. New York Historical Manuscripts, Dutch. Published under the direction of the Holland Society. Genealogical Publishing Co., Inc., Baltimore.

Cobb, Charles R., and Chester DePratter. 2012. "Multisited Research on Colonowares and the Paradox of Globalization." *American Anthropologist* 114 (3): 446–61.

Codwise, Edward B. 1915. *Map of the City of Kingston.* On file in City of Kingston, Office of Planning and Engineering, Kingston, NY.

Coe, Joffre. 1964. "The Formative Cultures of the Carolina Piedmont." *Transactions of the American Philosophical Society* 54 (5).

Cohen, David Steven. 1992. *The Dutch-American Farm.* New York University Press.

Cohen, Jay R. 2004. Preliminary archaeological testing at Matthewis Persen House proposed gardens, City of Kingston, Ulster County, NY. Letter report prepared for Kenneth Hewes Barricklo, Architect, Kingston, NY.

———. 2005. Archaeological data recovery for the Old Dutch Church east wall stabilization, City of Kingston, Ulster County, New York. Report prepared for Old Dutch Church and Kenneth Hewes Barricklo, Architect, Kingston, NY.

Combes, John D. 1974. "Ethnography, Archaeology, and Burial Practices among Coastal South Carolina Blacks." In *Conference on Historic Site Archaeology Papers, 1972,* edited by Stanley South. University of South Carolina.

Conners, Dennis, Lisa Cutten, Tammy Katzowitz, Lowell Thing, and Ed Pell. 2005. *New York Bluestone.* PDQ Printers.

Cordts and Hutton Brickyards. 1878. Map on file City of Kingston, Office of Planning and Engineering, Kington, NY.

Crane, Breed and Co. 1858. *Fisk's and Crane's Patent Metallic Burial Cases and Caskets, Air-Tight and Indestructable, for Protecting and Preserving the Dead for Vaults, Transportation, Ordinary Interment, or Future Removal*. Crane, Breed and Co., Manufacturers, Cincinnati.

Cross, John R. 1999. "'By Any Other Name . . .': A Reconsideration of Middle Archaic Lithic Technology and Typology in the Northeast." In *The Archaeological Northeast*, edited by Mary Ann Levine, Kenneth E. Sassaman, and Michael S. Nassaney. Bergin and Garvey.

Cultural Resource Group, Louis Berger and Associates. 1993. Iroquois Gas Transmission System Phase III data recovery excavations at Site 230-3-1. Prepared for Iroquois Gas Transmission System, LP, Shelton, Connecticut. Louis Berger and Associates, Inc., East Orange, New Jersey. Report on file at New York State Office of Parks, Recreation, and Historic Preservation, Waterford, NY.

Curry, Andrew. 2023. "Forging Connections: DNA from Enslaved Black Workers at a 19th Century Iron Forge Links Them to Living Descendants—But the Research Swirls with Ethical Questions." *Science* 381:472–77.

Custer, Jay F., and Conor J. Ewasko. 2022. "Not All 'Gorgets' Are Gorgets and Not All 'Pendants' Are Pendants: Actualistic Study of Gorget and Pendant Functions as Bullroarers." *Archaeology of Eastern North America* 50:109–40.

Dallal, Diane. 1996. "Van Tienhoven's Basket: Treasure or Trash?" In *One Man's Trash Is Another Man's Treasure*, edited by Alexandra Van Dongen. Museum Boymans-van Beuningen.

———. 2004. "The Tudor Rose and the Fleurs-de-Lis: Women and Iconography in Seventeenth-Century Sutch Clay Pipes Found in New York City." In *Smoking Culture: The Archaeology of Tobacco Pipes in Eastern North America*, edited by Sean Rafferty and Rob Mann. University of Tennessee Press.

Dann, Boyd. 1987. "Surface Analysis of the Ochee Spring Steatite Quarry in Johnston, Rhode Island." *Man in the Northeast* 34:85–98.

Deetz, James. 1977. *In Small Things Forgotten: The Archeology of Early American Life*. Anchor.

Deetz, James, and Edwin Dethlefsen. 1965. "The Doppler Effect and Archaeology: A Consideration of the Spatial Aspects of Seriation." *Southwestern Journal of Anthropology* 21 (3): 196–206.

———. 1967. "Death's Head, Cherub, Urn and Willow." *Natural History* 76 (3): 29–37.

———. 1971. "Some Social Aspects of New England Colonial Mortuary Art." In *Approaches to the Social Dimensions of Mortuary Practices*, edited by James A. Brown. Memoirs of the Society for American Archaeology 25. Cambridge University Press.

De Lisser, Richard Lionel. 1968. *Picturesque Ulster*. Twines Catskill Bookshop. Reprint of 1896–1905 publication.

De Roever, Margriet. 1987. "The Fort Orange 'EB' Pipe Bowls: An Investigation of the Origin of American Objects in Dutch Seventeenth-Century Documents." In *New World Dutch Studies: Dutch Arts and Culture in Colonial America, 1609–1776*, edited by Roderic H. Blackburn and Nancy A. Kelley. Albany Institute of History and Art.

Desse-Berset, Nathlie. 2011. "Discrimination of *Acipenser sturio, Acipenser oxyrinchus* and *Acipenser naccarii* by Morphology of Bone and Osteometry." In *Biology and Conservation of the European Sturgeon Acipernser sturio L. 1758: The Reunion of the European and Atlantic Sturgeons*, edited by Patrick Williot, Eric Rochard, Nathalie Desse-Berset, Frank Kirschbaum, and Jörn Gessner. Springer-Verlag.

Dethlefsen, Edwin, and Kenneth Jensen. 1977. "Social Commentary from the Cemetery." *Natural History* 86 (6): 32–39.

Diamond, Joseph E. 1990. Reconnaissance level survey of archaeological resources in the city of Kingston. Certified Local Government Program 1990. Manuscript on file at the City of Kingston and New York State Office of Parks, Recreation and Historic Preservation Bureau of Historic Sites, Peebles Island, Waterford.

———. 1996a. "The Catskill Rockshelter, Town of Olive, Ulster County, New York." *New York State Archaeological Association Bulletin* 110:16–25.

———. 1996b. Archaeological monitoring, Fred J. Johnston House, City of Kingston, Ulster County, NY. Manuscript on file, Friends of Historic Kingston.

———. 1998. "Terminal Late Woodland/Early Contact Period Settlement Patterns in the Mid-Hudson Valley." *Journal of Middle Atlantic Archaeology* 12:95–111.

———. 1999a. "The Terminal Late Woodland/Contact Period in the Mid-Hudson Valley." PhD diss., State University of New York Albany. University Microfilms.

———. 1999b. Archaeological survey and monitoring, Phase 1B/2, Company Hill Path and D&H Canal Company Office, Kingston, NY (EPF Grant #54-6083). Prepared for City of Kingston. Manuscript on file at the City of Kingston and New York State Office of Parks, Recreation and Historic Preservation Bureau of Historic Sites, Waterford.

———. 2004a. "The Guido Site: A Multi-component Pre-contact Site in Marbletown, Ulster County, NY." *North American Archaeologist* 25 (4):357–92.

———. 2004b. "Marbletown and Nachte Jan: Two Multi-component Rockshelters in the Esopus Drainage, Ulster County, NY." *Northeast Anthropology* 67:61–88.

———. 2004c. Phase 1 cultural resource investigation Sailors' Cove on the Hudson, City of Kingston, Ulster County, NY. OPRHP #04PR00377. Manuscript on file at the City of Kingston and New York State Office of Parks, Recreation and Historic Preservation Bureau of Historic Sites, Waterford.

———. 2004d. Archaeological excavations in the Matthewis Persen House, Kingston, NY. 2 vols. Prepared for the County of Ulster, Department of Buildings and Grounds, Kingston, NY. Manuscript on file at City of Kingston and New York State Office of Parks, Recreation and Historic Preservation, Waterford.

———. 2006. "Owned in Life, Owned in Death: The Pine Street African and African-American Burial Ground in Kingston, New York." *Northeast Historical Archaeology* 35:47–62. http://digitalcommons.buffalostate.edu/neha/vol35/iss1/22.

———. 2007a. Phase 1 Cultural Resource Investigation, Proposed Colony Liquor Expansion, City of Kingston, Ulster County, NY. OPRHP #07PR02718. Prepared for Colony Liquor and Wine Distributors, LLC, Kingston.

———. 2007b. Phase 2 cultural resource evaluation, proposed Colony Liquor Expansion, City of Kingston, Ulster County, NY. OPRHP #07PR02718. Prepared for Colony Liquor and Wine Distributors, LLC, Kingston.

———. 2008. Phase 1 cultural resource investigation, proposed Kingston Meadows Senior Residence, 191 Hurley Avenue, Kingston, Ulster County, NY. OPRHP #08PR01953. Prepared for Hudson Valley Housing Development Fund, Inc.

———. 2009. Phase 1B archaeological testing, proposed Millen's Recycling, LLC, Route 32, town of Ulster, Ulster County, NY.

———. 2010a. Phase 2 archaeological evaluation of precontact loci A11118.000072, A11118.000073, A11118.000074, and A11118.000075. Proposed Millen's Recycling, LLC, Route 32, town of Ulster, Ulster County, NY.

———. 2010b. Phase 2 cultural resource evaluation, proposed Kingston Meadows Senior Residence, 191 Hurley Avenue, Kingston, Ulster County, NY. OPRHP #08PR01953. Prepared for Hudson Valley Housing Fund, Inc.

———. 2013. "The Bear Trap Spring Rockshelter." *North American Archaeologist* 34 (2): 169–201.

———. 2014. Phase 1B archaeological monitoring and Phase 3 mitigations of Abeel Street Project and Abeel Street Pre-Contact Site #1, City of Kingston, Ulster County, NY.

———. 2018. SEQRA Phase 2 cultural resource evaluation, proposed Montano Project, US Route 32, town of Saugerties, Ulster County, NY.

———. 2023. "The Terminal Late Woodland/Contact Period in the Mid-Hudson Valley." In *Archaeology of New York State in the Twenty-First Century*, edited by Susan E. Maguire and Lisa Marie Anselmi. New York State Museum Record 9.

Diamond, Joseph E., and Thomas Amorosi. 2006. "A Middle-Archaic Reutilized Clovis Projectile Point from the Mid-Hudson Valley, New York." *Current Research in the Pleistocene* 23:91–92.

———. 2014. "A Preliminary Assessment of the Huyler Rockshelter; A Middle Archaic to Contact Period Rockshelter on the Hudson River, Town of Hyde Park, Dutchess County, NY." Paper presented at the 98th Annual Meeting of the New York State Archaeological Association, Oneonta, NY.

———. 2023. "A House within a House: Excavations Inside the Senate House State Historic Site, Kingston, Ulster County, N.Y." *Northeast Historical Archaeology*.

Diamond, Joseph E., Thomas Amorosi, and David Perry. 2016. "Late Woodland Subsistence the Wolfersteig Site: A Multi-component Site on the Esopus Creek." *Archaeology of Eastern North America* 44:131–60.

———. 2022. "The Van Deusen Site: A Multicomponent Precontact Site on the Esopus Creek, Ulster County, N.Y." *Northeast Anthropology* 89:1–40.

Diamond, Joseph E., and Susan O'Connell Stewart. 2011. "A Middle Woodland Pottery Stamp and Associated Middle Woodland Ceramics from the Indian Hill Site, Wawarsing, New York." In *Current Research in New York Archaeology: AD 700–1300*, edited by Christina B. Rieth and John P. Hart. New York State Museum Record 2.

Diamond, Joseph E., John R. Stevens, and James Decker. 2012. "Archaeological and Architectural and Investigations: Recreating the Original Roof-Lines of two Early 18th century Dutch Houses in Ulster County, NY." Paper presented at the 96th Annual New York State Archaeological Association Conference, Poughkeepsie, NY.

Dincauze, Dena F. 1976. *The Neville Site: 8,000 Years at Amoskeag, Manchester, New Hampshire*. Peabody Museum Monographs 4.

Dolan, Jean F. 1969a. "Test Digging Begins at Old Stockade Site." *Kingston Daily Freeman*, May 13.

———. 1969b. "Pay Dirt on Converse Street: Some Above-Ground Treasures." *Kingston Daily Freeman*, May 14.

Drillings, Rachel. 2024. "Nathan C. Bell's Kingston Ceramic Factory and Its Reflection on 19th-Century Consumer Trends in New York." Paper presented at the 105th Annual Meeting of the New York State Archaeological Association, Oswego.

Dumbrell, Roger. 1983. *Understanding Antique Wine Bottles*. Antique Collectors Club, Woodbridge, Suffolk, UK.

Dunn, Shirley. 1994. *The Mohicans and Their Land, 1609–1730*. Purple Mountain Press.

———. 2000. *The Mohican World, 1680–1750*. Purple Mountain Press.

Dunn, Shirley W., and Allison P. Bennett. 1996. *Dutch Architecture Near Albany: The Polgreen Photographs*. Purple Mountain Press.

Eisenberg, Leonard A. 1976. *Paleo-Indian Settlement Pattern in the Hudson and Delaware River Drainages*. Occasional Publications in Northeastern Anthropology, no. 4. Franklin Pierce College.

———. 1981. "A Preliminary Analysis of the Datum: A Multicomponent Prehistoric Site near the Hudson River, Ulster County, New York." *Man in the Northeast* 24:1–36.

———. 1989. "The Hendrickson Site: A Late Woodland Indian Village in the City of Kingston, Ulster County, New York." *Man in the Northeast* 38:21–53.

———. 1991. "The Mohonk Rockshelter: A Major Neville Site in New York State." In *The Archaeology and Ethnohistory of the Lower Hudson Valley and Neighboring Regions: Essays in Honor of Louis A. Brennan*, edited by Herbert C. Kraft. Occasional Publications in Northeastern Anthropology 11. Archaeological Services.

Ellis, Chris, James Keron, Darryl Dann, Joe Desloges, Ed Estaugh, Lisa Hodgetts, Kaitlyn Malleau, et al. 2014. "The Davidson Site, A Late Archaic, First Nations Ancestral Occupation near Parkhill, Ontario." Part1, "Coals, Site Setting and Site Investigations; part 2, "The Broad Point and Small Point Components." *Newsletter of the London Chapter, Ontario Archaeological Society* 14 (5–6, 7–8, respectively).

Evers, Alf. 1972. *The Catskills: From Wilderness to Woodstock*. Doubleday.

———. 1978. *Woodstock: History of an American Town*. Overlook.

———. 2005. *Kingston: City on the Hudson*. Overlook.

Every, Roger B. n.d. *Old Burial Grounds of Ulster County, N.Y*. Pamphlet, privately printed.

Fagan, Lisa A. 1978. "A Vegetational and Cultural Sequence for Southern New England 15,000 BP to 7000 BP." *Man in the Northeast* 15/16:70–92.

Faulkner, Alaric, and Gretchen Faulkner. 1987. *The French at Pentagoet 1635–1674: An Archaeological Portrait of the Acadian Frontier*. Special Publications of the New Brunswick Museum and Occasional Publications in Maine Archaeology, Maine Historic Preservation Commission, no. 5.

Fayden, Meta P. 1993. *Indian Corn and Dutch Pots: Seventeenth-Century Foodways in New Amsterdam/New York City*. PhD diss., City University of New York. University Microfilms.

Feister, Lois M., and Joseph S. Sopko. 2003. "Archaeology at Senate House State Historic Site, Kingston, Ulster County, New York, 1970–1997" Report on file at New York State Office of Parks, Recreation and Historic Preservation Bureau of Historic Sites, Waterford.

Fennell, Christopher C. 2007. *Crossroads and Cosmologies: Diasporas and Ethnogenesis in the New World*. University Press of Florida.

Feranec, Robert S., and Andrew Kozlowski. 2016. "Implications of a Bayesian Radiocarbon Calibration of Colonization Ages for Mammalian Megafauna in Glaciated New York State after the Last Glacial Maximum." *Quaternary Research* 85:262–70.

Ferguson, Leland. 1992. *Uncommon Ground: Archaeology and Early African America, 1650–1800*. Smithsonian Institution Press.

Fernow, Berthold, ed. 1881. *Documents Relating to the Colonial History of the State of New York*. Vol. 13. Weed Parsons.

Fisher, Charles. 1982. "Projectile Points from the First Avenue Site, Sleightsburg, New York: Implications from Multivariate Analysis." *Man in the Northeast* 23:61–65.

Fisher, Charles, and Karen Hartgen. 1983. "Glass Trade Beads from Waterford, New York." *Pennsylvania Archaeologist* 53 (1–2): 47–52.

Fisher, Charles, Karl J. Reinhard, Matthew Kirk, and Justin DiViriglio. 2007. "Privies and Parasites: The Archaeology of Health Conditions in Albany, New York." *Historical Archaeology* 41 (4): 172–97.

Fisher, Donald W., Yngvar W. Isachsen, and Lawrence V. Rickard. 1970. *Geologic Map of New York; Lower Hudson Sheet.* New York State Museum and Science Service Map and Chart Series 15.

Fitchen, John. 1968. *The New World Dutch Barn: A Study of Its Characteristics, Its Structural System, and Its Probable Erectional Procedures.* Syracuse University Press.

Fitting, James E. 1968. "Environmental Potential and the Post-glacial Readaptation in Eastern North America." *American Antiquity* 33 (4): 441–45.

Fitts, Robert K. 1996. "The Landscapes of Northern Bondage." *Historical Archaeology* 30 (2): 54–73.

Fleskes, Raquel E., Ade A. Ofunniyin, Joanna K. Gilmore, Eric Poplin, Suzanne M. Abel, Wolf D. Bueschen, Chelsey Juarez, et al. 2020. "Ancestry, Health, and Lived Experiences of Enslaved Africans in 18th Century Charleston: An Osteobiological Analysis." *American Journal of Physical Anthropology* 175:3–24.

Ford, Edwin Millard (with Friends of Historic Kingston). 2004. *Images of Kingston.* Arcadia.

———. 2010. *Street Whys: Anecdotes and Lore about the Streets of Kingston, New York.* Ford Printing.

Foster, Steven, and James A. Duke. 1990. *Peterson Field Guides: Eastern/Central Medicinal Plants.* Houghton Mifflin.

Fowler, William S. 1943. "Soapstone Bowl Making as Practiced at the Westfield Quarry." *Bulletin of the Massachusetts Archaeological Society* 4:42–44.

———. 1955. "The Stone Bowl Industry, Its Importance as Culture Diagnostic." *Bulletin of the Massachusetts Archaeological Society* 17:74–77.

———. 1969. "The Wilbraham Stone Bowl Quarry." *Bulletin of the Massachusetts Archaeological Society* 30 (3–4): 9–22.

Francaviglia, Richard V. 1971. "The Cemetery as an Evolving Cultural Landscape." *Annals of the Association of American Geographers* 61 (3): 501–9.

French, J. H. 1858. *Map of Ulster County, New York from Actual Surveys.* Taintor, Dawson.

———. 1860. *Gazetteer of the State of New York Embracing a Comprehensive View of the Geography, Geology, and General History of the State, and a Complete History and Description of Every County, City, Town, Village and Locality.* R. Pearsall Smith.

Fried, Marc B. 1975. *The Early History of Kingston and Ulster County, NY.* Ulster County Historical Society.

Funk, Elizabeth Paling, and Martha Dickinson Shattuck, eds. 2011. *A Beautiful and Fruitful Place: Selected Rensselaerwijck Papers*. Vol. 2. State University of New York Press.

Funk, Robert E. 1976. *Recent Contributions to Hudson Valley Prehistory*. New York State Museum and Science Service Memoir 22.

———. 1988. "The Laurentian Concept: A Review." *Archaeology of Eastern North America* 16:1–42.

———. 1991. "The Middle Archaic in New York." *Journal of Middle Atlantic Archaeology* 7:7–18.

———. 1993. *Archaeological Investigations in the Upper Susquehanna Valley, New York State*. Persimmon.

———. 1996. "Holocene or Hollow Scene? The Search for the Earliest Archaeological Cultures in New York State." *Review of Archaeology* 17 (1): 11–25.

Funk, Robert E., and Robert D. Kuhn. 2003. *Three Sixteenth-Century Mohawk Iroquois Village Sites*. New York State Museum Bulletin 503.

Furlow, David A. 2021. "Thank You for Smoking: The Archaeological Legacy of Edward Bird's Tobacco Pipes in New Netherland and Beyond." In *The Archaeology of New Netherland: A World Built on Trade*, edited by Craig Lukezic and John P. McCarthy. University Press of Florida.

Gade, Susan, Derrick J. Marcucci, and David W. Benn. 2021. Phase 1B archaeological investigations of the proposed Rondout Riverpoint shoreline stabilization and public access project and Phase II archaeological investigations of the Kingston Point site, Ulster County, New York (OPRHP #20PR02776).

Gall, Michael J., Richard F. Veit, and Robert W. Craig. 2011. "Rich Man, Poor Man, Pioneer, Thief: Rethinking Earthfast Architecture in New Jersey." *Historical Archaeology* 45 (4): 39–61.

Garman, James C. 1994. "Viewing the Color Line through the Material Culture of Death." *Historical Archaeology* 28 (3): 74–93.

Garvin-Jackson, Rose. 1993. "An Archaeological Analysis of Spatial Patterning in College Dormitory Rooms." *Northeast Historical Archaeology* 21/22:161–72.

Gates St-Pierre, Christian. 2001. "Two Sites, but Two Phases? Revisiting Kipp Island and Hunters Home." *Northeast Anthropology* 62:31–53.

Goddard, Ives. 1978. "Delaware." In *Handbook of North American Indians*, vol. 15, *Northeast*, edited by Bruce G. Trigger. Smithsonian Institution.

Goldberg, Arthur F., and James P. Witkowski. 2006. "Beneath His Magic Touch: The Dated Vessels of the African-American Slave Potter Dave." In *Ceramics in America*, edited by Robert Hunter. Chipstone Foundation.

Graeber, David. 2001. *Toward an Anthropological Theory of Value: The False Coin of Our Own Dreams*. Palgrave.

Gramly, Richard Michael, and Robert E. Funk. 1990. "What Is Known and Not Known about the Human Occupation of the Northeastern United States Until 10,000 B.P." *Archaeology of Eastern North America* 18:5–31.

Grimm, Claus, ed. 1984. *Gluck und Glas: Zur Kulturgeschichte des Spessartglases.* Verlag Kunst & Antiquitaten.

Grossman, Joel W. 1985. "The Excavation of Augustine Heerman's Warehouse and Associated 17th Century Dutch West India Company Deposits: The Broad Financial Center Mitigation Final Report." Report on file with the New York City Landmarks Preservation Commission, New York.

Grumet, Robert S. 1990. "A New Ethnohistorical Model for North American Indian Demography." *North American Archaeologist* 11:29–41.

———. 1991. "The Minisink Settlements: Native American Identity and Society in the Munsee Heartland, 1650–1778." In *The People of Minisink, Papers from the 1989 Delaware Water Gap Symposium*, edited by David G. Orr and Douglas V. Campana. National Park Service, Mid-Atlantic Region, Philadelphia.

———. 1994. "The Selling of Lenapehoking." In *Proceedings of the 1992 People to People Conference, Selected Papers*, edited by Charles F. Hayes III, Connie Cox Bodner, and Lorraine P. Saunders. Research Records 23. Rochester Museum and Science Center.

———. 1995. *Historic Contact: Indian People and Colonists in Today's Northeastern United States in the Sixteenth Through Eighteenth Centuries.* University of Oklahoma Press.

———. 2009. *The Munsee Indians: A History.* University of Oklahoma Press.

———. 2014. *Beyond Manhattan: A Gazetteer of Delaware Indian History Reflected in Modern-Day Place Names.* New York State Museum Record 5.

Gurcke, Karl. 1987. *Bricks and Brickmaking: A Handbook for Historical Archaeology.* University of Idaho Press.

Haines, Robert E. 2021. *Footprints: Selections from the Collection of Robert E. Haines.* Privately printed by the author.

Hall, Jerome L. 2005. "A Tobacconist's Dream: The Pipe Wreck, Monti Cristi, Dominican Republic." In *Beneath the Seven Seas: Adventures with the Institute of Nautical Archaeology*, edited by George F. Bass. Thames and Hudson.

Halliwell, David B., and Arthur E. Spiess. 2017. "Scute Differentiation between Atlantic and Shortnose Sturgeon: An Archaeological Investigation." *Archaeology of Eastern North America* 45:33–71.

Hamell, George R. 1983. "Trading in Metaphors: The Magic of Beads." In *Proceedings of the 1982 Glass Bead Conference*, edited by Charles F. Hayes III. Rochester Museum and Science Center Research Records 16.

———. 1987. "Mythical Realities and European Contact in the Northeast During the Sixteenth and Seventeenth Centuries." *Man in the Northeast* 33:63–87.

———. 1996. "Wampum: White, Bright and Light Things Are Good to Think." In *One Man's Trash Is Another Man's Treasure*, edited by Alexandra van Dongen. MuseumBoymans-van Beuningen.

Harney, Eadaoin, Steven Micheletti, Karis S. Bruwelheide, William A. Freyman, Katarzyna Bryc, Ali Akbari, Ethan Jewett, et al. 2023. "The Genetic Legacy of African Americans from Catoctin Furnace." *Science* 381 (6657): 500.

Harris, Edward C. 1975. "The Stratigraphic Sequence: A Question of Time." *World Archaeology* 7:109–21.

———. 1979a. *The Principles of Archaeological Stratigraphy*. Academic Press.

———. 1979b. "The Laws of Archaeological Stratigraphy." *World Archaeology* 11:111–17.

Harris, Wendy E. 2024. "Cruel Murder: A Story of Fear, Death, Childhood, and Enslavement in Early Nineteenth-Century Ulster County, New York." *New York History* 104 (2): 132–49.

Hart, John P., Lisa M. Anderson, and Robert S. Feranec. 2011. "Additional Evidence for Cal. Seventh-Century A.D. Maize Consumption at the Kipp Island Site, New York." In *Current Research in New York Archaeology, A.D. 700–1300*, edited by Christina B. Rieth and John P. Hart. New York State Museum Record 2.

Hart, John. P., David. L. Asch, C. Margaret Scarry, and G. W. Crawford. 2002. "The Age of the Common Bean (*Phaseolus vulgaris* L.) in the Northern Eastern Woodlands of North America." *Antiquity* 76:377–85.

Hart, John P., Jennifer Birch, Sturt W. Manning, and Brita Lorentzen. 2023. "Updating the Classic New York Lamoka Lake and Scaccia Sites: Refined Chronologies through AMS Dating and Bayesian Modeling." *Radiocarbon* 65 (3): 789–808.

Hart, John P., and Hetty Jo Brumbach. 2003. "The Death of Owasco." *American Antiquity* 68 (4): 737–52.

———. 2005. "Cooking Residues, AMS Dates, and the Middle-to-Late-Woodland Transition in Central New York." *Northeast Anthropology* 69:1–34.

Hart, John P., Hetty Jo Brumbach, Lisa M. Anderson, and Susan Winchell-Sweeney. 2017. "Maize and Pits: Late Prehistoric Occupations of the Hurley Site in the Esopus Creek Valley, Ulster County, New York." *Archaeology of Eastern North America* 45:133–60.

Hart, John P., Hetty Jo Brumbach, and Robert Lusteck. 2007. "Extending the Phytolith Evidence for Early Maize (*Zea mays* ssp. *mays*) and Squash (*Cucurbita* sp.) in Central New York." *American Antiquity* 72:563–83.

Hart, John P., and C. Margaret Scarry. 1999. "The Age of Common Beans (*Phaseolus vulgaris*) in the Northeastern United States." *American Antiquity* 64 (4): 653–58.

Hart, John P., Robert G. Thompson, and Hetty Jo Brumbach. 2003. "Phytolith Evidence for Early Maize (*Zea mays*) in the Northern Finger Lakes Region of New York." *American Antiquity* 68 (4): 619–40.

Hartgen Archeological Associates, Inc. (HAA). 1980. First Avenue site, town of Port Ewen, hamlet of Sleightsburg, Ulster County, New York. Archaeological

Mitigation Proceedings. Submitted to Brinnier and Larios, Kingston, NY.

———. 1981. Stage 1B archaeological field investigations of the City of Kingston and Town of Ulster proposed sewer system C-36-1037, Ulster County, NY.

———. 1994. Stage 1B field reconnaissance for the Sleightsburg Spit, Town of Esopus, Ulster County, NY.

———. 1995a. Report of archaeological potential and field reconnaissance, SEQR Parts 1 and 3, proposed Kingston Industrial Park, City of Kingston, Ulster County, NY.

———. 1995b. Stage 3 data recovery, Kingston Industrial Park prehistoric site, City of Kingston, Ulster County, NY.

———. 2002a. Phase 1A archaeological sensitivity assessment, Abeel Street project. Pin #8757.10. City of Kingston, Ulster County, NY.

———. 2002b. The Ulster County Jail Quarry site, Phase III data retrieval investigation, City of Kingston, Ulster County, NY.

———. 2005. End of field work letter, data retrieval investigation, Ulster Manor Precontact site, Town of Ulster, Ulster County, New York. Report on file at New York State Office of Parks, Recreation and Historic Preservation Bureau of Historic Sites, Peebles Island, Waterford.

———. 2009. Phase III archaeological data recovery, the pre-contact Manor site, Ulster Manor Residential Subdivision, Town of Ulster, Ulster County, NY (June 2009; OPRHP #03PR03925).

———. 2013. Phase II/III archaeological investigation, Reher Bakery building project, Reher historical site, 99 and 101 Broadway, City of Kingston, Ulster County, New York.

Hayes, Charles F. 1989. "An Introduction to the Shell and Shell Artifact Collection at the Rochester Museum and Science Center." *In Proceeding of the 1986 Shell Bead Conference, Selected Papers*, edited by Charles F. Hayes, Lynn Ceci, and Connie Cox Bodner. Research Records 20. Rochester Museum and Science Center.

Heckenberger, Michael J., James B. Petersen, Ellen R. Cowie, Arthur E. Speiss, Louise Basa, and Robert Stuckenrath. 1990. "Early Woodland Period Mortuary Ceremonialism in the Far Northeast: A View from the Boucher Cemetery." *Archaeology of Eastern North America* 18:109–44.

Hesse, Franklin J. 1968. "The Fredenburg Site: A Single Component Site of the Fox Creek Complex." *New York State Archaeological Association Bulletin* 44:27–32.

Historical Society, Newburgh Bay and the Highlands. 1900. *Centennial Number*. May 8. Newburgh Journal Printing House and Book-Bindery.

Hodder, Ian. 1986. *Reading the Past: Current Approaches to Interpretation in Archaeology*. Cambridge University Press.

———. 2012. *Entangled: An Archaeology of the Relationships between Humans and Things*. Wiley-Blackwell.

Holland, John D. 2004. "Lithic Types and Varieties of New York State." *NYSAA Bulletin* 120:17–36.

Holt, Henry M. R., and Hope E. Luhman. 2007. "Iroquois Pipeline Site 230-3-1: Lessons from a Hudson Valley Late Woodland Occupation." *Bulletin of the Archaeological Society of Connecticut* 69:59–75.

Huey, Paul R. 1981. "Archaeological Exploration of the Louw-Bogardus Site, Kingston, NY." *Bulletin and Journal of Archaeology for New York State* 82:4–24.

———. 1983. "Glass Trade Beads from Fort Orange, Albany, NY c. A.D. 1624–1676." In *Proceedings of the 1982 Glass Trade Bead Conference*, edited by Charles F. Hayes III. Research Records 16. Rochester Museum and Science Center.

———. 1987. "Archeological Evidence of Dutch Wooden Cellars and Perishable Wooden Structures at Seventeenth and Eighteenth Century Sites in the Upper Hudson Valley." In *New World Dutch Studies: Dutch Arts and Culture in Colonial America, 1609–1776*, edited by Roderic H. Blackburn and Nancy A. Kelley. Albany Institute of History and Art.

———. 1988. *Aspects of Continuity and Change in Colonial Dutch Material Culture at Fort Orange, 1624–1664*. PhD diss., University of Pennsylvania. University Microfilms.

———. 1998. "Schuyler Flatts Archaeological District National Historic Landmark." *NYSAA Bulletin* 114:24–31.

———. 2008. "From Bird to Tippet: The Archaeology of Continuity and Change in Colonial Dutch Material Culture after 1664." In *From De Halve Maen to KLM: 400 Years of Dutch-American Exchange*, edited by Margriet Bruijn Lacy, Charles Gehring, and Jenneke Oosterhoff. Nodus Publikationen.

———. 2015. "Bodkins in New Netherland." Unpublished manuscript.

———. 2021. "Marbles in Dutch Colonial New Netherland." In *The Archaeology of New Netherland: A World Built on Trade*, edited by Craig Lukezic and John P. McCarthy. University Press of Florida.

Hughes, G. Bernard. 1956. *English, Scottish and Irish Table Glass from the Sixteenth Century to 1820*. Bramhall House.

Hutton, George V. 2003. *The Great Hudson River Brick Industry: Commemorating Three and a Half Centuries of Brickmaking*. Purple Mountain Press.

Jackson, Fatimah L.C. 2023. "Community-Initiated Genomics." *Science* 381 (6657): 482–83.

Jacobs, Jaap. 2009. *The Colony of New Netherland: A Dutch Settlement in Seventeenth-Century America*. Cornell University Press.

———. 2015. *Dutch Colonial Fortifications in North America, 1614–1676*. New Holland Foundation.

Jacobs, Jaap, and Louis H. Roper. 2014. *The World of the Seventeenth-Century Hudson Valley*. State University of New York Press.

Jameson, J. Franklin, ed. (1909) 2010. *Narratives of New Netherland, 1609–1664*. Cosimo Classics.

Jamieson, Ross W. 1995. "Material Culture and Social Death: African American Burial Practices." *Historical Archaeology* 29 (4): 39–58.

Janowitz, Meta F. 1993. "Indian Corn and Dutch Pots: Seventeenth-Century Foodways in New Amsterdam/New York." *Historical Archaeology* 27 (2): 6–24.

Janowitz, Meta F., Kate T. Morgan, and Nan A. Rothschild. 1985. "Cultural Pluralism and Pots in New Amsterdam-New York City." In *Domestic Pottery of the Northeastern United States, 1625–1850*, edited by Sarah Peabody Turner. Academic Press.

Janowitz, Meta F., and Richard G. Schaefer. 2019. "The Humble Cookpot: Earthenware Evidence of Dutch Foodways and Commerce." In *The Archaeology of New Netherland: A World Built on Trade*, edited by Craig Lukezic and John McCarthy. University of Florida Press.

———. 2021. "By Any Other Name: Kookpotten or Grapen? Little Pots, Big Stories." In *The Archaeology of New Netherland: A World Built on Trade*, edited by Craig Lukezic and John P. McCarthy. University Press of Florida.

Jones, Olive R. 1983. "The Contribution of the Ricketts Mold to the Manufacture of the English 'Wine' Bottle, 1820–1850." *Journal of Glass Studies* 25:167–77.

Jonge, Caroline Henriette de. 1971. *Dutch Tiles*. Praeger.

Karklins, K. 1974. "Seventeenth Century Dutch Beads." *Historical Archaeology* 8:64–82.

———. 1983. "Dutch Trade Beads in North America." In *Proceedings of the 1982 Glass Trade Bead Conference*, edited by Charles F. Hayes III. Research Records 16. Rochester Museum and Science Center.

Kelly, Robert L. 2017. *The Lifeways of Hunter-Gatherers: The Foraging Spectrum*. Cambridge University Press.

Kenyon, Ian, and William Fitzgerald. 1986. "Dutch Trade Beads in the Northeast: An Ontario Perspective." *Man in the Northeast* 32:1–34.

Ketchum, William C. Jr. 1987. *Potter and Potteries of New York State, 1650–1900*. Syracuse University Press.

Kidd, Kenneth E., and Martha A. Kidd. 1970. "A Classification System for Glass Beads for the Use of Field Archaeologists." *Canadian Historic Sites: Occasional Papers in Archaeology and History* 1:45–89.

Kidd, W. S. F., A. Plesch, and F. W. Vollmer. 1993. "Lithofacies and Structure of the Taconic Flysch, Melange, and Allochton, in the New York Capital District." In *Field Trips for the 67th Annual Meeting of the New York State Geological Association*, edited by John I. Garver and Jacqueline A. Smith. Union College, Schenectady.

Klingelhofer, Eric. 1987. "Aspects of Early Afro-American Culture: Artifacts from the Slave Quarters of the Garrison Plantation, Maryland." *Historical Archaeology* 21 (2): 112–19.

Korf, Dingeman. 1981. *Nederlandse majolica*. DeHaan.

Kraft, Herbert C. 1975. *The Archaeology of the Tocks Island Area.* Archaeological Research Center, Seton Hall University.

———. 1989. "Evidence of Contact and Trade in the Middle Atlantic Region and with the Minisink Indians of the Upper Delaware River Valley." *Journal of Atlantic Archaeology* 5:77–102.

———. 1991. "The Indians of the Lower Hudson Valley at the Time of European Contact." In *The Archaeology and Ethnohistory of the Lower Hudson Valley and Neighboring Regions: Essays in Honor of Louis A. Brennan,* edited by Herbert C. Kraft. Occasional Publications in Northeastern Anthropology 11. Archaeological Services.

———. 2001. *The Lenape-Delaware Indian Heritage, 10,000 BC to AD 2000.* Lenape Books.

Kurlansky, Mark. 2007. *The Big Oyster: History on the Half Shell.* Random House.

Lacy, Margriet. 2013. *A Beautiful and Fruitful Place: Selected Rensselaerwijck Seminar Papers.* Vol. 3. New Netherland Institute.

LaPorta, Philip C. 1996. "Lithostratigraphy as a Predictive Tool for Prehistoric Quarry Investigations: Examples from the Dutchess Quarry Site, Orange County, New York." In *A Golden Chronograph for Robert E. Funk,* edited by Chris Lindner and Edward V. Curtin. Occasional Publications in Northeastern Archaeology 15. Arcaeological Services.

———. 1997. Quarry models and lithic analysis for the Phase II of the Iroquois Compressor Station project. Manuscript on file Hartgen Archaeological Associates, Troy, NY.

———. 2002. Geological catchment for the Ulster County Jail prehistoric quarry site, Town of Kingston, Ulster County, NY.

LaPorta, Philip. C, Scott A. Minchak, and Margaret C. Brewer LaPorta. 2018. "The Prehistoric Bedrock Quarries Occurring within the Chert Bearing Carbonates of the Cambrian-Ordovician Kittatinny Supergroup, Wallkill River Valley, Northwestern New Jersey-Southeastern New York, U.S.A." In *Between History and Archaeology, Papers in Honour of Jacek Lech,* edited by Dagmara H. Werra and Marzena Wozny. Archaeopress.

LeBreton, Greg T. O., F. William Beamish, and R. Scott McKinley. 2004. *Sturgeons and Paddlefish of North America.* Kluwer Academic.

Lee, Esther J., Lisa M. Anderson, Vanessa Dale, and D. Andrew Merriweather. 2009. "MtDNA Origins of an Enslaved Labor Force from the 18th Century Schuyler Flatts Burial Ground in Colonial Albany, NY: Africans, Native Americans, and Malagasy?" *Journal of Archaeological Science* 36:2805–10.

Lenig, Wayne. 1999. "Patterns of Material Culture during the Early Years of New Netherland Trade." *Northeast Anthropology* 58:47–74.

Lenik, Edward J. 1998. *Max Schrabish, Rockshelter Archaeologist.* Wayne Historical Commission, Wayne, NJ.

Lesniak, Matt. 2002. "'A Good Indian Commodity': Wampum on the Waterfront." In *At the Rivers Edge: Two-Hundred and Fifty Years of Albany History, Data Retrieval, SUCF Parking Structure, Maiden Lane, Albany, New York*. Vol. 1A. Hartgen Archaeological Associates.

Lewis, Ann-Eliza H., ed. 2001. *Highway to the Past: The Archaeology of Boston's Big Dig*. Massachusetts Historical Commission.

Lewis, Dylan. 2018. "The Perry Site: A Multi-component Pre-contact Site on the Rondout Creek, Kingston, NY." Master's thesis, Hunter College.

Lindner, Christopher R. 1992. "Grouse Bluff: An Archaeological Introduction." *Hudson Valley Regional Review* 9 (1): 25–46.

———. 1998. "Eight Rockshelters in the Ashokan Catskills and Comparison with Site Clusters in the Hudson Highlands and Connecticut." *Bulletin of the Archaeological Society of Connecticut* 61:39–59.

Lindner, Christopher R., and Lisa Folb. 1996. "Chert Microdrills from Eastern New York: Use-Wear on Bushkill Tools that might have made Middlesex Beads." In *A Golden Chronograph for Robert E. Funk*, edited by Chris Lindner and Edward V. Curtin. Occasional Publications in Northeastern Archaeology 15. Archaeological Services.

———. 1998. "Lopuch 3 and Microdrills: Site Report and Use-Wear Analysis." *Archaeology of Eastern North America* 26:107–32.

Lloyd, James T. 1864. *Lloyd's Topographical Map of the Hudson River from the Head of Navigation at Troy to Its Confluence with the Ocean at Sandy Hook*. J. T. Lloyd.

Lossing, Benson J. 1866. *The Hudson: From the Wilderness to the Sea*. Originally published by H. B. Nims. Reprinted in 2000 by Black Dome Press.

Lothrop, Jonathan C. 2023. "Paleoindian Peoples of the New York Region." In *The Archaeology of New York State in the Twenty-First Century*, edited by Lisa Anselmi and Susan Maguire. New York State Museum Record 9.

Lothrop, Jonathan C., Michael L. Beardsley, Mark L. Clymer, Joseph E. Diamond, Philip LaPorta, Meredith H. Younge, and Susan Winchell-Sweeney. 2017. "Paleoindian Landscapes in Southeastern and Central New York." *PaleoAmerica* 3 (1): 1–13.

Lothrop, Jonathan C., and James W. Bradley. 2012. "Paleoindian Occupations in the Hudson Valley, New York." In *Late Pleistocene Archaeology and Ecology in the Far Northeast*, edited by Claude Chapdelaine. Texas A&M Press.

Lothrop, Jonathan C., Adrian Burke, Susan Winchell-Sweeney, and G. Gauthier. 2018. "Coupling Lithic Sourcing with Least Cost Path Analysis to Model Paleoindian Pathways in Northeastern North America." *American Antiquity* 83 (3): 462–84.

Lothrop, Jonathan C., Philip LaPorta, Meredith Younge, Joseph Diamond, and Susan Winchell-Sweeney. 2018. "Paleoindian Occupations in Southeastern New York: New Data on Sites and Isolated Finds in the Wallkill/Rondout

Valley." In *The Eastern Fluted Point Tradition*, vol. 2, edited by Joseph A. M. Gingerich. University of Utah Press.

Louis Berger Group (LBG). 1987. *Druggists, Craftsmen, and Merchants of Pearl and Water Streets, New York: The Barclays Bank Site.* 2 vols. Cultural Resource Group.

———. 2008. *Subsistence and Subsidence: Archaeological Investigations at the Kingston Armory Site (A11140.001250), Kingston, Ulster County, New York.* 2 vols.

Lucas, Michael, and Matthew Kirk. 2023. "Enslavement and Autonomy in Late Eighteenth-Century Albany, New York." *Historical Archaeology* 57:885–911.

Luedtke, Barbara E. 1992. *An Archaeologist's Guide to Chert and Flint.* Institute of Archaeology, University of California, Los Angeles.

Marcoux, Jon Bernard, Corey A. H. Sattes, and Jeff Sherard. 2023. "Exploring the Materiality of Late Seventeenth-Century and Early Eighteenth-Century Lowcountry Colonoware through Practice-Based Analysis." *Historical Archaeology* 57:1031–63.

McCashion, John H. 1979. "A Preliminary Chronology and Discussion of Seventeenth and Early Eighteenth Century Clay Tobacco Pipes from New York State Sites." In *The Archaeology of the Clay Tobacco Pipe*, vol. 2, *The United States of American*, edited by Peter Davey. BAR International Series 60.

McClure Zeller, Nancy Anne, ed. 1991. *A Beautiful and Fruitful Place: Selected Rensselaerswijck Seminar Papers.* New Netherland Publishing.

McGuire, Randall. 1988. "Dialogues with the Dead: Ideology and the Cemetery." In *The Recovery of Meaning: Historical Archaeology in the Eastern United States*, edited by Mark P. Leone and Parker B. Potter, Jr. Smithsonian Institution Press.

McNulty, Robert H. 1971. "Common Beverage Bottles: Their Production, Use and Forms in Seventeenth and Eighteenth Century Netherlands. Part 1." *Journal of Glass Studies* 13:91–119.

———. 1972. "Common Beverage Bottles: Their Production, Use and Forms in Seventeenth and Eighteenth Century Netherlands, Part 2." *Journal of Glass Studies* 14:141–48.

Meeske, Harrison.1998. *The Hudson Valley Dutch and Their Houses.* Purple Mountain Press.

Meinsen, Jaime. 2011. "The Perry Site." Paper presented at the 95 Annual Conference of the New York State Archaeological Association, Johnstown, NY.

Miller, George L., Patricia Samford, Eileen Shlasko, and Andrew Madsen. 2000. "Telling Time for Archaeologists." *Northeast Historical Archaeology* 29:1–22.

Miller, John. 1695. *New York Considered and Improved, 1695.* Original ms. in the British Museum. Reprint published by Burt Franklin, 1970. Also adapted and changed for Fernow (1881, 84–85).

Milne, Claudia, and Pamela Crabtree. 2000. "Revealing Meals: Ethnicity, Economic Status, and Diet at Five-Points, 1800–1860." In *Tales of Five Points: Working-Class Life in Nineteenth-Century New York*, edited by Rebecca Yamin. 7 vols. John Milner Associates.

Mitford, Jessica. 1963. *The American Way of Death*. Simon and Schuster.

Moerman, Daniel E. 2004. *Native American Ethnobotany*. Timber.

Mouw, Dirk, trans. 2014. Final Senate House Dutch documents English translation. Translated for the New York State Office of Parks, Recreation, and Historic Preservation, Waterford.

Munsell Soil Color Charts. 1992. Rev. ed. Macbeth.

Murphy, Patricia O'Reilly (with Friends of Historic Kingston). 2013. *Kingston*. Postcard History Series. Arcadia Publishing.

Nash, J. M. 1972. *The Age of Rembrandt and Vermeer*. Holt, Rinehart and Winston.

National Register Bulletin. 1997. *How to Apply the National Register Criteria for Evaluation*. US Department of the Interior, National Park Service, Cultural Resources. National Register, History and Education.

Neve, Richard. (1726) 1969. *Neve's The City and Country Purchaser and Builder's Dictionary: The Compleat Builders Guide*. David and Charles Reprints.

Newkirk, E. B. 1887. Revised Map of 1867. On file at City of Kingston, Planning and Engineering, Kingston, NY.

New York Archaeological Council. 2000. *Cultural Resources Standards Handbook*. New York Archaeological Council.

New York Times. 1894. "Kingston's Old Cemetery: Where Lie Buried the Ancestors of Many a Famous Family." June 10.

Nicolls, Richard. 2002. *Richard Nicolls/Esopus Indian Treaty/1665*. Ulster County Clerk's Office, Kingston, NY.

Noël Hume, Ivor. 1961. "The Glass Wine Bottle in Colonial Virginia." *Journal of Glass Studies* 3:90–117.

———. 1962. "An Indian Ware of the Colonial Period." *Quarterly Bulletin, Archaeological Society of Virginia* 17:1.

———. 1970. *A Guide to Artifacts of Colonial America*. Knopf.

———. 2003. "Through the Lookinge Glasse: or, the Chamber Pot as a Mirror of its Time." In *Ceramics in America*, edited by Robert Hunter. Chipstone Foundation.

Norris, C. Sidney, and Company. n.d. *Illustrated Catalogue of Coffin Handles and Undertaker's Trimmings*. Baltimore, Maryland.

Nystrom, Kenneth C., Linda A. Amato, and Lindsay A. Jankowitz. 2011. "Strontium Isotopic Reconstruction of the Composition of an Urban Free Black Population from the 19th Century United States." *Journal of Archaeological Science* 38:3505–17.

Nystrom, Kenneth C., Joseph E. Diamond, and Tyrone E. Wilson. 2024. "Owned in Life, No Longer Owned in Death: Remembering our Ancestors by

Bringing to Light the Pine Street African Burial Ground." Paper presented at the 84th Annual Meetings of the Society for American Archaeology, New Orleans, LA.

O'Callaghan, Edmund Burke, ed. 1850a. *The Documentary History of the State of New-York*. Vol. 3. Weed, Parsons.

———. 1850b. *Census of Slaves, 1755 (Lower New York)*. Albany.

Olivier, Laurent. 2011. *The Dark Abyss of Time: Archaeology and Memory*. Rowman and Littlefield.

Olsen, Bjornar. 2013. *In Defense of Things: Archaeology and the Ontology of Objects*. Altamira Press.

Orr, David G. 2003. "Samuel Malkin in Philadelphia: A Remarkable Slipware Assemblage." In *Ceramics in America*, edited by Robert Hunter. Chipstone Foundation.

Osterberg, Matthew M. 2002. *The Delaware and Hudson Canal and the Gravity Railroad*. Arcadia Press.

Oswald, Adrian. 1975. *Clay Pipes for the Archaeologist*. British Archaeological Reports 14.

Parker, Arthur C. 1922. *The Archaeological History of New York*. New York State Museum and Science Service Bulletin nos. 235–238.

———. 1924. *The Great Algonkin Flint Mines at Coxsackie*. New York State Archaeological Association, Research Transactions 4 (4).

Parker Pearson, Mike. 1999. *The Archaeology of Death and Burial*. Texas A&M Press.

Patterson, Orlando. 1982. *Slavery and Social Death: A Comparative Study*. Harvard University Press.

Paxson, Comfort and Company. 1877. *Revised Wholesale Price List of Undertakers' Supplies*. Paxson, Comfort and Company, Philadelphia.

Pena, Elizabeth S. 1990. *Wampum Production in New Netherland and Colonial New York: The Historical and Archaeological Context*. UMI Dissertation Services.

———. 2006. "Wampum Diplomacy: The Historical and Archaeological Evidence for Wampum at Fort Niagara." *Northeast Historical Archaeology* 35:15–28.

Peteet, Dorothy, John Rayburn, Kirsten Menking, Guy Robinson, and Byron Stone. 2009. "Deglaciation in the Southeastern Laurentide Sector and the Hudson Valley—15,000 Years of Vegetational and Climate History." *New York State Geological Association Road Trip 4*.

Peterson, Harold L. 1956. *Arms and Armor in Colonial America, 1526–1783*. Stackpole Company, Harrisburg, PA.

Peterson, Lee Allen. 1977. *Peterson Field Guide Series: A Field Guide to Edible Wild Plants, Eastern/Central North America*. Houghton Mifflin.

Pfeiffer, John. 1984. "The Late and Terminal Archaic Periods of Connecticut's Prehistory." *Bulletin of the Archaeological Society of Connecticut* 47:73–88.

Pipes, Marie-Lorraine. 2021. "A Synthesis of Dutch Faunal Remains Recovered from Seventeenth-Century Sites in the Albany Region." In *The Archaeology* of New Netherland: A World Built on Trade, edited by Craig Lukezic and John P. McCarthy. University Press of Florida.

Poucher, J. Wilson, and Byron J. Terwilliger. 1931. *Gravestones of Ulster County*. Collections of the Ulster County Historical Society 1.

Pratt, Peter P. 1961. *Oneida Iroquois Glass Trade Bead Sequence, 1575–1745*. Fort Stanwix Museum.

Price, Richard, and Keith Muckelroy. 1977. "The Kennemerland Site: The Third and Fourth seasons 1974 and 1976, an Interim Report." *Nautical Archaeology* 6 (3): 187–218.

Remensnyder, John P. 1963. "Nathan Clark Bell, Potter of Kingston." *Ulster County Gazette* 7.

Reynolds, Helen Wilkinson. 1929. *Dutch Houses in the Hudson Valley before 1776*. Holland Society. Reprinted 1965 by Dover.

Rhoads, William B. 2003. *Kingston, New York: The Architectural Guide*. Black Dome.

Richards, Brandon. 2014. "Hier Leydt Begraven: A Primer on Dutch Colonial Gravestones." *Northeast Historical Archaeology* 43:1–22.

Rieth, Christina B., ed. 2008. *Current Approaches to the Analysis and Interpretation of Small Lithic Scatters in the Northeast*. New York State Museum Bulletin Series 508.

———. 2013. "Space, Time and the Middle Woodland 'Jack's Reef Horizon' in New York." *Archaeology of Eastern North America* 40:91–112.

Rink, Oliver A. 1986. *Holland on the Hudson: An Economic and Social History of Dutch New York*. Cornell University Press.

Riordan, Timothy B. 2000. *Dig a Grave Both Wide and Deep: An Archaeological Investigation of Mortuary Practices in the 17th-Century Cemetery at St. Mary's City, Maryland*. St. Mary's City Archaeological Series 3. Historic St. Mary's City.

Ritchie, William A. 1932. *The Lamoka Lake Site*. Researches and Transactions of the New York State Archaeological Association 7 (4).

———. 1949. "The Bell-Philhower Site, Sussex County, New Jersey." Prehistoric Research Series 3 (2). Indiana HistoricalSociety.

———. 1952. *The Chance Horizon, An Early Stage of Mohawk Iroquois Cultural Development*. New York State Museum Circular 29.

———. 1958a. *An Introduction to Hudson Valley Prehistory*. New York State Museum and Science Service Bulletin Number 367.

———. 1958b. *Traces of Early Man in the Northeast*. New York State Museum and Science Service Bulletin Number 358.

———. 1961. *A Typology and Nomenclature for New York Projectile Points*. New York State Museum and Science Service Bulletin Number 384.

———. 1969a. *The Archeology of New York State*. Natural History Press.

———, 1969b. "The K1 Site, the Vergennes Phase, and the Laurentian Tradition." *New York State Archaeological Association Bulletin* 42:1–5.

———. 1971. *A Typology and Nomenclature for New York Projectile Points.* New York State Museum Bulletin Number 384.

Ritchie, William A., and Robert E. Funk. 1973. *Aboriginal Settlement Patterns in the Northeast.* New York State Museum and Science Service Memoir 20.

Rockman, M., and J. Steele, eds. 2003. *Colonization of Unfamiliar Landscapes: The Archaeology of Adaptation.* Routledge.

Rorabaugh, W. J. 1979. *The Alcoholic Republic: An American Tradition.* Oxford University Press.

Rose, Peter G. 2009. *Food, Drink and Celebrations of the Hudson Valley Dutch.* History Press.

Rothschild, Nan A., and Diana diZerega Wall. 2014. *The Archaeology of American Cities.* University Press of Florida.

Rothschild, Nan A., and Arnold Pickman. 1990. "The 7 Hanover Square Excavation Report: A Final Report." Report on file Landmarks Preservation Commission, New York.

Rothschild, Nan A., Diana Rockman Wall, and Eugene Boesch. 1987. *The Archaeological Investigation of the Stadt Huys Block: A Final Report.* Report on file at Landmarks Preservation Commission, New York.

Rumrill, Donald A. 1991. "The Mohawk Glass Trade Bead Chronology, ca. 1560–1785." *Beads: Journal of the Society of Bead Researchers* 3:5–45.

Ruttenber, Edward M. 1872. *History of the Tribes of Hudson's River.* J. Munsell.

Salwen, Bert. 1975. "Post-glacial Environments and Cultural Change in the Hudson River Basin." *Man in the Northeast* 10:43–70.

Salwen, Bert, and Sarah T. Bridges. 1977. "Cultural Differences and the Interpretation of Archeological Evidence: Problems with Dates." In *Current Perspectives in Northeast Archeology: Essays in Honor of William A. Ritchie,* edited by Robert E. Funk and Charles F. Hayes III. New York State Archeological Association.

Sanborn Map Company. 1887. *Sanborn Fire Insurance Map.* On file in City of Kingston, Office of Planning and Engineering.

———. 1899. *Sanborn Fire Insurance Map.* On file in City of Kingston, Office of Planning and Engineering.

———. 1957. *Sanborn Fire Insurance Map.* On file in City of Kingston, Office of Planning and Engineering.

Sando, Anne, and Lucille Lewis Johnson. 2013. "The Upper Trapps Gap: Two Years of Excavation at a Prehistoric Rockshelter." *NYSAA Bulletin* 127:36–46

Sargent and Company.1883. *Coffin and Casket Trimmings, 1883 Appendix.* Sargent & Company, New Haven.

Sassaman, Kenneth E. 1999. "A Southeastern Perspective on Soapstone Vessel Technology in the Northeast." In *The Archaeological Northeast,* edited by Mary Ann Levine, Kenneth E. Sassaman, and Michael S. Nassaney. Bergin and Garvey.

———. 2006. "Dating and Explaining Soapstone Vessels: A Comment on Truncer." *American Antiquity* 71 (1): 141–56.

———. 2010. *The Eastern Archaic, Historicized*. Altamira.

Schaefer, Richard G. 1998. *A Typology of Seventeenth-Century Dutch Ceramics and Its Implications for American Historical Archaeology*. BAR International Series 702.

Schoonmaker, Marius.1888. *The History of Kingston, New York*. Burr Printing House.

Schrabisch, Max. 1909. Indian Rockshelters in Northern New Jersey and Southern New York. In *The Indians of Greater New York and the Lower Hudson*, edited by Clark Wissler. Anthropological Papers of the American Museum of Natural History 3.

———. 1919. "Indian Rockshelters in the Shawangunk Mountains." *Historic Wallkill and Hudson River Valleys* 26:43–58.

———. n.d. "Archaeology of Southern New York." Manuscript on file, New York State Museum, Albany.

Schulenberg, Janet K. 2002. "New Dates for Owasco Pots." In *Northeast Subsistence and Settlement Change, A.D. 700–1300*, edited by John P. Hart and Christina B. Rieth. New York State Museum Bulletin 496.

Sempowski, Martha L. 1989. "Fluctuations through Time in the Use of Marine Shell at Seneca Iroquois Sites." In *Proceeding of the 1986 Shell Bead Conference, Selected Papers*, edited by Charles F. Hayes, Lynn Ceci, and Connie Cox Bodner. Research Records 20. Rochester Museum and Science Center.

Short, Carolyn. 1982. "Discover Early 1800's Kingston Potteries." *Ulster County Gazette* 6, no. 306 (April 8): 1, 10.

Shorto, Russell. 2004. *The Island at the Center of the World: The Epic Story of Dutch Manhattan and the Forgotten Colony that Shaped America*. Doubleday.

Slater, Robert. 1983. Overlay of 1695 Miller map of Kingston showing Stockade additions from 1661–1677.

Smith, C. Lavett. 1985. *The Inland Fishes of New York State*. New York State Department of Environmental Conservation.

Snow, Dean R. 1980. *The Archaeology of New England*. Academic Press.

———. 1995. *Mohawk Valley Archaeology: The Sites*. Occasional Papers in Anthropology 23. Matson Museum of Anthropology, Pennsylvania State University, University Park.

Solecki, Ralph S. 1985. "Recent Field Inspections of Two Seventeenth Century Indian Forts on Long Island, Forts Massapeag and Corchaug." *NYSAA Bulletin* 91:26–31.

———. 1993. "Indian Forts of the Mid-17th Century in the Southern New England-New York Coastal Area." *Northeast Historical Archaeology* 21/22:64–78.

Solecki, Ralph S., and Robert S. Grumet. 1994. "The Fort Massapeag Archaeological Site National Historic Landmark." *NYSAA Bulletin* 108:18–28.

Sopko, Joseph. 1991. "The Stratigraphic Sequence of the Senate House Property Lot and the Evolution of the Structure on the Site." Paper on file New

York State Office of Parks, Recreation and Historic Preservation, Bureau of Historic Sites.

South, Stanley. 1977. *Method and Theory in Historical Archeology*. Academic Press.

———. 1978. "Pattern Recognition in Historical Archaeology." *American Antiquity* 43 (2): 223–30.

———. 1979. "Historical Site Content, Structure, and Function." *American Antiquity* 44 (2): 213–37.

Spence, Michael W., and William A. Fox. 1986. "The Early Woodland Occupations of Southern Ontario." In *Early Woodland Archeology*, edited by Kenneth B. Farnsworth and Thomas E. Emerson. Kampsville Seminars in Archeology 2. Center for American Archeology Press.

Spiess, Arthur E., D. Wilson, and James Bradley. 1998. "Paleoindian Occupation in the New England-Maritimes Region: Beyond Cultural Ecology." *Archaeology of Eastern North America* 26:201–64.

Starna, William A. 1979. "The Archaic Concept: Its Development in North American Prehistory." *NYSAA Bulletin* 75:67–77.

Staski, Edward. 1984. "Just What Can a 19th Century Bottle Tell Us?" *Historical Archaeology* 18 (1): 38–51.

Stelten, Ruud. 2013. *Archaeological Excavations at Schotsenhoek Plantation, St. Eustatius, Caribbean Netherlands: An Early- to Mid-Eighteenth-Century Slave Settlement at a Sugar Plantation on the Caribbean's "Historical Gem."* St. Eustatius Center for Archaeological Research.

Stessin-Cohn, Susan, and Ashley Hurlburt-Biagini. 2023. *In Defiance: Runaways from Slavery in New York's Hudson River Valley, 1735–1831*. 2nd ed. Black Dome.

Steuding, Bob. 1985. *The Last of the Handmade Dams: The Story of the Ashokan Reservoir*. Purple Mountain Press.

———. 1995. *Rondout: The Story of a Hudson River Port*. Purple Mountain Press.

Stevens, John. 2005. *Dutch Vernacular Architecture in North America, 1640–1830*. Society for the Preservation of Hudson Valley Vernacular Architecture.

Stone, Lyle M. 1974. *Fort Michilimackinac, 1715–1781: An Archaeological Perspective on the Revolutionary Frontier*. Michigan State University.

Strong, D., and Company. c. 1870. *Illustrated Catalog of Undertakers' Goods*. Connecticut Historical Society.

Theuerkauff-Liederwald, Anna-Elizabeth. 1968. "Der Romer, Studien zu Einer Glasform. Part 1." *Journal of Glass Studies* 10:114–55

———. 1969. "Der Romer, Studien zu Einer Glasform. Part 2." *Journal of Glass Studies* 11:43–69.

Thing, Lowell. 2015. *The Street That Built a City: McEntee's Chestnut Street, Kingston, and the Rise of New York*. Black Dome Press.

Tornes, Lawrence A. 1979. Soil survey of Ulster County, New York. US Department of Agriculture in Cooperation with Cornell University Agricultural Experiment Station.

Truncer, James. 2004. "Steatite Vessel Age and Occurrence in Temperate Eastern North America." *American Antiquity* 69 (3): 487–513.

Truncer, James, Michael D. Glascock, and Hector Neff. 1998. "Source Characterization in Eastern North America: New Results Using Instrumental Neutron Activation Analysis." *Archaeometry* 40:23–44.

Turnbaugh, William A., Sarah P. Turnbaugh, and Thomas Keifer. 1984. "Characterization of Selected Soapstone Sources in Southern New England." In *Prehistoric Quarries and Lithic Production*, edited by Jonathon E. Ericson and Barbara A. Purdy. Cambridge University Press.

van Dam, Jan Daniel, and Pieter Jan Tichelaar. 1984. *Dutch Tiles in the Philadelphia Museum of Art*. Philadelphia Museum of Art.

Van der Donck, Adriaen. 2008. *A Description of New Netherland*, edited by Charles T. Gehring and William A. Starna. University of Nebraska Press. Originally published 1655.

Van Der Poel's Hudson River Brick Collection. Andy Van Der Poel's complete list as of Summer 2023. brickcollecting.com.

van Dongen, Alexandra. 1996. "The Inexhaustible Kettle: The Metamorphosis of a European Utensil in the World of the North American Indians." In *One Man's Trash Is Another Man's Treasure*, edited by Alexandra Van Dongen. Museum Boymans-van Beuningen.

Van Tienhoven, Cornelius. 1851. "Information Relative to Taking Up Land in New Netherland." In *The Documentary History of the State of New York*, vol. 4, edited by Edmund Burke O'Callaghan. Weed, Parsons. Originally published 1650.

Veit, Richard, and Paul R. Huey. 2014. "'New Bottles Made with My Crest': Colonial Bottle Seals from Eastern North America." *Northeast Historical Archaeology* 43:54–91.

Venema, Janny. 2003. *Beverwijck: A Dutch Village on the American Frontier, 1652–1664*. State University of New York Press.

Vernon, Howard. 1978. "The Dutch, the Indians and the Fur Trade in the Hudson Valley, 1609–1664." In *Neighbors and Intruders: An Ethnohistorical Exploration of the Indians of Hudson's River*. National Museum of Man Mercury Series, Canadian Ethnology Service Paper 39. University of Ottawa Press, Ottawa.

Versaggi, Nina. 1999. "Regional Diversity within the Early Woodland of the Northeast." *Northeast Anthropology* 57:45–56

———. 2023. "The Transitional and Early Woodland Periods." In *Archaeology of New York State in the Twenty-First Century*, edited by Susan E. Maguire and Lisa Marie Anselmi. New York State Museum Record 9.

Vreeken, Hubert, Jan M. Baart, Thimo te Duits, Anna Lameris, and Margriet de Roever. 1998. *Glas in Het Amsterdams Historisch Museum en Museum Willet-Holthysen*. Amsterdams Historisch Museum; Waanders Uitgevers.

Waite, John G., and Paul R. Huey.1971. *Senate House: An Historic Structure Report*. New York State Historic Trust.

Walker, Iain C. 1977. *Clay Tobacco-Pipes, with Particular Reference to the Bristol Industry*. 4 vols. History and Archaeology 11. Parks Canada.

Waller, Joseph N., and Alan Leveillee. 1998. "Archaeological Investigations at Site RI2050 in Cranston, Rhode Island: A Native American Steatite Processing Site." *Bulletin of the Archaeological Society of Connecticut* 61:3–16.

Waterman, Kees-Jan, and Michael J. Smith. 2013. *Munsee Indian Trade in Ulster County, New York, 1712–1732*. Syracuse University Press.

Wellman, Beth. 1982. "A Survey of New York Fluted Points." *Archaeology of Eastern North America* 10:39–40.

Werner Archaeological Consulting. Twaalfskill Archaeological Survey: Twaalfskill Brook Drainage Outlet Cultural Resource Investigation Reports, State 1B Archaeological Field Investigation, State 2 Archaeological Survey. Werner Archaeological Consulting, Albany.

Werner, Dietrich, and Kurtis C. Burmeister. 2007. "An Overview of the History and Economic Geology of the Natural Cement Industry at Rosendale, Ulster County, New York." *Journal of ASTM International* 4 (6): 1–14.

White, Philip, Susan Stessin-Cohn, Ashley Hurlburt-Biagini, and Albert Cook. 2024. *Bearing Witness: Exploring the Legacy of Enslavement in Ulster County, New York*. Black Dome Press.

Whittaker, John C. 1994. *Flintknapping: Making and Understanding Stone Tools*. University of Texas Press.

———. 2003. *American Flintknappers: Stone Age Art in the Age of Computers*. University of Texas Press.

Wholey, Heather A., and Thomas D. Shaffer. 2014. "Prehistoric Steatite Acquisition and Transport: A Predictive Framework." *Archaeology of Eastern North America* 42:165–76.

Wilcoxen, Charlotte. 1987a. *Dutch Trade and Ceramics in America in the Seventeenth Century*. Albany Institute of History and Art.

———. 1987b. "New Netherland Ceramics: Evidence from Excavations of Fort Orange, 1624–1676." In *New World Dutch Studies: Dutch Arts and Culture in Colonial America 1609–1776*, edited by Roderic H. Blackburn and Nancy A. Kelley. Albany Institute of History and Art.

Williams-Myers, A. J. 1994. *Long Hammering: Essays on the Forging of an African American Presence in the Hudson River Valley to the Early Twentieth Century*. Africa World Press.

Williot, Patrick, Eric Rochard, Nathlie Desse-Berset, Frank Kirschbaum, and Jörn Gessner, eds. 2011. *Biology and Conservation of the European Sturgeon Acipernser sturio L. 1758: The Reunion of the European and Atlantic Sturgeons*. Springer-Verlag.

Wilson, Kenneth M. 1976. Window Glass in America. In *Building Early America*, edited by Charles E. Peterson. Chilton Book Company.

Wray, Charles Foster. 1948. "Varieties and Sources of Flint Found in New York State." *Pennsylvania Archaeologist* 18 (2): 25–45.

Wroth, Lawrence, C. 1970. *The Voyages of Giovanni Verrazzano, 1524–1528*. Yale University Press.

Wuertz, Sven, Stefan Reiser, Jörn Gessner, and Frank Kirschbaum. 2011. "Morphological Distinction between Juvenile Stages of the European Sturgeon *Acipenser sturio* and the Atlantic Sturgeon *Acipenser oxyrinchus*." In *Biology and Conservation of the European Sturgeon Acipernser sturio L. 1758: The Reunion of the European and Atlantic Sturgeons*, edited by Patrick Williot, Eric Rochard, Nathlie Desse-Berset, Frank Kirschbaum, and Jörn Gessner. Springer-Verlag.

Zawadzka, Dagmara. 2011. "Spectacles to Behold: Colours in Algonquin Landscapes." *Totem: The University of Western Ontario Journal of Anthropology* 19 (1): 6–32.

Index

Note: To better assist the reader, artifact finds with numerous mentions have largely been reduced here to those identified by a specific style/period or other importance. Dutch names follow standard alphabetization guidelines except where now-common use prevails (e.g., "Ten Broeck, Wessel" as opposed to "Broeck, Wessel ten"). Finally, terms or points of interest in the glossary and notes sections are also included in this index.

Abeel Street (Kingston, NY), 8, 14, 28, 34, 65, 76, 94–103, 301, 303, 360, 368–369, 405n12
Aboriginal Occupation of New York. See Beauchamp, William
abraders, 68, 79, 82, 88, 115, 253
Abraham Hasbrouck House. *See under* Hasbrouck
Abraham Masten House. *See under* Masten
Ackerman, Paul, 209
adzes, 29, 57, 115, 342–343, 396; definition, 371
African Americans, 8, 310; "free Blacks," 326–328, 334. *See also* enslaved people
Albany (NY), 16, 41, 123, 130, 143, 160, 198, 266, 293, 318, 326, 399
Albany Avenue (Kingston, NY), 124, 271, 305, 309
alder. *See under* trees
Alexander, Paul (Colonel), 275

Alsen (formation), 13
amaranth, 18, 388
American Museum of Natural History, 54, 56
Amorosi, Thomas, 83, 183, 248, 286
Andriaesen, Jacob, 126
Angstrom, Clement, 114
Angstrom site (Kingston, NY), 8m, 16, 19m, 40m, 65, 114–118, 360
animals. *See* birds, fish, mammals
antler tools, 18, 27, 71, 74, 116, 338, 381
anvils, 38, 104–105, 115, 117, 341, 392; definition, 371
Archaic period: Early 7, 25–28, 57, 78, 86, 340, 355, 360; Middle, 25–28, 54–55, 60, 65, 360; Late, 7, 28–31, 60, 66–67, 69, 78–79, 87–89, 91, 115, 117, 189, 340, 343, 352–353; Transitional, 31–32, 56, 62, 90, 115, 117, 232, 242–248, 289, 361, 395

Archeological History of New York. See Parker, Arthur C.
Archeology of New York State. See Ritchie, William
argillite, 89, 101, 378; definition, 373, 404n9
arquebus. *See under* muskets
artifact distribution/stratification, 88, 93, 108–113, 116
Ashokan Reservoir, 107
atlatls, 28, 374–376
Austin Glen formation, 13, 344, 351, 377, 404n
awls, 26, 68, 74, 90
axes, 62–63

Bagdon Environmental Associates, 85
bannerstone, 29, 33, 56, 352, 376, 384; definition, 374
barges: brick, 296, 298, 368; coal 303–304
Barmann, Peter, 311. *See also under* bottles
Barmann's Brewery, 311–312. *See also under* bottles
Bartmann Jug. *See* stoneware: Bartmannkrügge
bass. *See under* fish
bastion, 146, 156, 375
beads: Kidd types, 386; production, 29, 34, 229–230, 252–253, 338, 377, 399; for trade, 36, 76, 185, 210, 220, 251–252, 338, 366, 399. *See also* wampum
beans, 16, 18, 35, 117, 356, 402n9
bear. *See under* mammals
Beauchamp, William: *Aboriginal Occupation of New York*, 43–44
beaver. *See under* mammals
Becraft formation (NY), 13, 70–71. *See also under* chert

Beeckman, Wilhelmus M., 317, 365
Before Albany. *See* Bradley, James
Bell, Nathan C. *See* stoneware: Bell *and* Nathan C. Bell Pottery Factory
Bellarmine. *See Bartmannkrügge*
berries, 18, 35, 39, 41, 113
Beverwyck (Albany, NY), 143
birch. *See under* trees
Bird, Edward. *See under* pipes
Bird, Evert, 283
birds, 20, 41, 67, 83, 85; chicken, 83, 156, 164, 182, 183, 290, 292–293, 365; duck, 18, 179, 291–293, 367; pigeon, 20, 156, 183–184, 290, 293, 365; turkey, 18, 35, 75, 83, 113, 179, 183, 290–293, 367
birdstone, 33, 374; definition, 375
blockies, 97, 100, 105, 110–112, 121, 203, 352; definition, 375
Blom, Dominie, 269
bluestone, 301–303, 329, 333, 409n3
bodkins, 222–223, 280
Boerhans, Jacob, 148
Bogardus, Benjamin, 291, 324
Bogardus, Cornelis, 318
Bogart House (Albany, NY), 326
bolas stone, 115–116; definition, 376
bone tools, 18, 26, 67, 116
Booth, Henry, 54
bottles: Balsam of Honey, 211, 235; "case," 216, 220; Barmann's beer, 171, 332; crown closure, 396; English "onion," 172, 204, 216, 224, 240; George Hauck Brewing, 332; Jan Eltenge, 211, 235; "packer," 217; [J. W.] Reynolds soda water, 211, 225, 235; Ricketts-style, 207, 223, 225; shaft-and-globe, 210; Turlington Balsam of Life, 213, 326
bowery (*bouwerie*), 133, 136, 143; definition, 376

bracelets. *See under* jewelry
Bradley, James: *Before Albany*, 369
brass, 131, 185, 222, 253, 284, 338
bricks: Dutch red / Hudson Valley Flats, 156, 163, 171–172, 179, 187, 268–270, 315–316, 318, 381; Dutch yellow, 270–271, 381; Hutton, 188, 296–299; Terry, 296. *See also* industry: brickmaking
Bridges, Sarah, 8, 159–160, 163, 189–190, 264
British (colonists, settlers), 13–14, 150, 190, 366–367; food, 367; habitations, 130; soldiers, 150; trade, 366
Broadway (Kingston, NY), 94, 124, 300–301, 332, 369
Brodhed: Anna, 314; Wessel, 321–322
Broeck, Wessel ten. *See* Ten Broeck
Broyles, Bettye: *The St. Albans Site, Kanawha County, West Virginia*, 57
Bruyn, Jacobus, 155
buckles, 131, 188, 226, 279, 332
bullroarers, 75, 384
Burggraf, James, 355–356, 399
butternut. *See under* nuts
buttons, 5, 213, 215, 278–279, 324; bone, 171, 182, 221, 278–279; copper, 278; glass, 130, 224–225, 251; metal, 278; mother-of-pearl, 278

caches, 71, 86, 325, 333, 342; definition, 376
Canal Path Trail, 91–92
cannonballs, 209, 211, 275, 291, 407n8
Cantine's Island, 56, 64–65, 360, 368
carabines. *See under* muskets
caribou, 16–17, 20, 54
Catskill. *See under* Native American: Munsee speakers

cattails, 18, 41, 85, 113, 121–122, 134, 362, 388
cemeteries/graveyards: Comforter Reformed Church, 311; Houghtaling, 305, 307–308, 410n2; markers (or lack of), 167, 305–306, 309, 313–314, 327; Montrepose, 305, 309–311; Mt. Calvary, 312; Mt. Zion, 8, 305, 310–311; relocation of, 306–308; St. Mary's, 311; St. Peters, 311; Sharp Burial Ground, 309; Wiltwyck, 304, 308, 311. *See also* Old Dutch Church, Pine Street African Burial Ground
ceramics: Buckley-ware, 261–263; chargers/plates, 214, 255, 259, 261, 380; "Colono Ware," 161–162; creamware, 260, 397; delft, 187, 207, 219, 255–257, 274, 325–326, 364, 366, 380, 397; earthenware, 163–164, 175–178, 180; Hoogeboom, 16, 178, 185, 219, 261–262, 364; Jackfield, 171, 179–180, 182, 188, 201, 223, 225, 229, 261; *kookpots*, 224, 261, 263, 289, 387; majolica, 218–219, 255, 364, 366, 380, 397; Nottingham ware, 188; pearlware, 202, 210, 260, 325; pipkins, 224, 261, 289, 387; porcelain, 156, 179–180, 188, 207, 213, 216, 218, 221, 223–224, 226, 230, 243; porringers, 260, 390; Rockingham ware, 220, 225–226, 229; *Schüsselkachel*, 176–178, 270, 364, 408n9; tiles, 272–273, 315–316 (*See also* pan tiles). *See also* stoneware
chamber pots, 131, 223–224, 263, 289, 365
Chambers, Abraham Van Gaasbeck, 323

Chambers, Thomas, 91, 124–127, 129, 133–135, 144, 146, 149
Chance Horizon: An Early Stage of Mohawk Iroquois Cultural Development. See Ritchie, William
Chapel Street (Kingston, NY), 302
chert: Becraft, 70–71; Briarcliff, 104–106; Coeymans, 69–71; Eppler, 69–70, 82, 101; Esopus, 69–70, 82, 101, 248; Glenerie, 69–71; Harmonyvale, 74, 82, 101, 248; Indian River, 74, 82, 90, 101–102, 172, 248, 377; Kalkberg, 69–71; Knaderack, 70; Limeport, 69; Manlius, 70–71; Mt. Merino, 13–14, 41, 60, 70–71, 74, 82, 86, 88–90, 93, 101–102, 189, 248, 342, 344–345, 350, 352, 360, 375, 377, 404n; New Scotland, 69–71; Onondaga, 13–14, 54, 60, 69–70, 86, 88–89, 93, 96, 101–102, 110, 112, 172, 208, 248, 342, 352, 360, 375, 377, 405n14; Oriskany, 69–70, 101, 412n2; Port Ewen, 104–106, 248; Rickenback, 69–70; Schoharie, 248
chestnut. *See under* nuts
choppers, 82, 88, 377
Ciccone, Jay, 57
clams. *See under* shells
Clifton Avenue, 311
Clinton Avenue (Kingston, NY), 3, 5, 157, 159–165, 172–174, 186, 190, 248, 271, 279, 289, 364–366, 389
Cloonan, Edward, 300
clothing, 277–279. *See also* buttons, thimbles
coal, 151, 182, 284–285, 409n1
Coeymans (NY) formation, 13. *See also under* chert
Cohen, Jay R., 188–189, 293
Cohoes (NY), 31

coins: cents/pennies, 169, 210, 215, 225, 280, 333; dimes, 211, 280. *See also* wampum
Colony Liquors Precontact Site (Kingston, NY), 92–94
Comforter Reformed Church Cemetery. *See under* cemeteries
Converse Street (Kingston, NY). *See* Louw-Bogardus House
combs, 281, 332
copper, 29–30, 33, 36, 131, 212, 219, 224, 284, 362, 366, 388; beads, 221, 251–252; coins, 210, 280, 333; projectile points, 251, 253; sheet, 180, 185; thimbles, 223, 225, 278; wire, 279
coral, 175–176, 223, 267, 325, 408n6, 411n3
Cordts and Hutton Company, 296–297
corn. *See* maize
Cornell Agricultural Cooperative, 286
Corning Museum of Glass, 254
Cotton, John, 319
creamware. *See under* ceramics
Cregier, Martyn, 134, 146–148
Crown Street (Kingston, NY), 155, 190, 193, 195–197, 201–202, 230, 232
CRM. *See* cultural resource management
Cross, John, 28
cultigen, 35
cultural resource management (CRM), 3–4, 8–9, 44, 65, 68, 92–94, 153, 299, 301–302, 340, 369, 405n15; definition, 379
curated (reworked) artifacts, 28, 60, 71–72, 76, 90
curtain walls, 146–148, 150, 153, 157, 194, 219, 375

Davi[t]s, "Cit" [or Kit], 137–138
Dechker, Jacop, 317–318
deer (white-tailed), 18, 25, 35, 40, 67, 75, 83, 85, 113, 116–117, 180, 183, 291–293, 367
Deetz, James, 131–132
Delaware and Hudson Canal Company, 91–92, 151, 182, 285, 302, 413n5
Deschamps, Isaac, 317
Devonian period, 13, 101, 105, 248
Devries, David, 124, 164, 370
DeWitt, Andries, 167–170, 312, 323
DeWitt, Tjerk Classen, 166–170
DeWitt Family Association, 9, 166, 168, 170
DeWitt Plot. *See under* Old Dutch Church
Deyo, S. Dubois, 302
dikenga cosmograms, 326
Donck, Adriaen van der, 164
Drayton Hall (SC), 325–326
drills, 56, 62, 71, 79, 80–82, 88–89, 102, 115, 174, 248, 251, 355, 399; bone, 116; definition, 381; iron, 252
Duck Pond site, 112, 118–122, 360, 388
ducks. *See under* birds
Dutch (colonists, settlers), 2, 11, 13–15, 112, 128; farming, 108, 127, 131, 135, 143; food, 19, 128, 156, 164–165, 183–184, 362, 365; fortifications, 123, 129–135, 141–144, 146–149, 157, 189–190; home constructions/architecture, 155–156, 174, 196, 235, 267, 320, 362–364, 401–402n1; hunting, 275; settlements, 40–41, 112, 123–125, 127–132, 136–137, 183, 293; trade, 36, 121, 123–125, 127, 143–145, 185, 365–366; violence, *see* Esopus Wars

Dutch East India Company, 123
Dutchess County, 30
Dutch West India Company, 125–126, 141
Dykman, Johannis, 125

Early History of Kingston and Ulster County. See Fried, Marc
East Chester Street (Kingston, NY), 15, 312
Edgecliff (NY). *See* chert: Onondaga
Egbert Schoonmaker Stone Ware Factory, 296. *See also* stoneware: Schoonmaker
Eisenberg, Leonard, 8, 73, 76–77
elk. *See under* mammals
Elmendorf: House, 174, 408–409n9; Lucas, 308; Martin, 308; Street, 309
Eltenge, Jan. *See under* bottles
English (colonists, settlers). *See* British
enslaved people, 185, 313–335; personal items, 267, 325–326; purchase of, 317–321; records, 314–325; work, 139–140, 162, 172, 185, 319–321, 324, 335, 389. *See also* Pine Street African Burial Ground
Esopus (NY): 7, 13, 16, 125, 127–128, 151, 337, 352–354, 359, 406n1. *See also* Wiltwyck
Esopus Creek, 12, 15–16, 19, 107, 156, 354, 356, 383, 406n1; floodplain, 37, 40–41, 107, 113, 118, 354, 362
Esopus Wars: First, 127–128, 131–145, 209; Second, 145–150, 241, 356
Eubanks, Thomas, 300
Evans, William. *See under* pipes
extraction site. *See* quarries

Faith (ship), 155
fauna. *See* birds, fish, mammals

Index | 447

FCR. *See* fire-cracked rock
fir. *See under* trees
fire-cracked rock, 32–33, 75, 116; definition, 383
First Esopus War. *See* Esopus Wars
fish, 19, 35, 38, 41, 67, 113, 156, 179–180, 183–184, 290–293, 367; bass, 19, 39, 66, 83, 388; perch, 83, 184, 290–292, 365, 367–368; porgy, 83; shad, 19, 66, 184; shark, 291, 355; sturgeon, 19, 35, 39, 66–67, 75, 83, 117, 184, 291, 293, 355, 365, 383
Fisher, Charles, 353–354
fishhooks, 29
fishing. *See under* Native Americans
flakers, 71, 74
flasks, 224
Flatbush Avenue, 15, 311
flotation, 115, 383
Ford, Edwin, 158, 327
forests: boreal, 17, 26, 79, 360, 402n5; deciduous, 28, 79; pine, 25; mast, 28, 360
Forst Meat-Packing Plant, 95
Fort Albany (ON, Canada), 271
Fort Nassau (Albany, NY), 123
Fort Orange (Albany, NY), 41, 123–145, 160, 164, 198, 203, 218, 226, 267, 269, 271, 282–283, 362m, 399, 408n6
fox. *See under* mammals
Foxhall. *See* Chambers, Thomas
Foxhall Avenue (Kingston, NY), 124–125, 151, 271, 311
Franklin Street (Kingston, NY), 307, 327
Fred Johnston House (Kingston, NY), 166, 307; garden, 165
French (colonists, settlers), 13–14
Fried, Marc: *Early History of Kingston and Ulster County*, 125–126, 131, 155, 362

Friends of Historic Kingston, 155, 166, 188, 300, 369
Frog Alley. *See* Louw-Bogardus House

gamepieces: dominoes, 284; marbles, 131, 171, 213–216, 221, 223–224, 281, 284, 332
George Hauck Brewing Company, 332, 369. *See also under* bottles
Gerdes, Hendrik. *See under* pipes
glass: crown, 220, 224, 271–272, 378; *façon-de-Venise*, 212, 382; "firing glass," 216; goblets, 216, 225; *passglas*, 272, 389, 399; *roemers*, 175, 204, 212, 254, 272, 364, 391, 393, 399; syringes, 217, 220, 279, 332; *Waldglas*, 206, 254, 399. *See also* beads, bottles, buttons, windows
Glenerie (NY) formation, 14, 92, 248. *See also under* chert
gorgets, 33; definition, 383–384
goose, 18, 293, 367
gorgets, 33, 56, 74–75, 383
gouges, 29, 56–57, 62–63, 396; definition, 384
gravers, 26, 82, 90, 121, 189
graveyards. *See* cemeteries
gray literature, 1, 7, 9
Greenkill Avenue, 15
Green Street (Kingston, NY), 3, 143, 189–190
gunflints. *See* muskets: flints
guns. *See* muskets *and* cannonballs

Hallinan, Arthur, 309, 327
Hammel, George, 76
hammerstones, 38, 70, 82, 88–89, 95, 97, 100–101, 104–105, 114–115, 218–219, 248, 338, 341, 349–350, 352, 375; definition, 385
Hartgen, Karen, 7, 9

448 | Index

Hartgen Archeological Associates, 68, 85, 94, 104, 300, 308, 340, 352
Hasbrouck: Abraham, 319; House, 408; Park, 14
Helderberg group, 13
Hendrickson, Harmen, 138
Hendrickson site (Kingston, NY), 5, 8, 40, 71–77, 360, 368, 370
hickory. *See under* nuts
Hondersrae, Jan, 318
Hone Street (Kingston, NY), 95, 102
Hoogeboom, Cornelius Pietersen (and manufactories), 16, 172, 178, 185, 261–262, 269–271, 315–318, 364, 381, 389
Hudson, Henry, 36, 76; *Half Moon*, 36, 76, 123
Hudson River, 12–13, 19, 70–71, 124, 151
Huey, Paul, 130, 161–162, 194, 359
Huguenot Street (New Paltz, NY), 203, 268, 270, 283, 399, 409n
Hulter, Johan de, 125
Hurley (NY), 4, 13m, 16, 19, 151, 156, 174, 270, 303, 337, 355–356, 359
Hurley Avenue (Kingston, NY), 14, 16, 44, 107, 114–122, 156, 354, 383
Hutton Brick Company, 296–297
Hutton Brickyards, 4, 43, 57, 64, 151, 295–299, 304

Imbroch, Gysbert van, 144–146, 194, 219, 243, 275, 290, 293, 364–365
industry (colonial/modern): brickmaking, 4, 11, 15, 54, 64, 134, 151, 268–270, 295–299, 315–316; cement, 151, 302; mills, 19, 151, 156, 301–302, 320, 369; mining, 14, 16, 40, 43–44, 54, 57, 64–65, 69, 295–297
Indian River formation. *See under* chert
insects, 88
Ingarra Site (Kingston, NY), 103
Iroquois. *See under* Native Americans: Haudenosaunee
Island Dock, 92, 303, 368, 413n5
ivory, 212, 223, 225, 276–277, 281, 284

Jacobson, Harman, 126–127
Jacobson, Pieter, 155
Jacob's Valley, 15, 386
Jacobz, Andries. *See under* pipes
Jansen, Henry, 323
Jansen, Jacob, 134, 138
Jansen, Volkert, 143–144
Jansen, Willem, 136
jasper, 74, 90, 179, 378
javelins. *See* spears
jewelry: bracelets, 223; rings, 279, 290–291
John Street (Kingston, NY), 193, 196–197, 201, 227, 232
Jova Manufacturing Company, 296, 298
Juet, Robert, 123
Jury, Robert, 197–198

Kalkberg (NY) formation, 13, 71, 101. *See also under* cherts
Kennedy, David, 310
Kennemerland (ship), 222–223
Keppler, Joseph, 55
Kingston (NY): architecture, 198, 321; city government, 150–155, 158, 309; geology, 13–14, 87–88, 92; British, 198, 236, 285, 366
Kingston Armory, 16, 32, 86–91, 361, 392, 404n9
Kingston Business Park, 38, 69–71
Kingston Dutch Reformed churchyard, 155
Kingston Knolls, 85–86, 360

Kingston Landing (the Strand), 124–126, 128, 144, 151, 271, 303, 318
Kingston Meadows, 8, 37, 107–114
Kingston Point, 15–16, 34, 43–68, 76, 78, 124, 151, 295–296, 299–300, 304, 359–360
Kingston Stockade, 132–133, 142, 153–191, 197, 235, 271, 365
knives, 31, 36, 54, 56, 62, 71, 79, 81–82, 89, 100, 115, 326, 343, 355, 366 367; definition, 386; flake, 57, 79, 81; iron, 36, 229, 325, 366–367; jackknife, 223; slate, 29, 88; ulu, 29, 384, 398
kookpots. See under ceramics

Laet, Johannes de, 64–65
Lake Albany (glacial lake), 16–17, 54, 87
La Montagne: Johannes, 138–139, 145, 269; Rachel, 146
LaPorta, Philip, 69, 105–106, 405n14
Laurentian tradition. *See* Archaic period
Laurentide ice sheet, 17
Lawatsch, Anthony, 302
Laycock, Washington, 310
lead, 230, 271–272. *See also* quarrels
limestone (for construction), 11, 13–14, 40, 69, 74, 155, 196, 197, 227–228, 302, 304, 320
Linderman Avenue, 156
Lipton Street, 91
liquor, 135, 137–138, 144, 150
Long Island (NY), 17
Loughran House (Kingston, NY), 187
Louis Berger Group, 86
Lourissen, Andries, 136–138
Louw, P[i]eter Cornelissen, 155–156, 323
Louw-Bogardus House (Kingston, NY), 3, 5, 155–158, 366
Louwrens, Andries, 133–134, 136

Main Street: Hurley, 329, 408n9; Kingston, 165, 188, 244
maize, 16, 18, 35–36, 41, 116, 124, 131, 136, 338, 354, 356, 365, 403n9
mammals: bear, 18, 35, 40, 83, 292, 355, 367; beaver, 17–18, 20, 36, 85, 123, 127, 141, 338, 367; elk, 19–20, 40, 116; fox, 83; mammoth, 16, 20; mastodon, 17, 20; moose, 17, 20, 25; musk ox, 17, 20; muskrat, 75; otter, 18, 367; peccary (flat-headed), 17, 20; pig, 83, 128, 130–131, 365–368; rabbit, 18, 75, 367; raccoon, 18, 75, 116, 367; rat, 186, 201, 285–286, 290, 413n4; sheep, 83, 183, 365–368; squirrel, 18, 75, 83, 116, 291, 367; woodchuck, 18, 35, 75, 83
mammoth. *See under* mammals
Manlius (NY) formation, 13, 71. *See also under* cherts
Manor Avenue (Kingston, NY), 16, 91
Manor Site, 340–344
Mans, Willim, 320
maps: Beers, 296–297, 303, 327; Brink and Tillson, 296; Codwise, 297–298; Cordts and Hutton Brickyards, 297; French, 296, 327; Lloyd's, 296; Miller, 142, 154, 188–189, 209, 307; Newkirk, 298; Sanborn Fire Insurance, 198, 297–298, 302; Slater, 193–194; Ten Broeck survey, 172–173
marbles. *See under* gamepieces
Marbletown (NY), 33, 118, 186, 151, 361, 384
Marcelis, Geijssebert, 318
Mary Powell (ship), 295–296, 303, 368
Mary's Avenue (Kingston, NY), 309
Masten, Abraham: House, 187; Johannis, 323
mastodon. *See under* mammals
material culture, 2

Matthewis Persen House. *See* Persen House
Michigan. *See* copper
middens, 66–67, 73–76, 187, 237, 288, 362; definition, 387
Middle Woodland. *See under* Woodland
Millens Quarry, 8, 38, 344–352, 357, 392
Mohawk. *See under* Native Americans
Mohican. *See under* Native Americans: Munsee speakers
Montrepose Cemetery. *See under* cemeteries
moose. *See under* mammals
Morehouse (NY). *See under* chert: Onondaga
Mount Calvary Cemetery. *See under* cemeteries
Mount Merino (Greenport, NY). *See under* chert
Mount Zion Cemetery. *See under* cemeteries
mullers, 95, 97, 100, 115, 338; definition, 388
Muniz, Cara, 84
Museum of the American Indian, 54
muskets, 5, 137, 144–146, 366, 373, 382; arquebus, 146, 373; balls/shot, 149–150, 207, 220, 276; carabines, 146; flintlocks, 146; flints, 146, 207, 210, 213, 219, 223, 275–276, 382; fuses, 136; matches, 136
musk ox. *See under* mammals
muskrat. *See under* mammals
mussels. *See under* shells

nails, 131, 234, 236, 274–275, 385
Nathan C. Bell Pottery Factory, 296, 299–300, 368. *See also* stoneware: Bell
National Historic Preservation Act (NHPA), 3

National Register of Historic Places, 65–66, 68, 108, 153–154, 190, 299, 303, 309, 345, 351, 369–370, 379
Native Americans: Algonquians, 36, 229, 253, 402n8, 403n9, 412n3; ceremonial sites, 32–33, 41, 90; and colonists, 2; Esopus, 36, 65, 121–129, 134–137, 289, 354, 406n3 (*See also* Esopus Wars); farming/horticulture, 16, 18, 40, 356; fishing, 37–39, 66–67, 71, 76, 302; food processing, 32, 67, 88–90, 100–101, 289, 356; food sources, 18–20, 35, 39, 117–118; foraging, 18, 34, 122; Haudenosaunee, 35–36, 41, 138–140, 203, 210, 224–225, 229, 252, 283, 337–338, 402n9, 411n1, 412n3; hide processing, 38, 88–90, 100, 116; hunting, 20–21, 40, 54, 85, 88–90, 100, 102, 122; Mohawk, 136, 138, 140, 146, 338; Munsee speakers, 36, 76, 138, 140, 210, 224, 229; settlement pattern, 11, 21, 25, 33, 35–41, 75–77, 89, 106, 113, 117, 342, 355, 359–362, 394; stone extraction, *see* quarries *and* chert; tool-making, 7, 13–14, 38, 67, 100, 104–106, 345; trade, 33–34, 36, 76, 90, 121, 123–124, 253 (*See also* Dutch: trade); warfare, *see under* Dutch
needles, 29
netsinkers, 71, 79, 81–82, 121
New Amsterdam (Manhattan, NY), 124–125, 145, 149, 198, 269, 271
Newark Lime and Cement Company, 14, 44, 69, 151, 368
New Jersey, 17
New Paltz (NY), 203, 268, 270, 283. *See also* Abraham Hasbrouck House, Huguenot Street *and* State University of New York
New Scotland (NY) formation, 13, 69, 71. *See also under* cherts

New York City, 198, 285, 321, 377; artifacts found in, 203, 283, 332, 407n2
New York Department of Environmental Conservation, 153, 369
New York Parks, Recreation and Historic Preservation Law, 3
New York State Museum, 35, 56, 112, 118, 165–166, 168, 299, 340, 344, 355–356
New York State Office of Parks, Recreation, and Historic Preservation (OPRHP), 2, 3, 69, 118, 153, 155, 172, 187, 299, 315
New York State Preservation Act, 3
New York University. *See* Clinton Avenue *and* Green Street
NHPA. *See* National Historic Preservation Act
Nicolls, Richard (Governor), 149–150, 288
Niessen, Christiaen, 148
Niew Dorp, 143, 145, 156. *See also* Hurley (NY)
North Street (Kingston, NY), 295–297
North Front Street (Kingston, NY), 15–16, 153, 155–156, 158, 172, 187, 289, 364, 366, 369, 381, 389, 407n3
nutting stone, 62, 79, 82, 95, 97, 100–101, 114–116, 219, 251, 289, 353; definition, 388, 396
nuts (tree): butternut, 18, 28, 89, 101; chestnut, 18, 101, 117; harvesting, 18, 28, 39, 41, 113; hickory, 18, 28, 35, 89–90, 101, 116–117; oak, 35, 117–118; processing, 35, 37–38, 76, 89–90, 101–102, 117–118, 375, 388; storing, 89–90, 285–286, 289, 356, 388; walnut, 18, 28, 101, 116. *See also* nutting stone
Nystrom, Kenneth, 8, 330, 333–334
NYU. *See* New York University

oak. *See under* trees *and* nuts
Oak Hill, 73, 76, 116–117, 338
Old Dutch Church (Kingston, NY), 8, 188–189, 306–308; DeWitt plot, 166–172, 307, 312, 368; stabilization project, 4
Onondaga (NY) formation, 13–14, 60, 74, 82, 92–93, 101, 104, 185, 248, 269, 405n14. *See also under* cherts
Oots, Jan, 319
OPRHP. *See* New York State Office of Parks, Recreation, and Historic Preservation
Orange County (NY), 17, 74, 82
Ordovician era, 13, 344, 412n2
Ostrander, Jonathan D., 309
otter. *See under* mammals
oysters. *See under* shells

paintings, 165, 173–174, 177, 222, 230, 239, 269, 271–272, 280, 284, 367
Palen, Henry, 310, 327
Paleoindians, 7, 17, 20–26, 54–56, 359–360, 394–395. *See also* Native Americans
palisades. *See* Dutch: fortifications
pan tiles, 173, 178–180, 185, 238, 267–268, 315–316, 362, 408–409n9; definition, 389
Parker, Arthur C.: *The Archeological History of New York*, 43–44
Parslow, Frank, 56, 64, 73, 77–78, 403n1
passglas. See under glass
peccary. *See under* mammals
Pels, Evert, 125
pencils (slate), 215, 223, 225, 279–280, 332
Pennsylvania, 32–33, 151, 182, 285, 413n5
Perry, Roscoe, 77

Perry Site (Kingston, NY), 40, 77–84, 360, 368, 370
Persen: Adam, 234, 273, 277–279; Cornelius, 234–235, 273, 277–279; Matthewis, 278, 291, 323–324
Persen House, 4–5, 8, 143, 158, 174, 178, 193–294, 325, 364, 367–368, 389; construction, 194–196, 362
pestles, 55–56, 62–63, 82, 88–89, 115, 251, 289, 338, 352, 355, 396; definition, 389
Peter Barmann Brewing Company. *See under* bottles
pigeons. *See under* birds
pigs. *See under* mammals
pine. *See under* trees
Pine Street, 3, 307–308
Pine Street African Burial Ground (Kingston, NY), 3, 8–9, 170, 305, 307–310, 314, 327–335, 396
pintles, 131, 224, 274–275; definition, 389
pipes (tobacco): Andries Jacobz, 221, 283; Edward Bird, 208, 218–219, 224, 226, 228, 230, 264, 281–283, 369; *fleur-de-lis*, 159, 203, 218, 282; Hendrik Gerdes, 203, 283; Joan Tippet, 230; Native American, 115–116, 338, 340, 353, 355; Robert Tippet, 207, 210, 213, 215, 218, 221, 225–226, 228–230, 234, 281–282; Thomas Dormer, 182, 213, 234, 283; Tudor Rose, 221, 226, 282–283; William Evans, 212, 218, 283
pipkins. *See under* ceramics
Pleistocene period, 16–18, 20, 25, 44, 54, 87, 359
plummet stones, 29, 89, 115, 384; definition, 390
points. *See* projectile points

Ponckhockie (Kingston, NY), 3, 14, 43–44, 56, 71, 151, 303, 362, 368, 370, 404n7
porcupine, 18, 75, 83
Port Ewen (NY) formation, 13–14, 104, 106, 248. *See also under* chert
post molds: colonial/19thC, 160–162, 214, 218–220, 223, 238–241, 333; definition, 390; Native American, 66–67, 116, 180–181, 186, 242, 354–355
Post Street, 103
pottery (Native American), 36, 64, 73, 90; Bainbridge, 116–117; Black Rock, 185; Castle Creek, 112, 116–117; Cayadutta-Otstungo, 116, 355; Chance, 73, 75–76, 338, 353, 355, 412n1; coil-wound, 97, 103; cord-wrapped impressed, 36, 73, 83, 118, 185, 219; Jack's Reef, 73, 82–83, Kelso, 73, 116–117; Kingston Incised, 6, 75, 162, 186, 339, 355; manufactories, 44; Munsee Incised, 186, 355; Oak Hill, 73, 116–117; Otstungo, 355; Point Peninsula, 85; steatite, 82, 90; Vinette, 32, 75, 90; Wickham, 73, 83; Woodland, 73, 83, 113, 344, 353. *See also* ceramics, stoneware
projectile points, 21, 25–28; Adena, 62; Bare Island, 55, 65, 67, 82; antler/bone, 27; Beekman, 60, 89, 384; Brewerton, 30, 60, 65, 71, 79, 89, 91, 121, 340–341, 348, 350, 384; Charleston, 78–79, 86, 384; Dalton, 24, 26–27, 402n6; Frost Island, 32–33, 353; fluted, 21, 25–26, 54, 56–57, 402n3; Fox Creek, 34–35, 72, 80, 82, 384; Genesee, 57, 61, 384; Greene, 34–35; Jack's Reef, 35, 56, 62, 80, 115–116, 354, 384; Kanawha, 57, 60, 78, 86, 340; Kirk,

Index | 453

projectile points *(continued)* 57, 60, 78, 86, 384, 404n3; Lamoka, 30–31, 57, 61, 65, 82, 165, 174, 354, 384, 397; Levanna, 36, 57, 62–64, 71–72, 79–80, 82, 116, 118, 121, 204, 208, 251, 289, 332, 338, 343, 355, 384; Madison, 36, 62–64, 175, 338, 341, 352, 384; Meadowood, 33, 71–72, 80, 82, 175, 203, 211, 251; Neville, 28, 54, 60, 65, 76, 96 97, 121, 360, 384; Normanskill, 30–31, 61; Orient, 32–33, 62, 66, 80, 82, 90, 95–96, 204, 212, 223, 242, 251, 340, 342, 352, 354; Otter Creek, 29–30, 56, 60, 68, 79, 88, 384, 404n9; Perkiomen, 340–341; Rossvile, 62, 82, 360; slate, 68; Snook Kill, 31, 57, 60, 62, 82, 90, 95–96, 384; Stark, 28, 360, 384; Squibnocket, 352–353; Susquehanna, 30, 62, 90, 95–96, 341–342, 352; Sylvan, 30–31, 61, 71, 79–80, 85, 95, 100, 121, 165, 174, 341–342, 353, 384; Vosburg, 30, 57, 60, 79, 89, 91, 342, 384; Wading River, 66, 384

prunts. *See* glass: *roemers*

quarries, 7, 11, 13m, 21m, 38, 68–71, 104–107, 303, 342, 344–352, 357, 375, 382, 385, 387, 391–392; lithic scatters, 7, 37, 92–93, 113, 395. *See also* Millens quarry, Kingston Business Park, Ulster County Jail

quarrels. *See under* windows

Quarry Street. *See* Hurley Avenue

quartz, 74, 114, 225, 251, 345, 353, 378

quartzite, 70, 74, 101, 105, 349–350, 353, 378, 384, 412n2

rabbit. *See under* mammals
raccoon. *See under* mammals

rats. *See under* mammals

Ravine Street (Kingston, NY), 94, 97

Rayburn, John, 168, 328–329

Reher Bakery (Kingston, NY), 300–301, 368

Rhinehart, William, 296, 299

Ritchie, William: *The Archeology of New York State*, 6, 56; *Chance Horizon: An Early Stage of Mohawk Iroquois Cultural Development*, 337–338, 343, 397; *Traces of Early Man in the Northeast*, 56

Rochester Museum and Science Center, 35

Roggen, Frantz J., 324

Rondout (NY), 128, 151, 285, 300–303

Rondout Creek, 14–15, 56, 65–71, 74–76, 85–86, 92, 103, 124–125, 151, 182, 296, 301–303, 359, 368, 413n5

Rondout-Oswego Railroad, 309

Rondout Riverpoint Shoreline Project, 361

Roosa, Pet[er/rus], 324

Ryger, Henry Zeewant, 253

Sailor's Cove, 4, 64, 295–299, 368. *See also* Hutton Brickyards

St. Albans Site, Kanawha County, West Virginia. *See under* Broyles, Bettye

St. James Street (Kingston, NY), 307, 327–328

Saint Mary's Cemetery. *See under* cemeteries

Saint Peters Cemetery. *See under* cemeteries

Salwen, Bert, 8, 159

Saugerties, 16, 19, 151, 405

Schoharie (NY), 34. *See also under* chert

Schoonmaker, Egbert. *See under* stoneware

Schuyler, Arent, 318

scrapers, 26, 37, 56, 67, 71–72, 79, 81–82, 90, 95–97, 100, 110, 114–116, 248, 343, 355, 396, 405n17; definition, 393, 398; endscrapers, 85, 88–89
Sebrah, Clement, 317
Second Esopus War. *See* Esopus Wars
seeds, 11, 35
Senate House State Historic Site (Kingston, NY), 3, 5, 155–156, 159–160, 172–186, 315, 325, 361–368, 389
SEQRA. *See* State Environmental Quality Review Act
shad. *See under* fish
shale, 13, 15, 69, 101, 344, 404n6
Sharp Burial Ground. *See under* cemeteries
sheep/goats. *See under* mammals
shellfish, 28, 163–165, 248, 263–266, 367. *See also* shells
shells: clam, 83, 184–185, 253, 263, 266, 367–368, 399; mussel, 19, 74, 263, 266, 354; oysters, 159, 161, 163–165, 171, 179–182, 188, 206, 263, 265–266, 365, 367–368; turtle, 19, 281; whelk, 230, 253, 338, 366, 377, 399. *See also* beads, wampum
shotgun cartridges/shells, 5, 276
slate (tools), 68, 88
Slecht: Anthony, 235; Cornelis Barentsen, 125, 127, 129, 136, 138, 144, 148
Sleightsburg (NY), 4, 303, 352–354
Sluys, Andries van der, 127, 136
Smith, Ceazer, 330–331
Smith, Dirck, 134, 137–140
Smithsonian Institution, 55
soapstone (steatite), 32–33
soil strata/quality, 2, 14–16, 107–108, 115, 168–170, 199, 232–233, 371; acidity, 17, 74, 91, 102

South Wall Street (Kingston, NY), 8, 310–311, 335
Spada, Frank, 8, 95, 110
spears, 25–28, 31, 34, 54, 89–90, 113, 121, 402n3; in glossary, 374, 384, 391
spokeshaves, 114–116, 121
spruce. *See under* trees
squash, 16, 18, 35, 41, 131, 402n9
squirrel. *See under* mammals
Staples Brick Company, 296, 298
State Environmental Quality Review Act (SEQRA) of New York, 3, 104, 369–370, 394
State University of New York (SUNY) New Paltz, 3, 14, 40, 84, 103, 168, 171, 300, 328, 330, 334, 407n4
steatite (soapstone), 32–33, 82–83, 90, 174, 353; definition, 395
Stoll, Jacob Jansen, 125–129, 133, 135–137
Stoll, Jan Jacobson, 137
stoneware: Albany slipped, 221; Bartmannkrügge (German), 171, 175, 213, 216, 218, 223, 229–230, 240, 257–258, 365, 375, 407n7; Bell, 44, 296, 299–300; Crolius, 212, 216, 258; Derby, 223; "dot, diaper, and basket" pattern, 216, 220; Frechen (German), 164, 213, 218, 257–258, 407n7; Fulham, 226; production, 44, 65; salt-glazed, 156, 171, 179, 182, 187, 210, 216, 220, 225–226, 257–258; Schoonmaker, 44, 296; Westerwald, 163–164, 175, 226, 257–258, 364–365, 407n7
strike-a-lights, 79, 82; definition, 396
sturgeon. *See under* fish
Stuyvesant, Peter, 112, 125–126, 128–130, 132–141, 144–146, 157, 160, 181, 190, 269, 407n7
SUNY. *See* State University of New York
Swartout, Roeliff, 144, 209

Taconic Orogeny, 13, 404n
Tammany Street (Kingston, NY), 85
Tannery Brook, 16, 103, 156–157, 189–190
Tappen, Samuel, 310
Ten Broeck: Jacob, 323; Johan, 320; Wessel, 163, 172, 319, 323. *See also* Senate House State Historic Site
thimbles, 223, 225, 278–279, 324
tigerware. *See* stoneware: Bartmannkrügge
tiles. *See under* ceramics
Tippet, Robert. *See under* pipes
tobacco, 115, 135–136
tool-making. *See under* Native Americans
toothbrushes, 215, 223, 279–280
Topographical Map of the Hudson River from the Head of Navigation at Troy to Its Confluence with the Ocean at Sandy Hook. See maps: Lloyd
Traces of Early Man in the Northeast. See under Ritchie, William
trade. *See under* Dutch *and* Native Americans
trees: alder, 17, 25, 28; birch, 20, 28; fir, 17, 25–26; oak, 28, 118; pine, 20, 25, 117; spruce, 17, 20, 25–26; walnut, 88, 90
Troy (NY), 16
Turck, Thomas, 71, 73, 77–78
turkey. *See under* birds
turtles, 19, 35, 39, 67, 75, 83, 85, 113, 281, 290, 367. *See also under* shells
Twaalfskill Brook, 301–303, 368

Ulster (NY) city and formation, 4, 7, 13–14, 16, 38, 91–92, 337–352, 354–355, 359–360, 392, 404n7

Ulster County (NY), 155, 167, 196, 293, 296, 303, 408n9
Ulster County Jail, 8, 14, 38, 71m, 104–106, 357
Ulster Garden Club, 155
ulus. *See under* knives
United States Geological Survey (USGS), 11–12

Vanderlyn, John, 155
Van Coelen, Reyner, 269
Van Gaasbeek: Blandina (Ten Broeck), 320, 323; family, 178–179, 184, 186, 279; Peter, 323. *See also* Senate House State Historic Site
Van Sickle, George, 118
Van Tienhoven, Cornelius, 401–402n1
Van Valkenbergh, Ray, 54
Vermeer, Johannes: *The Little Street*, 230, 284
Verrazano, Giovanni da, 377

Wall Street (Kingston, NY), 8, 103, 166, 169, 172, 368
wampum, 127, 130, 137–138, 140, 208, 253, 338; definition, 399; manufacture, 184–185, 251–253, 266
walnut. *See under* trees, nuts
Waornecks. *See under* Native Americans: Esopus
Wappingers. *See under* Native Americans: Munsee speakers
Warranawankongs. *See under* Native Americans: Esopus
Washington Avenue (Kingston, NY), 16, 156, 172, 315, 364, 381
West Chester Street (Kingston, NY), 309
West Chestnut Street, 85–86
Westphaelen, Juriaen, 125

West Point Museum, 209
whistles, 212, 276–277, 281, 355, 407n8
whelk. *See under* shells
Wilbur Avenue (Kingston, NY), 301–303, 369, 402n2
Wiltwyck (Kingston, NY), 40–41, 123–150, 157, 194, 271, 286–288, 314, 321. *See also* Dutch: settlements, Esopus Wars
Wilson, Tyrone, 330–331, 333
Wiltwyck Cemetery. *See under* cemeteries
windows, 182, 271–272, 362; quarrels, 230, 272, 378. *See also* glass

Wisconsin Glacier, 20, 41, 395
Wolfersteig site (Hurley, NY), 19–20, 230
woodchuck. *See under* mammals
Woodland period/stage: definition, 395; Early, 33–34, 62, 79, 115, 361; Middle, 7, 34–35, 56, 62, 69, 79, 103, 115, 185, 353–354, 361; Late, 7, 16, 34–35, 40, 56, 64, 73, 79, 83, 113, 116–118, 162, 337–338, 340, 343–344, 353, 356–357, 361, 394
Woutersen, Cornelis, 155
Wurts Street (Kingston, NY), 94–95, 103, 369
Wynkoop, Johannes, 319, 323

www.ingramcontent.com/pod-product-compliance
Lightning Source LLC
Chambersburg PA
CBHW070746230426

43665CB00017B/2269